The
PRESIDENTIAL
RECORDINGS

—— LYNDON B. JOHNSON ——

The
PRESIDENTIAL
RECORDINGS

LYNDON B. JOHNSON

*Mississippi Burning and
the Passage of the Civil Rights Act
Volume Eight*

⊁⊁⊁JUNE 23, 1964–JULY 4, 1964⊰⊰⊰

Kent B. Germany and David C. Carter
Editors

Ashley Havard High
Associate Editor

Patricia Dunn
Assistant Editor

Timothy Naftali
General Editor

W. W. NORTON & COMPANY • NEW YORK • LONDON

The Presidential Recordings Program is supported in part by grants from the National Historical Publications and Records Commission.

Manufacturing by RR Donnelley Harrisonburg
Book design by Dana Sloan
Production manager: Julia Druskin

The Library of Congress has cataloged earlier volumes as follows:

Lyndon B. Johnson, the Kennedy assassination, and the transfer of power, November 1963–January 1964 / Max Holland, editor.
p. cm. — (The presidential recordings)
Includes bibliographic references and indexes.
Contents: v. 1. November 22–30, 1963 / edited by Max Holland—v. 2. December 1963 / edited by Robert David Johnson and David Shreve—v. 3. January 1964 / edited by Kent B. Germany and Robert David Johnson.
ISBN 0-393-06001-2 (set)
1. United States—Politics and government—1963–1969—Sources.
2. United States—Politics and government—1961–1963—Sources.
3. Johnson, Lyndon B. (Lyndon Baines), 1908–1973—Archives.
4. Presidents—United States—Archives. 5. Kennedy, John F. (John Fitzgerald), 1917–1963—Assassination—Sources. I. Holland, Max. II. Johnson, Robert David, 1967– III. Shreve, David, 1961– IV. Germany, Kent B., 1971– V. Series.
E846.L945 2005
973.923—dc22

2004066167

ISBN 978-0-393-08118-3 (for the set of two volumes)

W. W. Norton & Company, Inc.
500 Fifth Avenue, New York, N.Y. 10110
www.wwnorton.com

W. W. Norton & Company Ltd.
Castle House, 75/76 Wells Street, London W1T 3QT

1 2 3 4 5 6 7 8 9 0

In memory of Ernest R. May, 1928–2009

Contents

The Presidential Recordings Program

etween 1940 and 1973, presidents of the United States secretly recorded thousands of their meetings and conversations in the White House. Though some recorded a lot and others just a little, they all created a unique and irreplaceable source for understanding not only their presidencies and times but, indeed, the essential process of high-level decision making. These recordings by no means displace more traditional sources of historical knowledge such as official documents, private diaries and letters, memoirs, and contemporaneous journalism. Rather, they augment these sources much as photographs, films, and recordings augment printed records of presidents' public appearances. But they also do much more than that.

Because the recordings capture a series of formal meetings, informal office conversations, and telephone calls, and not just highlights recorded by a note taker or recalled afterward in a memorandum or memoir, they pierce the presidential veil created by staffers and image-makers. Presidents are human beings, with emotions, prejudices, and preferences, and the tapes are remarkable in the extent to which they convey that humanity, flaws and all. Left out of presidential statements and even many internal records are signs of indecision, uncertainty, anger, or alarm. And leaders are often not as decisive, implacable, and sure of their next step as they would like to be. Nor are they as in control of events as they would wish. The tapes offer a dynamic picture of how the various responsibilities of a president are constantly converging to test them—how a president could be simultaneously, not consecutively, a commander in chief worrying about war, a policymaker conscious that his missteps in economic policy could bring on a market collapse, a chief mediator among interest groups, a chief administrator for a myriad of public programs, a spokesperson for the interests and aspirations of the nation, a head of a sprawling political party.

The secret tapes also reveal how decisions and policies actually emerge. Presidential advisers can be heard debating with one another, adapting to the perspectives of others, and changing their minds. The president's own views are often reshaped as well, sometimes by a subtle but profound shift in the definition of an issue or the stakes involved. While participants rarely have a clear memory of such changes, the tapes record them word for word.

Finally, they provide audio snapshots of a dramatic era, both inside and outside of government. The White House does not exist in a vacuum. During the era that presidents were secretly taping, events in Congress and the Supreme Court were shaping the American story. So, too, were actions in the streets, at home or abroad, constantly challenging, worrying, or inspiring the occupants of those bugged rooms. Appearing on the tapes are some of the most influential individuals of the period—for example, A. Philip Randolph, Martin Luther King Jr., Jean Monnet, Golda Meir, Douglas MacArthur, Reverend Billy Graham—who also shaped the use of U.S. presidential power and authority.

Though Franklin D. Roosevelt, Harry S. Truman, and Dwight D. Eisenhower all made a few secret recordings, John F. Kennedy was the first president to install an elaborate taping system and to make extensive use of it. His family and aides removed the system almost immediately after his murder in 1963. Lyndon B. Johnson then installed a different system, of which he, too, made frequent use. Richard Nixon, after two years without using any recording devices, installed a voice-activated system that captured every conversation in a room containing a microphone.

The existence of Kennedy's taping system was known at the time only to the President himself, his private secretary (Evelyn Lincoln), and the two Secret Service agents who installed and maintained it. President Kennedy's brother Robert learned of the system at some point, and the circle probably eventually extended to include the President's close aide, Kenneth O'Donnell. Other senior White House officials like special counsel Theodore Sorensen or national security assistant McGeorge Bundy knew nothing about it. President Kennedy had to activate the system with a buzzer press, and he tended to use it as a kind of electronic diary to record meetings he considered important, probably with a view to memoirs that he never had the chance to write. He and his brother had the tapes from the Cuban missile crisis period transcribed in the summer of 1963. No records have turned up to explain why; perhaps the transcripts were made with an eye to their being compiled for the 1964 campaign. In general, however, President Kennedy paid little attention to the tapes while he was President, leaving them to Mrs. Lincoln to store away for later.

During the period covered by these volumes, President Johnson only recorded telephone conversations and the occasional office conversation caught while the speakerphone was activated. Johnson employed a system that used Dictaphone equipment. Originally produced as a Gramophone from patents by Thomas A. Edison, early Dictaphone recorders recorded sound by stylus cutting on wax-coated cylinders. During and after World War II, the Dictaphone Corporation developed electronic recording devices and in 1947 began to distribute Time-Master machines with reusable plastic dictabelts. These went into common use for dictation to be transcribed by stenographers. President Kennedy had used such a device to supplement his secret reel-to-reel taping system. President Johnson first taped telephone calls when he was majority leader in the Senate and then as Vice President, and he began to do so in the White House as soon as he became President. Later—though not in the period covered by these volumes—Johnson would install a system of his own for making secret recordings of meetings.

Richard Nixon created by far the largest collection of secret recordings. Between February 16, 1971, and July 12, 1973, Nixon taped over 3,700 hours of his meetings and telephone conversations. Eventually, the U.S. Secret Service installed microphones in five locations ranging from the Oval Office and Nixon's hideaway office in what is now the Eisenhower Executive Office Building to Camp David. An avid reader of history, Nixon had kept a recorded diary when he was Vice President. As President, he intended to make use of meeting and telephone tapes to write his memoirs.

On the premise that these and the other secretly made presidential recordings will remain important historical sources for years to come, the University of Virginia's Miller Center of Public Affairs is producing transcripts and annotations for these presidential recordings. This work is organized in the Center's Presidential Recordings Program (PRP), directed by David Coleman. For the Kennedy and Johnson presidencies, the recordings are arranged in reference volumes organized chronologically. In 2001 the first three volumes in the John F. Kennedy series appeared, covering all taped meetings and conversations between July 30, 1962, and October 28, 1962. This was followed in 2005 by the first three volumes of the Lyndon B. Johnson series, which included all taped meetings and conversations between November 22, 1963, and January 31, 1964. A second set of three Johnson volumes, covering February through May 1964, was published in 2007. The PRP also produces policy or thematic volumes in which scholars present a selection of transcripts to tell a particular story. Two of these books have appeared so far: *The Kennedy Tapes: Inside the White House During the Cuban Missile Crisis (the Concise*

Edition) by Ernest May and Philip Zelikow (2002) and *Kennedy, Johnson, and the Quest for Justice: The Civil Rights Tapes* by Jonathan Rosenberg and Zachary Karabell (2003). Finally, since 2006, the PRP has been working with the University of Virginia Press on producing digital thematic editions for publication in the Press's groundbreaking Rotunda digital imprint.

When the PRP began its work in 1998, it sought to build upon the methods and style developed by May and Zelikow to produce the original edition of *The Kennedy Tapes*, the first scholarly compilation of Cuban missile crisis transcripts. May and Zelikow had initially used court reporters and then settled on producing the transcripts themselves by listening to analog or cassette recordings without any amplification. Timothy Naftali, who led the PRP from 1998 to 2006, worked with George Eliades, then a scholar at the Center, to find better hardware and to develop a rigorous team method to produce transcripts. With principal editorial guidance from May and Zelikow, and the help of an editorial advisory board, PRP scholars subsequently developed a number of methodological guidelines for the preparation of the presidential recordings volumes:

First, the work is done by trained professional historians who are specialists on the period covered by the tapes and on some of the central themes of the meetings and conversations. Without such expertise, transcribing and interpreting presidential tapes can be a bit like trying to assemble a jigsaw puzzle without being able to see the picture on the puzzle box. Each volume has one or two lead editors, who write the daily introductions, conversation introductions, policy descriptions, and footnotes and are responsible for the final versions of the transcripts. The volume editors are listed on the cover. Assisting these editors are associate editors who also draft and critique transcripts and help with the research. The complete list of editors for each reference volume appears on the title page. These historians not only delve into documentary sources but sometimes interview living participants who can help us comprehend the taped discussions. Our voice identifications are based on samples we have compiled and on our research. We list only the names of the participants we can identify.

Second, the transcription process is built on the foundation of a team method. By having each transcript corrected and edited by several scholars, it maximizes the pool of expertise while at the same time minimizing some of the physical and psychological factors that complicate any transcribing effort (e.g., different people often hear slightly different things). By the time a transcript has passed through the process, it has been subjected to possibly hundreds of hours of listening and research by different scholars. The process is adaptable according to the degree of difficulty of the original recording, but every transcript has benefited from at least four listeners. The first stage is to generate raw, rough transcripts from the audio recordings. The PRP draws on the talents and enthusiasm of a team of carefully trained undergraduate and graduate student interns to construct a first draft. For office recordings, which are the most difficult to transcribe, usually one or two scholars painstakingly produce a primary draft (referred to as an A-version). Two or more scholars then carefully go over the transcript, individually or sometimes with two listening at the same time. They edit, correct, annotate, and update the transcript as they go (creating B- and C-versions). For telephone recordings, which are more audible and easier to understand because they typically involve only two participants, the A- and B-versions may be produced by student interns and then returned to Miller Center scholars for the C-, or third, review. In all cases, the transcript is then returned to the original scholar, who has the responsibility for pursuing any remaining annotation or research issues (creating a D-version). The reference volume editors remain accountable for checking the quality and accuracy of all the work in their set of transcripts, knitting them together with the annotations. We, as the general editors, then review this work. This method is by no means perfect, but it is the best we have been able to devise so far given available time and resources.

Third, the Program uses the best technology that the project can afford. As of 2006, the Program uses high-quality CDs made available by the National Archives and Records Administration. Using computer software and studio-quality headphones and amplification equipment, transcribers are able to examine each audio recording in minute detail and enhance the audio signal when necessary. The PRP made great strides in 2001 after the adoption of digital audio software, which had been introduced by Coleman, who had joined the PRP in 1999.

Fourth, we strive to make the transcripts accessible to and readable by anyone interested in history, including students. This requires a considerable amount of subjective editorial work. Since people often do not speak in complete and grammatically correct sentences, the transcriber has to infer and create sentence and paragraph structure, placing commas, semicolons, and periods. We omit the verbal stutters or tics such as the *uhs* that dot almost anyone's speech if they do not convey any information. This approach reflects the fact that listeners unconsciously filter out such debris in interpreting what someone is saying. But there are gray areas. If someone says, for example, "sixteen . . . uh, sixty . . . ," the editors have to decide whether this slip conveys anything about what the speaker was trying to say. These judgment calls are usually no more difficult than those involved in deciding whether to insert punctuation or paragraphing. In the effort to be exhaustive, sometimes there is the temptation to overtranscribe, catching every verbal fragment, however indistinct. Such attempts can add too much intrusive static, making the substance less understandable to readers now than it was to the hearers then. The goal is to give the reader the truest possible sense of the actual dialogue as the participants themselves understood it.

The tape quality varies and the scholars are occasionally unable to make out a word or a passage. In those instances, the editors have placed "[*unclear*]" in the text. The transcribers and editors aim for completeness. Rather than guess at an indistinct passage, however, it is their preference to indicate to the reader this lack of certainty. Over time, others using the transcripts and listening to the tapes or with access to better technology may be able to fill in passages marked as "unclear." Although the Miller Center volumes are intended to be reliable reference works, the transcripts will always be subject to amendments. The PRP welcomes suggestions and corrections and has in the past placed transcript updates on its website, whitehousetapes.net.

Fifth, the scholars seek to embed the transcripts in the political, international, cultural, and social context of the period. Each reference volume includes explanations and annotations intended to enable readers to understand the background and circumstances of a particular conversation or meeting. With rare exceptions, we do not add information that participants would not have known, and we comment on the significance of items of information only when necessary to make a conversation fully comprehensible. As with all historical sources, interpretations will have to accumulate over time.

For additional information on the Presidential Recordings Program and access to tapes and transcripts, see whitehousetapes.net.

The general editor wishes to make special mention of the work of Pat Dunn, who developed the style guide for the series and passes a keen eye over each volume.

Finally, a very sad note: Professor Ernest R. May died during the preparation of Volumes 7 and 8 of the Johnson series. In addition to inspiring the Miller Center's presidential tapes research effort with Philip Zelikow, Professor May served as a general editor for all previous PRP publications. The standards of academic rigor, accessibility, and good sense aspired to by all members of the PRP are a testament to Professor May's enduring legacy as a scholar, teacher, and editor. The PRP dedicates these new volumes to his memory.

Editors' Acknowledgments

The production of this volume was a massive undertaking that drew on the talents of many people and the resources of several institutions. In particular, this book would not exist without the Lyndon B. Johnson Library or the University of Virginia's Miller Center of Public Affairs. In both preserving historical records and providing access to researchers, the LBJ Library is a model institution. While there, the editors received assistance from Linda Seelke, Claudia Anderson, Shannon Jarrett, Laura Harmon, Regina Greenwell, Tina Houston, and Allen Fisher, each of whom graciously complied with extensive research requests and suggested possible locations of needed materials. In regard to the Johnson recordings, Regina Greenwell, Claudia Anderson, and Allen Fisher provided wonderful tutorials and readily shared their vast knowledge about and understanding of the tapes and the process of preserving them, and the editors are in their debt. Initial transcripts for this volume were made from digital audio files released by the LBJ Library. Afterward, exhaustive scholarly reviews of them were completed using state-of-the-art computer hardware, Cool Edit digital audio software, and studio quality headphones. The efforts of Linda Seelke and others allowed us to create recordings housed in Charlottesville and on whitehousetapes.net that are as close in quality to the original as possible. Final thanks must go to Harry Middleton, the former director of the Johnson Library, and to Betty Sue Flowers, the director from September 2001 to 2009. Director Middleton guided the library from its inception and contributed greatly to the creation of its culture of openness, its respect for scholars, and its dedication to professional standards, and Director Flowers continued these traditions admirably. For a long time to come, students of the 1960s will enrich their understanding by passing through the library's doors.

The editors also wish to express their appreciation to the Miller Center of Public Affairs. The administrative and technological infrastructure provided by the Center has sustained this work from the beginning. Philip Zelikow was director of the Center from 1998 to 2005 and provided steadfast support for the Presidential Recordings Program overall and, in the instance of this volume, for the Lyndon Johnson Project. His creation of an ambitious program dedicated to the open scholarly inquiry into the culture of the 1960s—at a time when support for the humanities and social sciences had been systematically undermined—served as an encouraging example of what can be accomplished in the academy. Gene Fife carried on this mission during his year as interim director, as has Gerald Baliles during his service as the current director. A former governor of the state of Virginia, Baliles has a unique perspective on American political history, and he has provided essential support for this ambitious effort to document part of it. Mike Mullen (now deceased) and Taylor Reveley also provided key advice and support during the years of production. Two other scholars deserve more thanks than these few lines can provide: Timothy Naftali and David Coleman. Naftali, the director of the Presidential Recordings Program from 1999 to 2006 and the general editor of this volume, was masterful at marshaling resources and recruiting scholars from around the world to participate in what became an invigorating and collegial intellectual community at the Miller Center. For this book, Tim read every line and offered crucial advice that transformed its substance and structure. Coleman, the current chair of the Recordings Program, has been the backbone of the program for several years. This book is a testament to his skills as a scholar and administrator, and the editors recognize with deep appreciation his influence, which is reflected on virtually every page.

Other scholars affiliated with the Miller Center have also greatly improved this work. David Shreve, Guian McKee, David Coleman, Marc Selverstone, and Robert David Johnson offered selfless assistance at varying stages of the work. Several other scholars contributed to this volume either through reading parts of the manuscript or discussing aspects of it and of Johnson's career with the editors. Taylor Branch was an invaluable member of the editorial advisory board, while Irv Gellman, Jeff Woods, Julian Bond, Holly Shulman, Thomas Jackson, Gareth Davies, Joe Crespino, Todd Moye, Bonnie Hagerman, Bill Miller, Will Thomas, Sidney Milkis, Brian Balogh, Andrew Morris, Matthew Holden, Kenneth Thompson, Jeffrey Turner, and members of the Presidential Recordings Program's editorial board have offered stories, thoughts, and suggestions that have shaped the thinking of the editors in their efforts.

A special recognition must be given to Ernest May, the longtime Harvard historian and general editor of the Presidential Recordings

Series who passed away in 2009. This book is dedicated to his memory and his contribution to the study of public policy, political power, and American governance.

One of the major challenges of this volume involved organizing the enormous amount of information represented by the tapes, the documentary record, and the secondary literature. In that regard, the editors also wish to acknowledge several people. First, Patricia Dunn and Ashley Havard High provided sturdy and relentless editorial assistance. Ashley listened to every second of the tapes covered in the volume several times over and went above and beyond the call of duty in suggesting annotations and raising questions about the material. Patricia is the kind of editor that all authors want. She copyedited every manuscript page and, with our gratitude, was unyielding in her commitment to the highest standards. Michael Greco, Sheila Blackford, and Roberta Ashmore provided key assistance in digitizing documents and audio and responding to a variety of requests. At Norton, Drake McFeely and Jeff Shreve were remarkable in moving the manuscript through publication.

At the Miller Center, the editors benefited from several research collections and from part-time student research assistants. The materials collected by the Miller Center's Scripps Library and Multimedia Archive made it easy to conduct research from afar. Additionally, the University of Virginia's Alderman Library has established easy-to-use systems that have opened up the vast resources of one of the nation's finest public research libraries. Their digital efforts are truly pathbreaking. The editors are particularly in debt to the arts and sciences librarians, the government documents librarians, the staff of the Library Express on Grounds, and the staff of Interlibrary Services. The editors were also blessed with a number of outstanding research assistants. In Austin, Matt Wood did much legwork in dubbing digital tapes at the LBJ Library. In Charlottesville, several students assisted with the project. They included Alice Anne Stephens, Robert DeRise, Mia Petrini, Leah Kuchinsky, Elizabeth Fife, Kate Bedingfield, Kerry O'Brien, Esther Brown, Christina Saunders, Irena Saric, Bill Tucker, Max Rosenthal, Daniel Lipton, David Reid, and Kyle O'Connor, as well as others in our team of talented interns who worked on various aspects of research and support. John Monahan has spent more hours exploring the life of Lyndon Johnson than perhaps any undergraduate anywhere and has left a formidable record of intelligence, diligence, and enthusiasm. At the University of South Carolina, graduate student Beth Sherouse provided key research assistance.

Kent Germany would also like to thank several people for their personal and professional support. His wife, Mary Glasgow Germany, and their three daughters, Elise Irene, Sarah Ruth, and Margaret Holt Germany, have been generously forgiving about the missed bedtimes, late nights, and the long working weekends. He also wishes to thank his parents, Raymond and Nelda Sue Germany, and to acknowledge the influence of members of his larger family who have added layers of understanding about southern people and life in rural Texas that could never have been gleaned from reading books. Special thanks should be extended to Kenneth Thompson, partly for relating his experiences with policy-makers such as Dean Rusk, but mostly for the richness of conversations held over his kitchen table. His legendary reputation for kindness and insight is well deserved. At the University of South Carolina, Kent wishes to thank a number of scholars for helping him think about a variety of aspects of this work. There are far too many to name each one here, but they include Cleveland Sellers, Dan Carter, Patrick Maney, Lacy Ford, Todd Shaw, Patricia Sullivan, Eric Bargeron, Kathy Roberts Forde, Sid Bedingfield, and Marjorie Spruill.

David Carter has benefited from the help of many of the individuals acknowledged above, particularly those at the LBJ Library and the Miller Center. He also owes a profound debt of gratitude to the dozens of under-graduates and graduate students whose perceptive questions and insights have contributed to his understanding of the Johnson years. He would like to thank the following individuals: Susan Youngblood Ashmore, Paul Betz, Jenny Brooks, Alicia Carter and Sam Warner, Bill Chafe, Joe Crespino, John Dittmer, Wayne Flynt, Frye Gaillard, Charles Israel, Tom Jackson, Joe Kicklighter, Steven Lawson, Earl and Kay Martin, Ken Noe, David Perry, John Salmond, Patricia Sullivan, Tim Thurber, Tim Tyson, Roger Wilkins, and Ben Wise. Kent and Mary Germany and their children have been like a second family, their generosity matched only by their patience. His parents, Dan and Jane Carter, taught him about the "beloved community" long before he began studying the civil rights era, and while his wife, Leslie Carter, and children, Philip and Anna, have spent many years competing for attention with the looming historical shadow of LBJ, he hopes they know that in the battle for his affections they easily won out over the "Johnson treatment."

In conclusion, the editors would like to thank the National Historical Publications and Records Commission for funding that made the volume possible. Their distribution of funding keeps critical parts of U.S. history alive and encourages deeper exploration of the nation's complicated past. They would also like to thank the Dillon Fund and the W. Alton Jones Foundation for generous grants that supported part of this book. Their philanthropic support of historical research is refreshing and important.

A Note on Sources

Several general references sources were used in this volume to verify details regarding dates, people, positions, and other matters. They include the Office of the Federal Register, National Archives and Records Service, *U.S. Government Organization Manual* (Washington, DC: GPO, 1963–1965); Joint Committee on Printing, *Official Congressional Directory for the Use of the United States Congress* (Washington, DC: GPO, 1964–1965); Charles B. Brownson, ed., *Congressional Staff Directory,* volumes 1963 and 1964 (Washington, DC: The Congressional Staff Directory, 1963–1964); Congressional Quarterly Service, *Congressional Quarterly Almanac,* volumes 19 and 20 (Washington, DC: Congressional Quarterly, Inc., 1964–1965); Congressional Quarterly Service, *Congress and the Nation, 1945–1964: A Review of Government and Politics in the Postwar Years* (Washington, DC: Congressional Quarterly, Inc., 1965); *Biographical Directory of the United States Congress, 1774–Present;* http://bioguide.congress.gov/biosearch/biosearch.asp; U.S. Department of State, Office of the Historian, www.state.gov/r/pa/ho; Federal Judicial Center, www.fjc.gov; and the LBJ Daily Diary compiled by the White House staff and preserved by the LBJ Library.

Conversation Participants
and Major Figures

Abell, Bess: White House Social Secretary

Albert, Carl B.: U.S. Representative, Democrat, from Oklahoma, 1947–1977, House Majority Leader, 1963–1970

Anderson, Clinton P.: U.S. Senator, Democrat, from New Mexico, 1949–1973; Chairman, Committee on Aeronautical and Space Sciences, 1963–1972, and Chairman, Federal Reconstruction and Planning Commission for Alaska, 1964

Bailey, Oriole Bunton: Elderly cousin of President Johnson's, lived on the LBJ Ranch

Ball, George: Under Secretary of State, 1961–1966

Boggs, Hale: U.S. Representative, Democrat, from Louisiana, 1941–1943, 1947–1973; House Majority Whip, 1961–1970

Boozer, Yolanda: Member of Lyndon Johnson's Senate, presidential, and post-presidential staffs

Brooks, Jack: U.S. Representative, Democrat, from Texas, 1952–1995

Bundy, McGeorge: Special Assistant to the President for National Security Affairs, 1961–1966

Busby, Horace: Former Senate aide to Lyndon Johnson and one of his top speechwriters

Carter, Cliff: Longtime friend and administrative assistant to Lyndon Johnson, 1937–1966

Chaney, Fannie Lee: Mother of slain COFO activist James Chaney

Chaney, James: COFO activist; murdered by white supremacists in conspiracy with local law enforcement

Clifford, Clark: Washington lawyer; adviser to Presidents Truman, Kennedy, and Johnson; Chairman, President's Foreign Intelligence Advisory Board since 1963

Clifton, C. V. "Ted": Senior military aide for Kennedy and Johnson administrations until 1965

Connally, John: Governor of Texas and one of Lyndon Johnson's closest advisers; joined Johnson's congressional staff in 1938 and managed

Johnson's campaign for the 1960 Democratic nomination; seriously injured during the assassination of President Kennedy

Conte, Silvio O.: U.S. Representative, Republican, from Massachusetts, 1959–1991

Daley, Richard: Mayor of Chicago, 1955–1976

Dean, Arthur: Senior partner, Sullivan and Cromwell; adviser to Johnson

Dillon, C. Douglas: Secretary of the Treasury, 1961–1965

Dirksen, Everett M.: U.S. Senator, Republican, from Illinois, 1951–1969; Senate Minority Leader, 1959–1969

Doar, John: Key attorney and local liaison in Civil Rights Division, U.S. Department of Justice

Dulles, Allen: Director of Central Intelligence, 1953–1961; Commissioner on the Warren Commission to investigate JFK's assassination

Dungan, Ralph A.: Special Assistant to the President, 1961–1964; U.S. Ambassador to Chile, 1964–1967

Eastland, James: U.S. Senator, Democrat, from Mississippi, 1941, 1943–1978; Chairman, Senate Judiciary Committee, 1954–1978

Farmer, James: National Director of CORE

Fehmer, Marie: Personal secretary to Lyndon Johnson

Feldman, Myer: Deputy Special Counsel to the President, 1961–1964; Counsel to the President, 1964–1965

Finney, Tom: Attorney in firm of Democratic adviser Clark Clifford; former aide to Senator and Commerce Committee Chair Mike Monroney of Oklahoma

Freeman, Orville: Secretary of Agriculture, 1961–1969

Friendly, Alfred: Executive vice president and managing editor, *Washington Post*, since 1955

Gargan, Ann: Niece and caregiver for Joseph Kennedy Sr.

Goldwater, Barry: Republican Senator from Arizona; front-runner for Republican presidential nomination

Goodman, Andrew: COFO activist; murdered by white supremacists in conspiracy with local law enforcement

Goodman, Robert: Father of Andrew Goodman, one of three civil rights activists who were murdered in Mississippi during the Freedom Summer

Gordon, Kermit: Director, Bureau of the Budget, 1962–1965

Graham, Jackson: Brigadier General of the Ohio River Division of the Army Corps of Engineers

Guthman, Edwin: Journalist who served as Robert Kennedy's Press Assistant, 1964–1965; recipient of Pulitzer Prize for National Reporting, 1950

Harriman, Averell: Under Secretary of State for Political Affairs, 1963–1965

Hodges, Luther H.: Secretary of Commerce, 1961–1965

Hoover, J. Edgar: Director of the Federal Bureau of Investigation, 1924–1972

Humphrey, Hubert: Democratic Senator from Minnesota since 1949; Senate Majority Whip; candidate for the presidential nomination in 1960 and a favorite of the party's liberal wing

İnönü, İsmet: Prime Minister of Turkey

Jenkins, Walter: Johnson's office manager, personnel chief, and administrative assistant; in point of continuous service his oldest employee, having served on Johnson's staff since 1939

Johnson, Lady Bird (née Claudia Alta Taylor): Wife of Lyndon Johnson since 1934

Johnson, Paul: Governor of Mississippi, Democrat, 1964–1968

Katzenbach, Nicholas: Deputy Attorney General, U.S. Department of Justice, 1962–1965

Kellam, Jesse: One of Lyndon Johnson's oldest friends and closest business associates; manager of the Johnsons' broadcasting properties

Kennedy, Edward: Youngest brother of President Kennedy; Democratic Senator from Massachusetts since 1962

Kennedy, Jacqueline Bouvier: Widow of President John F. Kennedy

Kennedy, Joan: Wife of Edward Kennedy, 1958–1982

Kennedy, Robert: Younger brother of President Kennedy and his campaign manager in 1960; Attorney General of the United States since 1961

King, Martin Luther, Jr.: President of the Southern Christian Leadership Conference; 1964 Nobel Peace Prize winner

Luce, Clare Boothe: Wife of Henry Luce; U.S. Representative, Republican, from Connecticut, 1943–1947

Mahon, George: U.S. Representative, Democrat, from Texas, 1935–1979; Chairman, House Appropriations Committee, 1964–1978

Mansfield, Mike: U.S. Senator, Democrat, from Montana, 1953–1977; Senate Majority Leader, 1961–1977

Marshall, Burke: Assistant Attorney General, Civil Rights Division, since 1961

McCormack, John W.: U.S. Representative, Democrat, from Massachusetts, 1928–1971; Speaker, U.S. House of Representatives, 1961–1971

McDonald, C. C. "Charley": Friend of Johnson; 1934 gubernatorial candidate in Texas Democratic primary

McDonald, Genie: Wife of Charley McDonald

McNamara, Robert S.: Secretary of Defense, 1961–1968

Moyers, Bill D.: Deputy Director, Peace Corps, 1961–1964; Special Assistant to the President, 1963–1967

O'Brien, Larry: Special Assistant to the President for Congressional Affairs, 1961–1965

Price, Cecil: Deputy Sheriff of Neshoba County, Mississippi; arrested for role in Chaney, Goodman, and Schwerner murders; convicted on federal conspiracy charges in 1967; never charged by the state of Mississippi

Rainey, Lawrence: Sheriff of Neshoba County, Mississippi; arrested for role in Chaney, Goodman, and Schwerner murders, acquitted on federal conspiracy charges in 1967; never charged by the state of Mississippi

Rains, Albert: U.S. Representative, Democrat, from Alabama, 1945–1965

Raupe, Craig: Top aide to House Speaker Jim Wright

Reedy, George E.: White House Press Secretary, 1964–1965

Reid, Ogden R.: U.S. Representative, Republican switched to Democrat in 1972, from New York, 1963–1975

Roberts, Juanita: Longtime personal secretary to Lyndon Johnson

Rooney, John J.: U.S. Representative, Democrat, from New York, 1944–1974

Rusk, Dean: Secretary of State, 1961–1969

Ryan, William Fitts: U.S. Representative, Democrat, from New York, 1961–1972

Schwerner, Anne: Mother of Michael Schwerner, one of three civil rights activists who were murdered in Mississippi during the Freedom Summer

Schwerner, Michael: COFO activist; murdered by white supremacists in conspiracy with local law enforcement

Schwerner, Rita: COFO activist; wife of slain activist Michael Schwerner

Smathers, George: U.S. Senator, Democrat, from Florida, 1951–1969; member of the Finance Committee

Smith, Jean Kennedy: Daughter of Joseph Kennedy; wife of Stephen Smith

Smith, Stephen: Husband of Jean Kennedy Smith; key adviser to Kennedy family

Stennis, John L.: U.S. Senator, Democrat, from Mississippi, 1947–1989; Chairman, Senate Select Committee on Standards and Conduct, 1965–1975

Sullivan, Joseph: FBI Inspector, a leader of Mississippi Burning investigation

Taylor, Jay: Texas businessman, friend of President Johnson, and president of the Texas Livestock Marketing Association

Taylor, General Maxwell: Former Chairman of the Joint Chiefs of Staff; incoming U.S. Ambassador to South Vietnam

Valenti, Jack: Special Assistant to the President, 1963–1966

White, Lee C.: Associate Counsel to the President, 1963–1965

Whittington, Gerri: White House secretary, December 1963–1965

Widnall, William B.: U.S. Representative, Republican, from New Jersey, 1950–1974

Wilkins, Roy: Executive Secretary, National Association for the Advancement of Colored People (NAACP), 1955–1964; Executive Director, NAACP, 1965–1977. In 1967, Johnson presented Wilkins with the Presidential Medal of Freedom.

The
PRESIDENTIAL
RECORDINGS

—— LYNDON B. JOHNSON ——

Tuesday, June 23, 1964

They've just disappeared from the face of the earth.
—Lee White to President Johnson

They can't disappear forever, can they?
—John McCormack to President Johnson

James Earl Chaney was 21 years old. Michael Henry "Mickey" Schwerner was 24. Andrew Goodman was 20. Chaney was a black Mississippian. Schwerner was a white New Yorker. Both men were seasoned activists with the Congress of Racial Equality (CORE) in Meridian, Mississippi, a small city near the Alabama border. Goodman was a white volunteer from New York on his first trip to the Magnolia State, one of approximately 800 mostly white, mostly northern students coming down to assist in voter education, freedom schools, and other organizing activities as part of Freedom Summer. Mississippi officials referred to the situation as the "Invasion of Mississippi by Northern College Students."[1] Adding to the wariness of many white Mississippians, Schwerner and Goodman—and many of the student volunteers—were Jewish. On June 21, two days after the Senate passed the historic Civil Rights Act of 1964, these three men kicked off Freedom Summer by investigating a church-burning in the Neshoba County community of Longdale. They expected to be back in

---

1. Virgil Downing, Mississippi Sovereignty Commission investigator, "Invasion of Mississippi by Northern College Students," 1 July 1964, Folder 1, July 1964, Box 136, Series II, Sub-Series 9: Sovereignty Commission, Johnson (Paul B.) Family Papers, in Collection M191, Manuscript Collection, McCain Library and Archives, University of Southern Mississippi (hereafter cited as Sovereignty Commission, Johnson Papers, University of Southern Mississippi).

Meridian by 4:00 P.M. (CST).[2] At approximately 3:30 P.M. (CST), however, they were arrested for allegedly going 65 miles per hour in a 30-mph zone and went to jail in nearby Philadelphia.[3]

A few hours before that incident, on the West Coast, President Johnson concluded a carefully orchestrated political trip to California, with the ending slightly tarnished by a hotel scheduling conflict that forced the relocation of 13-year-old Lyle Peskin's Bar Mitzvah. Johnson took the opportunity, however, to shake the boy's hand and greet his family as he left for the airport. President Johnson arrived back at the White House a little before 6:00 P.M. (EDT) and then shared dinner and a late-evening swim with Lady Bird, journalist William S. White, and two key White House aides.[4] While he relaxed in the nation's capital, tragic events were unfolding in the rural South. The Mississippi midnight would lead to the first major domestic crisis of his presidency. Like Dwight Eisenhower and John Kennedy before him, Johnson would be forced to redefine federal-local relations in the United States.[5] How would the federal government respond to the failure of local officials to provide equal protection of the laws and to adequately maintain law and order?[6]

---

2. To avoid possible confusion in time zone shifts between Mississippi and Washington, D.C., the editors of this volume use eastern daylight time (EDT) as the standard time reference from this point forward unless otherwise noted. In 1964, the choice to use daylight saving time was left up to the states and led to wide variation in implementation. Mississippi in 1964 was on central standard time (CST), two hours behind the EDT of Washington, D.C. After the passage of the Uniform Time Act of 1966, all but Michigan and Hawaii used daylight saving time. *New York Times*, 30 April 1967.

3. Federal Bureau of Investigation, "Miburn Prosecutive Summary" of the case "Bernard L. Akin, et al.; James Earl Chaney, Michael Henry Schwerner, aka Mickey, Andrew Goodman—Victims," 19 December 1964, File 44.25706, http://foia.fbi.gov/miburn/miburn3.pdf, pp. ii-iv, 7, 35–50.

4. To reconstruct President Johnson's day, the editors used several resources. The most important of these were the President's Daily Diary and the Daily Diary Backup, on which Johnson's office staff carefully noted where Johnson was during the day and night and with whom he spoke or met. Unless otherwise noted, references to Johnson's daily schedule came from the Daily Diary sheets found in Diaries and Appointment Logs of Lyndon B. Johnson, Special Files, 1927–1973, Lyndon B. Johnson Library.

5. On the role of federalism in the Little Rock school crisis in 1957, the Freedom Rides in 1961, the Ole Miss riots in 1962, and several incidents in Alabama in 1963, see Michal R. Belknap, *Federal Law and Southern Order: Racial Violence and Constitutional Conflict in the Post-Brown South* (Athens: University of Georgia Press, 1987), pp. 39–52, 70–105.

6. The state of Mississippi had given instructions to local law enforcement officers for Freedom Summer, encouraging them to do their "dead-level best to maintain law and order" as they had been "proud" to do in the past. The public safety commissioner recommended plans of action for "out-of-state" or "impostor" defense attorneys or for "agitators" or "intruders" who wished to worship at certain churches. He also pushed for them to create an "intelligence network," to update their riot gear, and to make sure they could handle "mass numbers of prisoners." T. B. Birdsong, Mississippi Commissioner of Public Safety, to All Law Enforcement Officers, 9 June 1964, Folder 7: "Highway Patrol Reports and Correspondence, June 1964," Box 144, Series II, Sub-Series 10: Highway Patrol, Johnson Papers, University of Southern Mississippi.

On this fateful night, President Johnson turned in at 11:15 P.M. About 45 minutes later in eastern Mississippi, the three civil rights activists paid a $20 bond for Chaney on the speeding charge and were released from the Neshoba County Jail. Escorted out of town by Deputy Sheriff Cecil Price and a Philadelphia patrolman around 12:30 A.M. (EDT), Chaney directed their 1963 Ford Fairlane station wagon along state Highway 19 toward Meridian. Within minutes, Price reappeared behind them, this time with a carload of violent white extremists at his rear. In an apparent attempt to outmaneuver Price, Chaney veered onto another road, Highway 492. Price soon turned on his flashing lights, and Chaney pulled over. The deputy transferred the activists to his cruiser and motored back to Highway 19. Not far ahead, he and the caravan made a left onto a dirt lane known as Rock Cut Road. Here, according to the FBI interviews of two conspirators, the gang that had followed behind Price took Schwerner, then Goodman, and then Chaney out of Price's car and shot them to death at close range. A few men placed the bodies back into the activists' Ford station wagon, with FBI witness Doyle Barnette claiming that his contribution was merely wedging Chaney's lifeless foot into the vehicle. The men buried them six miles southwest of Philadelphia in a new earthen dam at the Old Jolly Farm, a piece of property owned by a truck driver and entrepreneur.[7] Over the next six weeks, their disappearance became the central focus of the FBI's "Miburn" investigation, the shortened name for a case better known as "Mississippi Burning."

That same night in Williamsburg, Virginia, Prime Minister İsmet İnönü of Turkey settled into the first night of his first visit to the United States since John Kennedy's assassination. İnönü was in political turmoil at home and had flown to the United States to enlist Washington's support for his efforts to protect Turks on the Greek-dominated island in the Mediterranean.[8] In Massachusetts, 32-year-old Senator Edward Kennedy lay immobilized in a hospital room, confined to a Stryker spinal support

---

7. Grand Jury Charges in *U.S. v. Cecil Ray Price, et al.*, 23 January 1965, Folder 8, Box 2, M368, Michael J. Miller Civil Rights Collection, McCain Library and Archives, University of Southern Mississippi; Federal Bureau of Investigation, "Miburn Prosecutive Summary" of the case "Bernard L. Akin, et al.; James Earl Chaney, Michael Henry Schwerner, aka Mickey, Andrew Goodman—Victims," 19 December 1964, File 44.25706, http://foia.fbi.gov/miburn/miburn3.pdf, pp. ii–iv, 142, 170–90, 215–55 (principally the interviews of conspirators Doyle Barnette and James Jordan). A compelling, though often speculative, narrative of 21 June by two historical journalists is Seth Cagin and Philip Dray, *We Are Not Afraid: The Story of Goodman, Schwerner, and Chaney and the Civil Rights Campaign for Mississippi* (New York: Macmillan, 1988), pp. 278–301.
8. "Inonu to Seek Partition," *New York Times*, 21 June 1964.

machine after a tragic airplane crash on June 20. In response to this latest family tragedy, Robert Kennedy was debating whether to abandon his own plans to run for the U.S. Senate in New York. Half a world away, the U.S. presence in Saigon was undergoing two major changes. Outgoing U.S. Ambassador Henry Cabot Lodge was handing off his diplomatic duties to Maxwell Taylor, who would leave his position as chairman of the Joint Chiefs of Staff. Feeling the pull of the Republican Party in an election year, Lodge had decided to return to the United States to assist Pennsylvania Governor William Scranton's recently announced bid for the Republican presidential nomination. Meanwhile, General William Westmoreland was in the second day of his almost four-year command of U.S. military operations in Vietnam, taking over the Military Assistance Command, Vietnam (MACV), from General Paul Harkins.

It is not clear when Lyndon Johnson first heard about the missing civil rights activists, but news of their disappearance began moving slowly toward the White House when Chaney, Schwerner, and Goodman failed to check in promptly with fellow activists on the night of June 21.[9] Around 7:30 P.M. (EDT), staffers of the Council of Federated Organizations (COFO)—a coalition of civil rights organizations in Mississippi that had been the principal organizer of Freedom Summer—started making calls to local jails, including the one actually holding their colleagues. None of them proved fruitful, however.[10] At midnight (EDT) on June 22, according to a detailed chronology compiled by COFO workers, COFO reported Chaney, Schwerner, and Goodman as missing to FBI Special Agent H. F. Helgesen in Jackson, Mississippi. Thirty minutes later, a similar call went to Frank Schwelb, a Justice Department attorney with the Civil Rights Division who was in Meridian. At 1:00 A.M., John Doar, the administration's key liaison in several southern civil rights incidents and an assis-

---

9. A memorandum of a meeting between Lee White, Bill Moyers, Jack Valenti, and Richard Goodwin failed to mention the disappearance, but did list several detailed strategies for "generating an atmosphere of compliance and acceptance of the Civil Rights Bill." Lee C. White to President Johnson, 22 June 1964, "HU 2/ST 24 1/1/64–7/16/64" folder, Box 26, White House Central Files: Human Rights 2/ST, Lyndon B. Johnson Library. On Mickey Schwerner's tendency to report in promptly, see Rita L. Schwerner, Affidavit, *COFO v. L.A. Rainey, et al.*, 29 July 1964, p. 3, Folder 11: "Lauderdale County, 1964," Box 3, Council of Federated Organizations Records, Mississippi Department of Archives and History.

10. In addition to local groups from Mississippi, the primary organizations involved with COFO were the Congress of Racial Equality, the Student Nonviolent Coordinating Committee, the Southern Christian Leadership Conference, and the National Association for the Advancement of Colored People. This incarnation of COFO began in 1962 as part of the Voter Education Project (VEP) sponsored by the Southern Regional Council and encouraged by the Kennedy Administration.

tant to Assistant Attorney General Burke Marshall, first received word of the disappearance from the Atlanta office of the Student Nonviolent Coordinating Committee (SNCC), followed up by more contact early in the morning. At 8:00 A.M., he announced to SNCC, one of the chief components of COFO, that he had "invested the FBI with the power to look into this matter." Fifty-five minutes later, the Jackson COFO office reached the Philadelphia jail and were told that the men had been let go after supper at 8:00 P.M. (EDT), a time frame that the Neshoba County Sheriff Lawrence Rainey affirmed.[11] Rainey also claimed to have been caring for his hospitalized wife the night before and had known nothing about the disappearance until reporters called him early this morning.[12]

Communications intensified just before noon. At the White House just before noon, Associate Counsel Lee White received a request for an expanded investigation from CORE National Director James Farmer. A few minutes later, Doar took a brief break to receive the Distinguished Federal Civilian Service Award from President Johnson in a Flower Garden ceremony.[13] He and White remained busy with calls on the matter through the afternoon. At 7:20 P.M., some progress had occurred at the local level in Mississippi; Doar announced that the Mississippi Highway Patrol issued an all-points bulletin for Chaney, Goodman, and Schwerner. By 8:00 P.M., Lee White claimed that a "full scale search was on."[14] By 11:30 P.M., the FBI had four agents in Neshoba County, all of them from

---

11. Council of Federated Organizations, "COFO Contacts with Neshoba County Law Enforcement Officers in the Schwerner-Cheney [sic]-Goodman Case," and "The Philadelphia, Mississippi Case, Chronology of Contact with Agents of the Federal Government," Folder 16: "Depositions, Neshoba County, 1964," Box 3, Council of Federated Organizations Records, Z/1867.000/S, Mississippi Department of Archives and History. Other locations of the federal contact chronology are Lee White to Nicholas Katzenbach, 6 July 1964, "Civil Rights—Mississippi" folder, Office Files of Lee White, Box 6, White House Central Files, Lyndon B. Johnson Library; and Michal R. Belknap, *Civil Rights, the White House, and the Justice Department, 1945–1968*, vol. 10, *Racial Violence and Law Enforcement in the South* (New York: Garland, 1991), pp. 283–87.
12. A. L. Hopkins, Mississippi Sovereignty Commission investigator, "Continued investigation of the disappearance of the three civil rights workers after they were released from the Neshoba County jail at 10:30 P.M., Sunday, June 21, 1964," 3 July 1964, Folder 1, July 1964, Box 136, Series II, Sub-Series 9: Sovereignty Commission, Johnson Papers, University of Southern Mississippi. The FBI's heavily redacted report on Rainey's alibi is found in Federal Bureau of Investigation, "Miburn Prosecutive Summary," of the case "Bernard L. Akin, et al.; James Earl Chaney, Michael Henry Schwerner, aka Mickey, Andrew Goodman—Victims," 19 December 1964, File 44.25706, http://foia.fbi.gov/miburn/miburn8.pdf, pp. 880–908.
13. Other recipients were a naval researcher, the CIA's comptroller, and the executive secretary of the National Security Council.
14. Lee White, "Memorandum to the Files: Disappearance of Three Participants in Mississippi Project," 23 June 1964, "Civil Rights—Mississippi" folder, Box 6, Office Files of Lee White, White House Central Files, Lyndon B. Johnson Library.

the New Orleans office, with the United Press International news service soon reporting their arrival. The FBI's top inspector, Joseph Sullivan, arrived about the same time, making his way down from Memphis. The next morning, June 23, COFO's Meridian office notified its headquarters that two FBI agents had come around and that Mickey Schwerner's father was set to meet with White House Counsel Lee White.[15]

While communications flowed back and forth between COFO, CORE, Lee White, and the Justice Department on June 22, President Johnson seemed to remain insulated from events in the Magnolia State. Dominating his schedule was the visit of Prime Minister İnönü and other ceremonial duties, including a fete celebrating the 400th anniversary of Shakespeare's birthday. The major issues beyond the Turk-Greek tension were the decision to send Maxwell Taylor to Saigon, some federal appointments issues, the Medicare bill, and the timing of Johnson's anticipated signing of the Civil Rights Act.[16]

On June 23, almost a dozen other pressing matters divided Johnson's attention. The President found that he had to address squabbles in the Democratic Party ranks at the state level and fleshed out the agenda for the Democratic National Convention. Worried about both the fall election and southern racial violence, he also held several discussions about potential appointees to head the civil rights compliance agency known as the Community Relations Service. Concerned that Democrats might force Robert Kennedy onto him as a running mate, Johnson asked presidential confidant Clark Clifford and Democratic National Committee liaison Clifton Carter to gauge Robert Kennedy's political strength, especially in California, New York, Pennsylvania, and New Jersey. Johnson also took time to donate a swath of federal land to the state of New Jersey for a recreational park and conferred with Treasury Secretary Douglas Dillon about debt-limit legislation and congressional support for an excise tax amendment. Over the next ten days, Johnson spent much time in pitched struggles with Republicans and conservative Democrats on things such

---

15. Council of Federated Organizations, "The Philadelphia, Mississippi Case, Chronology of Contact with Agents of the Federal Government," Folder 16: "Depositions, Neshoba County, 1964," Box 3, Council of Federated Organizations Records, Z/1867.000/S, Mississippi Department of Archives and History; other locations of the chronology are "Civil Rights—Mississippi" folder, Office Files of Lee White, Box 6, White House Central Files, Lyndon B. Johnson Library; and Belknap, *Civil Rights, the White House, and the Justice Department, 1945–1968*, vol. 10, *Racial Violence and Law Enforcement in the South*, pp. 283–87.

16. See Guian A. McKee, ed., *The Presidential Recordings, Lyndon B. Johnson: Mississippi Burning and the Passage of the Civil Rights Act, June 1, 1964–July 4, 1964*, vol. 7, *June 1, 1964–June 22, 1964* (New York: Norton, 2011).

as foreign aid, mass transit, and the War on Poverty. In all, he was closely tracking 31 pieces of pending legislation with his typically meticulous eye for detail and mastery of the legislative process.[17] In foreign policy matters on this day, he continued to focus on Cyprus while also assessing ambassadorial candidates, touching base with Defense Secretary McNamara about defense appropriations and reconnaissance flights over Laos and ruminating over the direction of policy in Vietnam. In a blending of foreign and domestic policy battles, Johnson stood tough in a long-term struggle against conservatives who opposed foreign aid spending.

Toward the end of this day, he would ensure that pork barrel rewards went to Senate Minority Leader Everett Dirksen, the key Republican convert to the Civil Rights Act, while also haggling with the senator over excise taxes. To do so, the President personally lobbied an Army Corps of Engineers bureaucrat to check up on one of Dirksen's favored projects. Johnson's skills as a master legislator would be secondary today, however. A series of calls about Schwerner, Chaney, and Goodman dominated his agenda by the early afternoon, as he considered ways to intensify the investigation and to respond to anxious parents of children presumed to be dead.

8:45 A.M.: President Johnson began this Tuesday with his traditional sit-down breakfast with Democratic leaders from Capitol Hill.[18]

10:10 A.M.: Walked the group to the Oval Office, stopping briefly in the hall to take a picture with New Orleans Congressman Hale Boggs and Orleans Parish (Louisiana) District Attorney Jim Garrison, a man who would later gain national prominence as a driven investigator of the Kennedy assassination.

10:20 A.M.: Prepared for a morning press conference regarding Maxwell Taylor's appointment as U.S. Ambassador to South Vietnam. Attending the prep session were White House aides and advisers from the National Security Council, State Department, and Defense Department.

11:00 A.M.: Returned to the Oval Office with National Security Special Assistant McGeorge Bundy and close aide Jack Valenti. Johnson conferred with Press Secretary George Reedy before the press conference began.

---

17. Conversation between President Johnson and Larry O'Brien, 5:57 P.M., 1 July 1964, in this volume.

18. The leaders included Speaker of the House John McCormack, House Majority Leader Carl Albert, House Majority Whip Hale Boggs, Senate President Pro Tem Carl Hayden, Senator George Smathers, and Senate Majority Leader Hubert Humphrey. Also attending were aides Walter Jenkins, Bill Moyers, Larry O'Brien, Kenny O'Donnell, George Reedy, and Jack Valenti.

11:01 A.M.

From George Reedy[19]

McGeorge Bundy: . . . This is one that I put him up to.
Marie Fehmer interrupts to report that Reedy is on the line.
George Reedy: . . . set, Mr. President, should I bring them [the report-ers] in?
President Johnson: Well, let me see.
[*to Bundy*] Mac, are we ready to go?
Bundy: Yes, we are.
President Johnson: Give me my stuff there, then.
[*to Reedy*] OK.
Reedy: OK.

11:02 A.M.: President Johnson made an unrecorded call on his personal line to Jack Valenti (Valenti had gone to his nearby office).
11:04 A.M.–11:30 A.M.: Welcomed reporters to the Oval Office for an unannounced press conference.

Most of the questions at the press conference dealt with Vietnam, but toward the end, Johnson answered one about the missing civil rights activists from James "Scotty" Reston, the *New York Times* columnist and Washington bureau chief. The President asserted that he had ordered the FBI to "spare no effort" and that he had made requests for additional personnel several weeks earlier.[20]

Several times later in the day, Johnson would reiterate his claim that he had already requested a larger federal presence in Mississippi in antici-pation of Freedom Summer. Although many found that claim unconvinc-ing because that new federal presence was hard to find, Johnson offered a subtle explanation to Lee White and to the Speaker of the House: Most of the "FBI men" he had ordered were supposed to be there as under-

***

19. Tape WH6406.13, Citation #3814, Recordings of Telephone Conversations—White House Series, Recordings and Transcripts of Conversations and Meetings, Lyndon B. Johnson Library.
20. "The President's News Conference," 23 June 1964, *Public Papers of the Presidents of the United States, Lyndon B. Johnson, 1963–64* (Washington, DC: Government Printing Office [hereafter GPO], 1965), 1:802–8.

cover "informers" and infiltrators.[21] Johnson's claims remain a point of contention among historians, but there is additional evidence that at least one week before the Freedom Summer disappearances, he had asked Lee White to outline the legal and bureaucratic options available to the White House for a response to the "highly explosive situation."[22]

With the signing of the Civil Rights Act imminent, the Johnson administration had made serious efforts to try to limit white violence all over the South. In the previous week alone, Johnson and his advisers had pressured local officials to curtail brutal white attacks on blacks in St. Augustine, Florida. The potential for violence in Mississippi, however, dwarfed that of the Sunshine State. Over the past decade, the murders of Emmett Till, George Lee, Mack Charles Parker, Herbert Lee, and Medgar Evers—for which there had been no convictions—had been front-page news and were still well known to the Justice Department. In the past two years, activists in the federally supported Voter Education Project there had endured severe persecution and attacks. In the previous four months alone, Attorney General Robert Kennedy had identified 40 "instances of Klan-type activity or police brutality" in Mississippi. He was so concerned about the increase in "acts of terrorism" that he recently sent Assistant Attorney General Burke Marshall there on a fact-finding mission. Based on Marshall's findings, Kennedy suggested that the President have the FBI produce a detailed report on the Ku Klux Klan and other white supremacist groups before the end of June.[23]

For the Freedom Summer activists, though, the official word from the administration was that the federal government could guarantee them no protection, a message John Doar personally delivered to them. This information—and other internal Freedom Summer happenings— was quickly filtered to Mississippi officials through an informant in the

---

21. See conversations between President Johnson and John McCormack, 12:45 P.M., 23 June 1964, in this chapter; and President Johnson and Lee White, 12:35 P.M., 23 June 1964, in this chapter. On 8 April, Lee White had recommended adding more federal marshals to Mississippi as a "stabilizing influence." Lee C. White to President Johnson, 8 April 1964, "HU 2/ST 24 1/1/64–7/16/64" folder, Box 26, White House Central Files: Human Rights 2/ST, Lyndon B. Johnson Library.

22. Lee White to Burke Marshall, 17 June 1964, "PL/ST 24" folder, Box 53, White House Central Files: Political Affairs, Mississippi (Mississippi Freedom Democratic Party), Lyndon B. Johnson Library.

23. Robert F. Kennedy to President Johnson, 21 May 1964, "3/26/64–5/24/64" folder, Box 2, White House Central Files: Human Rights 2, Lyndon B. Johnson Library. For Marshall's list of incidents, see Burke Marshall to Dan H. Shell, 15 July 1964, Folder 1, July 1964, Box 136, Series II, Sub-Series 9: Sovereignty Commission, Johnson Papers, University of Southern Mississippi.

group working for the Mississippi State Sovereignty Commission, the state-sponsored antisubversive, anti–civil rights intelligence-gathering organization.[24]

> **11:35 A.M.–11:49 A.M.:** Off-the-record talk with Reston in the lounge. President Johnson also arranged for flowers to go to the son of Hubert Humphrey, who had recently had a cancerous tumor removed from his neck.
>
> **11:49 A.M.:** On his way back to the Oval Office, stopped to chat with Lee White, who was in Special Assistant Kenny O'Donnell's office.

White later recollected that he took this opportunity to tell Johnson that the parents of Schwerner and Goodman had requested a face-to-face meeting with the President and recommended that he comply. Only days earlier, White had marveled to President Johnson how "nearly incredible" it was that "those people who are voluntarily sticking their head into the lion's mouth would ask for somebody to come down and shoot the lion."[25] The disappearance of the three young men, though, had helped shift his thinking. Johnson responded by turning his attention to Jack Valenti and berating him for having his feet on his desk and talking on the telephone too much.[26] The politics of granting this request remained the major issue for the rest of the afternoon. With the considerable exception of Robert Kennedy, most of Johnson's advisers recommended that he avoid such encounters.

> **11:54 A.M.:** Before leaving for a noon-hour speech, met with Nevada Governor Grant Sawyer, the chairman of the National Governor's Conference. The governor delivered a report from the conference, offered his endorsement of Johnson for the fall election, and discussed Democratic Party matters.

---

24. Informant's report from Oxford, Ohio, and Jackson, Mississippi, 26 June 1964, Folder 10, June 1964, Box 135, Series II, Sub-Series 9: Sovereignty Commission, Johnson Papers, University of Southern Mississippi; Yasuhiro Katagiri, *The Mississippi State Sovereignty Commission: Civil Rights and States' Rights* (Jackson: University Press of Mississippi, 2001). The Sovereignty Commission files were made available to the public in March 1998 after two decades of litigation. They are available at the Mississippi Department of Archives and History (MDAH) in Jackson, Mississippi, and on the MDAH's Web site, http://www.mdah.state.ms.us/arlib/contents/er/sovcom/.

25. Lee C. White to President Johnson, 17 June 1964, "HU 2/ST 24 1/1/64–7/16/64" folder, Office Files of Lee White, Box 26, White House Central Files: Human Rights 2/ST, Lyndon B. Johnson Library.

26. Transcript, Lee C. White, Oral History Interview, 18 February 1971, Lyndon B. Johnson Library, p. 6–7.

12:02 P.M.: Left for Constitution Hall to speak to the Occupational Safety Conference, where he was met by Labor Secretary Willard Wirtz and Labor Assistant Secretary Esther Peterson.[27]
12:25 P.M.: Returned to the Oval Office.
12:30 P.M.: Called Walter Jenkins.

At some point, the Dictabelt recorder picked up the following fragment of a conversation about returning a call to CORE's national director, James Farmer. The secretary is most likely Juanita Roberts.

TIME UNKNOWN

With White House Secretary[28]

President Johnson: . . . Something like that. You oughtn't to—quit dealing in these murder cases. Because I—you make me call him back.
White House Secretary: Yes, sir.

12:35 P.M.

To Lee White[29]

The first lengthy civil rights–related recording of the day focused on the issues raised at the press conference and the disappearance of the three activists. Johnson and White discussed how to respond to a request for a meeting by James Farmer and how to approach the Mississippi issue with the National Association for the Advancement of Colored People (NAACP), which was then holding its annual meeting three blocks behind the White House at the Statler Hilton Hotel.

---

27. "Remarks to the President's Conference on Occupational Safety," 23 June 1964, *Public Papers, Johnson, 1963–64,* 1:808–10.
28. Tape WH6406.13, Citation #3817, Recordings of Telephone Conversations—White House Series, Recordings and Transcripts of Conversations and Meetings, Lyndon B. Johnson Library.
29. Tape WH6406.13, Citation #3818, Recordings of Telephone Conversations—White House Series, Recordings and Transcripts of Conversations and Meetings, Lyndon B. Johnson Library.

President Johnson: I asked [FBI Director J. Edgar] Hoover last . . . two weeks ago after talking to the Attorney General [Robert Kennedy] to fill up Mississippi with FBI [Federal Bureau of Investigation] men and infiltrate everything he could; that they haul them in by the dozens; that I've asked him to put more men after these three kids; that he hauled them in last night.

Lee White: Right.

President Johnson: That I've asked him for another report today; that I'm shoving it as much as I know how; that I didn't ask them to go, and I can't control the actions of Mississippi people. The only weapon I have for locating them is the FBI. I haven't got any state police or any constables, and the FBI is better than marshals, and I've got all of them I've got looking after them. I can't find them myself. That I think it's pretty dangerous that they'll overrun the White House. Because anybody that wants a conference with the President, all they've got to do is send his kid to Mississippi and then demand a conference with the President. And I think that's [an] awfully bad precedent for the President, to be seeing individual groups. I just think that . . . Every damn woman that gets indicted will be wanting to see him. Or everybody that gets arrested will be wanting to see him. And no telling where we'll ever stop it. Congressmen will get to come in, get their picture made coming in and out of the White House. And it'll just be *hell*.[30] But tell him [James Farmer] that we're doing everything we know how to do with the FBI and see if he's got any other constructive suggestion.

White: OK.

President Johnson: And then tell him if . . . you . . . I've got a luncheon on. Tell him the Prime Minister of Turkey [İsmet İnönü] is here, and I've got lots of problems, but if he [James Farmer] needs to talk to me after you've talked to him, that you'll get me to call him if you . . .

White: All right.

President Johnson: . . . if you can, and ask him—find out what I want to say to him because I want to be awful careful what I say to this fellow.

White: I agree. He seems fairly responsible, but it's murder dealing with these people on the telephone. But I've got the message, and I'll call him right away.

President Johnson: Here's what he said to [White House secretary] Juanita [Roberts]: "I want to express personally to the President my con-

---

30. The 30-second section from "That I think" to "be *hell*" was excised under deed of gift restriction until opened in October 2003.

cern about the disappearance of the three people in Mississippi. Familiar with the case?" Juanita: "Yes." "Two of them are our staff members, and I'm on my way down to Mississippi now to look at the situation personally. I'd hoped to be able to chat with the President about it."

White: Mm-hmm.

President Johnson: Juanita: "Yes, he's left a meeting to go to Constitution Hall to address the safety group [President's Conference on Occupational Safety]. How long would you be available?" See, she's trying to promote a meeting with us because she's dumb. "Well, I'll be here in my office until 2:00. That number is Columbia 7-6270." Juanita: "He's got an awful tight schedule. I want to get in touch with him, tell him of your call." [James] Farmer: "Well, I'll appreciate it, and I'll be here until 2:30. Thank you very much."

White: All right, I'll call him right away.

President Johnson: Tell him Mrs. Roberts has just called you and asked you to get in touch with him. You're trying to convey his message to the President, and what is it he wants to convey, and what have we done, and tell him these parents are wanting to see you and that we have made an appointment for him with the FBI and with [Burke] Marshall, who can do something about it.[31]

White: Right.

President Johnson: And that I've given them already a standing order to stay on it day and night. Now, have you . . .

What do they think happened? Think they got killed?

White: Uhh . . . This morning they had absolutely no trace. There's no sign of the automobile. They have found nobody who's seen the car or the three people.

So as far as they're concerned, they've just disappeared from the face of the earth.

President Johnson: Now, you're waiting to reply—

White: This means murder, as they see it.

President Johnson: You're waiting to reply to [William] Ryan and [Ogden] Reid?[32]

White: They'll probably be calling me as . . . about 1:30 . . .

President Johnson: When do they have appointments with the Justice Department and the FBI?

White: Sometime in the order of between 2 [P.M.] and 3 [P.M.],

31. Burke Marshall was assistant attorney general for civil rights.
32. Democrat William Ryan and Republican Ogden Reid were representatives from New York, the home of two of the three missing civil rights workers.

depending upon when the plane gets in, and we've, you know, agreed to be as responsive as Burke Marshall's schedule will permit, and he's— probably in the order . . . sometime around 2:30.

President Johnson: All right. Tell them after they get through there, if they still want to talk to me about anything to call you.

White: All right.

President Johnson: Tell them I'm not in the office, and I'm off making a speech and attending a luncheon.

White: OK.

President Johnson: And that you'll be glad to see them, or if there's anything you can do, but that *all* the power's over with Burke Marshall and the FBI, and that's who they ought to be talking to. And it'll set a bad example if they all start coming here because the White House will be overrun with everybody who wants to get their picture made with the President.

White: All right, and—

President Johnson: The other thing: I think we ought to be pretty careful to tell them that we don't see people who tell the newspaper before they get an appointment.

White: Yeah, well, that's—

President Johnson: We've had a rule against that for years, seeing people who get in the newspaper before they get an appointment.

White: That really does rankle.[33]

President Johnson: Now, what . . . what shape are we in with Roy Wilkins?[34]

White: Roy's hope is that either he could bring—no announcement was made last night, by the way. They . . . they said OK, no announcement. Roy did not call me. He was supposed to call me this morning, and I assume he's been tied up in his own meeting, but his assistant, a fellow by the name of [John] Morsell, did. And he said that, you know, if Roy can bring his whole [NAACP executive] board of 30 members, fine . . .[35]

President Johnson: That's good.

White: If he can't bring them, why, you know—

President Johnson: [*Unclear*] that's good. Tell him that'd be very good. I'd like to meet them, and we'll meet them in the Cabinet Room.

---

33. The 26-second section from "And it'll" to "does rankle" was excised under deed of gift restriction until opened in October 2003.
34. Roy Wilkins was executive director of the NAACP.
35. Johnson held an off-the-record meeting with the NAACP Board of Directors and vice presidents the next day at 5:48 P.M. in the Cabinet Room.

White: He says that they are Roy's employer, basically, that he's executive director, and . . .

President Johnson: That's fine. Well, I'd be glad to—

White: Makes sense.

President Johnson: I'd be glad to meet them, and tell him I want to tell them I think he's one of the most valuable citizens in this country, and I'll tell them that, my judgment.

White: I think that's wonderful.

President Johnson: And just tell him I'm anxious to meet with them. I want to help the cause, though, and to keep out of the newspapers. Just come on over, and we'll have a meeting like we did with [John] Kennedy on civil rights.[36]

White: Would you believe it desirable to send a little formal message to their meeting so it would be incorporated into their minutes of their convention?

President Johnson: I don't think so. I think the best thing to do is meet with them here.

White: OK.

President Johnson: Talk to them, and . . . Where is the best way to get them in without getting the press?

White: We can bus them in and bring them in through the Southwest Gate. There's enough of them that it'll warrant taking one bus, and—

President Johnson: Bring them in the Southwest Gate and take them to the Cabinet Room.

White: Yeah. And that's set for tomorrow at 5:30 [P.M.].

President Johnson: [*Unclear*] talk to him, and you tell him that let's keep out of the newspapers so we won't have every one of these groups coming in. Tell him every labor union comes [to Washington, D.C.] to have a convention, every bankers association, every one of them want to have a meeting with the President.

White: They sure do.

President Johnson: I'm meeting with them, but I'm keeping it off the record. Tell them there's 1,700 of them here.

White: That's right: They've got a big gang. There's no question about it—

President Johnson: I know all the labor unions want to meet with me,

---

36. For a 72-page report on Kennedy meetings on desegregation, see "List of Persons Who Attended Meetings With President Kennedy at White House With Respect to Voluntary Desegregation," "HU 2 7/28/64–8/20/64" folder, Box 3, White House Central Files: Human Rights, Lyndon B. Johnson Library.

and I've told them that I have to meet with the boards, but keep it out of the papers.

White: Fair enough, and they were extremely understanding and cooperative last night when I said that, you know, there wasn't any reason that we could see to announce an off-the-record meeting. It didn't help anything; it only added to the number of requests and the burdens, and they said no strain at all, they're glad to do it.

The high spot of Wilkins's speech last night was his statement about all of the . . . his people he's sure would remember Senator [Barry] Goldwater with a special vengeance, and apparently that stopped the whole [NAACP] convention right there.[37]

President Johnson: OK.

White: All right, sir.

President Johnson: You let me know, now, what we have to do about these other folks. I think I'll call the Speaker [John McCormack] and see if he can't talk to Ryan and Reid and ask them if they want to start the President's interviewing all these parents. I think that's pretty bad to see—

White: I'd say that this guy Ryan is a tough cookie to deal with. He was really unreasonable, and I'm not sure you've read it yet, but a memo to the files: He called at midnight last night to tell me that there were three kids missing in Mississippi and what were we doing about it.[38] And . . .

President Johnson: When did we have the FBI in there, yesterday afternoon?

White: Well, it really started yesterday morning about 11:30.

President Johnson: After the kids?

White: After the kids, yeah.

President Johnson: How many did they move in?

White: They began moving yesterday afternoon and moved in all night the extra people, but the people on the scene started at sometime around 11:30 [A.M.] or 12 [P.M.] yesterday.

President Johnson: Find out from Burke Marshall how many they got in, in response to my request the other day and how many they sent in yesterday.

---

37. Barry Goldwater (R-Arizona) was a front-runner for the Republican nomination for the fall presidential election.

38. Lee White, "Memorandum to the Files: Disappearance of Three Participants in Mississippi Project," 23 June 1964, "Civil Rights—Mississippi" folder, Office Files of Lee White, Box 6, White House Central Files, Lyndon B. Johnson Library.

White: All right, and what they have also arranged is to use the facilities and the equipment of the [Meridian] naval air base nearby.[39] They've got helicopters, and these are made available to the FBI for scouring the countryside. We've got quite a few things to report in the way of constructive action.

President Johnson: All right, tell Farmer what you've done and make a list of those things for me.

White: All right, sir.

President Johnson: OK.

White: Yes, sir.

12:40 P.M.

From George Reedy[40]

Since taking office, President Johnson had demonstrated frequent sensitivity to any criticism from the White House press corps and had taken an active role in responding to them. In this conversation, Johnson defended his handling of the morning's sessions.

President Johnson: Yeah?

George Reedy: Mr. President?

President Johnson: Yeah.

Reedy: I have a request whether you would do the [Henry Cabot] Lodge statement for film.

President Johnson: Yeah.

Reedy: You would, sir?

President Johnson: Yeah.

Reedy: OK, sir, about when?

President Johnson: Just put it on the tele[prompter] . . . put it on the teleprompter, [the] letter, the whole outfit. Yeah, I'll do it anytime you get it ready. Get it ready by teleprompter, right quick.

Reedy: OK, and how about the Southeast Asian policy statement too?

President Johnson: If they want it, yeah.

---

39. The Navy maintained an Auxiliary Air Station in Meridian, approximately 50 miles from Philadelphia.

40. Tape WH6406.13, Citation #3819, Recordings of Telephone Conversations—White House Series, Recordings and Transcripts of Conversations and Meetings, Lyndon B. Johnson Library.

Reedy: OK, sir.

President Johnson: But put in there a little bit different. Just say, "I have repeatedly stated our policy in Southeast Asia, as I . . . as General [Dwight] Eisenhower—as President Eisenhower did ten years ago. The policy has not changed. I repeat it again."

Reedy: Right. You bet.

President Johnson: [*to someone in the office*] OK. That's fine.

[*to Reedy*] Put that on [the] teleprompter right quick.

Reedy: Right.

President Johnson: Any other news?

Reedy: No, sir, I sent you in a list with all of the names on it who asked the questions, and . . .

President Johnson: All right. Now you be sure that you and [Mac] Kilduff get out [that] they had 19 questions.[41] And [if] any of them ask you anytime about a press conference, just say, "Now, when he has anything that justifies announcing, when he calls one and doesn't, y'all criticize him and say that it's not presidential caliber. Now, he doesn't want to dodge a question. If you've got any you want to ask him, I'll submit it right now. Get it for you in two minutes."

Reedy: Right.

President Johnson: "But until he has some announcement, he doesn't want to take your time. He doesn't mind taking his, but he doesn't want to just be calling, because you'll go out and write a story that he issued a bunch of announcements that the bureaus would normally issue." Just say, "We had a good deal of economic stuff this morning that he wanted to give. It's *very* significant. It's *very* important. But he didn't give it because he doesn't want you raising hell about . . ."

And I don't care: I'll give it to them fast or slow. I give it to them fast so that they won't say I used all the time, and they can have more questions, but when I do that, then they want me to go slow, so I went slow this morning. But they don't know what they want. And if they'll just tell me, I guess the thing—the rule now will be give them all opening statements real slow on the advice, the request, of Helen Thomas.[42] And let's let them know that we're going to go slow enough with them because . . . and they *always* refer to our press conferences as quickies. Well, we . . . when we have an announcement, we make it.

---

41. Malcolm "Mac" Kilduff was assistant press secretary.
42. Helen Thomas was a United Press International (UPI) White House correspondent.

We consider that a compliment, but they ought to quit acting like they're children. I don't know why we ought to give them a day notice to think up a question. They're supposed to be intelligent. They expect me to answer it on the spur of the moment, they ought to be able to ask it. Besides, they can accumulate their questions and put them in their ass pocket and write on them if they want to, accumulate them so when I do call on them, they're prepared. But there's no reason why I ought to give them a *day's* notice because I don't know a day ahead of time. Do they want me to delay the Lodge thing a day, or do they want me to give it to them when I got it?

Reedy: Well, this—

President Johnson: Both UP[I] [United Press International] and AP [Associated Press] spend a lot of time talking about the quickies, but I don't know why they don't want it as soon as I know it. Why they would want me to wait until tomorrow and give them all notice, I don't know why. OK.

Reedy: Yes, sir.

12:45 P.M.

To John McCormack[43]

Following up on McCormack's visit from this morning, Johnson spoke to the Speaker of the House about General Maxwell Taylor leaving the chairmanship of the Joint Chiefs of Staff to become ambassador to South Vietnam and U. Alexis Johnson's leaving his post as deputy under secretary of state for political affairs to be Taylor's deputy in Saigon. Johnson then spread the word about his proclaimed use of the FBI in Mississippi and addressed the pressure he was receiving from New York Democrat William Fitts Ryan and New York Republican Ogden Reid to see the parents of the missing white activists. Johnson also took the opportunity to complain about Republican obstructions to his Great Society agenda, particularly from House Minority Leader Charles Halleck.

---

43. Tape WH6406.13, Citations #3820 and #3821, Recordings of Telephone Conversations—White House Series, Recordings and Transcripts of Conversations and Meetings, Lyndon B. Johnson Library.

John McCormack: . . . secretary?

President Johnson: Alexis Johnson, same as the President, Johnson, J-o-h-n-s-o-n.

McCormack: E-l-i-x-i-s [*sic*]?

President Johnson: Yes. He is the outstanding, foremost expert in Southeast Asia, and it's going to be a real blow to us here, as is the chairman of the Joint Chiefs [of Staff, Maxwell Taylor]. But some of them will say it's too much military, so I put him out there to balance it, give us political, and I want the military to work with [Nguyen] Khanh because they got a military president and try to get his cooperation.[44] If he falls over, as he may any day, have another coup, we're through in Asia, and I'm trying to get a man [who] can lead him and give him advice.

I called you because we got a very dangerous and bad precedent shaping up, irresponsibility of some of these House members, a fellow named [William] Ryan and Ogden Reid. Uh . . .

McCormack: Who? Ryan?

President Johnson: Ryan.

McCormack: What Ryan?

President Johnson: Uh . . . from New York.

McCormack: What about him?

President Johnson: Well, he's a damn fool. That's first. [*McCormack attempts to speak.*] F-double-o-l.

McCormack: Well, [*unclear*] new to that.

President Johnson: F-double-o-l.

McCormack: He's one of the—He's nothing but [*unclear*].

President Johnson: He called at midnight last night. Midnight, now. And got ahold of my assistant [Lee White] and demanded we do something about these three kids that . . . these Jewish boys from New York. They went off to Mississippi—

McCormack: He just made a speech to the floor of the House.[45]

President Johnson: And . . . what we have done in Mississippi is this: About three weeks ago, I called in Edgar Hoover and told him to fill Mississippi—I can't say this publicly—but load it down with FBI men and put them in every place they anticipate they can as informers and put them in the [Ku Klux] Klan and infiltrate it. Get them to join up—we

---

44. General Nguyen Khanh was Prime Minister of the Republic of Vietnam (South Vietnam). Five months earlier, on 30 January, he led a successful coup d'etat against General Duong Van Minh.

45. The 31-second section from "a fellow named Ryan" to "floor of the House" was excised under deed of gift restriction until opened in October 2003.

can't advertise this—but get all the informers they need so we know what's going on and that we can protect these kids as best we can. We don't recommend it, don't advise it, but they're going to do it anyway, and so we're going to give them as much protection as we can. So he shipped the FBI in there, and he's got them joining up on everything, and they're trying to get in a position where they can be helpful.

When these kids didn't show night before last, yesterday morning we sent a new bunch of FBI in to supplement them in numbers. We got the Defense Department to turn over the helicopters and the whole facilities of the [Meridian] Naval Air Station to the FBI, and the FBI is using these helicopters to guard all roads and fly over them and take pictures and try to locate these people.[46] The FBI has got two big groups that have gone in at my request, although I don't want to be appearing to be directing this thing and appear that I'm invading the state and taking the rights of a governor or mayor.

Nevertheless, I've quietly shown plenty of firmness and put plenty of power. That's the only power I have. The marshals couldn't do much about it. The FBI is the best people. Marshals are not investigative in nature and can't locate anybody. We've asked them for a report as quickly as they can get it.

Now, [William] Ryan calls up and tells my assistant Lee White at midnight, "What are you doing about it?" And he tells him what we're doing. And so this morning he demands that we start interviewing these parents. The parents have given out a statement up in New York that they're heading down to see Ryan and Ogden Reid, and they're going to the President. So all you'll have to do to have a picture made at the White House and have an hour conference with the President is just to send somebody to Mississippi [*unclear comments by McCormack*] and not let them show up, then you get your picture made.

We told them the place they ought to go is talk to the Justice Department that's surveying this. The President can't personally look after each child when there [are] a thousand of them down there, and he oughtn't to be a babysitter anyway. [*Unclear word by McCormack.*][47] He

---

46. Johnson's speech trails off. This word may be "few" instead of "people." On the matter of the air station, Lee White reported that James Farmer had alerted the administration on 22 June to the possible equipment at the Meridian base. Lee White, "Memorandum to the Files: Disappearance of Three Participants in Mississippi Project," 23 June 1964, "Civil Rights—Mississippi" folder, Office Files of Lee White, Box 6, White House Central Files, Lyndon B. Johnson Library.

47. McCormack seems to say, "No."

ought to establish policies.[48] And I've got 1,700 organizations in this town. Every damn one of them want me to address them, from the Chamber of Commerce to the NAACP.

McCormack: Knight of Columbus. Knights of Columbus. [*Laughs heartily.*]

President Johnson: NAACP. NAACP, they got me today, and the Safety Council, I just came from there, and I've got the Turkish ambassador, and I've got Bill Benton and Governor Grant Sawyer ahead of the governors, and Governor Richard Hughes and [Robert] McNamara and [Dean] Rusk and [McGeorge] Bundy and the Prime Minister of Turkey.[49] Now, that's my day, but—

McCormack: How are you going to get along with Greece and Turkey? You'll be a master magician [*unclear*].

President Johnson: Well, I got Turkey going all right. I don't know what'll happen to Greece, but I've got Turkey. I got them signed on yesterday, just confidentially. The Greeks [are] going to be awfully tough, but there can't be anything but failure, but it does put off war, and I put it off every day as long as I can. They had their ships on the way, and they were going to invade. And by God, those Turks will fight.

McCormack: Oh, oh yeah, they'll fight [*unclear*].

President Johnson: And I stopped it, and it took guts, but I stopped it. And I don't know whether I can stop it anymore or not. [*Unclear comment by McCormack.*] But if I do, I'll have my conscience clear: I did all I could to avoid bloodshed.

Anyway, Ryan and Reid[50] . . . so I think what you ought to do—it's up to you, and you-all know the House members better than I do—I think you ought to tell them that you cannot publicly say this . . .

McCormack: I wouldn't trust Ryan.

President Johnson: But that—

McCormack: He's one of that reform group up in New York.[51]

President Johnson: But that you think they ought to know that the

---

48. The 35-second section from "And so this morning" to "establish policies" was excised under deed of gift restriction until opened in October 2003.

49. Raymond Hare was the U.S. ambassador to Turkey. Bill Benton, the former Democratic senator from Connecticut (1949–1953), was U.S. ambassador to the United Nations Educational, Scientific and Cultural Organization. Grant Sawyer, a Democrat, was governor of Nevada, and Richard Hughes, a Democrat, was governor of New Jersey.

50. The 26-second section from "Well, I got Turkey" to "Ryan and Reid" was excised under deed of gift restriction until opened in October 2003.

51. Congressman Ryan had been one of several politicians supported by the New York Committee for Democratic Voters, better known as the Reform Democrats.

FBI and the Department of Justice under instructions have put all the people in there that they can put in there, and they're on the job 24 hours a day. [*McCormack makes several unclear comments throughout.*] And that the president oughtn't to be put into the position of seeing every family that comes in. I can't even see the Kennedys and express sympathy to Teddy. I mean, this is not just a sympathy operation: It's a pretty tough one, to head the government. And if these two come in, every damn one of them are going to come right in here, in the White House. The President of the United States [is] going to be sitting down, sympathizing with mothers and fathers.

McCormack: [*Unclear.*]

President Johnson: I don't know . . . I made an appointment with the FBI for them. I made an appointment with Burke Marshall, the assistant attorney general in civil rights, who has all the information, all the knowledge, and all the power. And there's not anything I can do besides that. But after you feel it out, if you think I've got to see them, well, I'll just have the congressman. I don't want to turn him down, but it's sure a bad precedent.

McCormack: Well, you're dealing with an odd stick there. He . . . he . . . they're . . . they . . . He's one of the . . . one of that reform group up there [*unclear*] state of mind. He has no consciousness—"We don't care." And you're dealing with . . . I . . . I would . . . I wouldn't want to talk to them unless you give me permission to do so.

President Johnson: Well, I'd give you permission.

McCormack: [*Unclear*] . . . be impossible.

President Johnson: What would be your recommendation? Now, he and Reid are the ones that are doing the calling.

McCormick: Well—

President Johnson: They want to get all the attention they can.

McCormack: Well, you're a busy man.

President Johnson: That's right, and they say if . . . I'm afraid that if you tell them without explaining it to them . . . I'm afraid that they'll get out and say, "Well, the President is hard-hearted. He has no concern about them. He said, 'Let them eat cake. To hell with them.'" But I think . . . I think on the other hand, if the Speaker said to them "Now, I understand you're interested in these parents. They're coming down here. I was down at [the congressional leadership] breakfast this morning. The President has issued the orders. He's done everything he can. It's up to Burke Marshall and the FBI. The President told me to tell you that he'd made appointments for these folks over there, and it's bad—"

McCormack: Who's that? Burke Marshall?

President Johnson: Burke Marshall. He's the assistant attorney general, in charge of civil rights. He's the ablest man in the government. [*Unclear comment by McCormack.*] And the FBI—we've made appointments with both of them—that if they go to bringing each individual case into the President of the United States, pretty soon he won't have time to select General Taylor. And if they still think you got to do it and you recommend it, I'll see them.

McCormack: Yeah, the press—well, I won't go that far. I'll be damned if [*unclear*] I won't. I'm not going [*unclear*]—I won't. I'll talk with them, diplomatically. But . . . you're dealing with a fellow who's—why, he even went into another Democratic colleague's district and campaigned against him.[52]

President Johnson: What do you think, then, I ought to do?

McCormack: I wouldn't see them. Just diplomatically, you haven't got time. You can handle that. In a day or two, it'll—they'll catch those three. They can't disappear forever, can they?

President Johnson: No, unless they've killed them.

McCormack: Unless they killed them, and then if they killed them, then other action is necessary.

President Johnson: You talk to them and call me as soon as you do.

McCormack: [*with the President acknowledging*] By the way, the press told me that [Henry Cabot] Lodge resigned, and they asked me for a statement, so I said, oh, "Weeks ago, I expected it." [*Chuckles.*] That's all I said.

President Johnson: Well, he's coming back to try to rescue the [Republican] Party from [Barry] Goldwater, that's what he's doing.

McCormack: I mentioned before, you know, just about what he'd do. You under—I'm not surprised at all. Then he'll come back, he'll have some goddamn thing to nibble at.

President Johnson: Mr. Speaker, I think that we ought to tell Charlie [Halleck]—now, I want y'all to tell him whatever you want to, and I'll support you. That's a matter for the House. I can't determine when they adjourn and when they don't.[53]

McCormack: I—

President Johnson: But I think we ought to tell Charlie this: I think we ought to say [*speaking in rapid-fire fashion*], "Charlie, you've been

---

52. The 2-minute-and-41-second section from "And that the President" to "campaigned against him" was excised under deed of gift restriction until opened in October 2003.
53. See the conversation between President Johnson and Charles Halleck, 6:24 P.M., 22 June 1964, in McKee, *Presidential Recordings, Johnson*, vol. 7, *June 1, 1964–June 22, 1964*, pp. 535–43.

leader, and you've had a program. We've got 31 bills. These bills have been delayed. They've been held up here. We couldn't meet on Friday; we can't meet on Saturday; we can't meet on Monday. Now, we've got problems with our people, and we're to blame for some of this ourselves. The President's to blame for some of it. *But* we think that we ought to have action on these bills. Now, we're willing to give you one week or two weeks or three weeks if you want it, if you'll get us some action. Now come here and sit down and see what you can do without delaying and without procrastinating and without just being an obstruction."

McCormack: Well, I've already talked with him this morning about antipoverty, and I also talked about the civil rights because we have to have at least two, probably three, but at least two Republican members to sign that petition for a meeting.[54] And he's going to have a meeting with them. Apparently [Clarence] Brown went out to Ohio yesterday, and [Ray] Bliss ousted him as national committeeman [*unclear*]—[55]

President Johnson: He did. He did, and Brown walked out mad as hell.

McCormack: [*Chuckles.*] When Brown's mad, he's mad. And he's going to have a meeting, and he's going to let us know tomorrow. And we particularly—I—Carl [Albert] and I spoke to him about antipoverty.[56]

President Johnson: OK.

McCormack: I'll do the best I can.

President Johnson: Bye. OK.

McCormack: Fine.

12:55 P.M.: President Johnson made a quick, unrecorded call to Walter Jenkins before talking to his press secretary about filming an announcement of the Lodge departure from South Vietnam.

---

54. Passed by the Senate on 19 June, the civil rights bill had come to the House for final approval on 22 June and awaited action by Howard "Judge" Smith, chairman of the House Rules Committee.

55. Congressman Clarence J. Brown Sr. had been Ohio's Republican national committeeman for 20 years, but he had been replaced one day before, on 22 June, by Ray C. Bliss, the Ohio GOP's state chairman.

56. The administration's antipoverty bill was stalled in the House Rules Committee, where Clarence Brown was the ranking Republican. Carl Albert (D-Oklahoma) was House majority leader.

12:57 P.M.

From George Reedy[57]

President Johnson: Yes, yes?

George Reedy: Can we do the film at 2:30 [P.M.] in the Cabinet Room, Mr. President?

President Johnson: Yeah.

Reedy: And could you . . . would it be all right for you to do this one sitting down, just as you did it for the press?

President Johnson: [*Pauses.*] I don't know whether I can use teleprompter sitting down very well or not.

Reedy: [*to someone in room*] He can use teleprompter, can't he, [*unclear*]?[58]

Unidentified: [*Unclear*] hold the teleprompter directly over the camera.

Reedy: [*to Johnson*] Yes, you'll have it directly over the camera, sir.

President Johnson: Yeah. All right, OK.

Reedy: You bet.

1:01 P.M.: While traveling to a different taping in the Cabinet Room—a message for a Fourth of July celebration in Denmark—Johnson spent two minutes browsing the afternoon newspapers.

1:07 P.M.: Returned to the Oval Office and took a call from Treasury Secretary Douglas Dillon.

1:08 P.M.

From Douglas Dillon[59]

Dillon updated the President on two matters before the Senate Finance Committee. One was a bill to raise the limit on national debt from $315

---

57. Tape WH6406.13, Citation #3822, Recordings of Telephone Conversations—White House Series, Recordings and Transcripts of Conversations and Meetings, Lyndon B. Johnson Library.
58. Reedy may also have said, "He can use teleprompter, Kenny?"
59. Tape WH6406.13, Citation #3823, Recordings of Telephone Conversations—White House Series, Recordings and Transcripts of Conversations and Meetings, Lyndon B. Johnson Library.

billion to $324 billion. The other was the Excise Tax Extension Act, designed to continue the excise tax provisions in the $11 billion tax cut bill passed in February.[60] The excise tax issue had long been a problem for Johnson. In January, several members of the Finance Committee had tried to reduce excise taxes on a number of goods and services, but Johnson feared those reductions would cut revenue too greatly. In a flurry of phone calls on January 23, Johnson had been able to turn enough votes to save his preferred version of the legislation.[61]

Shortly after this call began, Kenny O'Donnell and Jack Valenti came into the Oval Office.

President Johnson: [*aside to someone in office*] Tell them . . . [*connecting to Dillon*] Thank you.

Douglas Dillon: I just wanted to tell you I spent the morning testifying on the debt limit before the Finance Committee. I don't think there'll be any trouble there. But they're taking up also tomorrow, without hearings, this excise bill, and we're just about where we were last winter with that. We have [a] problem with [Harry] Byrd and—who just won't make up his mind—and also with [Abraham] Ribicoff, and I didn't know if in the case of Byrd, if it wouldn't be possible for maybe for you to, oh, say something to him about your interest in it.[62] We haven't been able to get a commitment out of him one way or the other.

President Johnson: Mm-hmm. All right, I'll sure try.

Dillon: [*Unclear*] vote on it.

President Johnson: I'll sure try, Doug.

Dillon: Harry Byrd, I mean, that's about the only one, otherwise—

President Johnson: Yeah. . . . All right. I talked to [George] Smathers about it this morning.[63]

Dillon: Yeah, well, I think he's fine. He's—

President Johnson: I asked him to please get him. Larry [O'Brien]

---

60. *Congressional Quarterly Almanac*, 88th Cong., 2nd sess., 1964, vol. 20 (Washington, DC: Congressional Quarterly Service, 1965), pp. 540, 582.
61. See conversations on 23 January 1964 in Kent B. Germany and Robert David Johnson, eds., *The Presidential Recordings, Lyndon B. Johnson: The Kennedy Assassination and the Transfer of Power, November 1963–January 1964*, vol. 3, *January 1964* (New York: Norton, 2005), pp. 737–70.
62. Both Democratic senators, Harry Byrd represented Virginia and Abraham Ribicoff represented Connecticut. Byrd was also the chair of the Senate Finance Committee.
63. George Smathers was a Democratic senator from Florida.

gave me a list, and it looked like the only one out of line was [Vance] Hartke, according to Larry's statement.[64]

Dillon: Well, Hartke's wrong. Now, I'll tell you, they—Larry checked Byrd right off . . . [Mike] Man[atos] . . . He told Manatos a couple of months ago, about a month ago, that he was right, but I—[65]

President Johnson: Well, Manatos had a memo from me at the [congressional] leaders' meeting this morning that said he was right.

Dillon: Yeah, well, that's right, but I talked to him two days ago, and he said at that time he hadn't made up his mind how to vote on some of these individual things, and he had a lot of fur growers in his state, and maybe he was just giving me the razz, but he was . . .

President Johnson: I'll call him. I'll call him.

Dillon: He was [*unclear*] set that right.[66]

President Johnson: I'll call him, Doug.

Dillon: Thank you. Fine.

President Johnson: Bye.

1:11 P.M.: Standing in Kenny O'Donnell's office door again, the President talked to Defense Secretary Robert McNamara for one minute.

1:12 P.M.–1:29 P.M.: Came back to the Oval Office and met with former Connecticut senator William Benton. In the middle of the meeting, he received another call from the Speaker of the House.

1:20 P.M.

From John McCormack[67]

Johnson received advice from the Speaker about seeing the parents of the missing activists and then briefly discussed the upcoming Democratic National Convention.

---

64. Lawrence "Larry" O'Brien, special assistant to the President, was the Johnson administration's chief liaison on congressional matters. Vance Hartke was Democratic senator from Indiana.
65. Mike Manatos was O'Brien's deputy.
66. Dillon may have said, "He was upset that night."
67. Tape WH6406.13, Citation #3824, Recordings of Telephone Conversations—White House Series, Recordings and Transcripts of Conversations and Meetings, Lyndon B. Johnson Library.

President Johnson: Go ahead, John? Yes, Mr. Speaker.

John McCormack: I just talked with [William] Ryan, and he said that that initiated in New York through the press, where the press said that he was going to try and make—get an appointment with the parents for *you*, with you, rather. And I told him everything humanly possible is being done, and he could rest content on that, and I said he can tell the parents and use me as a quote if he wants to.

President Johnson: Mmm.

McCormack: And he realizes the difficulty, and he talked with Lee White, I think.

President Johnson: Yeah.

McCormack: And the parents are going to call Lee White.

President Johnson: Mm-hmm.

McCormack: And that's according to apparently what he said was Lee White's . . . was White's suggestion.

President Johnson: Yeah.

McCormack: [*with the President acknowledging throughout*] Now, what I . . . might I think—and of course, he realizes how busy you are and so forth. I told him everything humanly possible was being done. And I can tell you that now, and Bill . . . because that's the result of your . . . Your one-minute speech, I said, interested me. . . . I made some inquiries.

Now, might—what I might suggest is you might have the parents reach someone of your administrative [*unclear*]—

President Johnson: All right, I'll tell Lee White to get them over to Justice and see FBI and the—Burke Marshall, who are tops, and then if they still want to, they can come see him.

McCormack: That's what I'd suggest.

President Johnson: OK. Can you talk to [Ogden] Reid, tell him the same thing?

McCormack: Oh, I won't talk to Reid. No, he's a Republican.[68]

President Johnson: Fine. . . . All right.

McCormack: I'll leave it with Ryan.

President Johnson: OK.

McCormack: You don't mind, do you?

President Johnson: Not at all, you're the boss.

McCormack: I think if you talk with him, you make . . . you would make a mistake.

President Johnson: You're the boss. Say, I want to talk to you. We

---

68. Eight years later, in 1972, Reid switched to the Democratic Party.

are not going to do anything on conventions until after the Republicans meet to see what the story is.[69] We'd like to have you as permanent chairman [of the Democratic National Convention] if you'd like to do it. If not, we'd like to have your suggestion, and we have nobody picked out for anything, and I'd like for you to be thinking about who you think would be good. And I'm going to talk to some of the boys in the Senate, but I'm not going to until after we get . . . see whether it's [Barry] Goldwater or who it is, because we've got plenty of time. We don't have to move until six weeks after they do. We've got [until] the end of August, and we really won't do any campaigning until after Labor Day. And [John] Kennedy set it back [to] August, and I think he did it very wisely. So we'll let them show all their hold cards, and then we'll come in and trump them.

McCormack: All right, Mr.—
President Johnson: You be just—you just be—
McCormack: Whatever you want is OK with me.
President Johnson: You just be thinking.
McCormack: Whatever you want is OK with me.
President Johnson: OK.
McCormack: Thank you.
President Johnson: OK.

> **1:30 P.M.:** President Johnson walked to the Fish Room to preside over the ceremony marking the U.S. Army's donation of land to New Jersey's Sandy Hook State Park. Among the dignitaries in attendance were New Jersey Governor Richard Hughes, Senator Harrison Williams, Senator Clifford Case, Interior Secretary Steward Udall, and Army Secretary Stephen Ailes.[70]
>
> **1:35 P.M.:** Made a quick, unrecorded call to George Reedy, then took a call from Democratic National Committee liaison Cliff Carter.

---

69. The Republican National Convention was set for 13–16 July, with the Democratic National Convention to follow, 24–27 August.
70. "Remarks on the Transfer to New Jersey of Lands for the Sandy Hook State Park," 23 June 1964, *Public Papers, Johnson, 1963–64,* 1:810–11.

1:36 P.M.

From Cliff Carter[71]

Carter, in Detroit preparing for a Johnson fund-raiser on June 26, called to report on trouble within the Nevada Democratic Party. Johnson used the opportunity to press him to get information on the level of support for the President among the biggest state delegations. Johnson was particularly concerned about enthusiasm for Robert Kennedy in California, New York, New Jersey, and Pennsylvania.

President Johnson: Yes?

Juanita Roberts: Cliff Carter is calling in from Detroit, if you still need him.

President Johnson: OK.

Roberts: Thank you.

Johnson leaves the line briefly.

President Johnson: [*to operator*] Give me Cliff Carter.

[*to someone in office*] They over there now? Have we got anything else?

White House Operator: There you are.

President Johnson: [*to someone in office*] When do I have to come back here?

[*over phone*] Hello?

Cliff Carter: Yes, sir.

President Johnson: Cliff?

Carter: Yes, sir.

President Johnson: The governor of Nevada [Grant Sawyer] was in here this morning and just raising hell about this fellow Brown that said I had named as LBJ coordinator, and said he wasn't well thought of, and he got hell beat out of him 2 to 1 for the [Democratic] National Committee's job, and that [Alan] Bible and the governor did not feel that we were taking them into the picture.[72] And if we didn't want them that's all right, but they'd like to go for us, and they thought that [Barry] Goldwater had a chance to carry Nevada because of the conservatism but that we had to

---

71. Tape WH6406.13, Citation #3826, Recordings of Telephone Conversations—White House Series, Recordings and Transcripts of Conversations and Meetings, Lyndon B. Johnson Library.
72. Alan Bible (D-Nevada) had served in the Senate since 1954. The first name for Brown was not identified.

include them in on the plans if we wanted to have any hope of it. I told him I never had heard of Brown, didn't know anything about it. Did we name him?

Carter: No, sir. Senator Bible—Senator [Howard] Cannon . . . It was my understanding that Senator Bible concurred in this . . . selected him.[73]

President Johnson: Well, you better check that, and you better call. I don't know where he is, but have your office, when he calls, tell him to call you at whatever place you are so you can talk to him and try to explain to him and see what we do about it.

Carter: Yes, sir.

President Johnson: Now, we want to also see how many of these people . . . I don't think there's anything to this, but they tell me yesterday a newspaperman, who's *very* reliable, says that our friend Bobby [Kennedy] met with Pierre Salinger and the whole group two weeks ago, and they decided that they could get about 40 percent of themselves for the top job [of president].[74] We don't want to express that at all, but they've talked to [Richard] Daley and to the various leaders: California and Illinois and Pennsylvania and Massachusetts and New York.[75] And they counted about 40 percent, but they were going back and survey and have another meeting. They met two weeks ago at Hyannis Port [Massachusetts]. I would think it's about the vice presidency, and I don't know they had had a meeting at all, I would doubt it, but Walter [Jenkins] said that Salinger was here two weeks ago on *Meet the Press.* I don't know what our contact is with Daley, but we ought to have a friendly one, talk about general things, what we can do to help Chicago and so forth, and then we ought to see if he's, without being blunt like New Jersey . . .

[*to someone in the Oval Office*] See if we can get Dick Hughes before he leaves.[76] I want to talk to him.

[*returning to Carter*] If we can see if he is going to go with us; if he's not, well, maybe we ought to just let them pick their whole outfit.

Carter: Yes, sir.

President Johnson: And you ought to find out from Dave Lawrence

---

73. Howard Cannon (D-Nevada) had served in the Senate since 1959.
74. Pierre Salinger, the former press secretary for John Kennedy and for Johnson, had resigned on 19 March 1964 to campaign for the U.S. Senate seat in California.
75. Richard Daley was the Democratic mayor of Chicago from 1955 until his death in 1976.
76. Richard Hughes, the governor of New Jersey, had met with Johnson a few minutes earlier as part of a ceremony to donate 271 acres of Army land to New Jersey's Sandy Hook State Park. Hughes's state was hosting this year's Democratic National Convention.

who's going to run the Pennsylvania delegation.[77] Who *is* going to run it?

Carter: He's still got a big hand in it—

President Johnson: All right, find out who's going to run it and if they're with us all the way. Now, do you know who's handling New York?[78] We sent a wire this morning to somebody up there—[Stanley] Steingut at Brooklyn.[79]

Carter: Yes, sir.

President Johnson: But you ought to talk to Eddie Weisl, and we ought to see if they're going to be with us or if they're going to be some other way. Now, we're told . . . Dick Goodwin told me that Jesse Unruh told him in California that he didn't want to be quoted, but if he had to, he'd have to go with Bobby.[80]

Carter: Yes, sir. [*Unclear.*]

President Johnson: And I don't know whether he's got the delegation or not. We ought to see if [Governor Pat] Brown's got it, or he's got it, or who's got it.[81] Now, you are the one that's got to do these things, and we've been there seven months, and I just want to be sure that we're on top of these things.

Carter: Yes, sir.

President Johnson: Are we?

Carter: Yes, sir, I think so.

President Johnson: Have they got any of this stuff staked out besides Massachusetts?

Carter: Uh . . . A couple of them I'm not sure of.

President Johnson: Who?

Carter: Those areas that you mentioned.

---

77. David Lawrence, a former governor of Pennsylvania (1959–63), was a special assistant to the President. Otis Morse was the Democratic State Committee chairman.

78. William McKeon was the chair of the New York Democratic State Committee. The national committeeman for New York was Carmine G. De Sapio, a Tammany Hall leader from Manhattan. Two months later, Johnson replaced him with Edwin Weisl Sr., a Johnson friend from the days of the Senate Preparedness Committee and former director of Paramount Pictures. *New York Times,* 23 August 1964. For Weisl's earlier discussions of New Jersey and New York politics, see David Johnson and Kent B. Germany, eds., *The Presidential Recordings, Lyndon B. Johnson: Toward the Great Society, February 1, 1964–May 31, 1964,* vol. 4, *February 1, 1964–March 8, 1964* (New York: Norton, 2007), pp. 224–27.

79. Stanley Steingut was a Democratic member of the New York State Assembly from 1955 until 1977.

80. Richard Goodwin was one of Johnson's chief speechwriters. Jesse "Big Daddy" Unruh was the leader of a powerful faction in the California Democratic Party and the Speaker of the California State Assembly. In the California race for the U.S. Senate, Unruh was backing Salinger.

81. Edmund "Pat" Brown was the Democratic governor of California.

President Johnson: Well, that's where the votes are. You better be sure of them. Better get busy and go to seeing them, because all this detail stuff and this . . . it's not worth a damn if you haven't got those big ones. We found that out in Los Angeles in '60.[82]

Carter: Yes.

President Johnson: What you want to do is get New Jersey and get New York and—have you got New Jersey? Is that delegation with us? I would gather not, from the way they wouldn't put in the resolution up there.

Carter: No, no, sir, they're with us.

President Johnson: You think that they would be for Mr. Pat Brown if I wanted him for vice president?

Carter: Yes, sir.

President Johnson: All right. All right. Now, but you don't know who New York would be for?

Carter: I think they're . . . who you are.

President Johnson: All right, well, you visit around and get close enough to them where you know.

Now, I think it's bad for you to be in on any money-raising things. You try to stay as far away from it as you can.

Carter: All right.

President Johnson: Let Dick [Richard Maguire] handle that.[83]

Carter: All right, sir.

President Johnson: And just tell him you don't know, you've never had any experience with it, you don't have anything to do with it, and that he's the best one, and you do other things because . . . you got a big write-up in the [*Washington*] *Star* here today about you and Maguire meeting with a bunch of people from Cleveland was it, Ohio?

Carter: Yes, sir.

President Johnson: And who let that out?

Carter: I don't know.

President Johnson: Tell them over at the [Democratic] National Committee to quit claiming they're picking up all this money that they're not picking up. They claim they picked up a million dollars out yonder. They don't do it. They didn't pick up 500,000 [dollars] net. And I'd put the net figure because if we pick up that, people are not going to want to give money. Do you follow me?

---

82. Johnson failed to capture the Democratic nomination in 1960 and had to settle for being running mate to John Kennedy.
83. Richard Maguire was treasurer of the Democratic National Committee.

Carter: Yes, sir. Yes, sir.

President Johnson: And I'd just quit telling them all this stuff that we do tell them. Somebody over at that committee talks too much to these reporters. This fellow [Walter] Pincus of the *Star*. But you look into it, and you get back, that's what I wanted to tell you.

Carter: Yes, sir.

President Johnson: Any other news?

Carter: No, sir.

President Johnson: Have you got any idea how many votes we got up to now?

Carter: Uh . . .

President Johnson: How many in the convention . . . total?

Carter: [There are] 2,580.

President Johnson: All right, so that means we've got to have roughly 1,300.

Carter: Yes, sir, 1,250.

President Johnson: How many do we have?

Carter: I think over a thousand.

President Johnson: Mm-hmm.

Carter: Actually, you've got more than that, but over a thousand definite.

President Johnson: Mm-hmm. Let's be positive, now, [that] we wrap up the number that we need right away. He's [Robert Kennedy's] going to announce, probably this afternoon, [that] he's not going into New York.

Carter: Mm-hmm. [*Pauses.*] OK, sir.

President Johnson: OK. Bye.

Carter: Bye.

1:52 P.M.

From Clark Clifford;
preceded by Office Conversation with Richard Hughes[84]

New Jersey Governor Hughes dropped by for two minutes, then Johnson asked longtime Democratic presidential adviser Clark Clifford to find out

---

84. Tape WH6406.13, Citation #3828, Recordings of Telephone Conversations—White House Series, Recordings and Transcripts of Conversations and Meetings, Lyndon B. Johnson Library.

more about the Robert Kennedy situation. Johnson also updated Clifford on the replacement of Ambassador Lodge.

Before Clifford comes on the line, Johnson speaks apparently to New Jersey Governor Richard Hughes about Democratic Party politics.

President Johnson: . . . going to try to meet with any of these other leaders [*unclear*]?

Richard Hughes: Not too many, no. [*Unclear.*]

President Johnson: If I were you, I think I'd go on and call [David] Lawrence and talk to [Richard] Daley, and—

Hughes: All right, sir.

President Johnson: —put yourself in a position. Talk to John Connally, ask him what's happening in the South.[85]

Hughes: I shall indeed.

President Johnson: Kind of look after my . . .

The operator interrupts to announce that Clifford is on the line. The recording captures almost 40 seconds of silence before picking up on the phone conversation.

President Johnson: . . . called me up and asked me if I wanted him to go to Poland.[86] He thought I knew about it, and I said, "No, I haven't heard of it, don't know anything about it, don't know what the merits are. I'd be guided by your judgment: If you think you ought to go, I'll go with you; if you don't think you ought to go, I'd stay." So I just checked it back to him, and . . .

Clark Clifford: All right.

President Johnson: I'd called two or three times to ask about his brother [Ted Kennedy] and been very friendly.[87]

Bill Benton came in just now and said he'd been talking to [Averell] Harriman and some of them and that he urged me to send Bobby to Moscow as ambassador with some ideas because [Nikita] Khrushchev

85. John Connally was the governor of Texas who was shot while riding with John Kennedy in Dallas on 22 November 1963. A leader of the state's conservative Democrats, he had recently taken a major step in his reelection bid by winning the Democratic Party primary. Although he was an old friend and ally of Johnson's, the two had feuded over Texas politics earlier in the year. See 1 February 1964, 3 February 1964, and 8 February 1964 in Johnson and Germany, *Presidential Recordings, Johnson*, vol. 4, *February 1, 1964–March 8, 1964*, pp. 131–33, 332–40, 795–98.

86. See the conversation between President Johnson and Robert Kennedy, 8:58 P.M., 18 June 1964, in McKee, *Presidential Recordings, Johnson*, vol. 7, *June 1, 1964–June 22, 1964*, pp. 452–55.

87. Senator Edward Kennedy had suffered severe back injuries during a 19 June airplane crash.

wanted to get along, and he hoped I'd send Sargent Shriver to Paris.[88] I didn't comment either way. I don't know whether there's a plant. He said Harriman had suggested this, and Harriman met him. Harriman and Bobby are pretty close.

Clifford: Yeah.

President Johnson: He may be wanting that kind of world experience, but I don't have any idea.

[*with Clifford acknowledging throughout*] Anyway, that's your department, and I just thought you ought to have all this background in case you got called or talked to. I assume he'll tell me about it this afternoon. If he does, I'll just say fine, whatever you want to do in regard to New York, that's your business, and I . . . if you would decide you'd want to do it, I'm prepared to go with you; if you don't, that's all right too.

There's talk . . . A newspaper man came in yesterday, said they had a meeting two weeks ago up at Hyannis Port, and [Pierre] Salinger came in, and Ken O'Donnell and a number of them, and that they said that they had Massachusetts and New York and Illinois and Ohio and . . . California, and they've had about 40 percent of them that thought he'd make the best president, but they decided to have Tydings in from Maryland, and they'd go back and have a little survey, and they'd meet again about the time of the Republican convention.[89] I don't believe anything like that happened. They might have talked about the vice presidency, but the . . . we checked it, though, Walter Jenkins did, and Salinger was here, and they did . . . there were some . . . they did have . . . he was up there during that weekend.

Clifford: Hmm.

President Johnson: [*with Clifford acknowledging*] Now, I don't know. This newspaperman told the fellow on the Judiciary Committee of the Senate, and he told me. I don't know how much truth there is in it. Larry O'Brien told me he definitely wanted the second place. He has been to California on TV and meeting with a group out there and has been in New York a good deal as you know, and I think has had some contacts with Pennsylvania and Illinois. I think it's something that we ought to look into, and I don't know who ought to look into it, but anyway, that's the picture, and you keep that to yourself.

Clifford: [*Unclear.*]

---

88. Averell Harriman was under secretary of state for political affairs. Director of the Peace Corps, Sargent Shriver was coordinating the President's antipoverty efforts.

89. This person is probably Joseph Tydings, the son of deceased Maryland senator Millard Tydings. He was a federal attorney in Maryland and a Democratic candidate for the U.S. Senate.

President Johnson: I named [Maxwell] Taylor and Alex Johnson, assistant secretary of state, in the number one and two places this morning to take over for [Henry Cabot] Lodge, and Taylor's a wonderful civilian, and among the military he's the best. And we think he can hold this general [Nguyen Khanh] in line too. We have to have somebody who can hold him up because he may go under any day, and if they do, we go under. Alex Johnson, on the other hand, can take care of the political thing. He's the best expert we have on Southeast Asia.

Clifford: Great.

President Johnson: So we thought both of them is a good signal to Hanoi and Peiping.

Kay Graham's all right. [Al] Friendly's a little worried because we don't want a military man, and he thinks it's his job to protect the virtue of that young girl, and he's probably raising hell because I got a military man.[90] That may kick off a little trouble, but Taylor's not a rambunctious military man.

Clifford: Not at all; not at all.

President Johnson: And I believe it will be pretty well received.

Clifford: Mm-hmm.

President Johnson: You got any knowledge or anything you want to tell me?

Clifford: No, I'm interested in these reports you get, and I'll see if I can't take a—

President Johnson: You might wish them [the Robert Kennedy party] good-bye, at least, before they leave. They're leaving tonight, and—or in the morning—and you might just say, "I see where you're leaving, just wanted to pay my respects and . . ."

Clifford: And see what I pick up.

President Johnson: What have you decided in New York? Be good. Call me.

Clifford: Thank you very much.

President Johnson: Call me when you hear anything.

Clifford: I will.

1:59 P.M.: Johnson held an off-the-record lunch in the Mansion with Secretary of State Dean Rusk, Secretary of Defense Robert

---

90. The reference to "that young girl" is unclear but was most likely about Katharine "Kay" Graham, who succeeded her husband as the president of the *Washington Post* in 1963 after his suicide. Alfred Friendly was executive vice president and managing editor.

McNamara, Special Assistant McGeorge Bundy, and a few other White House aides, likely to discuss Maxwell Taylor.
2:56 P.M.: Returned to the Oval Office with Bundy and Jack Valenti.

2:59 P.M.

From Luther Hodges[91]

Johnson had been experiencing difficulties in finding a director for the Community Relations Service, the entity to be created by the Civil Rights Act to mediate disputes in the South. Since the new bureaucracy was slated to fall under the jurisdiction of the Commerce Department, Secretary Hodges had been leading the search for Johnson, and the two men had discussed a number of candidates on June 19.[92] In this call, Hodges, the former governor of North Carolina, reported that Atlanta Mayor Ivan Allen had turned it down. The two men then considered Charlotte Mayor Stanley Brookshire and former Florida Governor LeRoy Collins. In this section of tape, Johnson set out some of his rationale for a Community Relations director's qualifications and the danger of using too much federal power in the South. Collins eventually got the job, despite a warning later today from Mississippi Senator James Eastland, who railed against Collins as a "damn cheat, double-crosser, and a liar" and a "goddamn, lying, son of a bitch."[93]

President Johnson: Yes?
Luther Hodges: Hello, Mr. President.
President Johnson: Yes.
Hodges: Luther Hodges.
President Johnson: Yes.
Hodges: Mr. President, I've had Mr. [Ivan] Allen here for a half an hour or so from Atlanta. He simply will not give the mayor's job up to come here or to be with us on a full-time basis.

---

91. Tape WH6406.13, Citation #3829, Recordings of Telephone Conversations—White House Series, Recordings and Transcripts of Conversations and Meetings, Lyndon B. Johnson Library.
92. Conversation between President Johnson and Luther Hodges, 2:28 P.M., 19 June 1964, in McKee, *Presidential Recordings, Johnson*, vol. 7. *June 1, 1964–June 22, 1964*, pp. 463–68.
93. Conversation between President Johnson and James Eastland, 3:59 P.M., 23 June 1964, in this chapter.

President Johnson: Hmm.

Hodges: I put a lot of heat on him and told him what a sacrifice it would take, and he said well, he's just committed to that. He'd give us [one-]third time or half time [to] help us organize whatever it was. He simply *couldn't* take the job. Now, I had mentioned the directorship to him over the phone, but he didn't quite get it over the phone. He's working here with us now on committees and things of that character, but I didn't see any use to bother you to bring him over unless he's willing to do it.

President Johnson: No . . . no.

Hodges: Now, I'd like to talk with you for a few minutes maybe this afternoon if you could fit it in. I've got one or two ideas about which way we move now.

President Johnson: All right. I've got a TV program, and then I've got a meeting of 300 over at the House, and I've got to come back with the Prime Minister of Turkey at 5:00 [P.M.]. It could be sometime late, maybe in the evening. Why don't you try that [mayor of] Charlotte [Stanley Brookshire] fellow? Or anybody else that you have in mind that you think will—

Hodges: Well, I can find out from the Charlotte fellow.

President Johnson: We've got to find somebody . . .

Hodges: I know that.

President Johnson: . . . that will go along, that the Negro groups know and has some record with them as being friendly, that would—according to my idea, the best man would be somebody that could meet that qualification and still be fair and just for the South [*Hodges acknowledges*] and know something about them.[94]

Hodges: I talked with [*unclear*]—

President Johnson: And I think you just [are] almost going to have to stay on the road with these southern governors as soon as we sign this bill, taking your conciliation man and getting people like Buford Ellington that—they won't rate high with the Negroes up here, but they can talk to the southern governors, and we're going to have to get these men to quit preaching violence and start asking for observance.[95]

Hodges: Right.

---

94. For cross-reference and context, see Johnson's search in February–March for replacements to the Civil Rights Commission in Johnson and Germany, *Presidential Recordings, Johnson*, vol. 4, *February 1, 1964–March 8, 1964*, pp. 113–14, 528–30, 864–83.

95. Buford Ellington was the former governor of Tennessee and one of Johnson's troubleshooters on political and racial matters in the South. In March 1965, Ellington became the director of emergency planning in the Johnson administration.

President Johnson: Because if we don't, we're going to have more problems than we got in Mississippi, and I've got all this—father and mother—they're wanting to come in and see me this afternoon, with these three children that are lost.

Hodges: Is that right?

President Johnson: [*with Hodges acknowledging*] I told them I couldn't see them. I sent them to see the FBI and see Burke Marshall, but . . . the only other candidate I know outside of the man, if we could get the Charlotte man to consider it, would be this fellow they suggested over in [Secretary of Labor] Bill Wirtz's shop. You might ask Wirtz if he knows—

Hodges: William Simkins [*sic*]?[96]

President Johnson: Yeah. If you don't like him, you better ask him if he knows any other negotiators or mediators in this field. It's . . . need somebody to take some . . . have some experience. I don't know, we may look back over the WTB files in the old days where we had professors come in from the South that might . . .[97] We got to have someone in enough standing, though . . .

Hodges: Exactly.

President Johnson: . . . that the Negroes will accept.

Now, Roy Wilkins is about ready to get upset with me because I won't go and address the NAACP. And I just tell him this is not the time to do it, but . . .

Hodges: Right, right.

President Johnson: We've got to get a man on that, and I thought that Atlanta man [Ivan Allen] was the last word.

Hodges: Well, I thought so too, and I talked to him about [Harold] Walker, by the way, and he said that we were right about Walker: that he wasn't quite persuasive enough; he's a little too technical.[98] So he's the one, you know, that you felt like that there's . . .

President Johnson: Well, they felt that he would be industry's man and that they didn't know him, and even though he was their friend, that

---

96. William E. Simkin was director of the Department of Labor's Federal Mediation and Conciliation Service.

97. The WTB was the War Trade Board, a bureaucracy created during World War I.

98. Harold Walker, Atlanta native and general counsel for Lockheed, had been suggested as a person to head the Community Relations Service. See the conversation between Ralph McGill and Juanita Roberts, 11:40 A.M., 17 June 1964; Luther Hodges to Johnson, 11:45 A.M., 18 June 1964; and Johnson to Roy Wilkins, 5:20 P.M., 19 June 1964, in McKee, *Presidential Recordings, Johnson*, vol. 7, *June 1, 1964–June 22, 1964*, pp. 384–86, 425–28, 478–84.

the . . . even old Roy Wilkins and Whitney Young would support him.[99] You got fellows like this James Farmer.

Hodges: Mm-hmm.

President Johnson: And they [are] outlaws—Martin Luther King—and you just got to be awful careful.[100]

Hodges: Well—

President Johnson: Maybe this Charlotte man, we could look at him, and . . .

Hodges: I'll call him. But can you take a couple minutes now on the phone? I'll tell you [unclear]—

President Johnson: Yeah, oh, yeah. Yeah, sure, sure.

Hodges: Here's what I run into. The other day—and I hope you're not . . . understand I'm not beating this man's drum; I'm trying to do the best job.

President Johnson: No . . . no. I know that.

Hodges: We can get [Le]Roy Collins to do this job if you would be willing to make a telephone call to his board to let him off for about a year or more.[101] As N . . . you know, as NAB [National Association of Broadcasters]. I know you don't have much to do with them, the broadcasters, but I asked him, as I've asked two or three other people, [for] any suggestions. This is the kind of thing that he would do a great job on, and this is the kind that Burke Marshall and all the rest of them, I know, would go crazy about. I checked him also . . . what Allen—

President Johnson: Well, check that out, and if you think . . . talk to Burke Marshall and let's see, and if you do, I'll call the board. I'll call anybody I need to that'll help you.

Hodges: All right. I think we might as well get as close to the top one—

President Johnson: You better check with the Florida senators first, though.[102] Say if you got him to take a leave and if he'd do it, if they would have any objection, because there's no use in getting him to say so. If one of them say[s] "I don't like him," that's the end of it.

Hodges: Well, of course, you know . . . you probably know that what's-

---

99. Young was the executive director of the National Urban League.
100. The nine-second section from "You got" to "awful careful" was excised under deed of gift restriction until opened in October 2003.
101. Florida governor from 1955 to 1961, LeRoy Collins had been serving as president of the National Association of Broadcasters since 1961. Later in 1964, he took the position as director of the Community Relations Service.
102. Democrats George Smathers and Spessard Holland were Florida's junior and senior senators, respectively.

his-name, George [Smathers], has probably . . . has been afraid that [Le]Roy would someday run against him, so you don't [*unclear*] any.

President Johnson: Well, if I wanted him, that's why I'd put him in here.

Hodges: Yeah. [*They both chuckle.*]

President Johnson: Yes, sir.

Hodges: I know exactly what you mean.

President Johnson: This is not going to be any place to win any popularity contests.

Hodges: Not at all, and this guy would sacrifice anything in the world for the principle of doing a job for his country. This man—Collins. No question about it. Well, I'll . . . Let me . . . I'll check Brookshire, and then let me check—

President Johnson: Then if you can get Collins, call up them, say, "Now, we've had his name suggested. We want to try to draft him, but before I ever approach a man on anything, or the President does, I check with the senators, and I just want to be sure he wouldn't be obnoxious to you."

Hodges: Yeah. You're willing for me to check that.

President Johnson: Yeah, yeah, yeah, I'd call them.

Hodges: Well, I'll do it and stay in touch with you.

President Johnson: And you'd better be thinking like this fellow in Georgia, the Atlanta man. You better be thinking of Buford [Ellington] in Tennessee. And you ought to be thinking who you can get in North Carolina and South Carolina.

Hodges: We're doing that.

President Johnson: And we ought to try to get 10, 11 topflight people that you can direct and get out and see these governors and see these leading publishers of the papers. Make you up a list of opinion makers and go to them and say, "What we want is observance instead of enforcement. We don't want to send troops in here to enforce something. We want to get you-all to appeal to them to observe it, and Johnson and I are going to do all we can to stay out of your way and keep off your neck. But we can't do it unless you help us a little bit."

Hodges: Right.

President Johnson: That's—

Hodges: When do you think this bill would become law?

President Johnson: I'd think July the Fourth.

Hodges: July Fourth. [*Johnson belches noticeably.*] Well, then we would have to go right to work on it—

President Johnson: Yes, sir, but if I don't have one, you going to have to be the conciliator because you've got enough humaneness about you and understanding and enough judgment and brains about the South, and I'm just not going to let them move these seven divisions in the South. I'm just going to withstand it long as I can. I moved a bunch of FBI people into Mississippi last night, but I'm not going to send troops on *my* people if I can avoid it. That they've got to help me avoid it, and they've got to know it. Now, I want to sit down and talk to this governor of Mississippi [Paul Johnson]. I know his problem, and he's got a *hell* of a problem, and I want to be . . .

Hodges: It's not going to be easy, Mr. President, in the Deep South.

President Johnson: Oh, it's going to be awful. It's just going to be awful. You just don't know how bad it is.

Hodges: No question about it.

President Johnson: Well, you do know. You're the only one in the administration that does know.

You go on, though, and talk to the two senators and then let me know what you want me to do, and I'll do it, and if you want to come over late in the evening, you call me and we'll get together anytime.

Hodges: Thank you, Mr. President.

President Johnson: Bye.

3:11 P.M.

Between Jack Valenti and Robert Kennedy[103]

While Johnson had been attending matters of foreign policy and finding a suitable southern civil rights mediator, Robert Kennedy had been meeting at the Justice Department with Andrew Goodman's mother and father and Michael Schwerner's father. He told them that he was using the "maximum resources" available, including personal ones. The parents emphasized that they wanted the administration to protect the civil rights workers, not just to commit to investigate when things happened to them.[104] He phoned the President immediately after that session to

---

103. Tape WH6406.13, Citation #3831, Recordings of Telephone Conversations—White House Series, Recordings and Transcripts of Conversations and Meetings, Lyndon B. Johnson Library.
104. Council of Federated Organizations, "The Philadelphia, Mississippi Case, Chronology of Contact with Agents of the Federal Government," Folder 16: "Depositions, Neshoba County, 1964," Box 3, Council of Federated Organizations Records, Z/1867.000/S, Mississippi Department of Archives and History.

petition the President to make a statement of personal concern for the activists, but Jack Valenti took the call. According to the Daily Diary, two minutes after this call began, Johnson headed to the Cabinet Room to tape his message about Ambassador Lodge, telling secretary Vicki McCammon, "Sure is a fancy outfit you have on there."

Jack Valenti: Mr. Kennedy?

Robert Kennedy: Yeah?

Valenti: He is in the Cabinet Room recording on television some of his statements in the press conference today, and I'll have him call you just as soon—

Kennedy: Well, now, let me—should I tell you what the problem is?

Valenti: All right.

Kennedy: And this, the . . . I've just seen these parents, you know, of these kids that have been picked up or lost down in Mississippi, and I think that two things: Number one, I think he should probably make a statement about that, and I heard he said something at the press conference this morning.

Valenti: Right.

Kennedy: But I think it should really be more formalized, although I haven't seen the statement, and perhaps it's satisfactory. Second, I think he should consider seeing them, the parents. And third, I think he should consider making a call to Governor [Paul] Johnson and expressing concern so it would be said that he had made that call.

Valenti: All right.

Kennedy: Do you know the facts about the case?

Valenti: Yes, sir, I'm very well acquainted with them, sir.

Kennedy: Yeah. And now, you see, yesterday, I told them to use the . . . you know, the helicopters, and they—get the FBI in as if it's a kidnapping, so we're doing all we can. But I think that people are going to get . . . there's going to be more of this, and people are going to wonder . . .

Valenti: Let me read you his answer:

The question was: "Mr. President, do you have any information about the three kids that disappeared in Mississippi?"

The answer: "The FBI has a substantial number of men who are closely studying it and investigating the entire situation. We have asked them to spare no effort to secure all the information possible and report to me as soon as possible. We believe they are making every effort to locate them. I have had no report since breakfast, but at that time I understood they had increased their forces in that area. Several weeks ago, I asked them to anticipate the problems that would come from this and to send extra FBI personnel into the area. They have substantially augmented their personnel in the last few hours."

That was his statement on it.

Kennedy: You see, I think that to express sort of concern . . .

Valenti: Right.

Kennedy: You know, personal concern for them and for their families. Now, I don't know whether he wants—I've seen their families. It might not be necessary, but . . . we're going to have more of this, and that's a hell of a problem.

Valenti: Yes, sir . . . that it is.

Kennedy: But I think at least he—I think that the—what he . . . I do think he should call the governor.

Valenti: All right, sir.

Kennedy: And just say that how concerned he is.

Valenti: Will you be in your office for a while, sir?

Kennedy: Yeah.

Valenti: All right, sir.

Kennedy: And would you have him think about those three possibilities, and while he's on television, he might just, you know, just supplement that answer by expressing personal concern about them and that he's—

Valenti: Well, the two things that they're doing on television right now is his rereading his statement on [Henry Cabot] Lodge and [Maxwell] Taylor—

Kennedy: I see . . . I see.

Valenti: —and second, rereading his restatement of U.S. policy on Vietnam.

Kennedy: Yeah.

Valenti: Those are the two things that he's reading on television. They wanted that for the TV audiences. And—

Kennedy: Yeah. . . . I'd like to have him say something also, you know, even if just a paragraph on—so it got on television about his concern about this thing.

Valenti: All right, sir.

Kennedy: I think it'd make them feel . . . and that's not as important as just the fact that he's on top of all these things.

Valenti: Right.

Kennedy: I think it's the human equation that's damn important for everything.

Valenti: All right, sir.
Kennedy: OK.
Valenti: Thank you, sir.

3:31 P.M.: President Johnson returned to the Oval Office with McGeorge Bundy. Johnson tried to return Attorney General Robert Kennedy's call, but had to settle for the deputy attorney general.

3:35 P.M.

To Nicholas Katzenbach[105]

In this almost nine-minute call, they addressed the most pressing issue of the afternoon: how to deal with the parents of the missing young men. Katzenbach worried about setting the precedent of a presidential meeting and argued for sending a message through Lee White. In this call, Katzenbach speculated that the activists were dead.

White House Operator: Mr. President?
President Johnson: Yes.
White House Operator: He's [Robert Kennedy] gone to a TV studio, and he should be back in about an hour. Could I reach him, or have him call you?
President Johnson: Let me talk to Katzenbach.
White House Operator: Thank you.
President Johnson: [*to someone in Oval Office*] He's gone to a TV studio.
The President holds for approximately one minute and fifteen seconds before Katzenbach comes to the line. While holding for Katzenbach, he instructs someone in the office, "Tell the girls to get Senator [James] Eastland on the phone for me."
White House Operator: Ready, sir.
President Johnson: Nick?

---

105. Tape WH6406.13, Citation #3832, Recordings of Telephone Conversations—White House Series, Recordings and Transcripts of Conversations and Meetings, Lyndon B. Johnson Library.

Nicholas Katzenbach: Yes, sir.

President Johnson: The Attorney General called me. Were you around when he called me?

Katzenbach: No, I was gone just before he called you.

President Johnson: He . . . I was in the TV studio on my statement on Laos and Vietnam, and when I called him back ten minutes later, he'd gone to a TV studio and [is] going to be gone an hour.

Katzenbach: Yes.

President Johnson: [*with Katzenbach acknowledging throughout*] Now, he talked to Jack Valenti and suggested that he thought I probably should make a statement on these three boys that are missing down in Mississippi and I ought to consider seeing their parents. I've been considering that all day. I talked to the Speaker [of the House John McCormack] about it. A little Republican congressman, Ogden Reid, is trying to get it in here. I'm afraid that if I start housemothering each kid that's gone down there and that doesn't show up, that we'll have this White House full of people every day asking for sympathy and congressmen too, because they want to come over and have their picture made and get on TV, and I don't know whether the President of the United States ought to be busy doing that or not.

I told them that we . . . what we'd done, and we had called in the Defense Department, and the Navy turned them over helicopters, and we'd called in all the FBI two weeks ago and asked them to put on extra people and sent in extra ones yesterday. So there's not anything new I can tell them except to let this be a forum, and I thought I better talk to you before I cleared that request. [*Katzenbach attempts to interject.*] The Speaker talked to [William] Ryan, explained it to Ryan, and he understood it.

Katzenbach: I think both Reid and Ryan understand that, although for the reasons that you indicate, they're both, you know, always anxious as any congressman would be [*chuckling*] [to] do what he can for constituents. Now, they might see Lee White.

President Johnson: Well, I thought Lee ought to come over there, and then they don't have this as a bunch of television cameras. The White House, the President's assistant, could sit in on it, but they busted up. I told him to get his tail over there, and he messed around here and didn't do it. And—

Katzenbach: Well, they're going back over it with the congressmen now. Why doesn't he hightail it up there and see them up there?

President Johnson: Where?

Katzenbach: At the—

President Johnson: Over where?

Katzenbach: —They're going back to Congressman Ryan's—I'll make sure where it is, but I think it's Congressman Ryan's office.

President Johnson: I thought they were going to the FBI?

Katzenbach: No, the FBI doesn't want to interview them at this time because all the press is around, which I understand. They would rather let that go for a couple of hours and then talk with them when the press is gone. Now, the press will be finished when they leave here. They're talking to some press, and I think what they say will be all right.

President Johnson: Now, is Ryan and Reid with them?

Katzenbach: Yeah. [*Pause.*]

President Johnson: Well, what do you think we ought to do?

Katzenbach: Well, I think if you'd—I haven't seen your statement this morning, Mr. President.

President Johnson: I haven't made any statement on it.

Katzenbach: All right, I thought you said something in the press conference.

President Johnson: No, I said that . . . Oh, I did make some mention of it by saying that the FBI [*Katzenbach acknowledges*] . . . let me read it to you. But, I mean I'm . . . I put out no statement since the Attorney General made this suggestion.

[*reading*] "Do you have any information about the kids that disappeared in Mississippi?" That's Scotty Reston.[106]

[*reading*] President: "The FBI has a substantial number of men who are closely studying and investigating the entire situation. We've asked them to spare no effort to secure all the information possible, to report to us as soon as possible. We believe they're making every effort to locate them. I've had no report since breakfast, but at that time I understood they had increased their forces in that area. Several weeks ago, I asked them to anticipate the problems that'd come from this and send extra FBI personnel into the area. They have substantially augmented their personnel in the last few hours."

Katzenbach: Well, that pretty much covers everything you can say, really. The only—I think if Lee were to see them and to carry an expression of personal concern from you to give to them, say that he had talked to you and that you had expressed your personal concern and sympathy with them in this difficult time for them with their children missing, that that would do.

---

106. James "Scotty" Reston was the Washington, D.C., bureau chief and a columnist for the *New York Times*. Johnson had held a private meeting with him after this morning's press conference.

Now, I think whether Lee sees them at the White House, or I think it'd be just as good if Lee saw them in Congressman Ryan's office. I think that could be—I don't . . . be done without any press around. I think I could arrange that.

President Johnson: Ask them. Tell them that . . . call them and tell them that Lee White's been handling this and that he's been directing the Defense Department and talking to you-all about it for the White House and for the President. And he handles these matters for him, and he'd like if they'd like for him, he'll have him come right up and meet with them, and see what they say.

Katzenbach: All right.

President Johnson: And then call me back.

Katzenbach: All right, Mr. President.

President Johnson: OK.

Now, you think that's just as good as having them up in Lee's office? That avoids all the press?

Katzenbach: Well, that avoids the press if you have them in Lee's office, I suppose, but the press will be on the outside and want—

President Johnson: Oh, yeah, yeah, I say, but—

Katzenbach: Yeah. I think this way I can find out if there's any press there and . . . and the congressmen understand the difficulties of the press on this—

President Johnson: Just tell them that they're going to bring them in from every damn kid that goes down there. He's going to hide out to get his mama's picture in the paper if he needs to.

Katzenbach: That's right.

President Johnson: What do you think happened to them?

Katzenbach: I think they got picked up by some of these Klan people, be my guess.

President Johnson: And murdered?

Katzenbach: Yeah, probably, or else they're just being hidden in one of those barns or something, you know, and getting the hell scared out of them. But I would not be surprised if they'd been murdered, Mr. President. Pretty rough characters.

President Johnson: How old are these kids?

Katzenbach: Twenty, and twenty-four, and twenty-two.[107]

President Johnson: Mm-hmm. What did you say to them, and what'd the Attorney General say to them?

---

107. The press was reporting the ages of Goodman as 20, Schwerner as 24, and Chaney as 21. Chaney had his 21st birthday less than a month earlier.

Katzenbach: Simply that we were doing everything that we possibly could to find out what had happened and essentially what you just said: The FBI was there; we had helicopters out, we are doing everything we could. And if they had any suggestions as to what ought to be done, to get in touch with us and tell us what ought to be done. And an expression of sympathy, and then some discussion of the general difficulty of the federal government being involved beforehand in protection and why the Constitution didn't permit this.

President Johnson: What did they say?

Katzenbach: And they reacted quite favorably to this. They said they understood the problem, and they just were distressed and just hoped that everything was being done that could be done, and they're . . . They were not dissatisfied with anything, Mr. President. I think they felt everything was being done, that could be done.

President Johnson: Now, if you think . . . if they've got any preference and they're raising hell, tell them to come on down and see Lee right now and just let me know.

Katzenbach: All right.

President Johnson: And if you don't think it's the thing to do. If you don't think going to the Hill is better, but you think down here would suit them better, just tell them to come on down and see him, and I may just walk in his office and say a word to them.

Katzenbach: All right, Mr. President.

President Johnson: Would you advise that or not advise it?

Katzenbach: [*with the President acknowledging*] Your seeing them? I think you have the problem of every future one, and I think you've got an awful good reason today to be tied up. I'm inclined to think that a personal message from you via Lee would be sufficient. I'm trying to look out for the future because this is not going to be the only time this sort of thing will occur, I'm afraid.

President Johnson: OK.

Katzenbach: All right.

President Johnson: Thank you.

After the Katzenbach conversation, Johnson attempted to place a call to Lee White, but decided to meet with him in person.[108]

---

108. Tape WH6406.13, Citation #3833, Recordings of Telephone Conversations—White House Series, Recordings and Transcripts of Conversations and Meetings, Lyndon B. Johnson Library.

3:40 P.M.: The President made an unrecorded call to Walter Jenkins.

3:45 P.M.: Met with Lee White in the Oval Office.

3:50 P.M.: Accepted some material sent by George Reedy before speaking to the assistant attorney general for civil rights.

3:51 P.M.

To Burke Marshall[109]

President Johnson sought advice from Marshall on the disappearance of the COFO workers. He also followed up on a suggestion given to him an hour earlier by Commerce Secretary Luther Hodges, who said that Burke Marshall "would go crazy" in support of LeRoy Collins serving as head of the Community Relations Service.

President Johnson: [*to someone in office*] Tell [George] Reedy I would say no to that. Tell Walter [Jenkins] to be sure that John Connally knows that he got that.

[*on phone*] Burke?

Burke Marshall: Yes, Mr. President.

President Johnson: The Attorney General is going to see me later, but I talked to [Nicholas] Katzenbach, and he left a message about our talking to these families. I want to—Katzenbach's going to get Lee White to run up and see them in [William] Ryan's office and tell them what all we've done and how interested we are so we don't open up . . . have every boy that gets missing, his parents come down to the White House and have a platform and these congressmen come along with them.

Marshall: Yes.

President Johnson: If we can't catch them in the office, why, we'll have them come to see Lee White there. Now, I want to talk to you about the conciliation thing. First, do you think I ought to call the governor

---

109. Tape WH6406.14, Citations #3834 and #3835, Recordings of Telephone Conversations—White House Series, Recordings and Transcripts of Conversations and Meetings, Lyndon B. Johnson Library.

[Paul Johnson] on this?[110] The Attorney General indicated he thought
maybe I ought to.

Marshall: The governor—

President Johnson: And I thought I'd call Senator [James] Eastland
and ask him what he thinks we can do here on these three boys.[111]

Marshall: Oh, I think the senator could tell you, Mr. President, better
than I could if you ask him that question.

President Johnson: You think that's the thing to do, then, is talk to
him?

Marshall: Yes. I talked to Attorney General [Joe] Patterson down
in—

President Johnson: That's Mississippi?

Marshall: [*with the President acknowledging*] Yes, this morning. I know
him, and I've always . . . he's always been honest with me, you know, as
Senator Eastland always is. And so I've done that, and he's probably told
the governor about that call. I told him that the bureau [FBI] was in
there, and that we wanted to cooperate and not fight with the state over
this, which was the matter of finding three kids that had disappeared.
And so he was . . . as he always is, he was perfectly friendly and said
that he'd see what he could do to help, and—but I think on whether you
should call the governor, which I think maybe you should do, I think the
senator would give you better advice than anyone else on that.

President Johnson: What would you say to the governor if you talked
to him? Just ask him to try to help find them?

Marshall: Yes.

President Johnson: Wouldn't he say I'm already doing that? Probably.

Marshall: Probably.

President Johnson: Mm-hmm. Uh—

Marshall: I think that if you did do it, Mr. President, I think it would
have to be in a way that wasn't public. I mean, I think we couldn't do that
to the governor. It wouldn't . . . we wouldn't . . . I mean, it would make it
so tough on him to be helpful at all on any other—

---

110. In a series of recommendations about Mississippi on 8 April, Lee White had recommended
that Johnson reach out to Governor Paul Johnson either by phone or by intermediary to make
him more accessible in situations such as this one. Lee C. White to President Johnson, 8 April
1964, "HU 2/ST 24 1/1/64–7/16/64" folder, Box 26, White House Central Files: Human
Rights 2/ST, Lyndon B. Johnson Library.

111. First elected in 1942, James Eastland was a Democratic senator from Mississippi and the
powerful chair of the Senate Judiciary Committee.

President Johnson: Did you tell the kids that—tell their parents that you'd talked to the Attorney General?

Marshall: Yes, I did tell them that.

President Johnson: Mm-hmm. Uh—

Marshall: But he won't mind that. But the governor would . . .

President Johnson: Resent it?

Marshall: I would think that he might, Mr. President. Again, I think Senator Eastland could give you the best advice on that. We need . . . That governor needs . . . We need to keep him.

President Johnson: Sir?

Marshall: *[speaking louder]* We need to keep him helpful if we can, Mr. President.

President Johnson: Mm-hmm. Mm-hmm. And you don't think my calling him would be . . . make him helpful if it got out?

Marshall: I wouldn't think so.

President Johnson: Mm-hmm. That's my judgment.

Now, on this conciliator, we got the mayor of Atlanta [Ivan Allen] in, and he just said [under] no circumstances would he resign. He'd give us a third of his help or half-time help, but he couldn't resign. So I told [Luther] Hodges to pursue it with the mayor of Charlottesville [*sic*, Charlotte, North Carolina]—that was the other suggestion he made. And if he failed there, to give some thought to LeRoy Collins. What would you think of that?

Marshall: Oh, I think he'd be first-rate, Mr. President, although he's awfully . . . he's cashed in a lot of chips down there, of course. That is, he's spoken out so strongly on this subject in the past. But I think in all areas, except the very, very difficult states, he'd be first-rate.

President Johnson: Mm-hmm. All right, now, if we fail there, they talked to Dave Lawrence [of Pennsylvania]. He doesn't want to do it, but would you think that he's a little too old? Or would you . . . Do you know anybody [who] would be better? We've got to get somebody pretty quick.

Marshall: That's right, Mr. President. I'd . . .

President Johnson: The South likes Dave Lawrence.

Marshall: Do they?

President Johnson: They respect him, every one of them. The Dick Russells, the Lyndon Johnsons, everybody that he was against.[112] He's

---

112. Senator Richard Russell (D-Georgia) was one of the most powerful figures on Capitol Hill and a leading foe of civil rights legislation. He was also a close friend and confidant of President Johnson's.

never been for us, I mean, he was strong for Jack Kennedy against Lyndon Johnson. But he does it in such a way that you respect him.

Marshall: Mm-hmm.

President Johnson: You like him?

Marshall: Well, he's a very fine man, Mr. President.

President Johnson: Well, will you explore that and give me some other names if you think of them? I want to be sure that we get somebody that you think the Negroes will accept, that you-all will think will be fair and work with you and under your leadership, and that Hodges will appoint.

Marshall: All right, Mr. President.

President Johnson: And you give me two or three more names of southerners that we can explore. Now, I wouldn't be hesitant to make Ted Kheel do it, if he'd do it, although he's a New Yorker.[113]

Marshall: Yes, I think he has some identifications with the NAACP and other groups that would make it difficult for him, and . . .

President Johnson: Mm-hmm. May be that.

Marshall: He was identified—I think he may have been a founding member of a thing called the Gandhi Society [for Human Rights] [*Johnson acknowledges*], which is . . . was—which [Martin Luther] King was involved in.[114]

President Johnson: Now, Hodges doesn't like him, but Dr. [George] Taylor recommended this fellow [William] Simkin over at the . . . Sitkin or Sinkin, what is it, over at Labor Department, conciliator, head of the conciliation service?[115]

Marshall: I don't know him.

President Johnson: Simkin or Sitkin? You might look at him. He's the director of conciliation for [Willard] Wirtz, and I might suggest you talk

---

113. Theodore "Ted" Kheel was a New York attorney who had helped mediate railroad labor negotiations in April 1964. He had also assisted Johnson with the Civil Rights Act of 1957. See also the conversation between President Johnson and Luther Hodges, 2:28 P.M., 19 June 1964, in McKee, *Presidential Recordings, Johnson*, vol. 7, *June 1, 1964–June 22, 1964*, pp. 463–68.

114. Kheel's name, along with those of Harry Belafonte and A. Philip Randolph, was mentioned in a 20 April 1962 memorandum from FBI Director Hoover to Attorney General Kennedy. Hoover had been tracking the activities of Stanley Levison, the associate of Martin Luther King Jr. that Hoover claimed was a former Communist, and reported on Levison's role in the formation of the Gandhi Society. David Garrow, *The FBI and Martin Luther King, Jr.: From "Solo" to Memphis* (New York: Norton, 1981), pp. 46–47.

115. A professor at the Wharton School of Business at the University of Pennsylvania, George Taylor had also assisted in avoiding a railroad strike earlier in the year. William Simkin was director of the Department of Labor's Federal Mediation and Conciliation Service.

to Wirtz and see if he's got any good people that . . . He may have some good conciliators, you know, that . . . [*unclear*].

Marshall: Yes. I think that . . . I think he might, Mr. President. I'll talk to him, if you want.

President Johnson: Yeah, I sure do. Now, anything else?

Marshall: No—

President Johnson: The Attorney General suggested I might want to say something in a statement. Now . . .

Marshall: On these people in Mississippi?

President Johnson: Yeah. Here's what I said this morning—he didn't know it:

[*reading*] "Mr. President, do you have any information about these kids that disappeared in Mississippi?" The President:—that's Scotty Reston—"The FBI has a substantial number of men who are closely studying, investigating the entire situation. We have asked them to spare no efforts, to secure all the information possible, report to us as soon as possible. We believe they're making every effort to locate them. I've had no report since breakfast, but at that time I understood that they had increased their forces in that area. Several weeks ago, I had asked them to anticipate the problems that would come from this and to send extra FBI personnel into the area. They have substantially augmented their personnel in the last few hours."

I don't know what else I can say.

Marshall: No, I think that's fine, Mr. President. I think if Lee is going to see them and . . . and . . . When they were over here, we said that you were concerned about it, and I think that's all they want.

President Johnson: Mm-hmm. OK. Much obliged.

Marshall: Thank you, Mr. President.

3:59 P.M.

To James Eastland[116]

Hoping to gain an entrée to the Mississippi governor, the President reached his old Senate friend James Eastland in the senator's hometown of Ruleville, Mississippi. Johnson kept Eastland on the speakerphone for

---

116. Tape WH6406.14, Citation #3836, Recordings of Telephone Conversations—White House Series, Recordings and Transcripts of Conversations and Meetings, Lyndon B. Johnson Library.

the entirety of this conversation, literally shouting into what he called the "squawk box" for over eight minutes. Eastland, in his thick Mississippi Delta accent, mocked the idea that any violence had occurred and gave voice to a prevalent white southern belief that the disappearance was a "publicity stunt," declaring confidently that there was "nobody in that area to harm them."

President Johnson: Jim?

James Eastland: Hello, Mr. President, how you feel?

President Johnson: I'm doing all right. I hope you are. You got a lot of sunshine down there?

Eastland: Need some rain—we need rain mighty bad.

President Johnson: Well, we're so dry in my country that we're going to have to sell off all of our cattle if we don't get rain.

Eastland: Well, I'm in the same shape: got a cotton crop just burning up.

President Johnson: I'll be darned. I thought you'd be harvesting cotton pretty soon. When is it, July?

Eastland: Yeah.

President Johnson: I guess they're harvesting in the valley right now.

Eastland: Uh-huh.

President Johnson: Jim, we've got three kids missing down there. What can I do about it?

Eastland: Well, I don't know. I don't believe there's . . . I don't believe there's three missing.

President Johnson: We've got their parents down here.

Eastland: I believe it's a publicity stunt.

President Johnson: They say that their parents are here, and they've come down to see the Attorney General, and they've seen Burke Marshall, and they're going to be interviewed by the FBI—the parents. And they've got some newspaper people and some photographers with them and a couple of congressmen: Congressman [William] Ryan and this Republican, Congressman Ogden Reid, whose folks used to own the *Herald Tribune* in New York.[117]

Eastland: Yeah?

President Johnson: They want to come to the White House to see the

---

117. Lee White recounts that he pointed out the *Herald Tribune* connection to Johnson while standing in the doorway of Kenny O'Donnell's office just before noon. Lee White, transcript, Oral History Interview, 18 February 1971, Lyndon B. Johnson Library, pp. 8–9.

President, and I told them that I thought that that would be better to let Lee White—who handles matters like that for me—to talk to them, and he'd go up to Ryan's office and talk to them. I don't know whether that's going to be satisfactory or not.

The Attorney General called over while I was out. He thought I ought to make a statement on it. I made one at my press conference this morning. Scotty Reston said, "Mr. President, do you have any information about those three kids that disappeared in Mississippi?" I said [*reading*]: "The FBI has a number of men who are studying it, and we've asked them to spare no efforts to secure information and report to us. I've had no reports since breakfast, but at that time I understood that the FBI had forces in that area looking into it. Several weeks ago, I asked them to anticipate the problems that would come from this, and they have sent extra FBI personnel into the area. They have substantially augmented their personnel in the last few hours." And that's all I said.

Eastland: Well, that's all right. Now, I'm going to tell you why I don't think there's a damn thing to it. They were put in jail in Philadelphia, in East Mississippi, right next to . . . the county right next to John Stennis's home county, and they were going to Meridian.[118] There's not a Ku Klux Klan in that area; there's not a Citizen's Council in that area; there's no organized white man in that area, so that's why I think it's a publicity stunt.[119] Now, if it had happened in other areas, I would pay more attention to it, but I happen to know that some of these bombings where nobody gets hurt are publicity stunts.

This Nigra woman in Ruleville that's been to Washington and testified that she was shot at 19 times is lying.[120] Course, with anybody that gets shot at 19 times [*chuckling*] is going to get hit, and she hasn't been shot at a *time*, and nobody's tried to bother her. They let her sit in on the Democratic . . . in the Democratic county convention this morning.

---

118. Democratic Senator John Stennis was from Starkville in Oktibbeha County, home to Mississippi State University. It was approximately 70 miles north of Philadelphia, Mississippi.

119. Eastland's plantation was in Sunflower County in the Mississippi Delta. The county seat was Indianola, where in 1954 the first Citizen's Council was formed two months after the *Brown v. Board* Supreme Court decision.

120. Eastland was referring to Fannie Lou Hamer, the sharecropper who had become one of the most influential civil rights leaders in Mississippi. In late-August 1962, Hamer lost her job as a timekeeper for a plantation and was evicted from her home. On the night of 10 September 1962, 16 shots were fired into the home where she had been staying since her eviction, but apparently unknown to the shooters, she was not in the house. That same night, two women were shot in Ruleville and another home was fired upon. To profound effect two months after this call, Hamer repeated her story to the Credentials Committee of the Democratic National Convention.

President Johnson: Uh-huh.

Eastland: I don't think there's anything to it.

President Johnson: Well, now, here's what I'm calling you about as my friend: Number one, they said I ought to make a statement. I've made this statement, and I think I'll stand on it. Do you see any need of my going any further?

Eastland: No!

President Johnson: All right, that's number one. Number two, they've suggested I see these parents. I've told them I thought that'd be a bad precedent. I'm going to try to get them to see an assistant of mine and get by with that if I can, so I don't add to the fuel. Uh, do you . . . you . . . you . . . Don't you think that's the thing to do?

Eastland: Sure, and I think it's going to turn out that there's nothing to it. Now, I don't know, but . . .

President Johnson: Now, number three, the Attorney General suggested that I probably ought to call the governor [Paul Johnson]. I found out that Burke Marshall called the attorney general, [Joe] Patterson of Mississippi, this morning. He was quite cooperative, and he said they were going to do everything they could to help. If I call the governor, it might put him on the spot a little bit, particularly if it got public, and he might resent it. Now, what's your judgment?

Eastland: Well, my judgment is that he's going to do everything he can, and is doing everything he can, to enforce the law.

President Johnson: All right, now, should I call him or not?

Eastland: Well, it'd be all right.

President Johnson: Would you advise it or not advise it?

Eastland: No, I'm not going to advise you. I don't think it would mean anything either way. He's going . . . I can call *him,* and . . .

President Johnson: You just do that, and I'll say I've communicated with the proper people, and I'm doing everything I can with everybody I know.

Eastland: All right. I'll call him and talk to him about it [*unclear*]—

President Johnson: I'd rather work with you. Now you tell him that I want to see him anytime he wants to now. I told you and John Stennis we want to get this bill out of the way so they couldn't say I was trading and filling out.[121] Now, it's out of the way, and you tell him anytime he wants to meet—

Eastland: Well . . .

---

121. Presumably, Johnson meant the Civil Rights Act, which he would sign on 2 July.

President Johnson: —I'm ready.

Eastland: This boy in the . . . What's—[Nicholas] Katzenbach said to arrange it one day next week after the sixth.

President Johnson: All right, that's good. Well, you just—

Eastland: And I'm going . . . I was going to talk to him this afternoon.

President Johnson: All right. You just tell him anything—

Eastland: Well, let me ask you this question about these three that are missing: Who is it there to harm them? There's no organ—there's no white organizations in that area of Mississippi. Who would . . . who would—could possibly harm them?

President Johnson: Well, might have some crank, or some nut, like . . . They locked [*talking over Eastland*] a man up in Minneapolis today for saying he's going to kill me Friday when I go out there.[122]

Eastland: [*Unclear.*][123] . . . It'll take a crowd to handle . . . make three men disappear.

President Johnson: Well, it depends on the kind of men, Jim.

Eastland: Huh?

President Johnson: It depends on the kind of men.

Eastland: Well, there's nobody in that area to harm them.

President Johnson: They might take a big crowd to take three like you.

Eastland: [*chuckling*] Ah, well—

President Johnson: I imagine it wouldn't take many to capture me.

Eastland: [*continuing to chuckle*] Well, I'd run.

President Johnson: All right. Well, now you get that rain for both of us and send it on east when you get through using it.

Eastland: I'll do it.

President Johnson: Now you tell the governor I send my regards. I want to work with him.

Now, we got a party conciliator under this law, Jim. I've got to have some southerner that knows something about the South and that the Negroes will have confidence in and won't say that I've fixed them. If you've got any ideas or anybody that's worth a damn, I wished you'd let me know.

Eastland: I'll do it.

---

122. Johnson had several speaking engagements in Minnesota on 27–28 June.
123. Eastland seemed to say, "Naw, it'll take a bear."

President Johnson: I tried to get the mayor of Atlanta [Ivan Allen] today, and he wouldn't take it.

Eastland: I didn't know that.

President Johnson: Well, I asked him, and he said he wouldn't take it. Some of them have suggested that I try to get Dave Lawrence of Pennsylvania, but he's been governor, and he wouldn't want to take it. Some of them have suggested that I get a mayor from North Carolina; I don't know him [Stanley Brookshire]. One of them suggested that I get LeRoy Collins. I don't know whether he'd get out of the association he works for or not.

Eastland: Well, he's a damn cheat, double-crosser, and a liar, and he's a . . . strictly dishonest. Now, he agreed that the convention . . . before he was to recognize us to vote for you, and he went back on his word, and I called him a goddamn, lying, son of a bitch out there.[124]

President Johnson: Well, we don't want him, then, do we?

Eastland: Hell, no!

President Johnson: All right, I'll tell them that. Now, get some—

Eastland: You couldn't retain your self-respect and vote a—and support a man that fought you like he did.

President Johnson: All right. OK, much obliged.

Eastland: Well, I think—

President Johnson: You think of anybody you can and give me a ring.

Eastland: I'll do it.

At 3:32 P.M. (EDT), the FBI had located the 1963 Ford Fairlane station wagon driven by Chaney. The burned car rested 15 miles northeast of Philadelphia. It was 48 feet off of Highway 21 and just over 100 feet east of the languid Bogue Chitto Creek. The FBI found the vehicle through tips from the superintendent at a nearby Choctaw Indian Reservation and a local man who had seen ten-foot-high flames in the area at approximately 4:00 A.M. (EDT) on June 22 (a little over three hours after the

---

124. LeRoy Collins was chairman of the 1960 Democratic National Convention in Los Angeles. During the nomination roll call, the Mississippi delegation proved notable for its early morning submission of arch-segregationist governor Ross Barnett as their candidate, a move met by loud boos from surprised Democrats in the Convention Hall. *Washington Post*, 14 July 1960.

murders). Arriving on the scene were Neshoba County Sheriff Lawrence Rainey and an estimated 20 FBI agents.[125]

4:05 P.M.

From J. Edgar Hoover[126]

Shortly after Johnson's exchange with Eastland, the FBI director called with the startling news about the car, adding that the men had "been killed." During the call, Johnson remained on the speakerphone.

A conversation between the White House operator and Marie Fehmer precedes the call in which they decide to put Hoover on the line before Luther Hodges.
J. Edgar Hoover: Mr. President?
President Johnson: Yeah.
Hoover: I wanted to let you know we found the car.
President Johnson: Yeah?
Hoover: Now, this is not known. Nobody knows this at all, but the car was burned, and we do not know yet whether any bodies are inside of the car because of the intense heat that still is in the area of the car.[127] The license plates on the car are the same that was on the car that was in Philadelphia, Mississippi, yesterday, and apparently this is off to the side of the road. It wasn't going toward Meridian, but it was going in the opposite direction.

Now, whether there are any bodies in the car, we won't know until we can get into the car ourselves. We've got agents, of course, on the ground, and as soon as we get definite word, I'll of course get word to you. But I did want you to know that apparently what's happened: These men have

---

125. Federal Bureau of Investigation, "Miburn Prosecutive Summary" of the case "Bernard L. Akin, et al.; James Earl Chaney, Michael Henry Schwerner, aka Mickey, Andrew Goodman—Victims," 19 December 1964, File 44.25706, http://foia.fbi.gov/miburn/miburn6.pdf, pp. 427, 458, 465–78; Chief A. D. Morgan, Mississippi Highway Patrol, Report, Folder 7: "Highway Patrol Reports and Correspondence, June 1964," Box 144, Series II, Sub-Series 10: Highway Patrol, Johnson Papers, University of Southern Mississippi.
126. Tape WH6406.14, Citations #3837 and #3838, Recordings of Telephone Conversations—White House Series, Recordings and Transcripts of Conversations and Meetings, Lyndon B. Johnson Library.
127. The activists had been driving a recent-model, blue Ford Fairlane station wagon.

been killed. Although, as I say, we can't tell whether there are any bodies in there in view of the intense heat.

President Johnson: Well, now, what would make you think they'd been killed?

Hoover: Because of the fact that it is the same car that they were in, in Philadelphia, Mississippi, and the same license number is on the outside of the car. Now, as I say, the heat is so intense you can't tell—on the inside everything's been burned—whether there are any charred bodies or not. It is merely an assumption that probably they were burned in the car. On the other hand, they may have been taken out and killed on the outside.

President Johnson: Or maybe kidnapped and locked up.

Hoover: How's that?

President Johnson: Or maybe kidnapped and locked up.

Hoover: Well, I would doubt whether those people down there would even give them that much of a break. But of course, we're going to go into that very thoroughly: not only as to the fact as to whether they're still alive. If they're not in the car, then they maybe have been killed and their bodies buried in one of those swamps down there.

President Johnson: Where did you find the car? How far from Philadelphia?

Hoover: The car was about, I'd say, eight miles from Philadelphia, but not in the direction of Meridian. It was in the opposite direction. Now, they had left Philadelphia—according to the reports that we had earlier—to go to Meridian, which is about 20 miles. This, however, was on state Highway 21, and the car was off to the side of the highway, although it could be seen from the highway. And an Indian agent—there's an Indian [Choctaw] reservation down in that area, although the car is not on the reservation—an Indian agent saw the car and immediately notified us, and we went there, and there we found this condition.[128]

President Johnson: How long had the car been burnt, you reckon, six or eight hours?

Hoover: Well, we . . . we frankly don't know. The intense heat would have indicated that the car probably had been burning for nearly six hours, or five or six hours.

---

128. According to two journalists' accounts, Special Agent John Proctor had received a report from Lonnie Hardin, the superintendent of the nearby Choctaw Reservation. In the days after the car's discovery, finding the identity of the person reporting the car to the FBI was a top priority of the Mississippi Highway Patrol. Cagin and Dray, *We Are Not Afraid*, p. 338; Gwin Cole, Assistant Chief, Mississippi Highway Patrol, "Report RE: Philadelphia Situation, 1:05 P.M., 1 July 1964," Folder 1, July 1964, Box 136, Series II, Sub-Series 9: Sovereignty Commission, Johnson Papers, University of Southern Mississippi.

President Johnson: What would you indicate? They filled it with gasoline, and . . .

Hoover: I would think so, yes. There wasn't any indication of any explosion like dynamite or anything of that kind. And, of course, dynamite wouldn't have caused the intense heat and fire that kerosene or gasoline would have.

President Johnson: Well, looks like a poor fellow would jump out of a car that [was] burning.

Hoover: Well, you would think they would, unless they'd been bound and were locked in that car and then the car set afire.

President Johnson: Well, why wouldn't an agent be able to look at a car and see if there's any bones in it?

Hoover: See whether there are any bodies in it?

President Johnson: Any bones, yeah.

Hoover: Well, the reason for that is the car is so burned and charred with heat that you can't get close to it, except that we did get the license number, which is on the outside of the car.

President Johnson: You mean it's still burning?

Hoover: Well, the car is still burning, yes.

President Johnson: You mean you think this happened in the last few minutes, then?

Hoover: No, I don't think it's the last few minutes. I think it's something that's happened within the last maybe five or six hours. You see, they didn't leave there until sometime yesterday, I think it was.[129]

President Johnson: OK, you call me as soon as you can.

Now, this group's coming down here to see Lee White, my assistant.

Hoover: Yes?

President Johnson: You think in the light of this that this congressman —both of them are raising hell for me to see them. You think I ought to step in and just tell them I've talked to you, and you're doing everything you can?

Hoover: I think it would be all right. I don't like to have you having to see these people because we're going to have more cases like this down South, and every time that it occurs, they're going to have these fami-

---

129. Hoover's early report here on the car's temperature was likely erroneous, particularly since it had been seen aflame almost 36 hours earlier. The Mississippi highway patrolman on the scene reported that the car had been "burned sometime before and was now cold." Chief A. D. Morgan, Mississippi Highway Patrol, Report, Folder 7: "Highway Patrol Reports and Correspondence, June 1964," Box 144, Series II, Sub-Series 10: Highway Patrol, Johnson Papers, University of Southern Mississippi.

lies come on here to Washington, and of course the congressmen, being politically minded, they'll want you to see them.

Now, they've seen [Nicholas] Katzenbach, as I understand, over here.

President Johnson: Yeah.

Hoover: And politically, it might be wise for you to just step in and say that you've been in communication with the bureau [FBI], somewhat along the statement that you issued this morning. [*Unclear comment by Johnson.*] I wouldn't give the details of the number of agents that we've got. You said it was substantially augmented, and I think that's . . . that's entirely sufficient. And that you're being kept advised of any progress that is being made.

President Johnson: That's good. OK. Thank you a lot.

Hoover: Fine.

President Johnson: You let me know as soon as you hear anything.

Hoover: Yes, I'll call you, Mr. President. OK.

4:14 P.M.

To Luther Hodges[130]

Johnson's next call was a quick follow-up to Hodges on Eastland's complaints about LeRoy Collins. The President was still talking through the speakerphone.

The President asks for Nicholas Katzenbach before the operator connects the Hodges call.

President Johnson: Hello?

Luther Hodges: Yes, sir.

President Johnson: Luther?

Hodges: Yes, sir.

President Johnson: I talked to Jim Eastland about this Mississippi thing.

Hodges: Yes?

President Johnson: And it's pretty bad down there, and he . . . I mentioned [LeRoy] Collins to him, and he said he's a goddamn, lying,

---

130. Tape WH6406.14, Citation #3839, Recordings of Telephone Conversations—White House Series, Recordings and Transcripts of Conversations and Meetings, Lyndon B. Johnson Library.

son of a bitch. He wouldn't trust him on oath and not to even think of naming him.

Hodges: Oh, really?

President Johnson: Yeah, he said that he lied to them, and they don't— they hate him pretty much, so I think you better not name him.

Hodges: Really? That's a . . . that's a shocker.

President Johnson: Said they tried to get him to recognize him at the convention. He promised to do it, and then he wouldn't let Mississippi vote for me.

Hodges: Oh, for heaven's sake.

President Johnson: Real vicious about it.

Hodges: Really?

President Johnson: We better think of a . . .

Hodges: Well, you think I better . . . should I double . . . Should I check on the other two of the Florida senators [George Smathers and Spessard Holland] just to see what their reaction is before I move?

President Johnson: I believe that it'd be out, though, if Eastland felt that way. I wouldn't want him. I think that they're very bitter, and if a fellow feels that way about me, why . . .

Hodges: Well, he doesn't feel that way about you.

President Johnson: Well, Jim Eastland said that they had a bound agreement with him at the convention to recognize him so Mississippi could vote for me, and said, by God, he wouldn't recognize him, said he called him a damn liar.

Hodges: Well, I—of course, I don't suppose either you or I could argue that at a distance, but I can't believe that's true, Mr. President. [*Unclear.*][131]

President Johnson: Well, Mississippi was pledged to me, and they told me they changed before they got to the end of roll call, and they did ask for recognition. They couldn't get it.

Hodges: Hmm.

President Johnson: He was chairman.

Hodges: Yeah. Well, I just don't know the details of that, do you?

President Johnson: No. No, that's all I know.

Hodges: I have talked with this man, and I know he has the very highest regard, and I don't believe he would have premeditatedly done a thing like that. I'd like, if you don't mind, like to get to the bottom of that.

President Johnson: All right, ask him and without telling him [about]

---

131. Hodges may have said, "Coming from him."

Eastland, just tell him some people say that Mississippi had an agreement with him.

Hodges: I'll do that.

President Johnson: [*Unclear*] what it is. But in the meantime, you pursue that North Carolina man [Stanley Brookshire].

Hodges: I'll do that. I'll know by tonight.

President Johnson: Bye.

Hodges: See what else we can do. Thank you.

4:16 P.M.

To Nicholas Katzenbach[132]

The news from Hoover changed the handling of the Mississippi situation, as Johnson firmed up plans to see the parents. Continuing to speak on the speakerphone, he informed the deputy attorney general about the burned car.

An office conversation with Lee White precedes the Katzenbach call.

Lee White: [James] Farmer was headed down there to—

President Johnson: Can you get Farmer now? It's 3 [P.M.] . . . 4:00. He said he'd leave at 2:30.

White: [*talking over Johnson*] I'm sure he's on . . . I'm sure he's en route.

President Johnson: Where was he, at the hotel?

White: No, he was in his office. He was planning to leave New York City at 2[:00] or 2:30 for Meridian.

President Johnson: Well, I guess he's already gone.

White: I think he is, sir.

President Johnson: I'd place a call for him at his home anyway to tell him this . . . found the car. You won't get him, but you can tell him you tried to get him.

I think if Katzenbach hasn't gotten them [the parents], what you'd better do is just tell them to come on down at your office and come in that side door from the EOB [Executive Office Building]. Get word out there

---

132. Tape WH6406.14, Citation #3840, Recordings of Telephone Conversations—White House Series, Recordings and Transcripts of Conversations and Meetings, Lyndon B. Johnson Library.

and bring them to your office, and then you tell them what all we've done, and let me come over and say a word, and I may just—I guess I ought to tell them we found the car, don't you think so?

White: Unless there's any reason for . . . [*unclear*] . . . from [J. Edgar] Hoover's point of view that it would harm things. I don't think it would.

President Johnson: Well, he didn't tell me to keep it confidential.

White: No, he [*unclear*]. That's right, he didn't. Of course, if you know it and they don't tell them . . . [if] you don't tell them, you're [*unclear*].

President Johnson: I'd have to tell them.

White: Yeah, going to be rough.

President Johnson: I don't think we ought to tell anybody else until Hoover tells [*unclear*]—[133]

The operator announces the Katzenbach call.

President Johnson: Yes, Nick?

Nicholas Katzenbach: Yes, Mr. President.

President Johnson: What'd you find out about those fellows?

Katzenbach: I haven't found out anything yet.

President Johnson: Are they still in [William] Ryan's office?

Katzenbach: They're still there, went back over there, and I guess that's where they are. I asked Burke Marshall to try to follow it because I had a group in my office and couldn't talk. And so I asked Burke to try to do it and . . . and see if the press was over there. And I suspect they are, since they tailed out [of] here after them. So I think under those circumstances, it'd be better for Lee to see them in the White House, Mr. President.

President Johnson: All right. Well, I'd just tell Lee to call them, and . . . I understand they found the car burned up down there.

Katzenbach: Did they? I didn't . . . hadn't heard that information.

President Johnson: I don't know what that means. If a car is burned up, they say they can't tell whether there are any bodies in it or not. Sounds like somebody put a lot of gasoline in it and touched it afire.[134]

---

133. White apparently took notes from this meeting and others in the day on the back of a civil rights task force report. Task Force Issue Paper, 17 June 1964, "Civil Rights Legislation" folder, Office Files of Lee White, Box 3, White House Central Files, Lyndon B. Johnson Library.

134. Johnson was apparently correct about the flame accelerant. FBI witness Doyle Barnette claimed that one of the conspirators at the Old Jolly Farm dam site had produced a "glass gallon jug" of gasoline for burning the station wagon. Federal Bureau of Investigation, "Miburn Prosecutive Summary" of the case "Bernard L. Akin, et al.; James Earl Chaney, Michael Henry Schwerner, aka Mickey, Andrew Goodman—Victims," 19 December 1964, File 44.25706, http://foia.fbi.gov/miburn/miburn3.pdf, pp. 176.

Katzenbach: Yes.

President Johnson: But I don't believe three men would burn up in it. I believe they'd run out. You might find some bodies around it. They'd be . . .

Katzenbach: Well, they may have . . . They might could have . . . They could have been killed first and left in there. Then burned it.

President Johnson: What would be the point in doing that?

Katzenbach: Destroy as much evidence as they could in the fire, Mr. President. [*Pauses.*] Make it as difficult to trace as possible.

President Johnson: Well. [*Pauses.*] What else can we do to forestall the reoccurrence of this?

Katzenbach: That's what I've been trying—

President Johnson: And what other things can we do besides ask FBI to be every damn place they can [*unclear*]?

Katzenbach: My—I think that's the major thing that we can do, Mr. President, and that . . . And the only other thing is to attempt to make the appeals that can be made quietly to the governor. I mean, I know Jim Eastland. I've talked at length with him on this, and he doesn't want violence down there and swears [Governor] Paul Johnson doesn't, and he's never misled me on anything.

I don't know what else we can do, and you can work with the groups that we have: the decent citizens, try to get them aroused. You've been doing that, sir. And it's hard to . . . it's just hard to think of anything else, Mr. President. I've been sitting here. We've spent endless times over here trying to think of things that can be done. That's all we've come up with. [*Pause.*]

President Johnson: OK, much obliged. You let me know if there's anything else.

Katzenbach: Yes.

4:21 P.M.

To J. Edgar Hoover[135]

To clarify the confidentiality issue raised with Lee White, Johnson checked with Hoover about what information he could relay to the parents.

---

135. Tape WH6406.14, Citation #3841, Recordings of Telephone Conversations—White House Series, Recordings and Transcripts of Conversations and Meetings, Lyndon B. Johnson Library.

An office conversation with Lee White precedes the call.

President Johnson: You just ask them what time they want to come down and tell—[*Loud feedback on the line can be heard.*] What'd you do over there?

Lee White: I just pushed a button that went down. You mean the line here on this . . .

President Johnson: You can come talk right into this one.

White: [*Unclear.*] [*Pauses for ten seconds.*] I've got a memo, Mr. President, over to the [*unclear*]—

The operator interrupts to announce that Hoover is on the line.

President Johnson: Yes, Edgar?

J. Edgar Hoover: Mr. President?

President Johnson: Yeah.

Hoover: I think this can be done when you see these people. I think it's proper that you can now say that the car has been found and has . . . that the car was burning, has been found, and that agents are endeavoring now to get inside of the car. What I find now, on the last word I just got, was that the inside of the car, from the intense heat, has melted and burned everything into ashes. Now, we've got to therefore pry the doors open, which we're doing, and getting into the inside to examine to see whether there's any human bones inside the car. If there are, we know the bodies, then, were in the car. But everything has been consumed in the car, even to the metal inside the car being melted.

President Johnson: Mm-hmm.

Hoover: Now, this Indian agent that first flashed this information to us said that he saw this car *yesterday* burning, and then he reported it to us today. So therefore the car has been extremely hot, and it's . . . the agents now are able to—have gotten the tools there—able to pry open the doors of the car to examine the inside. Whether we find any human bones or ashes of human bones that can be examined from that point of view we won't know until we can have the experts in the laboratory examine that down there.

President Johnson: Fine, Edgar. Much obliged.

Hoover: Fine.

President Johnson: You have to keep me informed.

Hoover: OK.

Time Unknown

Between Lee White and William Ryan[136]

White used Johnson's phone to set procedures for the parents' visit to the White House.

The President asks the operator to get Congressman Ryan for Lee White. The recording apparently is captured through the President's speaker-phone: Only White's side of the conversation is recorded.

Lee White: Hello? Congressman, this is Lee White. I heard your meeting went well with the Justice Department, and I had hoped to get down there myself to participate, but unfortunately, I was at the White House and couldn't make it. Are the parents still with you and with your people? [*Pause while Ryan responds, with White acknowledging.*]

Well, this is an awfully rough day for the President, so let me suggest then—if you have some transportation—if you'll bring them through the Southwest Gate to the West Basement in my office, and I'll be glad to meet with them. And, you know, I know it's not the same as the President is. I have been working on it, and I'll be glad to hear them and give them the benefit of whatever information I have. [*Pause while Ryan responds.*]

Southwest Gate. [*Pause while Ryan responds.*] That's the gate ... [*Pause while Ryan responds.*] That's right, around the south side, that big old, shaped fence in between the West Wing and the Executive Office Building. My office is the second floor, and you just bring them or have them come to the West Basement [*unclear*].

The recording of the conversation continues unclearly in the background as an unidentified male and the operator come on the line and discuss that the Oval Office telephone was apparently left off the hook. White hangs up and resumes his office conversation with the President while an operator continues to attempt to get the attention of someone on the line. The President finally realizes that the intercom is on and instructs White to turn it off.

4:24 P.M.: Johnson took an unrecorded call from Walter Jenkins.

---

136. Tape WH6406.14, Citation #3842, Recordings of Telephone Conversations—White House Series, Recordings and Transcripts of Conversations and Meetings, Lyndon B. Johnson Library.

4:25 P.M.

From James Eastland[137]

Heeding Johnson's request, Senator Eastland had called Mississippi Governor Paul Johnson. Early on in this report on his findings, Eastland relayed the governor's belief that the disappearance was a hoax, but Johnson stopped him with the news of the burned station wagon.

James Eastland: . . . [*unclear*] impartial observer down here to advise you whether there's any violence, whether or not everything's not being handled exactly as it ought to be—that he [Governor Paul Johnson] would welcome it.

President Johnson: All right. All right.

Eastland: Now . . . and he says he'd be glad to cooperate. He'd give them . . . send them anywhere they want to go, see anybody they want to see, that he thinks you ought to know what the facts are. He says that these people [COFO activists] that are in the state haven't scratched the . . . and that they've got to do something to attract attention. [*Johnson acknowledges.*]

Now, here's what he says about this thing at Philadelphia: He said those people were in Meridian. They left Meridian to go to Philadelphia, which is 45 miles away. Before they got to Philadelphia, they were announced missing by the headquarters of this organization in Jackson. And then they showed up in Meridian and were put in jail after that and kept a few hours and turned loose. Now, he says he expects them to turn up and claiming with bruises and claiming that somebody's whipped them, when that . . . he doesn't believe a word of it. And it is peculiar from what he said that they were reported missing, he said, 45 minutes after they left Meridian and before they got to Philadelphia, and they served . . . were put in jail in Philadelphia after that.

President Johnson: OK, now, here's the problem, Jim. [J. Edgar] Hoover just called me one minute ago, and—oh, I guess five minutes ago—and told me that they had found the car. It wasn't headed toward Meridian; it was headed a different direction out at a Indian reservation . . .

---

137. Tape WH6406.14, Citation #3845, Recordings of Telephone Conversations—White House Series, Recordings and Transcripts of Conversations and Meetings, Lyndon B. Johnson Library.

Eastland: Well, there's all kind of Indian reservations between Philadelphia and Meridian.[138]

President Johnson: Well, he said it was headed away from Meridian, but an Indian found it, saw it burning yesterday.

Eastland: Oh.

President Johnson: And he reported it to them, and his agents have gone out there, and the car is still burning. And it's so hot they can't get inside of it, and they don't know whether the people are inside of it or not, but it's the same car they were in because it's got the same license numbers.

Eastland: Well, I know nothing about that. But the governor says you can send some impartial man down here and that you'll get the surprise of your life, and there is, now . . . now, all around me, there are . . . in Ruleville—it's one of the headquarters—and there's just nothing. There's no violence or no friction of any kind.

President Johnson: Mm-hmm. OK, much obliged. And you've communicated my wishes to him, so there's no use in my calling him?

Eastland: Yeah, now, what . . . I'm going to have to call the Justice Department. They—Bobby [Kennedy] suggested an agenda of what you were going to talk about, and he wants that.

President Johnson: All right. That's good.

Eastland: That's something we can arrange.

President Johnson: Yeah, that's good. I haven't seen it, but I . . . anything suits me, and I want to be guided by you-all's suggestions, you and Attorney General.

Eastland: Well . . . that's fine.

President Johnson: OK.

Eastland: Bye.

President Johnson: Bye.

For the next 20 minutes, concerns about tax policy, ambassadorial appointments, Cyprus, and Henry Cabot Lodge momentarily interrupt the focus on the Mississippi crisis.

---

138. That area of Mississippi had several Choctaw reservations.

4:29 P.M.

From Douglas Dillon[139]

Dillon followed up on his earlier discussion (at 1:08 P.M. this day) about the Senate Finance Committee and reported on new developments in the excise tax–extension deliberations.

President Johnson: Yes?

Douglas Dillon: Mr. President, I just had quite a long talk on the phone with Russell Long, and for this excise thing tomorrow, we've lost . . . [Albert] Gore and [Paul] Douglas, and so we need to have . . . [Vance] Hartke's vote.[140] And both our own people from talking to him and Russell Long from talking to him thinks that if *you* talk to him, we can get it; otherwise, we won't get it. And with that, we'll have nine votes, counting [Harry] Byrd, and we'll be all right. Without it, they think we may lose anything up to a billion dollars in revenue in what the committee will do.

President Johnson: All right, I'll try to talk to him. They don't know anything about my relationship with Hartke, and I don't think that I'm the one to talk to him, but I'll go ahead and do it just so they—

Dillon: Well, they felt that—

President Johnson: [*Unclear*] try. They don't know a damn thing. They don't know how I stand with Hartke, and . . . but I'll do it. I don't . . . I don't . . . I wouldn't be very optimistic about it, though.

Dillon: Well, we'll see—

President Johnson: What is the vote on that committee? How's it—

Dillon: It would be 9 to 8 if we have Hartke and Byrd. We'll have nine. We'll lose six Republicans and Gore and Douglas.

President Johnson: Well, I understood Douglas is just going to make one motion: that's to strike out some excise and substitute oil or something.

Dillon: No. . . . No, he's . . . [Mike] Manatos misunderstood him, and he now has told Manatos that. He's going to make that motion, but then

---

139. Tape WH6406.14, Citation #3846, Recordings of Telephone Conversations—White House Series, Recordings and Transcripts of Conversations and Meetings, Lyndon B. Johnson Library.
140. Russell Long, Democrat of Louisiana, had been the Senate floor leader of Johnson's tax bill in January and February 1964. Albert Gore and Paul Douglas were Democratic senators from Tennessee and Illinois, respectively. Douglas, an economist and tax specialist, chaired the Joint Economic Committee.

he'll go along with [Everett] Dirksen anyway, no matter what happens to his motion.[141] So we've lost him. Because he was against us before, so it's nothing new.

President Johnson: OK. All right. Much obliged.

Dillon: All right, thank you.

President Johnson: Bye.

4:30 P.M.: Using his personal line, the President made an unrecorded call to Walter Jenkins.

4:43 P.M.

To Dean Rusk[142]

Johnson continued to wrap up the details of his seven-month search to find a replacement for Carl Rowan as ambassador to Finland. Earlier in the year, Democratic fund-raiser Mary Lasker had turned him down. Art critic Aline Saarinen seemed to be in line to accept, but later withdrew. Tyler Thompson, a career Foreign Service officer, would be appointed to the post on July 31.

Dean Rusk: Hello?

President Johnson: Dean—

Rusk: Yes, sir.

President Johnson: —I want to ask you: We sent some career person to Finland, and I got a little bit fuzzed up. It got by me without my knowing it, and we haven't notified him yet, although we asked the country if he'd be acceptable. Some of your career people—I just wondered if there's any reason why we couldn't change it and put this boy Sam Gilstrap to Finland and give this career man something else.[143]

---

141. Everett Dirksen, a Republican senator from Illinois, was the Senate minority leader and a member of the Senate Finance Committee.
142. Tape WH6406.14, Citation #3847, Recordings of Telephone Conversations—White House Series, Recordings and Transcripts of Conversations and Meetings, Lyndon B. Johnson Library.
143. Sam Gilstrap, an Oklahoman, had been the U.S. consul general in Singapore, but was set to become the first ambassador to the newly independent African nation of Malawi. The United States would create an embassy in Singapore in 1966.

Rusk: Well, my understanding was, Mr. President, that this name was on a list that apparently we were notified that you had approved—

President Johnson: Yeah.

Rusk: —and the Finnish government was very pleased with it when they were asked for the agrément. There is considerable disadvantage in shifting gears. It is not impossible to do it. Let me look at the . . .

President Johnson: I don't believe the fellow's been told. If he hadn't, I would like to switch him some other place. I don't know him, and I[′d] like to send Gilstrap to Finland if I could.

Rusk: Uh-huh, let me check on that.

President Johnson: Gilstrap was consul, you know, out at Hong Kong, and he's being promoted to an ambassadorship.

Rusk: Mm-hmm.

President Johnson: And he's young and able and attractive and shrewd and smart, and if you can, I'd sure like to.

Did you ever talk to [George] Aiken?[144]

Rusk: I have not been able to reach him yet, but I will. I've been in a meeting this afternoon. I'll get him, though, before I come over for this 5:00 meeting with [Turkish Prime Minister İsmet] İnönü. There was an agreed communiqué, by the way. [Under Secretary of State] George Ball will be in to see you a few minutes before the meeting.

President Johnson: Is it any good? What does it say, nothing?

Rusk: It says much of nothing, but I think the Turks are reasonably pleased with it.

President Johnson: Mm-hmm.

Rusk: But—well, I'll—Let me look into this other matter and advise you tomorrow on it.

President Johnson: All right.

Rusk: Right.

President Johnson: Aiken says that he's sure that there's some difference or something out there, and a good many of them are leaving the impression that [Henry Cabot] Lodge is in a fight with us. So I wished you would quote to Aiken that Lodge said he was coming back to campaign, that he thought he had to stand up and be counted for [William] Scranton.[145]

Rusk: Right, I surely will. I'll be—I'll call him before I come over.

---

144. George Aiken was a Republican senator from Vermont.
145. William Scranton was governor of Pennsylvania and one of the major challengers to Barry Goldwater's bid for the presidential nomination.

President Johnson: All right.

Rusk: Thank you.

4:49 P.M.

From Lee White[146]

Lee White called to plan the White House's handling of the news about the burned car, but Johnson had encountered another problem that was at least as problematic: The NAACP convention had voted at 2:30 P.M. to picket the Justice Department to protest the lack of protection in the South.[147] Afterward, Johnson intensified his efforts to arrange a visit with the parents.

President Johnson: Hello?

Lee White: Mr. President?

President Johnson: Yeah.

White: It just occurred to me as I sat here trying to figure out what in the world we could do when this information breaks. I haven't come up with any particularly spectacular, but it seems—

President Johnson: NAACP has just voted to picket the White House tomorrow because they want protection for their people in Mississippi.[148]

White: No kidding?

President Johnson: Yeah.

White: Well, that's really great, isn't it? [*Pauses.*]

What I was thinking was this would be an absolutely perfect time for Governor [Paul] Johnson to make a strong statement about what he intends to do to apprehend these . . . the people who perpetrated whatever crime this turns out to be, and if he could be prepared with some sort of a position, I think—and perhaps even get some other southern governors and statesmen to speak out and to decry this. I'm sure they're going to

---

146. Tape WH6406.14, Citation #3850, Recordings of Telephone Conversations—White House Series, Recordings and Transcripts of Conversations and Meetings, Lyndon B. Johnson Library.
147. Louis Martin to Lee White, 24 June 1964, "Civil Rights—Mississippi" folder, Office Files of Lee White, Box 6, White House Central Files, Lyndon B. Johnson Library.
148. The vote was for a protest at the Justice Department, not the White House. Two Mississippians led the push for action: Charles Evers, the brother of slain Mississippi NAACP Director Medgar Evers, and Dr. Aaron Henry, the president of the Mississippi NAACP. *New York Times*, 24 June 1964.

be as shocked and as badly battered as I feel and perhaps could do a great deal to . . . if the timing were right.

I just wondered how that struck you as at least somewhat a way of trying to bring order out of that . . . the chaos that could emerge when this information becomes public.

President Johnson: Yeah, I think it would be good. What would we do, suggest that Eastland get him to make a statement or something?

White: Yes, sir. And that he himself could say that people of Mississippi are not violent, that this is shocking. I mean, Senator [James] Eastland's got some stature and standing, and if everybody began to speak out, I think that would be of tremendous assistance because—

President Johnson: Well, get me two or three sentences that each one of them might say along the line you think.

White: All right.

President Johnson: I think you ought to try to get ahold of Roy Wilkins and ask him what in the hell we've done. Tell him I've been on the phone all day long. I've talked to [Nicholas] Katzenbach and [Burke] Marshall and Jim Eastland twice, the Attorney General and [J. Edgar] Hoover four or five times.

White: Yeah, this . . .

President Johnson: Ask him what else he wants us to do. Tell him we don't know . . . if they're going to picket, they'll destroy . . . people won't think we've done any . . . the people we try to help for will think we're—if we don't have their confidence, there isn't . . . nobody going to do anything. I don't see what good they think it'd do by picketing the White House. They must think they can do some good, though.

White: Well, I have a hard time figuring out what benefits they'll pull from that. It doesn't strike me as very beneficial. I'll try to get in touch with Roy and find out.

Now, I—you may recall in one of my memos, I specifically raised this question with him very early in the game, and he said no sir, he figured they were just absolutely pleased with everything and the way it was going and that he would certainly do his best to head off anything that came along that might look like it was critical of the administration or of you personally. But he—

President Johnson: Well, doesn't picketing of the White House imply that they're very angry with us?

White: Does to me. It doesn't strike me as being a very complimentary or very flattering thing. I'd say—

President Johnson: You call Roy, and then you call Burke Marshall and ask him what we ought to do about it.

White: All right.

President Johnson: I think maybe you ought to think about getting me a statement on this Mississippi thing, too.

White: All right, sir, I will. All right, I'll bring them down.

President Johnson: All right. Have you heard from these people yet?

White: No, sir, apparently they're en route.

President Johnson: We ought to get them down here. You ought to call [William] Ryan again and ask him if they've left.

White: All right. I will.

4:59 P.M.

To Mike Mansfield[149]

Johnson called the Senate majority leader about Henry Cabot Lodge's leaving South Vietnam to take a greater role in the Republican Party and about the impending excise tax vote. In the middle of those topics, Johnson dropped in the news about the burned car.

President Johnson: Mike?

Mike Mansfield: Yes, sir.

President Johnson: George Aiken said that he was sure that Lodge must be coming back because of some difference of opinion.

Mansfield: Yes.

President Johnson: Lodge announced that—he agreed to let me announce it first—but Lodge announced that the reason he was coming back was, quote, "because I believe it is my duty to do everything I can to help Governor [William] Scranton to win for president," unquote.

Mansfield: Uh-huh.

President Johnson: That's the only reason he's coming back. He frankly says he wants to get up and help before the [Republican] Convention.

Now, I wonder if you wouldn't tell Aiken that those are the facts. He told us that's why he's coming. He told them publicly, so there's no use of

---

149. Tape WH6406.14, Citation #3851, Recordings of Telephone Conversations—White House Series, Recordings and Transcripts of Conversations and Meetings, Lyndon B. Johnson Library.

leaving the impression with the people that there's been any argument, because there has not. He—

Mansfield: I would be glad to, sir.

President Johnson: He praises me in the letter, and we praise Lodge. And there's no quarrel: We wanted him to stay on, but his own people just raised so much hell, he thought he ought to come back and help Scranton, or he would be considered as not standing up and being counted when he was needed.

Mansfield: I'll tell George Aiken right away.

President Johnson: Tell him that, because he's got it all over the tickers, and he evidently put it out before he knew why Lodge was quitting.

Mansfield: I see.

President Johnson: Now, second, Douglas Dillon tells me we're in [a] very serious situation, that . . . that [Paul] Douglas is quitting us and [Albert] Gore is quitting us and that if we don't get [Vance] Hartke's vote, [Everett] Dirksen is going to repeal all these excess [*corrects himself*] excise taxes, and that'll just wreck us. Now, can you talk to Hartke and ask him to vote with the Democrats instead of the Republicans?

Mansfield: Yes, sir, I can.

President Johnson: Now, he's running this year, and while this may help him with a little group of banjo players, if he defeats his President and the Republican wins out, it's going to hurt me enough that he's liable to go down with me.[150]

Mansfield: Yes, sir, I'll be glad to talk to him.

President Johnson: Now, we've had a bad situation in Mississippi.

Mansfield: Mm-hmm.

President Johnson: Looks like they may have murdered those three kids.

Mansfield: Oh, God!

President Johnson: We found the car burning—that's confidential— we're trying to confirm it, but the car has been burnt.

Mansfield: Uh-huh. Oh, my lord.

---

150. In January 1964, Vance Hartke, a Democrat from Indiana, had pushed for a reduction of excise taxes on musical instruments, partly because a major instrument manufacturer was located in his state. The President applied personal pressure via the telephone and told him not to worry about the "goddamned band and musical instruments" but to consider the "big credit" that the Democratic Party would receive for the fall election. See the conversation between President Johnson and Vance Hartke, 1:11 P.M., 23 January 1964, in Germany and Johnson, *Presidential Recordings, Johnson*, vol. 3, *January 1964*, pp. 743–44.

President Johnson: But let me give you this statement again. I'm quoting from the ticker now. . . .

Mansfield: Yeah. I'd like to copy it down then. OK.

President Johnson: Let me find it. [*Pauses.*] Wait a minute. [*Pauses.*] Lodge said in Saigon he resigned as ambassador because he believed it his duty, quote, "to do everything I can to help Governor Scranton to win for president," unquote.

Mansfield: Mm-hmm . . . I can to . . .

President Johnson: "Help." That's the UP[I] [United Press International]. The AP [Associated Press] says, "Because I believe it is my duty to do everything I can to help Governor Scranton to win for president."

Mansfield: OK—

President Johnson: So both of them carry the same thing, and it's AP number 125.

Mansfield: Yes?

President Johnson: And it's filed at 12—at 2:12 [P.M.].

Mansfield: 2:12.

President Johnson: Yeah.

Mansfield: OK, [*unclear*].

President Johnson: Thank you.

Mansfield: Thank you.

5:00 P.M.

**From George Reedy; preceded by Office Conversation
with Jack Valenti**[151]

Press Secretary Reedy checked with Johnson about details that could be released regarding Mississippi.

Jack Valenti: Mr. [George] Ball and Mr. [Robert] Komer are here to give you a brief briefing before you meet the Prime Minister [İsmet İnönü].[152]

---

151. Tape WH6406.14, Citation #3852, Recordings of Telephone Conversations—White House Series, Recordings and Transcripts of Conversations and Meetings, Lyndon B. Johnson Library.
152. Robert Komer was a member of the National Security Council staff.

A secretary interrupts to report that Reedy is on the line.

President Johnson: Yeah?

George Reedy: One quick one, sir. Did you talk to the Attorney General about this Mississippi thing?

President Johnson: Mmm. Yeah, Attorney General called and talked to Jack Valenti. [*Pauses.*] I've talked to [Nicholas] Katzenbach in his absence, and I've talked to Burke Marshall.

Reedy: Yes, sir, and to the people in Mississippi—

President Johnson: I'd just say—

Reedy: —and to J. Edgar Hoover.

President Johnson: [*with Reedy acknowledging*] Yeah. I've been in touch with Hoover three or four times. Been in constant touch with him the last several days and three or four times today, if they ask you the question. And I'd say we've been in touch with the Attorney General and Katzenbach and Burke Marshall, because the Attorney General talked to Jack Valenti.

Reedy: That's enough. "We've been in touch on it" is OK, sir.

President Johnson: Anything else?

Reedy: That's all I need.

President Johnson: All right.

5:02 P.M.: Under Secretary George Ball and NSC staffer Robert Komer came into the Oval Office for the Turkey briefing.

5:10 P.M.: Johnson received an unrecorded call from Walter Jenkins.

5:15 P.M.: Walked to the Cabinet Room with Ball and Komer to meet Dean Rusk and the Turkish delegation.

5:25 P.M.: Made an unrecorded call to George Reedy from the Cabinet Room.

5:29 P.M.: Walked to the Oval Office with Prime Minister İsmet İnönü and others to present him with an autographed copy of *A Time for Action,* a published collection of Johnson's speeches and writings from the previous decade.[153] Afterward, the President took İnönü to Kenny O'Donnell's office and introduced him to several people there.

---

153. Lyndon B. Johnson, *A Time For Action: A Selection from the Speeches and Writings of Lyndon B. Johnson, 1953–1964* (New York: Atheneum, 1964).

5:33 P.M.: Made an unrecorded call to Jenkins. Two minutes later, Johnson called the FBI director in anticipation of the visit by the parents of the missing civil rights activists.

5:35 P.M.

To J. Edgar Hoover[154]

Johnson clarified details about the burned car while the parents were brought into the office, who had apparently heard the news about their children for the first time.

While the President waits for Hoover to come to the line, he speaks to Walter Jenkins.

President Johnson: You better comb your hair, Walter, looks like you been sleeping on it. Run in my office, right quick there. Put some water on it. You're worse than George Reedy these days.[155]

The operator connects the call.

J. Edgar Hoover: Hello?

President Johnson: Edgar?

Hoover: Yes, Mr. President.

President Johnson: [*reading*] "NAACP votes to demonstrate in front of the White House tomorrow to protest the worsening civil rights situation in Mississippi. In unanimous vote, during a special meeting of the NAACP, members voted to stage a demonstration at the Justice Department."

Hoover: Yes.

President Johnson: "[To] urge stronger federal action. The vote came as the FBI continued a full-scale re—search."

Have you-all put out any announcements yet?

Hoover: No, we haven't. We haven't put out any announcement

---

154. Tape WH6406.14, Citation #3853, Recordings of Telephone Conversations—White House Series, Recordings and Transcripts of Conversations and Meetings, Lyndon B. Johnson Library.
155. A few months earlier, Johnson told the generously proportioned Reedy, "You come in, in a damned old wrinkled suit, and you come in with a dirty shirt, and you come in with your tie screwed up. I want you to look real nice—get you a corset if you have to." Conversation between President Johnson and George Reedy, 2:25 P.M., 25 January 1964, in Germany and Johnson, *Presidential Recordings, Johnson,* vol. 3, *January 1964,* p. 829.

here. There has come out from New Orleans word that the car has been found.

President Johnson: Mm-hmm.

Hoover: The . . . We notified the Mississippi Highway Patrol, which has been cooperating and which had out a three-point alarm to locate the car. So in order to terminate that, we asked the Mississippi Highway Patrol to assist us in roping off this area where the car's found. What we want to try to do now down there is to locate any footprints or any car tread prints that may be in the mud or dirt on the side of the road of the persons who took the car there.

President Johnson: Mm-hmm. What can I tell the parents?

Hoover: I think you can tell the parents that the car has been found and that it was burned and that the agents are proceeding with intensive investigation to determine any evidence that would aid in—

President Johnson: Car's been found and it's burned.

[*to someone in the room, or to someone who picks up the line and then puts the receiver back down*] [*Unclear.*] No, but I just want you to take this.

[*to Hoover*] The car's been found, and it's been burned, and—

Hoover: Yes.

President Johnson: —the agents are proceeding with intensive investigation.

Hoover: To find out . . . to find the—

President Johnson: [*to someone in room*] Bring them on in.

Nathan Schwerner, Robert and Carolyn Goodman, Congressman William Ryan, Congressman Ogden Reid, the parents' attorney Martin Popper, Lee White, Walter Jenkins, and Jack Valenti begin the process of entering the Oval Office.

Hoover: —perpetrators of the crime.

President Johnson: To find the perpetrators. Any indication they're in the car yet?

Hoover: There's no indication as to whether they are because the entire inside of the car is melted into molten metal.

President Johnson: But wouldn't there be some bones there if . . .

Hoover: We have sent laboratory experts there to make examination of the ashes and of the inside to see whether there is any human bones or human evidence of ashes that would enable us to determine whether the bodies *were* in the car.

President Johnson: Mm-hmm.

Hoover: We do not know that they were, and we do not know that they were not.

President Johnson: Do you have any idea when I'll know that?

Hoover: We will probably get word on that sometime this evening.

President Johnson: Mm-hmm. You are sure, though, that you have found the car?

Hoover: We are sure we found the car in that it is the same make, the same color, and the same license numbers that were on the car when the car was in Philadelphia, Mississippi, yesterday.

President Johnson: Same car, same make, same license number, same color and everything?

Hoover: Yes.

President Johnson: All right. Now, where was it found from Philadelphia?

Hoover: It was found about . . . I think it was on highway, on state Highway 21, which is northeast of Philadelphia, about eight miles northeast of Philadelphia.

President Johnson: State Highway 21, eight miles northeast of Philadelphia?

Hoover: That's correct.

President Johnson: But it was not headed toward Meridian?

Hoover: No, it was not headed toward Meridian; it was in the opposite direction of Meridian.

President Johnson: Now, I talked to Mississippi. They told me that they had an announcement that the car and the people in it were missing prior to their arrival in Philadelphia and that when they later arrived and they were jailed, then . . . that this announcement had been made before that. Do you know whether that's true or not?

Hoover: No, I [*unclear*] . . . No, that couldn't have been true.

President Johnson: Couldn't have been true?

Hoover: No, it couldn't have been true because this car was burning yesterday.

President Johnson: Now, are you in touch with all the local officials and—

Hoover: Oh, yes.

President Johnson: Are they cooperating with you?

Hoover: They're cooperating thoroughly. This is the Mississippi Highway Patrol, and we have . . . we've had in the air, of course, the helicopters trying to locate the car. That will be no longer necessary now. But the local authorities are, of course, cooperating thoroughly.

[*with the President acknowledging*] Now, what's going to complicate the picture is, is going down there, some of these leading agitators of the Negro movement, to investigate this matter themselves. For instance, Palmer is— [James] Farmer is—of CORE—is flying down to

Philadelphia, Mississippi. And the . . . this Mrs. [Anna] Diggs, I think she's the wife of the congressman from Illinois.[156] She's a lawyer; she's going down there also. Now, of course, as soon as they arrive in those little towns, there's going to be even more disturbance. But I've issued orders to our men that they are to allow *no one* to come within the boundary of the roped-off area in which we are working.

President Johnson: I wonder if you oughtn't to ask one of your best people to communicate to the governor and suggest maybe that he make a statement that . . . a pretty strong statement that he's . . . what he's going to do, so that we can be sure that he gives us all the protections we can.

Hoover: I think it'd be a very good idea.

President Johnson: See if one of your men won't—can't talk to him and indicate that.

Hoover: I'll take care of that right away.

President Johnson: Thank you, Edgar. And keep me informed, now. The first thing you hear, you call me.

Hoover: Yes, I will.

5:40 P.M.

From Robert McNamara[157]

Immediately after the Hoover call, Johnson took one from the Secretary of Defense. Most of the conversation was about replacing Maxwell Taylor as chairman of the Joint Chiefs of Staff, reconnaissance flights in Laos, and Appropriations Committee business. McNamara hung up before Johnson could ask about military efforts in Mississippi.

During this call, the President is meeting with three of the parents of Andrew Goodman and Michael Schwerner.

Robert McNamara: [*with Johnson acknowledging*] Two points, Mr.

---

156. Anna Johnston Diggs (later Taylor) was the wife of Charles Diggs, the prominent black congressman representing a Detroit, Michigan, district. During this summer in Mississippi, she assisted the National Lawyers Guild. In 1979, she was appointed a federal judge for the Eastern District of Michigan.
157. Tape WH6406.14, Citation #3854, Recordings of Telephone Conversations—White House Series, Recordings and Transcripts of Conversations and Meetings, Lyndon B. Johnson Library.

President. First, on the chief of staff of the Army: I mentioned at lunch, I believe, we had two men under consideration.[158] One was [Creighton] Abrams, who's about 49½, and the other is a man named [Harold] Johnson, who is about 52½. General [Earle] Wheeler strongly recommends General Johnson for the post, with Abrams as his vice-chief. Johnson was formerly commander of the Command and General Staff School at Leavenworth [Kansas]. He's known as one of the ablest of the Army generals. We'd be reaching down rather far to pick him up; he's currently deputy chief of staff operations. Wheeler believes that Abrams and Johnson are about equal in ability, that to take the younger man over the older man, even though the older one's only three years older, would be undesirable from the point of view of morale in the Army. In either case, we're reaching down very far below all of the four-star generals to pick one or the other of these. I would support General Wheeler's conclusion, as does Cy Vance.[159]

President Johnson: All right, get me a little note transmitting that and give me their biographical background and let me look at it tonight, and I'll be in touch with you in the morning.

McNamara: I will do that.

Secondly, the State Department and we would recommend a reconnaissance mission at medium level—that is to say around 6[000] to 10,000 feet, one reconnaissance aircraft plus two fighter escorts—over Route 13 in Laos plus the Plaine des Jarres area—either tomorrow night or the next night depending on weather. [Leonard] Unger has recommended such a mission; State concurs in it.[160]

President Johnson: Mm-hmm. Now, why is that necessary again? Intelligence and psychological?

McNamara: I think, yes. Well, it's both. Unger is particularly interested in the movements along Route 13. You may have re—noticed that [General] Kong Le is talking about some kind of an offensive action down around Vang Vieng, which is on Route 13, in the event that the Pathet

---

158. President Johnson had to fill the Army position because General Earle Wheeler was vacating it to take over for Maxwell Taylor as chairman of the Joint Chiefs of Staff.

159. Cyrus Vance had been deputy secretary of defense since January 1964. Johnson took his and Wheeler's advice and announced General Johnson as the new Army chief of staff and General Abrams as the new vice-chief. According to Carroll Kilpatrick of the *Washington Post*, the President passed over 31 other higher-ranked officers to appoint Harold Johnson, and 32 others for Abrams. *Washington Post*, 25 June 1964.

160. Leonard Unger was U.S. ambassador to Laos.

Lao move towards Muong Soui up in that other Route 7.[161] [*Johnson acknowledges.*] And Unger is interested in finding out as much as he can about Pathet Lao dispositions along Route 13 for that reason.

President Johnson: Hmm. Wonder if you would get, just for my information, get the military aide and tell him to bring me those maps and point out to me—[162]

McNamara: I will. I'll do that.

President Johnson: —what you recommend, and you go over that with him, and then that's OK unless you hear from me.

McNamara: Very good. Thank you.

President Johnson: All right. Anything else?

McNamara: No, that's all for the time.

President Johnson: Now, they tell me we had a war in the Appropriations Committee this afternoon, but I'll talk to you about it a little bit later on, on the [foreign] aid thing.[163]

McNamara: I heard there was one vote in issue and that . . . I haven't heard the result.

President Johnson: Mm-hmm. OK, thank you.

McNamara: Thank you.

President Johnson: Bob? Bob? Bob? [*McNamara had already hung up.*]

---

161. Featured on the cover of this week's *Time* magazine, Kong Le was a general in the Royal Armed Forces in Laos. He commanded the Lao neutralist military forces until October 1966. *Time*, 26 June 1964.

162. Major General Chester V. Clifton was the White House military aide.

163. Since taking office, President Johnson had battled with Louisiana Congressman Otto Passman over foreign aid funding, referring to him as a "caveman." In today's round, Passman, the chair of the House Appropriations Subcommittee on Foreign Operations, had tried to cut $515 million from Johnson's $3.5 billion aid package. Passman's bid failed, but the subcommittee did trim $200 million. The full Appropriations Committee sent the appropriations bill to the House floor on 25 June, and it passed on 1 July. Robert David Johnson and David Shreve, eds., *The Presidential Recordings, Lyndon B. Johnson: The Kennedy Assassination and the Transfer of Power, November 1963–January 1964*, vol. 2, *December 1963* (New York: Norton, 2005), p. 567; *Congressional Quarterly Almanac*, 1964, vol. 20, p. 313.

5:44 P.M.

To Robert McNamara[164]

The President continues to meet with the parents of Andrew Goodman and Michael Schwerner.

President Johnson: [*to people in office*] Y'all pardon me, but I'm selecting the Joint Chiefs of Staff and the secretary of staff and secretary of the Army and gotten them on the way to Saigon, and [Henry Cabot] Lodge is coming out, and we're having all kinds of problems today.

Unidentified: We know.

The operator announces that McNamara is on the line.

President Johnson: Mr. Secretary, I'm here with the parents of these boys that have not been heard from in Mississippi since night before last. You have . . . are making available everything that you have to the FBI for . . . in their rescue and search, I assume.

Robert McNamara: Yes, sir, we have.

President Johnson: You be sure, now, to tell [J. Edgar] Hoover—

McNamara: We have helicopters that are being used at present along with some naval security cars.

President Johnson: Well, you be sure to let them know that every facility of the Department [of Defense] is available to them, and see that Hoover knows that, and see that he utilizes it to every extent possible.

McNamara: I will indeed, and we've had people working with Burke Marshall today on it.

President Johnson: Uh . . . Uh . . . So . . . OK, thank you.

McNamara: All right, thank you.

5:55 P.M.: Commerce Secretary Hodges arrived for an eight-minute meeting.

5:56 P.M.: During the meeting with Hodges, the President took an unrecorded call from Walter Jenkins, and four minutes later, took a call from a powerful Illinois Republican.

---

164. Tape WH6406.14, Citation #3855, Recordings of Telephone Conversations—White House Series, Recordings and Transcripts of Conversations and Meetings, Lyndon B. Johnson Library.

6:00 P.M.

From Everett Dirksen[165]

Johnson stepped away from the situation in Mississippi to tend to the interests of Everett Dirksen, the Senate minority leader, who had been essential for the passage of the Civil Rights Act and remained a key figure for the passage of a wide range of proposed legislation. Here, Dirksen pressured Johnson to accelerate the Corps of Engineers' approval process for the Kaskaskia River Navigation Project, a series of locks and dams in southern Illinois designed to make the river navigable by barges. After that, Johnson took the opportunity to pressure Dirksen on the excise amendment.

Everett Dirksen: . . . [*unclear*] civil works. He's going to appear before the Public Works Appropriations Subcommittee tomorrow morning. There is planning money in the bill for the Kaskaskia River Navigation Project.

President Johnson: How do you spell it?

Dirksen: K-a-s-k-a-s-k-i-a. Kaskaskia River Navigation Project. Now, all I want him to do is to have [General Jackson] Graham say to the committee that the [Army Corps of] Engineers do have construction capability for fiscal 1965, and if it's only 25[,000] or 50,000 dollars, that'll be enough to nail the thing down.[166]

President Johnson: How big's the project?

Dirksen: Huh?

President Johnson: What's the total cost?

Dirksen: The total cost of the project, I think, is $30-some million. Now, it's in that area of Illinois that's distressed. And already, Kaiser Aluminum and a half a dozen other plants have optioned sites in that area, just waiting for the time when this thing can be finished so that they can

---

165. Tape WH6406.14, Citation #3856, Recordings of Telephone Conversations—White House Series, Recordings and Transcripts of Conversations and Meetings, Lyndon B. Johnson Library.
166. General Jackson Graham was director of civil works for the Army Corps of Engineers until 1967.

barge coal out of there and raw materials.[167] And it's going to be the making of the southern 30 counties of the state.

President Johnson: Let me get on to it. I'll call you back.

Dirksen: Yeah.

President Johnson: All right.

Dirksen: I just want to be sure that General Graham will say—

President Johnson: All right. . . . Now, you're not going to beat me on excise taxes and ruin my budget this year. [*Unclear comment by Dirksen.*] I've got Ways and Means holding hearings, and we're going to come up with a recommendation one way or the other, but don't beat me on that, now. You can do it if you want to, and you can ruin my budget, but you're hollering "economy" and trying to balance it, and I cut the deficit 50 percent under what [John] Kennedy had it. Now, if you screw me up on excise taxes and get that thing going, I'll have hell. Now, let my Ways and Means Committee—

Dirksen: Now . . . Now, look at the pressure I'm under.

President Johnson: No, you're not under—

Dirksen: [*Unclear*] damn trade associations.

President Johnson: Well, I know it, but God, you're also for good fiscal prudence, and you know . . . you know that the way to do this is through the House committee, and you know if you put it in, you're not going to get it. They're not going to let you-all write a bill over in the Senate on taxes.

Dirksen: I don't suppose we are.

President Johnson: Now, please don't press me on that.

Dirksen: Well, I got to press it [*unclear*]—

President Johnson: Well, who are you going to take? You going to take all your Republicans? Give me one or two of them and let them be prudent. You've got people on there that can . . .

Dirksen: Well, you've got enough votes to beat it.

President Johnson: No, I haven't. I haven't. You can beat me, and if you . . . you oughtn't to do it. And you see how I'm—how you're going to let me win by one vote in there, and I'll call you back in a little bit on this.

Dirksen: You never talked that way when you were sitting in that front seat.

President Johnson: Yeah, well, I did—

Dirksen: You always had [*unclear*].

---

167. Among the companies purchasing tracts of land near the river in anticipation of the $28 million project were Kaiser Aluminum, Illinois Power Company, and Humble Oil. *Chicago Tribune*, 19 November 1967.

President Johnson: I did if my country's involved. I voted for Ike [Dwight Eisenhower] one time when [William] Knowland voted against him. I cast the vote on his foreign aid and brought it out of the committee.[168]

Dirksen: You're a hard bargainer.

President Johnson: And—No, I'm not.

Dirksen: Yes, you are.

President Johnson: But you just take care of them, and I'll look at this and see what I can do and call you right back.

Dirksen: All right.

6:07 P.M.: President Johnson held a meeting with Secretary of State Dean Rusk and Under Secretary of State George Ball that lasted until approximately 6:30 P.M. J. Edgar Hoover called during the meeting with more news about the burned car.

6:15 P.M.

From J. Edgar Hoover[169]

J. Edgar Hoover: . . . car was so hot and had been burned down that it's just like molten metal, so that the ashes, and when—things in the bottom of the car have got to be analyzed by laboratory experts before we can determine whether there are any human bones or flesh or anything of that kind.

President Johnson: Mm-hmm. Well, why in the hell can't they take a crowbar and break into that car?

Hoover: We've broken into the car; we're at work on that now.

President Johnson: Mm-hmm.

Hoover: We got the crowbars there within, I guess, about a half hour ago and broke open the doors, which couldn't be opened any other way.

---

168. The President had used this example when discussing the foreign aid bill the week before. William Knowland was a Republican senator from California (1945–1958). See the conversation between President Johnson and James "Scotty" Reston, 6:58 P.M., 17 June 1964, in McKee, *Presidential Recordings, Johnson*, vol. 7, *June 1, 1964–June 22, 1964*, pp. 395–400.

169. Tape WH6406.14, Citation #3857, Recordings of Telephone Conversations—White House Series, Recordings and Transcripts of Conversations and Meetings, Lyndon B. Johnson Library.

And now they're, as I say, are working on the matter of getting the particles of the inside of the car out and preserving such parts that can be preserved.

Now, of course, what's happened down there is the community has learned that the—of the car being found, and we have asked the Mississippi Highway Patrol to put out . . . to give us enough men that we can surround the area to keep away sightseers and newspapermen and all that type of individual that will cause us a trouble. What we want to preserve are any footprints or any tire prints of persons who might have come there with this car and then left the car there because they set it afire. Obviously, whoever did it didn't walk away, I would imagine, except to get into another car and drive away. So therefore, we are trying to preserve whatever evidence we can find on the outside there.

[*with the President acknowledging throughout*] But so far, as to whether the bodies were in the car or not, we can't say that definitely yes or no. We can say it is *the* car and that is . . . and the license numbers that were on the car in Philadelphia, Mississippi, are the license numbers on this burned car, because the burning of the car occurred inside. The outside of it was not burned. It was scorched, of course, and then burned, but was not destroyed.

Now, I understood—I conveyed your suggestion that we get in touch with the governor and see whether he would issue a statement. He could not be reached for 20 minutes because he was holding a press conference. I would surmise that that may be dealing with this particular thing because the Mississippi Highway Patrol told us that they had had a flash that the car had been found and they were sending some of their men down to where it was in order to be of any assistance that they could, since it is both a federal and a state violation of law. I told them, however, to still keep after the governor and then to let me know what the governor was . . . what the governor said—if it was a . . . if . . . if he was dealing with this subject—what he said in his press conference. I suggested to them that they tell the governor that it might be desirable for him to indicate that not only would the full facilities of the law enforcement agencies of Mississippi be extended to the federal authorities, but he would see that everything was done to bring the perpetrators of this crime to justice. Now, whether he'll say that or not, I don't know.

President Johnson: Mm-hmm. OK, much obliged. You call me when you get anything.

Hoover: I will. Yeah.

6:18 P.M.

To Jackson Graham[170]

Attesting to Johnson's interest in helping Everett Dirksen, the President found the director of civil works for the Army Corps of Engineers in less than 15 minutes.

President Johnson: General?

Jackson Graham: Yes, sir, Mr. President.

President Johnson: Senator [Everett] Dirksen, the Republican leader, has called me about a project, Kaskiakaskia River [*sic*]. Do you know anything about it?

Graham: Yes, sir, I do . . .

President Johnson: He wants you to testify . . . When if you . . . When you're testifying tomorrow.

Graham: Yes, sir, I go up tomorrow.

President Johnson: It says the [Army Corps of] Engineers do have construction capability for 1965, and he's going to try to get the committee to put in 35[000] [to] 40,000 dollars of construction money. He's got planning money.

Graham: Right.

President Johnson: Is that correct?

Graham: Well, we're actually making an economic restudy now for about a hundred thousand [dollars], and if that comes out favorable, we would have a construction capability.[171]

President Johnson: When will you have that study available?

Graham: About September, Mr. President. We're hopeful that it's going to come out all right, but—

President Johnson: But you can't say until September?

Graham: Well, I think we'll have a pretty good idea by July, but the final answer would come in September or—

President Johnson: How could you testify tomorrow that the [Army Corps of] Engineers believe it has a construction capability for '65?

---

170. Tape WH6406.15, Citation #3858, Recordings of Telephone Conversations—White House Series, Recordings and Transcripts of Conversations and Meetings, Lyndon B. Johnson Library.
171. The Corps of Engineers required that a project's potential economic impact justify its expense.

Graham: I would have to make this contingent on favorable outcome of the restudy. I certainly could indicate a capability of about the figure you indicate with that proviso.

President Johnson: Contingent on . . .

Graham: Contingent on favorable restudy of the economics of the project. What's happened is the railroads have gone in with unitized trains, are taking coal out of this Kaskaskia area into the Chicago area, so that we couldn't very well compete with that on a . . . with barges. We think we can justify this by figuring barging out into the lower river and generally moving the coal south rather than north into the Chicago area.

President Johnson: All right. Now, will you . . . will you say that, then: that you believe that it has a construction capability, and you'd go along with 25[000] or 35,000 [dollars] construction money if it's contingent on the favorable restudy of economics?

Graham: I'm perfectly willing to say that, sir.

President Johnson: All right.

Graham: And, actually, we probably could use a little bit more.

President Johnson: How much? Fifty, a hundred? What do you say?

Graham: I would—let's settle on 60,000 [dollars], [*unclear*].

President Johnson: 60[000], OK.

Graham: This [*unclear*]—

President Johnson: I'm going to say that you'll say that you will testify that the [Army Corps of] Engineers do have a construction capability for 1965 contingent on the favorable restudy of the economics of the project.

Graham: That's correct, sir.

President Johnson: Thank you.

Graham: I'll be happy [to]. Thank you.

6:22 P.M.

From Everett Dirksen[172]

Johnson and Dirksen continued their conversation about the Kaskaskia River Navigation Project.

---

172. Tape WH6406.15, Citation #3859, Recordings of Telephone Conversations—White House Series, Recordings and Transcripts of Conversations and Meetings, Lyndon B. Johnson Library.

President Johnson: ... General [Jackson Graham], I guess at home. He says that if I want him to, that he'll testify ... He said he's got a hundred thousand [dollar] restudy going on that won't be out until September.

Everett Dirksen: Yeah.

President Johnson: That he can't tell, that if the railroads haul this coal out of there and the economics are such that it won't justify, that he'd be in a hell of a shape. So—

Dirksen: Yeah, but there's no reason—

President Johnson: —he's says that what—

Dirksen: [*Unclear*]—

President Johnson: He says what he'll testify is this: that the [Army Corps of] Engineers have a construction capability for 1965 contingent on favorable restudy of the economics of the project.

Dirksen: Yeah.

President Johnson: That he believes that it will be a favorable restudy, that he believes that they can get barges out of there, but he can't see positively because he's got a hundred thousand [dollars] wrapped up in this study—it's coming out in September—and said if it came out the wrong way, he'd be in a hell of a shape. But he'll put it in. He'll say that they have a capability contingent on the restudy, and you can put the money in contingent on the restudy, and then he ... If the restudy goes against it and the project's no good, he'll just have to not spend it.

Dirksen: Yeah, except his division engineer in St. Louis told us today that they *did* have this construction capability.[173]

President Johnson: Well, he says they'll have a construction capability if the thing ought to be built at all, but if—

Dirksen: Yeah.

President Johnson: —if the economics of it are not justified—and they'll know when they get through with this hundred thousand [dollar] study, which will be through in September. So he says put your money in contingent upon it being justified.

Dirksen: OK.

President Johnson: And I told him to go as strong as he could, and he said he'd go 60,000 [dollars]. So ...

Dirksen: OK.

President Johnson: He'll testify for 60,000 [dollars] for you, and don't

---

173. Colonel James B. Meanor Jr. headed the Corps' St. Louis District. Michael J. Broadhead, historian, U.S. Army Corps of Engineers, to Kent Germany, 9 June 2006, in possession of the editors.

you tell anybody, now, that you've got a back door to the White House, but you go up there, and don't you kill my goddamn tax bill tomorrow. And quit messing around in my smokehouse.

Dirksen: You forget . . . You forget that I bought a key at Peoples Drug Store.[174]

President Johnson: Well, I know it.

Dirksen: It's got a label on it: back door at the White House.

President Johnson: What Republicans are going to vote against you tomorrow [on the excise tax extension]?

Dirksen: [*Chuckles.*] Against what?

President Johnson: Against your raid on the Treasury.

Dirksen: I don't know whether anybody's going to vote [*unclear*].

President Johnson: Well, how many will you let vote against you?

Dirksen: Well, I don't know. I'll have to do a little worshipping.

President Johnson: I'm going to lose a bunch of people on my side, so I've got to get two or three of your men.

Dirksen: You're a hard bargainer.

President Johnson: Well, you get them for me.

[*talking over Dirksen, with Dirksen then acknowledging throughout*] Now, here's what Joe Fowler says.[175] Joe Fowler says that the position [Wilbur] Mills is taking is the correct position.[176] That his committee [*reading*] "will make a full, definitive study of the present taxes immediately, and that study should be continued. That is my strong feeling. I would like to—I would have to stick with the colleagues in the Treasury. Once you uncork this thing just a little bit, you're a little bit pregnant and you'll never know where it ends. You'll have great difficulty with Mills if you try to take off *some* of the taxes. He wouldn't allow that. Whatever was said at the time the big tax bill was up about hearings was not to give any indication that the administration subscribed. Furthermore, no statement was made that hearings would be held before June the 30th." Some of them said they was made, so I called him.

Now, you offer your amendment, but don't you . . . don't you . . .

Dirksen: Wilbur's got time on his side. He can kill it in conference.

President Johnson: No, don't kill it in conference. That gets everybody upset, and you get every damn outfit in the country, and don't make it cruel and inhuman punishment. That's unconstitutional.

---

174. Peoples Drug was a national chain store.
175. Henry "Joe" Fowler had been under secretary of the Treasury since 1961.
176. Democrat Wilbur Mills of Arkansas chaired the House Committee on Ways and Means.

Dirksen: Why, everybody's upset all the time.

President Johnson: No.

Dirksen: What do you think about me?

President Johnson: Sure enough, now. Hmmph. Hell, I just got you straightened out: [*talking over Dirksen*] 30 million dollar's worth.

Dirksen: You let me [be] upset for a hundred days on our damn civil rights bill.

President Johnson: Thirty million dollars. You got yourself into that. You're the hero of the hour now. Hell, they've forgotten that anybody else is around. Every time I pick up a paper, it's Dirksen—magazine.[177]

Dirksen: Yeah, I—

President Johnson: NAACP is flying Dirksen banners and picketing the White House tomorrow.

Dirksen: I couldn't even get you to change your tune about that damn House [civil rights] bill.[178]

President Johnson: Oh, the hell you couldn't.

Dirksen: No, you didn't. You never did [*unclear*]—

President Johnson: I told them that I—was the first thing they asked me. I said whatever Dirksen and the Attorney General agree on, I'm for. [*Dirksen chuckles.*] That's what I sent him up there to agree for. You know, you never got a call from me during the whole outfit, and you know it.

Dirksen: I know.

President Johnson: But don't mess up that tax bill tomorrow now, Everett. Please don't.

Dirksen: Well, I got to offer this, but—

President Johnson: Well, offer it, but don't—John Williams is not for raiding the Treasury, so get him to save you.[179]

Dirksen: [*Chuckles.*] Well, he's been my savior before.

President Johnson: Well, get him to do it.

Dirksen: Well, we'll see.

President Johnson: OK.

Dirksen: Bye.

---

177. Dirksen's portrait was on the cover of the previous week's *Time* magazine. *Time*, 19 June 1964.

178. Dirksen had tried to weaken the bill's equal employment provisions.

179. John Williams was a Republican senator from Delaware with whom Johnson had sparred over the tax cut bill and the Bobby Baker investigation.

6:26 P.M.

From George Reedy[180]

On the heels of his cajoling of Everett Dirksen, Johnson chastised his press secretary for releasing information about the burned car.

George Reedy: . . . whether these parents knew about the burned car when they went in to see you.

President Johnson: Well, ask them that, or you'll have to ask—tell them you don't know about that. You don't know what the parents had in their mind. That's what I'd say.

Reedy: Of course, they'll probably say that you told them.

President Johnson: Well, if they do, let them tell them. Just say, "Boys, I don't know what the parents had in their mind. I don't know what the parents knew. I just don't plain don't know."

Reedy: Mm-hmm.

President Johnson: Do you?

Reedy: No, I don't—

President Johnson: How would you know?

Reedy: —know. I just know what Lee White told me happened: that you were the one that told them.

President Johnson: Well, he shouldn't have told you because when you get information, you get in trouble. Long as you don't know, you do wonderful, but . . . Every time [McGeorge] Bundy or Lee White or them go out and go talking big, tell you what they know, and that gets you in trouble, see. I'd just tell them that I surely don't know because we asked those people not to talk, you see. [*Reedy acknowledges.*] And if we go to talking, it makes us look pretty bad, don't you think so?

Reedy: [*sighing*] I don't think so in this particular case, sir—

President Johnson: Well, because—

Reedy: —but I'm not going to argue with you.

President Johnson: I don't want to be announcing it anyway.

Reedy: Oh, OK.

---

180. Tape WH6406.15, Citations #3860 and #3861, Recordings of Telephone Conversations—White House Series, Recordings and Transcripts of Conversations and Meetings, Lyndon B. Johnson Library.

President Johnson: I . . . I'd . . . They don't know what they found yet. They're still looking. I just hung up talking to [J. Edgar] Hoover.

Reedy: Well, they asked me if you had known about it, since it had cleared the wire. I said yes, you knew about it. I [*unclear*]—

President Johnson: Well, I wouldn't say that. You don't know what I know about it. I'd say, "I don't know. I haven't talked to him. I'll find out." I just can't . . . I'm going to call Lee and just cuss him out for going and telling you, because he oughtn't to do that. That just gets us real messed up.

Reedy: Well, I didn't say anything that Lee told me, sir.

President Johnson: No, I know it, but how'd you know I know about it?

Reedy: Well, I didn't want the wire knowing something that you didn't, frankly, sir.

President Johnson: Well, I'd just say, "I don't know. I'll check with you, but let me check." They tell me it's always good business to say, "Let me check on that one." "Gee, fellows, I'd like to help you, but I'll have to check it."

Reedy: OK, sir.

President Johnson: Because you're not supposed to read my mind. [*Pauses.*]
OK.

Reedy: OK, sir.

After the conversation with Reedy, Johnson placed a call to Lee White. While waiting, he continued his session with Secretary Rusk and Under Secretary Ball.

TIME UNKNOWN

From Yolanda Boozer; followed by Jack Valenti and Dean Rusk[181]

President Johnson: Yes?
Yolanda Boozer: Congressman Jack Brooks, [line] 9-2.[182]
President Johnson: Who?

---

181. Tape WH6406.15, Citation #3863, Recordings of Telephone Conversations—White House Series, Recordings and Transcripts of Conversations and Meetings, Lyndon B. Johnson Library.
182. Texas Democrat Jack Brooks and his wife, Charlotte, were good friends of President and Mrs. Johnson.

Boozer: Congressman Jack Brooks.

President Johnson: Tell him I've got the Secretary of State with me, and I'll come on, but I can't be but a minute.

Boozer: Yes, sir.

A 22-second pause ensues.

Dean Rusk: You want me to slip out and try and get four or five [*unclear*]?

Unidentified: I don't know that I can—

President Johnson: Yes, I think you better. You've—got any further suggestions before we go on this?

Rusk: Mr. President, I may be off base, but on this matter of the director of conciliation and so forth, but is the Justice Department working [*unclear*]—

A buzzer sounds; Rusk continues to talk in the background while Valenti comes on the line.

Jack Valenti: The Attorney General is here, sir.

Rusk: —the human relations council [*unclear*] community council [*unclear*]—

While Rusk continues to talk, someone says something unclear about the Department of Commerce. As that occurs, the following conversation takes place on the line.

Boozer: Hello?

Valenti: I was waiting to get the President.

Boozer: Jack?

Valenti: Yeah?

Boozer: Are you in your room?

President Johnson: Yes?

Valenti: Mr. President?

President Johnson: [*louder*] Yes?

Valenti: The Attorney General is here, sir.

President Johnson: All right, I'll be ready in just a minute.

Valenti: All right.

6:30 P.M.

To Lee White[183]

Johnson calmly chided White for talking to Reedy.

President Johnson: Lee? George [Reedy] wants to know now. He said you had told him that we had talked to these people.

Lee White: Mm-hmm.

President Johnson: When you tell George anything you get in trouble, so don't ever [*White chuckles*] do that, please don't.

White: No, I'm sorry.

President Johnson: I just can't stand him, because he's ready to issue a press release on it now. What can I do about it?

White: Mmm . . . Inasmuch as—

President Johnson: I told him not to talk.

White: Inasmuch as the story had broken on the wires about the automobile having been found at the time when they were known to be in your office, struck me, Mr. President, that you'd carry that off so. . . . so [*unclear*]—

President Johnson: How do they know that . . . how do they know they were in the office? Did they give that out? They get reporters with them, or what?

White: Apparently, they brought some photographers with them who were separated when they came into the building, and photographers stayed in the West Lobby. And so we didn't let the photographers follow them around the building, but apparently the word had—

President Johnson: Didn't they come in the side door? They didn't come like you told them, huh?

White: [*with the President acknowledging throughout*] They did come in the side door, but they brought the photographers with them. The guards didn't let the photographers come by; their names weren't on the list. The photographers then went around and got into the West Lobby, I believe, and they're the ones. But I think the word had filtered through that they were in the building, that they wanted to come in the building, and [Assistant Press Secretary] Mac Kilduff had had inquiries about it as

---

183. Tape WH6406.15, Citation #3864, Recordings of Telephone Conversations—White House Series, Recordings and Transcripts of Conversations and Meetings, Lyndon B. Johnson Library.

early as 1:00 this afternoon. So that the prospects of their being here was always pretty good.

But I'd say, sir, my own reaction is that there's something bold and dramatic and really courageous about your having told those people, and it turned out that it was the best thing you could have done because as soon as they got in their automobile, they must have heard on the radio the bulletin that the car had been found. So I'd say that [it] strikes me as something that if George is asked he could say, yes, that they heard it from you because it's a courageous thing, and it went off so smoothly.

President Johnson: All right. OK.

White: I sure didn't envy you. [*Chuckles lightly.*] You did it beautifully.

President Johnson: All right . . . All right.

White: Yes, sir.

6:30 P.M.: President Johnson made unrecorded calls to George Reedy and Jack Valenti on his private line.

6:33 P.M.: Met with Robert Kennedy, Nicholas Katzenbach, and Burke Marshall. The three men remained for the next three hours.

6:34 P.M.

From Clark Clifford[184]

As Bobby Kennedy arrived, Johnson received a call from Clark Clifford, the adviser that Johnson had asked to gather information from Kennedy almost six hours earlier.

Clark Clifford: This is Clark.

President Johnson: Mm-hmm.

Clifford: [*with the President acknowledging throughout*] I had a brief conversation with the man [Robert Kennedy]. He was in a great hurry, getting ready to fly to New York to get a plane to Europe. He said the

---

184. Tape WH6406.15, Citation #3865, Recordings of Telephone Conversations—White House Series, Recordings and Transcripts of Conversations and Meetings, Lyndon B. Johnson Library.

event that had decided him was the [airplane] accident to his brother Teddy. He says that he wants to spend time with him. He's going to have a very serious morale factor—he's always been so active, and he's got to lie there on that fracture bed for maybe six months. And also, he expects to devote a very substantial amount of time to campaigning in Massachusetts in Teddy's behalf because Teddy can't do a thing. He'll be in the fracture bed from now until November, and he wants to be free to go campaign for his brother and see that nothing happens up there. At least, those were the two reasons that he gave to me.

So he said, "I'm off in a hurry," said, "I just wanted to tell you I thought it all over with great care," and he said, "I was really continuing to be undecided until the terrible thing happened to Teddy." And he said, "That decided me. I think that I've got to stick closer to him and help him and get him through. And I'll look after myself later on."

So I wanted to pass that on to you. That may be part of it; the other part is a sneaking notion that he might be there when the lightning struck for number two, which, of course, was his choice when he came here last week. I thought maybe he'd gotten out of it by the time he left.

President Johnson: Thank you, much obliged.

Clifford: Thought I'd just pass it on.

President Johnson: Thank you, appreciate it.

Clifford: All right.

6:40 P.M.: Johnson made a quick, unrecorded call to Walter Jenkins on the private line.

6:40 P.M.

From George Mahon[185]

Johnson spoke to the Texas congressman about the afternoon's foreign aid showdown with Louisiana Congressman Otto Passman. Mahon, the chair of the full House Appropriations Committee, had sided with the majority on the Foreign Operations Subcommittee to reduce the size of Passman's desired cut.

---

185. Tape WH6406.15, Citation #3866, Recordings of Telephone Conversations—White House Series, Recordings and Transcripts of Conversations and Meetings, Lyndon B. Johnson Library.

The President is meeting with Robert Kennedy, Nicholas Katzenbach, and Burke Marshall at the time of the call.

President Johnson: [*to people in the office*] . . . [*unclear*] word, so I called him back and told him. He said in the meantime, he had called the governor—no, what he did, he called me back.[186] [He] said he had talked to the governor. Governor said he didn't want any violence, that he was going to do everything he could, that he was looking forward to coming up here next week. He's looking forward to getting an agenda from you on what we'd talk about. Said you would send him an agenda. I told him all [*unclear*] assuming we can work it out. He wanted to come next week and talk to me, and that he—Eastland didn't want any violence—

The recording cuts directly to the phone conversation.

George Mahon: We didn't do so well. Have you seen the ticker?

President Johnson: No.

Mahon: Well, Mr. [Otto] Passman stormed out and announced to the press that he was—

President Johnson: I heard that: said he wasn't a prostitute.

Mahon: Yeah, he wasn't a prostitute—

President Johnson: I disagree with him.

Mahon: Yes, I do, and he said if you were so infallible, why didn't we elect you for life?

President Johnson: Mm-hmm. Well, I'm for that.

Mahon: [*Laughs.*] I don't see anything wrong with that.

President Johnson: I don't believe anybody could hold this job for life. I don't know whether I can go until November or not. [*Mahon continues to laugh.*]

[*to people in office*] Passman said if I was so infallible I ought to have been elected for life. [*Laughs.*]

Mahon: But now . . . listen now, this is not all roses. [*Johnson acknowledges.*] This is the beginning of the . . .

President Johnson: Oh, of course it is.

Mahon: But—

President Johnson: I told him to get the list of all the Republicans [who] voted for us last time and try to see that we can hold those and get all the Democrats [who] voted against us and see if we can change some of them.

Mahon: Yes, and . . . you see, the point is that you haven't won this victory: We took a 200 million–dollar cut.

---

186. Presumably, the "he" in this paragraph is Senator James Eastland.

President Johnson: Yeah . . . that's right.

Mahon: And we by—actually we took a 229 million–dollar cut. We moved to reconsider, and we got that out of the way, and we had a lot of flare-ups and the rough edges, but—

President Johnson: Who stayed with you?

Mahon: Oh, I'll tell you right now: Old [William] Natcher really did go to town.[187]

President Johnson: He did?

Mahon: He saved the day for us.

President Johnson: Well, that's wonderful. Did—

Mahon: I was—

President Johnson: Did [Joseph] Montoya and does [John] Flynt stand up?[188]

Mahon: Montoya and . . . Montoya and old Jack Flynt, they stayed right in there.

President Johnson: And you and [Vaughan] Gary and . . .[189]

Mahon: Gary.

President Johnson: And Johnny Rooney?[190]

Mahon: Johnny Rooney.

President Johnson: All right. That made you seven, didn't they?

Mahon: Yeah, we had the seven.

President Johnson: And [Silvio] Conte?[191]

Mahon: And Conte. Don't overlook Conte.

President Johnson: No other Republicans?

Mahon: No other Republicans. But that Conte is like a [*unclear*]—

President Johnson: All right, Passman and what—what Democrat did we lose besides Passman? Any?

Mahon: Well, of course, George Andrews.[192]

President Johnson: George Andrews couldn't—why? Can't he ever go with us?

Mahon: No, no, no. He—

President Johnson: Not be reelected in Alabama, huh?

---

187. William Natcher was a Democratic representative from Kentucky.
188. Both Democratic representatives, Joseph Montoya was from New Mexico and John Flynt was from Georgia.
189. Vaughan Gary was a Democratic congressman from Virginia.
190. Democrat John Rooney was a representative from New York.
191. Silvio Conte was a Republican representative from Massachusetts. The *New York Times* called him a "maverick Republican" who was the "nearest thing" in spirit and outlook to former New York mayor Fiorello La Guardia. *New York Times,* 26 June 1964.
192. Democrat George Andrews had served in the House from Alabama since 1944.

Mahon: Yeah, not in Alabama. He, you know, no—

President Johnson: Well, I salute you. You rolled him. Now, what do you . . . will you have any problem in your full committee?

Mahon: We may have. We may have, but . . .

President Johnson: Well, you look after—

Mahon: He [Passman] has denounced the President and denounced the majority of the committee, and he in effect called us all prostitutes. This . . . this is . . . this is . . . Just the statement he made is going to help us a lot. It'll help solidify us on the House floor.

President Johnson: You better get—in the morning—you better get on that committee of yours and don't take any chances on him rolling you there.

Mahon: Oh, I've been on that committee for two or three days.

President Johnson: Well, you just—

Mahon: I've got only one man I know of who's with us [who's] going to be absent, and that's Joe Evins of Tennessee.[193]

President Johnson: Well, when does the vote come?

Mahon: Well, the vote comes at . . . on Thursday morning.

President Johnson: Can't you make him stay there?

Mahon: [*slightly chuckling*] Well . . . he's [*unclear*]—

President Johnson: Can you vote proxies in your committee?

Mahon: [*with the President acknowledging*] Well, we don't have proxies. But we're going to count every nose. You see, I've got the subcommittee chairmen, including Jamie Whitten, working with me.[194] And so we're going to count every nose, and we're going to be OK. I know the reason why.

President Johnson: God bless you. And then we'll get to work on the House, and I'll get with you, and we'll work on it.

Mahon: Yes, well, I tell you, I hated to have to call on you so much in this, but you pulled it out of the fire when you talked to Natcher. That's what did the trick.[195]

President Johnson: Yeah, mighty proud of you.

Mahon: Thanks a lot.

President Johnson: Absolutely.

---

193. Joseph Evins had served as a Democratic representative from Tennessee since 1947.

194. Jamie Whitten, the Mississippi Democrat, chaired the Appropriations Agriculture Subcommittee.

195. Johnson apparently spoke to Natcher on the evening of 22 June. For discussions about Natcher, see the conversation between President Johnson and Walter Jenkins, 9:15 A.M., 20 June 1964; and between President Johnson and Larry O'Brien, 5:10 P.M., 22 June 1964, in McKee, *Presidential Recordings, Johnson*, vol. 7, *June 1, 1964–June 22, 1964*, pp. 500–503, 518–23.

7:05 P.M.

To Allen Dulles; President Johnson joined by Robert Kennedy[196]

Earlier in the day, Governor Paul Johnson had requested that Johnson send an "impartial observer" to Mississippi. Here, Johnson and Kennedy asked former CIA director Allen Dulles to be that person.

Allen Dulles: How are you? [*Tape skips.*] Very well.

President Johnson: We got the ox in the ditch, and we need a little help.

Dulles: You have what?

President Johnson: The ox in the ditch.

Dulles: [*Chuckles.*] I didn't catch the first word.

President Johnson: [*Chuckles.*] Ox, o-x. [*Dulles laughs heartily.*] Uh . . .

Dulles: What can I do?

President Johnson: The Attorney General and I are sitting here talking and . . .

Dulles: Yeah?

President Johnson: [*slowly*] The governor of Mississippi this afternoon sent me word that he would like for me to pick some impartial, objective observer that would represent the President and come down and talk to him and let him show my representative what he was doing to try to prevent violence and what the state police were doing, what the local officials were doing, and review what his problem was and what we were doing. We wanted to . . .

Dulles: Yeah.

President Johnson: . . . get someone that we thought all the country would respect, and I want to be careful who represents me, and Attorney General and I have talked about it. We concluded that you were about the best and only fellow that we knew that'd get that job done for me, and we wanted to talk to you about it.

Dulles: Well, I'm certainly, any time I'm at your disposition. Whether I'm the best man for this or not, I don't know.

President Johnson: Oh yes, you are. Let—[*Dulles laughs.*] I know you are. Now, let the Attorney General tell you what he thinks about it, and I'll be back on in a minute.

196. Tape WH6406.15, Citation #3868, Recordings of Telephone Conversations—White House Series, Recordings and Transcripts of Conversations and Meetings, Lyndon B. Johnson Library.

Dulles: Yeah. . . . All right.

Attorney General Kennedy comes on the line.

Robert Kennedy: Oh, Allen?

Dulles: Bob?

Kennedy: How are you?

Dulles: Very well, but I—

Kennedy: Good.

Dulles: —feel terribly about your brother, you know. [*Unclear, tape skips.*]

Kennedy: Yes. Well, he's coming along now, and he's going to recover.

Dulles: Good, good. . . . When you see him next, give him my respect and regard.

Kennedy: I'll do that; I'll do that.

I think this is . . . could be awfully important. You know, the situation is extremely explosive in Mississippi [197]

Dulles: Oh, I know it is.

Kennedy: [*with Dulles acknowledging*] And there's very little contact and has been for the last few years between the authorities down there and the federal authorities, and the fact that the governor said that this was a possibility that he'd accept and have some impartial person go down there and look at the situation, I think could, you know, be a big help and give us some breathing space. And also somebody with your reputation around the country and around the world, I think, could perform a real service. I think it would be a question of going down and talking to him, talking to some of these students, talking to some of the Negro people down there, talking to some of the FBI, and then coming in and talking quite frankly with the governor and talking quite frankly with President Johnson about what you think needs to be done.

Dulles: I'm not a great expert on this subject, though.

Kennedy: [*with Dulles acknowledging*] I don't think that's—I think it's just a question of decency, really, and just looking at the facts and us, and we'd obviously give you a briefing on what we . . . how we found the

---

197. Robert Kennedy and Allen Dulles had been involved in another explosive situation during his brother's administration, the Bay of Pigs fiasco in 1961. President Kennedy made a joke during the 1962 Ole Miss crisis about Dulles having to step down as director of the CIA, saying that he had not had as "interesting a time since the Bay of Pigs," while Robert mockingly worried that he would soon have to resign and join Dulles at Princeton University. "Meeting on Civil Rights," September 30–October 1, 1962, Timothy Naftali and Philip Zelikow, eds., *The Presidential Recordings, John F. Kennedy: The Great Crises,* vol. 2, *September–October 21, 1962* (New York: Norton, 2001), p. 274.

situation, and then you could talk to him and see what you think. But I think it'd be, you know, it's something that we don't have and never have had, and the fact that you have no communication in such an explosive situation is very, very dangerous for the country.

Dulles: Oh, I realize it is.

Kennedy: And I think that you could . . .

Dulles: I realize it.

Kennedy: This is not a question of needing a great deal of expertise on civil rights or on the—

Dulles: I understand.

Kennedy: —problems of Negroes. I mean, hell, you could get that.

Dulles: Yeah. Yeah.

Kennedy: It's just a question of whether, you know . . . people—

Dulles: [*with Kennedy acknowledging*] Why wouldn't it—wouldn't it be best for me to sit down with you—

Kennedy: Yes.

Dulles: —or with the President just as he wants?

Kennedy: Yes.

Dulles: And both of you and talk and see whether I can be of service.

Kennedy: Yes, I think that the . . . you see, we . . . we had these three students down there who have been missing for 48 hours.

Dulles: Yeah, I know it.

Kennedy: And they found this car, which is burning, and they haven't been able to find out if the students were in there or not.

Dulles: Ah.

Kennedy: But I think it would be helpful if the President could say sometime tonight that he talked to the governor and talked to you and that he's taking that step so it doesn't look like . . . you know, I think that it's important to get on w[ith]—

Dulles: My job would be purely advisory, I mean—

Kennedy: That's right.

Dulles: I'd . . .

Kennedy: That's right, and I think you'd go down and report on what the facts are and make suggestions.

Dulles: Yeah.

Kennedy: And you make suggestions—

There is a break in the tape.

Kennedy: —and that we . . . you know, there'd be somebody that would go with you and . . .

Dulles: Right. Somebody from your office?

Kennedy: [*with Dulles acknowledging*] Well, or that, or we could pick out a young lawyer who, you know, was satisfactory to you. I have a little hesitation about our office because—

Dulles: Yeah. I see your point. See your point [*unclear*]—

Kennedy: [*talking over Dulles*]—they might think it was suspect, but I think you could get some young lawyer. You know, this fellow [Tom] Finney from Clark Clifford's office is one possibility, but somebody like that.

Dulles: Yeah. Yeah. Yeah.

Kennedy: Somebody that you had confidence in [*Dulles agrees*] who could, you know, we could fill in on all the facts.[198]

Dulles: And that would be with the governor and then with all the elements—

Kennedy: Yes, yes.

Dulles: Yeah.

Kennedy: I think it could be, you know . . . we've worked together for a long time, and so I know what you could do, and I know you'd do this well, and I know that you could do it, Allen.

Dulles: You want to announce it right away?

Kennedy: Well, I think it'd be well if—

Dulles: Now, what is the timing on this? I'm on this other commission [Warren Commission], you know, and we're trying to finish up our work, and I wouldn't want the . . .[199]

Kennedy: No, but I think if you could—

Dulles: . . . the Chief Justice [Earl Warren] to think I'd run out on him.

Kennedy: No, I think—what I think is that if you could go down there for a day or so [*Dulles makes unclear sound*] or a couple of days and then come back up here.

Dulles: Yeah.

Kennedy: And I think just to be—go down and talk to the governor and talk to some of the other people down there, and then you could come back up, but I think just to get it started, it would be helpful.

Dulles: Go down pretty soon you mean?

Kennedy: Yes.

---

198. Tom Finney, a former aide to Senator and Commerce Committee Chair Mike Monroney of Oklahoma, had been briefly considered in January 1964 as a possible appointee to the Securities and Exchange Commission. See Mike Monroney to Johnson, 1:00 P.M., 24 January 1964, in Germany and Johnson, *Presidential Recordings, Johnson*, vol. 3, *January 1964*, p. 783–86.

199. Dulles was also serving on the President's Commission on the Assassination of President Kennedy, better known as the Warren Commission.

Dulles: Something like day after tomorrow or tomorrow [*unclear*].

Kennedy: Yes, and then just talk to them, and . . . but you wouldn't have to—

Dulles: Yeah, yeah. . . . Do you think the governor's in good faith?

Kennedy: [*with Dulles acknowledging*] Yes. Now, of course this is all subject to that. And if the governor wasn't, you know, then we—it certainly wouldn't be announced, but I think that even if you found out that he wasn't, it would—

Dulles: I don't think I know him personally.

Kennedy: No, we don't know him, but I think that if he found out he wasn't, Allen, even that's helpful to the country and helpful to the President, just to—

Dulles: I see. . . . Well, you know him, don't you?

Kennedy: I don't know him.

Dulles: Don't you really?

Kennedy: I've talked to him on the phone. You see, we really don't have any communication with him down here, and the fact that he's opened this door is very important.

Dulles: He's suggested it?

Kennedy: Yes. And that—

Dulles: This is [George] Wallace, is it?[200] I got [*unclear*]—

Kennedy: No, this is [Paul] Johnson.

Dulles: Oh, it is Johnson.

Kennedy: Yeah.

Dulles: Oh, yes, certainly. Johnson, yes. Yeah.

Kennedy: Yeah . . . So . . .

Dulles: Has he a fairly good reputation with [*unclear*]?

Kennedy: No, we just don't know. Well, they say he's better than his predecessor, [Ross] Barnett.[201]

Dulles: Yeah. Oh, yeah. Better than Barnett.

Kennedy: [*with Dulles acknowledging*] But I think even, you see, even if that's not true, the fact that you could report that or, I mean, that you found it. Just if President Johnson has to take some steps later on, you know, and these things have such an effect across the country: It's not just

---

200. George Wallace, the governor of Alabama, was one of the most visible defenders of segregation in the South. One year earlier, he made his stand in the schoolhouse door to prevent the matriculation of two black students at the University of Alabama.

201. Ross Barnett had been the Democratic governor of Mississippi from 1960 to 1964 and was an arch-segregationist who, in September and October 1962, had defied the Kennedy administration's orders to desegregate the University of Mississippi.

Mississippi, but just have an effect across the country. I mean, this is not just a local m[atter]—

Dulles: Why did you pick me for this?

Kennedy: Because I know you. [*Chuckles.*]

Dulles: [*Laughs heartily.*] I've been a little mad at you, you know, a little bit on this Bay of Pigs book, but I'd like to forget that very easily.[202]

Kennedy: Well . . . Oh, well, I'm glad. [*Dulles laughs.*] But anyway, you know I . . .

Dulles: [*chuckling*] I don't stay angry long.

Kennedy: [*not reciprocating Dulles's amusement*] Yeah. Well, fine. But I think it could be . . . and I think the President feels it could be a big help.

Dulles: Well listen, I'd do anything for the nation, you—

Kennedy: Yes.

Dulles: —know, anytime. I've never refused. I just have a little question of my . . .

Kennedy: Well, I'm sure you could do it.

Dulles: . . . wise, wise thing to do.

Kennedy: But he—

Dulles: He wants to announce this tonight, the President wants to announce it tonight?

Kennedy: Yeah, I think he'd like to if it works out with Pre[sident]— Governor Johnson. Here he is back again.

Dulles: Yeah.

President Johnson comes back on the line.

President Johnson: Mr. Dulles?

Dulles: Yes, Mr. President.

President Johnson: I'll tell you what I'll do: I'll talk to the governor, and then I'll give you a ring back and perhaps we can get together in the morning.

Dulles: Right. I'll be at your disposition.

President Johnson: Do you know—

Dulles: If you think I can do it?

President Johnson: Oh yeah.

Dulles: [*with the President protesting*] I'm not so sure that—this is a field that I'm not . . . no expert in. I've . . . I go along—

---

202. Dulles may have been referring to a book published a month earlier that directed blame at the CIA for the failure of the Bay of Pigs operation. Haynes Johnson, Manuel Artime, José Pérez San Román, Erneido Oliva, and Enrique Ruiz-Williams, *The Bay of Pigs: The Leaders' Story of Brigade 2506* (New York: Norton, 1964).

President Johnson: No, you're the man for it. Now, we want to get you some . . . any assistance you want. I don't know who you may want. Anybody I know that I can get, I will.

Dulles: Yeah.

President Johnson: I don't think it'd be good to get somebody from the Justice Department. They'll have plenty of—

Dulles: No, I'd [*unclear*] have a private citizen probably—somebody from private life.

President Johnson: Now, this boy John [*sic*] Finney is pretty knowledgeable, able, young lawyer, very brilliant young fellow. He was Mike Monroney's administrator for a while, and he's gone in Clark Clifford's law firm.

Dulles: Yeah.

President Johnson: And . . .

Dulles: I have great respect for Clark. I know him very well.

President Johnson: I don't know whether he'd let him go or not, but I'd ask him if you thought it'd be helpful. The Attorney General and I are rather agreed he'd be a good one.

Dulles: [*with the President acknowledging*] You remember that I'm on . . . you put me on this commission that I'm working on with the Chief Justice and the others.

President Johnson: Yes, I know that.

Dulles: And that is now reaching a point where I wouldn't want to neglect that work.

President Johnson: I know that. . . . No. No, I understand that.

Dulles: For anything.

President Johnson: I understand that.

Dulles: Yeah.

President Johnson: [*with Dulles acknowledging*] And . . . But you'll have to go down there and stay a day or two and then come right on back, and I'll put a plane at your disposal, and you can take one of the Jetstars and go down in the morning and come back in the evening after a couple days there. Go in and out. And I'll call Clark and see about John [*sic*] Finney, and then I'll call you as soon as I talk to the governor.

Dulles: You might do that. . . . Someone that Clark thought was good, I'd be very glad—he's got some very able men in his office.

President Johnson: Fine, thank you.

Dulles: Very able.

President Johnson: Thank you so much, Mr. Dulles.

Dulles: Thank you, Mr. President, for the confidence.

President Johnson: All right, thank you.

7:15 P.M.

From J. Edgar Hoover[203]

Hoover, a man who had a long professional rivalry with Dulles, checked in with President Johnson to let him know that no bodies were in the car.

President Johnson: Yes?

J. Edgar Hoover: This is Edgar Hoover, Mr. President.

President Johnson: Mm-hmm.

Hoover: I wanted to let you know first, the governor has issued the statement along the lines suggested.

President Johnson: Good.

Hoover: And has also indicated that he will give every assistance, that even to the extent of calling out the National Guard, to aid in any search that we might desire.

President Johnson: Good.

Hoover: And that he'll support us in every way he possibly can.

President Johnson: Good.

Hoover: Now, the . . . the . . . the . . . I talked to the Secretary of Defense, and he's placed at our disposal a plane which has taken the two laboratory men, and they will arrive at Meridian, Mississippi, at midnight; otherwise, we couldn't have gotten down there until tomorrow morning.

President Johnson: Good.

Hoover: [*with the President acknowledging throughout*] We have moved all the inside of the car from the place the car was found to Meridian, where the experts will make the examination immediately upon their arrival.

Now, it's the impression of the agents who have removed the material, most of which are ashes and all kinds of debris, there were no bones that could be found, although bones would burn [in] a fire as hot as that. However, there were no dental plates or anything of that type that would normally would not burn, so the offhand presumption is that the bodies were not in the car. However, we will not know that definitely until the laboratory men tomorrow by—at midnight will make the determination, and I'll have word the first thing in the morning.

---

203. Tape WH6406.15, Citation #3869, Recordings of Telephone Conversations—White House Series, Recordings and Transcripts of Conversations and Meetings, Lyndon B. Johnson Library.

President Johnson: Fine, thank you.

Hoover: Then we'll, of course, have to start the search for where they are or who did this thing.

President Johnson: Any information they get, if they call you tonight or in the morning, you call me.

Hoover: Yes, I will, Mr. President.

President Johnson: Thank you. Thank you very much.

Hoover: Thank you.

After this call, Johnson asked a White House operator to place calls to Clark Clifford and Governor Paul Johnson. Shortly after that, while meeting with Nicholas Katzenbach and Robert Kennedy, he asked to be connected to the deputy attorney general's office.[204] During that time, Jack Valenti spoke to Congressman Ryan.

7:25 P.M.

Between Jack Valenti and William Ryan[205]

After Hoover reported that no bodies were in the burned car, Johnson asked Jack Valenti and Lee White to find the phone numbers for the parents. One minute into this conversation, Johnson received a call from Walter Jenkins (see conversation below).

Jack Valenti: Where may we reach these parents? Where are they located?

William Ryan: Well, I'll give you—I have the phone number for the Goodmans.

Valenti: All right, the Good—Mr. [Robert] and Mrs. [Carolyn] Goodman.

Ryan: Mr. and Mrs. Goodman.

---

204. Tape WH6406.15, Citation #3870, Recordings of Telephone Conversations—White House Series, Recordings and Transcripts of Conversations and Meetings, Lyndon B. Johnson Library.
205. Tape WH6406.15, Citations #3871 and #3872, Recordings of Telephone Conversations—White House Series, Recordings and Transcripts of Conversations and Meetings, Lyndon B. Johnson Library.

Valenti: All right.

Ryan: It's Endicott-2 . . .

Valenti: Endicott-2.

Ryan: . . . 7-2-6-5.

Valenti: All right. Is that a hotel?

Ryan: No, that would be their home in New York.

Valenti: That's in New York. Are they here now?

Ryan: No, they've gone back to New York.

Valenti: They've gone back to New York.

Ryan: Right.

Valenti: All right. What about the other ones? Do you know anything about the other ones?

Ryan: Other . . . now, wait a minute. The other number, if you can't get the Goodmans there, is Endicott-2 . . .

Valenti: Endicott-2 . . .

Ryan: . . . 7-1-7-5.

Valenti: . . . 7-1-7-5. Both New York numbers?

Ryan: Right, that's the same—there are two phones in the same house.

Valenti: I see. What about—

Ryan: I'll have to get you Mr. Schwermer's [*sic*]—Schwerner's number.

Valenti: All right, would you call me back on that?

Ryan: I'll get that for you.

Valenti: All right.

Ryan: It's in the Westchester phone book, and I'll pull it out and get it for you.

Valenti: Hold on just one second, would you? Would you hold on there, Congressman?

Ryan: Yes.

Forty-five seconds elapse while Valenti is away from the line.

Valenti: Bill?

Ryan: Yes.

Valenti: Hello?

Ryan: Yes.

Valenti: No, I was just—I'm sorry, I had to get the other phone there. Mr. and Mrs. Goodman, Endicott-2, 7-2-6-5.

Ryan: Right.

Valenti: Endicott-2, 7-1-7-5.

Ryan: Right.

Valenti: Would you call me back and let me know where the other people—When did these people go to New York?

Ryan: Well, they left right after being with the President.

Valenti: I see.

Ryan: And they took whatever the first plane was when they got to the airport.

Valenti: I understand. . . . Now, wasn't the other one Mr. Schermer?

Ryan: Schwerner.

Valenti: How do you spell that?

Ryan: S–c–h–w–e–r–n–e–r. Schwerner.

Valenti: S–c–h–w–e–r–n–e–r, Schwerner.

Ryan: Right; right.

Valenti: Do you think that—is that Congressman [Ogden] Reid's people?

Ryan: Yes.

Valenti: Well, maybe I could call . . . [*unclear*] . . . if you—

Ryan: Well, we are just trying his office.

Valenti: All right, fine. Would you call me—

Ryan: I know he's not here.

Valenti: Would you call me back?

Ryan: Yes.

Valenti: Thank you.

Ryan: Right.

Valenti: Good-bye, sir.

Ryan: Any further word?

Valenti: No, nothing else yet. I just want to have it just in case that we want to talk to them, that's all.

Ryan: Fine.

Valenti: Thank you, Congressman.

Ryan: Hold it just a minute.

[*to someone in his office*] You got it there, [*unclear*]?

[*on phone*] Hold on one minute, Jack.

Valenti: All right.

Ryan: All right, I got it right here. P-e . . .

Valenti: P—

The recording is interrupted by the operator reporting to the President that J. Edgar Hoover is calling the Attorney General, who is meeting with Johnson in the Oval Office. Kennedy's side of the conversation, consisting of a greeting and two affirmations, are recorded before cutting back to the Ryan call.

Ryan: . . . about finding the car. Apparently it's been on—

Valenti: He was hoping to talk to his wife.[206]

Ryan: He wanted to talk to his wife before she heard it.

Valenti: Yes.

Ryan: So he was headed right back.

Valenti: All right. Thank you, Congressman.

Ryan: All right. We—Listen, I want to tell you how much I appreciate the President seeing them and your—

The recording is interrupted by a brief exchange between Yolanda Boozer and an operator.

Ryan: . . . thought reacted very well.

Valenti: Thank you, sir. We'll be in touch with you.

Ryan: OK.

Valenti: Bye.

Ryan: Bye.

7:26 P.M.

From Walter Jenkins[207]

Amid the rush to deal with the news from Hoover, Johnson took the time to give Jenkins some instructions to pass along to A.W. Moursund, Johnson's business partner, who was being pursued by the *Wall Street Journal.* Three months earlier, the newspaper had published a series of articles outlining the sources of the Johnson family's wealth and their broadcast stations. The reporting focused in depth on the favorable relationship between the Johnsons and the Federal Communications Commission.[208]

President Johnson: Yes?

Walter Jenkins: Well, I have A.W. [Moursund] on the other line, and I thought maybe I ought to make a report before I let him go. He said he was in Blanco [Texas] at the hearing all morning, and when he got

---

206. Nathan Schwerner's wife (the mother of Michael), Anne, was not in the parents' group that had met with Johnson earlier in the afternoon. Michael Schwerner's wife was fellow COFO activist Rita Schwerner.

207. Tape WH6406.15, Citation #3874, Recordings of Telephone Conversations—White House Series, Recordings and Transcripts of Conversations and Meetings, Lyndon B. Johnson Library.

208. Louis M. Kohlmeier, "The Johnson Wealth," *Wall Street Journal,* 23 March 1964; "President Johnson, as Well as His Wife, Appears to Hold Big Personal Fortune," *Wall Street Journal,* 23 March 1964; Kohlmeier, "Johnson and the FCC," *Wall Street Journal,* 24 March 1964.

back, he got trapped: that Ray Shaw of the *Wall Street Journal*, Dallas, and Mr. E. [Ed] Cony of the *Wall Street Journal*—[209]

President Johnson: Now, we'll have to send a guard [*unclear*].

Jenkins: —were sitting in his office when he walked in. And that Jesse [Kellam] tells him that [Louis] Kohlmeier is in Austin trying to talk to Don [Thomas], but they're dodging him.[210] But he said that he just walked in, and they were there.

President Johnson: Hmm.

Jenkins: [*with the President acknowledging*] He said that he told them first off that he was busy and couldn't spend all—any of his time talking to newspapermen, that Abe Fortas had written the trust instrument and any details that they could get out of him, that'd be fine.[211] And they said that they'd been told that before, but wanted to ask him a few little questions, and he said he would doubt that he would answer any of them. And they said, "Well, we'd like to ask them anyway." And—

President Johnson: [*Unclear*] please, oh, those boys. How can we tell them to avoid that?

Jenkins: He said they could go to 20 people on the opposite side, and they'd be glad to talk to them, but they wanted to try to stick to what was accurate and what was right. And he said the only thing he could tell them at all would be very general. And they started out onto the [LBJ] Foundation, wanted to know if the President was a principal contributor, and he said, "I said all I could tell them about that is that doubtless, he had contributed, but I wasn't going into names and amounts. And [they] wanted to know about the stocks that the foundation owned, and I said I didn't think it was proper of me to talk about that with them. [They] said they had gone into the Kennedy Foundation. I said I had never seen any report on that, what the Kennedy Foundation's stocks are, on the things they owned. I did volunteer that the foundation is a little charitable institution that we're mighty proud of and that we hope will amount to something someday. We're trying to build it up where it will be good for some worthwhile causes, and he jumped on that and said that then I guess that accounts for the fact that you're not paying out all the income

---

209. Blanco, Texas, was a small Hill Country town just south of Johnson City.

210. Jesse Kellam and Don Thomas were overseers of Johnson's blind trust while he was President. Louis Kohlmeier, a reporter for the *Wall Street Journal*, had been writing articles about Johnson's business holdings. On 30 June, he published another piece on the Johnson City Foundation (formerly the Lyndon B. Johnson Foundation). Louis Kohlmeier, "How President Uses Family Foundation to Donate to Charity," *Wall Street Journal*, 30 June 1964.

211. Abe Fortas was a partner in the prestigious Washington, D.C., firm of Arnold, Porter, and Fortas and was perhaps the closest legal-political adviser to President Johnson.

in contributions. And I said I don't know that to be a fact. I said I'm sure that maybe some years may have paid out more and perhaps some years less, wouldn't know unless I had the statements before me, but we were trying to make something out of it besides just a pipeline and wanted to be really good to do some worthwhile good.

"He got off the foundation and jumped me on Brazos-Tenth [Street Corporation] and wanted to know the connection between the President and Brazos-Tenth.[212] I told him there was no connection, looked him right in the eye. He looked at me like he thought I was lying, wanted to know about an exchange between Texas Broadcasting and Brazos-Tenth. Have 19 parcels of land. I said you're talking about something covered by the trust, and I'm not going into anything that would inform Mrs. [Lady Bird] Johnson through the newspapers of what I'm not supposed to tell her at all, and I let him read the paragraph out of the trust that told me what all I could say.

"And then he said the records show that I had a large hand in the Moore State Bank along with Brazos-Tenth, a large interest in the Moore State Bank along with Brazos-Tenth, and there'd been some rumble about the bank paying me a thousand-dollar-a-month retainer.[213] I said I do practice law, and I do try to render value received, and . . . that there's no concern of anyone about my practice. And I said you're talking about my business now, and not somebody else's, and I'm not a public figure at all.

"Asked about the Haywood [Ranch].[214] Said he'd seen in the newspapers that the President and I owned the Haywood together, and I told him that that was correct. He wanted to know about some Lake Forest lots the President and I are supposed to have together, and I told him there were some little lots that a fellow had been trying to sell and they weren't worth much, said they'd probably cost us 4[00] or 500 dollars, each of us.

"And he wanted to know if my job was a tough job. I said if it's hard for me to carry out the instructions in the trust instrument: no, that it's not hard, it's easy. And asked me about the telephone line. I made the same

---

212. Ostensibly owned by Don Thomas, the Brazos–Tenth Street Corporation was housed in the same building as the LBJ Company and was suspected of being a front corporation for LBJ. Alfred Steinberg, *Sam Johnson's Boy: A Close-Up of the President from Texas* (New York: Macmillan, 1968), pp. 574–76.

213. Moore State Bank was located in nearby Llano, Texas.

214. Situated along the Llano River, the approximately 4,500–acre Haywood Ranch was owned by Johnson and Moursund through their Comanche Cattle Company. Hal K. Rothman, *LBJ's Texas White House: "Our Heart's Home"* (College Station: Texas A&M University Press, 2001), p. 153.

statement that I've made before. I said, 'Now look here, fellow. I'm not seeking any publicity. We have an awfully good man; let's try to uphold him.' He said, 'If you're telling us not to use your name, we just can't do that.' They grinned, and were very friendly and all that, but I guess they'll go off and cut my guts out."

President Johnson: That's right, and tell him that we sure—

Jenkins: "Did the best I could and tried not to make any mistakes."

President Johnson: Tell him that's all right, but we strongly recommend from here that when they catch him, wait like they did Don, or catch him, to just never say but one thing and that is under the—"Let me read you the trust instrument. I can't divulge it, and you talk to the attorney." That's the only advice I can give him, because they get the interview. Doesn't make any difference whether it's accident or not, Walter.

Jenkins: Yep.

President Johnson: They've got it, and they've got it by a bad thing, and they've got him admitting it, all this, and he oughtn't to do it. Just tell him that you've talked to the boss, and he says he doesn't know anything except to read them the . . . put a paragraph on his desk and read it if they're in his office. They don't have to let them come in, and . . . but just read them that and say that's all I can tell you. Refer them to him, that's all I know to do. Don't make him feel bad, because he's just played hell, but none of them know how to avoid it.

Jenkins: All right, sir.

President Johnson: Just as long as there are people that talk, why, we'll . . . they'll have stories. Just tell him I said as long as anyone would say yes to them that . . . they'd do it now.

Did they ever say they talked to Abe?

Jenkins: Never did say for sure that they would, said they'd been told before to do that, and he hopes they will, but . . .

President Johnson: Well, just tell him that if any more else come in, please don't talk to them. Just don't talk to them. Just say, "I'm sorry, but here's the trust instrument, and I can't do it."

Jenkins: All right.

President Johnson: Kohlmeier and who?

Jenkins: Well, Kohlmeier was not here. Kohlmeier was in Austin trying to see Don [Thomas]. This was Ray Shaw, *Wall Street Journal,* Dallas, and E. Cony of the *Wall Street Journal,* New York, has—

Fifty seconds excised under deed of gift restriction.

President Johnson: Anything else?

Jenkins: No, I believe that's all. I'll get back and talk to A.W.

President Johnson: All right. Just—

Jenkins: Nothing else you want to tell A.W., is there?

President Johnson: Just tell him, though, that that's a real problem with us and he'll have to talk to Don and . . . them and make it abundantly clear that . . . that they don't talk to them.

Jenkins: All right, sir.

President Johnson: OK.

Jenkins: All right, sir.

7:30 P.M.: Lee White returned to join the civil rights advisers in the Oval Office, and President Johnson received another call from Clark Clifford.

7:30 P.M.

From Clark Clifford[215]

President Johnson: Hello?

Clark Clifford: Yeah. Hi, Mr. President.

President Johnson: Clark, I'm here with the Attorney General and some of these boys on this Mississippi thing. The governor of Mississippi told Senator [James] Eastland today that he'd like for me to send an impartial observer down there to . . . that he could go over with a federal . . . with my observer, communicate with us what he was doing to try to maintain law and order, doing everything including calling out the National Guard if necessary.

These three missing boys, they found the car burned today that they were in. They don't believe they were in the car when it was burned; they can't find any bones or teeth or plates or anything like that. But they don't know. Their parents were in to see me.

So I'm going to call him back this evening, and—governor—and tell him that I'm anxious to send that observer, and I'm going to ask Allen Dulles to go. [*Unclear comment by Clifford.*] And he is agreeable to do it. I need a young man to go with him to help him. He says you've got a bunch

215. Tape WH6406.15, Citation #3875, Recordings of Telephone Conversations—White House Series, Recordings and Transcripts of Conversations and Meetings, Lyndon B. Johnson Library.

of good, bright, young men in your firm. I suggested we might ask you to lend us John Finney . . . what—not Finney, whatever his given name is.

Clifford: Tom.

President Johnson: Tom Finney.

Clifford: Yeah.

President Johnson: Because he's not anti-southern, and he's knowledgeable. He's worked in Oklahoma a lot, and he knows Dulles. Dulles is up in years.[216] I can put them in a Jetstar and let them fly down there for a day or two and talk to the governor and talk to the FBI and talk to the local officers and talk to the churches and talk to the others, and they can make a report back.

Clifford: Very good.

President Johnson: And I didn't want to say that until I talked to you, and I didn't want to talk to Tom until I talked to you.

Clifford: Fine.

President Johnson: Maybe you want to talk to him before I do.

Clifford: Well, I—what I'll do is call him immediately and tell him that he will hear from you—

President Johnson: All right. . . . That's fine.

Clifford: [*with Johnson acknowledging*]—and that it's perfectly agreeable with me for him to do it because I think his sense of obligation to the firm would be such that he would say that he would have . . . that he felt he would have to check with me, so I will do that ahead of time and tell him that he can expect a call, and he is to agree at once to do it, and he will do an excellent job. He's a very, very bright and mature young man.

President Johnson: Thank you a lot. Thank you a lot. And I'll call, be back in touch with you. And I'll call him. Thank you.

Clifford: All right.

7:40 P.M.: Johnson made an unrecorded call to George Reedy on the private line.

---

216. Allen Dulles was 71 years old; he died five years later, in 1969.

8:00 P.M.

Between J. Edgar Hoover and Robert Kennedy[217]

While in the Little Lounge with the President and the President's tailor, the Attorney General asked FBI Director Hoover to check out a CBS report that the bodies had been found.

White House Secretary: Hello?
Robert Kennedy: Hello? Yes.
White House Secretary: Do you want to take it down?
Kennedy: Yeah.
White House Secretary: Thank you.
[*to Hoover*] There you are.
Hoover comes on the line.
J. Edgar Hoover: Hello?
Robert Kennedy: Oh, Edgar?
Hoover: Yes, Bobby.
Kennedy: CBS just had a report that the bodies have been found.
Hoover: I haven't received word on that.
Kennedy: No. So could—
[*checking with someone in the office*] Who was it, Gerry Waters?[218]
[*to Hoover*] Gerry Waters. I thought maybe somebody could take a . . . find out what . . . basis of his information is. It's Gerry Waters, G—
Hoover: Is he with CBS?
Kennedy: Yeah.
Hoover: I'll take care of that right away.
Kennedy: Thanks a lot.
Hoover: Fine.

---

217. Tape WH6406.15, Citation #3876, Recordings of Telephone Conversations—White House Series, Recordings and Transcripts of Conversations and Meetings, Lyndon B. Johnson Library.
218. This CBS reporter was Gerald A. Waters.

8:10 P.M.

Between Edwin Guthman and Robert Kennedy[219]

Using a phone in the Oval Office, Kennedy called his assistant to talk about delaying their trip to Europe.

Edwin Guthman: Bob?
Robert Kennedy: Hi.
Guthman: Well, the plane has not landed yet. They think it's overhead, and it's, you know, and it's coming in.
Kennedy: Yeah.
Guthman: Now, we can—can you stand by over—
Kennedy: Yeah, that's right. Well, I don't see how I'm going to go to New York now, tonight.
Guthman: Oh . . .
Kennedy: We haven't said I'm not going yet, have we?
Guthman: Haven't done a thing yet. So you'll stand by?
Kennedy: Don't you think?
Guthman: Well, yeah, except . . . umm . . .
Kennedy: God, it'd make it much more . . . better if I could go, wouldn't it?
Guthman: Tomorrow morning?
Kennedy: Yeah.
Guthman: Well, yeah.
Kennedy: But I think it's better not to, don't you?
Guthman: Yeah, and I think that if you delay once and then go, that indica[tes]—and, you know, depending on how things go tomorrow, then it looks more like, you know . . .
Kennedy: Yeah. . . . On top of it.
Guthman: Yeah. Another thing is that you have to fly all night; that's the hell of it.
Kennedy: Yeah.
Guthman: But I would . . . then, you know, I wouldn't think it'd be too wrong to go ahead and say that you're going to . . . you've delayed your trip, or you, you know, could make the morning papers with it.

---

219. Tape WH6406.15, Citation #3877, Recordings of Telephone Conversations—White House Series, Recordings and Transcripts of Conversations and Meetings, Lyndon B. Johnson Library.

Kennedy: OK. [*Unclear comment by Guthman.*] OK. That's fine, then.
Guthman: All right.
Kennedy: OK.
Guthman: Thanks a lot. Talk—stay—we'll call you just as soon as we know something.
Kennedy: All right.
Guthman: We'll call you.

8:20 P.M.: Lady Bird arrived at the Oval Office for a brief visit before the President phoned the governor of Mississippi.

8:21 P.M.

To Paul Johnson[220]

While President Johnson is being connected, Lady Bird speaks in the background.
President Johnson: Hello?
Yolanda Boozer: Governor Paul Johnson, 9-0.
President Johnson: All right, are you on—Attorney General in there?
Boozer: Yes, sir, he's on the other line.
President Johnson: Tell him that I'm talking on that call now.
Boozer: Yes, sir. Thank you.
The operator then connects the call.
President Johnson: Hello, Governor?
Paul Johnson: Hello?
President Johnson: Governor?
Paul Johnson: Yes.
President Johnson: Lyndon Johnson.
Paul Johnson: Yes, sir, Mr. President, how are you?
President Johnson: Fine; hope you are.
Paul Johnson: Getting along fine, thank you.
President Johnson: I was talking to Jim Eastland this afternoon, and he told me—after he talked to you he called me back and said that you had . . . you were deeply concerned about this situation, as I was, and—

---

220. Tape WH6406.16, Citation #3878, Recordings of Telephone Conversations—White House Series, Recordings and Transcripts of Conversations and Meetings, Lyndon B. Johnson Library.

Paul Johnson: Yes, we've been doing everything that we possibly could to solve it as quickly as possible.

President Johnson: He said that . . . He said you had suggested that [you would] be glad if I'd send an impartial, objective observer down to talk to you so you could tell him what you were doing and see themselves what all was happening.

Paul Johnson: Just exactly what the situation is.

President Johnson: And I'll tell you what I thought: I thought that . . . I think that's a good idea, and I asked Allen Dulles—who is the brother, you know, of the former secretary of state [John Foster Dulles] and a very able man—to fly down there and told him that you had asked us to do that, had been told that you . . . and I'm going to ask him to go down there tomorrow or next day, and I'll have him give you notice beforehand.

Paul Johnson: All right.

President Johnson: I want him to talk to you and any people that you suggest that might be desirable for him to talk to. Send him to anyone that you think he ought to see, any local officials or state official—

Paul Johnson: Right. We'll send him anywhere he wants to go.

President Johnson: Or state officials, and I think he also ought to, before he comes back, see some of the Negro groups so that he can hear anything they've got to say or talk to them. I think he ought to talk to the FBI people that are in there.

Paul Johnson: Yes.

President Johnson: I'm deeply concerned about this situation, as I know you are.

Paul Johnson: [*with the President acknowledging throughout*] Yes. The real danger in it, Mr. President, is these youngsters who come into a situation where you already have a hard-core group of people with long police records that are professional agitators, and these youngsters don't realize what they're getting into. And they've been in here a good while, and they've stirred up a great deal of tension, and now these youngsters come in when the tension is getting toward the boiling point.

On this matter over there of these three that have disappeared, we've had investigators in there, of course, since yesterday morning checking it out. Then we have, of course, our people over there at the scene of this automobile, and I have been in touch with the FBI resident agent—or the district agent, [Harry] Maynor, down at New Orleans—and my people and his have been working very closely together.[221]

---

221. The governor was referring to Harry G. Maynor. John Proctor was the resident agent for Meridian, an area that fell under the control of the New Orleans office.

President Johnson: Yes. See, Edgar Hoover told me that a couple times this afternoon.

Paul Johnson: Right. . . . And then I told him that I thought that our people should get with his group and make a decision as to whether or not that big swamp [Bogue Chitto] should be searched. And if they needed to do so, or determine that was the thing to do right away, that we would be glad to furnish some additional personnel to get in there and to search that swamp out.

I, frankly, don't think that they will find them anyway, except perhaps in another part of this country. [*President Johnson acknowledges.*] From what we could determine, it looked like that they went out of there on foot to the highway, which is only about a hundred yards away. So . . .

President Johnson: Mm-hmm. . . . From the car?

Paul Johnson: [*with the President acknowledging*] Yes. And that's a tremendous swamp in there, particularly on the south part of the road, and it would take a large number of men to really scour that swamp closely. But we're willing to do it if they feel that that would, you know, be beneficial.

President Johnson: Mm-hmm. You issued a statement this afternoon, didn't you?

Paul Johnson: That's correct, sir.

President Johnson: What'd you say in that statement?

Paul Johnson: Well, in that statement—and incidentally, the CBS crowd were there and filmed it.

President Johnson: Mm-hmm.

Paul Johnson: I said that my people had been in there on assignment since yesterday morning. That I had not received any official notice or request to search for these people or to run this down until last night, but despite that, as quick as we heard about it yesterday morning, we sent investigators over. And then we also alerted our patrol units over in that area to be on the lookout also. And that the car had been found; that it was in the swamp about 12 miles northeast of Philadelphia; that it was on the north side of the highway in the Bogue Chitto swamp, about a hundred yards off the highway. That the FBI agents were there on the scene, that some of our personnel were there on the scene, that there were no bodies found in the car, and that the area had been roped off. That news personnel, I felt certain, would not be permitted in the area until an investigation had properly been carried out by the FBI and by our state investigators and by the local sheriff, and that every effort was being made, through a coordinated movement between all three of the law enforcement branches, to see that the ends of justice are met.

President Johnson: Mm-hmm.

Paul Johnson: That was more or less the statement that I [*unclear*].

President Johnson: Mr. Hoover told me that you had made it, and it pleased me very much. [*Unclear comment by Governor Johnson.*] We want to cooperate with you in any way in the world that we can. We know what a problem it is, and we want to make available all facilities that the federal government has that we can to you and work . . .

Paul Johnson: Did you see where—

President Johnson: . . . work with all of our people there and our equipment to try to locate these boys.

Now, CBS has got out a report that they'd located the bodies, and they'd found the bodies. You know anything about that?

Paul Johnson: I know nothing whatsoever about that, and if that were true, the investigators over there would have contacted me immediately.

President Johnson: I believe so. CBS called to say the student bodies have been found. [*Unclear comment by Governor Johnson.*][222] I don't know whether—I just got that since I started talking to you.

Paul Johnson: No, I . . . we do not know if they have.

President Johnson: Mm-hmm.

Paul Johnson: We haven't found out.

President Johnson: Mm-hmm.

Paul Johnson: But I'll certainly be delighted to give you a ring or to give someone that you may designate a ring—

President Johnson: Wait just a minute: Hoover's calling us on the other phone now. Let me see what he says. . . .

Paul Johnson: Sure.

There is a 15-second pause as the President apparently checks with Hoover.

President Johnson: This CBS man says that it's an unconfirmed report from a UPI [United Press International] stringer in Jackson.[223]

Paul Johnson: Uh-huh.

President Johnson: UPI still has not carried the story.

Paul Johnson: No. I feel that if they had located the bodies that they would have notified me immediately.

President Johnson: Mm-hmm. The parents were down. I've got to say something at night, and I don't want to . . .

Paul Johnson: Right.

---

222. Governor Johnson speaks too faintly here to make a definitive judgment, but he seemed to say "uh-oh."
223. A stringer is a freelance reporter.

President Johnson: I want to contribute to a solution and not add to a problem.

Paul Johnson: Well, certainly. You see what the big problem is down here is this: Suppose we had a half million marshals in here. You could not have prevented such a thing as happened in this particular incident. It's an isolated proposition that could happen anywhere in the state because of its size and because of the wooded areas and because of the fact that it is a rural state with a lot of small communities. And you're going to have this sort of a thing in New York City or anywhere else. It's a matter of when these things do happen that we run them to earth and bring them to justice.

President Johnson: Mm-hmm.

Paul Johnson: But this sort of thing could not have been prevented, regardless of what anyone had done.

President Johnson: Mm-hmm.

Paul Johnson: That's our big problem here, and it would be in Texas or Arkansas or anywhere else.

President Johnson: Yes, that's right. Now—

Paul Johnson: But you can have an individual incident or isolated incident like that.

President Johnson: Mm-hmm. Well, I think that we're going to have a long summer, and as I said before—

Paul Johnson: Yes, it is.

President Johnson: —we're—I'm deeply concerned about what's going to happen day to day, and I think it's just imperative that we work together as closely as we can, and all the resources of the state, and—

Paul Johnson: That's correct.

President Johnson: —the local people and the folks that we have be put together to try to see if the law's observed and see that we can avoid any violence.

Paul Johnson: Well, we have been doing that . . . we have been doing that for about six months, and we've just kept the lid on this thing. How we've done it, I don't know, but we've kept it all suppressed, and I've just looked for the dynamite keg to go off any minute, you know, and me sitting on it. But we have—I think the FBI agents and any of your people here in the state will tell you the same thing.

President Johnson: Mm-hmm.

Paul Johnson: That we've made a tremendous effort to try to keep the people calm, and so far they have been. There have been no demonstrations at all.

President Johnson: [*with Governor Johnson acknowledging through-*

out] Well, I wanted to tell you that . . . what I said before: that I was very pleased with your statement, that I appreciate your invitation to have this objective observer. I'm going to send Mr. Dulles; I'll notify you when he comes. I'm very anxious to—repeat, anxious—to cooperate with you and the local people, and all the facilities I have available *are* available for that purpose.

The governor [*sic,* Dulles] will come and talk to you and any people that you desire he talk to—and I'd suggest that you figure out various parts of the state [if] there are any people you think who could give him helpful suggestions and report on what's happening so we can get a pretty complete picture.

Paul Johnson: Certainly.

President Johnson: [*with Governor Johnson acknowledging*] Give him any guidance you can on any of the leaders that you think he might ought to talk to, to get all sides of the picture. We'll—He'll talk to the FBI people who are familiar, as you suggest, and then I'll want him to come back and give me some information because they're [the NAACP's] picketing us tomorrow, and [*chuckles slightly*] they'll say that we're not taking steps that we ought to, and so forth. So we want to be sure that we do everything we possibly can consistent with getting results.

Paul Johnson: [*with the President acknowledging*] Well, regardless of what had been done, Mr. President, an incident like this cannot be obviated anywhere in the United States or anywhere in the world. And those people who do criticize, they realize that, but they are just trying to stir up a storm, you know.

President Johnson: Well, we've got to . . . we've got to put everything we've got behind it because the summer's going to be long and a difficult one, Governor, and I know how you feel about it, and you know my problem too. And let's just work together as closely as we can, and my phone's always ready for you, and I'll consider yours the same way, and we'll be back in touch with each other.

Paul Johnson: [*Unclear*] . . . fine, and I do appreciate your calling me so very much.

President Johnson: Thank you. I'm looking forward to seeing you next week.

Paul Johnson: On anything that you think that I *can* do [*President Johnson attempts to speak*] to help suppress this situation, I wish you'd let me know.

President Johnson: I'll sure do it, and I just hope you appeal to all of them to continue, as you did today, to observe the law, and everybody follow it, and let's have no violence. [*Unclear comment by Governor Johnson.*] That's fine.

    Paul Johnson: We will require it.

    President Johnson: Thank you.

    Paul Johnson: Yes, sir.

Immediately after the call with the governor, Johnson tried to reach Tom Finney to invite him to accompany Allen Dulles.[224] The next recorded call went to the mother of Michael Schwerner.

8:35 P.M.

To Anne Schwerner[225]

Johnson began phoning parents with the news that the FBI had found no bodies in the burned car. Anne Schwerner had not accompanied her husband, Nathan, to the meeting with the President earlier in the day. Johnson reached her at home in Pelham, New York.

    President Johnson: Mrs. Schwerner?

    Anne Schwerner: Hello, President Johnson.

    President Johnson: Are you the mother of the . . .

    Schwerner: Of Michael.

    President Johnson: Yes. We have received word from Mr. [J. Edgar] Hoover that the investigation in the car indicates that there were no people in the car, and it's very likely that none of them were burned as could have been possible under the early information.

    Schwerner: Yes, thank you.

    President Johnson: And I have talked to the governor there, and he is making all the facilities of the state available in the search. And they have seen some tracks leaving the car.

    Schwerner: Yes.

    President Johnson: And they're going to try to continue. We're flying

---

224. Tape WH6406.16, Citation #3880, Recordings of Telephone Conversations—White House Series, Recordings and Transcripts of Conversations and Meetings, Lyndon B. Johnson Library.

225. Tape WH6406.16, Citation #3882, Recordings of Telephone Conversations—White House Series, Recordings and Transcripts of Conversations and Meetings, Lyndon B. Johnson Library.

people in from the FBI tonight, and I just wanted you to know that, and that was a little hope that we didn't have earlier, and I thought that we would enjoy it as long as we could.

Schwerner: [*emotionally*] Thank you so much, President Johnson. I appreciate this. Thank you very much.

President Johnson: Thank you, ma'am.

Schwerner: [*emotionally*] Thank you.

President Johnson: Bye.

8:45 P.M.

To Tom Finney; President Johnson joined by Robert Kennedy[226]

Johnson finally reached Finney to invite him to join Dulles.

Tom Finney: Yes, sir.

President Johnson: Has Clark [Clifford] talked to you?

Finney: Yes, I talked to him just a minute ago.

President Johnson: I hope you can be helpful to us.

Finney: I'm at your disposal.

President Johnson: All right. I'll have Jack Valenti call you in the morning and get you with Mr. [Allen] Dulles. We'll see if he can get off to go down there tomorrow. I'd like for him to go if he can.

Finney: All right, sir.

President Johnson: And we'll get a plane set up for you, and you better think about your . . . any stenographic facilities you might need [*Finney acknowledges*], and . . . we'll fly you down to see the governor. What we want to do is: I've told the governor that you're coming, and he's asked for an objective observer. I'm telling him I'm sending Mr. Dulles, but he's up in years, and I want some young man that's got some imagination and initiative and go with him and kind of support him. And I told the governor how deeply concerned we are, and we want to cooperate and make all the facilities available that we have. And I want the governor to talk—Dulles to talk to the governor, and then I want him to talk to any people the governor wants him to talk to. And then I'm very anxious for him to talk to

---

226. Tape WH6406.16, Citation #3883, Recordings of Telephone Conversations—White House Series, Recordings and Transcripts of Conversations and Meetings, Lyndon B. Johnson Library.

the FBI people we've got there and, over the state, the Negro leaders and some of the church leaders that are on the other side and get a picture and be sure that they're doing everything they can do and that we're doing everything we can do to bring about law observance and to prevent these things that happen, like burning this car today, and so forth.

Finney: Has there been any further word on the three boys?

President Johnson: No, they haven't located—they haven't located them. They have seen . . . They found some tracks leading away from the car, but that's all. The Attorney General's here with me, and I want you to talk to him about it before we get off the line.

Finney: All right, sir.

President Johnson: Now, do you have anything else you want to say?

Finney: No, sir. You think . . . what, I'll leave tomorrow, you believe?

President Johnson: Yeah, I would think so.

Finney: Yeah.

President Johnson: I want to get you to meet with the people over there like Burke Marshall or the [Attorney] General, anybody that would be helpful, and then we'll . . . we'll get you off just as quickly as you can. I think the quicker, the better.

Finney: I think that's right.

President Johnson: OK. Here's the A.G.

Finney: All right, sir.

Attorney General Kennedy comes on the line.

Robert Kennedy: Hello?

Finney: Hi, Bob.

Kennedy: Hi, how are you?

Finney: Fine.

Kennedy: I think, maybe, if you could come by some time tomorrow morning. You want to give me a ring?

Finney: Sure.

Kennedy: And then we could chat about it.

Finney: All right. Or if you'd like, I can just be at your office at whatever time.

Kennedy: Why don't you come by at 10 [A.M.], then?

Finney: All right.

Kennedy: And I'll try to get hold of Allen Dulles, too.

Finney: All right, fine.

Kennedy: And if there's any change, I'll give you a ring.

Finney: OK, fine.

Kennedy: Fine, Tom.

Finney: All right. Thank you, Bob.

8:50 P.M.

To Robert Goodman[227]

Johnson reached the father of Andrew Goodman in New York City. Robert Kennedy was with Johnson in the Oval Office.

A brief, unclear office conversation precedes the call.
President Johnson: . . . threw their hats at each other.
Robert Kennedy: God . . . that . . . When did I come on? [*Unclear.*]
President Johnson: [*Unclear*] came on after [*unclear*].
Yolanda Boozer then announces Robert Goodman.
Robert Goodman: Hello, Mr. President.
President Johnson: The FBI got in the car.
Goodman: Yes.
President Johnson: And think that there's a . . . there are reasons to believe that no people were in the car because they've been unable to find any evidence of that, and there are indications that there were tracks leading from the car back to the highway.
Goodman: That's wonderful news, Mr. . . .
President Johnson: And we don't know where we'll go from there, but I thought you should have that information as soon as we had it.
Goodman: [*emotionally*] Thank you so much.
President Johnson: We've talked to the governor, and he's agreed to make available all the facilities at his command to search that entire area, and he and the FBI together are working up a plan to go through the area and see if they can find any further information and give it to us. So we're making arrangements to send additional people in tonight and tomorrow.
Goodman: [*emotionally*] Mr. President, I can't express my words to thank you for what you're doing: for these boys and for us. Thank you so much.
President Johnson: Thank you, sir.
Goodman: [*emotionally*] Thank you.
President Johnson: Good-bye.

---

227. Tape WH6406.16, Citation #3884, Recordings of Telephone Conversations—White House Series, Recordings and Transcripts of Conversations and Meetings, Lyndon B. Johnson Library.

8:53 P.M.

To Allen Dulles; President Johnson joined by Robert Kennedy[228]

Johnson and Kennedy updated Dulles on the details of the Mississippi fact-finding trip.

President Johnson: . . . men that have been very close to this situation—

Allen Dulles: I would like that very much.

President Johnson: —before you go, and we'll set a plane up hopefully for tomorrow afternoon, a Jetstar, to take you to Jackson, hoping you can see the governor tomorrow, late.

Dulles: Right.

President Johnson: [*with Dulles acknowledging*] They tell me if you leave here at 4 [P.M.] you get there at 4—there's two hours' change in time. It's about the same thing. [Tom] Finney said he'd be available to meet you in the morning anytime that you want to meet him. He's a young lawyer from Clark [Clifford]—I talked to Clark; he thought he'd be—

Dulles: All right. If there's any possibility, I'd like to meet him tonight.

President Johnson: All right, I'll call him back and see if he . . . [*unclear*]—

Dulles: All right, but why don't I call him and save you the trouble?

President Johnson: All right . . . fine. Tom Finney. F-i-n—

Dulles: If I start into this situation cold, you know, and I'd like to get as much as soon as I can—

President Johnson: Well, now, he won't know any more about it than you do, hardly. He's just going to be a fellow that'll dig up things for you—

Dulles: That's fine.

President Johnson: [*with Dulles acknowledging*] —and work with you, but the Attorney General's here, and he will tell you what he wants you to do in the morning about meeting with Burke Marshall and some of these people that . . .

Here's a statement that I'm going to make:

---

228. Tape WH6406.16, Citation #3885, Recordings of Telephone Conversations—White House Series, Recordings and Transcripts of Conversations and Meetings, Lyndon B. Johnson Library.

[*reading*] "As I said in my press conference this morning, we have been concerned about the whereabouts and physical safety of the three young people that are still missing in Mississippi. At the present time, although their car has been found burned, we have no definite information on what has happened to them. We share the anxiety and deep distress of the parents of these young men.

"I talked to Governor [Paul] Johnson of Mississippi and expressed my deep concern. He reaffirmed to me what he said publicly this afternoon to the people of Mississippi: that law enforcement facilities of that state will be utilized to their full extent to prevent acts of violence or public disorder from any source. By arrangement of Governor Johnson, I've asked Allen Dulles to go to Mississippi to meet with the governor, other officials of the state, and others who have information on the law observance problems that exist there and are a matter of great concern to the governor and to us. Mr. Dulles will leave shortly and will keep me fully advised on these matters.

"We're basically a law-abiding nation. All the forces of our society, both state and federal, must be directed to preserving law and order. I call for cooperation and restraint of all the citizens of this country in maintaining a society free of anarchy, violence, and disdain for the law."[229]

Here's the Attorney General. You got any suggestions on that?
Dulles: No, that's fine.
President Johnson: Fine.
Robert Kennedy comes on the line.
Robert Kennedy: Oh, Allen?
Dulles: Yes, Bob.
Kennedy: Would it be at all possible to see you in the morning?
Dulles: Surely.
Kennedy: Would you have any time?
Dulles: Oh, I'll give you any—all the time you want.
Kennedy: Fine. Well, maybe, what if we meet in my office at 10:00?[230]
Dulles: 10:00.
Kennedy: That'd be all right with you?
Dulles: That is wise, is it, to meet there?
Kennedy: I don't think there's any problem about it.

---

229. The White House released this statement shortly after this call.
230. Kennedy had already arranged for Tom Finney to meet there at the same time.

Dulles: All right.

Kennedy: Wait a minute.

[*to Johnson*] Do you think we can get Tom Finney to see him before he comes in?

[*to Dulles*] No, I think it's logical that you would do that.

Dulles: Of course.

Kennedy: So I don't think there's any . . . I mean, there's no mystery about the fact you [*unclear*] see [*unclear*]—

Dulles: I understand.

Kennedy: Yeah, I think it was good to raise the point, but I think it's all right.

Dulles: All right, I'll be in your office at 10:00.

Kennedy: And I'll just have these people go over. As I say, I don't think it's . . . it's not that complicated or difficult, and we could just tell you what we found, and then you can talk to—

Dulles: Yeah, I'd start on this cold, you know—

Kennedy: I know, but I don't think it's . . . it's not—

Dulles: If there's anything I could be working on tonight, I'd be glad to do it.

Kennedy: I don't think that—

[*to Johnson*] Is there anything that he can read tonight?

[*to Dulles*] Where are you, Allen?

Dulles: I'm in my home . . . 2723 Q Street.

Kennedy: [*to Johnson*] Well, I could send over some . . . we could send over some of the FBI reports.

[*to Dulles*] I could send over some FBI reports that you might take a look at.

Dulles: I'd like that, and a biography of [Governor] Johnson and so forth and so on for background.

Kennedy: And a biography of Johnson.

Dulles: Yes.

Kennedy: Well, why don't we do that, and I'll send some material over.

Dulles: Right.

Kennedy: And that'll be over in another 45 minutes.

Dulles: That's fine.

Kennedy: Thanks a lot, Allen.

Dulles: Thank you.

Kennedy: Bye.

Dulles: Right.

TIME UNKNOWN

With William Ryan and Ogden Reid;
President Johnson joined by Jack Valenti[231]

Johnson provided assurances that the White House would stay in charge of the investigation.

President Johnson: . . . taking pictures of those. I'm sending down some experts by jet plane tonight. They'll arrive there a little after midnight, and they are examining them carefully, but it gives us some hope that they were not in the car.

William Ryan: [*Unclear.*]

President Johnson: And of course, you know, I don't know any more than you do. I just thought I ought to give you the information as soon as I have it because—

Ryan: Well, I am certainly grateful to you, Mr. President, for taking the time from your very onerous duties.

President Johnson: Well . . .

Ryan: And I deeply appreciate it.

President Johnson: I've called the governor of Mississippi, and I've asked him to put all of the facilities of his people to search immediately, and he's agreed to do that, and I'm sending additional people there tonight and tomorrow to join with them. I've had a number, just had dozens of them there for several weeks now, but they can't—they don't know what happens out on the highway, you know, and there are hundreds of miles of highways all over that state.

Ryan: Right.

President Johnson: And so . . . and then, the governor's asked me to send in an impartial observer that I'm sending down tomorrow. It'll probably be Mr. Allen Dulles, former head of the Central Intelligence [Agency]. And he's a great, able fellow, you know, and—

Ryan: [*Unclear*] aware of that.

President Johnson: —the [former] secretary of state's brother, and I've called him tonight, and he's going to go as my representative.

So we're going to stay right on top of it. I'm still at the office, and I'll

---

231. Tape WH6406.16, Citation #3886, Recordings of Telephone Conversations—White House Series, Recordings and Transcripts of Conversations and Meetings, Lyndon B. Johnson Library.

be here through the evening, and I want you to leave word here where I can reach you at any time, and you—

Ryan: I'll be at this number all the time, and I'm sure that your office will know how to break through if there's another call.

President Johnson: Wait just a minute here.

[*to Valenti*] Jack, come get this number here so we can see where to get him.

[*to Ryan*] Here's Mr. Valenti, and you give him the number where you can be reached.

Ryan: I will—

President Johnson: Thank you.

Ryan: Thank you. And thank you ever so much. I'm *most* grateful, Mr. President.

President Johnson: Fine. Tell Ogden about it, and tell him I'll see him a little later.

Ryan: Yes. Mr. Reid asked that I convey his thanks, Mr. President.

President Johnson: OK. Thank you. Just a minute, here's Valenti.

Ryan: Could he do so himself?

President Johnson: Yes.

Ryan: Just a moment.

President Johnson: [*to Valenti*] I want you to get his—

Congressman Reid comes on the line.

Ogden Reid: Mr. President?

President Johnson: Yes, Ogden.

Reid: Thank you very, very much. And we'll stand by for anything we can do or any word here.

President Johnson: Thank you, Ogden. Here's Jack Valenti. I want to get the number where you can be reached.

Reid: Thank you, sir.

Valenti comes on the line.

Jack Valenti: Congressman?

Reid: Yes.

Valenti: Let me have the number.

Reid: The number, the code is 914 . . .

Valenti: Now, is this the number where you can be reached?

Reid: This is the Schwerner's home.

Valenti: Schwerner's home: area code, 914.

Reid: And the number is Pelham-8, P-E-8 . . .

Valenti: 8.

Reid: . . . 3718.

Valenti: 1-8. How do you spell their name?

Reid: S-c-h-w-e-r-n-e-r.

Valenti: All right.

Reid: The address is 34 5th Street.

Valenti: 34 *5th* street.

Reid: 5th, F-i-f-t-h Street, Pelham, New York.

Valenti: *Pelham*, New York.

Reid: Pelham, P-e-l-h-a-m. My number is White Plains-9-1-2—

Valenti: White Plains . . .

Reid: 9.

Valenti: 9.

Reid: 1291.

Valenti: 9-1.

Reid: And I will be at the Schwerner's probably for the next hour, and then I'll be back at my home.

Valenti: All right.

Reid: And we appreciate any word that you might have. I'll stay up all night.

Valenti: All right.

Reid: Thank you.

Valenti: All right, Congressman.

Reid: Thank you.

Valenti: You're at the Schwermer [*sic*] number now?

Reid: That is correct.

Valenti: All right, and if you're not there, you'll be at your own number: White Plains-9-1291.

Reid: That's correct.

Valenti: Their number is Pelham-8-3718.

Reid: That is correct.

Valenti: 34 5th Street.

Reid: That is correct, and the code for both numbers is 914.

Valenti: All right. Thank you very much.

Reid: Thank you very, very much.

Valenti: Bye.

Reid: Bye.

TIME UNKNOWN

Between White House Operators and Lee White[232]

Whereas congressmen William Ryan and Ogden Reid had given the White House the contact information for the parents of the two missing white activists, Lee White had to depend on the press and AT&T.

White House Operator #1: Hello?

Lee White: Lee White. Do you have any luck with that family by the name of Chaney in Meridian?

White House Operator #1: Wait a minute.

There is an approximate 15-second pause.

White House Operator #2: Hello?

White: Yes?

White House Operator #2: I haven't—can't find out anything, sir. I'm trying now for little towns outside of Meridian to see if they might have anything listed.

White: I'd appreciate it if you would, and if you could keep at it.

White House Operator #2: Yeah, I have the long-distance operator on the line trying for me.

White: If—

White House Operator #2: You haven't . . . You're sure of the spelling, C-h-a-y-n-e-y?[233]

White: Well, that's what came to us out of the paper. It could possibly be C-h-e-n . . . C-h-e-y-n-e-y.

White House Operator #2: C-h-e-y-n-e-y, OK.

White: I guess that would be an alternative spelling.

White House Operator #2: I'll try either way.

White: If you can't catch me here, if you'd catch me at home, I'd appreciate it.

White House Operator #2: All right, Mr. White, I'll be glad to.

White: Thank you.

---

232. Tape WH6406.16, Citation #3887, Recordings of Telephone Conversations—White House Series, Recordings and Transcripts of Conversations and Meetings, Lyndon B. Johnson Library.
233. This spelling of Chaney's name was the one that White used in his memorandum of the day's events. Lee White, "Memorandum to the Files: Disappearance of Three Participants in Mississippi Project," 23 June 1964, "Civil Rights—Mississippi" folder, Office Files of Lee White, Box 6, White House Central Files, Lyndon B. Johnson Library.

9:10 P.M.: Johnson made an unrecorded call to Walter Jenkins on the personal line.

9:20 P.M.–9:25 P.M.: Press Secretary George Reedy came to the Oval Office for five minutes.

9:30 P.M.: Went to the Little Lounge with Jack Valenti; joined by secretary Yolanda Boozer.

9:45 P.M.: Called Bill Moyers to set up a doctor's visit at the Mayo Clinic during a trip to Minnesota.

10:15 P.M.: Lady Bird brought the President his supper, which he did not eat for another half hour.

10:20 P.M.

To Dean Rusk[234]

In the last recorded call of the day, the two men discussed Henry Cabot Lodge's departure from Saigon and the situation in Vietnam.

President Johnson: Dean?

Dean Rusk: Yes, sir.

President Johnson: Did you have a chance to talk to [George] Aiken?

Rusk: I haven't been able to reach him, but I've talked to Bill Fulbright here, and he has talked to Aiken, and Aiken says he was misquoted.[235] But I have a date to call him at quarter of 8 in the morning before he has a breakfast, and that has been set up.

President Johnson: [*with Rusk acknowledging*] OK. Now, [Henry Cabot] Lodge goes into a good deal of detail in his statement tonight. He said, "I have resigned as ambassador to Vietnam because I believe it's my duty to do everything I can to help [William] Scranton to win his contest for the Republican nomination [for] president. I have accepted an invitation to address the Resolutions Committee of the Republican Party. I'm deeply grateful for the many courtesies extended to my wife and me. [It] truly makes us sad to leave, but Vietnam is on the right track, and

---

234. Tape WH6406.16, Citation #3889, Recordings of Telephone Conversations—White House Series, Recordings and Transcripts of Conversations and Meetings, Lyndon B. Johnson Library.
235. J. William Fulbright, Democrat of Arkansas, was chairman of the Senate Committee on Foreign Relations.

with persistence its freedom and independence will surely be achieved. I shall"—so he says we're on the right track, and "I shall continue to be—"

Rusk: I have that . . . I have that quotation.

President Johnson: I can—

Rusk: I will use that with Aiken, but . . . but he was talked to today, and he said that he had been misquoted, but I will . . . I have a date to talk to him at quarter of 8 before he has an 8:00 breakfast with a number of senators.

President Johnson: That's good . . . fine. Thank you, Dean.

Rusk: All right.

President Johnson: Bye.

10:25 P.M.: President Johnson made his last call of the night (unrecorded) to aide and speechwriter Horace Busby to chastise Busby for his wordy speeches. According to the Daily Diary, Johnson felt that this morning's address to the Occupational Safety Conference had "too many long phrases."

10:45 P.M.: Went to the Mansion with Lady Bird to eat dinner at last, then turned in at midnight, awaking the next morning with a sore throat.

Wednesday, June 24, 1964

A local colored man had been making himself obnoxious, a smart-aleck troublemaker. I'm afraid somebody's after him and just got the others along with him. . . . Out in those rural areas, you know how hard it is.

—John Stennis to President Johnson

In Mississippi, the hunt for James Chaney, Michael Schwerner, and Andrew Goodman intensified. According to the *New York Times*, approximately 60 local, state, and federal law enforcement officials were actively searching key areas. The Johnson administration continued to pressure local officials to maintain law and order, while the Federal Bureau of Investigation put more agents on the ground. Civil rights activists were working tirelessly to pressure local, state, and federal authorities. Some of them were set to spread out in clandestine search parties of their own, scouring the countryside after midnight to avoid detection by the Ku Klux Klan or the local police. Cleveland Sellers, a veteran of the Student Nonviolent Coordinating Committee (SNCC), recalls rummaging through ditches and holes with sticks and "with our hands and feet," frequently fighting off snakes and spiders in the dark.[1] In Philadelphia, Mississippi, the state police prevented a group of over 30 black activists from visiting the site of the burned station wagon. Mississippi Highway Patrol Assistant Chief

---

1. Cleveland Sellers, *The River of No Return: The Autobiography of a Black Militant and the Life and Death of SNCC* (New York: William Morrow, 1973; repr., Jackson: University Press of Mississippi, 1990), pp. 84–92, quotation from p. 91. Citations are to the University of Mississippi edition.

Gwin Cole stopped the group's leaders at the Philadelphia line and told them "to go back to where they came from."[2]

A few hours after lunch, Allen Dulles and Tom Finney arrived in Mississippi to begin their special mission as "impartial observers" for the White House. Mississippi Governor Paul Johnson was "delighted" that the men would finally be able to see the "domestic tranquility between the races" in the Magnolia State.[3] Rita Schwerner, the Council of Federated Organizations (COFO) activist and wife of Michael Schwerner, arrived as well and immediately set out, in her words, to "find my husband." The day before, she had called the White House and left a message with a Secret Service agent that she would consider President Johnson "lax" if he did not take a "personal interest" in the investigation.[4] Coincidentally, on the way down to Mississippi, she was comforted in the Cincinnati airport by fellow activist Fannie Lou Hamer, who happened to be on her way back from the Freedom Summer training sessions in Oxford, Ohio (two months later at the Democratic National Convention, Hamer's testimony about white supremacist intimidation in Mississippi became the defining moment in Atlantic City).[5] In Meridian, at the E. F. Young Hotel, Fannie Lee Chaney, the mother of James Chaney, explained that she was "just hoping and not thinking."[6]

---

2. Those leaders included Council of Racial Equality (CORE) national director James Farmer, SNCC chairman John Lewis, comedian and activist Dick Gregory, and Mississippi CORE activist George Raymond. "Information from Charlie Snodgrass," 3:35 P.M., 24 June 1964, Folder 7: "Highway Patrol Reports and Correspondence: June 1964," Box 144, Series II, Sub-Series 10: Highway Patrol, Johnson (Paul B.) Family Papers, in Collection M191, Manuscript Collection, McCain Library and Archives, University of Southern Mississippi (hereafter cited as "Highway Patrol Reports and Correspondence, June 1964," Johnson Papers, University of Southern Mississippi). Quote by Gwin Cole, assistant director of the Highway Patrol's Bureau of Identification, in William Chapman, "Hunt Gives No Lead to Rights Aides," *Washington Post,* 25 June 1964.

3. David Halberstam, "Governor Greets Dulles Warmly," *New York Times,* 25 June 1964; Al Richburg, Assistant Director, Mississippi Highway Patrol Safety Responsibility Bureau, to Colonel T. B. Birdsong, "Mr. Dulles Timetable," 26 June 1964, "Highway Patrol Reports and Correspondence, June 1964," Johnson Papers, University of Southern Mississippi. (In this report, Richburg mistakenly writes July 23 and July 24 when he almost certainly meant June 24 and June 25.)

4. "Vain Hunt for Rights Aids," *Chicago Tribune,* 25 June 1964; Rita L. Schwerner, "Caller's Statement," 23 June 1964, "Mississippi Summer Project Voter Registration" folder, Office Files of Lee White, Box 6, White House Central Files, Lyndon B. Johnson Library.

5. Jerry Mitchell, "Rita's Story," *The Clarion-Ledger,* 18 June 2000.

6. Mrs. Chaney lived until 24 May 2007 and was able to testify at the trial of Edgar "Preacher" Killen in 2005. Claude Sitton, "Hope for 3 Wanes," *New York Times,* 25 June 1964; Douglas Martin, "Fannie Lee Chaney, 84, Mother of Slain Civil Rights Worker, Is Dead," *New York Times,* 24 May 2007.

Lyndon Johnson remained actively engaged in the investigation, but also had to continue his role as an international diplomat. Still nursing a cold, Johnson met with Greek Prime Minister George Papandreou about the Cyprus situation, while hosting Australian Prime Minister Robert Gordon Menzies. President Johnson believed that the Turks were supportive of peace measures in Cyprus, but had less confidence in his chances to corral the Greeks.[7] The President also had to balance the personalities of two powerful Washington figures. Late in the previous evening, Robert Kennedy, one of the top contenders for the vice presidential nomination and a possible presidential nominee, had announced his decision not to run for the Senate in New York. With that on his mind, Kennedy met with the national leadership of the National Association for the Advancement of Colored People (NAACP) at the Justice Department and then greeted Myrlie Evers, whose husband, Medgar Evers, had been murdered by a white supremacist a year earlier. In a well-received move, Kennedy waded into the crowd of NAACP protesters outside his building before leaving for his trip to Europe. The *Washington Post* headline called it a "touching scene." In another part of the Justice Department, J. Edgar Hoover worried about the role being played in Mississippi by former CIA director Dulles and by the military. Over the next few days, Johnson had to step in to soothe the FBI director's concerns. In the biggest non-Mississippi news of the day, the Federal Trade Commission ordered cigarette manufacturers to place health warning labels on their packaging by 1 January 1965 and in their advertisements by 1 July 1965.[8]

> **8:20 A.M.:** President Johnson had breakfast in bed, received treatment for his sore throat, did a few exercises, and spoke to Jack Valenti about the upcoming day.
>
> **9:25 A.M.:** Made an unrecorded call from the Mansion to legislative liaison Larry O'Brien.
>
> **10:00 A.M.:** Made an unrecorded call from the Mansion to Senator Hubert Humphrey.
>
> **10:01 A.M.:** Headed to the South Lawn with Lady Bird Johnson to

---

7. Conversation between President Johnson and John McCormack, 12:45 P.M., 23 June 1964, in this volume.

8. Robert E. Baker, "Touching Scene at Justice Dept.," *Washington Post*, 25 June 1964; Nate Haseltine, "Health Warning Label Ordered for Cigarettes," *Washington Post*, 25 June 1964.

greet Prime Minister Papandreou, where both men offered brief remarks to the press.[9]

10:20 A.M.–11:31 A.M.: Johnson and Papandreou left the press and proceeded to the Oval Office for a meeting with Under Secretary of State George Ball and the Greek delegation.

Johnson gave the Prime Minister the same set of gifts that Turkey's Prime Minister received the day before, and much of the same advice. Johnson let them know that he had no "formula or recommendation" for a solution except a desire for the Greeks and the Turks to sit down and work out a compromise, offering the services of former Secretary of State Dean Acheson as a mediator.

11:34 A.M.: Had an anesthetic sprayed on his ailing throat.

11:35 A.M.: Made unrecorded calls on the personal line to Walter Jenkins and George Reedy.

11:44 A.M.: In an East Room ceremony with Defense Secretary Robert McNamara and White House military aide General Chester Clifton, gave the Distinguished Service Medal to General Paul D. Harkins, the 60-year-old former protégé of George Patton. Harkins had served as commander of the Military Assistance Command, Vietnam (MACV) from 13 February 1962 until 20 June 1964, when he was replaced by General William Westmoreland.[10]

11:53 A.M.: Walked to the upstairs quarters in the Mansion to meet with Attorney General Robert Kennedy and to brief former CIA Director Allen Dulles and attorney Tom Finney about their trip to Mississippi.

12:04 P.M.: Australian Prime Minister Menzies arrived at the White House and was brought upstairs by Ambassador Angier Biddle Duke, where they exchanged greetings with Allen Dulles and Tom Finney.

12:12 P.M.: The President met privately with Prime Minister Menzies while still upstairs in the Mansion instead of moving to the Oval Office, as the Prime Minister was not feeling well.

---

9. "Remarks of Welcome at the White House to Prime Minister Papandreou of Greece," 24 June 1964, *Public Papers of the Presidents of the United States: Lyndon B. Johnson, 1963–64* (Washington, DC: GPO, 1965), 1:811–12.

10. "Remarks Upon Presenting the Distinguished Service Medal to General Harkins," 24 June 1964, *Public Papers, Johnson, 1963–64*, 1:813–14.

1:00 P.M.: Walked downstairs with Prime Minister Menzies to greet guests in the Red Room.

1:15 P.M.–2:20 P.M.: Attended luncheon in the State Dining Room honoring Prime Minister Menzies, along with 80 other guests.[11]

2:20 P.M.: Retired to his bedroom for his customary afternoon rest and remained there for almost three hours. While in his bedroom, the President made several unrecorded calls: to Walter Jenkins (2:25, 2:38, 3:16, and 4:24 P.M.), Jack Valenti (2:35 P.M.), George Reedy (3:03 P.M.), Larry O'Brien (3:45 P.M.), Congressman Carl Albert (4:31 P.M.), and Secretary George Ball (4:55 P.M.).

5:14 P.M.: Returned to the office and told White House secretary Marie Fehmer to get Secretary Robert McNamara, who had called the President earlier. The first recorded call of the day came one minute later.[12]

5:15 P.M.

To Myer Feldman[13]

White House Special Counsel Myer Feldman updated Johnson on a Cabinet-level committee on fuel policy.

Myer Feldman: Mr. President.

President Johnson: What happened to that Bob McNamara commission on coal?

Feldman: That's been formed already. You signed the letter. Bob McNamara has—and I've sent copies to each of the government departments that are serving on the commission with him and called them on the telephone to tell them the purpose. I sent back [to] Bob McNamara

---

11 "Toasts of the President and Prime Minister Menzies of Australia," 24 June 1964, *Public Papers, Johnson, 1963–64*, 1:814–16.

12. See conversation between President Johnson and Myer Feldman, 8:17 P.M., 5 June 1964, in Guian A. McKee, ed., *The Presidential Recordings, Lyndon B. Johnson: Mississippi Burning and the Passage of the Civil Rights Act, June 1, 1964–July 4, 1964*, vol. 7, *June 1, 1964–June 22, 1964* (New York: Norton, 2011), pp. 109–11.

13. Tape WH6406.16, Citation #3890, Recordings of Telephone Conversations—White House Series, Recordings and Transcripts of Conversations and Meetings, Lyndon B. Johnson Library.

a copy of the letter they sent in. I talked to the National Coal Policy Conference and told them what they—what we were doing, and they heartily approved it, so I think we're in business.[14]

President Johnson: OK. When did you send this to McNamara?

Feldman: Well, I did it—you signed it the day before yesterday. I guess it went out last night.

President Johnson: OK. Thank you.

Feldman: Yes, sir.

5:16 P.M.: The President tried to reach Secretary McNamara again, but left a message for McNamara to return his call after learning from Marie Fehmer that the Defense Secretary was meeting with the Australian Prime Minister.

5:20 P.M.: Over the next quarter hour, made an unrecorded call to George Reedy on the personal line, nominated a candidate for U.S. marshal for Puerto Rico, and presented gifts to Prime Minister Menzies.

5:29 P.M.: Touched base with Walter Jenkins in an unrecorded call, then reached the FBI director.

5:30 P.M.

To J. Edgar Hoover[15]

Hoover reported some of the latest theories on the Mississippi Burning investigation. The conversation ended abruptly when Mississippi Senator John Stennis was patched through.

White House Operator: Yes, please?

President Johnson: Shall I hold on, or are you going—

White House Operator: I could call you back, Mr. President—

President Johnson: All right, get Edgar Hoover for me, and—

White House Operator: I will.

---

14. The National Coal Policy Conference, Inc., was a joint effort by coal companies and miners' unions to expand coal consumption.

15. Tape WH6406.16, Citation #3891, Recordings of Telephone Conversations—White House Series, Recordings and Transcripts of Conversations and Meetings, Lyndon B. Johnson Library.

President Johnson: —then if you get Senator [John] Stennis, cut in on me.[16]

White House Operator: I will.

The President holds for approximately 50 seconds while waiting for Hoover to come on the line.

J. Edgar Hoover: Hello?

President Johnson: Edgar?

Hoover: Yes, Mr. President.

President Johnson: Any other news on Mississippi?

Hoover: No, there's no additional news on that. I sent over the two memorandums to [Walter] Jenkins today, giving in substance what we had developed last night and the fact that our laboratory men found no evidence of any human bones or indication of human beings in that car when it was burned.[17]

President Johnson: That sheriff's [Lawrence Rainey's] a pretty bad fellow down there, isn't he?[18]

Hoover: Yes, he is, and we [*unclear*] have been going over him pretty thoroughly.

President Johnson: Mm-hmm.

Hoover: There are several theories that have been advanced, and of course we're running out all leads—some of them are cranks, but we're running out all of them.

One is that this may have been done by these three fellows as . . . in order to create an incident that would inflame the situation. The basis for that is that the setting this car afire within sight of a highway—it was only a few feet off a highway—and burning it, leaving the license tags on the car, was not a thing a person would do who probably had committed a murder and had killed the three, but that these three fellows may have done it themselves. And there've been several reports, which we're running out down there, of two in—two white men resembling these two

---

16. John Stennis was the junior senator from Mississippi.

17. Special Agent Jay Cochran led the survey of the car on 24 June. Jay Cochran, Report, 29 June 1964, Federal Bureau of Investigation, "Miburn Prosecutive Summary" of the case "Bernard L. Akin, et al.; James Earl Chaney, Michael Henry Schwerner, aka Mickey, Andrew Goodman—Victims," 19 December 1964, File 44.25706, http://foia.fbi.gov/miburn/miburn6.pdf, pp.446–49.

18. Lawrence Rainey was sheriff of Neshoba County and was a central target in the FBI investigation. On 3 October 1964, the FBI arrested him and four other officers for violating the civil rights of seven other black residents over the past two years. On 4 December, they took him, Deputy Cecil Price, and 17 others into custody on charges of conspiracy to violate the civil rights of Chaney, Schwerner, and Goodman. Rainey eventually escaped conviction, receiving acquittal on 20 October 1967.

fellows—two of these three fellows—who were seen at an airport trying to board a plane going west to the . . . to Los Angeles. That, of course, is one of these cases where people phone in and imagine that they've seen something, but we've got to run all of that out anyway.

President Johnson: Mm-hmm.

Hoover: On the other hand, I . . . the thing that we lean strongly to here that these three may have gotten rather fresh in the—[*the operator attempts to interject*]—when they were in the—[19]

White House Operator: I beg your pardon.

President Johnson: Yeah?

Hoover: When they were in—

President Johnson: Thank you, that's what—Edgar?

The exchange ends here as Johnson takes the expected call from John Stennis. He continues the Hoover conversation after hanging up with Stennis.

5:32 P.M.

To John Stennis[20]

On the Senate floor today, Senator Stennis asked the White House to use its authority to stop students from coming to Mississippi and blamed the civil rights activists for the violence against them. Any "blood," he declared, "will be on the hands of those who formed and led this invasion into a state where they were not welcome nor invited." In response, New York Republicans Jacob Javits and Kenneth Keating called on the White House to send federal marshals to Mississippi.[21]

White House Operator: I have Senator Stennis.

President Johnson: All right. Tell Edgar Hoover that I had another call emergency, and I'll call him right back.

White House Operator: Fine.

President Johnson: That you cut in. Hello? Hello?

White House Operator: Yes, Mr. President.

Stennis comes on the line.

---

19. Hoover seemed to begin saying "custody."
20. Tape WH6406.16, Citation #3892, Recordings of Telephone Conversations—White House Series, Recordings and Transcripts of Conversations and Meetings, Lyndon B. Johnson Library.
21. *Washington Post,* 25 June 1964.

John Stennis: Hello?

President Johnson: John?

Stennis: Yes, sir, Mr. President.

President Johnson: I've been wanting to call you, but I had two prime ministers on my hands.

Stennis: [*Unclear.*] I know.

President Johnson: The Greece fellow [Prime Minister Papandreou] until noon and then Australia [Prime Minister Menzies], and I just got out.

Stennis: Well, you have [*unclear*]—

President Johnson: [*with Stennis acknowledging*] Now, last night I talked to the governor of Mississippi [Paul Johnson] and had a very fine talk with him and kind of along the line you talked about three or four weeks ago, and he said he was doing everything in the world he could, and he would like for me to send an impartial observer that I had confidence in, and that he—that I thought the nation would have confidence in, that he wanted to show him some of the problems that he had and try to have a little better understanding, a little better communication than we—both of us put . . . pool our facilities to try to see that we had observance of the law. And we can't people . . . keep them from traveling, or people from talking, and . . .

Stennis: I know.

President Johnson: [*with Stennis acknowledging*] But that we can watch them and be as careful as we can. So I decided I'd think about it, and I tried to get somebody that I thought would have the confidence of the country, and I picked Allen Dulles, a Republican—that I thought was judicious and fair and not an extremist. And so he's going to fly down and talk to the governor, and the governor is going to send him to see several other people in various places in the state. And he'll talk to the FBI, and he [will] come back and talk to me in a day or two about it.

Stennis: Oh, [*unclear*].

President Johnson: And I just . . . I know how this troubles you . . .

Stennis: Yes.

President Johnson: And it's just an awful thing.

Stennis: Yes.

President Johnson: But I've got Edgar Hoover on the other line. He tells me they've looked in the car very carefully, and there's no indication that the bodies were in the car at all.

Stennis: Yeah, yeah. Well, I'm awfully, awfully worried about it, Lyndon. You know—

President Johnson: Oh, it's just a—

Stennis: [*with Johnson acknowledging*]—there's [a] colored man. A local colored man had been making himself obnoxious, a smart-aleck troublemaker. I'm afraid somebody's after *him* and just got the others along with him.

President Johnson: Yeah, I'm afraid that's right too.

Stennis: Out in those rural areas, you know how hard it is. Well, my—

President Johnson: Yeah, I sure do. . . . [*talking over Stennis*] I just wanted you to know, my friend, and I love you, and I know your heart's bleeding, and mine is—

Stennis: Yeah, I know.

President Johnson: —too, and maybe somehow we'll work out of it.

Stennis: All right. Well, I'll keep—you call me anytime.

President Johnson: I will. I'll just—

Stennis: Anything I can do. I'll—

President Johnson: I know that.

Stennis: —I'll have it myself—

President Johnson: Well . . . I'm going to see him next week, you know. I'm going to see the governor next week.[22]

Stennis: Are you?

President Johnson: Yeah.

Stennis: Oh, fine. That's good.

President Johnson: Yeah . . . yeah.

Stennis: [*with the President acknowledging*] Listen, after . . . Those boys over in the House called me, John Bell Williams called me this morning, wanted to come down there to see you with them, you know, and I put him off.[23] And I'd tell him now you've sent Dulles down there at Governor Johnson's request and [*unclear*] going to wait until you get—

President Johnson: He didn't request Dulles, but he said he'd like for me to send a—

Stennis: Send someone.

President Johnson: "Impartial, objective observer." That's his language.

Stennis: Well, I tell you, when I heard that this morning, I immediately tried to call Mr. Dulles. I missed him, but he called me just before he left.[24]

---

22. The editors found no record of a meeting between the two men during the next week.

23. John Bell Williams was a Democratic representative from Mississippi.

24. Stennis was the second-ranking Democrat on the Senate Armed Services Committee and was on that committee's Central Intelligence Subcommittee.

President Johnson: Well, that's good.

Stennis: And I had already talked to the governor about it, Governor Paul Johnson, you know, we just talked quite briefly.

President Johnson: [*with Stennis acknowledging*] Well, he . . . Dulles is . . . Dulles put out a—he's a pretty good—said [*reading*] "I'm not . . . I'm not going down there as a sleuth or as a spy or as an investigator. There are competent people down there out doing that." He said he's going as envoy to President Johnson, to get the views of the governor and other leaders in Mississippi.

Stennis: Well, he can give you a valuable report.

President Johnson: [*reading*] "Asked—"

Stennis: Let me say this about Governor [*unclear*]—

President Johnson: "Asked whether he thought there was a possibility when he came back he'd recommend marshal law, he said he saw no such prospect whatever."

Stennis: Yeah, yeah. All right, old fellow.

President Johnson: OK.

Stennis: Well, I thank you very deeply—

President Johnson: Thank you, John. . . . Thank you, John.

Stennis: —for what you're doing.

President Johnson: Thank you, John.

Stennis: God bless you, too.

President Johnson: Bye.

TIME UNKNOWN [25]

To J. Edgar Hoover [26]

Johnson reconnected with Hoover and took the time to carefully explain the rationale for sending Allen Dulles to Mississippi.

The President asks the operator to reconnect him with Hoover.

J. Edgar Hoover: Yeah?

President Johnson: Edgar, I'm sorry we got interrupted.

---

25. This conversation with J. Edgar Hoover took place shortly after the Stennis conversation.
26. Tape WH6406.16, Citation #3893, Recordings of Telephone Conversations—White House Series, Recordings and Transcripts of Conversations and Meetings, Lyndon B. Johnson Library.

Hoover: That's all right.

President Johnson: I . . . Walter [Jenkins] told me that Deke [DeLoach] was upset some because . . . that somebody had indicated that [Allen] Dulles was supposed to go down there and be an investigator, and I told him that that never had—that was the furthest thing from my mind.[27] [*Hoover attempts to interject, then acknowledges throughout.*]

What happened was after we talked yesterday, and you got the governor to have that press conference—he gave out a wonderful statement—then he called [Senator] Jim Eastland, who is my friend and your friend, and told Eastland that he would like for me to see some of the problems that they were confronted with down there, with all these damn fellows parading all over every place, and that he would like for me to send an impartial observer to come and talk to him.[28] And he would like to see . . . send him to talk to a few of the businessmen and try to see how we could avoid some of this. I think what he's going to want Dulles to do is to explain to the folks here what's happening to their state with everybody coming into it.

Hoover: Exactly.

President Johnson: So I tried to figure out somebody that I could send that . . . get to go down there, and so I finally decided this—I'd get this boy with [Mike] Monroney and Dulles, and I got him on the phone, and he said he'd go.[29] And so they asked him what if he's going down there to take over the investigation, and he said he wanted to make it clear that he wasn't going to spy or [as] an investigator of any kind, that there are already competent investigators on the spot. He's going as my personal envoy to get the views of the governor and other leaders of Mississippi.

Now, I felt like if the governor asked me to send an impartial observer and I didn't send it, I'd be in a little bad shape later on if I had to do something—

Hoover: Sure . . . sure you would.

President Johnson: —and if I had of thought for one moment that it was something that would affect you in any way, I'd have picked up the phone and called you because I haven't got a better friend in this government than you, and I always will have.

---

27. Cartha "Deke" DeLoach was deputy director of the FBI.
28. Democrat James Eastland was the senior senator from Mississippi.
29. Tom Finney had once been a key aide for Mike Monroney, the Democratic senator from Oklahoma.

Hoover: [*Unclear*] question.

President Johnson: [*with Hoover acknowledging*] And so I told them to plant a question in my press conference today, and George Reedy told them where to head in.

Hoover: [*with the President acknowledging*] Yes. Well, I . . . Allen Dulles stopped by to see me this morning, and he told me that he had several inquiries from the press as to whether he was going to take over the investigation. He made it very clear—

President Johnson: Well, there ain't nobody here who['s] going to take over anything from you as long as I'm living. Now, you just forget—

Hoover: [*with the President acknowledging*] He said that he made it very clear that he was just . . . that he was there to confer with the governor and to see that the . . . what the general atmosphere was. He—

President Johnson: Well, I felt a little bit last night that [*unclear*] . . . I might be asking you to do a little too much, but I had to get somebody to do it, and . . .

Hoover: Well, certainly.

President Johnson: And when you got him [Governor Johnson] to make that statement, that's the best thing that's happened to us, and if you just repeat that every day or so, it'll help, you see.

Hoover: That's right.

President Johnson: But . . .

Hoover: He's been very decent with us; we've gotten along fine with him. And I told Allen Dulles . . . that is, Allen asked me whether he might quote me to the governor as to what I had to say about the Mississippi Highway Patrol and about the attitude of the governor. I told him he could.

President Johnson: That's good. Well, nobody's ever going to take anything between us.

Hoover: I know that. I know.

President Johnson: And you just be sure of that and if we do, we may make a mistake of the head sometimes—I make a lot of them over here every day—if it is, you just tell Deke what the score is, and we'll get it straightened out so damn quick it'll make your head swim.

Hoover: Don't . . . don't [*unclear*]—

President Johnson: Ain't nobody going to take our 30-year friendship and mess it up *one* bit.

Hoover: Well, don't you have any concern about that, Mr. President.

President Johnson: [*chuckling*] I won't. God bless you.

Hoover: Bye. Fine. Thank you.

5:40 P.M.: While en route to the Cabinet Room, President Johnson spoke to Walter Jenkins on Marie Fehmer's telephone outside the Oval Office, then paused briefly to complain to Lee White about the addition of UAW President Walter Reuther to the upcoming meeting with the NAACP board of directors. "We've got Dulles down there [in Mississippi]," he explained, "and we just can't meet with the head of every group in town." Johnson instructed White to have Reuther tell the press that he was at the White House to discuss "strike negotiations" and not Mississippi.[30]

5:48 P.M.: Held his off-the-record meeting in the Cabinet Room with the NAACP Board of Directors and vice presidents (a group of over 30 people), Walter Reuther, Lee White, and the powerful black adviser and deputy chairman of the Democratic National Committee, Louis Martin. White advised Johnson to note Roy Wilkins's "tremendous leadership" in the nation, to highlight the passage of the Civil Rights Act, and to emphasize the "four or five hours" of meetings that Johnson had spent on Mississippi from the day before.[31]

6:36 P.M.: After the NAACP meeting, spoke with Lee White in Juanita Roberts's office.

6:39 P.M.: Left to attend a reception at the Blair House for Prime Minister Papandreou. Accompanying him were Jack Valenti, Ambassador Duke, and Charles Tillinghast, the president of Trans World Airlines, who was there to discuss restrictions on flights to Greece and the overall situation in Africa. The group stayed briefly at the reception and headed back to the White House.

7:04 P.M.–7:17 P.M.: Back at the White House, met off the record with Tillinghast.

7:17 P.M.: While alone in his office, read the news ticker. A few minutes later, he contacted Lee White.

---

30. Quoted material from Daily Diary, 24 June 1964.
31. Lee White to President Johnson, 24 June 1964, "HU 2 5/25/64–7/16/64" folder, Box 2, HU 2 Equality of the Races, White House Central Files: Human Rights, Lyndon B. Johnson Library.

7:21 P.M.[32]

To Lee White[33]

Johnson had received word that the *Washington Post* was working on a piece about Mississippi. Lee White was trying to make sure they had the White House perspective.

President Johnson: Lee?

Lee White: Yes, Mr. President.

President Johnson: What did you find out about the [*Washington*] *Post*?

White: I got ahold of Carroll Kilpatrick, who was the guy who told us about it.[34] He'd already had . . . got a few points himself. He said he would take those that I gave him and see what he could do about it.

A telephone begins ringing in the background and continues throughout the remainder of the conversation.

White: He'd gotten the information about it being written somewhere in the editorial shop and wanted to see if he could give them some information that would help them make up their minds. He wasn't sure what he could do, but he had—he wrote it down and said he'd get in touch with them.

I asked him what it was that they objected to, and he said he didn't know. All he had, was that it was that they objected to it. And I told him I couldn't think of any reason why they would have. He said, "Well, maybe they thought that you should have sent [J. Edgar] Hoover." I said, "God, that's when they really would have objected, if you'd have done that." He agreed, and said he'd see what he could do and would let us know.

President Johnson: Well, Hoover's already in there and all his people. This is just a . . .

White: Sure.

President Johnson: . . . issue.

White: Well, it's disturbing. I don't know what they had in mind, and Carroll promised to do what he could on it. He was trying to help all the way, and it was he who, you know, brought it to us, and he said he

---

32. The Daily Diary notes the Lee White call at 7:27 P.M. The time slip for the recording, however, listed 7:21.

33. Tape WH6406.16, Citation #3895, Recordings of Telephone Conversations—White House Series, Recordings and Transcripts of Conversations and Meetings, Lyndon B. Johnson Library.

34. Carroll Kilpatrick covered the White House and presidential politics.

appreciated the information. I'd given him a few points that he had not put together on his own, so—

President Johnson: Had they talked to anybody? Had the Attorney General [Robert Kennedy] left?

White: I'm not sure whether he has or not. I suggested, you know, that if he wanted more information he might try those people, or I could have him call. He said, well, he thought that he had enough material, and he would call him as quickly as he could and not waste any more time.

President Johnson: Did you talk to Burke [Marshall] about it?[35]

White: No, I haven't yet, sir. I assume that, you know, that Carroll's timing was such that he had all the information he could, although I had the impression from Carroll that he had talked to somebody in Justice. He didn't specify, and I don't know that he did, but he said, well, he'd had some contact down there, and he thought it was a good appointment, couldn't understand why . . . what the basis for the objection might be. For the life of me, I can't either.

President Johnson: [*Unclear*] . . . I want you to call Burke Marshall and tell him about it, Lee. Didn't I make that clear?

White: I tried to get ahold of Burke, but he wasn't there. But I told Carroll if he needed more information that, you know, we would do our best. He said, well, he had a time problem, and he was going to get in touch with them right now, and if he needed anything more, he'd be in touch with me. But I'll call Burke again; see if I can get him.

President Johnson: Burke's probably in Mississippi. Call [Nicholas] Katzenbach, tell him what's happening.[36] He may know somebody— Carroll's just a working boy. He may know somebody in the editorial department.[37]

White: All right. Well, I'll call Nick right now. All right.

7:30 P.M.–7:55 P.M.: Mary Lasker, the Democratic fund-raiser and health research philanthropist, joined the President in the Oval Office. Due in part to Lasker's lobbying, Johnson had created the President's Commission on Heart Disease, Cancer, and Stroke on February 10, 1964. Lady Bird was hosting a reception for the Commission on June 29.

---

35. Burke Marshall was assistant attorney general for civil rights.
36. Nicholas Katzenbach was deputy attorney general.
37. The next day's editorial was on Freedom Summer. "Mission to Mississippi," *Washington Post*, 25 June 1964.

7:56 P.M.: Johnson left his meeting with Lasker feeling the effects of his cold, asking Marie Fehmer, "Do you feel as bad as I do?" The two arranged for Johnson to see the White House physician after having a drink.

7:59 P.M.: Made an unrecorded phone call to Walter Jenkins on the private line.

8:02 P.M.: Went to the lounge for drinks with Fehmer and Jack Valenti. Walter Jenkins and Valenti's wife Mary Margaret, who had served as one of Johnson's secretaries before marrying Valenti, came later.

At approximately 8:40 P.M. (EDT), Allen Dulles and Tom Finney checked into rooms 415 and 416 at the Sun-n-Sand Hotel in Jackson, Mississippi. They soon left for the Governor's Mansion for an almost four-hour meeting.[38]

9:00 P.M.: Fehmer and the Valentis leave the lounge; the President and Jenkins stay awhile longer.

9:30 P.M.: Johnson returned briefly to the Oval Office, then asked his secretary Juanita Roberts to have Dr. George Burkley come to the Mansion and to tell Zephyr Wright, Johnson's longtime cook, that he was coming to the Mansion for supper.

9:45 P.M.: Arrived at the Mansion to dine with Barbara Ward (also known as Lady Jackson), the popular economist and author of the influential 1962 book *The Rich Nations and the Poor Nations* whose advice Johnson sought regarding his Great Society agenda.[39]

9:55 P.M.: During dinner, made an unrecorded call to House Majority Leader Carl Albert.

10:20 P.M.: Took a call from Lady Bird Johnson who was in Detroit, Michigan, where she had spoken to the American Home Economics Convention.

10:23 P.M.: Made a quick unrecorded call to Speaker of the House John McCormack.

10:45 P.M.: Took an unrecorded call from Bill Moyers.

11:15 P.M.: Turned in for the evening.

---

38. Al Richburg, Assistant Director, Mississippi Highway Patrol Safety Responsibility Bureau, to Colonel T. B. Birdsong, "Mr. Dulles Timetable," 26 June 1964, "Highway Patrol Reports and Correspondence, June 1964," Johnson Papers, University of Southern Mississippi.
39. Barbara Ward, *The Rich Nations and the Poor Nations* (New York: Norton, 1962).

Thursday, June 25, 1964

I imagine they're in that lake, my guess. . . . Three days now.
—President Johnson to Luther Hodges

On this day in Mississippi, Allen Dulles and Tom Finney left the Sun-n-Sand Hotel at 10:00 A.M. (CST) to begin their much-publicized domestic diplomatic mission for the White House, with Justice Department official John Doar serving as a liaison between them and various people in Jackson. About 80 miles away, near Philadelphia, Mississippi, the FBI continued to lead the search for Chaney, Schwerner, and Goodman.[1] To assist the effort, President Johnson ordered approximately 200 sailors from the Meridian Naval Auxiliary Air Station into the field. Confusion over his noontime request created a shock wave in the region because many people believed that Johnson was sending in the Marines. According to J. Edgar Hoover, at least one planeload of soldiers took off from Camp Lejeune in North Carolina heading to Meridian. Later in the day, the FBI and the White House clarified the situation, and the Marines returned to their previous duties. Despite increasing pressure, the President continued to resist requests to send in federal marshals to protect civil rights workers.

Also in Mississippi, Rita Schwerner struggled in her quest to find out what had happened to her husband. She and Bob Zellner, a white SNCC

---

1. Al Richburg, Assistant Director, Mississippi Highway Patrol Safety Responsibility Bureau, to Colonel T. B. Birdsong, "Mr. Dulles Timetable," 26 June 1964, Folder 7: "Highway Patrol Reports and Correspondence, June 1964," Box 144, Series II, Sub-Series 10: Highway Patrol, Johnson (Paul B.) Family Papers, in Collection M191, Manuscript Collection, McCain Library and Archives, University of Southern Mississippi.

(Student Nonviolent Coordinating Committee) activist from Alabama, confronted Neshoba County Sheriff Lawrence Rainey, who reluctantly consented to show them the burned station wagon. Governor Johnson refused to meet with her, but later that day, Schwerner, Zellner, and Jackson, Mississippi, activist Reverend Edwin King were able to catch him with Alabama Governor George Wallace and Jackson Mayor Allen Thompson outside the governor's mansion. Upon seeing the activists, the segregationist leaders fled into the mansion.[2] In a widely reported exchange, Schwerner did speak with Allen Dulles at a meeting of civil rights activists. With little hesitation, she told him, "I don't need your sympathy. I want my husband."[3]

On Capitol Hill, Congress moved ahead with tax amendments and mass transit legislation, while Johnson and his allies tried to wrest War on Poverty legislation from the House Rules Committee. In overseas matters, the White House prepared to send its new diplomatic team to Saigon and passed along the Cyprus negotiations to the United Nations and to former secretary of state Dean Acheson. Late in the day, citizens in the Florida beach town of St. Augustine led a race riot. A mob of nearly 300 white protesters attacked a group of almost 200 black activists, putting almost 20 black citizens in the hospital. Before the outbreak of violence, Martin Luther King Jr. had contacted Lee White for assistance in managing the situation. According to White, King "wanted to find some means of pulling out of St. Augustine and 'saving face' in the process."[4]

> **9:40 A.M.–11:51 A.M.:** President Johnson spent most of the morning in the Mansion, holding unrecorded telephone conversations with Burke Marshall (9:40 A.M.), Walter Jenkins (11:10 A.M.), George Reedy (11:19 A.M. and 11:31 A.M.), J. Edgar Hoover (11:34 A.M.), George Reedy (11:40 A.M.), Walter Jenkins (11:45 A.M.), and Larry O'Brien (11:51 A.M.).

---

2. Rita L. Schwerner, Affidavit, *COFO v. L.A. Rainey, et al.*, 29 July 1964, p. 3, Folder 11: "Lauderdale County, 1964," Box 3, Council of Federated Organizations Records, Mississippi Department of Archives and History; Jerry Mitchell, "I'm not giving up until I find out," *Jackson Clarion-Ledger*, 18 June 2000.

3. Quote from David Halberstam, "Dulles Gets Appeal to Send Marshals," *New York Times*, 26 June 1964. COFO documents record Rita Schwerner's response as, "I don't want your sympathy. I want much, much more." See Council of Federated Organizations, "The Philadelphia, Mississippi Case, Chronology of Contact with Agents of the Federal Government," Folder 16: "Depositions, Neshoba County, 1964," Box 3, Council of Federated Organizations Records, Z/1867.000/S, Mississippi Department of Archives and History.

4. Lee White, "Memorandum to the Files," 26 June 1964, "Civil Rights–St. Augustine" folder, Office Files of Lee White, Box 6, White House Central Files, Lyndon B. Johnson Library.

11:55 A.M.: Arrived at the Oval Office and almost immediately took a call from Commerce Secretary Luther Hodges.

11:56 A.M.

From Luther Hodges[5]

Johnson was close to naming former Florida governor LeRoy Collins as the inaugural director of the Community Relations Service. Collins had expressed interest in taking the job, but was waiting to get clearance from his current employers, the National Association of Broadcasters.

Luther Hodges: Mr. President?

President Johnson: Yeah.

Hodges: Governor [LeRoy] Collins is here with me, and I think if we had a few minutes with you sometime whenever you can, early afternoon, I would . . . I think we can work this thing out, and we would need to—you or I, [either] one—that can get ahold of five people that would have to decide it for him was his executive board. But he's willing to make this kind of sacrifice because of what he thinks you and I are trying to do.

President Johnson: OK, I'll try to do it. It'll probably be about 4:30. I've got the Prime Minister of Greece [George Papandreou]. I've got to communicate with him, and got a dinner, a luncheon for him. I've got three ambassadors set up.[6]

Hodges: Oh, yes.

President Johnson: So I'll try. Let's shoot at 4:30 at my office.

Hodges: 4:30 at your office?

President Johnson: Mm-hmm. Come in the Southwest Gate, the back door [*Hodges acknowledges*], and come up to my office.

Hodges: All right, Mr. President.

President Johnson: OK. Thank the governor.

---

5. Tape WH6406.16, Citation #3896, Recordings of Telephone Conversations—White House Series, Recordings and Transcripts of Conversations and Meetings, Lyndon B. Johnson Library.
6. In addition to the meetings about Vietnam and Cyprus on this day, Johnson took photos with Ambassadors William Blair (Philippines), Henry Labouisse (Greece), and Raymond Hare (Turkey) at 6:10 P.M.

12:00 P.M.: Johnson walked to the Fish Room (later known as the Roosevelt Room) to take a photograph with the leaders of the Knights of Columbus, the Catholic service society. In a brief exchange, they presented the President with a resolution proclaiming their loyalty to him.

12:03 P.M.–12:23 P.M.: Returned to the Cabinet Room to meet with several high-level politicians and conservationists about his proposal to create the Redwoods National Park in northern California. Among those in attendance were Interior Secretary Stewart Udall, National Geographic Society President Melville Grosvenor, and the former California governor and current U.S. Supreme Court chief justice, Earl Warren.[7]

12:24 P.M.: On his way to the Oval Office, stopped at his secretary's desk to receive a message from Lee White that Martin Luther King Jr. had called. According to the Daily Diary, Johnson told White to tell King that "I've sent eight helicopters down there this morning, and 200 marines . . . have made available every facility of the Federal Government and the Defense Department and the FBI has."

12:26 P.M.: Back at the Oval Office, took up the matter of Cyprus with former secretary of state Dean Acheson, Under Secretary of State George Ball, National Security Council staffer Robert Komer, and National Security Special Assistant McGeorge Bundy.

12:39 P.M.: Headed to the Mansion with George Ball for a session with Greek Prime Minister Papandreou and his official party.

12:55 P.M.: The group went to the East Room for a brief reception.

1:10 P.M.–2:10 P.M.: They proceeded to the State Dining Room for an hour-long lunch for 112 guests.

2:15 P.M.–4:06 P.M.: Returned to the second floor of the Mansion. Over the next two hours, he held a series of unrecorded phone conversations with McGeorge Bundy (2:25 P.M.), Walter Jenkins (2:40 P.M. and 3:36 P.M.), Hubert Humphrey (2:47 P.M.), George Reedy (3:00 P.M. and 3:37 P.M.), Larry O'Brien (3:39 P.M.), John McCormack (3:45 P.M.), Lee White (3:55 P.M.), and Larry O'Brien (4:06 P.M.)

---

7. "Remarks on the Proposed Redwoods National Park in Northern California," 25 June 1964, *Public Papers of the Presidents of the United States: Lyndon B. Johnson, 1963–64* (Washington, DC: GPO, 1965), 1:817.

4:13 P.M.: Arrived back at the Oval Office to start the second half of his day, soon making a call to the director of the FBI.

4:18 P.M.

To J. Edgar Hoover[8]

Published reports that Johnson was sending in the Marines to help with the missing persons case had caused a stir in Washington and in Mississippi. Here, the FBI director tried to set the record straight.

President Johnson: Hello.
J. Edgar Hoover: Hello?
President Johnson: Yes, Edgar.
Hoover: Yes, Mr. President.
President Johnson: Did you talk to the governor [Paul Johnson]?
Hoover: Yes, I talked to the governor—
President Johnson: Get him straightened . . .
Hoover: —and got him all straightened out.
President Johnson: Now, you're going to use the Navy if they can do it, and if not, you're going to get the Marines, is that right?
Hoover: [*with the President acknowledging throughout*] I'll be put— We're not going to get the Marines at all. What happened on that thing: They had told us down there at Meridian that this [naval auxiliary air] base outside of there was a Marine base, and then we made the request of the Defense Department for access to have those Marines assist in the search. Meantime, your noon press statement came out saying Marines were going to be used, so the Defense Department, being sticklers for protocols, understood that to be an order for Marines and therefore ordered Marines in from Camp Lejeune [North Carolina]. I got in touch with them as soon as I got this word from Walter Jenkins about the concern of Governor Johnson, and the Defense Department said that they had read this statement of yours, and therefore they'd have to send the Marines in since you had used the word *Marines* unless it was countermanded. I said, "I'll take the responsibility for countermanding it."

---

8. Tape WH6406.16, Citation #3897, Recordings of Telephone Conversations—White House Series, Recordings and Transcripts of Conversations and Meetings, Lyndon B. Johnson Library.

They had one plane already in the air en route to Meridian with Marines from Camp Lejeune. I said, "Send that plane back to Camp Lejeune and keep the Marines at Camp Lejeune. What we want are the . . . is manpower, and these Navy men that are at Meridian, we'll use them." So that was then straightened out, and that has been done.

So we've got now 200 Navy personnel at the Navy base there, and then we've got our own, then, and we've got the Mississippi Highway Patrol. I explained all that to the governor, and he's thoroughly satisfied with it. He said that the National Guard was entirely available, and it would be subject to our call if we wanted them. I said we had given some thought to that this morning, and that, very frankly, we felt that it would be better to use the local military people, the naval people there, at Meridian because the National Guard are all natives of the state, and it's not integrated, and the extremists of the Negro movement would begin to holler that we had brought the anti-Negro National Guard into this picture to make the search. I said they claim that the FBI is anti-Negro also, but I said in order not to add any more fuel to the fire, I said we decided to use the local naval personnel, and I said they are the ones that are now going to be used.

There are no Marines coming into Mississippi. The sailors will be under our direction. They are merely to make the search. He said that was fine, and I said I'll see that in the future if there is anything that develops that a statement is going to be made on that is of any significance, I'll call you or have our man down there be in touch with you so as to alert you, so you'll be informed. He said that would be fine. He wanted us to still know that he wanted to extend full cooperation, et cetera.

Then I called [John] Stennis and explained the same thing to him, and he was thoroughly satisfied. He said they'd been after him to make some kind of a press statement, and I told him, I said, "Well, you can make a press statement to the effect that I have said—as I told Allen Dulles yesterday, and he could tell the governor—that the governor has been most cooperative, and the Mississippi Highway Patrol have been most helpful, and that they've been of great assistance in the progress we've made so far in this case." So Stennis said that was what he was going to say on TV this afternoon. So he's satisfied.

President Johnson: All right, now, I understood you told me this morning it *was* Marine personnel, or was it—

Hoover: Yes, sir, and we were told that too. But—

President Johnson: Uh-huh . . . Who told you that, your local people that are down there, or the Defense people?

Hoover: The Defense people down there had told us that it was this Marine base outside of Meridian.

President Johnson: What is it, a naval base?

Hoover: It's a naval base, yes.[9] And then when we got clearance up here to call on that . . . to call on them for personnel. [In the] meantime, your statement came out, mentioning the word *Marines*, and they—

President Johnson: Mm-hmm. . . . That's what you told me.

Hoover: Yes, that's what I told you; that's what I sent over in the memoranda.

President Johnson: Yeah.

Hoover: And the Defense Department is saying that since you had used the word *Marines*, then they would have to bring Marines in.

President Johnson: Well, we can just—we've got to correct it with the press. So I think the thing we ought to say is that we were notified from local authorities that they had some personnel near Meridian at a naval installation.

Hoover: Yes.

President Johnson: And there's . . . it would be fine that they're going to use Navy boys instead of Marine boys because that's what they have there.

Hoover: That's correct . . . that's correct.

President Johnson: OK.

Hoover: That's correct.

President Johnson: All right, OK.

Hoover: Fine.

President Johnson: Bye.

4:28 P.M.: Johnson placed an unrecorded call to George Reedy on the personal line. He then received news from Capitol Hill.

4:31 P.M.

From Larry O'Brien[10]

On this day, the House of Representatives passed their version of the Urban Mass Transportation Act, which provided $375 million worth of grants to

---

9. They were referring to the Meridian Naval Auxiliary Air Station.
10. Tape WH6406.16, Citation #3898, Recordings of Telephone Conversations—White House Series, Recordings and Transcripts of Conversations and Meetings, Lyndon B. Johnson Library.

state and local organizations to improve their mass transit systems. The Senate accepted this House version on June 30, and President Johnson signed it on July 9.

Larry O'Brien: Mr. President?
President Johnson: Yeah.
O'Brien: 212 [to] 189, 3 present.
President Johnson: That's wonderful: 212 [to] 189.
O'Brien: Three present.
President Johnson: What should we say about that in the press conference?
O'Brien: Well, I think that certainly this represents a major recognition on the federal level of the tremendous problems of urban America; that the great need for cooperative action in the federal-state level has been apparent for several years, and this represents a breakthrough in this area that is bound to be beneficial to every American.
President Johnson: Thank you.
O'Brien: OK, Mr. President.
President Johnson: All right.

> 4:32 P.M.: The President made another unrecorded call to George Reedy on the personal line.
> 4:36 P.M.: Took a few minutes for a haircut at the White House barbershop.

4:52 P.M.

To Nicholas Katzenbach;
preceded by Office Conversation with Luther Hodges[11]

Johnson called Katzenbach to discuss LeRoy Collins's qualifications for being director of the Community Relations Service. As the call was being

---

11. Tape WH6406.16, Citation #3899, Recordings of Telephone Conversations—White House Series, Recordings and Transcripts of Conversations and Meetings, Lyndon B. Johnson Library.

connected, Johnson spoke in the office to Commerce Secretary Luther Hodges about Collins and about the Mississippi case.

The audio for the Hodges conversation is poor.

Luther Hodges: This issue [*unclear*].

President Johnson: Huh?

Hodges: It's in commerce—it's in the commerce clause, and I'm pretty sure [*unclear*] and that he deals with them anyhow. You'll have no problem there. [*Unclear section.*] It's taking a lot to persuade him [*unclear*] this is. But he's a . . . he's a *very* patriotic person, most thankful to do a job [*unclear*]—

The White House operator interrupts with a message.

White House Operator: Mr. President?

President Johnson: Yeah?

White House Operator: Mr. [Burke] Marshall is en route to the Pentagon. He just left.

President Johnson: See if Mr. Katzenbach is there.

White House Operator: Katzenbach, thank you.

The office conversation resumes.

Hodges: Did you send people in to see if we could find the people?

President Johnson: I imagine they're in that lake, my guess.

Hodges: No evidence [*unclear*].

President Johnson: Three days now.

Hodges: They drown in a body of water? [*Pause.*] That's tough. [*Unclear.*] This man that—I think when we're going to decide. I had a little question about. He's talking about—

White House Operator: Mr. Katzenbach, sir.

Hodges: —coming clean August 1st.

President Johnson: Nick?

The deputy attorney general comes on the line.

Nicholas Katzenbach: Yes, sir.

President Johnson: This . . . I got this list of names. Now, I told you the other night we had Governor [LeRoy] Collins under consideration.

Katzenbach: Yes.

President Johnson: I assume if we can get him, well, we ought to get him without taking any of these others, don't you?

Katzenbach: Yes, I thought . . . I was under—

President Johnson: This is in case he didn't come, isn't that right?

Katzenbach: Yes, sir, and I had unders—I had mistakenly understood that . . . that . . . that he was not acceptable with some of the . . . for political reasons.

President Johnson: Well, [James] Eastland had some—raising hell about it, but I don't believe it'd go before his [Judiciary] Committee.[12] Wouldn't it go before Commerce?

Katzenbach: It'd go before Commerce, yes, sir.

President Johnson: And he's acceptable to the two senators from the state [Florida].[13] So it's a national job, and I would imagine that we could get him confirmed, wouldn't you?

Katzenbach: Would they testify for him?

President Johnson: Well, they both cleared him with [Luther] Hodges.

Katzenbach: Yeah, yeah. Well, that ought to . . . that'd be fine.

President Johnson: OK. And then who would be first on . . . would you think the labor secretary next if we failed on that one?[14]

Katzenbach: I would think so. He's a prominent Republican, and . . . but, you know, out of politics now, and that has its advantages.

President Johnson: You think he'd be preferable to Collins?

Katzenbach: I don't know the gentleman personally, and Arthur Goldberg spoke highly of him; Ralph Dungan spoke highly of him.[15] [Secretary of Labor] Bill Wirtz spoke highly of him. The only question with Collins that I have is whether or not he would be regarded in the South as one who had . . . was a turncoat of some kind. That's probably Eastland's objection. But if he would be effective, I think that the southerner understands the problem much better than northerners do.

President Johnson: He . . . you think he'd be satisfactory, though, with the Negro groups?

Katzenbach: Collins? Yes, sir, no question.

President Johnson: Yeah, that's been checked out. Somebody checked it, didn't they?

---

12. Two days earlier, Eastland, the chair of the Senate Judiciary Committee, had recommended against Collins, telling Johnson that he was a "damn cheat, double-crosser" and a "goddamn, lying, son of a bitch." Conversation between President Johnson and James Eastland, 3:59 P.M., 23 June 1964, in this volume.

13. Spessard Holland and George Smathers were the senators from Florida.

14. The President had been considering William E. Simkin, director of the Department of Labor's Federal Mediation and Conciliation Service, as an alternative. See the conversation between President Johnson and Burke Marshall, 3:51 P.M., 23 June 1964, in this volume.

15. Former secretary of labor Arthur Goldberg was an associate justice on the Supreme Court. Ralph Dungan was a special assistant to the President who handled appointments matters.

Katzenbach: Yes. . . . Yes, no question. No question about that.
President Johnson: OK. . . . All right.

4:55 P.M.–5:00 P.M.: President Johnson met with Luther Hodges and
LeRoy Collins, who then departed.

  Although Johnson had not officially nominated Collins to
direct the Community Relations Service and continued to lobby
the National Association of Broadcasters to release him from
his duties, the press would report the next day that Collins was
Johnson's choice.

5:04 P.M.: Spoke with NSC staffer Robert Komer in the hallway outside the Oval Office about a Greek interpreter and then went
into the Oval Office for a five-minute meeting with Komer,
Secretary of State Dean Rusk, and Under Secretary of State
George Ball. He then held a series of quick, unrecorded telephone conversations with George Reedy (5:11 P.M.) and Walter
Jenkins (5:14 P.M. and 5:15 P.M.) on the personal line.

5:16 P.M.: With Rusk, Ball, and Ambassador Henry Labouisse, met
in the Cabinet Room with Greek Prime Minister Papandreou
and his advisers.

5:55 P.M.: Returned to the Oval Office, speaking to Juanita Roberts
on the way about an invitation to a party being held by Senator
Eugene McCarthy of Minnesota.[16] In the office, he picked up
the phone to discuss the day's reporting on the situation in
Mississippi.

5:57 P.M.

To Lee White[17]

Earlier this day, a group of concerned parents had held a press conference
to lobby for more protection for students going to Mississippi. In this call,
Johnson conferred with his chief civil rights aide about the matter.

----

16. Johnson was scheduled to speak in Minneapolis on 27 June at an event hosted by Senator
McCarthy.
17. Tape WH6406.17, Citation #3900, Recordings of Telephone Conversations—White House
Series, Recordings and Transcripts of Conversations and Meetings, Lyndon B. Johnson Library.

President Johnson: [*reading*] . . . "Summer project today expressed shock"—[*the line clicks*].

Hang up, whoever—

[*continues reading*]—"over the fact that federal marshals have not been sent to Mississippi. They conferred with several federal officials and pleaded that the federal protection be ordered for their children and other civil rights crusaders. Later at a news conference, they called—challenged the Attorney General's position that the law does not authorize preventive action in Mississippi. They offered in support of their argument a letter to Professor Johnson—President Johnson sent June 9 by Mark DeWolfe Howe, a Harvard law professor, and other legal authorities.[18] It urged that participants in the Mississippi project be furnished federal protection and said it would be legal.

"Norman Blum of Great Neck, New York, chief spokesman of the group, was asked if he felt President Johnson was partially responsible for the disappearance of three of the youths. 'It could be interpreted that way,' he said. Another parent, Sydney Rufeld of New York, said the situation in Mississippi demands action by [Robert] Kennedy or some other official. Kennedy was accused by Blum of taking a very narrow interpretation of the law. Lillian Gruber of Great Neck said it was ironic that Kennedy should fail to send marshals in view of the death of his brother—fate of his brother. Another parent said she felt Kennedy should have delayed his current trip to Germany. The parents said they'd conferred with presidential assistant Lee White and Assistant Attorney General Nicholas Katzenburg [*sic*], among others."

Lee White: Well, that was a group of parents that Mrs. Rabinowitz brought in yesterday.[19] I don't remember the . . .

President Johnson: Well, did they—

White: Norman Blum, but there was a Mrs. Rabinowitz, and about—

President Johnson: What questions did they raise with you? Did they want marshals?

White: They wanted marshals, 2,000 armed marshals, to be sent into the area—

President Johnson: 200 marshals, he says, and 200 FBI agents.[20]

White: Well, at that point in the little session we had, the woman

---

18. Mark DeWolfe Howe was a devotee of former President Kennedy and an expert on constitutional law who supported civil rights causes.

19. The spellings of Sydney Rufeld, Lillian Gruber, and Mrs. Rabinowitz are phonetic.

20. Civil rights activists in Mississippi had made similar requests this day to Allen Dulles, adding to the ones by New York senators Jacob Javits and Kenneth Keating the day before.

suggested—this was a 45-minute discussion—one of the recommenda-tions was that 2,000 federal marshals armed and in Mississippi would show the people down there that the federal government really means business. And my response was that the relationships between the fed-eral government and the state are such that we can't send armed people into states unless there is a determination and a finding that the, you know, the law has [gone] outside of the control of the state authorities. We have just received—and your conversation with Governor [Paul] Johnson would indicate—a bona fide attempt on their part to control the situation, and that we . . . just struck me that was an idea that we would have to hold in mind and watch as the situation unfolded.

President Johnson: All right. Now, why don't you get Katzenbach to call his attention to this UPI [United Press International] release 148?

White: UPI 48 . . . 148?

President Johnson: Yeah, and we ought to find out who [is] this law-yer running around with them. He's a Washington lawyer here.

White: Was that 148, Mr. President?

President Johnson: Yeah, UPI 148.

White: All right.

President Johnson: It cleared the wire at 3:57 [P.M.].

White: What was the lawyer's name?

President Johnson: William Higgs, an attorney in Washington.[21]

White: Oh, that guy. William Higgs—he's a white fellow from Mississippi who's a very liberal civil rights lawyer who's been sort of kicked out of the state. Bill Higgs has been a thorn in our side for . . . for, oh, at least a couple years. He's—

President Johnson: Is he a Republican?

White: No, sir, he's a wild, liberal Democrat and not very well regarded at home. His wife had to leave him; she couldn't . . . the pres-sures got so intense in Mississippi. I think he's well meaning and good in—good-hearted and well-motivated fellow, but he is able to generate 14 wild ideas in an hour. And this makes a little more sense. He's not stupid by any stretch of the imagination, and, as I said, I think his intentions are good, and he would love to, you know, to press and to push and to goad us into doing something like going into Mississippi.

He's exactly the sort of guy that is just a total danger because he is bright, he knows the law, and, as I say, I believe his heart is pretty

---

21. Among other things, William Higgs was a civil rights attorney who represented the Student Nonviolent Coordinating Committee, one of the key sponsors of Freedom Summer.

good. He sticks with these SNCC boys from the . . . they're the roughest of all. He's been in Washington, I would guess, about six months or eight months and is just really . . . been a thorn in the side of the Justice Department ever since he's been in town. He has some pretty good ideas, I have to admit. As I say, he's the mixed sort of a fellow.

President Johnson: Mm-hmm . . . yeah. I think that somebody . . . I think Katzenbach ought to put out a statement as to what the Justice Department [has] done, everything we've done, someway or other, and explain why we can't get marshals in there.

White: Well, on June 17, a week ago yesterday, I sent a memo to Burke [Marshall] raising eight of these kind of questions we could tell were coming up.[22] Typical are this: Under what conditions can federal marshals or federal troops be sent into Mississippi to protect the college students? What has the Justice Department or the entire federal government done so far by way of preparing? What additional steps, preliminary actions, various alternatives would be available to the federal government in the event of widespread disorders? Are there any steps that the President could consider taking between now and the first outbreak of violence? Any precedents to guide us? And, in addition to formal steps, are there any way[s] we can establish informal liaison with the state or local enforcement?

Now, some of these have already been taken care of. I think—

President Johnson: You talk to him and see what he can do to get out so that the people know. Every senator and congressman that calls up and says "marshals," we ought to tell them why and tell them we've got FBI men in lieu of it, and let these people know that we don't know whether there are 200, but we know there are plenty of them.

White: Well, I think the number ought to be classified, but I . . . your description of them as greatly augmented, I think, is pretty good, and [unclear]—

President Johnson: I'd tell them that and tell them we don't want to expose our hand—who they are and where they are—because they're in all these various groups.

White: Right. Well, we can have a . . . you know, a formal legal opinion, and I think it'd be useful for everybody to have in mind here and the circumstance [unclear] too good.

---

22. Lee White to Burke Marshall, 17 June 1964. "PL/ST 24" folder, Box 53, Political Affairs/ Mississippi (Mississippi Freedom Democratic Party), White House Central Files, Lyndon B. Johnson Library.

President Johnson: You get on that, will you? . . . I got to go to a 6:00 meeting. Would you get on that with them and see that whatever we need to do is done?

White: I certainly will. We had a call, Mr. President, from this fellow, Martin Popper, who's a lawyer for the Goodmans. He said that the Goodmans are . . . have suggested that they would like to see Governor [Paul] Johnson. They'd like to go down there to Jackson to meet with him and to call for the people in the state to come forward with any information they may have about their son. I said, well, that would really be between the Goodmans and Governor Johnson. He said, well, yes, but first of all, they didn't want to do it if we thought it was not a good idea. Second, if we did think it was a good idea, they wanted some . . . whatever assistance we could give in getting in touch with the governor.

[*Unclear*] . . . It sounds to me a little bit like a trap. Strikes me that if the governor wants to see them that they . . . their names are well known to him and that they could use whatever resources that are available to them.

President Johnson: Yeah, that's right. We can't make . . . be making appointments.

White: I hate to try to make an appointment, and I hate to even say it's a good idea or a bad idea.

President Johnson: Mm-hmm.

White: Frankly, I don't think it would be one bit of help. I hate to see those parents dragged through some more, and I don't really know whether it's their idea or this lawyer's idea. I was really uncomfortable with their bringing a lawyer with them. If they'd have brought a friend or a minister or something, I'd have felt better, but a lawyer—

President Johnson: What, did they come in and see you today?

White: No, sir, on the telephone.

President Johnson: Well, what do you mean "their bringing a lawyer with them"?

White: [*with the President acknowledging*] When they met with you in your office, I didn't know it, but the guy that they brought as their friend and their comforting fellow was a lawyer who, you know, I don't know if he's been retained or whether he's a personal friend or what. But now he's calling me on the phone like, you know, we're old, long-lost buddies, and he's their counsel.

President Johnson: Tell him that that's a matter between them and whoever he wants to see, that the President doesn't make appointments for people.

White: If you don't mind, I'd just as soon not even put you in it. Just tell them, you know, that I . . .

President Johnson: Yeah, I don't—that's good. OK.

White: OK, sir.

6:05 P.M.: President Johnson made an unrecorded call to Walter Jenkins.

6:10 P.M.: Went to the Fish Room for a photo session with the ambassadors to Philippines, Greece, and Turkey.

6:14 P.M.: Returned to the Oval Office to take more photos, this time for *Ebony* magazine with Hobart Taylor, the Houston attorney who served as Johnson's chief aide on the President's Commission on Equal Employment Opportunity. During that session, George Reedy called to report on a recent press briefing.

6:15 P.M.

From George Reedy[23]

Johnson's press secretary reported on his afternoon encounter with the press. Johnson tried to clarify the Marine/naval personnel issue that J. Edgar Hoover had raised two hours earlier and then carefully walked Reedy through the administration's reasoning for not sending in federal marshals.

President Johnson: How'd you go with your briefing?

George Reedy: I think it went fairly well. The . . . of course, a lot of amusement about these Marines suddenly becoming sailors, but I think they all realized this came to us from the FBI.[24] The main question I have now is *if* [Allen] Dulles comes back tonight, and I don't know whether he's coming or not, are you going to meet with him?

---

23. Tape WH6406.17, Citation #3901, Recordings of Telephone Conversations—White House Series, Recordings and Transcripts of Conversations and Meetings, Lyndon B. Johnson Library.
24. See the conversation between President Johnson and J. Edgar Hoover, 4:18 P.M., 25 June 1964, in this chapter.

President Johnson: Tell him we have no plans to, that we don't know. I have no word when he's coming, and don't know anything about it, and have no plans to. I wouldn't want to forgo it or foreclose it. If he does, and there's any news in it, why, we'll call them.

Reedy: Right.

President Johnson: But . . . didn't you explain to them that the FBI said that they were Marines from this station, that they—

Reedy: Yes.

President Johnson: —were Marine helicopters, and the other people are going to be Navy boys?

Reedy: Right.

President Johnson: And what . . . did they raise hell with you about it?

Reedy: No, they didn't raise hell about it.

President Johnson: Mm-hmm. [*Pause.*] OK, you read these—

Reedy: The main thing they're trying to push on right now is a policy statement on this letter that we're supposed to have gotten from these parents last June 9. I never heard of the letter until I saw it in the wire today.

President Johnson: Mm-hmm.

Reedy: And . . . well, whether we're going to send troops into Mississippi or not. That's what it comes down to.

President Johnson: Well—

Reedy: I told them I have not seen that letter, and that all I know is . . . [*unclear*]—

President Johnson: [*with Reedy acknowledging throughout*] I think you can go back and say that we have had a good many of these things brought to our attention, but we have all . . . we took action back [in] the early part of June to send in additional forces of FBI people, and we think that in the light of the situation that that's all that the Justice Department—I'd talk to [Nicholas] Katzenbach and get him to give you a statement on that.[25]

But . . . we don't want to get you in a legal argument because the more you talk, the more trouble you'll get in. But they have no authority under law to send in marshals until the law has been flouted or until an

---

25. Katzenbach's policy paper on this issue argued that such proposals for law enforcement "raise mixed problems of law, morality, and practicality." Nicholas Katzenbach, "Memorandum for the President: Use of Marshals, Troops, and Other Federal Personnel for Law Enforcement in Mississippi," 1 July 1964, "Civil Rights—Mississippi" folder, Office Files of Lee White, Box 6, White House Central Files, Lyndon B. Johnson Library.

emergency has been declared. And the fact that people are missing, we don't know whether law has been violated or not, we're investigating it.

Reedy: Right.

President Johnson: And we can't send in marshals, but we can send in FBI, and we've got them in there by the dozens.

Reedy: Right.

President Johnson: We don't want to say by the dozens—

Reedy: No.

President Johnson: But we've got them in by substantial numbers, and the President stated it was greatly augmented some time ago. And that was the answer to these letters.

Reedy: Right.

President Johnson: We ordered in everything we could.

Reedy: OK, sir.

President Johnson: They're going back and tying it in to the Little Rock thing.[26] We've got to be awfully careful about that.

Reedy: I know that that's what they're after.

President Johnson: All right. . . . Did [George] Ball do all right with his group?[27]

Reedy: Yes, sir, he did quite well, I think. They just left. He briefed them in here on a background basis, and we got the communiqué out to them as they left.[28]

President Johnson: Mm-hmm . . . mm-hmm. OK.

Reedy: OK, sir.

> **6:20 P.M.:** In preparation for U. Alexis Johnson's leaving for Saigon, the President met with the departing diplomat and several top-level administrators in the Cabinet Room.[29] Twenty-five minutes into the meeting, President Johnson asked for George Reedy to bring him J. Edgar Hoover's report on the use of Marines.

---

26. Johnson was referring to Dwight Eisenhower's sending in the 101st Airborne in 1957 to implement Little Rock's school desegregation order.

27. Under Secretary of State George Ball was handling the Cyprus matter for the administration.

28. See "Joint Statement Following Discussions with the Prime Minister of Greece," 25 June 1964, *Public Papers, Johnson, 1963–64*, 1:818–19.

29. Included in this group were McGeorge Bundy, Robert McNamara, Maxwell Taylor, U.S. Agency for International Aid Director David Bell, Assistant Secretary of State for East Asian and Pacific Affairs William Bundy, National Security Council staffer Michael Forrestal, United States Information Agency Director Carl Rowan, Central Intelligence Agency Director John McCone, and the Secretary of State's special assistant for Vietnamese affairs and director of the Vietnam Coordinating Committee, William Sullivan.

6:50 P.M.–7:15 P.M.: Defense Secretary Robert McNamara remained at the White House for a session with the President. Fifteen minutes later, they strolled outside along the White House Colonnade.

7:15 P.M.: Johnson returned to the Oval Office with Jack Valenti.

7:40 P.M.: On the personal line, Johnson placed an unrecorded call to George Reedy. At some point before the next call, the President tried to locate an unknown person. The exchange with the White House operator was captured on tape, as was a brief one with McGeorge Bundy.

TIME UNKNOWN

With White House Operators[30]

President Johnson: . . . and I've been waiting a long time.

White House Operator #1: Just a moment, please.

White House Operator #2: He's in the car, Mr. President, and I thought I could reach him for you.

President Johnson: Well, is he on the way home?

White House Operator #2: Well, they're not sure.

President Johnson: Well, ask his car where the hell is he and when he'll be home, that I'm trying my best to talk to him before *I* go to a dinner.

White House Operator #2: Yes, Mr. President.

7:42 P.M.

From McGeorge Bundy[31]

McGeorge Bundy: . . . night and talk about it in the morning, because it's a complicated little problem. Would that be easier for you?

President Johnson: No, you better come and explain them.

---

30. Tape WH6406.17, Citation #3902, Recordings of Telephone Conversations—White House Series, Recordings and Transcripts of Conversations and Meetings, Lyndon B. Johnson Library.
31. Tape WH6406.17, Citation #3903, Recordings of Telephone Conversations—White House Series, Recordings and Transcripts of Conversations and Meetings, Lyndon B. Johnson Library.

Bundy: All right, I'll bring them up, and I'll bring my expert [Francis Bator].[32]

President Johnson: All right.

7:45 P.M.

From Chester V. "Ted" Clifton[33]

President Johnson was scheduled to give speeches in Detroit and Minneapolis on June 26 and June 27. Concerned about possible press coverage of a planned trip to the Mayo Clinic and the high cost of taking the Boeing 707 that normally served as Air Force One, he preferred to make the trip in a Jetstar, a small jet built by Lockheed and favored by Johnson for its versatility.[34] When his military aide explained the resistance to Johnson's plan, the President revisited his long-running battle with the Secret Service, at one point telling General Clifton that "they do everything except kill you."

President Johnson: Why do we have to have a backup plane go to Detroit?

Chester V. "Ted" Clifton: The two reasons are: One, is you have very bad communications on this thing, and if you decide to go someplace else or were called to, why, you wouldn't have any Secret Service with you. You'll have three—

President Johnson: Well, I've got more than I need now. So I'm not going to charge these poor, little ole government people that work for civil service to make a lot of big, foolish plans. I've been flying that plane for years around here, and I don't see any reason why you got to have another one coming around messing us up that's got no better communications on it.

Clifton: No. . . .

---

32. Francis Bator was the other special assistant for national security affairs and an expert on Europe and economic policy.
33. Tape WH6406.17, Citation #3904, Recordings of Telephone Conversations—White House Series, Recordings and Transcripts of Conversations and Meetings, Lyndon B. Johnson Library.
34. Air Force One was the radio call sign for the plane carrying the president and applied to whatever plane the president happened to fly.

President Johnson: We're not going to be but an hour or so on either of these trips: going from Detroit to Minneapolis is not over an hour or so, and from here to Detroit. Now, what I want to do is take . . . I want to go out . . . Mrs. [Lady Bird] Johnson, I'll pick her up. I can take . . .

Clifton: Right.

President Johnson: I can take three Secret Service with me . . .

Clifton: Right, sir.

President Johnson: . . . and the rest of them can go out in the morning.

Clifton: Right.

President Johnson: Let them pay their own damn way. [*Clifton attempts to interject.*] I think it's a waste of time. I think they're going to get me killed. If they don't get me killed, they're going to let the gun go off, one of them, and kill me because they've got so damned many around you that you can't ever do anything. And I think that we ought to make an economy study there and see how many of them you can get out of your way because they never do anything but endanger you: They notify everybody in town what time you're coming, *how* you're coming, *where* you're coming, and how to kill you if you want to. They do everything except kill you. And if they'll just let us go, and they get in the car and keep their damn mouth shut, we'll go down a back road and nobody ever knows we're there. But they get their sirens going, 40 cops leading you, and all that kind of stuff.

So I don't care about hauling any more of them than necessary because the most I've ever been in danger was when I'm with a bunch of Secret Service men. They don't know how to operate their guns. Hell, I tried to . . . I had ten of them out there one day, tried to kill a snake, and they couldn't kill him. They just emptied their gun at my ranch. So, I don't— [*talking over Clifton*]—that argument don't appeal to me that I need more than three in a Jetstar.

Clifton: Right.

President Johnson: So that's the first argument. Now, what's the second one?

Clifton: Well, the communications are—

President Johnson: Well, the communications are not any better on—

Clifton: —[unclear] better, and you don't worry about that hour and 15 minutes.

President Johnson: Not at all, they're not going to be any better in the backup than they are in the one I'm in.

Clifton: No, sir. And . . .

President Johnson: And I never had—

Clifton: You think you can get along with the doctor [George Burkley] and the rest of us in one Jetstar?

President Johnson: I can take . . . I can take the two senators, Clifton, and the doctor.[35]

Clifton: Right, sir.

President Johnson: I don't think the doctor's necessary, but I'll yield to you-all's judgment on that. I think it'd be just as well if he wanted to go out commercial. I don't think I'll miss him that hour.

Clifton: And they all—my other point, and this is not a problem to you, then, is the alternate in case something happened to the first one when we're on the ground and a valve didn't work or something.

President Johnson: Well, that's all right. It's not going to bother me. It's a pure political campaign trip. Hell, I haven't got to the point where I can't wait an hour.

Clifton: All right, sir. Well, then we can go with one plane.

President Johnson: I just don't like for these little civil service people that are buying these $100 tickets to have to waste 16[000] or 18,000 dollars that I've raised on this kind of crap.

Clifton: Right, sir, and incidentally to this whole subject, I am getting a reexamination of these charges because they charged two different rates, and I've asked the Air Force to come up and show me the justification for this 1958 decision.[36] So I'm looking this all over. It may be charging us a lot more than we should be paying for these aircraft.

President Johnson: Mm-hmm.

Clifton: Mr. [Cyrus] Vance and Mr. [Robert] McNamara's viewpoint is that the political thing should be paid for, for four or five passengers, those who are going for political reasons, and because you're the commander in chief and you need communications things, they'd rather have you take the big plane and take the people that are supposed to be on your staff.[37]

President Johnson: [*with Clifton acknowledging*] Of course they had, but they're not running for office, and they don't have to get elected, and they're not the taxpayers, and a lot of other of these things. Just like . . . [Jack] Valenti came into me awhile ago and said that the military is

---

35. Johnson was referring to Patrick McNamara and Philip Hart, both Democratic senators from Michigan.

36. The Democratic National Committee eventually paid the Air Force $149,000 for Johnson's 1964 campaign trips. The Boeing 707 traditionally known as Air Force One cost $2,350 per hour, while the Jetstar was $524 per hour. Published reports indicated that Johnson was charged using the same formula as Eisenhower in 1956. *New York Times*, 15 April 1965.

37. Cyrus Vance was deputy secretary of defense.

going to order this plane, and I said, "Well, we're going to see whose order prevails: mine or theirs. Damned if I'm going to have the military ordering anything to go to a political meeting with me unless I approve it."

Clifton: Well, that's right. We weren't going to do that without your approval—

President Johnson: All right. Well, I sure as hell don't approve it. I just don't think that you ought to be sending along a bunch of extra guys, and I don't want to create any excitement about it. I'm going to Mayo's hospital, my judgment, on Saturday morning.[38]

Clifton: Right, sir.

President Johnson: And if I've got to have . . . I've got to have that bag with me [at] all times, is that right?[39]

Clifton: Yes, sir, you have to.

President Johnson: All right.

Clifton: Yeah, that's essential, and one aide can bring it on the plane.

President Johnson: All right.

Clifton: And we'll put the rest of the people to help us on that press plane—buy them a ticket—that we need. I'm talking about a courier to help me.

President Johnson: Yes, or the Secret Service.

Clifton: On the trip to Rochester, we want to do this sort of quietly, as I understand.[40]

President Johnson: We do until we go in there. Now, you'll have to tell George [Reedy] in the morning so the press plane can get into Rochester.

Clifton: You're going to take them with you?

President Johnson: Well, I don't give a damn whether they—I don't want them to go with me, but I imagine they'll want to.

Clifton: Well, my thought was if you wanted to do this quietly, the Coast Guard has a plane up there in that area, and we could ride out the back of the hotel and out to the Coast Guard plane and go in there, and nobody [would] know the difference for a long time.

President Johnson: [*with Clifton acknowledging throughout*] Well, they'll know it, and they'll give us unshirted hell. No, I think we better

---

38. One of Johnson's longtime personal doctors, James Cain, was at the Mayo Clinic. See Transcript, James C. Cain Oral History, Interview I, 22 February 1970, by David G. McComb, Internet Copy, Lyndon B. Johnson Library.

39. Johnson was apparently referring to the case containing nuclear launch procedures. A later generation would refer to it as "the football."

40. The Mayo Clinic was in Rochester, Minnesota, approximately 90 miles southeast of Minneapolis.

tell them. I think my judgment is, we'll decide on it after I talk to Mrs. Johnson tonight. She's in Detroit.

My guess is that we'll leave here tomorrow in time to get downtown Detroit at the time they think we'll have the biggest crowd. And I'd like to be later, but they say that they've got to get there by 4:30 or something, and we'll move up the time of departure. We'll stay through the meeting and get away as early as we can tomorrow night. And we'll tell George Reedy in the morning so he can tell the press plane. They can get a plane—he won't have to tell them—but he [can] get a press plane that can get in to the Rochester airport. Then they can go on, and the Secret Service can go on that press plane, buy them a ticket, and they'll have plenty of people in Detroit anyway. I mean, they got an office there, and they can have two or three there.

But if they want to bollix it up, you can just put whatever number on there, there. Then when we go to Rochester, if the press plane goes with us, the Secret Service can go on it. And then we go on out to Minneapolis. But that's a lot different than the 60—

Clifton: We'll go straight to Rochester to Minneapolis on Saturday.

President Johnson: Yeah, we go to Detroit tomorrow night. I'd stay all night there. Now, I don't know whether the press will want to go with me or not.

Clifton: Well, if they do, we'll have to get them the right kind of plane in the morning, and I think that's all right. I don't know what they'll do in Rochester, but they may want to just send a pool and get a small plane to go out there. I'll talk to Mr.—

President Johnson: [*with Clifton acknowledging*] But I'm just going by and pay a social visit to my friends and schoolmates and family. This is kind of like my sister, Doctor [James] Cain, and I'm going to get a thorough examination of Mayo's while I'm there. Not going to be any secret about it, I'll just tell them; just like I told them I had a heart attack. And then I would get there tomorrow night, say at midnight. The only information we don't have is how far it is from Detroit to Rochester. We got everything else.

Clifton: I'll check that out.

President Johnson: [*with Clifton acknowledging*] And then . . . the next—Saturday morning, I'll get an examination, stay there all day Saturday, get into Minneapolis, the last time I need to, to make my first date. Then we'll show them that I'm physically fit by making the DFL [Democratic-Farmer-Labor Party] speech and then making the dinner speech. Then we'll stay all night in Minneapolis. Then we'll get up the next morning and go to the church that [Hubert] Humphrey wants us to and waste time around there, and then we'll go to the Swedes he wants to, and then we'll get on back to Washington.[41]

Clifton: Right, sir. All right—

President Johnson: And let's don't tell the press, though, that we're going to Rochester in case I cancel it out.

Clifton: No, sir.

President Johnson: Just get them a plane that'll go to Rochester. Check whatever plane it is, and it won't be very much longer to Detroit anyway, regular . . .

Clifton: No, sir. . . . I think an Electra will go in there, and that's one of their favorite planes.[42] And I'll check it out . . .

President Johnson: The press [would] like an Electra as well as a jet?

Clifton: Yes, sir. And it's a very comfortable plane, and it goes very, not jet speed, but very fast, and I'll check that Rochester airport.

President Johnson: Mmm. . . . Now, how many can we take? You see, I guess the Secret Service will have to have baggage.

Clifton: Well, they've got some baggage, and my honest opinion is—and I've got that study, you know, that's eight-pages long that you asked me to get for you that tells you exactly how much everybody can weigh and so forth, and I got it done by Major [unclear], so I didn't talk through my hat on it.[43] And you can take—Mrs. Johnson will have some baggage, of course.

President Johnson: Yes, and I'll have some.

Clifton: And you'll have some, and the rest of us can send our baggage on the press plane. We won't have any problems with our bags because all we need is a pencil and paper when I'm with you, and so we can take 10 people, possibly 11, depending on—

President Johnson: All right, you'll have the President and Mrs. Johnson . . .

Clifton: The Secret Service.

President Johnson: You have, let's see: the President, three Secret Service—that's going to Detroit, now. That's four. [Patrick] McNamara and [Philip] Hart, six; [Neil] Staebler, seven; Valenti's eight; Clifton's nine; [Dr. George] Burkley's ten.[44]

---

41. On 28 June, President Johnson and Lady Bird went to church at the Mt. Olivet Lutheran Church in Minneapolis with Senator Humphrey, Governor Karl Rolvaag, and two Minnesota congressmen. President Johnson then gave a speech to an estimated 85,000 spectators at the Swedish Day festival, known as Svenskarnas Dag.

42. Lockheed's Electra was a propeller-driven aircraft that could carry close to 70 passengers.

43. General Clifton may have said Major "Croft" or "Cross."

44. Neil Staebler was a Democratic representative from Michigan.

Clifton: Right, sir. And then we'll have a place for Mrs. Johnson when she gets on.

President Johnson: When she gets on, we may have to cut off a Secret Service, be 11 going to Minneapolis. If you can carry 11 with baggage, all right; if not, we'll cut off a Secret Service and let him go on the press plane.

Clifton: Well, we'll work that out. All right, sir.

President Johnson: So the only two musts are Burkley, Clifton, and Valenti.

Clifton: That's right. Those are three—

President Johnson: That's three, and then tell Secret Service they can have three, but if they want to, they can go out on the press plane.

Clifton: All right, sir.

President Johnson: OK.

Clifton: All right.

President Johnson: [*to Valenti, while hanging up*] Now, Jack—

8:00 P.M.

To John McCormack[45]

With the civil rights bill waiting for action by the House Rules Committee and well on its way to becoming law, Johnson was placing more pressure on Congress to pass legislation for the War on Poverty. The House Committee on Education and Labor had reported the bill out on June 3, but it had languished in the House Rules Committee since then. The administration was trying to put more pressure on Howard "Judge" Smith, the conservative Virginia Democrat who chaired the Rules Committee, to allow the bill to go to the floor of the House for a vote. At the beginning of this call to the Speaker of the House, McGeorge Bundy and Francis Bator arrived for a short meeting. According to the Daily Diary, they exited at 8:05 P.M.

President Johnson: I want to thank you for that mass transit [bill].

John McCormack: Well, thanks, Mr. President, it was a nice victory.

---

45. Tape WH6406.17, Citations #3905 and #3906, Recordings of Telephone Conversations— White House Series, Recordings and Transcripts of Conversations and Meetings, Lyndon B. Johnson Library.

President Johnson: Well, I'm going to call two or three of them, and I just got through with some meetings and I'm still here at the office. I have a note here from [Sargent] Shriver [that] says he called at 2:15.[46] He visited with [Charles] Halleck and [Howard] Smith.[47]

[*reading*] "Smith says he's not opposed to giving a rule. He insists that any congressman wanting to testify should be allowed to do so. He said four Republicans are declaring that they want to testify. Rules Committee is going to meet Tuesday. If the testimony is completed and the rule given on civil rights on Tuesday, then we'd hope we could get a meeting Wednesday and Thursday. Shriver asked Halleck to urge Republican congressmen to complete their testimony on Wednesday and Thursday, if Smith would give them a hearing then. Halleck said that he would talk to Republicans and see if he can limit their testimony, then Judge Smith is willing to accept a motion to give a rule at the end of the Thursday session. Judge Smith said that he would vote against the rule but he would not block it. He seemed to be extremely friendly to Shriver."

I don't know how accurate that is. That's just a memo that I'm just getting—

McCormack: Well, I asked him if he'd give . . . I asked him if he'd start hearings on the antipoverty on Wednesday, and he said he wouldn't give me any promise. He told me how Shriver was up to see him.

President Johnson: Yeah.

McCormack: And I said, "Well, I'm asking you to do this," I said, "now." And just before he was leaving the chamber I called him up to the chair again, I said, "Judge," I said, "I'm making the request with you to start hearings on antipoverty." I said . . . "And on Wednesday, and I'm going to be terribly disappointed if you don't. And I'll be very pleased if you do." So that's . . .

President Johnson: Mm-hmm. That's good. Now—

McCormack: That's the way I left it with him.

President Johnson: I don't know how to get Halleck to get his men ready to be a quorum.

McCormack: Now, the only thing is this: If there's going to be a vote on Thursday, we got to get Dick Bolling back.[48]

President Johnson: Yeah, yeah.

---

46. Sargent Shriver, the director of the Peace Corps, was also heading the administration's task force for the War on Poverty.
47. Charles Halleck was the House minority leader.
48. Richard Bolling, a liberal Democrat from Missouri, was a member of the House Rules Committee.

McCormack: Got to be watched very closely, because if you have a vote when there's 14 there, it'll be 7 [to] 7.

President Johnson: Yeah . . . yeah. Yeah, that's good. Well, we'll do that, and we'll get him back.

McCormack: It wouldn't—

President Johnson: And I hope that Halleck will get his congressmen there. I don't want any of them to go unheard, but they've got all week to hear them, and if we get—

McCormack: Oh, listen, Mr. President, I said to Halleck, I said, "Listen, your committee is not supposed to hear every witness that wants to appear before it."

President Johnson: No, of course not, we know that.

McCormack: "You're not a standing committee."[49]

President Johnson: We know that . . . we know that. We know that, but he wants to hear them, and we don't object to him hearing if they'll go on and hear them. But if they want to be heard and then won't speak, why, we can't do that. Maybe you can ask Halleck tomorrow, say, "Now, we want to accommodate you, and we want to get out of here."[50]

McCormack: Yeah.

President Johnson: "But get your men up there where they can be heard Wednesday and let them testify, and—"

McCormack: No, I haven't agreed on next Saturday [*unclear*].

President Johnson: I know it; I know it. OK.

McCormack: [*Unclear*], no, they haven't got any agreement out of me.

President Johnson: No, but they—that's right—but they think if we don't get this bill, why, that we won't have anything to bring up.

McCormack: [*with the President acknowledging*] Of course, Phil felt . . . Phil was frank. He's a wonderful fellow, Phil Lannum—Landrum. But of course, I've got that Georgia delegation over, and they've been the difference you know, very valuable.[51]

President Johnson: Yeah, that's right. . . . That's right . . . that's right. Well, you talk to Halleck in the morning and see if he won't help us to that extent and then we can help him.

McCormack: When are you leaving for Michigan?

---

49. The Rules Committee had no subcommittees.

50. See the conversation between President Johnson and Charles Halleck, 6:24 P.M., 22 June 1964, in Guian A. McKee, ed., *The Presidential Recordings, Lyndon B. Johnson: Mississippi Burning and the Passage of the Civil Rights Act, June 1, 1964–July 4, 1964*, vol. 7, *June 1, 1964–June 22, 1964* (New York: Norton, 2011), pp. 535–43.

51. Democrat Phillip Landrum of Georgia was the floor manager for the antipoverty bill in the House.

President Johnson: I'm leaving tomorrow afternoon.

McCormack: Fine. What are you going to do out there?

President Johnson: I'm going to make a speech—tomorrow, I'm going to make a speech to Detroit, tomorrow night, $100 [per person] dinner.

McCormack: Oh, yeah.

President Johnson: Then I'm going on out to Minnesota the next day.

McCormack: Mmm. How's your throat feeling?

President Johnson: OK.

McCormack: Fine.

President Johnson: Bye.

8:20 P.M.

From Larry O'Brien[52]

The day before, on June 24, the Senate Finance Committee reported out the Excise Tax Extension Act to the floor. Today, the Senate considered eleven amendments to exempt certain items and accepted seven of them. These exemptions were expected to lead to a loss of $525 million in federal revenue.[53] O'Brien, the White House's chief legislative liaison, gave Johnson the news on those amendments, as well as the transit bill and the War on Poverty.

President Johnson: Larry?

Larry O'Brien: Yes, Mr. President.

President Johnson: Well, you had a good day, didn't you?

O'Brien: Yeah, we had a pretty good one, until the boys started playing excise tax games over in the Senate.

President Johnson: Well, did they mess you up?

O'Brien: Yeah, but we're just getting the pieces together to figure it out, but they reversed the committee action on putting the taxes at the manufacturers' level and then proceeded to, in substance, get their 500 million [dollar] cut. [John] Pastore on jewelry opened up the door, and

52. Tape WH6406.17, Citation #3907, Recordings of Telephone Conversations—White House Series, Recordings and Transcripts of Conversations and Meetings, Lyndon B. Johnson Library.
53. *Congressional Quarterly Almanac*, 88th Cong., 2nd sess., 1964, vol. 20 (Washington, DC: Congressional Quarterly Service, 1965), p. 542.

then a few others came in there.[54] I haven't gotten from Treasury yet just how much it means in revenue lost, but I understand that [Douglas] Dillon isn't awfully concerned about it. I haven't talked to [Wilbur] Mills either to determine just what his position will be in conference.[55] What was the—

President Johnson: Well, hell, I was reading the ticker, and I thought it was going fine. They were knocking the hell out of the amendments, even by one or two votes, some of them.

O'Brien: Yeah, they were damn close [*unclear, the President coughs*] when they got to Pastore—

President Johnson: Why in the hell would [Mike] Mansfield run off when they got a bill like that up?[56] Where in the hell is he?

O'Brien: Well, he's up in Massachusetts, I believe.

President Johnson: What's he doing?

O'Brien: He's speaking up there tonight, I think.

But they were taken somewhat by surprise. I think the total votes seem to be running around 86—

President Johnson: 42 to 41 is what I saw.

O'Brien: Yeah, that was 83, and I think the highest they went is 85 or [8]6. And they get . . . what the hell, the dike opened. There just was . . . I talked to them yesterday afternoon and pointed out, if they hadn't remembered, the difficulty we had in holding those taxes, you know, the last time around. We won by two votes after Ev[erett] Dirksen wound up in the hospital and wasn't there to present his case on the floor.[57] So in any event, what the hell, that's it, and—

President Johnson: You passed renegotiation and the debt limit, didn't you?

O'Brien: No, the debt limit is coming up tomorrow.

President Johnson: Oh, hell.

---

54. Senator John Pastore, Democrat of Rhode Island, and Kenneth Keating, Republican of New York, had introduced an amendment to eliminate the duties on cosmetics, handbags, and perfume and to exempt the first $100 on jewelry and furs. *Congressional Quarterly Almanac*, 1964, vol. 20, p. 542.

55. Best known for his control of the House Ways and Means Committee, Arkansas Democrat Wilbur Mills of Arkansas also chaired the Joint Committee on Internal Revenue Taxation.

56. Mike Mansfield had Johnson's old job as Senate majority leader.

57. In early February, the Senate minority leader received emergency treatment for bleeding ulcers. See the conversation between President Johnson and Oliver Dompierre, 5:50 P.M., 3 February 1964, in Robert David Johnson and Kent B. Germany, eds., *The Presidential Recordings, Lyndon B. Johnson: Toward the Great Society, February 1, 1964–May 31, 1964*, vol. 4, *February 1, 1964–March 8, 1964* (New York: Norton, 2007), pp. 99–100.

O'Brien: Yeah, because, see, this thing went on all afternoon.

President Johnson: I'll—

O'Brien: We checked out the debt limit with them, and [Hubert] Humphrey and [Frank] Valeo just insist that there's no problem, and I guess they're right in that. That's an entirely different matter.[58]

President Johnson: Why in the hell don't they bring it up and pass it?

O'Brien: Pardon?

President Johnson: Why in the hell didn't they bring it up and pass it, if there's no problem?

O'Brien: Well, they kept running late. They ran damn late tonight. Once the boys smelled blood, they went at it pretty good.

So, I must say that I thought we'd wind up the day saying it was a damn good day, and then that thing hit us from the rear, but . . .

President Johnson: Mass transit, will the Senate take the House amendments?[59]

O'Brien: Now, we've talked to [John] Sparkman.[60] They're consulting with Pete Williams, and I can see no reason why they wouldn't.[61] But they wanted to talk to Pete Williams, and we've already told Hubert, of course, obviously, that that's the route we should travel. Sparkman says he does want to look at the bill before he makes a decision, but he doesn't know of any reason why he wouldn't. I talked to Al Rains, and he said, "God Almighty, I hope you can sell them that idea," and the Speaker [McCormack] too, and I'm sure we can. So they've got a good bill. In fact, Rains and I—he's an objective guy—he said that the House bill is somewhat better than the Senate bill anyway and that they'll just pick it up and run with it. But—

President Johnson: [*reading*] "[Sargent] Shriver called in and said he asked [Charles] Halleck to urge Republican congressmen to testify on Wednesday and Thursday if [Howard] Smith would give them a hearing [on War on Poverty legislation]. Halleck said he would talk to the Republicans, see if he can get . . . limit their testimony, then Judge Smith's willing to accept a motion to give a rule to end the Thursday session.

---

58. Francis "Frank" Valeo served as secretary for the majority in the Senate from 1963 to 1966.

59. The House passed the transit bill on this day with seven amendments, six of them introduced by Albert Rains of Alabama. Three of the most notable involved expanding job protection provisions, requiring the use of U.S.-made parts, and reducing the appropriation from $500 million to $375 million. On 30 June, the Senate passed the House version of the bill, 47–36. *Congressional Quarterly Almanac*, 1964, vol. 20, p. 559.

60. John Sparkman was a Democratic senator from Alabama.

61. Harrison A. "Pete" Williams Jr. was a Democratic senator from New Jersey.

Judge Smith said he would vote against the bill, but would not block it. He's extremely friendly to Shriver."

That's the memo I got, according to what Shriver recalled of it. You better check that in the morning.

O'Brien: Well, now, I talked to Shriver. He reported verbally the same way to me. But hell, that's an extremely optimist memo.

President Johnson: That's what I would think.

O'Brien: Yeah.

President Johnson: That'd be my judgment from what I [can] tell.

O'Brien: Because Halleck has either gotten back to him or will get back to him when Sarge wants to check him just to tell him that hell, he talked to his boys and they're not buying. You know, hell, Charlie isn't about to agree with Sarge on that.

President Johnson: Well, what does Halleck have to gain by just not letting them testify? He wants them to testify; he knows they're going to pass it, and he knows in time they'll get to it. What . . .

O'Brien: Oh, God, you know, Mr. President, you remember how we couldn't figure that guy's mind back at the holiday [unclear].

President Johnson: What about the foreign aid now, are we in pretty good shape on that?[62]

O'Brien: Pretty good. Pretty good. There's—

President Johnson: Did they give them a rule on it this afternoon that would make that amendment in order?

O'Brien: Yeah, they straightened out the amendments.

President Johnson: Mm-hmm.

O'Brien: They straightened out the rule, rather. I would say the spirit is pretty good up there. I've talked to some of the fellows. I didn't get into it much with them because of the mass transit thing, but the general spirit is pretty good. I think that some of the boys that have felt in the past that this was a dreary, dreary road are now saying to me, "God, I think we can hold it." So I think we got a little bit of spirit going for a change.

President Johnson: [with O'Brien acknowledging] Well, you better put your best researcher on the Republicans that voted with you last time, and then you better put your best man to take this Eisenhower wire to them and ask them if they'll stand with us and show them how we asked—[63]

---

62. On this day, the House Appropriations Committee reported the foreign aid appropriations bill out to the House floor. The House passed it on 1 July.

63. Eisenhower's telegram to Johnson warned that any drastic cuts to foreign aid would harm "the vital interests of the United States." *New York Times*, 25 June 1964.

There ought to be about three points made: This is less than Eisenhower asked any year he was in; that's number one. Number two, it's a billion, 400 million [1.4 billion dollars] less than [President] Kennedy asked. And it's approximately what they gave us last year. And we've got a hell of a lot more problems in Greece and Turkey and Brazil and India because of the change in government and every other place.[64] And we get those Republicans. Then we ought to look at the southerners and see which ones we can get to absent themselves or to help us in Texas by changing, or something like that, because we can't let him [Minority Leader Halleck] defeat us on the floor now.

O'Brien: No, we're not going to let him. That's—

President Johnson: Did he take his whipping pretty bad?

O'Brien: He did, very bad.

President Johnson: Is he still raising hell?

O'Brien: Yeah, he's very bad. He told [Hale] Boggs, of course, last night to his face, he said, "We've got you by at least 10."[65]

President Johnson: That what?

O'Brien: Halleck told Boggs that he had us licked by at least 10 [on the mass transit bill]. Of course, we pulled a pretty good surprise on him, Mr. President. God, you know, there was a real effort put into that thing, and he never figured us for . . . to get up to the 180 mark on Democrats.[66] Now, those Republicans, the key motion or the key vote, of course, was the recommit, and by God, I sort of kept saying that I didn't think they could get over 30, and I thought they'd be at 25, and I'd be happy with that.

President Johnson: Got 39.

O'Brien: No, that was on the final passage.

President Johnson: Yeah?

O'Brien: No, on the key one they got 32 or [3]3, which is right on the button.

President Johnson: Well, that's good.

O'Brien: Yeah.

President Johnson: Well, now, Charlie told Hale what? That he had him beat 10 votes on the mass, or on the foreign aid?

---

64. In Brazil, Humberto Castelo Branco had become president in the wake of a coup against João Goulart in March–April 1964. In India, Lal Bahadur Shastri had succeeded Prime Minister Jawaharlal Nehru, who died on 26 May.

65. Hale Boggs, a Democrat from Louisiana, was House majority whip.

66. There were 256 Democrats in the House. *Congressional Quarterly Almanac*, 1964, vol. 20, p. 24.

O'Brien: No, no, mass transit. No, no, that's what's got him disturbed. Because he was bragging all over the Hill this morning about mass transit and how he was going to send us down the drain good. No, he was so—

President Johnson: Well, you ought to brag to two or three of these reporters so that you can say, "Old 'gut fighter Charlie' has lost his ass all year," because that's what's happened.[67] He started out on foreign aid, and you beat him Christmas, and you brought him down. You ought to let one or two of them say, "Old 'gut fighter Charlie,' there's talk that they're going to replace him. Whupping his ass on every vote."

O'Brien: [*sounding amused*] Well, you mention that, I just wanted to in passing tell you what—did you hear about Al Rains?

President Johnson: No.

O'Brien: Well, Al Rains, as soon as the vote was over, stepped across the aisle, and he said, "Charlie, kiss my ass." [*Both chuckle.*]

President Johnson: What'd Charlie say?

O'Brien: Jesus, he blew sky-high!

President Johnson: Can't you go to Charlie in the morning from me and tell him that I want him to . . . these people, they're telling me [who] want to be heard, and I want to get them heard Wednesday and Thursday, and please let us do it, and then he can go on to his . . . go fishing?

O'Brien: I will. I'll talk to him in the morning. He—

President Johnson: Tell him, now, he talks about [us] both being old pros, and let—I don't . . . first, I think it's a goddamn bunch of foolishness for all of his people that got their ass whipped fair and square in the committee to want to go testify after they've done had testimony for six months up there. And I don't think that's fair play.[68] But if they want to testify, we're glad to have the meetings for them Wednesday and Thursday and let them testify, bring the damn bill up Friday, and we'll pass it Friday, and he can go on home Saturday.

O'Brien: Yeah, I'll try him out in the morning.

President Johnson: Now, just tell him this means something to me, and this is something I want. Now, what he wants: I took care of his man over in [the Senate Banking] Committee yesterday, Mr. [Hamer]

---

67. Halleck referred to himself as a "gut fighter." "The Congress: The Gut Fighter," *Time*, 8 June 1959.
68. Presumably, Johnson meant the House Education and Labor Committee, which had approved the poverty bill on 26 May. All 19 Democrats favored it, while all 11 Republicans opposed. *Congressional Quarterly Almanac*, 1964, vol. 20, p. 222.

Budge, and I [would] tell him I'll try to take care of him on everything he wants, but this is something *I* want.[69]

O'Brien: All right. I'll take a whirl at him.

President Johnson: OK.

O'Brien: All right, Mr. President.

8:30 P.M.

From Hale Boggs[70]

Johnson spoke to the Democratic whip about the House's reaction to the Senate excise tax amendments.

President Johnson: Hale?

Hale Boggs: Yes, Mr. President.

President Johnson: I don't guess there's any chance of y'all accepting all this crap the Senate did on these reductions and excises is it?

Boggs: God, no.[71] I—

President Johnson: They just—well, Mike Mansfield went off to Massachusetts. [*Unclear comment by Boggs.*] They just got up there, and they were doing fine, and something went wrong, and they ran over [Hubert] Humphrey, I guess. I haven't talked to him.

Anyway, I want to thank y'all on mass transit.

Boggs: We're not going to take—we're not going to take those amendments.

President Johnson: I wouldn't think so.

Boggs: We'll knock them all out—

President Johnson: Thank you for what you did on mass transit.

Boggs: Say, didn't we do all right?

---

69. Halleck had been pushing for President Johnson to appoint the conservative former Idaho congressman Hamer Budge to a federal commission. Johnson settled on placing Budge on the Securities and Exchange Commission, and for the past three weeks had been taking extensive criticism from liberals. Budge's appointment took affect the next day, 26 June. See the conversation between President Johnson and Charles Halleck, 6:15 P.M., 3 February 1964, in Johnson and Germany, eds., *The Presidential Recordings, Johnson*, vol. 4, *February 1, 1964–March 8, 1964*, p. 104.

70. Tape WH6406.17, Citation #3908, Recordings of Telephone Conversations—White House Series, Recordings and Transcripts of Conversations and Meetings, Lyndon B. Johnson Library.

71. The Senate amendments did not survive the Conference Committee.

President Johnson: Yeah, mighty proud of you. [*Boggs chuckles.*] We're moving now.

Boggs: Let me tell you another thing.

President Johnson: Yeah.

Boggs: We're going to do all right on foreign aid, too.

President Johnson: Well, we just got to. That's one we can't—

Boggs: But the mass transit vote, Mr. President, was terrific. Charlie Halleck sat there, and . . . you know, I figured we'd win by 10 votes last night. We really worked hard on this, just like everybody else did, but today we had it going, and we wouldn't let them debate. We knew we had them going. We beat every amendment. We had it on the floor, and Halleck called the roll three times. He insisted on calling it. Each time we won the thing. It was a good day, really.

President Johnson: Good-bye. Thank you.

Boggs: OK, Mr. President.

President Johnson: Bye.

Boggs: Thank you.

TIME UNKNOWN

Between Gerri Whittington and Jack Valenti[72]

The last exchange recorded this evening was between one of Johnson's aides and one of his secretaries, an African American woman whose appointment had received extensive press attention in December and January.

Gerri Whittington: Ms. Whittington.

Jack Valenti: Gerri?

Whittington: Yes?

Valenti: Is he still in his office?

Whittington: Yes, Jack.

Valenti: Just want you, as he gets ready to leave, put him a little note in his hand saying that Barbara Ward is probably still in her room sort of standing by for him.[73]

---

72. Tape WH6406.17, Citation #3911, Recordings of Telephone Conversations—White House Series, Recordings and Transcripts of Conversations and Meetings, Lyndon B. Johnson Library.
73. Barbara Ward was the British writer and economist who was staying at the White House and was advising Johnson on the Great Society.

Whittington: OK.

Valenti: OK?

Whittington: Yes, Jack.

Valenti: What's he doing?

Whittington: He's sitting in the lounge.

Valenti: By himself?

Whittington: Uh-huh.

Valenti: Well, I'll be damned. Well, OK.

Whittington: Do you want me to buzz him and tell him?

Valenti: No, no, no, no, no. No, no.

Whittington: Mm-hmm.

Valenti: But if he talks to you, just say that Jack just wanted me to remind you that Barbara Ward is probably in her room waiting for you to . . . well, you know, standing by for you.

Whittington: Yes.

Valenti: OK.

Whittington: OK, thank you.

9:00 P.M.: After signing some documents, Johnson departed the Oval Office and went to the Mansion.

9:05 P.M.: Called his dinner guest, Barbara Ward.

9:10 P.M.: Called J. Edgar Hoover.

9:45 P.M.–10:45 P.M.: Either during dinner or afterward, he held the following unrecorded telephone conversations: Texas Congressman Wright Patman (9:45 P.M.), White House Aide Bill Moyers (9:52 P.M.), Jack Valenti (10:15 P.M.), *New York Times* reporter Max Freedman (10:45 P.M.).

10:55 P.M.: Asked the operator to send "chief" to the Mansion, likely meaning Navy Chief Warrant Officer Tom Mills, the assistant to White House physician George Burkley, who normally gave the President his rubdowns.[74]

11:00 P.M.: Johnson had a prominent guest staying in the Lincoln Room overnight—former Democratic presidential nominee Adlai Stevenson—but Stevenson did not arrive until 11:00 P.M.

11:30 P.M.: Johnson went to bed.

---

74. Others who frequently gave rubdowns to the President were Stuart Baltimore and (first name unavailable) Martinelli. Bill Gulley, with Mary Ellen Reese, *Breaking Cover* (New York: Simon and Schuster, 1980), p. 90.

While Johnson was spending the evening in the White House, events in St. Augustine turned brutal, and for a moment, white violence in America's oldest town drew some attention away from the mysteries of Philadelphia, Mississippi. In response the next day, Farris Bryant, Florida's Democratic governor, made an unplanned visit to St. Augustine and added another 80 state police officers to maintain order.[75]

75. Homer Bigart, "St. Augustine Aides Say They Cannot Keep Peace," *New York Times,* 27 June 1964.

Friday, June 26, 1964

You ought to review the number of agents that you have in that state [Mississippi]. They're not really going to enforce this business, I'm afraid, unless they have somebody looking over their shoulder a bit, and I think you're the only fellow that can do it.

—Allen Dulles to J. Edgar Hoover

For Lyndon Johnson, most of this day involved the Mississippi civil rights investigation and a campaign trip to the Upper Midwest. Around noon, Allen Dulles and Tom Finney briefed him and his key civil rights aides. Johnson then had Dulles participate in calls to Mississippi Governor Paul Johnson and FBI Director J. Edgar Hoover.[1] President Johnson pressured Governor Johnson to work with the White House in putting a stop to the "acts of terror." Governor Johnson agreed, but blamed the leaders of the Freedom Summer project for the trouble, calling them a "nucleus of your hard-core, Communist-leaning type people with police records." The governor also foresaw "lots of acts of violence." During a call to FBI Director J. Edgar Hoover, Allen Dulles quietly laid the foundation for creation of a permanent FBI office in Mississippi. Later in the day, Dulles would tell the press that the authorities must punish people who participate in "terroristic activities" and warned that activists were in "great danger" whenever they went into "unprotected areas."

---

1. "Briefing by Mr. Alan [*sic*] W. Dulles Re His Trip to Mississippi for the President," 26 June 1964, "HU 2/ST 24 1/1/64–7/16/64" folder, Box 26, White House Central Files: Human Rights 2/ST, Lyndon B. Johnson Library.

Dulles would also publicly request that the FBI send more agents to the Magnolia State.[2]

In the early afternoon, McGeorge Bundy and Robert McNamara delivered disturbing reports about Laos. For at least the second time in a month, U.S. reconnaissance aircraft had been shot at. The lengthiest call of the day, however, came after Johnson had arrived at the Sheraton-Cadillac Hotel in Detroit. He and Walter Jenkins, in a typical exchange between the two men, talked for almost a half hour about a wide variety of things. This day's call included discussion about the *Wall Street Journal*'s investigation into Johnson's finances, a Treasury Department investigation into Johnson's foreign aid nemesis Otto Passman, some questionable fund-raising practices in Barry Goldwater's campaign, a proposed Army Corps of Engineers project that would flood some of Johnson's Texas property, an inquiry into the influence of Haitian sugar interests on Capitol Hill, an expected round of corruption charges from Texas Republicans, and a plan to improve the air conditioning in the White House guest quarters.

> **8:30 A.M.:** Johnson awoke, had breakfast in bed, tea with Jack Valenti and Barbara Ward, and then did his calisthenics routine.
>
> **9:05 A.M.–11:05 A.M.:** Held the following 11 unrecorded phone conversations in the Mansion: Nicholas Katzenbach (9:05 A.M.), Sargent Shriver (9:23 A.M.), Douglas Dillon (9:30 A.M.), Walter Jenkins (9:55 A.M.), Bill Moyers (10:10 A.M.), J. Edgar Hoover (10:15 A.M.), Dean Rusk (10:24 A.M. and 10:26 A.M.), George Reedy (10:32 A.M.), and Walter Jenkins (11:00 A.M. and 11:05 A.M.).
>
> **11:15 A.M.:** Arrived at the office, took a quick unrecorded call from Walter Jenkins, and then spoke to his press secretary in his first recorded conversation of the day.

---

2. Conversation between President Johnson and Paul Johnson, preceded by Allen Dulles, 1:05 P.M., 26 June 1964, in this chapter; Richard L. Lyons, "Dulles Sees Johnson on Racial Issue," *Washington Post*, 27 June 1964.

11:24 A.M.

From George Reedy[3]

Johnson discussed plans for his upcoming speech at the Democratic fund-raiser being held in Detroit this evening.

George Reedy: A couple of things: First of all, we have the . . . we've been—received a copy of the speech for tonight. Can we put that out for A.M. release?

President Johnson: I haven't gone over it. Can you do it on the plane?

Reedy: Yes, sir, we can put it out in the plane.

President Johnson: That's what I'd do. I haven't gone over it, and I need to go over it and check it, and if I make some corrections, they'll play them up big, and I'd just let them write it when they get in the plane or get out there. I don't care about getting any publicity. The least publicity I get on it, the better, because it's a political speech. By announcing both of them together, all the stories today on the wires are how many political speeches we're making, so I don't care about much publicity on it.

Reedy: OK, sir, the . . . well then, just as soon as you give it—we'll hold it until we get word.

President Johnson: Yeah, I'd just tell them that you'll . . . that I'm still working on it and that you'll give it to them just as soon as you get it.

Reedy: I've checked out, and [Patrick] McNamara, [Philip] Hart, and [Neil] Staebler are going with you.[4] [*Unclear*]—

President Johnson: Yeah, McNamara just got mad, said he wouldn't go on account he couldn't carry a suitcase. You better check with Walter [Jenkins] and see if he got him back in a good humor. I told him he could carry his suitcase now.[5]

Reedy: OK, sir. Now, what should I tell them about tonight?

President Johnson: About their going?

Reedy: Yeah.

---

3. Tape WH6406.17, Citation #3913, Recordings of Telephone Conversations—White House Series, Recordings and Transcripts of Conversations and Meetings, Lyndon B. Johnson Library.
4. All Democrats from Michigan, Patrick McNamara (no relation to the Secretary of Defense) and Philip Hart were the state's senior and junior senators, respectively, and Neil Staebler was a representative from Ann Arbor.
5. On Johnson's use of the smaller Jetstar airplane, see the conversation between President Johnson and Chester V. "Ted" Clifton, 7:45 P.M., 25 June 1964, in this volume.

President Johnson: I'd just . . . just if you think it helps you any, just tell them. Do you have to tell them anything? Why don't we just go on, and go on out in a little plane, and not . . . just tell the [press] pool? Or you think you got to tell them that, though, so they'll be satisfied with not having a pool?

Reedy: Well, I've got to tell them that—

President Johnson: All right.

Reedy: —because otherwise they'll wait here for your time of departure. So I've got to tell them that there's not going to be any pool flying out there, that the pool will be in the cavalcade in Detroit in the wire car, but not in the plane. I've got to tell them that.

President Johnson: Yeah. OK.

Reedy: And also, I'm thinking of the Rochester thing, too.[6]

President Johnson: Well, I don't think I'm going to Rochester. I think you about talked me out of that. I think there's too many problems. I'll just go back out there sometime if I can or wait until some other way. I haven't figured it out. Maybe I can get him to come down here and get the X-rays made here without having to go through all that torment and all that speculation.

Reedy: That would probably be best, sir.

President Johnson: All right.

Reedy: Now, shall I tell them we're staying out there tonight, or coming back?

President Johnson: I'd tell them that we—my present plan is to stay.

Reedy: OK, sir.

President Johnson: And . . . But don't create any emergency if I come back because it just depends on how early we get through, and my present plan is I think it'll be so late that I'll want to stay all night.

Reedy: Right.

President Johnson: But don't speculate on any emergency, any troubles, if he does decide to come back.

Reedy: OK, sir.

President Johnson: Anything else?

Reedy: No, sir. Should I tell them that [Allen] Dulles . . . you're going to see Dulles in a few minutes? I could [*unclear*]—

President Johnson: I wouldn't. Just as soon as I sees [*sic*] Dulles, I want—I thought you'd wait until I saw him and—

---

6. Johnson was making a side trip to the Mayo Clinic in Rochester, Minnesota.

Reedy: Either way, sir.

President Johnson: —ask him if he'd see him. Didn't we agree that we'd—[that] I'd ask him, and if he'll see him, then tell you—I'll call you the moment he walks in.

Reedy: OK, sir.

11:28 A.M.

To Larry O'Brien[7]

Following up on the conversation from the previous evening, O'Brien updated Johnson on the status on the Urban Mass Transportation Act and the struggle with House Minority Leader Charles Halleck and Virginia Democrat Howard "Judge" Smith to get the poverty bill out of the House Rules Committee.

Larry O'Brien: Hello?

President Johnson: Larry?

O'Brien: Yes.

President Johnson: I see Pete Williams says that he believes that they'll have a conference, but there won't be any trouble.[8]

O'Brien: Yeah.

President Johnson: I would sure warn him that we're [as] close to getting his bill as possible and he better accept those amendments because [if] it gets back in that Rules Committee, anything in the world can happen there.

O'Brien: I agree totally, and [John] Sparkman, as I told you, feels quite strong about it.[9] He wanted to read the bill this morning, and he and Pete—and I've got Mike [Manatos] on it—are going to talk.[10] I can't believe that we'll have any great difficulty with Pete. I think that was off the top of his noggin after he was asked for a comment after the vote. But they looked that thing over this morning and, God, any reasonable guy

---

7. Tape WH6406.17, Citation #3915, Recordings of Telephone Conversations—White House Series, Recordings and Transcripts of Conversations and Meetings, Lyndon B. Johnson Library.
8. Harrison A. "Pete" Williams Jr. was a Democratic senator from New Jersey. O'Brien was referring to the urban mass transportation bill.
9. John Sparkman was a Democratic senator from Alabama.
10. Mike Manatos was an administrative assistant to the President working as a congressional liaison under O'Brien.

that wants to see a bill enacted is just going to have to buy Senate action on this. And Pete wants that bill, you know, he can taste it.

President Johnson: Well, you better talk to him yourself.

O'Brien: Yeah.

President Johnson: Have you talked to [Charles] Halleck?

O'Brien: Yes, I talked to Halleck. No go.

President Johnson: What does he say?

O'Brien: Well, he simply says that this pitch that's being given by some of our people about four members of that committee, Republican members of that committee, still on the list to testify is not an accurate one; that for . . . he has two additional, among others, that insist upon testifying and at some length. One of them is [William] Widnall, and the other is Tom Curtis. And that, by God, if this is the way we're going to try and strong-arm, then maybe we have troubles next week on civil rights.[11]

And he isn't about to buy it, and I said, "Well, Charlie, you ought to buy a rule. What in the hell?" And we talked for a half an hour, and he's still . . . very honestly, he referred to what he could have done to us yesterday if he wanted to, and all that sort of stuff. He just left burning off yesterday. And while we—

President Johnson: What could he have done yesterday?

O'Brien: Well, according to him, he could have held us down to less than 12 Republicans if he wanted to swing his weight, and we would have lost the bill. But he didn't—he's not that kind of fellow. [*Chuckles.*] But, you know, I didn't do any bragging on the thing at all, and I told him that that's probably true: that if Charlie wanted to swing around yesterday and really be miserable, maybe he could have dumped us, but what we're talking about is today, and I'm not discussing yesterday with him, and what have you. Now—

President Johnson: But he won't let those that want to testify go on and testify. He wants to hold it up, huh?

O'Brien: No, he said that there are so many people that are on his side that are scheduled to testify and insistent upon it and will testify at some length and then question the jurisdictional aspects of the bill and everything else, that if we insist on Wednesday and Thursday of next week to get a rule, that it just is not possible. It isn't going to happen.

And he said, "I talked," he said, "with Judge [Howard] Smith," he said,

---

11. Both Republican members of the House, William Widnall represented New Jersey and Tom Curtis represented Missouri.

"after [Sargent] Shriver talked to him." He said, "I learned that Shriver had had a conversation with Smith, so Smith and I compared notes, and we've gone over this thing." He said, "I know you fellows resent me talking to a Democratic Rules [Committee] chairman." I said, "We don't resent you talking to him. We'd like to have you talk to him once in a while in the interests of a little bit of bipartisanship in this stuff."

And he said, "Well, by God, I suggest that you . . . you and Carl [Albert] and John McCormack get together, and now let's clean this thing up and let us out of here.[12] We'll get that civil rights bill down there and let him sign it, and we'll worry about these other things after the 20th." And I said, "Well, God, what would be much better is to get this rule, Charlie, and we'll calendar it after the 20th. What the hell are you concerned about? It isn't going to make that much difference." And he said, "Well, no," but he said, "I'll talk to you later today." But he said, "Why don't you talk to your boys," and he said, "by nightfall, we ought to be in consultation because," he said, "if you fellows are going to try and strong-arm this thing next week," he said, "we want to know it before Tuesday morning when we agreed to meet on a rule for civil rights." So that's where it was left.

President Johnson: Well, hell, I'd let him run out on civil rights if he wanted to.

O'Brien: See, what has happened is, as I told you last night, Mr. President, the guy . . . he . . . he's steaming. You know, he really did more bragging in advance on this thing yesterday than he's ever done on anything. He's got a tendency to do that. He said, well, he thought maybe you were a little peeved at him because he had a conversation with you the other night, and maybe he was a little rough, but he had had a couple of pops and all that, so I don't know what that's all about.[13]

President Johnson: No, every time I talk to him he's drinking.

O'Brien: Yeah. Well, you catch him after noontime, that's the way it has to be. You know—

President Johnson: OK.

O'Brien: OK, Mr. President.

---

12. Carl Albert and John McCormack were the House majority leader and Speaker of the House, respectively.

13. See the conversation between President Johnson and Charles Halleck, 6:24 P.M., 22 June 1964, in Guian A. McKee, ed., *The Presidential Recordings, Lyndon B. Johnson: Mississippi Burning and the Passage of the Civil Rights Act, June 1, 1964–July 4, 1964*, vol. 7, *June 1, 1964–June 22, 1964* (New York: Norton, 2011), pp. 535–43.

11:36 A.M.

To Bess Abell[14]

Abell was the White House social secretary.

President Johnson: Bess?

Bess Abell: Yes, sir.

President Johnson: Has the July African reception been announced yet?

Abell: The dinner? I believe so. I have it on all the things from the State Department.

President Johnson: You've got a suggested guest list for a reception honoring the members of the Organization for African Unity—[15]

Abell: Oh, no, no, that has not been announced yet.

President Johnson: Let's hold it, because I . . . we may want to postpone it in the light of developments.

Abell: All right.

President Johnson: Remind me of it next week.

Abell: OK.

President Johnson: Bye.

Abell: Thank you.

TIME UNKNOWN

From Ralph Dungan[16]

Dungan, returning the President's earlier call, was instructed to speak with Walter Jenkins.[17]

---

14. Tape WH6406.17, Citation #3917, Recordings of Telephone Conversations—White House Series, Recordings and Transcripts of Conversations and Meetings, Lyndon B. Johnson Library.
15. An outgrowth of African liberation movements, the Organization for African Unity (OAU) was formed in May 1963 and contained almost 40 African nations. The OAU held a summit in Cairo, Egypt, in mid-July.
16. For Johnson's earlier attempt to reach Dungan, see Tape WH6406.17, Citation #3918, Recordings of Telephone Conversations—White House Series, Recordings and Transcripts of Conversations and Meetings, Lyndon B. Johnson Library.
17. Tape WH6406.17, Citation #3916, Recordings of Telephone Conversations—White House Series, Recordings and Transcripts of Conversations and Meetings, Lyndon B. Johnson Library.

11:38 A.M.–12:50 P.M.: Johnson placed a quick call to Walter Jenkins on the personal line and then welcomed Allen Dulles and Tom Finney for their debriefing. The meeting was also attended by Lee White, Burke Marshall, and Nicholas Katzenbach, with Lee White remaining until 12:54 P.M.

12:55 P.M.: Luther Hodges and several associates arrived for a 10-minute session with the President.

1:05 P.M.: Johnson reconvened his meeting with Dulles, Katzenbach, Marshall, and White and made a call to the governor of Mississippi. One of Dulles's main recommendations was to ensure good communication between President Johnson and Governor Johnson.

1:05 P.M.

To Paul Johnson; President Johnson preceded by Allen Dulles[18]

Dulles briefed the governor on the findings from his recent trip. Then the President tried to address the antagonism aroused by tapping the Navy to search the Bogue Chitto swamp instead of relying on local officials or the Mississippi National Guard. For his part, the governor predicted more violence unless the student activists stopped coming into Mississippi.

Allen Dulles: Governor?

Paul Johnson: Yes, sir, Mr. President. How are you?

Dulles: This is Mr. Dulles. The President is with me, sir.

Paul Johnson: Oh, yes. . . . Well, I should have recognized your voice.

Dulles: Well, we've seen quite a bit of each other the last couple of days.

Paul Johnson: We certainly have, and it's been a real pleasure.

Dulles: The President wanted me to speak to you, and then he will talk with you.

Paul Johnson: All right, sir.

Dulles: I wanted to give you just an outline of the informal report I made to the President and the points that I . . . of recommendation that I made to him that he now has under consideration and will discuss briefly with you.

---

18. Tape WH6406.17, Citation #3919, Recordings of Telephone Conversations—White House Series, Recordings and Transcripts of Conversations and Meetings, Lyndon B. Johnson Library.

Paul Johnson: All right.

Dulles: [*with Governor Johnson acknowledging*] My first point was that . . . contact should be maintained between the President and you to facilitate the local, state, and, as appropriate, federal action to control and, where necessary, punish terroristic activities, particularly the activities of clandestine groups in the state, which I outlined to the President. That's point one.

Paul Johnson: Yes, sir.

Dulles: Point two was to review the role of the FBI in the state and its staff to see whether the security situation could be improved by any beefing up of the staff of the FBI.

Paul Johnson: Yes, sir.

Dulles: The third point that I made was the desirability of maybe quiet and informal discussions with the National Council of Churches, pointing out to them the security problems which have been created by these groups going in and to make sure that they understand the nature of their responsibility in connection with that.[19]

Paul Johnson: Yes.

Dulles: Now, I have outlined the whole situation as we saw it in talking with these several groups and gone into it in much more detail and added certain other things that are rather not a part of the recommendations itself.

Paul Johnson: Yes.

Dulles: And I think the President would like to have a word with you, sir. I have told him of your great courtesy—

Paul Johnson: All right.

Dulles: —to me and of all the facilities you extended to me in connection with the mission the President has given me.

Paul Johnson: Well, thank you, sir. Now, did I understand that the President was going to talk with the Council of Churches' leaders?

Dulles: Well, I don't know that the President is. You might discuss that with him. I was going to see one of their leaders personally on behalf of the President this afternoon.[20]

---

19. The National Council of Churches (NCC) was one of the organizations supporting Freedom Summer, in particular the Freedom Schools initiative.

20. Assisted by Justice Department officials Burke Marshall and John Doar, Dulles held a meeting at his home the next day, 27 June, with Robert Spike, the executive director of the NCC's Committee on Religion and Race; and John Pratt, attorney for the NCC. Dulles's public response after the meeting was to suggest that Freedom Summer activists "go to areas not so dangerous." *New York Times,* 28 June 1964.

Paul Johnson: Fine. All right.

Dulles: And he's in Washington today.

Paul Johnson: I think that would be good.

Dulles: The President . . . I'll put the President on, sir.

Paul Johnson: Fine, sir.

President Johnson comes on the line.

President Johnson: Morning, Governor.

Paul Johnson: Yes, sir. How are you feeling, Mr. President?

President Johnson: Fine. I'm very sorry about the misunderstanding yesterday.[21] The request came to us from the FBI, and we were under the impression—the boy that handled it here—that locally the . . . that the—It had originated in Mississippi from the local FBI there, and their people and your people were all aware of it. But I hope we finally got it corrected, and I asked [J. Edgar] Hoover to call you personally.

Paul Johnson: Yes. Actually what happened, Mr. President, I called them Tuesday night, the FBI group and our group, and told them to . . . that they should make a decision as soon as possible whether or not they would search that big swamp.

President Johnson: Yeah.

Paul Johnson: [*with the President acknowledging*] And if so, my units of the National Guard were available to them for it, and we had units that have had a lot of experience in that particular swamp. And evidently the people there in Washington did not know that I had already offered the National Guard facility, which would have been much better.

President Johnson: Well, I'll tell you what—

Paul Johnson: These sailors, some of these boys [*chuckles*] are real landlubbers, and they've never been off the concrete.

President Johnson: [*Chuckles.*] That's right. Well, Hoover did, Governor, know about it, but he thought that in view of the hysterical and the deep concern that a lot of folks here had and the pressure that they were bringing on us and me and him and everybody else, that they would say that local people in Mississippi weren't conducting the investigation they ought to be. And he thought by taking the Navy that he would not put that problem on the [National] Guard and that criticism on them.

Paul Johnson: Well, of course—

President Johnson: That's what Hoover—

Paul Johnson: [*with the President acknowledging*]—the National Guard

---

21. Johnson was referring to the mix-up over whether the Marines were joining the search for the missing activists. Naval reserves from a nearby auxiliary base did join the search.

down here serves the President a whole lot better than it serves me. And they carry out their federal assignments, or a federal assignment that is even made or acquiesced to by the state itself. They never fail. And of course, there would be none of that. Those boys would get in there and find those people if they were in the swamp.

President Johnson: [*with Governor Johnson acknowledging*] Yeah, well, what . . . when I heard of it was when Senator [John] Stennis called after your conversation with him, and I got ahold of Hoover and asked him to straighten it out, call you and explain to you what his problem was. [*Unclear comment by Governor Johnson.*]

Now, before Mr. Dulles left here, I thought that I should tell you what—he should tell you what he's recommending. The first point: that the state and the federal government to cooperate in attempting to avoid these acts of terror. The only real help that we can be at the moment, we are being, is providing all the FBI people that we can there to work closely with your people, and that's . . .

Paul Johnson: We've been working together on every act of terrorism that has come about.

President Johnson: I think that we ought to do everything we can to . . . they come in and say there have been 30, 40 of them, and none of them have been prosecuted, and all that kind of stuff.[22] And I think that the FBI boys ought to work with your boys, and we ought to do what we can to prevent them, and then where they're not preventable, we ought to try to get some action on them because I don't want this thing to build up. And they're putting more pressure on me: Every one of them are writing; the lawyers are writing me this morning and telling me I've got to have marshals and troops and all that kind of stuff, and I want to—

Paul Johnson: Well, they can [*unclear*] down here.

President Johnson: I want to show them that we are going to have a state-federal relationship like we've got now and that the FBI's going to work very closely, and if they need any more of them, why, we'll try to get them. And that we're going to not only try to work with you to try to prevent the acts, but if they are committed, we're going to do what we can to see that they're convicted.

Paul Johnson: Right. Well, of course, these acts that we have had,

22. Robert F. Kennedy to President Johnson, 21 May 1964 and 5 June 1965, "3/26/64–5/24/64" folder, Box 2, White House Central Files: Human Rights 2, Lyndon B. Johnson Library; Burke Marshall to Dan H. Shell, 15 July 1964, Folder 1, July 1964, Box 136, Series II, Sub-Series 9: Sovereignty Commission, Johnson (Paul B.) Family Papers, in Collection M191, Manuscript Collection, McCain Library and Archives, University of Southern Mississippi.

every one of them has been immediately investigated by the state, and they have been investigated by the FBI, and our people have alerted the FBI on many of these [*the President whispers to someone*] matters. I say many; there are probably about 12 or 15, you know, little acts of intimidation or . . . two or three of them were acts of real violence. But they've all been working together on it.

These kinds of matters are the very devil to try to solve. An activity on the part of the Klan, as you well know, they don't use local people. They'll use somebody from outside to come in and to administer a whipping to someone, and that's what throws you off and makes it very, very difficult to ever run down. That's one reason that these people have not been brought to trial. [*The President acknowledges.*] It's a very difficult proposition.[23]

President Johnson: Well, what I wanted to do: I thought—I didn't want you to read about it in the paper—I thought I ought to call you and tell you what he is suggesting, and if it's all right with you, I'll tell Mr. Hoover to check his men and have his head man down there [Joseph Sullivan] get in touch with your people and see if they have adequate people; if they don't, give him whatever else he needs.[24] And your people will be instructed by you to cooperate closely with them and maybe we can rely [*Governor Johnson attempts to speak*] on that and Mr. Dulles's recommendation instead of having to act at the moment on other . . . other . . . sources.

Paul Johnson: [*with the President acknowledging*] Sure. Well, we are beefing up our group down here, and for the first time, frankly, first time in the history of the state, our state police do have general state police powers under proclamation. You see, in the past we've not even been permitted to arrest a person for speeding on a gravel road or a country road, you see? And then too, we have beefed up the patrol to an additional 200 men, and then we are now setting up a police training academy and trying to train these local law enforcement officers in the various counties, you know, these little constables and people who know practically nothing about law enforcement, or matters of courtesy, or anything else. And we are trying to—

President Johnson: Is it all right for Mr. Dulles to say he talked to you—is it all right for Mr. Dulles to say he talked to you about that, and he assured me the governor was adding additional men and was going to stay on top of it?

---

23. The people arrested and tried for this particular crime were local citizens from Mississippi.
24. Joseph Sullivan, the FBI's top inspector, was heading up the investigation. Also sent to Mississippi was Alex Rosen, the assistant director for the investigative division.

Paul Johnson: Yes siree!

President Johnson: All right. What I wanted you to know, I just didn't want you to get by surprise what he was recommending. I wanted you to be the first one while he was here in the office. He's going over and talk to Mr. Hoover and the Justice Department officials after he leaves, and he's going to say that he's urging us to maintain contact with each other and have a joint state and federal cooperation against any further acts of terror; that he's asking the FBI to review their needs and asked to . . . supply any additional needs they may have; and third, he's asking the National Council of Churches to look at their problems and to be aware of their responsibility and conduct themselves accordingly.

Paul Johnson: Right. I think that is where our real danger lies.

President Johnson: Fine, and fourth, he's going to say that he's talked to you and that you have arranged for a couple hundred extra patrolmen and to beef up your operation and that you're going to make every possible effort of the state to see that there's no further acts of terrorism, and if there are, they're prosecuted promptly.

Paul Johnson: Right.

President Johnson: OK.

Paul Johnson: And then too, one other thing. I'd like to get this across to you: If they continue to send these youngsters in here, without them properly being oriented and realizing what they're getting into, with a nucleus of your hard-core, Communist-leaning-type people with police records, unless that comes about and the Council of Churches keeps these youngsters out of here the best that they possibly can, we're going to have lots of acts of violence.[25]

President Johnson: Yeah. I know it.

Paul Johnson: And I wanted you to know that because they are— those are things that you couldn't prevent if you had a thousand FBI in each county in the state.

President Johnson: That's right. Thank you, Governor, and I'll be back in touch with you next week.

Paul Johnson: Thank you very much, Mr. President.

President Johnson: Bye . . . bye.

While Dulles was in the office, Johnson got the FBI director on the line.

---

25. Governor Johnson made similar charges, verbatim in places, when speaking to President Johnson on 23 June. See the conversation between President Johnson and Paul Johnson, 8:21 P.M., 23 June 1964, in this volume.

1:17 P.M.

From J. Edgar Hoover; President Johnson joined by Allen Dulles[26]

Dulles relayed his recommendation for Hoover to add more agents and to apply more pressure on the agents on the scene. Hoover agreed, but also explained the difficulties faced by the FBI.

Hoover was able to report one bit of progress to the President. Today, agents had arrested three white men for their involvement in a kidnapping of Freedom Summer activists. The day before, in the small Delta town of Itta Bena—which Hoover initially called "Teeny-Weeny"—those white men had seized two Freedom Summer volunteers and local COFO project director William McGee, took them to a bus station, and warned, "If you speak in town tonight, you'll never leave here." According to historian Taylor Branch, the white men took the volunteers hostage, but McGee escaped and alerted other activists, who found the two volunteers being held at a gas station. One of the volunteers asked McGee to take him to St. Louis later that night.[27]

J. Edgar Hoover: Yes, Mr. President.

President Johnson: Edgar?

Hoover: Yes, Mr. President.

President Johnson: Mr. Dulles is in here making his report.

Hoover: Yes.

President Johnson: And I wanted him to go over with you his recommendations to me before you read about them, and I wanted to talk to you and the governor of Mississippi. I think they're rather good. What he does—well, I'll let him tell you. Here it is, and then I'll get back on the phone.

Hoover: All right, fine. Thank you.

---

26. Tape WH6406.17, Citations #3921 and #3922, Recordings of Telephone Conversations—White House Series, Recordings and Transcripts of Conversations and Meetings, Lyndon B. Johnson Library.

27. Council of Federated Organizations (COFO), "Mississippi Summer Project Running Summary of Incidents," Folder 25: "Depositions Summary, 1964," Box 3, Council of Federated Organizations Records, Z/1867.000/S, Mississippi Department of Archives and History; Bob Moses to Parents of All Mississippi Summer Volunteers, [n.d., before 6 July 1964], "Civil Rights—Mississippi" folder, Office Files of Lee White, Box 6, White House Central Files, Lyndon B. Johnson Library; *New York Times*, 27 June 1964; Taylor Branch, *Pillar of Fire: America in the King Years, 1963–65* (New York: Simon & Schuster, 1998), pp. 371–72.

Dulles comes on the line.

Allen Dulles: Edgar?

Hoover: Yes, sir, Allen.

Dulles: [*with Hoover acknowledging*] I felt after reviewing the situation down there that, as the President concurred, I realize it's difficult for you, but that you ought to review the number of agents that you have in that state. They're not really going to enforce this business, I'm afraid, unless they have somebody looking over their shoulder a bit, and I think you're the only fellow that can do it. I write an excess number on account of this Philadelphia business.

Hoover: That's correct.

Dulles: [*with Hoover acknowledging throughout*] But I think that when you come to withdraw those, there should be a look at the whole situation because there are a half a dozen other situations down there that are full of difficulty, and there might be terroristic activities of any kind unless they felt that somebody's really looking at them.

Now, I was going to make that recommendation—I have made that recommendation to the President—and the President wanted me to repeat it to the press. I didn't want to do it without getting your views.

Hoover: Well, of course, that's going to be an almost superhuman task, don't you think, Allen?

Dulles: I realize.

Hoover: In other words, there will be about a thousand of these youngsters who are going to be going down there within the next 30 days. I think you've got down there now . . . well, there are . . .

Dulles: There are 2[00] or 300 now.

Hoover: There are 2[00] or 300 now, and—

Dulles: I understand that thousand is cut down very substantially in the last . . . well, days and hours almost.

Hoover: Yeah. Well, of course, maybe some fear has gone into them on what's happened down there.

Dulles: [*with Hoover acknowledging*] That's right. . . . And one of the other recommendations I made to the President that he has so far approved is that we have a talk immediately with the National Council of Churches to impress them with their responsibility: that they're sending people into a situation where, despite all attempts at law enforcement, there may be . . . because of the ingrained situation there, there may be really serious attempts on their lives.

Hoover: Yes. The thing that's going to make it physically difficult is, as I understand it, after these people have been trained at . . . I think there's a college at Oxford [Western College for Women].

Dulles: That's right, Oxford, Ohio.

Hoover: Yeah. After they've been trained there, they're then going down and are going to live in the homes of the colored population.

Dulles: Oh, that stirs up the . . . Yeah, that's the case.

Hoover: [*with Dulles acknowledging throughout*] And that, of course, is what's riling a lot of these [*unclear, take skips*] and, in addition there too, they will hold meetings in each community, large and small, to give them the education that they are supposed to have in order to be able to be registered.

Now, it practically means, in order to prevent any one of them—in view of the nature of the territory, geographical nature of it, the physical condition of the land down there—you've got to almost keep a man, keep an agent, with these individuals as they come into the state, because this Klan crowd—and you've got down there—

Dulles: Oh, yes. I know. I know.

Hoover: —members of the Mississippi Highway Patrol—

Dulles: Yeah, yeah.

Hoover: —some of those are Klansmen, a number of the chiefs of police are, many of the sheriffs are—

Dulles: Yeah, I realize that. That I know.

Hoover: —and therefore you can't count upon the local people to really extend any enforcement.

Dulles: Yeah, yeah.

Hoover: And when you get back into those rural areas, and that's where these things would occur—

Dulles: I realize you can't be perfect on this, but I think that . . . I know from my little experience down there that if you have a few more people down there, it's going to make differences . . . a tremendous difference, if—

Hoover: The only thought in my mind is whether it ought to be the FBI or whether there ought to be United States marshals in there.

Dulles: Yeah.

Hoover: As was done down in Alabama.[28]

Dulles: Yeah, yeah.

Hoover: I—

Dulles: Well that, you and the Department of Justice ought to work out, I think. Which is the best way.

---

28. On 20 May 1961, John Kennedy sent approximately 400 marshals to Montgomery, Alabama, after Freedom Riders received savage beatings.

Hoover: [*with Dulles acknowledging*] Because the United States marshal in there is a symbol of authority, of course, out of the Department of Justice, and at the same time he doesn't have to conduct any investigative work, which we have to do, and—

Dulles: I understand. I'm in the President's office now, and I think he wants this office for other purposes. Maybe I better call you on another phone.

Hoover: All right. Fine. Fine, Allen.

Dulles: But I appreciate very much, Mr. Hoover.

Hoover: That's all right, fine.

Dulles: Thank you, J.

Hoover: Thank you.

Dulles: One second?

Hoover: Yeah.

Dulles: Hello?

Hoover: Yeah.

President Johnson returns to the line.

President Johnson: Edgar?

Hoover: Yes, sir, Mr. President.

President Johnson: What he's doing there in substance is saying we want to cooperate with the local officials. We've told the government we'd do it, and we're going to cooperate [with] them through your people down there. That's the first thing.

Hoover: We have them . . . we have the Mississippi Highway Patrol participating in the search along with the Navy people, and—

President Johnson: Yeah, that's right. . . . That's right. We want to do that to avoid the marshal thing, the troops thing. We want to do it through your people, number one.

Hoover: Yes.

President Johnson: Number—and the governor's agreeable to it. We've—

Hoover: And the governor's agreeable to it.

President Johnson: —talked [*unclear*]. And you just have your top man stay in close touch with him on everything.

Hoover: We're doing that.

President Johnson: [*with Hoover acknowledging*] So that anything we do, when we're going to use sailors or helicopters or anything, that he . . . tell them [to] be sure to tell the governor. The second thing, we want to review to be sure that we have an ample number of people down there. And I rather think we ought to send some more in, if for no other reason [than] to say to these groups that are pressuring us all the time that we have reviewed it several weeks ago when I talked to you and you sent in people anticipating it; you've sent in more following these three; sent—Mr. Dulles went down; you're going to send in some more, so that we can let those people know that we mean business. Maybe we can prevent some of these acts of terror by the very presence of your people.

Hoover: [*with the President acknowledging*] I'm hoping that this case that we've developed down at this place called Teeny-Weeny [Itta Bena]—it's a peculiar name they got—but I'm hoping that if we can get the [Justice] Department—we're going to submit it to them this afternoon—to authorize us to arrest those hoodlums down there . . .

President Johnson: Well . . . I'll tell [Nicholas] Katzenbach to . . .

Hoover: . . . and have a complaint filed in the federal court down there on them, that that will be a deterrent because they told these two white boys, "Now, if you don't get out of town, the same thing is going to happen to you as happened up at that Philadelphia."

President Johnson: Yeah. . . . Well, you just go on. I'll tell Katzenbach about it, and I'm sure the department will give you that authority. But you consider sending some other people down there so we can say we supplemented it following this report.

Hoover: I'll—

President Johnson: And the more you have there, the more they're going to prevent things, and I don't want to send troops in there and marshals, Edgar. [*Hoover attempts to speak.*] I'd rather you send another 15, 20 people there.

Hoover: I'll send some additional men in there right away.

President Johnson: All right, OK. . . . All right, now, then the . . .

[*to Dulles*] What was the third thing?

[*to Hoover, with Hoover attempting to interject*] He's going to talk to National Council of Churches, Mr. Dulles is, and tell them to try to control their people a little better.

Hoover: Yeah, because they're playing with fire in this thing.

President Johnson: Mm-hmm. Fine. Well, you think these recommendations, then, are all right—

Hoover: I think those recommendations are all right.

President Johnson: All right, you get your men in there now and—

Hoover: I will.

President Johnson: —tell your man to tell the governor that you're sending some extra in, so that word will get around.

Hoover: [*with the President acknowledging*] I've already . . . also, just as a collateral matter, they're planning a large picketing of you at Cobo Hall in Detroit this evening.[29] Starting at 4 P.M., and to demand that President Johnson send federal marshals to Mississippi to protect civil right[s] workers. Now, we've notified the Secret Service of that, so that they will have the necessary protection there at Detroit.

President Johnson: All right. Well, what we want to do is . . . well, we'll say to—here . . . here we've asked for additional men, and you're going to send them.

Hoover: Yes, that's right.

President Johnson: OK.

Hoover: That's right. OK.

President Johnson: Bye.

Hoover: Fine, thank you.

1:30 P.M.: Johnson made two unrecorded calls on the personal line to Jack Valenti (the second at 1:37 P.M.) and then contacted Silvio Conte, the Massachusetts Republican who had helped in beating back Otto Passman's cuts to the foreign aid appropriations bill. Conte was the only Republican on Passman's Foreign Operations Appropriations Subcommittee who supported the Johnson administration.

1:41 P.M.

To Silvio Conte; preceded by Jack Valenti[30]

Jack Valenti: Mr. President?

President Johnson: Is Mac Bundy out there?

Valenti: He went downstairs and told me to call you before [*unclear*].

President Johnson: [*Unclear.*] [*Long pause.*]

White House Operator: There you are.

President Johnson: Yes?

Conte comes on the line.

---

29. Cobo Hall was a relatively new downtown convention space named for the city's Republican mayor, Albert E. Cobo, during the 1950s. One of the sources of former Mayor Cobo's political strength were conservative white homeowners' associations that strongly resisted racial integration of their neighborhoods. Thomas J. Sugrue, *The Origins of the Urban Crisis: Race and Inequality in Postwar Detroit* (Princeton, NJ: Princeton University Press, 1996), pp. 83–87 and 222–25.

30. Tape WH6406.18, Citation #3923, Recordings of Telephone Conversations—White House Series, Recordings and Transcripts of Conversations and Meetings, Lyndon B. Johnson Library.

Silvio Conte: Mr. President?

President Johnson: Yes. Hello?

Conte: Hello. Mr. President?

President Johnson: Yes.

Conte: It's Silvio Conte.

President Johnson: Sil, I wanted to tell you, you did a great job, and I appreciate your help for your country. I read the *New York Times* this morning, and they had a mighty good story about it.[31]

Conte: It was wonderful, Mr. President, and I hope we'll prevail Tuesday and Wednesday.[32]

President Johnson: Well, George Mahon told me what a tower of strength you were, and we've talked to some of the folks on the *Times*.[33] I just think you did an excellent job, and I'm proud of you.

Conte: Well, I can't tell you how much I appreciate this call. It's the greatest thing that ever happened in my life.

President Johnson: Well, it's one of the greatest things ever done for your country because we are . . . just like General Eisenhower said, we have got more problems now than we've ever had, and we're trying to do our best, and the only weapons we got is this little [foreign aid] thing, and you stood up and put your country first, and I'm mighty grateful.[34]

Conte: Well, I agree with you wholeheartedly. I just hope—I want to see George—the strategy will be that Otto [Passman] will make a move on [a] developing grant cut, and he'll cry and say that this is the only cut he's going to make, and then, of course, [John] Rhodes and [Gerald] Ford and [William] Minshall will make the other moves and the other cuts, so that we—we have to hold them on that first one.[35] That's the one that would be [*unclear*].

President Johnson: Yeah. . . . You talk to George and give him a judg-

---

31. The *New York Times* had two articles on 26 June 1964: "Maverick Republican: Silvio Otto Conte," and Felix Belair's "Full Committee Balks Passman." The *Times* also had an editorial on the matter, "Defeat for Mr. Passman."

32. The vote before the full House came on Wednesday, 1 July, and the House passed the Appropriations Committee version without changes.

33. George Mahon, Democrat from Texas, chaired the House Appropriations Committee. See the conversation between President Johnson and George Mahon, 6:40 P.M., 23 June 1964, in this volume.

34. Eisenhower sent his telegram on 24 June 1964.

35. John Rhodes from Arizona, future president Gerald Ford from Michigan, and William Minshall from Ohio were all Republicans on the Foreign Operations Subcommittee who sided with Passman. On the floor, Passman and Rhodes put forward several amendments to cut the appropriations, but were beaten back. *Congressional Quarterly Almanac*, 88th Cong., 2nd sess., 1964, vol. 20 (Washington, DC: Congressional Quarterly Service, 1965), p. 313.

ment, and I think you ought to give—make him give you a copy of that wire of General Eisenhower's—[it's] a good, strong wire, and—

Conte: Right, [*unclear*]—

President Johnson: —people ought [to] pay some attention to it.

Conte: And what I'll do is see that every Republican, I'll mail one out to every Republican Tuesday or Monday before the debate, so they'll all have a copy of it.

President Johnson: Thank you, Sil.

Conte: Thank you, Mr. President.

President Johnson: Bye.

Conte: I hope I get to see you soon.

President Johnson: Sure, anytime you want to, you just whistle.

Conte: Thank you very much, Mr. President.

> **1:43 P.M.–1:54 P.M.:** McGeorge Bundy arrived for a briefing on world events. The conversation below was apparently recorded during that time.

TIME UNKNOWN

Office Conversation with McGeorge Bundy[36]

President Johnson: Mac, how are you?

McGeorge Bundy: Just fine, Mr. President, and you?

President Johnson: Well, I've had Mississippi all morning.

Bundy: It's fantastic what you've got there. Make any progress?

President Johnson: No, we haven't [*unclear*] things to report, and I've got the board's [*unclear*] release to [LeRoy] Collins.[37] And I just talked to [Silvio] Conte to thank him for that foreign aid.

Bundy: Good man, Conte.

President Johnson: [*Unclear*] doing it and passed today. Set it so he can come on down here now.

Bundy: That's a great victory.

President Johnson: We got a [excise] tax bill in [House-Senate] conference. I've got a . . . I talked to Larry [O'Brien] [*unclear*] get our transit

---

36. Tape WH6406.18, Citation #3924, Recordings of Telephone Conversations—White House Series, Recordings and Transcripts of Conversations and Meetings, Lyndon B. Johnson Library.
37. Johnson was referring to the governing board of the National Association of Broadcasters.

bill, mass transit, without going to conference, I hope. So we're going to have lots of legislation [*unclear*] I don't get a poverty [*unclear*]—

Bundy: Not at all?

President Johnson: Well, they'll go over there to the [Republican National] Convention [*unclear*] still at stake. Can't get these boys—

Bundy: You've got a tremendous record on what you've done so far. I know it's your right not to be satisfied.

Three things, Mr. President: Laos—

The recording ends abruptly.

1:45 P.M.: Johnson made an unrecorded call to Walter Jenkins on the personal line.

2:05 P.M.: Met with Jack Valenti and speechwriter Richard Goodwin. He then received a report on Laos from the Secretary of Defense.

2:10 P.M.

To Robert McNamara[38]

Robert McNamara: We ran a recon mission over Route 13—which is west and south of Muong Soui and then across the Plaine de Jarres—last night, with one recon plane and two escort aircraft. And the recon plane apparently—and I'm not absolutely certain of this—but the recon plane apparently went in at about 20,000 feet, along with the two escort aircraft. They were fired upon, but of course this was far beyond the range of the antiaircraft, and they did not fire back.[39] And that's the only mission we've run. [*Johnson acknowledges.*] And this mission was, of course, coordinated with State and everybody else.

President Johnson: Yeah, yeah. . . . But . . . it says that [*reading*] "the planes, their number undisclosed, are reported to have come from a U.S. carrier in the South China Sea off South Vietnam."

---

38. Tape WH6406.18, Citation #3926, Recordings of Telephone Conversations—White House Series, Recordings and Transcripts of Conversations and Meetings, Lyndon B. Johnson Library.
39. U.S. reconnaissance aircraft over Laos were attacked earlier in the month. Johnson held 11 recorded conversations about the incident on 8 June and 9 June, two on 11 June, two on 12 June, and one on 13 June. See McKee, *The Presidential Recordings, Johnson,* vol. 7, *June 1, 1964–June 22, 1964.*

McNamara: This was a recon plane from the carrier, plus the two escort aircraft. No firing by our aircraft to the best of my knowledge. We've had our mission report, a flash report, in this morning.
President Johnson: OK, then. Thank you.
McNamara: All right, sir. Thanks.

2:21 P.M.: Johnson left with Jack Valenti and Richard Goodwin for lunch at the Mansion.[40]

3:05 P.M.: With a small party, took a helicopter to Andrews Air Force Base, arriving at 3:15 P.M. and leaving Andrews at 3:20 P.M. (EDT) on a Jetstar.

3:35 P.M. (CST): Touched down in Detroit and arrived at the Sheraton-Cadillac Hotel at 4:17 P.M. (CST). In the presidential suite, met up with Lady Bird , who had been visiting the wives of Senator Philip Hart and former Michigan governor and current Assistant Secretary of State for African Affairs G. Mennen "Soapy" Williams. Within the hour, the President called Walter Jenkins in Washington to talk about matters both personal and political. The rest of this day's recordings were taped in Detroit.

5:30 P.M. (CST)

To Walter Jenkins[41]

The two men spoke for approximately 25 minutes.

The opening one minute and ten seconds of this call are excised under deed of gift restriction.
President Johnson: Any other news?

---

40. At some point after the McNamara call, the recorders picked up a brief conversation between McGeorge Bundy and Marie Fehmer in which Bundy inquired about foreign aid paperwork that needed President Johnson's signature. Tape WH6406.18, Citation #3928, Recordings of Telephone Conversations—White House Series, Recordings and Transcripts of Conversations and Meetings, Lyndon B. Johnson Library.
41. Tape WH6406.18, Citations #3929 and #3930, Recordings of Telephone Conversations—White House Series, Recordings and Transcripts of Conversations and Meetings, Lyndon B. Johnson Library.

Walter Jenkins: Now, let's see here . . .

President Johnson: Abe's [Fortas] gone for the week, isn't he?[42]

Jenkins: Yes, sir.

President Johnson: Mm-hmm. Where's he gone?

Jenkins: Well, he's still here in town today. He's going to Switzerland, but he's leaving tonight. I've gone over everything with him.

President Johnson: Yeah. Did he have any suggestions?

Jenkins: [*with the President acknowledging*] Well, he thought this was all . . . thought every—thought it was all right. We haven't . . . I haven't got any problem with it.

Let me see, John Sparkman called on behalf of Stevens for the [Federal] Parole Board.[43]

President Johnson: Who is Stevens?

Jenkins: He's the one that Mrs. [Lady Bird] Johnson . . . this friend of Edwina.[44] Mrs. Johnson's friend came up to see her. [*Unclear comment by Johnson.*] Jesse [Kellam] called and said—

President Johnson: Doesn't . . . Doesn't [Everett] Dirksen want somebody for the parole board?

Jenkins: Well, he wants the fellow that's there from Illinois to be reappointed, but it's a Republican . . . he's a Republican, and the board already has a majority of Republicans on it. It's not required to have *any*. He does have . . .

President Johnson: Mm-hmm. Well . . .

Jenkins: And I was hoping maybe we could do something for him on one that *had* to be a Republican.

President Johnson: Yeah. Well, I imagine he'll make us do it because he's [minority] leader. [*Pauses.*] How many are on the board?

Jenkins: Eleven.

---

42. Abe Fortas was one of Johnson's closest legal and political advisers and was intimately aware of Johnson's business arrangements.

43. The Federal Board of Parole was an eight-person commission appointed by the President. Two members retired in 1964: former Republican Nebraska senator Eva Bowring left on 30 September, and Republican George J. Reed on 30 November. Ziegel Neff from the Pentagon succeeded Bowring, and Charlotte Paul Groshell (later Reese) of Washington State replaced Reed. Charles Casey of California had been tapped for Reed's slot, but Groshell was the final appointee. Groshell was supported by Washington's Democratic Senator Warren Magnuson. Peter B. Hoffman, *History of the Federal Parole System* (Washington, DC: GPO, 2003), pp. 44–51; Sue Cronk, "She Believes Women Are the Cause of Men's Downfall," *Washington Post*, 20 December 1964; George Dixon, *Washington Post*, 9 October 1964; *New York Times*, 10 September 1964.

44. Jesse Kellam was Johnson's business manager in Texas. Stevens is a phonetic spelling. Edwina was not positively identified.

President Johnson: And how many are Republicans?

Jenkins: Seven.

President Johnson: Well, how come that there are?

Jenkins: Because they're four-year appointments, and a good many of them were appointed near the end of the Eisenhower administration.

President Johnson: And none of them are required to be?

Jenkins: No, sir.

President Johnson: Mm-hmm.

Two minutes and fifteen seconds excised under deed of gift restriction.

Jenkins: Shel Cohen, Sheldon Cohen, called me two minutes ago and said that one of their lawyers, Saul [Mitchell] Rogovin, got a long-distance call from a law firm in New York on Wall Street earlier today asking him whether it was a violation of law for a publication to publish information other than that what [was] authorized by law on pages three and four of a foundation return.[45]

President Johnson: I wished he'd have told them it damn sure was.

Jenkins: He did. Now, he asked him who he represented, and he said, "Well, I'm asking this as just a sample case, not representing anybody in particular." We looked him up in Martindale-Hubbell.[46] The . . . Its . . . Nu—His office is at #1 Wall Street. It does not list his . . . some lawyers list their clients, some don't. He doesn't, but we figured it's [*chuckles*] probably the *Wall Street Journal* because it's a Wall Street lawyer.[47] [*Pause.*]

President Johnson: Well, is it . . .

Jenkins: They've now reached the conclusion that it is. But they think it would not be very [*Johnson blows his nose*] official to move against them, or Sheldon thinks that.

President Johnson: Well, I . . .

Jenkins: He thinks you get more publicity out of it than the value you'd get from it.

President Johnson: Yeah, but I think we ought to scare hell out of them.

---

45. Sheldon Cohen at age 36 was chief counsel for the Internal Revenue Service and a former attorney with Arnold, Porter, and Fortas. Johnson elevated him to IRS commissioner in December 1964. The Saul Rogovin mentioned by Jenkins is Mitchell Rogovin, Cohen's assistant, who took over as chief counsel when Cohen moved up.

46. Martindale-Hubbell was a legal directory.

47. See the conversation between President Johnson and Walter Jenkins, 7:26 P.M., 23 June 1964, in this volume.

Jenkins: That's exactly what I told him. [*Pause.*]

Now, did Secretary [Luther] Hodges tell you that [Hubert] Humphrey worked it out where that can go to the Commerce Committee?[48]

President Johnson: No.

Jenkins: He did.

President Johnson: Good.

Jenkins: Secretary [Douglas] Dillon came by to see me to . . . this afternoon to tell me that they let, he was sorry to say, they let [Otto] Passman get off the hook.[49] They made an investigation. There's no question about the facts: It was smuggling. But in connection with the investigation, they had the interviews from some of the people that knew about it, including the fence.

President Johnson: Including *de*fense?

Jenkins: *The* fence. The fellow who was used to sell the pearls.

President Johnson: What is a fence? What does that mean?

Jenkins: Well, that's an underground word meaning that if somebody brings something in, smuggles something in, he's gives it to a fence; a fence then sells it out to somebody for legitimate enterprise. He's the liaison man between the smuggler and the final purchaser.

And word got back apparently, they assume, to Passman, because he bundled them all back, just a few days ago, and shipped them all back to Hong Kong by diplomatic pouch, he said. [*Chuckles.*] And they're investigating some other cases earlier where they think that the same thing may have happened, but he says if they can't move against him on . . . get a conviction, because he didn't actually carry it out, why, they [will] work out some way to see that it's known at least.

President Johnson: Oh, that's a zoo. Why did they accept them and send them back?

Jenkins: [*Pause.*] Well, they didn't know what was in it. Apparently.

President Johnson: Well, how do they know he sent them back, then?

Jenkins: Well, that's what the . . . that's what the dealer that they interviewed that told them that it happened. They're checking it, but that's what they're led to believe has happened. [*Pause.*]

---

48. Jenkins was likely referring to the nomination of LeRoy Collins as director of the Community Relations Service. The Senate Commerce Committee approved Collins on 9 July, the full Senate on 20 July.

49. Charges of corruption and influence-peddling haunted Passman as his career ended in the mid-1970s. Shortly after leaving office, he was tried and acquitted for allegedly receiving over $200,000 in bribes from South Korean businessman Tongsun Park. This specific allegation by Jenkins was not identified, but the later investigation into Park's dealings revealed that Passman reportedly sold antique jewelry to Park at inflated prices. *Time*, 17 April 1978.

President Johnson: Well, they ought to have somebody interview him. [*Pause.*]

Jenkins: Bert Harding sent me over this afternoon a letter that was going out to doctors over in California for the [Barry] Goldwater Committee saying that here's how you can scheme, legally called a third-party beneficiary contract.[50] It's not tax evasion, and all the doctors are told that when the patient comes to write their check, all they have to do is hand them the check and say, "Make this to the Goldwater for President Committee, and I will not enter the call in my books." And then have some addressed envelopes handy. Says this way, if you're in the 75 percent [income tax] bracket, you can give four times as much to Goldwater without it costing you." And they've sent him a letter, Internal Revenue has, saying this is strictly illegal and that they ought to notify anybody that's got this letter that the information is incorrect.

President Johnson: Sent the letter to who, Goldwater?

Jenkins: No, they sent it to the fellow who signed the letter, the chairman of the Doctors for Goldwater [Committee]. His name is William Hawkins, in California. Santa Ana, California.

President Johnson: All right.

Jenkins: Got a letter from Jim Rowe, who's finished his physical exams now and says that:[51]

[*reading*] "I'm in good shape"—here's what the doctor says—"I'm in good shape a year and a half after a serious heart attack, primarily due to an otherwise healthy constitution. In fact, I've been an unusual patient in the sense I've done exactly what the doctors told me. The tests are all good. As for going over the Democratic National Committee, Doctor Miller says I must first get a 10-day rest. I must then get a short rest every day and have some long weekends. I should not work long hours, and I should not do too much traveling. *If*"—and he underlines if—"the President thinks it's worthwhile, under these rather strict circumstances, I'm available, pursuant to the doctor's orders. I'll take 10 days at Cape Cod, where my family is, beginning July 1 and be back in town July 10. Will you talk to the President and let me know? P.S.: The President might be interested in Doctor Miller's comments about him. Quote, 'Don't be contaminated by the President. He's had good luck, and he's eight years

---

50. Bertrand Harding had been serving as the interim IRS commissioner since Mortimer Caplin's resignation in late May.
51. James Rowe, a partner in Corcoran, Youngman, and Rowe, was a prominent Democratic political adviser and Johnson's friend from the New Deal era. His law firm had been representing interests in the Haitian sugar industry.

down the road, which is a lot farther than you are, which is only one and a half years. As a doctor and a citizen, I wish he'd take better care of himself because we're in a hell of a mess if he doesn't,' unquote.[52] There is a doctor who's terrified of Goldwater."

President Johnson: [*to his valet in the office*] Get me some ice water, Paul [Glynn].[53]

Jenkins: The FBI are making some arrests this afternoon in [Itta Bena] Mississippi, not in connection with that other case, but with the new ones.[54]

President Johnson: Yeah. [*Pause.*]

Jenkins: I've got a memorandum from Elmer Staats where he confirms this *New York Times* story about a reservoir which would cover up part of the Scharnhorst [Ranch]; not until 1975, though.[55]

President Johnson: Well, where'd they get . . . who's going to do it? Army [Corps of] Engineers?

Jenkins: Yes, sir, it's a part of their long-range plan developed in this Texas Water Study Commission that we had down there and the Colorado River Program. And it's for use long range to supply municipal water for San Antonio.

President Johnson: Who's going to build it, Army [Corps of] Engineers?

Jenkins: Yes, sir.

President Johnson: On the Pedernales [River]?

Jenkins: Yes, sir.

President Johnson: Where's the dam?

Jenkins: Four miles downstream from the main LBJ Ranch. [*reading*] "The upstream limit of the maximum pool would be about four miles downstream from the main LBJ Ranch, which would be unaffected. The President was shown the site or a nearby one on the ground by the district engineer, we are told. About a third of the Scharnhorst Ranch would

---

52. Dr. Miller was not identified.

53. Sergeant Paul Glynn was the President's assistant and valet. Transcript, Marie Fehmer Chiarodo Oral History Interview II, 16 August 1972, by Joe B. Frantz, Internet copy, Lyndon B. Johnson Library, pp. 22–23.

54. See the earlier conversation between President Johnson and J. Edgar Hoover, 1:17 P.M., 26 June 1964, in this chapter.

55. According to the *New York Times,* Johnson owned approximately 15,000 acres of ranch land near his Texas home, including the Scharnhorst property, a parcel that was reportedly one of Johnson's favorite hunting grounds and that occupied over a mile of the Pedernales River. In October 1965, he told the *New York Times* that he wanted to give it to Lynda Bird someday. The lake was not built. Elmer Staats was the deputy director of the Bureau of the Budget. *New York Times,* 3 November 1965.

lie in the maximum pool. Under present land acquisition policies a somewhat larger portion of the ranch would have to be acquired." This is information supplied by the Corps. "Survey report will not be completed this
summer or fall." The story is basically correct except in one respect: It
says the survey will be completed this summer or fall. It will not be. [It
will] be completed sometime next year.

President Johnson: Well, I'll be damned. The dam is going to be down
below the Scharnhorst then, and back water up on it.

Jenkins: Yes, sir. I have a memo from [Bureau of the] Budget saying
GSA [General Services Administration]—

President Johnson: Send that to A.W. [Moursund].[56]

Jenkins: Send it to A.W.? All right.

President Johnson: Yeah, photostat it and keep copies of it. Send him
a copy of the *Times* article.

Jenkins: All right.

President Johnson: And that—and I wonder how the *Times*, where'd
they get it?

Jenkins: They studied this Texas Water Study Commission reports,
Staats thinks, because it's a big book, but it's buried down in there.

President Johnson: All right. All right.

Jenkins: Got a memo from Budget saying GSA has now completed
their study of air-conditioning in the East Room and the third floor. They
plan to go ahead with the work that needs to be done.

President Johnson: What needs to be done?

Jenkins: A new compressor, cooling coil, increased capacity, fan's
motor—that's for the East Room, 10,000 [dollars]. And then the third
floor is increase window fan coil units, individual controls for each room,
30,000 [dollars]. One construction contract. GSA will coordinate the
schedule with Mr. West in order to complete the project [by] the earliest date.[57]

President Johnson: All right. [*Pauses.*] Need any authority, does it
show?

Jenkins: No, sir.

President Johnson: Anybody know it?

Jenkins: No, sir. It's going to be used out of GSA money that they
already had.

---

56. A.W. Moursund and President Johnson owned the Comanche Cattle Company, which ran
livestock on several ranches near Johnson's Texas home.
57. West was not identified. The spelling is phonetic.

President Johnson: Make them fix those rooms up there where we can have guests right away. Go on and get them fixed up.

Jenkins: All right.

President Johnson: What else?

Jenkins: I have a memo from [McGeorge] Bundy—the one person I didn't go to see, I didn't think of him—asking to use Camp David on the weekend of the 4th. We'll just decline him.

President Johnson: No, go on and let him use it. We can't stop them because we just don't know how to do it, Walter. I give up on our staff. We've got the worst staff in the United States. I told Jack [Valenti] last night to call out here and tell them what time we'd be here, and he didn't do it until today. He just said I didn't tell him. We just don't do those things. I asked him to tell every human being that. We argued it out. [*Pause.*]

Jenkins: I believe that's about it, sir.

President Johnson: Is [there] any way you can do it, say to the Navy to get those ships back, those boats back?

Jenkins: I have said that.

President Johnson: All right. Do you reckon they've got them?

Jenkins: I don't know. I'll find out.

President Johnson: All right, find out. Now, what are you going to do about the . . . Camp David?

Jenkins: I've told the general not to . . . to notify everybody that it be not used for staff anymore.

President Johnson: And what'd he do, say he hadn't notified Bundy?

Jenkins: Well, I don't know for sure. I'm sure that's right, and I told all of our people myself. [*Pause.*]

President Johnson: Well, we ought to, after the Bundy thing, just arrange for—

Jenkins: Well, I think—

President Johnson: —them to close it up and send the people on back somewhere and just maintain it somewhere and—

Approximately 17 seconds excised as classified information.

Jenkins: . . . here.

President Johnson: All right. Well, just get them out. Clean that whole outfit out. Just have a maintenance man go and take care of it. Tell them I want the whole thing cut out and never used unless I personally say so, and I don't plan to use it and don't want anybody else to use it. I think it's a waste, and there's no reason we ought to have a luxury hotel for a few special people.

Jenkins: All right.

President Johnson: See that he tells people so they won't—or just say that we have agreed to close it down.

Jenkins: All right.

President Johnson: And don't say why, and don't say the President, or anything else. Just say it's closed for repairs. Not going to be available this summer. I'm not going to have it as a campaign issue.

Jenkins: All right. I've got a copy of [Jim] Rowe's correspondence with Jock Whitney.[58]

President Johnson: What happened there?

Jenkins: Well, Rowe just felt it was a story [that] was not true: that he never had represented the Haitian government, and he didn't anymore represent even a sugar company. He used to. And . . . Whitney writes back [*reading*], "Dear Jim, The lot of a publisher is never unhappier than in a case like this. I personally regret giving you this kind of difficulty, and I've asked that a full report be made to me. Even if we can't undo things this time, we can make sure there isn't a repeat performance because I don't like it one bit either. Anyway, I'm glad you're still friends with Betsey [Whitney]. All the best, Jock."[59]

President Johnson: Well, now, what—did he publish it?

Jenkins: Yes. In his note to me, Rowe said it's a very small item on page eight, minor reference, and while he didn't think it'd amount to anything, he didn't agree with George Reedy, who talked to him, that it was quite wrong, so he had written a letter to Jock Whitney, a rather cross letter about the inaccuracy of the story.

President Johnson: [Did] he send you the letter he wrote Whitney?

Jenkins: Yes, sir.

President Johnson: Let me read it.

Jenkins: [*reading*] "Dear Jock, The lot of a publisher is an unhappy one. I regret adding to your unhappy lot, but I think the [*New York*] *Herald Tribune* has treated me outrageously. When I returned today from a week's trip to my home state Montana, I found on my desk the enclosed story from the *Herald Tribune* of June 18, 1964, about Haiti. The casual reader would certainly receive the impression that I and my associate, Richard O'Hare, are quote 'spies for [François "Papa Doc"] Duvalier.'[60]

---

58. John Hay "Jock" Whitney was one of the wealthiest businessmen in the United States and had served as ambassador to Britain under President Eisenhower. This matter concerned his role as publisher of the *New York Herald Tribune*.

59. Betsey Cushing Roosevelt Whitney was the wife of Jock Whitney and the ex-wife of James Roosevelt.

60. François Duvalier was President of Haiti.

Even the careful reader would conclude that Mr. O'Hare and I are agents for the Haitian government. This is a flat misstatement of the facts. It seems to me any competent reporter could have ascertained the truth by looking at the Department of Justice file.

"The fact is, we no longer are attorneys for the Haitian-American Sugar Company. I cannot fault your reporter on this particular point, however, because we only recently informed our clients that we did not intend to continue, and we have not yet made our final filing with the Department of Justice. One of the considerations for not continuing was my feeling that publicity such as that from your reporter was hardly worth the 50 to 75 dollars a month take-home pay I received after office expenses and income taxes. The fact also is, we refused to represent the Haitian Government and Duvalier on sugar matters some years ago.

"The Haitian-American Sugar Company is just what it sounds like: a company engaged in raising sugar. It was formerly a Delaware corporation but a few years ago became a Haitian corporation for either tax or internal policy reasons of which I am not aware. The officials of the company are American businessmen with offices and residences in New York City, some of whom you may know. I do not know their politics, but I assume, from my casual conversations with them, that they belong to the same political party you do. It is my understanding that most of the stockholders are Americans. A quick reference by your reporter to Moody's or some other obvious reference work could have ascertained these facts.[61]

"As you may imagine, the company has confidentially had considerable difficulty over the past few years with Duvalier. In fact, I was instrumental in securing legislation in the last Sugar Act which would protect the company from discrimination on sugar allotments by Duvalier in favor of the government-owned mill.[62]

"My records show that Mr. [Dom] Bonafede telephoned my office at 4:55 P.M. on June 17.[63] As I have said, I was in Montana. Mr. O'Hare had

---

61. Moody's was a financial reporting service.

62. The Jones-Costigan Act of 1934 and its successors, the Sugar Acts of 1937 and 1948, established a system of sugar import quotas as a way to protect the domestic U.S. sugar industry. Its most recent amendments had come in 1962.

63. Dom Bonafede was a reporter for the *New York Herald Tribune*. See the conversation between President Johnson and Bill Moyers, 6:28 P.M., 3 February 1964; and the conversation between President Johnson and Walter Jenkins, 9:16 P.M., 9 February 1964, in Robert David Johnson and Kent B. Germany, eds., *The Presidential Recordings, Lyndon B. Johnson: Toward the Great Society, February 1, 1964–May 31, 1964*, vol. 4, *February 1, 1964–March 8, 1964* (New York: Norton, 2007), pp. 108–9 and 399, respectively.

left for the day. No effort was made to reach him at home. There is nothing in the story Bonafede got from Congressman [Cornelius] Gallagher
which could not have kept for a day or so if he really wanted to confirm
its accuracy.[64] I can conclude, therefore, that the 4:55 P.M. call was for the
record only, since he must have written his story immediately afterward.
This is either outrageous or sloppy reporting.

"It has been suggested to me that being accused of working for the
Haitian government is today actionable. I think this is nonsense. In any
event, I would not sue Jock Whitney. I do not want a public retraction
because that merely compounds the injury, but I do want to tell you that
I don't like it one bit. As ever, Jim Rowe. Despite all this, please give my
best to Betsey."

President Johnson: All right. [*Pause.*]

Jenkins: I have a note that you wanted to talk to me about a letter
to Governor [William] Guy on the Garrison Diversion Unit [Water
Project] in North Dakota.[65]

President Johnson: Yeah, it was in there, and I want the letter rewrit-
ten. [*The recording skips.*] It's some fool . . . the letter, it says that you
can tell the committee that I'm for something. No president ought to be
having—

Jenkins: No.

President Johnson: —a governor tell a committee something like
that. Hobart [Taylor] wrote the letter.[66]

Jenkins: Yeah.

President Johnson: And it's just an amateur letter. We've got to
have . . . get him out; we can't let him write letters. And you oughtn't to
let a letter like that get to my desk because I sign them in a hurry.

Jenkins: Right. That's . . . you're entirely justified.

I've got a memo from Liz [Carpenter] about doing an advance trip
[that] they're going to do for a trip Mrs. Johnson's going to do in the
Goldwater-leading western states.[67] The invention . . . at the invitation of
[Stewart] Udall to dedicate a dam, visit impoverished Indians—along

---

64. Cornelius Gallagher, a Democrat from New Jersey, served on the House Foreign Affairs
Committee.
65. In February, the Senate had approved almost $250 million for an irrigation project to divert
water from the massive, Missouri River–fed Garrison Reservoir, but it died later this year in
the House Rules Committee.
66. Hobart Taylor, an African American attorney with deep roots in Houston, had been serving
as associate White House counsel since April. Before that, he had been executive vice chairman
of the President's Committee on Equal Employment Opportunity.
67. Liz Carpenter was Lady Bird Johnson's press secretary.

with [Frank] Moss, [Gale] McGee, and [Mike] Mansfield—very shortly after the Republican Convention closes.[68] And since it's a public function trip, she's asking if they could use a Jetstar for the event.

President Johnson: No, tell her absolutely not.

Jenkins: All right.

President Johnson: Under no circumstances.

Jenkins: [*Pause.*] General [Carl] Phinney came by and said—of course, there's nothing to do about much of this—he said that he . . . a man in Dallas that's close to the Republican Campaign Committee told him that there were three items that they were putting out on a quiet basis.[69] One, that George Parr had had a transaction with you that involved $32,000, didn't know what for. Second, that they made a deal with Coke Stevenson to make a nationwide campaign. They're going to ship him around the country explaining how he lost the [1948] election—Box 13.[70] And third, that some people very closely related to us have purchased large tracts of real estate near the space center in Houston before the location was announced and then sold it at a huge profit. [*Pauses.*]

President Johnson: Well, none of them true. Coke might do it, but the others—

Jenkins: No, the second one could be, but I doubt he's well enough. I believe that's all, sir.

President Johnson: Who's he say . . . Where's he say he gets that?

Jenkins: I asked him. He said it was from a man whose name we wouldn't know and he's promised not to use, but he's a high-up fellow in the Republican circles in Dallas.

President Johnson: Well, so what? Does the fellow believe it, or . . .

Jenkins: He thinks he does. At least he told him that that's what they had been told down there to spread. [*Pause.*]

---

68. Lady Bird dedicated the Flaming Gorge Dam in Utah on 17 August. Stewart Udall was secretary of the interior. Frank Moss and Gale McGee were Democratic senators from Utah and Wyoming, respectively. Mike Mansfield, from Montana, was Senate majority leader. Morris Udall was a representative from Arizona, but Jenkins almost certainly meant the interior secretary.

69. A World War II hero, Major General Carl Lawrence Phinney had retired from the service in 1961 to a life as an attorney and investor in Dallas. Texas House of Representatives, Resolution No. 128, 5 April 2001.

70. This incident is one of the most widely reported of Johnson's early career. George Parr was the powerful leader of a south Texas political family who figured in the controversial 1948 Senate election. In that race, Johnson earned his nickname "Landslide Lyndon" by defeating Coke Stevenson by a mere 87 votes. Helping Johnson secure victory was the mysterious appearance of a ballot box from Precinct 13 in Parr-controlled Alice, Texas, which contained only one vote for Stevenson and over 200 for Johnson.

President Johnson: Well, did he tell him that he didn't . . . that he knew anything about it?

Jenkins: He told him he didn't know anything about any of it, but he felt sure none of it was true, unless the part about Stevens.

President Johnson: Well, you can tell him it's not. Did you?

Jenkins: I did. [*Twenty-second pause.*]

President Johnson: OK, any other news?

Jenkins: I believe that's all, sir.

President Johnson: OK. [*Hangs up.*]

Jenkins: Hello? [*Pauses.*] Hello?

White House Operator: Operator.

Jenkins: Did he hang up?

White House Operator: Yes, sir, he did.

Jenkins: I guess he's through. OK, thank you.

6:23 P.M. (CST)

To Walter Jenkins[71]

Johnson next turned to Jenkins for assistance on the appointment of LeRoy Collins to the Community Relations Service.

Jenkins is on hold before the President comes on the line.

President Johnson: Walter?

Walter Jenkins: Yes, sir.

President Johnson: We're trying to get Governor [LeRoy] Collins.

Jenkins: Yes, sir.

President Johnson: Would you mind calling Johnny Hayes and just say to him that we've looked the nation over and this is the toughest job we've got—we've got them in St. Augustine; we've got them in Mississippi; we've got them every place—and that everybody's looked at it and says that Johnny Hayes could—I mean that Governor Collins could do it: his southern background and his experience as governor and his northern viewpoint and the fact that he's got all the radio stations and television stations helping him, and the press. And see if Hayes would mind put-

---

71. Tape WH6406.18, Citation #3931, Recordings of Telephone Conversations—White House Series, Recordings and Transcripts of Conversations and Meetings, Lyndon B. Johnson Library.

ting in a good word with the head of that NAB [National Association of Broadcasters]. And if you'd mind talking to Al Friendly about it and getting them to support him if he's in Maine.[72]

Jenkins: All right. [*Pause.*]

President Johnson: OK.

Jenkins: I'll do it right now.

President Johnson: He'd be for him, wouldn't he?

Jenkins: I'm sure he will if we ask him to.

President Johnson: OK.

Jenkins: Yes, sir.

6:30 P.M. (CST)

To Al Friendly[73]

Johnson reached the managing editor of the *Washington Post* to talk about LeRoy Collins. The President was eating during parts of the call.

President Johnson: Al?

Al Friendly: Hello?

President Johnson: Al?

Friendly: Yes, sir.

President Johnson: Hello, Al.

Friendly: Yes?

President Johnson: Lyndon Johnson.

Friendly: Mr. President.

President Johnson: That was a wonderful story this morning.[74]

Friendly: Was that all right?

President Johnson: Couldn't have been better.

Friendly: Good, I hope I didn't reveal any confidences I shouldn't—

---

72. John S. Hayes had been president of WTOP radio and television in Washington, D.C., a company co-owned by the *Washington Post* and the Columbia Broadcasting System. He was currently chairman of the executive committee and president of the *Post-Newsweek* stations. Alfred Friendly was executive vice president and managing editor of the *Washington Post.*

73. Tape WH6406.18, Citation #3932, Recordings of Telephone Conversations—White House Series, Recordings and Transcripts of Conversations and Meetings, Lyndon B. Johnson Library.

74. This story was not positively identified, but the *Post*'s editorial page ran a column that morning praising Johnson's legislative skill while belittling Otto Passman. "The Unkindest Cut," *Washington Post,* 26 June 1964.

President Johnson: Not a bit. It couldn't have been better if you had worked on it for a year.

Friendly: Fine . . . thank you.

President Johnson: [*with Friendly acknowledging throughout*] We got a good deal of problems, and I think I've got them going all right, but I need a little help on them. I told Walter [Jenkins] to call Johnny Hayes, and if you feel like it, maybe you would feel like talking to him. We've searched the country for the last two or three weeks to try to get a top man to handle the toughest job we'll have, not even excepting Cabinet, and that's this conciliation service.

We've . . . think we're going to get St. Augustine worked out, but we're kind of having to do some of these things ourselves.[75] And this [civil rights] bill, when we sign it, it provides for a top conciliator. That was in my original bill back in '57, and they took it out in the Senate, but it was recommended by this boy Ted Kheel in New York and . . . Phil [Graham] and Kheel and Ben Cohen and all of us [who] worked on it thought it was one of the most important parts of the bill.[76]

He's . . . he organizes people like the mayor of Atlanta and the mayor of Charlottesville [*sic*, Charlotte] and good people. And where you have one of these questions like St. Augustine, you send him in, and he calls them together and winds up by having a community council where he can get communications going and so forth.

I tried to get Dr. [George] Taylor at University of Pennsylvania, who settled a railroad strike, to do this for me, and his doctor wouldn't let him.[77]

Friendly: Great guy, but he's worked a long time at that.

President Johnson: That's right. Now, we've got LeRoy Collins, and he's very dedicated and very willing to take it and going to have a great sacrifice. But I had his board in today, five members of it, and they're all willing to help him do it, and I think they'll give him leave and give him a little money to . . . as a severance pay so he can start it because this doesn't pay much, and it's the meanest job in the government.

---

75. Governor Farris Bryant had come to St. Augustine in person to try to assure the maintenance of order.

76. Ted Kheel was a New York attorney who had helped mediate railroad labor negotiations in April 1964. Philip Graham was publisher of the *Washington Post* until his suicide in 1963. Ben Cohen was a Democratic Party insider and had been a close adviser to President Franklin Roosevelt. See William Lasser, *Benjamin V. Cohen: Architect of the New Deal* (New Haven, CT: Yale University Press, 2002).

77. George Taylor was a professor at the Wharton School at the University of Pennsylvania and had been chairman of the War Labor Board during World War II.

Friendly: Right.

President Johnson: But they've got to go back to the various television and radio people on this NAB [National Association of Broadcasters] board. Now, I think Johnny Hayes is on it. If he's not, he's influential with it.

Friendly: I'm sure of the latter, and I'm not sure of the former. He may or may not.

President Johnson: Anyway, if you don't mind putting in a word, I know that if you'll just kind of help me a little bit. I know if Phil [Graham] was here, he'd do it, and I've just got to have this—the country's got to have this fellow if we can.

Friendly: Mr. President, you know, of all your problems I think that's the least one as far as getting LeRoy Collins sprung or at least as far as John Hayes is for it. I'll do it immediately, but I don't think they'll be any problem anyway.

President Johnson: Fine, if you can just help a little, I'll appreciate it.

Friendly: Wonderful.

President Johnson: Bye.

Friendly: Thank you.

The fund-raising event took up the rest of the evening. After a series of receptions and handshaking events—with many of the nation's most powerful automobile executives—President Johnson and Lady Bird arrived at Cobo Hall for the Democratic fund-raising dinner around 8:30 p.m. The President gave his remarks at 9:30 p.m. and departed at 10:14 p.m. Five minutes later, Johnson and the First Lady settled in at their hotel suite. Johnson's day was not over, however, as he placed a call (unrecorded) to CORE Director James Farmer at 10:58 p.m.

Saturday, June 27, 1964, and Sunday, June 28, 1964

President Johnson was still on his fund-raising/political trip to Detroit. He recorded only one call on Saturday and no conversations on Sunday.

12:55 P.M.

To McGeorge Bundy[1]

This entire two-minute-and-thirty-nine-second conversation is closed as classified information. The Lyndon B. Johnson Library notes that Bundy reported on progress in the U.N. mediation of the Cyprus situation, on Greece, on Turkey, and on an unidentified air mission, possibly in Laos.

After the call, the President and his delegation flew from Detroit to Minneapolis–St. Paul, arriving at 3:00 P.M. Forty-five minutes later, he was standing before 8,000 members of the Democratic Farmer-Labor-Party at the St. Paul Auditorium. He spent the rest of the day attending receptions and related events, finishing off the night at the "Salute to President Johnson Dinner" with a speech to approximately 2,000 supporters.[2] At

---

1. Tape WH6406.18, Citation #3933, Recordings of Telephone Conversations—White House Series, Recordings and Transcripts of Conversations and Meetings, Lyndon B. Johnson Library.
2. "Remarks Upon Arrival at the Minneapolis–St. Paul International Airport," "Remarks in St. Paul at the Minnesota State Democratic-Farmer-Labor Party Convention," and "Remarks at a Fundraising Dinner in Minneapolis," 27 June 1964, *Public Papers of the Presidents of the United States: Lyndon B. Johnson, 1963–64* (Washington, DC: GPO, 1965), 1:823–30.

10:09 P.M., the President and Lady Bird left for the Sheraton-Ritz's presidential suite. They turned in for the night at 10:15 P.M.

On Sunday, the Johnsons went to services at the Mt. Olivet Lutheran Church and then traveled to Minnehaha Park for the Svenskarnas Dag picnic. Johnson spoke to approximately 85,000 in attendance and then left for the airport.[3] Airborne by 2:25 P.M., the contingent arrived back in the nation's capital around 5:30 P.M. Although the President apparently recorded no calls, he did make a number of unrecorded ones from the Mansion, including calls to Jack Valenti (7:58 P.M.), Chief Warrant Officer Tom Mills (9:00 P.M.), and Walter Jenkins (9:05 P.M.). Johnson then dined with Lady Bird and Barbara Ward, made another unrecorded call to Jenkins at 9:30 P.M., and went to bed at 10:45 P.M.

---

3. "Remarks at the Annual Swedish Day Picnic, Minnehaha Park, Minneapolis," 28 June 1964, *Public Papers, Johnson, 1963–64*, 1:830–33.

Monday, June 29, 1964

God, today's an awful one.

—President Johnson to Myer Feldman

Back from a successful trip to the Midwest, Johnson spent much of today giving official welcomes and good-byes, while taking a few moments in the evening to catch up with old friends from Texas. One good-bye in the morning was a politically complicated, front-page send-off for Massachusetts Republican Henry Cabot Lodge, the other a more sedate Oval Office exit for John Badeau, the departing ambassador to the United Arab Republic. Among the welcomes for the day, he met Mary Bunting for the first time at her swearing-in ceremony for her post on the Atomic Energy Commission. The scientist and Radcliffe College president was one of Johnson's prize recruits in his efforts to expand the number of women in the federal government.

Johnson had less success in his dealings with another woman, Rita Schwerner. The Council of Federated Organizations (COFO) staffer and wife of missing COFO activist Mickey Schwerner met with the President briefly this afternoon in her ongoing efforts to expand the investigation into the disappearance of her husband and two other activists. Johnson came away from the encounter agitated and upset with her (coincidentally, he immediately went to a National Security Council meeting and agreed to a small military escalation against Communist nationalists in Laos). Compounding his bad reaction to Rita Schwerner was J. Edgar Hoover's incendiary allegations an hour later that she was a Communist and "no good at all." The FBI director also claimed that both her husband and her attorney were Communists and had been for "many years." Besides attacking the Schwerners, Hoover had little to report to

Johnson today. The search for Chaney, Schwerner, and Goodman had yielded no breakthroughs in finding their bodies or catching their assailants. Hoover, however, did inform the President that he planned to open a permanent FBI office in Jackson and promised to send in up to 400 agents to supplement the 200 that he asserted had already been sent to Mississippi.[1]

In Mississippi, the search had expanded to the Pearl River, a clay-stained stream that passed under State Highway 19 just north of Philadelphia. Downstream, the waters of the Pearl filled the new Ross Barnett Reservoir (named for the segregationist governor who had in 1962 repeatedly refused to allow the admission of James Meredith to Ole Miss) before rolling through Jackson and southward to the sea. Two days earlier, the FBI had begun leading an effort to drag the river for human remains.

7:40 A.M.: The phone calls began early today. Unrecorded calls from the living quarters went out to Bill Moyers at 7:40 A.M. and then to Walter Jenkins at 7:45 A.M.

8:00 A.M.: President Johnson received a checkup from White House physician George Burkley for his cold, then did his exercises and ate breakfast. Jack Valenti reviewed plans for the day ahead.

10:40 A.M.–10:58 A.M.: Arrived at the Oval Office, met with McGeorge Bundy (10:47 A.M.), then made unrecorded calls to Valenti (10:50 A.M.) and George Reedy (10:58 A.M.) on the personal line.

11:00 A.M.: The President and Secretary Dean Rusk met with Ambassador Henry Cabot Lodge, who had flown in from Saigon the day before.

11:36 A.M.: The group went to the Cabinet Room for Lodge's send-off to the press. Johnson thanked Lodge for his service to two presidents and for the quality of his "performance on a most difficult assignment." The President exited the room after his remarks, and Lodge held the floor. Among other things, Lodge declared that "the whole thing" in Vietnam "is on the right track." He took the opportunity to press his support of Pennsylvania Governor William Scranton, making

---

1. Conversation between President Johnson and J. Edgar Hoover, 6:47 P.M., 29 June 1964, in this chapter.

some not-so-subtle criticism of Barry Goldwater's impetuous style.[2]

11:40 A.M.: Johnson and Rusk returned to the Oval Office. Five minutes later, Johnson made an unrecorded call to Walter Jenkins on the personal line. Then the Speaker of the House called to arrange an appointment for leaders of the American Jewish Committee.

11:50 A.M.

From John McCormack[3]

President Johnson: . . . [*unclear*] hasn't been. Got an advisory committee on labor management, got Ambassador [John] Badeau, and I'm just running out of my ears today, and . . .[4]

John McCormack: All right, Mr. President.

President Johnson: Myer Feldman talked to them, why, if they . . . I know I can't see them today, but if it's something that requires my attention, I'll get with them tomorrow or the earliest possible moment.

McCormack: All right, thank you.

President Johnson: OK.

McCormack: Bye.

11:54 A.M.

To Myer Feldman[5]

Johnson followed up on McCormack's request with a call to Myer Feldman, a holdover from the Kennedy administration. In April 1964,

---

2. "Remarks Upon Introducing Henry Cabot Lodge to the Press Upon His Return from Viet-Nam," 29 June 1964, *Public Papers of the Presidents of the United States: Lyndon B. Johnson, 1963–64* (Washington, DC: GPO, 1965), 1:437; Conversation between President Johnson and George Reedy, 12:50 P.M., 29 June 1964, in this chapter; Carroll Kilpatrick, "Lodge Blasts at Goldwater," *Washington Post*, 30 June 1964.

3. Tape WH6406.18, Citation #3934, Recordings of Telephone Conversations—White House Series, Recordings and Transcripts of Conversations and Meetings, Lyndon B. Johnson Library.

4. John S. Badeau was U.S. ambassador to United Arab Republic (Egypt). Johnson met with him and Phillips Talbot, assistant secretary of state for Near Eastern and South Asian affairs, at 1:02 P.M.

5. Tape WH6406.18, Citation #3935, Recordings of Telephone Conversations—White House Series, Recordings and Transcripts of Conversations and Meetings, Lyndon B. Johnson Library.

Johnson had elevated him to special counsel to the President, filling the slot left by Ted Sorensen's departure.

Myer Feldman: Hello?

President Johnson: Myer?

Feldman: Yes, Mr. President.

President Johnson: The American Jewish Committee, [Morris] Abrams [*sic*] and somebody else, is up [in] John McCormack's office and wanted to come right on down here to see me.[6] I told them that I had the Committee on Labor Management, and I had Dr. [Mary] Bunting, and I had Mrs. America [Desree Jenkins], and I had a [National] Security Council, and [Henry Cabot] Lodge is still in the Cabinet Room [in a press conference], and I just couldn't see them, [but] to talk to you about whatever their problem was.[7]

Feldman: All right.

President Johnson: And if you couldn't handle it, which I think you can [*Feldman acknowledges*], that then you could talk to me about it.

Feldman: Yes, sir. I think they want to talk to you about the trip they're making to Latin America.[8] I think I can handle it, though, Mr. President.

President Johnson: You just call them right now in the Speaker's office and tell them I asked you to get in touch with them because I'm in a meeting of labor management group.

Feldman: Yes, sir.

President Johnson: Tell them that.

Feldman: Yes, sir.

President Johnson: Any other news?

Feldman: No, sir. I sent some memoranda down to you, which I'll talk to you later—I wonder if you could see Dr. [Edward] Dempsey sometime today, the fellow Mary Lasker—[9]

---

6. Morris B. Abram was a Rhodes Scholar from Georgia who was a civil rights attorney and had been the chief legal adviser for the Peace Corps. In February 1964, he had become president of the American Jewish Committee. "Jewish Unit Picks National Leader," *New York Times*, 16 February 1964.

7. Johnson was recounting his upcoming schedule for today. Mary Bunting's swearing-in was at 12:10 P.M., the President's Advisory Committee on Labor-Management Policy was meeting at 12:20 P.M., and Mrs. America was coming by for photos at 1:20 P.M.

8. The American Jewish Committee sent a delegation to South America in late July and August 1964 to investigate conditions for Jewish populations there.

9. Edward Dempsey was a member of the President's Commission on Heart Disease, Cancer, and Stroke that was the pet project of Democratic fund-raiser Mary Lasker.

President Johnson: No, not today. I might tomorrow, but God, today's an awful one.

Feldman: All right.

President Johnson: What ever happened? Did they ever fill that place?

Feldman: The Bo Jones place?[10]

President Johnson: Yeah.

Feldman: No, Dr. Dempsey is ... [Anthony] Celebrezze will take him.[11] Mary Lasker thinks he's good. I'm sure he's good. He's really an outstanding person. He's the head of the medical school at St. Louis University, and he's our man above all, so I think he's a good appointment.

President Johnson: Good. . . . OK, well, we'll take a look at him tomorrow, then.

Feldman: Yes, sir.

President Johnson: Bye.

11:56 A.M.

To Lee White[12]

Johnson continued to get updates on the missing civil rights activists, James Chaney, Michael Schwerner, and Andrew Goodman. White let Johnson know that Rita Schwerner, the wife of Michael, was in Washington, D.C., and had requested a meeting with the President. After the call, White arranged a late-afternoon session. In this call, White also passed along a suggestion from Carolyn Goodman, the mother of Andrew Goodman, for Lady Bird to ask help from mothers in Mississippi.

President Johnson: . . . [Fannie Lee] Chaney?[13]

Lee White: I talked to her, and apparently she was under the impression that you had attempted to make a call to her yesterday. I checked with—

---

10. Boisfeuillet Jones Sr., a Georgia native, had resigned (effective 30 June) his position as special assistant for health and medical issues at the Department of Health, Education, and Welfare. His son, Boisfeuillet Jones Jr., later became the president of the *Washington Post*.

11 Anthony Celebrezze was secretary of health, education, and welfare.

12. Tape WH6406.18, Citation #3936, Recordings of Telephone Conversations—White House Series, Recordings and Transcripts of Conversations and Meetings, Lyndon B. Johnson Library.

13. Fannie Lee Chaney, the mother of James Chaney, was the parent that White could not locate on 23 June. See the conversation between Lee White and White House Operator, time unknown (after 8:53 P.M.), 23 June 1964, in this volume.

President Johnson: No . . . no.

White: —Jack [Valenti], and apparently that was not the case. And I think I assured her that we were doing everything and that you had asked me to keep her advised of any information that came, and she, I think, was quite happy with the way it had gone.

President Johnson: All right. Do you know how to get in touch with her from time to time now?

White: We do have her number.

President Johnson: Now, have you heard anything from Mississippi?

White: Nothing in terms of information, but we got a new little bit of a problem. This fellow [Michael] Schwerner's wife [Rita] is going to be in Washington this afternoon. She's coming here from New York City in the company of Congressman [Ogden] Reid. And Congressman Reid's office called to say that she was coming and had requested a meeting with *you.* Now, I'm . . . don't know anything about it other than that.

"She wants"—I'm reading now from a note that came from Reid's office—"She wants to see the President, or you [Lee White] if she can't see the President. They will be seeing Nick Katzenbach at 3:00." Once again, the things . . . people do things the most peculiar way. An additional note I get from Reid's office is this, "The main purpose of the visit is to see the President." Apparently, she did not get to see Governor [Paul] Johnson. *Time* and *Life* magazine[s] called Congressman Reid's office in Washington saying they understood Mrs. Schwerner was coming to see the President.[14] Apparently she gave out the story in New York. It's [*chuckles*] another one of those thoughtless acts on the part of them. My intention was to meet her personally, but I thought I'd mention it to you to—

President Johnson: Have we met with her before?

White: [*with the President acknowledging*] No, sir, she's the young . . . she's the wife who was down in Mississippi herself. She was in western Ohio at Oxford when her husband disappeared. She then went on to Mississippi and attempted to see the governor, but that didn't work very well. He refused to see her. She then went to New York to be with her parents over the weekend and is now en route back to Mississippi and is going to stop here in Washington. She will be in the . . . accompanied by Ogden Reid. There's no indication of, you know, of why she wants to see you or what information she has.

President Johnson: Well, I would see her and ask her everything she's

---

14. On this incident, see the introduction to 25 June 1964 in this volume.

got and just tell her that my schedule has been full for a week. And read her what it is: [Henry Cabot] Lodge—

White: Sure.

President Johnson: —and Dr. [Mary] Bunting and Committee on Labor Management and ambassador [John Badeau] from the Arab countries and Senator [Olin] Johnston and the [National] Security Council meeting, and [tell her] that you'll bring her in. You bring her in and out and leave Reid and the rest of them outside. Just bring her in and out and let you be a witness to what happens, but you just bring her in while I have somebody else in here.[15]

White: Just so you can shake her hand and tell her you're doing everything you can.

President Johnson: Yeah, yeah, yeah . . . yeah.

White: All right.

I had one other call from Mrs. [Carolyn] Goodman today. It was an interesting one. She's been sitting around trying to think of things that would be helpful, and one she hit upon was to have Mrs. [Lady Bird] Johnson issue a statement calling on all the mothers of Mississippi to be of help.[16] I've checked it out with Liz [Carpenter] who, I believe, talked to Mrs. Johnson about it, and the reaction there was they'd much rather stay out of it.[17] You're doing everything you can and that Mrs. Johnson never interferes when you're . . . you have a major matter before you and are actively engaged in it. I haven't returned Mrs. Goodman's call yet. That's roughly what I intended to tell her, as nicely as I knew how.

---

15. Johnson met with Rita Schwerner later this day, at 5:25 P.M., in the Mansion's Green Room. Congressman Reid, however, did not wait outside, and attended the session.

16. One group of women with backgrounds similar to Carolyn Goodman was already engaged in quiet efforts to organize mothers and other women in Mississippi. Sponsored by the National Council of Negro Women (NCNW) and a number of women's religious organizations, the Wednesdays in Mississippi (WIMS) program flew in teams of affluent, activist northern women for three-day trips to the Magnolia State. Led by Dorothy Height, the president of the NCNW, and by Polly Spiegel Cowan, an activist from a prominent Jewish family who was married to former CBS president Louis Cowan, these women arrived on Tuesdays, spent Wednesdays fanning out across the state, and then returned home on Thursdays. Some of the women's travel information was passed along from the FBI to the Mississippi Highway Patrol. "Information Received from Bill Cullen of F.B.I.," 11:25 A.M., 17 August 1964, Folder 8: "Highway Patrol Reports and Correspondence, August 1964," Box 144, Series II, Sub-Series 10: Highway Patrol, Johnson (Paul B.) Family Papers, in Collection M191, Manuscript Collection, McCain Library and Archives, University of Southern Mississippi; Robert J. Spivack to Jack Valenti, 8 June 1964, "1/1/64–6/30/64" folder, White House Central Files: Human Rights—Equality of the Races, Lyndon B. Johnson Library.

17. Liz Carpenter was Lady Bird's press secretary.

President Johnson: Yeah. Tell her they'd consider that interference. Then they'd have the problem of all the other wives of government officials wanting to get in, and it'd create lots of problems.

White: [*with the President acknowledging*] Right, and I can, of course, indicate the deep concern that not only Mrs. Johnson, but everybody else, shares with her.

Our St. Augustine thing is not fallen apart yet, but we've had [an] extremely difficult time getting four principals who we could get together. One of the Negroes that Mr. [Herbert] Wolfe offered was perfectly acceptable, the other one is not.[18] We're now—Governor [Farris] Bryant's been trying to work out a package deal where they add a white member and a Negro member and come up with six, and he's exceedingly . . . personally involved in the thing and spending most of his time doing it.[19] He said yesterday that he was fearful that Governor—that Judge [John] Simpson, the federal district judge, was going to issue a ruling holding him in contempt and barring the state from interfering with nighttime demonstrations.[20]

Now, our information from Justice [Department] is it may not be that way at all. I don't think the judge wants to have it happen, and in any event, I think the governor was just saying that he may be in a position soon when he doesn't think he can control it. Now, he hasn't said that, and he hasn't used his National Guard yet. He's got a few places to go, but he's beginning to look like the pressure's getting him, and he's not sure he can control the situation. He had to say that apparently in his hearing in order to justify his position of ruling out nighttime demonstrations. It doesn't

---

18. On 25 June, Reverend Dr. Martin Luther King Jr. had asked the Johnson administration to send a representative to mediate the troubling situation in the oldest town in the United States. That night, white attacks on a nighttime demonstration put 19 activists in the hospital. In response, Florida Governor Farris Bryant issued an order banning night marches, which civil rights leaders fought. Although the exact identities of the four people mentioned here are unclear, the strong possibilities were Reverend King, Governor Bryant, Mayor Joseph Shelley, Robert Hayling (a local dentist and NAACP official leading the attempts to integrate public spaces), and Herbert Wolfe, the chairman of St. Augustine's Quadricentennial Commission. Wolfe was a powerful local businessman who had served as a chief fund-raiser for Senators George Smathers and Spessard Holland. *New York Times* reporter John Herbers characterized him as a "one-man power structure." *New York Times*, 7 June 1964.

19. Reverend King had met resistance to his call for a biracial committee to facilitate negotiations between the white and black communities. Governor Bryant did form such a committee on 30 June, with two black and two white members, but refused to release the names of the participants to protect them. *New York Times*, 1 July 1964.

20. The 61-year-old John Milton Bryan Simpson was the chief judge for the U.S. District Court for the Middle District of Florida. President Johnson elevated him to the Fifth Circuit Court of Appeals in October 1966.

look very good if he says that he can't control it if there are nighttime, and the court says, "OK, there're going to be nighttime anyhow."

But still quite possible though, even with [*unclear; the President coughs and obscures the word*] and looks like the makings of an agreement is there. Mr. Wolfe was very discouraged yesterday. This morning [*Johnson blows his nose loudly*] he's back in an optimistic frame of mind and willing to . . . and much more willing to meet with people today than he was yesterday. [Martin Luther] King is still *extremely* anxious to be out of the city. He just wants to get out as much as he can, and it looks like he's going to be able to. But the damn solution is always *just* two inches outside of our grasp, it seems. You always think you just about got it, and it slithers away, but everybody's got a little more optimistic attitude down there today in the situation.

And of course we will be kept advised, but we have tried to get out of it, in the direct sense, in that for about, oh, 24 hours the governor would call me, I'd call Burke [Marshall], Burke would call King, and now we've kind of got one of King's men talking to one of the governor's men, and they're negotiating kind of directly, and it looks like they will get all of the people to agree sometime today to sit down. In the meantime, King has had his people for three nights in a row. They did not march, and nobody's been hurt, and I have a feeling this situation has eased just a little tiny bit, but I am keeping right in close touch with the governor.

President Johnson: Where is he going to break out next when you get Mississippi and St. Augustine—Maryland or someplace?

White: [*Chuckles.*] Mr. President, I wish I knew. I'll swear, it's like trying to walk around on a dozen eggs. . . .

President Johnson: Is there anything else Burke Marshall or you can figure out we could be doing in Mississippi so we show a little concern without . . . without starting any fight? I guess we ought to call the governor and ask how things are going, but there's no . . .

White: Wouldn't hurt. One thing Nick Katzenbach reported this morning was that he had talked to Governor Johnson, I think Saturday or Sunday, and had offered him to use this fellow by the name of [Floyd] Mann.[21] He was a guy who had been the Alabama highway commissioner,

---

21. Floyd Mann, Alabama's commissioner of public safety, had worked closely with the Kennedy administration during the 1961 Freedom Rides. When George Wallace became governor in 1963, he replaced Mann with a hard-liner, Al Lingo. In a May 1963 conversation with President Kennedy about the Birmingham crisis, Robert Kennedy referred to Mann as "our friend in Montgomery." Oval Office Meeting Between President John Kennedy and Robert Kennedy, 12 May 1963, JFK Meeting Tape E-1/86.2, Recordings, John F. Kennedy Library.

or state police commissioner, and the governor was fairly interested in it if he thought he could get away with it: that he would have this fellow Mann sort of be attached to [Allen] Dulles and serve as a liaison between the state law enforcement people—they have a Colonel [T. B.] Birdsong who's in charge of their operation in Mississippi—and with the FBI and the Justice Department.[22]

The governor was thinking that over, over the weekend, as to whether he thought he could do it. He believed that there might be some problem, but he figured that it made a little sense to him to have a fellow like that who's a southerner, who's experienced, and who is not in any way a bad name. The only strike he had against him was that this fellow had been let out by Governor [George] Wallace, but apparently with no hard feelings. It was just a political reshuffling of his cabinet when he came—took over.

Nick had, therefore, been in touch with the governor, and I'd see no reason why you couldn't—

President Johnson: Ask Nick and Burke Marshall to figure out something I ought to be doing today, if anything, to keep in touch with it.

White: All right. Burke had—

President Johnson: And you three—

White: Burke and Mr. Dulles met Saturday with the National Council of Churches [NCC] in an effort to get them to have a much tighter control over these kids to give us an itinerary so—[23]

President Johnson: Do any good?

White: Apparently it did pretty much good because they asked Burke to go up to New York today to meet with the council—what is it—the National Council of Churches there and with the people who are actually controlling the situation, and Burke is in New York this morning trying to work out specific details with them.

President Johnson: You ask Nick. Just tell him you want to come up with a report to me each day and any recommendations of anything else I ought to be doing.

White: All right, and I'll . . .

President Johnson: Bring that girl by.

White: I'll check—yeah, with your office and bring Mrs. Schwerner by.

---

22. T. B. Birdsong was commissioner of public safety in Mississippi and oversaw the Mississippi Highway Patrol.

23. Robert Spike, the executive director of the NCC's Committee on Religion and Race, and John Pratt, attorney for the NCC, had met with Dulles, Katzenbach, and Marshall at Dulles's home on 27 June. Jack Raymond, "Dulles Confers on Rights Drive," *New York Times*, 28 June 1964.

President Johnson: All right . . . all right. All right.
White: All right.

> **12:03 P.M.–12:06 P.M.:** Johnson made a quick unrecorded call to Jack Valenti, welcomed McGeorge Bundy, and made an unrecorded call to Walter Jenkins.
>
> **12:10 P.M.–12:15 P.M.:** Went to the Cabinet Room for the swearing-in ceremony for Dr. Mary Bunting, the president of Radcliffe College, who was taking a seat on the Atomic Energy Commission. Since Johnson did not know her, he asked Bundy, the former dean of the faculty at Harvard (Radcliffe's co-institution), to accompany him and "point her out."[24] Just before 12:15 P.M., the President gave brief remarks on the value of Bunting's roles as scientist, university leader, and mother.
>
> **12:20 P.M.:** Moved quickly to the Fish Room for a meeting with the President's Advisory Committee on Labor-Management Policy.
>
> **12:45 P.M.:** Returned to the Oval Office and took a phone call from George Reedy, the White House press secretary, who was seeking guidance on the Mississippi Burning case.

12:50 P.M.

From George Reedy[25]

George Reedy: Mr. President, this one question might bob up: whether you've talked to Mr. [J. Edgar] Hoover this morning about Mississippi.

President Johnson: No, but I've talked to staff members here about it, and maybe I ought to before you talk to them. You think I ought to?

Reedy: I think it might be good. I've got . . .

President Johnson: How did [Henry Cabot] Lodge do?[26]

Reedy: [*with the President acknowledging*] He talked politics entirely. He didn't talk it. He had no option, but he could have said, "Of course, I'm

---

24. Quote from Daily Diary, 29 June 1964, Lyndon B. Johnson Library.

25. Tape WH6406.18, Citations #3937 and #3938, Recordings of Telephone Conversations—White House Series, Recordings and Transcripts of Conversations and Meetings, Lyndon B. Johnson Library.

26. Lodge had spoken to the press in the Cabinet Room after his earlier remarks.

not here to talk politics," but he didn't. And what he said, in effect, was that . . .

We have got three leads: the AP [Associated Press] said that—has him declaring that he considered a higher duty of him to return home and fight for the Republican presidential nomination for Governor [William] Scranton than to remain as ambassador to South Vietnam. He told a White House news conference that he felt "the war in South Vietnam was on the track, while I feel the Republican Party is not in the track." Another, UPI [United Press International] has him saying that he will try to enlist former President Dwight D. Eisenhower's help on behalf of Governor William Scranton's GOP presidential bid. Agence France Presse has him saying that he feels that the problem in Vietnam is to try to find new steps and that he minimizes the dangers of stepping up the war. And . . . then they say that in response to questions, he, after taking farewell of you, that he declared again that a military effort in Vietnam should be able to succeed with perseverance. Reuters hasn't moved a lead on it yet, or may have one moving at the moment. [*Pause.*]

I have here an FBI statement just saying that "the intensive search and investigation involving the three missing civil rights workers is continuing in Philadelphia and Mississippi. [*Unclear*] have a circular containing photographs and descriptions of the missing workers . . . been prepared and will be distributed today throughout Mississippi and the surrounding states of Alabama, Tennessee, Arkansas, and Louisiana."[27] I can just say, "We have been informed that this has happened." [*Pause.*]

It's not necessary that you call Mr. Hoover, I can just say the White House has been informed by the FBI, and of course you're keeping close touch with all developments—

President Johnson: No, I'll call him right now and see if I can get him. OK.

Reedy: OK, sir.

The President tried to call Hoover next, before Reedy's press conference. After holding for over two minutes, he was informed that the FBI director was away from his desk.[28] At 12:55 P.M., he made an unrecorded call to Walter Jenkins on the personal line and then took another call from Reedy.

---

27. These notices became iconic images of the civil rights movement.
28. Tape WH6406.18, Citation #3939, Recordings of Telephone Conversations—White House Series, Recordings and Transcripts of Conversations and Meetings, Lyndon B. Johnson Library.

1:00 P.M.

From George Reedy[29]

A brief office conversation precedes the call.

Jack Valenti: . . . that's what he wants.

President Johnson: Tell him to see Mac Bundy. I suggested he see Mac Bundy. My schedule's running out of my ears, and tell Mac if he needs to, to bring him up.

Valenti: OK. Now, you've got the [*unclear*] waiting out—

A secretary reports that Reedy is on the line.

President Johnson: . . . call me back, but he [J. Edgar Hoover] hadn't, so I guess you have to go ahead.

George Reedy: Right. Now, one thing, Mr. President—

President Johnson: We have been in touch with him: Walter [Jenkins] has talked to Deke DeLoach two or three times this morning.[30]

Reedy: Sure. . . . Right, and I have also, sir. Should I lid them immediately? I was wondering about this [Olin] Johnston thing, if you'd want photographers to come in afterward or anything.[31] That's off the record, and they don't know about it.

President Johnson: What?

Reedy: This Mrs. America [Desree Jenkins] and Olin Johnston, they do not know about it, but I wanted to be sure that I could brief them and lid them.

President Johnson: Oh, God, I never knew about it either. I don't know what it is.

[*to Valenti*] Olin Johnston, you want photographers for that?

Valenti: Not unless—it's off the record.

President Johnson: No. [*Unclear.*]

Reedy: They do not know about it, so it's no problem.

President Johnson: That's all right.

Reedy: I'll just brief them, then, and lid.

---

29. Tape WH6406.18, Citation #3940, Recordings of Telephone Conversations—White House Series, Recordings and Transcripts of Conversations and Meetings, Lyndon B. Johnson Library.
30. Cartha "Deke" DeLoach was assistant director of the FBI and the chief liaison to the White House.
31. Olin Johnston, the Democratic senator from South Carolina, had arranged a photo opportunity at the White House for one of his constituents, the new Mrs. America.

President Johnson: All right, and then tell Cecil [Stoughton] to stay around.[32]

Reedy: Yeah, OK.

President Johnson: All right.

Reedy: You bet.

1:02 P.M.: The President met with John Badeau, U.S. ambassador to the United Arab Republic, in the Oval Office. Badeau was leaving his position to take a job at Columbia University. President Johnson discussed the matter with him and Assistant Secretary of State for Near Eastern and South Asian Affairs Phillips Talbot. Badeau's replacement was Lucius D. Battle, the assistant secretary of state for educational and cultural affairs.[33] While they were in the Oval Office, Johnson was finally able to get through to the director of the FBI.

1:09 P.M.

To J. Edgar Hoover[34]

President Johnson: Edgar? Anything new on Mississippi?

J. Edgar Hoover: No, nothing new. We, of course, are expanding the search down there, extending it. I've got about 110 additional men in there now.

[*with the President acknowledging*] And they made those arrests that I spoke to you about before you left Washington and arraigned them before the commissioner, and they were released on bond. That case will be tried in due time.[35]

---

32. Cecil Stoughton was a White House photographer. His best-known photograph is of President Johnson's swearing-in aboard Air Force One after John Kennedy's assassination. See serial number: 1A-1-WH63, Photo Image Archives, Lyndon B. Johnson Library.

33. "Memorandum of Conversation," 29 June 1964, 12:45 P.M., U.S. Department of State, *Foreign Relations of the United States (FRUS), 1964–1968: Arab-Israeli Dispute, 1964–1967*, ed. Harriet Dashiell Schwar (Washington, DC: GPO, 2000), 18:176–78.; "The President's News Conference of July 10, 1964," *Public Papers, Johnson, 1963–64*, 2:851–58.

34. Tape WH6406.18, Citation #3941, Recordings of Telephone Conversations—White House Series, Recordings and Transcripts of Conversations and Meetings, Lyndon B. Johnson Library.

35. See the conversation between President Johnson, Allen Dulles, and J. Edgar Hoover, 1:17 P.M., 26 June 1964, in this volume.

President Johnson: How are you expanding your search? You mean away from the lake?

Hoover: [*with the President acknowledging*] Oh, yes, away from the lake and we've dragged the river. There's a river in the area—that was being dragged yesterday and today—and we are gradually going farther and farther away from the place where the burned car was located. And then I've also issued today a circular with the photographs of the three men that we're looking for, and we're distributing that in Mississippi and the adjacent states. The adults are [*unclear, Johnson coughs*][36] for those [to] be placed in post offices and local police departments and so forth.

President Johnson: Mm-hmm. But nothing new? They're just going ahead, same stuff?

Hoover: Same stuff, yeah.

President Johnson: OK. Thank you.

Hoover: Fine.

President Johnson: Bye.

    1:10 P.M.–1:11 P.M.: Immediately after the Hoover conversation, the President place unrecorded calls on the personal line to Walter Jenkins and George Reedy.

    1:20 P.M.: Met with South Carolina Senator Olin Johnston and Johnston's wife on the White House porch to take photographs with Mrs. America, Desree Jenkins, a 34-year-old woman described by the Universal Press International as a "curvaceous belle from Columbia, South Carolina, who can cook a luscious pound cake."[37] Jenkins and her two children, Teresa Ann and Barry Lee, gave Johnson a beach towel with his famous monogram. Johnson then returned to the office to call his press secretary.

    1:50 P.M.: Headed off for a short lunch with Jack Valenti.

    2:20 P.M.: Back in the Oval Office, the President sought advice on an opening on the Securities and Exchange Commission.

---

36. Hoover may have said "calling," or possibly "crying."

37. *Washington Post*, 14 April 1964.

2:25 P.M.

To Ralph Dungan[38]

After being on hold for approximately one minute, President Johnson connected with one of his White House aides who handled federal appointments issues.

Ralph Dungan: Yes, sir.

President Johnson: Ralph.

Dungan: Yes, sir, Mr. President.

President Johnson: Walter [Jenkins] talked to me over the weekend while I was away in Denver . . . I mean in Minneapolis or Detroit . . .

Dungan: Yes, sir.

President Johnson: . . . about some fellow that'd been recommended that was dean of Southern California for the Securities [and] Exchange Commission.[39] Would you talk to him about it and look at him and compare the two?

Dungan: Right, sir. He's sitting right here, and we'll talk about it.

President Johnson: I would doubt that he's a Republican, but he may be. Anyway, you-all look at him very carefully, and then I'll talk to you today, later today or tomorrow.

Dungan: Will do. . . . Did you get that note that I sent down from Don Cook on [Francis] Wheat?[40]

President Johnson: No.

Dungan: Don Cook wrote a letter in—I sent it down there this morning—saying that he had heard that Wheat was in the contention and he was very high on him. But in any event, I'll talk to Walter right now and we'll check this other fellow.

President Johnson: Mm-hmm. . . . Mm-hmm. Now, we'll have [Hamer] Budge and our man from Oklahoma, what's his name?[41]

---

38. Tape WH6406.18, Citation #3943, Recordings of Telephone Conversations—White House Series, Recordings and Transcripts of Conversations and Meetings, Lyndon B. Johnson Library.

39. Robert R. Dockson was dean of the Graduate School of Business Administration at the University of Southern California.

40. Donald Cook was president of the American Electric Power Company and a close friend of Johnson's. Francis Wheat was an attorney from Los Angeles who would be appointed to the Securities and Exchange Commission (SEC) in July.

41. Johnson appointed Hugh F. Owens of Oklahoma to the SEC in February 1964. Over the past week, House Minority Leader Charles Halleck had successfully pressed Johnson to appoint Hamer Budge, the conservative former Republican congressman from Idaho, to replace the outgoing Republican commissioner Jack Whitney.

Dungan: Right. Owens, Hugh Owens.

President Johnson: Owens. And this will be three. How many, five [*unclear*]?

Dungan: Five, sir. Five, right.

President Johnson: Mm-hmm.

Dungan: But you've got—

President Johnson: That leaves [Manuel] Cohen and who else?

Dungan: Cohen and a guy by the name of [Byron] Woodside.[42]

President Johnson: Is Woodside a Democrat?

Dungan: He's in the middle. He's an old career fellow. He came up from the staff, kind of a neuter . . .

President Johnson: Well, he must be a Democrat because . . .

Dungan: Well, you got Owens—

President Johnson: You got Budge. You got Budge, a Republican, and this Wheat will be a Republican, so that'd be two out of five.

Dungan: Right, but you've also got Cohen.

President Johnson: Well, Cohen's a Democrat.

Dungan: Cohen's a Democrat, right.

President Johnson: And Woodside's a Democrat—

Dungan: Cohen, Wheat, and Owens.

President Johnson: No, Wheat's a Republican.

Dungan: No, sir, he's a Democrat.

President Johnson: Wheat is going to be our Democrat?

Dungan: Yes, sir.

President Johnson: Well, I thought this was another Republican.

Dungan: No, sir. This is a Democratic vacancy. You've got Woodside and Hamer Budge that are the Republicans.

President Johnson: Well, that changes it, then. I thought that this was another Republican vacancy.

Dungan: No, sir, this is a Democratic vacancy.

President Johnson: Mm-hmm. OK, then this fellow from Southern California doesn't have to be a Republican; he can be a Democrat.

Dungan: Correct, sir.

---

42. Manuel F. Cohen was a 22-year employee of the SEC who had been confirmed as a commissioner by the Senate in May 1964. In July 1964, Cohen became chair of the SEC, replacing William Cary, a Democratic appointee. Byron Woodside, a career official who had been with the SEC since its creation in 1934, had served as commissioner since 1960. Coincidentally, Woodside was elevated to the commission from his position as director of the SEC's Division of Corporation Finance. His replacement in that position was Cohen. "New S.E.C. Member Had Start in Field Before Agency Existed," *New York Times*, 18 July 1960; "S.E.C. Fills High Post," *New York Times*, 19 July 1960.

President Johnson: And Wheat is a Democrat.

Dungan: Yes, sir.

President Johnson: Well, why—we were wanting to get the Republicans' endorsement, just because he's a Republican senator; that's the reason why.

Dungan: That's right. Right. And that's going to be on its way very shortly: three prominent Democrats—the county chairman and the state chairmen—have all wired [Thomas] Kuchel, and I expect to have that in a day or so.[43]

President Johnson: Thank you.

Dungan: Yes, sir.

2:35 P.M.

To Hubert Humphrey; President Johnson joined by Jack Valenti[44]

President Johnson's speech in Minneapolis the day before was the lead story in most of the morning newspapers, picking up on the President's line that nations that wanted to remain free "must be prepared to risk war."

President Johnson is on hold for approximately one minute before the operator announces Senator Humphrey.

President Johnson: Hubert?

Hubert Humphrey: Hello, Mr. President.

President Johnson: Well, we had a wonderful day, and I just want to thank you for it.

Humphrey: Oh, listen, they just loved it. You ought to see the follow-up stories in the morning press out there. They were—

President Johnson: I hope they didn't play that war like this paper here did.[45]

Humphrey: No, they didn't.

---

43. Republican Thomas Kuchel, an alumnus of the University of Southern California, had been serving as a senator from California since 1953.

44. Tape WH6406.18, Citation #3945, Recordings of Telephone Conversations—White House Series, Recordings and Transcripts of Conversations and Meetings, Lyndon B. Johnson Library.

45. The lead headline in this morning's *Washington Post* read, "President Blunt on Risks of War in Viet-Nam."

President Johnson: It was a peace speech, and I said sometimes we have to risk war to get peace—

Humphrey: Yeah.

President Johnson: —but as long as I'm in office, my job is going to be a quest for peace, and damn if they didn't take the sentence right out of the paragraph.

Humphrey: Oh, I know it, they took it. [*The President chuckles.*] But they ran the full text out there, and they had a wonderful, wonderful story.

President Johnson: That's good.

Humphrey: In all the papers. And the St. Paul paper had you speaking to a 150,000; the Minneapolis just a 100,000.

President Johnson: Mm-hmm! Well, somebody here cut it down to 50[000].[46]

Humphrey: Oh, that damn outfit here, they don't know anything about it.

President Johnson: The *Chicago Tribune* cut it to 50[000].[47]

Humphrey: Yeah. . . . Yeah, well, you can expect that. [*Johnson laughs.*] But everybody was—it was such good feelings, you know, everybody.

President Johnson: Oh, they were happy.

Humphrey: Yeah.

President Johnson: They were in better shape than I ever saw them, and I never saw a crowd as good.

Humphrey: Well, they loved you.

President Johnson: Thank you. I'll see you in the morning [at the legislative leaders' breakfast]. You-all get your list of things that we're going to get up, that list, and let's see which ones we can pass.

Humphrey: Yeah. . . . I talked to Sarge [Shriver]—

President Johnson: [*to Valenti*] I'll call you.

Humphrey: —today.

President Johnson: Wait a minute.

[*to Valenti*] Jack, wait a minute.

[*to Humphrey*] Go ahead.

---

46. Johnson's own people estimated the crowd at 85,000. Daily Diary, 28 June 1964, Lyndon B. Johnson Library.

47. This estimate came in the *Tribune's* front-page story on the Minneapolis speech. The banner headline was in large, all capital letters. Robert Young, "Will Risk War: Johnson," *Chicago Tribune*, 29 June 1964.

Humphrey: [*with the President acknowledging*] I say, I talked to Sarge Shriver today. And . . . about the poverty bill.[48] I'll tell you about—

President Johnson: We want to wait until the rule . . . get through on.

Humphrey: Yeah, they're a little concerned about that.

President Johnson: Here's Jack. He said he didn't think you had as many as you thought you were going to have.

Humphrey: [*chuckling*] Yeah. Listen . . .

Jack Valenti: [*laughing*] Now, Senator . . .

Humphrey: Valenti, [*they both laugh heartily*] you listen you, I just saw those nice [*unclear*] folks.[49]

Valenti: Oh, they're nice people, they really are. I appreciate it.

Humphrey: They've had a wonderful tour here of the Capitol. I had them down for lunch, and . . .

Valenti: That's wonderful.

Humphrey: They've really enjoyed it.

Valenti: Senator, I do want to tell you that one newspaper said 50,000. I do want to point that out.

Humphrey: That goddamn newspaper said—

Valenti: That's the *Chicago Tribune.*

Humphrey: They flunked the third grade in arithmetic.

Valenti: The *Chicago Tribune* gave you 50[000], and you know they were exaggerating a little bit, too.

Humphrey: Yeah, you know they were. [*Valenti laughs.*] You damn right. And you never went to a town where you had less gripes, boy, let me tell you.

Valenti: Oh, I'm happy. I'm a Minneapolis man myself.[50]

Humphrey: [*laughing*] Are you?

Valenti: I'm a Humphrey, Minneapolis man. [*Humphrey continues to laugh.*] Just a minute, sir.

President Johnson: OK.

Humphrey: All right, Mr. President.

President Johnson: Bye.

Humphrey: Thanks a million. Bye.

---

48. Shriver was heading up the federal task force in charge of planning the War on Poverty. The House version was slowed down in the House Rules Committee, but the Senate's Select Subcommittee on Poverty (of the Labor and Public Welfare Committee) had been holding hearings on the bill.

49. Humphrey may say "Wickman."

50. Valenti was speaking figuratively here. His hometown was Houston, Texas.

Before walking over to the Mansion, President Johnson stopped for a few minutes at the lounge off of the Oval Office, where he took a call from an aide on a religious matter.

2:45 P.M.

From Myer Feldman[51]

Almost two hours earlier, Johnson had decided not to add the American Jewish Committee to this day's schedule. Here, his special counsel updated him on the Second Vatican Council's attempt to change the Catholic Church's position condemning Jews for the death of Jesus.

President Johnson: Hello.

Myer Feldman: Mr. President.

President Johnson: Yeah.

Feldman: I met with the people—you called me earlier. Were you calling me about my meeting with those people [American Jewish Committee]?

President Johnson: Yeah, yeah. . . . Yeah, yeah.

Feldman: They came to suggest that the Ecumenical Council had reached an impasse in the proposal before them which called for a revision of the rights of the Catholic Church against the deicide.[52] I don't know how familiar you are with it, but Pope John had suggested that the rituals would be changed so that the charges against the Jews for deicide would be removed from it.[53]

Now, everybody in the Catholic Church in the United States apparently —and most of the Protestant churches and so on—all agree with this. In fact, if it came up for a vote before the Ecumenical Council, it would pass overwhelmingly; however, they have something that's like our Rules Committee which is called the Curia, which schedules things for votes before the Council. The Curia will not put it on the agenda for a vote and

51. Tape WH6406.19, Citation #3946, Recordings of Telephone Conversations—White House Series, Recordings and Transcripts of Conversations and Meetings, Lyndon B. Johnson Library.

52. This Ecumenical Council of the Catholic Church, the meeting of over 2,000 cardinals and bishops also known as Vatican II, was the first in over a century.

53. On 20 November 1964, the council approved language absolving Jews of blame, but the debate within the Church raged for another year. Pope Paul VI did not publicly announce his support until 28 October 1965. *New York Times*, 21 November 1964 and 29 October 1965.

have given the agenda to the Pope [Paul VI] now, and the Pope—he's much weaker than Pope John was—is inclined to go along with the Curia and not put it on the agenda.

I've talked to Mac Bundy about this. Dean Rusk has asked—Dean Rusk I've talked to about this too—Dean Rusk asked our ambassador to intercede with the Pope and suggest that it be put on the agenda. It has wide ramifications, because if it is not passed by the Ecumenical Council, it will amount to a reaffirmation of the deicide or be construed in that way. There'll be a good deal of hostility, certainly in the Jewish community. The Catholics don't like it. In fact, Speaker [John] McCormack is very incensed about it.[54] Cardinal Spellman and others are incensed about it and are anxious that it *be* put on the agenda and that there *be* a vote.[55]

And the suggestion is—and Mac Bundy agrees with this suggestion —that it seems that if the President of the United States would send a message to the Pope indicating his interest in it, it might be very useful. There are no disadvantages to this so long as it can get kept quiet, and Mac's suggestion is that we use John McCone for this purpose because he says the Pope has indicated he'd be glad to receive any message through McCone that you wanted to send to him.[56] I think you could either do that or use somebody like Andrew Courtier—who used to be the assistant to Dag Hammarskjöld at the United Nations—who is very familiar with this problem, and who's a prominent Protestant layman.[57]

President Johnson: Give me a little note on it, then, and let me talk to him about it, and I'll get right back to you with it, and we'll pick out somebody.

Feldman: Yes, sir.

President Johnson: OK. Did you satisfy them?

Feldman: What's that, sir?

President Johnson: Were they happy?

Feldman: Yes, they were. They . . . I told them I would give you the whole story and that I felt sure that you'd have some response by tomorrow.

President Johnson: All right. OK, you give me a little note on it.

Feldman: Yes, sir.

---

54. John McCormack represented a district in Massachusetts, a state with a strong Catholic constituency.
55. Francis Joseph Cardinal Spellman was the powerful archbishop of New York.
56. John McCone was director of the Central Intelligence Agency.
57. Dag Hammarskjöld was secretary-general of the United Nations from 1953 until his death (in a plane accident while on a peace mission in the Congo) in 1961.

2:53 P.M.: Johnson told his staff to "turn my lights off" and prepared to head to the Mansion for his afternoon rest. Shortly after, however, he caught up with an old friend and Democratic ally.

3:00 P.M.

To Richard Daley[58]

Richard Daley, Chicago's mayor since 1955, was arguably the most powerful mayor in the United States. Here, the President reviewed several situations with him, including the Wisconsin trip, the Mississippi Burning investigation, the situation in Vietnam, and the presidential campaign. Daley emphasized his faith in prosperity and in fighting unemployment.

President Johnson: Dick?

Richard Daley: Mr. President, how are you?

President Johnson: I'm just a little worn out. I've had a long trip. I came back, and I came over to read the paper and get a little nap, and I was just thinking of you and thought I'd give you a buzz.

Daley: Well, that's very nice, and I [unclear] following you with great interest. You really are having some terrific crowds and meetings, and that's the way it should be.

President Johnson: Well—

Daley: You're really giving them some issues to think about, and you're really carrying on the leadership of our party with great distinction and honor to all of us. We get prouder every day of what you're doing and what you're trying to do.

President Johnson: Well . . .

Daley: We love it and watch you with great interest, and we've seen the great reception you had up in Minneapolis. Also, you're enjoying it: that's the greatest part too. [*Laughs.*]

President Johnson: [*Unclear*] sure am.

Daley: [*laughing*] I [*unclear*] remark about the [*unclear*].

President Johnson: [*Chuckles.*] You going to be down here anytime soon?

---

58. Tape WH6406.19, Citation #3947, Recordings of Telephone Conversations—White House Series, Recordings and Transcripts of Conversations and Meetings, Lyndon B. Johnson Library.

Daley: I'm going to try—I'm trying to get down sometime after the holidays. Will I be able to see you all right?

President Johnson: Yeah . . . you'll be able to see me. Bring your wife, stay all night, and let's visit a little bit.

Daley: No. No, we know you're pretty busy.

President Johnson: No, no. No, no. You just come. Whenever you come, you come—If you can get away from Chicago some morning, why, come down in the afternoon and stay all night, and let me know a day or so ahead of time so I'll be sure I won't have something else, and I'd like to sit down. I need to talk to you. I need a . . . I need some advisers, and I don't think I've got a better one in America than you, and I just want to give you some of my thoughts and get some of yours.

Daley: Very nice.

President Johnson: This Mississippi thing is awful mean, and I'm—

Daley: Yes, it is.

President Johnson: —going to have to walk a tightwire there. I don't know what in the world is going to happen. Every day—I talked to [J. Edgar] Hoover about an hour ago, and it's . . . I don't have any authority to do anything but send the FBI, and I've got over a hundred in there now [*Daley acknowledges*], about 120, and the governor is cooperating. He's put 200 extra ones on, but all these folks going in and no telling what's going to blow up.

Daley: That's right. Pretty serious situation.

President Johnson: It really worries me.

Our war thing, South Vietnam, we think that we've got a couple of good men in charge out there [*Daley acknowledges*], and it's really good that [Henry Cabot] Lodge came back. Lodge is going to get in this [William] Scranton thing, and . . .

Daley: Looks that way.

President Johnson: And I don't mind. I don't believe they can stop [Barry] Goldwater. What do you think?

Daley: [*with the President acknowledging*] I think you're right. I don't think they can. I think he's done his groundwork too well. While all these fellows were sitting on the sidelines waiting for the moment to be called, I think he was out for the last couple of years making his contacts and getting the people that mean something. And up to date, I don't see any evidence of them budging very much here.

President Johnson: Mm-hmm. That's—

Daley: Out in the Middle West. I don't know what it is all over the country, but I imagine it's the same thing all over the country.

President Johnson: Will [Everett] Dirksen wind up going for him?[59]

Daley: [*with Johnson acknowledging*] I think he will. Sure. I think that's definite.

President Johnson: What are our problems in Chicago and Illinois?

Daley: Well, I think—

President Johnson: How are we going to—how are we going to get the—

Daley: [*with the President acknowledging*] —[the] greatest problem is employment. If we can get work for these people, all these other things are secondary. They might be doing a lot of shouting about it, but the more our prosperity continues, but . . . some of the prosperity, as you know, doesn't rub off on a certain segment of our population. We have to get more and more of it into them. And we've got to get rid of some of this persistent and hard—You've done a pretty good job on it in reducing the figures on unemployment, but I still think we have to get it below what it is now. And if we could get a couple of million people to work over the next couple of months, many of these other problems go out the window. We are—everyone is trying. I know you are, and business is trying, but maybe they can do a little more on this employment.

We're caught between this cross fire of automation and also modernization and cost and all of this. And in it, of course, the people that are least able to take care of themselves are the ones that you've been saying constantly are the people that are really affected and are really affected badly, because they're the ones that haven't got the qualifications, they haven't got the education, and therefore, they can't qualify for the job.

President Johnson: That's sure the truth—

Daley: We—my humble opinion—if we can only get . . . if you get a fellow a job, all this other agitation goes out the window because then he starts thinking about himself and his family and his pocketbook, and he's a pretty good citizen. But while you have just large numbers of unemployment in some of the large communities and the cities, you'll have a little of this problem.

One of the things we find, however, is they're not selling out here, the average person, and in their own neighborhoods and their own communities. They realize that in Chicago we have given opportunity after opportunity to many, many people, and they are not so much inclined. Although we also have this situation, where those people will not speak out. It's generally the agitator that continues to lead the force. And again,

---

59. Dirksen announced his support for Goldwater the next day, 30 June.

you have the complications, as you know it, of the overemphasis of the small news by the mediums of communication. Hell, this is one of the real problems that—

President Johnson: How in the hell do you survive with those papers you've got out there? I don't understand it.

Daley: We just fight them, and so forth. [*Laughs.*]

President Johnson: They're the meanest damn papers, meanest papers I ever saw.

Daley: [*chuckling*] Well . . . they're like yourself: You just have to be tough to fight them back, that's about all. [*Both laugh.*] But I do think you've been moving in great directions and in great shape. The business community out here, predominantly Republican, reflects favorable attitudes on everything you're doing and saying. Labor people are all happy. Professional people and academic people also express admiration and confidence in the way you're handling things.

President Johnson: What are they saying about our vice president? What are we going to do about that?

Daley: Well, everyone is waiting for you, and they're saying that, as we know, although he . . . in the past many of them never made the decision —they did, but it wasn't known—but everyone feels that the president generally selects or has some inclination to select the vice president, and it will be his decision ultimately as to who the vice president will be. There hasn't been too much conversation about, you know, too many people.

President Johnson: I want you to think about it a little bit, and you keep it that way, and then I want to talk to you before—after this Republican convention.[60]

Daley: Yeah.

President Johnson: You tell the missus that we want to pay her back for being so nice, and—

Daley: Well, you're always—

President Johnson: —you see if you can't get away one night and come down and see . . . and visit with me.

Daley: Fine, Mr. President. I'll call you.

President Johnson: After the 4th, you give me two or three days' notice—

Daley: We sure will.

President Johnson: —and see if there's somebody here you want to have in. Any of the departments you want to talk to about any of—

---

60. The Republican National Convention was to begin on 13 July in San Francisco.

Daley: Some of your poverty thing we're getting a lot of reaction on.

President Johnson: You come down here, and I'll have all of my people: I'll have Willard Wirtz and Sargent Shriver and some of them meet in with you, and let's get something going out your way.

Daley: Fine. Thanks, Mr. President.

President Johnson: All right. Bye, Dick.

Daley: Good to talk to you.

President Johnson: Bye.

Daley: Good luck to you and your health, you and Mrs. [Lady Bird] Johnson.

President Johnson: Bye. . . . You know how much I think of you, Dick.

Daley: OK, Mr. President.

President Johnson: Bye . . . bye.

3:15 P.M.: After the call with Daley, Johnson requested that his blood pressure be checked by the White House doctor. The numbers for the 55-year-old Texan with a history of heart problems came in at a healthy 126 over 76.

4:40 P.M.: Lee White had his conference with Rita Schwerner, the wife of missing COFO activist Mickey Schwerner.[61]

5:06 P.M.: White phoned Johnson at the Mansion (unrecorded), and the group prepared to head over to the Mansion's Green Room.

5:15 P.M.: The President attended Lady Bird's reception for the Heart, Cancer, and Stroke Commission.

5:25 P.M.: Lee White, New York Congressman Ogden Reid, and Rita Schwerner met President Johnson for a brief—and, according to Johnson, unpleasant—session.

5:30 P.M.: Johnson headed back to the Oval Office for a few minutes.

5:35 P.M.: Had pictures taken in the Fish Room with outgoing IRS Commissioner Mortimer Caplin and family.

5:38 P.M.–6:00 P.M.: Attended a NSC Executive Committee meeting in the Cabinet Room.

The United States had been conducting aerial reconnaissance flights over the Plaine Des Jarres in Laos in an effort to strengthen Prime Minister Souvanna Phouma's military for-

---

61. Lee White to President Johnson, 4:40 P.M., 29 June 1964, "HU 2/ST 24 1/1/64–7/1/64" folder, Box 26, White House Central Files: Human Rights 2/ST, Lyndon B. Johnson Library.

tunes. Since June 6, attacks on American planes had caused
serious concern in the White House and Pentagon.[62] Recently,
the North Vietnamese–linked Pathet Lao had stepped up hos-
tilities and threatened the town of Muong Soui. Johnson con-
vened a quick, off-the-record meeting of the National Security
Council's Executive Committee to explore a course of action.
The President decided to offer more military assistance, particularly in the availability of aircraft. Publicly, however, the
United States and four allies called for a cease-fire from the
Pathet Lao.[63]

6:00 P.M.: Strolled along the Colonnade with Defense Secretary
Robert McNamara, Treasury Secretary Douglas Dillon, and
White House Press Secretary George Reedy.

6:08 P.M.: Returned to the Oval Office eight minutes later with Dillon
and received a call from Reedy concerning an Associated Press
inquiry about the flurry of NSC arrivals and departures at the
White House.

6:10 P.M.

From George Reedy[64]

President Johnson: Yeah?

George Reedy: Mr. President, Karl Bauman of the AP [Associated
Press] saw [Dean] Rusk, [Robert] McNamara, and [John] McCone in
the White House and has sent in a note asking me if I can say why they're
here.

---

62. "Summary Record of the 533d Meeting of the National Security Council," 6 June 1964, U.S.
Department of State, *Foreign Relations of the United States (FRUS), 1964–1968: Laos*, ed. Edward
C. Keefer (Washington, DC: GPO, 1998), 28:141–42; John McCone, "Memorandum for the
Record," 6 June 1964, ibid., 28:142–44.

63. The instructions on the military buildup went out to the U.S. embassy in a little under two
hours after this meeting. The McCone memorandum also contained material on the reported
successes of the United States' OPLAN 34A, a project involving support for raids and sabotage
against North Vietnam that Johnson had approved on 16 January 1964. The operations plan
played a key role in the Gulf of Tonkin Incident in August 1964. John McCone, "Memorandum
for the Record," 29 June 1964, ibid., 28:218–19; Dean Rusk, "Telegram from the Department
of State to the Embassy in Laos," ibid., 28:219–20; "Laos Cease-Fire and Withdrawal Urged by
Envoys," *New York Times*, 30 June 1964.

64. Tape WH6406.19, Citation #3948, Recordings of Telephone Conversations—White House
Series, Recordings and Transcripts of Conversations and Meetings, Lyndon B. Johnson Library.

President Johnson: Just . . . I'd just say that people come in all day long. They're in and out of here all day long.

Reedy: You think I should say they're here to bring you up to date on . . .

President Johnson: No, no, I'd just say—

Reedy: Since you've been away over the weekend.

President Johnson: No, I'd just say that they're in and out all day long with [McGeorge] Bundy and with the rest of them. We've got a Situation Room here, and that's what they're working.[65]

Reedy: Right. OK, sir. You bet.

President Johnson: Bye.

6:22 P.M.–6:33 P.M.: The President met with Commerce Secretary Luther Hodges.

6:45 P.M.

Office Conversation with Lady Bird Johnson[66]

While the President was on hold for a call to be placed to an unidentified person, he engaged in an office conversation with the First Lady about the Johnson family business. This conversation had been closed under deed of gift restriction until it was opened in October 2003.

Immediately after this exchange with the First Lady, Johnson reached J. Edgar Hoover by phone.

Lady Bird Johnson: Hello, darling.

President Johnson: Hello, sweetheart. How are you?

Lady Bird Johnson: I'm fine. [*Unclear.*]

President Johnson: Come here. You're just in time.

Lady Bird Johnson: To look at what?

President Johnson: Sign your name right there to this $25,000 [*unclear*].

---

65. The White House Situation Room was in the lower levels of the West Wing and was generally the province of the National Security Council.

66. Tape WH6406.19, Citation #3950, Recordings of Telephone Conversations—White House Series, Recordings and Transcripts of Conversations and Meetings, Lyndon B. Johnson Library.

Lady Bird Johnson: What am I sign—What are we buying, darling?

President Johnson: Nothing. I'm just renewing on a note we're offering [*unclear*]. I'm going to pay for all of it.

Lady Bird Johnson: Hmm. [*Unclear statement.*]

President Johnson: I don't see yours. You've got one for 5,000 [dollars].

Lady Bird Johnson: Well, mine is on my desk, waiting for me to sign. Am I sign—am I borrowing at a loan, or is it something [*unclear*] . . .

President Johnson: No, it's just 5,000 separate so you [*unclear*].

The operator breaks in and the recording ends abruptly.

6:47 P.M.

To J. Edgar Hoover[67]

Johnson reported on his 5:25 P.M. meeting with Rita Schwerner to the FBI director.

J. Edgar Hoover: Mr. President.

President Johnson: I saw this Mrs. [Rita] Schwertner [*sic*] this evening.

Hoover: Yes.

President Johnson: The wife of the missing boy.

Hoover: Yes. She's a Communist, you know.

President Johnson: No, but she acted worse than that.

Hoover: Is that so?

President Johnson: Yeah. She was awfully mean, and very ugly, and . . .

Hoover: Well, she and her husband both have been active members of the Communist Party in New York for some years.

President Johnson: Is that true? Is that so?

Hoover: Oh, yes.

President Johnson: Well, I'll be damned. I didn't know that.

Hoover: I sent a report over to you . . . uh . . . yesterday.[68]

---

67. Tape WH6406.19, Citation #3951, Recordings of Telephone Conversations—White House Series, Recordings and Transcripts of Conversations and Meetings, Lyndon B. Johnson Library.

68. The 21-second section from "She's a Communist" to "yesterday" was excised under deed of gift restriction until it was opened in October 2003. Hoover routinely made such accusations about civil rights activists.

President Johnson: Well, she came in this afternoon and saw Lee White, and he brought her down to see me.

Hoover: Yeah.

President Johnson: She wants thousands of extra people put down there and said I'm the only one that has the authority to do it. [*An unidentified voice says "hello" over the line.*] I told her I put all that we could efficiently handle, and I was going to let you determine how many we could efficiently handle.

Now, I talked to [Robert] McNamara this afternoon. He said he's got plenty of airmen and plenty Army people in Mississippi, without moving them in, and plenty of Navy people.

Hoover: That's right.

President Johnson: So, if you don't mind, you figure out what we can do because if we don't, they're going to m—They're going to want us to go in with big troops and stuff like that.

Hoover: That's right.

President Johnson: And I'd utilize as many as I could and add a few each day until we give up hope.

Hoover: I'll do that.

President Johnson: Talk to McNamara yourself. He says that if you'll let him know how many you can use.

Hoover: OK.

President Johnson: And it wouldn't be a bad thing to put another hundred on somewhere to search other places, wherever they think they can do it, so we show the country that we *are* really working at it and being very diligent, and we stay just ahead of the hounds [*unclear comment by Hoover*] because if they don't, this crowd is going to demand everything in the world.

Hoover: Now, the . . . there's one possibility that we haven't used: We can call upon the governor down there to put in the National Guard, if you have that . . . if you think that's all right. He's offered that to us several times.

President Johnson: I don't see any harm in it. They might say that it wasn't worth a damn, but I—

Hoover: [*with the President acknowledging throughout*] Well, at least it shows that the people of Mississippi are—and the National Guard are of course natives of there—that they are actually doing it.

Now, what I'm also planning to do, which I'll have effective within the next day or two, I'm opening a main office of the Bureau at Jackson. There are 52 offices in the service; I'm increasing it to 53 [*Johnson coughs loudly*] and putting in a full-time office at Jackson, Mississippi, with an [Special] Agent in Charge and a full staff as we would have it at New York or San Francisco and those places.[69] But that won't be able to be effective before probably three or four days.

President Johnson: Yeah, that's all right. Well, now, what I would do, I'd follow your judgment: If you think it's good to tell the governor that you want some of the National Guard, fine, but I'd sure ask McNamara for some more people in the next day or two and announce them in about two different groups. I'd announce that we're going to have a hundred from the Air Force and maybe another 50 or 75 from the Navy or something, so whatever your men can profitably employ.

Hoover: Well, you see, they've got down there 1,200 naval personnel.

President Johnson: Good.

Hoover: We've got 200. I can immediately order another 200 in, wait a couple of days, and order another 200 in.

President Johnson: That's what I'd do; that's what I'd do. I'd have them patrolling every damn thing in that country and that'd at least keep these kids scared.

Hoover: Yeah. [*Johnson coughs loudly.*] This woman is no good at all.

President Johnson: Yeah.

Hoover: And her husband's the same way, and her lawyer's the same way.

President Johnson: Mm-hmm.

Hoover: They've been tied in with Communist activities for years.

President Johnson: Is she actually a member?

Hoover: Oh, yeah. She's an actual member—[70]

The recording cuts off immediately.

---

69. To much fanfare, Hoover opened the Jackson field office on 10 July.
70. The 16-second section from "This woman is no good" to "an actual member" was excised under deed of gift restriction until it was opened in October 2003.

6:55 P.M.

To Lee White; preceded by Office Conversation
with Jack Valenti and Lady Bird Johnson[71]

Jack Valenti: I thought you might like to read this telegram and then tell me . . .

A 30-second pause ensues, as the President apparently reads. Midway through, Johnson blows his nose noticeably.

President Johnson: Yeah, I'll have to see him.

Valenti: Mr. President, [*unclear*]—

White House Operator: I'll have him in just a moment.

President Johnson: Yes?

White House Operator: I'll have him in just a moment.

Valenti: But I suspect that he will, as soon as he gets back to Los Angeles, he will make . . . have a press conference. Tell them he saw the President and everything else, as long as we understand that. Here is the schedule for [*unclear.*]

[*to Lady Bird*] Are you going over to this [Walter] Jenkins thing, Mrs. Johnson?[72]

Lady Bird Johnson: Uh . . . I think I am. I'm waiting to see if maybe Lyndon might go with me. [*A 13-second pause follows.*]

Valenti: [*to the President*] They want to talk about the inter—[*the tape is garbled*] memorandum on it. [*Pause.*]

President Johnson: Who was it that was so interested in [*unclear*] the other day? I want to know whether [*unclear*] Pat Brown, if he [*unclear*].[73] [*Pause.*] [*Unclear.*]

Valenti: That's all. I [*unclear*].

All right, if you're going over to that [*unclear*] tonight, we'll ride with you. Otherwise, I'll [*unclear*]—

President Johnson: All right. I think I'll change. [*Unclear*] be signing stuff, I'll go ahead and change shirts [*unclear*]. [*Unclear*] ride with me [*unclear*].

Valenti: I just thought you might . . . [*Unclear*]—

President Johnson: What is this?

---

71. Tape WH6406.19, Citation #3953, Recordings of Telephone Conversations—White House Series, Recordings and Transcripts of Conversations and Meetings, Lyndon B. Johnson Library.
72. Johnson's congressman, Jake Pickle, was hosting a reception for Walter Jenkins and his wife, Marjorie. The President and Lady Bird arrived at 7:34 P.M.
73. Edmund G. "Pat" Brown, a Democrat, was the governor of California.

Valenti: [*Unclear.*] An old friend of mine at the Ford Motor Company took these pictures of you. I think this was at the . . . Irvine. [*Pause.*]

An unclear section follows.

President Johnson: Ford Motors?

Valenti: This [*unclear*][74] who is with Ford Motors had his own photographer out there. He's the general manager of Ford up in [*unclear*]. He [*unclear*] I thought you might send Pat [*unclear*][75]—

While the operator tries to get the President's attention to announce that White is on the line, Mrs. Johnson tells her husband that she would wait for him while he changed shirts. The President then takes the call.

Lee White: Hello?

President Johnson: Lee?

White: Yes, Mr. President.

President Johnson: [*with White acknowledging*] I've talked to Edgar Hoover and Secretary [Robert] McNamara. I had McNamara over here this afternoon, and he said he would make available whatever people they could profitably use.

White: Good.

President Johnson: Hoover said he might ask for another 100, maybe for even 200, that he'll look into it, that he's opening an office in Jackson, Mississippi.

White: I see.

President Johnson: And that he's going to thoroughly and methodically and diligently follow through until they locate what's happened to these boys. That they think they know better how to do it than some little scrubby woman that's a Communist. [*White laughs heartily.*] And he said she is a member of the Communist Party and her husband is too.

White: Really? I declare.

President Johnson: So I think you ought to call Reid and tell him.

White: I will.

President Johnson: I immediately checked on . . . uh . . . and we oughn't to bring those Communists in to see me. I expect I better not see them if they're Communists.

White: No, I agree. This . . . That's a little—

President Johnson: We'd better check these people before they come in. Ask the FBI. He said he notified us yesterday.

White: Is that right?

---

74. Valenti may have said "Fred Klein."
75. Valenti may have said "Brown."

President Johnson: I guess Walter Jenkins got it and didn't tell me. In any event, you call Reid and locate him at home, wherever he is.

White: All right.

President Johnson: Tell him, number one, I talked to Hoover, and Hoover said he was opening his office, and he was going to use as many as he possibly could. That you have a feeling that he'll probably use an extra hundred to two hundred right away. And I've already had McNamara over here, and McNamara's checking to see that they be made available.

White: Right.

President Johnson: We don't want any announcement on that before it's done, but that [I] want him to know it.

White: All right.

President Johnson: Tell him, number two, this woman is a Communist, and it's very bad for him to be bringing Communists in to see the President. And just tell him he'd better be careful about it, and you just wanted to know. That's what the FBI tells us.

White: All right. All right, I will indeed. I think from what Congressman Reid reported before, she's about to have a press conference herself, or had one. And Reid himself issued a statement saying that you were doing all that you could and that he was totally impressed. He's been very good in this whole thing, by the way, except for this one. And then I could . . . Maybe he was under such pressure he couldn't resist.

And I'm sorry we didn't have that information before, although it may be just as well. Then we'd to had to . . . had to admit that they're deeply involved in this whole program.

Ah, boy. I'll tell you. She . . . she was *terrible*. Although . . .

President Johnson: Tell him that. And tell him, "Of course, Congressman, I know you wouldn't want the congr—the President to be seeing the Communists, because he'd be criticized pretty severely for that." [*Johnson coughs noticeably again.*]

White: Yeah.

President Johnson: Say, "He saw them because you wanted him to. [*White attempts to interject.*] Before we see any more of them, you better check them very carefully." And tell him to be sure not to announce it ahead of time because it just makes us run crazy. All of them go to running into the [National] Security Council this afternoon, wanting to know if I saw Mrs. Schwertner [*sic*].[76]

---

76. At 5:38 P.M., Johnson held a meeting of the NSC Executive Committee, which was approximately ten minutes after meeting with Rita Schwerner and Ogden Reid.

White: Yeah . . . we got one break: We can always say that this was at his request, because it was.

President Johnson: Yeah, yeah.

White: And he was there too. So that . . . you know, if it becomes that kind of an issue—

President Johnson: Tell them if they request me—I'm not going to say anything, but if they do—I'm going to say that I saw her at his request.

White: OK.

President Johnson: Tell him that so he'll know, and . . .

White: Oh, well, it's as clear as a bell. Not only does his office call, but he asked me personally, in her presence, if it could be arranged. So, I mean there's no doubt about it. He is in it . . .

President Johnson: Well, just tell him that that . . . if . . . that, and get him straightened out and let him know who he is dealing with.

White: I sure will, right now.[77]

7:17 P.M.: The President left for the Mansion with Lady Bird. A few minutes after arriving, he took a call from Secretary Robert McNamara and made a call to Lee White (both unrecorded). He and Lady Bird then rode to a Women's National Democratic Club event in honor of Walter Jenkins and his wife, Marjorie.

7:55 P.M.–8:53 P.M.: The Johnsons traveled to McGeorge Bundy's home and attended a dinner in honor of new AEC Commissioner Mary Bunting.

9:10 P.M.: They returned to the White House for dinner with Texas friends and economic writer Barbara Ward (also known as Lady Jackson).

10:02 P.M.: The President's last order of business before getting a massage and going to sleep was an unrecorded call from legislative liaison Larry O'Brien.

11:20 P.M.: President Johnson retired for the night.

---

77. The 3-minute-and-22-second section from "that they think they know better" to "right now" was excised in accordance with the agency that originated the information and under deed of gift restriction until opened in October 2003.

Tuesday, June 30, 1964

Well, you got a bad break, but it'll . . . My mother used to tell me that things like that develop character. It'll make you stronger when you get older.

—President Johnson to Edward Kennedy

Considering the past week's intense travel schedule and the civil rights episodes in Mississippi and Florida, this busy Tuesday at the White House was almost routine. Demanding most of the President's attention was the official state visit of Costa Rican President Francisco José Orlich. Between the 19-gun salutatory greeting in the morning and the lavish State Dinner in the evening, however, Johnson did spend considerable time on domestic issues. In particular, he gathered tallies on expected votes for the House foreign aid bill, fielded advice on investigating the low prices that ranchers were getting for their animals, and weighed in on the tricky international trade issue of wool textile imports. On civil rights matters, Philadelphia, Mississippi, and St. Augustine, Florida, were filtering out of the national spotlight, falling off the front page of the major daily newspapers and taking up less time in Johnson's schedule. Attention was shifting to the expected Civil Rights Act and the implementation challenges it would present. That legislation moved closer to adoption on this day as the House Rules Committee agreed to send the Senate version of the bill to the floor for a vote. On June 22, Rules Committee Chair Howard "Judge" Smith had set the committee's vote for June 30, the latest date allowed by House rules. Once out of that body, it would go to the full House. In a related matter, the food stamp bill—another prominent initiative that had begun under the Kennedy administration—was passed by the Senate. It, however, would languish in the House until August.[1]

In Republican Party news today, Illinois delegates were deciding whether to back Arizona Senator Barry Goldwater or Pennsylvania Governor William Scranton for the presidential nomination. Hoping to improve Scranton's standing, Henry Cabot Lodge was openly courting support from former President Dwight Eisenhower.

> **7:00 A.M.:** An early morning for the President began with tea, cereal, and calisthenics, followed by a checkup for a nagging cold and cough by Dr. George Burkley. Before his regular Tuesday legislative leaders breakfast, he chatted with Jack Valenti and Barbara Ward, his guest from the night before.
>
> **8:50 A.M.:** Before leaving the Mansion, the President made an unrecorded call to Arkansas Senator J. William Fulbright, the chair of the Senate Foreign Relations Committee.
>
> **8:55 A.M.:** Began his breakfast with the Democratic leadership and his top White House aides.
>
> **9:40 A.M.:** The group moved to the Oval Office. The first recorded call of the day came thirty minutes later.

10:10 A.M.

To George Mahon; preceded by Office Conversation with Walter Jenkins[2]

Mahon, Johnson's longtime acquaintance from Texas, was chair of the House Appropriations Committee and had been vital to the administration during the recent foreign aid appropriations battle with Otto Passman. Before Mahon came on the line, Walter Jenkins reported on the support in the Texas Democratic congressional delegation for the July 1 foreign aid vote in the House.

---

1. For Johnson's reaction to the setback leading to this delay, see the conversation between President Johnson and George Smathers, 4:59 P.M., 1 July 1964, in this volume.
2. Tape WH6406.19, Citation #3956, Recordings of Telephone Conversations—White House Series, Recordings and Transcripts of Conversations and Meetings, Lyndon B. Johnson Library.

President Johnson: . . . after your reception?[3]

Walter Jenkins: Well, both before and after. I called him—the last call I made before I went to the reception then during the . . . after the line broke up, I went back and talked to him awhile.

President Johnson: He was there?

Jenkins: Yes, sir.

President Johnson: I never could get past the door; they just mobbed me.

Jenkins: Yeah, they had too many people. It was too big a party, but it was nice of them to do it. [*Pauses.*]

He thinks he's in good shape, but he's not sure. He thinks he's in good shape with the Texans, but he's not sure. I talked to all of them I could get yesterday. I changed one, [Joe] Pool, who . . . last time they had a vote, we had 16 and lost 5: Pool was one of the five.[4] So we polled the 16, which I think we can, all of them but [Jake] Pickle, and I guess we can him too.

Twenty-eight seconds excised under deed of gift restriction.

President Johnson: George?

George Mahon: [*to someone in room*] The President's on the other line.

[*on phone*] Yes, Mr. President.

President Johnson: How you getting along?

Mahon: Oh, I'm just . . . I just called Dean Rusk to ask him to send a good speechwriter to my office to help me work on a speech that I think would have some very good ideas. I want a little documentation and help on it.

I think we're going to do fine on this [foreign aid] bill. I think we'll beat down amendments and defeat the motion to recommit, whatever it is. They've gotten off their sights with respect to the additional 300 million dollar cut, making a total of 500 million [dollars]. I think they're down now to about an additional 175 million. This is what I hear. I want to . . . well, of course I want Mr. [J. Vaughan] Gary to be out in front.[5] I don't want to get Mr. [Otto] Passman to be a martyr and thereby help him in that respect.

---

3. Texas Congressman Jake Pickle, the representative for the district encompassing the LBJ Ranch, had hosted a party for Walter Jenkins and Jenkins's wife, Marjorie.

4. The next day, eleven Texas Democrats voted for the foreign aid bill, nine opposed it, and one was paired against it. Pool ended up voting no, while Pickle supported Johnson. *Congressional Quarterly Almanac*, 88th Cong., 2nd sess., 1964, vol. 20 (Washington, DC: Congressional Quarterly Service, 1965), p. 637.

5. J. Vaughan Gary was a Democratic representative from Virginia.

I want to only say what is necessary to say, and nothing maybe in general debate, but I want to have a little trial on the issue of whether or not we should have foreign aid, and I want to call to the stand Mr. [Nikita] Khrushchev. "Mr. Khrushchev, do you think we should have it?" And he'd say, "No, this is ridiculous; interfering with other countries." "Well, Mr. Khrushchev, if you're so strong on foreign aid to the United States, why did you build the Aswan Dam?[6] Don't you know that the people in Egypt don't love you too much, and so forth? And why have you helped India, because isn't it true that Mr. [Jawaharlal] Nehru used to throw Communists in jail? Why, then, are you against foreign aid for the United States, which you have used it yourself?" You see what I'm . . . I'm trying to work up a novel idea here. I don't know whether it would work or not.

Anyway, we're doing our best. What can I do?

President Johnson: Nothing. I think that's all right. I—just fine. You better talk to Jake Pickle, sound like he's getting off a little bit.

Mahon: Well, I'm going to talk to all of the boys that are sort of off the reservation—that is, in our delegation. I wrote a letter yesterday to all members who voted with us on the authorization.

President Johnson: Well, we lost five votes last time in Texas. I don't imagine you can get any help from them, but they oughtn't to vote against you and me too, particularly after you've really cut it 500 [million dollars] and I cut it a billion-four [$1.4 billion].

Mahon: That's right.

President Johnson: That's [Omar] Burleson and [John] Dowdy and [Ovie] Fisher . . .

Jenkins: [*in the office*] And Pool.

Mahon: Pool.

Jenkins: [*in the office*] One other.

Mahon: And Pool. Pool, I think, is going to go with us—somebody was telling me—on the motion to recommit.

President Johnson: I believe so, but you got Dowdy and Fisher and Burleson . . . and one more. I've forgotten who the other one [Robert Casey] is.

Mahon: Yeah. Well, I've got . . . I don't have the list before me, but I know what you're talking about.

President Johnson: You got any chance to get Dowdy or Burleson?

---

6. In the 1950s, the building of the Aswan High Dam on the Nile River was a key source of competition and conflict between the United States and the Soviet Union, with the Soviet Union eventually funding a major portion of its completion. The dam was finished in 1970.

Mahon: I think we might get Burleson, and I'm going to . . . I worked on Burleson a little, and he hasn't said, but I haven't worked on Dowdy at all.

President Johnson: What about Fisher?

Mahon: Oh, Fisher is impossible. Impossible, unless you had some real bait for him, which I do not have. I think he is. But anyway, we'll do our best. [Bob] Poage is trying to help us. [*Johnson coughs, so Mahon repeats.*] Poage's trying to help us. He's not going to vote for the bill, but he's going to try to help us.

President Johnson: Do you feel reasonably good about it?

Mahon: Yes, I do.

President Johnson: I sure hope you're right, because it'd be tragic if they whipped us both on that floor.

Mahon: Oh, this would be . . . this would be a real humiliation, real humiliation to get defeated at this stage.

President Johnson: Are you getting any Republicans at all?

Mahon: Yes, we're going to get about 10 or 15 Republicans.

President Johnson: What about [Robert] Casey?[7]

Mahon: Casey, I don't know. He's one that you should have included awhile ago.

President Johnson: Yeah. Better talk to Casey.

Mahon: Yes, I will talk to all of those boys.

President Johnson: OK.

Mahon: Well . . .

President Johnson: Congratulations.

Mahon: Good. Thank you, Mr. President.

TIME UNKNOWN

Between Horace Busby, Jack Valenti, and President Johnson[8]

Johnson and Valenti were in the Oval Office preparing for the ceremony to greet Costa Rican President Francisco José Orlich at 11:00 A.M. Here, Valenti called one of the President's longtime speechwriters to clarify the source of a quote in Johnson's toast to be given later this evening at dinner. Johnson spoke in the background.

---

7. Burleson, Dowdy, Fisher, Casey, and Poage all voted against the final aid bill.

8. Tape WH6406.19, Citation #3958, Recordings of Telephone Conversations—White House Series, Recordings and Transcripts of Conversations and Meetings, Lyndon B. Johnson Library.

Horace Busby: Hello?

Jack Valenti: Buzz, in your remarks for the Costa Rican arrival—

Busby: Mm-hmm.

Valenti: —you quote a great Central American on "et cetera, rags."[9] Who made the quotation?

Busby: This is from the State Department, and what I—it's Georgè, Georgé [or Jorgè, Jorgé] somebody, and I just eliminated the name, Jack.

Valenti: All right, we need to find out about it: Who is he, and then, in case . . . Any time the President quotes somebody, even if you don't put the man's name, he needs to know the source and who the guy is.

Busby: Well, I'll have to inquire at State because I was simply rewriting their material.

Valenti: All right.

Busby: In that instance.

Valenti: Would you call me right back?

Busby: Yeah.

Valenti: Is he anyone that you know?

Busby: No, but I don't know anybody in . . . I don't know Central American figures.

Valenti: Right. See if he's a poet or writer or statesman, a Marxist or . . .

President Johnson: Wait just a second, hold it.

Valenti: All right, just a second, Buzz.

President Johnson: He asked me to join in the toast. I thought this was a walk-in.

Busby: It is.

Valenti: It is.

Busby: Just reading the wrong one.

Valenti: [*to the President*] Just get the wrong one. I'll get you the other one.

[*on phone*] Hold on, Buzz.

Busby: Uh-huh.

Valenti: I'll be back in touch with you.

11:00 A.M.: After walking to the South Portico with Lady Bird and White House military aide General Chester V. Clifton, Johnson greeted Costa Rican President Francisco José Orlich and

---

9. The line Johnson delivered quoted was: "To have rights but live in rags is bitter living."

his wife and then presided over their military welcome. Both men delivered brief prepared remarks.

11:24 A.M.: Johnson and Orlich sat down by themselves in the Oval Office—in their "shirt-sleeves," as recorded by Johnson's secretaries.

11:30 A.M.: The two men proceeded to a more formal affair with their top aides in the Cabinet Room.

11:50 A.M.: President Johnson returned to the Oval Office. At noon, he caught up with the Secretary of Agriculture on some foreign and domestic issues.

12:00 P.M.

To Orville Freeman[10]

Better known as the Food for Peace program, PL 480 was part of the broader foreign aid framework. In 1964, the Johnson administration wanted Congress to extend its legislation (the Agricultural Trade Development and Assistance Act of 1954) for five years.[11] In this call to his Secretary of Agriculture, Johnson opened with a discussion of the House's consideration of the extension of the Food for Peace program and then turned to the National Commission on Food Marketing, a 15-person group appointed by the President. The House had approved a $1.5 million appropriation for the commission, and Johnson would sign it into law on July 3. In making appointments to the commission, the President had to balance the concerns of farmers who wanted higher prices for their raw products with those of retailers and consumers who worried about those higher prices.

Johnson was quite familiar with one of the major interest groups upset about the current market: ranchers and other cattle growers. In addition to Johnson's experience as a rancher himself, he had received extensive pressure over the past several months to curb meat imports. On February 17, Australia, New Zealand, and Ireland had agreed to a voluntary reduction, but those measures were not enough to stop the House from passingstiffer import quotas nine days later. In May, Johnson delivered news

---

10. Tape WH6406.19, Citations #3959 and #3960, Recordings of Telephone Conversations—White House Series, Recordings and Transcripts of Conversations and Meetings, Lyndon B. Johnson Library.

11. Congress did extend two sections, but only until 1966.

that New Zealand and Australia had agreed to a formula that dropped their exports to the United States by 22 percent (New Zealand) and 29 percent (Australia) of their 1963 level. This action did little to stop the Senate from taking up the House quota bill. Despite the administration's desire not to antagonize its GATT (General Agreement on Tariffs and Trade) partners at the Kennedy Round of trade negotiations, the Senate Finance Committee was considering the legislation. By an overwhelming vote on July 1, they reported out a bill limiting imports to an average of the imports from the previous five years.[12]

President Johnson was on the speakerphone.

Orville Freeman: These are the big things. We've got some other little ones we're working on, and . . .

President Johnson: Well, you don't have to do anything on sugar. You can just let it lay, can't you?

Freeman: That's what I'm trying to do, but they—[Bob] Poage doesn't want to bring out PL 480 [Food for Peace] until sugar is decided, and I've got to go up and put the arm on him once more.[13]

President Johnson: Why? Why is he wanting to do that?

Freeman: Because he thinks he'll have more pressure on sugar to make the administration do what he wants because he knows that PL 480 is important. Just that simple. He doesn't even make any bones about it. You want PL 480 and Food for Peace Program, why, you be nice boys where sugar is concerned, which . . .

President Johnson: Why is he so interested in sugar?

Freeman: Well, because the House Agriculture Committee likes to play State Department, and this is one place where they got every country in the world running up there—[Harold] Cooley has—wining, dining, and courting in order to allocate out what country gets what sugar quota. And they love every minute of it. And that's what it comes down to, and every lobbyist in town, courting them on the same basis. And he just runs a little court of royalty over there on this basis.

And, as you know, this time particularly, it's a real knotty . . . has

---

12. *Congressional Quarterly Almanac,* 1964, vol. 20, pp. 133–36; "Remarks to the Newspaper Farm Editors Association," 12 May 1964, *Public Papers of the Presidents of the United States, Lyndon B. Johnson, 1963–64* (Washington, DC: GPO, 1965), 1:686–89.
13. Chaired by Harold Cooley of North Carolina, the House Agriculture Committee was having to revise sugar import quotas. Poage was the ranking Democrat behind Cooley.

some additionally difficult overtones because of the quick switch world-wide from a critical position of short supply and high price a year ago to one now where our prices currently are higher than the world prices. We urged increased production from other countries *and* our own domestic producers to try and keep the price from going through the roof, and now it's completely turned around on us. Well, you know all this. And also it overlaps with the beef situation because the same bastards that are screaming at us in some of the beef areas are just waiting and already have started to scream on the beef thing.[14]

So I've urged them very, very strongly to go ahead and open hearings, and this is going to be a fight, and that we would come in at the appropriate time when we could do some good. And let's not be exposed early and have everyone jumping on us.

President Johnson: Have they had any hearings on 480?

Freeman: Yes, Poage has completed his hearings on 480. And now I'm working on [Allen] Ellender.[15] So far, Ellender has said he doesn't want to move on 480 until the House does. If I can't move Poage, I'll go back to Ellender and try and get him to move ahead so we can start hearings on the Senate and get them out of the way as quick as possible.

President Johnson: When does it expire, 48[0]?

Freeman: It expires . . . well, it expires . . . at the end of this calendar year. This one runs on a calendar-year basis.

President Johnson: Well, Poage won't let it expire, will he? He—

Freeman: I don't think so, no. I don't think so. But the one thing they're talking about on both sugar and on PL 480 that worries me just a bit is that they're talking about one-year extensions because it's an election year. [There's] some merit in this. On the other hand, next year, we'll get socked with all our commodity programs, plus PL 480, plus sugar, and they'll have a dollar figure dancing around on agriculture that will break the bank. And I'd rather get some of them out of the way this year. And PL 480, if we're going to operate with these countries and as a part of our foreign policy and advance planning, why, we need a five-year program, and at the very least a three-year program, so we can do it properly.

President Johnson: [Mike] Mansfield says that Gale McGee wants

---

14. Pressure from the beef lobbyists had complicated the administration's handling of a fight over meat imports from Australia and New Zealand. Johnson had recorded dozens of calls on the matter since December 1963.

15. Allen Ellender, the senior senator from Louisiana, chaired the Senate Committee on Agriculture and Forestry.

to be chairman of that study group.[16] I wouldn't think that'd be very good for a senator to be chairman, would you?

Freeman: No, sir, I wouldn't think it'd be very good: number one, for a senator to be chairman, and number two, because Gale identified himself very early in the game as being anti–chain store. And I think that the validity and the effectiveness and the usefulness of this study would be compromised if we had anyone as a chairman who would be considered on one side or another or as having strong preconceptions.[17] I say that with great respect for Gale McGee, who I like and who ran the [*unclear*] thing and who I think probably would do a pretty good job.[18] But I think on this basis that it would be bad. But he's running a hell of a campaign, and he's suggesting that if the chairman is not a member of Congress, why, it means that really this is going to be kind of a whitewash in the chain stores, and he's been a little bit nasty this way.

President Johnson: What . . . Who would be the outstanding man for this?

Freeman: Well, we've gone into this very, very carefully, as you instructed, and I think at this point we would recommend Marvin Jones as the chairman.[19] I've got a little reservation, Mr. President, in terms of his age—if he's got the real vigor and drive this would take—but checking with a number of people, why, he seems to have a hell of a lot of bounce, and he knows something about agriculture, although he hasn't been exposed to it for many, many years. If his mind is quick enough to pick it up, he's got a background, and, as you say, he's a fellow that would be for the folks and would tend to satisfy the producers.

I think we've got to have someone on there also that, if you'll pardon my language, has got a little cow shit on his shoes, and—but I think we ought to be careful that it's someone that is not too highly identified with any one or another side in this beef wrangle business between the chain

---

16. Gale McGee, a former history professor, was a Democratic senator from Wyoming. He had pressed the Senate and the Federal Trade Commission to investigate the role of chain grocery stores in keeping down prices paid to farmers, particularly cattle growers. In 1966, he endorsed a national boycott of the chain stores. "Chain Stores Blamed for Low Farm Prices," *Los Angeles Times*, 24 March 1964; "Supermarket Boycotts Backed by Sen. McGee," *Chicago Tribune*, 2 November 1966.

17. The National Association of Food Chains was one of the key lobbying groups on this issue.

18. Freeman may have said "humanity."

19. John Marvin Jones, a 78-year-old Democrat from Texas, had chaired the House Agriculture Committee during the 1930s and then went on to a long career as chief judge of the Court of Claims, a position from which he was retiring on 14 July. Johnson appointed him as chairman of the Food Marketing Commission.

stores and the producers either, because I envisage this study as having the status that the [*unclear*] one had years ago in giving us some of the information that we're going to have to have if we're going to make really sensible and thoughtful and accurate appraisals of what goes on so plans will be based upon sensible foundations that are publicly acceptable.[20] And, of course, that's going to require people who are just like Caesar's ghosts, especially on the President's appointees.

President Johnson: What about . . . who else, if you can't get Jones?

Freeman: Well, I think we can . . . from all we find out, that Jones is available.

President Johnson: Well, suppose we didn't want to name him? Who would be your second choice?

Freeman: If we weren't going to name Jones at this point, the second—

[*aside, to himself*] Where the hell is that sheet?

[*to the President*] We had a second one that's over there now. I should have it on the tip of my tongue. Oh yeah, here: Our second choice was Clark Kerr.[21]

President Johnson: Well, everybody wants him for everything.

Freeman: That's correct.

President Johnson: He's got—he's so damn busy, he can't do anything.

Freeman: But I have some reason to believe that possibly on this thing, for a number of reasons, that he would be interested.

President Johnson: Well, have you [had] anybody talk to him?

Freeman: Well, I've had this sounded out indirectly from people that are around him. I haven't talked to him directly, wouldn't want to, obviously, because . . . until you had an idea of whether you were serious.

President Johnson: How many do we name?

Freeman: We name five. And I think we should have two nominal Republicans among that group. [*Pauses.*] Now, in terms of a producer representative, I've made the recommendation of—I think I mentioned this before—of someone like former congressman Fred Marshall, who

---

20. Freeman may have said "humanity."

21. Chancellor of the University of California, Clark Kerr had been recommended to the President earlier in the month as a potential replacement for Henry Cabot Lodge as ambassador to Vietnam. See Johnson to Richard Russell, 12:26 P.M., 11 June 1964, in Guian A. McKee, ed., *The Presidential Recordings, Lyndon B. Johnson: Mississippi Burning and the Passage of the Civil Rights Act, June 1, 1964–July 4, 1964*, vol. 7, *June 1, 1964–June 22, 1964* (New York: Norton, 2011), pp. 227–41.

would command in the circles, who would tend . . . who might say, if when you had professional people on this, that they would be chain-store oriented, a guy like Fred Marshall would command real producer support and also real congressional support.[22] [*Pauses.*]

There's two women up before you on this too: one that Mrs. [Dorothy] Jacobson recommended from here, Mrs. Erma Angevine, who I know just casually; and also, Esther Peterson strongly recommended a Dorothy Brady.[23]

President Johnson: Dorothy who?

Freeman: Brady, who is an economist and statistician from the University of Pennsylvania and apparently a very, very competent woman with some consumer background. Both of these women would have a rather broad acceptance in consumer circles.

President Johnson: OK. Well, we'll get in it and get back to you and may want you to call Kerr and Marvin Jones, too.

Freeman: Whatever you say, Mr. President.

By the way, did Jack [Valenti] give you on the way back from Minneapolis the other night the little memoranda about this meeting which is going to be held late in July on international development directed towards strengthening our coordinated approach between the land-grant colleges, AID [Agency for International Development], and [Department of] Agriculture? We'll have about 300 people in here from the land-grant colleges that will be the cream of the crop. I asked Jack to ask you to look at a memo on that, if I dropped in at the banquet in a few words on this, could be a very strategic occasion to point out to the world, food and agricultural-technical assistance, and what we've done and need to do.

President Johnson: OK. All right, I'll check into it.

Freeman: Very good, sir. Thank you.

---

22. A farmer and former state-level agriculture bureaucrat, Fred Marshall served as a Democratic representative from Minnesota from 1949 to 1963. Johnson appointed him to the Food Marketing Commission.

23. Dorothy H. Jacobson was assistant secretary of agriculture for international affairs. Esther Peterson was Johnson's special assistant for consumer affairs and chair of the President's Committee on Consumer Interests. Earlier in the spring, she had pressed for the investigation of the chain store practices. Erma Angevine was a leading consumer advocate who became executive director of the Consumer Federation in 1968. See Orville Freeman to Johnson, 4:10 P.M., 10 March 1964, in David Shreve and Robert David Johnson, eds., *The Presidential Recordings, Lyndon B. Johnson: Toward the Great Society, February 1, 1964–May 31, 1964*, vol. 5, *March 9, 1964–April 13, 1964* (New York: Norton, 2007), pp. 102.

12:10 P.M.: President Johnson made an unrecorded call to Walter Jenkins on the personal line before his next call to the director of the Bureau of the Budget.

12:18 P.M.

To Kermit Gordon[24]

Since taking office, Johnson had been on a campaign to reduce wasteful expenditures and had even pressed his administration to turn out unneeded lights at the White House. Gordon gave him some new information in the fight.

Kermit Gordon: Hello?
President Johnson: Kermit?
Gordon: Mr. President.
President Johnson: There's a mean story going around written by the *Chicago Daily News* about those White House bills, and it said, "Is President Johnson getting careless with the light switches?" Said, "The monthly budget statement for May showed that 83,445 [dollars] was spent on Executive Mansion and grounds, $6,562 more than the same month a year ago. Other spending under the Executive Office of the President is also up: the Bureau of the Budget, the Council of Economic Advisers, even the White House office itself, all spent more. Total Executive Office expenditures for May '64: 2,454,376 [dollars]."
Gordon: Mm-hmm.
President Johnson: "Total for May '63 under President Kennedy: 1,969,720 [dollars]."
Gordon: Mm-hmm.
President Johnson: Now, I've given Walter Jenkins hell and told him to keep our personnel down. I don't know what else is running. He said there must be some improvements he doesn't know anything about. You know what this could be?
Gordon: Offhand, I don't, Mr. President, but I'd be happy to look into it and give you a report on it promptly. It can be . . . it can be . . . let's see

---

24. Tape WH6406.19, Citation #3961, Recordings of Telephone Conversations—White House Series, Recordings and Transcripts of Conversations and Meetings, Lyndon B. Johnson Library.

now, a higher level of salaries, of course. There's been a salary increase which could affect the Executive Office picture. I doubt if total employment in the Executive Office is significantly higher today than it was a year ago. It may, in fact, be a little bit lower.

President Johnson: Ought to be, if not, I'm going to just put in a 10 percent slash or something. I'm not going to have this. This is going to ruin my whole image if I have more than they do, so just find out what it is and let me know what we can do about it.

Gordon: I'll get into this right away, Mr. President. Thank you.

12:20 P.M.: President Johnson and Bill Moyers spent a little over ten minutes with John Bartlow Martin trying to "nail down" his commitment to the campaign.[25] The well-known journalist and biographer had close ties to Robert Kennedy and had served as ambassador to the Dominican Republic under John Kennedy.

12:33 P.M.: Johnson called George Reedy and then Moyers two minutes later on the personal line, both calls unrecorded.

12:45 P.M.–1:03 P.M.: Met briefly with Anthony Buford, a Kansas politico and old friend of Harry Truman. Shortly after Buford arrived, the President connected with one of his old friends from the cattle trade.

12:47 P.M.

To Jay Taylor[26]

Johnson checked with Taylor, the president of the Texas Livestock Marketing Association and an old acquaintance of President Johnson, on the appointment of another Texan to head the National Food Marketing Commission.

President Johnson: Jay?

Jay Taylor: Yes, sir.

President Johnson: Two things I wanted to talk to you about confidentially.

---

25. Quote from Daily Diary, 30 June 1964, Lyndon B. Johnson Library.
26. Tape WH6406.19, Citation #3963, Recordings of Telephone Conversations—White House Series, Recordings and Transcripts of Conversations and Meetings, Lyndon B. Johnson Library.

Taylor: All right.

President Johnson: One is your friend, our friend, Marvin Jones.

Taylor: Yes, sir.

President Johnson: Is he active enough, and would he make a good chairman of this study commission of the chain stores and the producers and so forth?

Taylor: I talked to him quite a long time about it, and I'm convinced that he is. He's a rather young 70, or whatever he is, Lyndon, and, as you know, he's better fitted for it and [*unclear*], and I said to him, "What about this? Several people [*unclear, Johnson coughs*]?"[27] He said, "Well, I don't know what to say. I'm [*unclear*] interested in it." But he says, "It's something I've done all my life. I think I could do it." And he told me this just a month ago.

President Johnson: Mm-hmm. All right. Now, you remember a fellow you brought down to my apartment, fifth floor one time, from New York? [*Pauses.*] Fred [Kappel]?[28] Hello? Hello? Oh, hell. [*Noises on the line.*] Hello?

White House Operator: Hello? Hello?

President Johnson: How do I get to finish my call? I got disconnected and . . .

White House Operator: Oh, I'm sorry, Mr. President.

President Johnson: [*to unknown person in office*] Isn't that hell? [*Unclear question by unknown person.*] You locate a fellow after chasing him all over the world, and then you get him in Montana, and then he gets one sentence and they cut him off.[29]

The President reconnected with Taylor a few minutes later, at 1:09 P.M.

---

27. Marvin Jones was 78 years old.
28. Frederick Kappel was chairman of the board of AT&T.
29. Taylor was in Ennis, Montana.

12:55 P.M.

To William Widnall[30]

Johnson thanked Widnall, a Republican congressman from New Jersey, for helping the urban mass transportation bill pass the House on June 25. The Senate passed it later this day.

Unidentified: Jesse's [Kellam's] got a heart [*unclear*]—
A secretary interrupts the office conversation to report that Widnall is on the line.
President Johnson: Goddamn that thing. [*Fumbling noises can be heard.*]
[*on phone*] Hello?
William Widnall: Hello?
President Johnson: Bill?
Widnall: Yes?
President Johnson: Lyndon Johnson.
Widnall: Well, good to talk to you, Mr. President.
President Johnson: I tried to reach you since, oh, God, I don't know how long—four or five days now—to thank you and tell you what a wonderful job I thought you did for the country on that mass transit thing.
Widnall: Well, thank you very, very much. I appreciate your call.
President Johnson: I missed you, and it was in the evening. And I've been out in Michigan and Minnesota and just got back, and I didn't want to let it go. I wanted to tell you that I thought you did a real public service, and I'm proud of you.
Widnall: Well, thank you very, very much, Mr. President. It was a pleasure to work with you on it.
President Johnson: Well, I want to work with you anytime I can. Thank you a lot.
Widnall: All right, thank you, now.
President Johnson: Bye.
Widnall: Bye.

---

30. Tape WH6406.19, Citation #3964, Recordings of Telephone Conversations—White House Series, Recordings and Transcripts of Conversations and Meetings, Lyndon B. Johnson Library.

1:00 P.M.

To Albert Rains[31]

Johnson continued to thank representatives who had helped on the transit bill. This call went to a key Democrat from Alabama.[32]

The unidentified person in the office with the President is talking when the secretary buzzes.

President Johnson: Yes?

Office Secretary: They have Congressman Rains for you, but they got him in Gadsden, Alabama.

President Johnson: Well, I just want him if he was here, and I want Jay Taylor. I had him in Montana and I got cut off. And ask them what the hell happened to me.

Office Secretary: All right, sir.

White House Operator: Ready.

President Johnson: Albert?

Albert Rains: [*Unclear*], Mr. President.

President Johnson: I didn't know you were in Alabama. I've been trying to call you for two or three times to tell you what a superb job I thought you did on mass transit, and I've been gone in Minnesota and Michigan. I just got back, and I ask them where in the hell Albert Rains was, and they said they'd get you, and now they tell me I bothered you down home.

Rains: I'm on my way back to Washington this afternoon. I've had an illness in my family, my wife's mother's been ill, so I had to come down here and see about them. I appreciate your call, Mr. President.

President Johnson: Well, I just wanted to say thank you and tell you I thought you did a superb job.

Rains: It was quite a battle. It was a good one, and I was greatly pleased to win it. We won it in pretty good fashion, to tell you the truth, by 23 votes.

President Johnson: Well . . . yeah. Well, I'm mighty proud of you.

Rains: I appreciate it, Mr. President, very much. So I'll be back to Washington this afternoon.

---

31. Tape WH6406.19, Citation #3965, Recordings of Telephone Conversations—White House Series, Recordings and Transcripts of Conversations and Meetings, Lyndon B. Johnson Library.
32. See the conversation between President Johnson and Larry O'Brien, 8:20 P.M., 25 June 1964, in this volume.

President Johnson: Well . . . thank you, Albert.

Rains: Thank you much, Mr. President.

President Johnson: Bye. . . . Let me hear from you.

Rains: Thank you.

1:09 P.M.

To Jay Taylor[33]

Johnson continued his earlier conversation with the cattle lobbyist.

President Johnson: Jay?

Jay Taylor: I'm sorry we got cut off.

President Johnson: Yeah, they tell me you got a short on your line in . . .

Taylor: Yes.

President Johnson: I wanted to tell you: You remember this fellow [Frederick] Kappel you brought down to see me?[34]

Taylor: Yes, sir.

President Johnson: I'm going to name a couple of outstanding men from business, give them the freedom medal this month, and one of them is going to be Tom Watson, one's going to be Fred Kappel.[35]

Taylor: Wonderful. I'm delighted to hear it.

President Johnson: That's a presidential medal, and there's just 30 or 40 in the—

Taylor: Well, I think they both deserve it.

President Johnson:—30 or 40 in the United States that get it, so I thought [if] you wanted—if you ever—some of these days I'll get your man [Thomas] McCabe in, if you can keep him from politicking too long.[36] [*Taylor laughs.*] That's the damnedest fellow.

Taylor: He's politicking, I think, for a lost cause.

---

33. Tape WH6406.19, Citation #3966, Recordings of Telephone Conversations—White House Series, Recordings and Transcripts of Conversations and Meetings, Lyndon B. Johnson Library.

34. Frederick Kappel served as chairman of the board of AT&T.

35. Thomas J. Watson Jr. had been chairman of the board of IBM since 1961.

36. Thomas McCabe, chairman of the Philadelphia-based Scott Paper Company, had chaired the Federal Reserve during Truman's administration from 1948 to 1951. He had been actively campaigning for Pennsylvania Governor William Scranton for the Republican presidential nomination.

President Johnson: Yeah, you better get him for Johnson.

Taylor: Well, I think I had him for Johnson [*unclear*] thought [*unclear*] made that run.

President Johnson: All right. OK. Well, we—

Taylor: Now listen, on Marvin [Jones]: I don't know if you heard or not, but when I heard that he might be considered, I went up there and took him out to dinner, spent a lot of time with him, because I thought maybe you might ask me, and I'm convinced that he can do this job. He knows what he's talking about, he's spent his life in it, and he's plenty active to do it.

President Johnson: OK, we'll see.

Taylor: Now listen.

President Johnson: Yeah?

Taylor: One more thing: When will—I've got these kid ponies ready for your youngsters down there. [*Johnson acknowledges.*] When will you be at the ranch?

President Johnson: I don't know, it might be the Fourth of July, but if not, I don't know when.

Taylor: Well, I'll check—

President Johnson: You're not going home until the seventh, they told me.

Taylor: You're not?

President Johnson: You're not, are you?

Taylor: Oh, I'm going home tomorrow.

President Johnson: You are? Well, if I go, I'll let you know sometime before I go.

Taylor: Let me know, and we'll have . . . we'll send the little ponies down.

President Johnson: OK. All right. How you doing, all right? [*Taylor hangs up.*]

White House Operator: Are you through?

1:12 P.M.–2:45 P.M.: President Johnson walked to the Mansion for an off-record lunch with Secretary of State Dean Rusk, Secretary of Defense Robert McNamara, and National Security Special Assistant McGeorge Bundy. He made unrecorded calls to Hubert Humphrey (1:18 P.M.), Jack Valenti (2:40 P.M.), and Walter Jenkins (2:45 P.M.).

2:50 P.M.: Napped until 4:30 P.M.

4:31 P.M.: Called Walter Jenkins (unrecorded).

4:32 P.M.: Donald Thomas, the Johnsons' business manager in Texas, visited his boss in the President's bedroom.

4:36 P.M.: Made an unrecorded call to Walter Jenkins.

5:04 P.M.: Received an unrecorded call from Larry O'Brien.

5:26 P.M.: Returned to the Oval Office.

5:35 P.M.

To Edward Kennedy[37]

On June 19, Senator Kennedy's airplane crashed on its way to the state Democratic convention, killing the pilot, Edwin Zimny, and Kennedy aide Edward Moss. Indiana Senator Birch Bayh and Bayh's wife, Marvella, survived the impact with minor injuries, with Senator Bayh reportedly able to pull Kennedy's body from the wreckage. This call was Johnson's first recorded conversation with the young Massachusetts leader since the accident. Kennedy had broken his back and was confined to a Stryker spinal support apparatus at the Cooley Dickinson Hospital in Northampton, Massachusetts.[38]

President Johnson: Hello?

Edward Kennedy: Oh, Mr. President?

President Johnson: My friend, I'm sure glad to hear your voice.

Kennedy: Well, thank you so much. Listen, I wanted to call and tell you how much we appreciate it. Joan [Kennedy] appreciates everything you've done, and your—[39]

President Johnson: Haven't done anything. I haven't done anything, but I'm sure ready and willing.

Kennedy: Well, no. Well, you sent all those wonderful people up from the Army, and . . . [Deputy Defense] Secretary [Cyrus] Vance did. They made a great deal of difference, and everyone's been so, so kind down there, and they've taken great care of me. So I've been really, really coming along now, making progress.

---

37. Tape WH6406.19, Citation #3967, Recordings of Telephone Conversations—White House Series, Recordings and Transcripts of Conversations and Meetings, Lyndon B. Johnson Library.

38. "Sens. Kennedy, Bayh Hurt," *Chicago Tribune*, 20 June 1964; John H. Fenton, "Edward Kennedy Takes First Steps," *New York Times*, 4 December 1964.

39. Kennedy had been married to Virginia Joan Bennett since 1958.

President Johnson: Well, you got a bad break, but it'll . . . My mother used to tell me that things like that develop character. It'll make you stronger when you get older.

Kennedy: Well, I don't know [*Johnson chuckles*], I'll tell you, you know, you're ready to trade a little of that for a few weeks right now, I should say. But anyway, that's what I keep reading in all that mail. They say, "Well, you're going . . . after all that, you get down on that back a little while, and think and do a little suffering, you'll be a better man." So, I guess I'll take my chances with that, anyway.

President Johnson: Well, you're a great guy, and you got lots of guts, and stay in there and pitch, and anything we can do, we're ready.

Kennedy: Well, really appreciate it, Mr. President, and Joan wants to thank you for everything. Mrs. [Lady Bird] Johnson called, and you've been awfully kind during this, and we're very much appreciative and my parents are, too.

President Johnson: You just tell them we're ready to do anything and everything that you want done. And we'll elect you by a bigger vote than you got before.[40]

Kennedy: I know it. God, now we're really going to have to . . . you're going to have to pull me through up here.

President Johnson: Well, just tell them that I'll fill your speaking engagements.

Kennedy: [*Laughs.*] Well, I certainly shall. That was awful kind of you, but we'll be looking forward to getting back down there.

President Johnson: Thank you. Give Joan a hug for me.

Kennedy: Certainly will, Mr. President.

President Johnson: Bye.

Kennedy: Thank you very much.

President Johnson: Bye. Thank you for calling.

5:45 P.M.–6:13 P.M.: Lee White joined the President briefly before the two men met off the record with Secretary of the Interior Stewart Udall, Washington Senator Warren Magnuson, Nevada Senator Alan Bible, and Arizona Senator Carl Hayden. At stake were details of an electric power transmission system

---

40. In a special election in 1962, Edward Kennedy defeated George Cabot Lodge to fill the seat vacated by his brother John. In November 1964, he was reelected to a full term, defeating Republican Howard Whitmore Jr. by an almost 3-to-1 margin (1,716,908 to 587,663). John H. Fenton, "Edward Kennedy Takes First Steps," *New York Times*, 4 December 1964.

being called the Pacific West Coast electrical intertie. A number of power-hungry western states wanted to have the federal government link federal hydroelectric power production in the Pacific Northwest to other parts of the West. After the meeting, Johnson asked Congress for $45 million to kick-start the massive project to build power lines from Washington to California, Nevada, and Arizona.[41] After the session broke up at 6:13 P.M., Senator Magnuson stayed for another two minutes and Lee White remained for a solo session that lasted six minutes.

Afterward, Johnson waited for a call to be placed to Myer Feldman and engaged in an office conversation about paperwork with an unidentified person.[42] He then took a call from Capitol Hill.

6:26 P.M.

From Carl Albert[43]

The House minority leader reported on the progress of the foreign aid bill and discussed some delicate scheduling matters involving the final vote on the civil rights bill after it came out of House Rules Committee.

President Johnson: Hello?

Carl Albert: Mr. President?

President Johnson: Yeah, Carl.

Albert: The Speaker [John McCormack] and I are here together. The Speaker sent for George Mahon. It looks like we're going to wind up general debate on the foreign aid bill. Walter [Jenkins] called me about the civil rights bill.

Now, we had planned to go on with the foreign aid bill tomorrow because civil rights will hold them here for foreign aid. It'll hold—

---

41 "Johnson Requests Funds for Start of Power Intertie," *Wall Street Journal*, 30 June 1964; John H. Allan, "Big Power System in West Spurs Capital Issues," *New York Times*, 3 September 1964.

42. Tape WH6406.19, Citation #3968, Recordings of Telephone Conversations—White House Series, Recordings and Transcripts of Conversations and Meetings, Lyndon B. Johnson Library.

43. Tape WH6406.19, Citation #3969, Recordings of Telephone Conversations—White House Series, Recordings and Transcripts of Conversations and Meetings, Lyndon B. Johnson Library.

President Johnson: Yeah. Yeah. Yeah.

Albert: It'll hold the people we need here, too.

President Johnson: Yeah.

Albert: And there's no problem on civil rights *after* tomorrow. We could pass it within, I'd say, two hours after—Here's George now. [*Consults briefly with Mahon.*] Oh, George says he has to go answer [Otto] Passman.

[*to Mahon*] I'm talking to the President. [*Unclear comments by Mahon in background.*]

[*to Johnson*] George is very much of the opinion we should not put—

[*to Mahon*] Run it in the middle of—

President Johnson: No, no. Nobody—no. Hell, no. I wouldn't suggest that at all.

Albert: And then, we've got one other thing: We've got Rules Committee on Thursday . . . are going to meet to give us some rules, which we're just running out of rules. And if we adjourn tomorrow night, which we would do after, in effect, after passing both bills, why, we wouldn't be able to hold these members here for the Rules Committee on Thursday morning.

President Johnson: Mm-hmm.

Albert: Now, if this is all right with you, what we *can* do, I think without any problem, is to pass this foreign aid bill tomorrow. And I don't think it'd take over . . . I think we can have the other one passed by 2:00 Thursday and down to you by—we ought to have it down to you by 3:00.

President Johnson: That's good; that's good. That's wonderful.

Albert: We'll have one . . . we'll probably have . . . we may have two or three roll calls, but I doubt it. We've only got one hour of debate, so there's a limit to what they can do, and I would think, with luck, we could have it down to you by 3 [P.M.].

President Johnson: That's good.

Albert: Because it's enrolled: All we have to do after we pass it is for the Speaker to sign it and Mr. [Carl] Hayden, Senator Hayden, to sign it.[44] Send it right over to the Senate—they'll be in session waiting for it—and then buck it right down to you, and we will do everything necessary to expedite it. Of course, we'll come in at 12 [noon], we'll have a roll call. We'll have one hour of debate, and then we'll have a vote, and I think that'll be it. That'll be two roll calls plus an hour of debate.

President Johnson: All right, now, what . . . does it take a lot of time to get it over to the Senate? How long after—

---

44. Carl Hayden, the 86-year-old senator from Arizona, was Senate pro tempore.

Albert: It shouldn't take 15 minutes to get it over to the Senate after we've passed it.

President Johnson: Mm-hmm.

Albert: It shouldn't take 15 minutes. [*Unclear*]—

President Johnson: All right, now you just check that with the parliamentarian [Lew Deschler]. Be sure that's right. Then I can announce the ceremony Thursday afternoon, then.

Albert: [*with the President acknowledging*] You could announce it Thursday after—or Thursday evening late, you know, like the 6:00 [hour], or something like that. You did on that . . . you know, you had one down there at night one time with all the cameras there. When was that? I don't know [*unclear*].

President Johnson: Tax bill, wasn't it?[45]

Albert: It was the tax bill. That's your other big bill you had at night. So I'm sure you can have it Thursday night without . . . I wouldn't . . . I wouldn't announce it publicly until after we get passed the foreign aid bill, though.

President Johnson: Well, you see, you won't do that until Wednesday, will you?

Albert: We'll pass the foreign aid bill tomorrow, but what if we ran into an engrossed copy?[46]

President Johnson: Yeah. Yeah.

Albert: And they might demand an engrossed copy, if they knew we were doing this, you see?

President Johnson: Yeah.

Albert: But all these southerners don't want it signed on the Fourth of July.

President Johnson: That's right.

Albert: And all these people [who] are for it don't give a darn, so I don't think we have any real problem.

President Johnson: Well, if you get it to me Thursday where I can have a ceremony Thursday evening, that's good, because everybody'll be leaving town then.

Albert: All right, sir.

---

45. Johnson signed the tax bill at 6:30 p.m. on 26 February 1964 and spoke to a national audience at 6:45 p.m.

46. According to the *Guide to the Records of the United States Senate at the National Archives*, the engrossed copy is a bill after it "has passed both Houses together with its engrossed amendments." It then becomes the "official working copy from which an enrolled bill is prepared." http://www.archives.gov/legislative/guide/senate/appendix-e.html.

President Johnson: And that'll just be wonderful. All I told Walter was I want to be sure that you get it to me as soon as you can, but I don't want to set aside foreign aid: That's the one that they could really damage us on if they beat us on that.

Albert: That's right.

President Johnson: How's the debate going? How does it look to you? How does it feel?

Albert: The debate looks all right. The . . . Vaughan [Gary] did real well.

President Johnson: Is Passman giving you hell?

Albert: [*with the President acknowledging*] Passman raised a little hell, but he didn't have an audience, didn't have much audience. We just kept 100 on the floor to keep from getting a quorum call. They tried about four or five times to get a quorum call and never were able to get one. So, he didn't have a full house. And George is going out now to close the debate on just a—he's just going to make a two-minute speech to close the debate.

President Johnson: Do you—are you getting any Republicans?

Albert: Yes, we've had one Republican to speak for the bill from the committee: that was [Silvio] Conte.[47]

President Johnson: That's Conte.

Albert: Yeah.

President Johnson: But any of the rest of them going to vote with you?

Albert: I think so. We're told we'll get about . . . we ought to get at least 12 Republicans.[48]

President Johnson: Who tells you that, Conte?

Albert: Well, Conte has told Vaughan and these fellows that we ought to get at least 12. I think we will.

President Johnson: We had 16 last year. Have you got anybody that's changing, that's helping us this year, that didn't last year?

Albert: Well, we've got these that . . . I've had a list made of those who voted this year for the authorization bill who didn't vote for the appropriation bill last year, and I think all of those are going to go with us. Now, that includes mostly members from the Committee on Appropriations.

---

47. On 26 June, Johnson had praised Conte for his support on foreign aid. See the conversation between President Johnson and Silvio Conte, 1:41 P.M., 26 June 1964, in this volume.
48. The bill passed the House the next day 231 to 174, with 55 Republicans in support. *Congressional Quarterly Almanac*, 1964, vol. 20, p. 636.

President Johnson: Mm-hmm. OK, God bless you.
Albert: All right.
President Johnson: Bye.

6:38 P.M.–6:50 P.M.: White House Counsel Myer Feldman brought in several bills for Johnson's signature. Before Feldman exited, Johnson held his final recorded call of the day.

6:45 P.M.

To George Ball[49]

Johnson asked the under secretary of state to review a personnel matter regarding wool textiles negotiations. Ball learned that Johnson did not approve of Ball's preferred negotiator.

A brief office conversation precedes the call.
Myer Feldman: Excise tax, though, will be over late tonight.[50] Should we interrupt your [State] Dinner [*unclear*]?
President Johnson: Yes, sir, anything. Anything. I hope that mass transit's over too. We won't sign it, but they're debating it now [in the Senate].
The call is then connected.
George Ball: Hello?
President Johnson: George?
Ball: Yes, Mr. President.
President Johnson: Where did we get ahold of Wilson Wyatt on these negotiations?[51]

49. Tape WH6406.19, Citation #3970, Recordings of Telephone Conversations—White House Series, Recordings and Transcripts of Conversations and Meetings, Lyndon B. Johnson Library.
50. This evening, the Senate approved the House-Senate Conference Committee's version of the excise tax extension bill and sent it to the White House for Johnson's signature.
51. In May 1963, President Kennedy had sent Wilson Wyatt, the lieutenant governor of Kentucky who had lost a close race for the U.S. Senate in 1962, as his special envoy in a dispute over oil interests with Indonesian President Achmed Sukarno. He helped broker a compromise that prevented the complete nationalization of Indonesia's oil and allowed outside oil companies to continue operating there. A. M. Rosenthal, "Western Oil Men Reach an Accord with Indonesians," *New York Times*, 2 June 1963.

Ball: I brought him in originally, Mr. President, to do a negotiation with [Achmed] Sukarno, and he did an extremely good job.[52] I . . . the only thought that we had of using him—he's now going over on a . . . he went over on a wool negotiation for us, and he's going . . . the plan is to send him back again to try to negotiate a wool textile agreement. We thought a little of using him in South Africa. The only reason is that he's an experienced fellow. He's got a little . . . a certain amount of political sense, and he's a good lawyer, and he's been an effective negotiator.

I haven't had thoughts beyond that, but that's . . . these spot jobs, the ones he's had so far, he's done a very good job on. I—

President Johnson: Well, now, they don't think he did a very good one on his last wool job, and they're going back again, and they'd much prefer to have somebody else. And it seems to me like [if] we're going to not get very far anyway, we ought to send somebody that would please them.

Ball: Well—

President Johnson: The Congress doesn't want him, and the industry doesn't want him, and . . .

Ball: Well, in fairness to him, I should say, Mr. President, that on this wool textile business, he did what his instructions were, which was to go over and do a kind of preliminary reconnaissance and then come back and report. And then we made a decision that we would go ahead, although Chris Herter is very much opposed to it, and we've had problems on the . . .[53]

President Johnson: I don't want to send this wire "at the request of the President they're doing this," and I wouldn't ever request Wilson to be negotiating for me. You-all—I like him, but I just I think he's as out of place as he could be, and I'd try to get somebody that knows something about the industry.

Ball: Well, the other man we could get is Eddie Gudeman, who was under secretary of commerce and, of course, was in the [*Johnson seems to whistle softly*] business for a good many years.[54] Now, the reason that we didn't—I had signed him up to go over on this mission, and John Pastore indicated that he thought that Gudeman hadn't been sympathetic

---

52. Achmed Sukarno had been President of Indonesia since 1945.
53. Christian Herter, a former secretary of state under Eisenhower, was serving as a presidential special assistant on trade matters.
54. Edward Gudeman was under secretary of commerce in the Kennedy administration and had been an executive at Sears, Roebuck & Company.

with him when he was at Commerce.[55] It's awful hard to find somebody that . . . that meets the . . .

President Johnson: Let's get them to make some recommendations, and let's look at two or three of them before they go and see if we can't find somebody that suits them.

Ball: Now, there's a fellow [Warren] Christopher that we've sent is the man who negotiated the long-term cotton textile agreement.[56]

President Johnson: Yeah. . . .

[*whispering to someone in the office*] Christopher Warren?

Ball: He's a Los Angeles lawyer. He's a very, very competent fellow. If they would accept just him, we can send him. He . . . he is supposed—they have said that he has their confidence in that he was the . . . did a very, very effective job of negotiating an agreement they're entirely satisfied with.

President Johnson: All right, we'll check him, and if he's not—if that doesn't make them happy, we'll tell them to submit a half a dozen names of somebody that has some experience, and we'll look at them and see if we can't find one that would suit them, so they'll be pleased with it.

Ball: Your own[57] . . . your own impression of [Wilson] Wyatt is that you don't think he's very effective, or . . .

President Johnson: [*with Ball acknowledging*] I don't want anybody to know that but me. No, *hell no*, I wouldn't have him represent me on anything.

Ball: Right.

President Johnson: I know him, like him, and was with him with the housing administrator, but he's out of place.[58]

Ball: Yeah.

President Johnson: He's out of place. And he may be a good lawyer in the courtroom, but he's lost in some of this other stuff. And I've known him for 25 years.

---

55. John Pastore was a Democratic senator from Rhode Island.

56. The future secretary of state for the Bill Clinton administration was a partner at the New York–based law firm O'Melveny & Myers; Johnson would appoint Christopher as deputy attorney general in 1967.

57. This section below had previously been closed under deed of gift restriction.

58. Appointed on 12 December 1945, Wilson Wyatt was the housing expeditor for the Office of War Mobilization and Reconversion and led a controversial federal building program to reduce postwar housing shortages for veterans. He resigned under significant criticism a year later. "Letter Accepting Resignation of Wilson Wyatt as Housing Expediter," 5 December 1946, *Public Papers of the Presidents of the United States: Harry S. Truman, 1946* (Washington, DC: GPO, 1962), 1:490.

Ball: Well, I . . . this was an . . . uh . . . a reading I wanted to get from you.

President Johnson: Yeah. OK.

Ball: Right, thanks.

7:00 P.M.–7:45 P.M.: President Johnson spoke to Walter Jenkins several times before leaving for the Mansion to prepare for the Orlich State Dinner.

8:10 P.M.–8:25 P.M.: At the White House's North Portico, President Johnson and Lady Bird extended greetings to President and Mrs. Orlich and then proceeded upstairs to give the Costa Rican leader a western saddle, an Accutron desk clock with the presidential seal, a signed copy of Johnson's book of speeches *A Time for Action*, and a signed, framed photograph of Johnson himself. Fifteen minutes later, the couples went to the East Room to say hello to guests before the State Dinner.

8:50 P.M.: The 186-guest State Dinner began in the State Dining Room and the Blue Room. Guests feasted on dishes such as Cream Baltimore, Filet Mignon Orlich, creamed spinach, green salad, Mousse of Roquefort, and coffee parfait.

10:05 P.M.–10:30 P.M.: Attendees mingled over coffee as after-dinner guests arrived and then gathered for dancing in the East Room and the East Terrace.

12:45 A.M.: The President and Lady Bird went to the second floor, with the President heading to bed over an hour later at 1:50 A.M.

Wednesday, July 1, 1964

Before it's over with, you're going to get all of it, and it's going to be because you just rode everybody's ass to do it.
—George Smathers to President Johnson

Don't you be too damn kind to that guy [Otto Passman], because he's awfully mean, and we've got to let people know it. They can't be that way and play on the team.
—President Johnson to George Mahon

Lyndon Johnson was on familiar ground this day. With the exception of a meeting about California energy needs, some ceremonial matters, and a quick session with Costa Rica's President Jose Orlich, almost all of his time was dedicated to Capitol Hill. The major development was the final showdown on the foreign aid bill with Congressman Otto Passman, a man who was responsible for drastically reducing every foreign aid appropriation for the past ten years. Today, Passman made one final attempt to trim almost $250 million from the bill. By the end of the afternoon, however, the President claimed victory, defeating the Louisiana politician's amendment by 20 votes. "That's the first time anybody's ever rolled Mr. Passman," he bragged to an aide.[1] The *Washington Post* agreed, proclaiming in a front-page story that "an era ended on Capitol Hill" because of

---

1. Conversation between President Johnson and Ralph Dungan, 5:37 P.M., 1 July 1964, in this chapter.

Johnson's "special touch."[2] Not content to rest on that success, Johnson immediately turned to the food stamp bill (which had passed the Senate the day before) and other pending legislation.

In other political developments, Barry Goldwater was celebrating an important victory of his own. He carried 48 of Illinois's 58 Republican delegates—including the biggest prize, the vote of Senate Minority Leader Everett Dirksen. Pennsylvania Governor William Scranton, his most formidable challenger, got none. Chalmers Roberts of the *Washington Post* called it a "smashing victory" and declared that Goldwater was "very probably" going to get the Republican nomination.[3]

> **9:25 A.M.–11:25 A.M.:** Before coming into the Oval Office, President Johnson held a number of unrecorded calls with aides. Calls were made to Walter Jenkins (9:25 A.M.), Bill Moyers (9:35 A.M.), Larry O'Brien (10:00 A.M. and 11:05 A.M.), George Reedy (10:29 A.M. and 11:25 A.M.), McGeorge Bundy (10:55 A.M.), and Senator Hubert Humphrey (11:15 A.M.). He also saw two doctors at 10:30 A.M., and did his exercises at 11:00 A.M.
>
> **11:45 A.M.:** Arrived at the Oval Office with Jack Valenti.
>
> **11:50 P.M.:** Called Special Assistant for National Security McGeorge Bundy.
>
> **11:52 A.M.:** Had a three-minute, off-the-record session with Massachusetts Congressman James Burke.
>
> **12:05 P.M.:** Went to the Cabinet Room with Jack Valenti to tape some statements for the Democratic National Committee.
>
> **12:11 P.M.:** Made an unrecorded call to Walter Jenkins on the personal line.
>
> **12:14 P.M.:** With aide Lee White, began a meeting that lasted approximately 20 minutes with several congressmen from California about the Pacific West Coast electrical system. While they were there, the President made several phone calls, including unrecorded calls to Bill Moyers (12:16 P.M. and 12:19 P.M.), George Reedy (12:17 P.M.), Walter Jenkins (12:18 P.M.), and Jack Valenti (12:20 P.M.).

---

2. Richard L. Lyons, "Full $3.3-Billion for Aid Passes House, 231–174," *Washington Post*, 2 July 1964.

3. Chalmers M. Roberts, "Illinois Gives Barry Big Boost," *Washington Post*, 1 July 1964.

12:24 P.M.

From George Reedy[4]

The President rebuffed a request from a film crew to shoot footage at his Texas ranch. At the time of the call, Johnson was meeting with several California congressmen.

Unidentified: . . . professionals. It is impossible to analyze prior to the hearing—[*unclear, continues talking in the background*].
The secretary reports that Reedy is on the line.
George Reedy: . . . and Hyman Fillmore are part of a camera crew headed by a man named George Stevens [Jr.], who is doing a film for USIA [United States Information Agency] under contract.[5] This is a film that we review before anything ever goes out.
President Johnson: Did you give them any such authority?
Reedy: No, sir, I—
President Johnson: All right.
Reedy: —did not. But I've given them authority to do other things, and I guess they just assumed that—
President Johnson: Well, no, we don't want assuming, because that [LBJ] Ranch is private property.
Reedy: I said I guess *they* just assumed.
President Johnson: Well, they ain't got no business around the ranch. Why should they be there?
Reedy: Well, I think the . . . I think in this case we should let them because—
President Johnson: Well, I haven't got anybody to support them, not "let them." Somebody's got to guide them and take over the thing. [We] haven't got the manpower. It's a question of whether A.W. [Moursund] throws down his thing and goes and takes them. You're not going to turn them loose up there.
Reedy: Um . . .

---

4. Tape WH6407.01, Citation #4101, Recordings of Telephone Conversations—White House Series, Recordings and Transcripts of Conversations and Meetings, Lyndon B. Johnson Library.
5. George Stevens Jr. was director of the Motion Picture Service of the United States Information Agency. His father was George Stevens Sr., the legendary director of such Hollywood films as *Shane* (1953), *Giant* (1956), and *Diary of Anne Frank* (1959). Hyman Fillmore is a phonetic spelling.

President Johnson: And if you're going to do that and you just think you should, why, give me the dough to do it with.

Reedy: No, sir, this is a last minute thing that just came up to me, sir.

President Johnson: Yeah, yeah.

Reedy: This is the first I've heard of it.

President Johnson: Well, I know it, but I've got to make a deciding . . . I'd just say that we haven't given them any authority and let them come on back. Got no business down there. We don't want this kind of stuff ballooned up. And we have—see, we've got those guards there, and we've got no facilities.

Reedy: I understand, sir.

President Johnson: When somebody goes on there, you got to go with them, you got to take them.

Reedy: I understand, sir. It was a bad slip up on their part. They should have checked it out with us. But the overall control that we have is that no film ever goes out until we've reviewed it.

President Johnson: Yeah, I don't care about that. All I'm talking about is I haven't got the manpower to furnish—

Reedy: Right.

President Johnson: —them, to escort them. Now, what do I do about it?

Reedy: Well, if you don't have the manpower then, sir, I'll just tell them to tell them come on back.

President Johnson: [*talking over Reedy*] Yeah, I'd sure would. I'd just say we have no facilities there available to them. We don't want that played up; we don't want it in the picture; [they've] got no business doing it. And they cleared it with no one. That's what I'd tell them.

Reedy: Right. OK, sir.

President Johnson: Bye.

12:26 P.M.: President Johnson made an unrecorded call to Walter Jenkins on the personal line.

12:45 P.M.: Lee White had remained after the meeting with the California congressmen. Kenny O'Donnell joined them for one minute before Johnson met off the record with former Pennsylvania Governor David Lawrence. Lawrence remained until 1:04 P.M.

1:05 P.M.: Went to the Flower Garden for the official swearing-in of four top administrators at the Pentagon. Solis Horwitz, a former aide to Johnson in the Senate, became assistant secretary of defense for administration. Dan Luevano, a Californian and Mexican American, was taking the position of assistant secretary of the Army for installations and logistics. Johnson had targeted him in January and February to expand the number of minorities in high-ranking federal positions.[6] Robert Morse was the new assistant secretary of the Navy for research and development. John McNaughton was the highest-ranking appointment, replacing William Bundy as assistant secretary of defense for international security affairs.[7]

1:10 P.M.: Returned to the Cabinet Room to greet a number of guests from the ceremony.

1:16 P.M.: Texas Senator Ralph Yarborough, a one-time rival to the President who had recently become an important ally, brought a friend to Johnson for a photo opportunity and a brief tour.

1:36 P.M.: Met with McGeorge Bundy and Jack Valenti.

1:50 P.M.

To Jack Brooks[8]

Calling from the cloakroom, Johnson's good friend from Texas kept him abreast of the House votes on foreign aid appropriations. Brooks had been one of the President's dinner guests on June 29.

A brief office conversation precedes the call.
Unidentified: . . . or crisis.
President Johnson: I think anybody that's important in this country,

---

6. See the conversation between President Johnson and Thomas Mann, 12:23 P.M., 25 January 1964, in Kent B. Germany and Robert David Johnson, eds., *The Presidential Recordings, Lyndon B. Johnson: The Kennedy Assassination and the Transfer of Power, November 1963–January 1964*, vol. 3, *January 1964* (New York: Norton, 2005), pp. 821–25.

7. In 1967, John McNaughton was elevated to secretary of the Navy, but was killed in July in a midair collision before taking that office. "Remarks at the Swearing In of John T. McNaughton, Daniel Luevano, Solis Horwitz, and Robert W. Morse as Key Officials in the Department of Defense," 1 July 1964. *Public Papers of the Presidents of the United States: Lyndon B. Johnson, 1963–64* (Washington, DC: GPO, 1965), 2:839.

8. Tape WH6407.01, Citation #4102, Recordings of Telephone Conversations—White House Series, Recordings and Transcripts of Conversations and Meetings, Lyndon B. Johnson Library.

I don't know of any better way to spend the evening than spend them with—

The secretary interrupts to report that Brooks is on the line.

President Johnson: Jack?

Jack Brooks: Mr. President.

President Johnson: How's it look up there?

Brooks: Looks pretty good. It looks pretty good. We've got . . .

President Johnson: Somebody told me [Charles] Halleck made an awful mean speech.

Brooks: Yeah, but I—

President Johnson: Did you hear it?

Brooks: No, but I heard it was pretty mean, but we've got the votes. I think we're going to keep them.

President Johnson: When [are] they going to vote?

Brooks: I don't know. They're just battling away. [Otto] Passman just screaming a little while. But he made a fool out of himself. He's not helping. I think that we're going to win it. [George] Mahon is working good. I talked to him about 30 minutes ago, and we're staying on the floor pretty well. That's the problem: keeping people here, you know.

President Johnson: Are they still offering amendments?

Brooks: Yeah.

President Johnson: Are there any—have they adopted any of them?

Brooks: Nothing that's significant, no. I don't think they've adopted *any.*

President Johnson: When are they going to vote on recommittal?

Brooks: Sometime this afternoon. And we're going to get almost every vote in Texas. We're going to lose [Joe] Pool, but he'll vote with us in the well if we need him. [Ovie] Fisher says he's got to vote for it, that he just can't change. He was nice about it, and I talked to him. [John] Dowdy is on the fence, and we got [Robert] Casey and [Omar] Burleson going to vote right for a change.[9]

President Johnson: Well, they ought to. They're going to be there a long time with George Mahon, and they ought to support him on his first bill.

Brooks: They sure ought to. I've been telling them that they're going to print that record vote, just sort of touching them up.

How you feeling?

---

9. None of these Texas House Democrats supported the bill on the final vote. Only four of Texas's twenty-one Democrats did.

President Johnson: Pretty good. I'm still anxious to hear on this thing. So I—

Brooks: I'll call—

President Johnson: —thought you-all would be about to stage your voting now.

Brooks: I will call back and give you a current report—I'm in the cloakroom now—and I will call you immediately on the vote.

President Johnson: All right. Don't tell anybody I called you.

Brooks: Aye, aye, sir.

2:00 P.M.

To Craig Raupe[10]

Johnson sought more information about the foreign aid situation from Craig Raupe, a Texan who was the chief congressional liaison for the Agency for International Development. Before that, Raupe had served as an aide to Texas Democrat Jim Wright.

Unidentified: [*Unclear.*]

President Johnson: Excuse me one second. I hear them calling.

The secretary announces Raupe's call.

Craig Raupe: Doing real well, Mr. President.

President Johnson: You got those votes?

Raupe: I think we're . . . we probably got 10 to 15.

President Johnson: That's not enough.

Raupe: Margin.

President Johnson: That's not enough. Your absentees show up?

Raupe: Yes, sir. We've got every absentee that we can find. It looks we got about seven on our side.

President Johnson: How many people told you that they'd vote with you if they had to have you? Two or three? Four?

Raupe: No, sir, we've got more than that. Must have ten.

President Johnson: Mm-hmm, all right.

Raupe: Must have ten.

---

10. Tape WH6407.01, Citation #4104, Recordings of Telephone Conversations—White House Series, Recordings and Transcripts of Conversations and Meetings, Lyndon B. Johnson Library.

President Johnson: Be sure to watch that, then. When you going to vote?

Raupe: [*with the President acknowledging*] Within . . . they've said they'd be real generous—they're on this five-minute rule—they said they'd be real generous. I'd figure in the next—before 3:00. The first one will be on tellers.[11] The tellers . . . we can win that one pretty good, and then on the recommittal, I think we got 15 Republicans and maybe a 199 or 200 Democrats. Now, that's including an awful lot of real redneck folks that normally wouldn't be with us on final passage.

President Johnson: Well, but you'll still have enough to pass it because you'll get some Republicans in, won't you?

Raupe: On final passage, we'll get about 60 Republicans, and we'll drop off on Democrats to 170.

President Johnson: So you know what you're doing then?

Raupe: Well, hope we do.

President Johnson: Halleck very mean with you? And Passman?

Raupe: No, Halleck was real good. We got in kind of a little wrangle with him the other night talking about this, and he was going to offer a straight motion to recommit without money. Then awhile ago, he got up on the floor, and he made kind of a dramatic statement that I'm for this amendment. Then, it looked like he was going to lay low because we prepared this material for [Carl] Albert. Albert, of course, was going to stay out of it unless Halleck got in it, and then [John] Rooney, who's pretty raucous and pretty loud, got up and attacked Halleck. That in turn got [Gerald] Ford and a bunch of them to defending Halleck, and at that juncture Albert took the floor and, in fact, his entire speech was a defense purely of you as much as it was the bill.[12] But he just sat down, so . . .

President Johnson: [Albert] Thomas?[13]

Raupe: No, Albert.

President Johnson: Carl Albert.

Raupe: This is Carl Albert.

President Johnson: Yeah.

Raupe: They're all gathered round him over there: the Speaker [John McCormack] and Albert are gathered around, and [Thomas] Morgan

---

11. In a teller vote, a House member walked past tellers who then counted them either in support or in opposition. The teller counted the votes, but did not record the identity of the voter.

12. John Rooney was a Democrat from New York, Gerald Ford a Republican from Michigan.

13. Albert Thomas was Johnson's friend from Texas, one of the four Texans who supported the final bill.

and Mahon and [Vaughan] Gary are all gathered together.[14] They're showing a real show of strength.

President Johnson: Mm-hmm. Well—

Raupe: But it's going to be pretty much party line, though.

President Johnson: Mmm. What . . . who had attacked me? Was it Passman?

Raupe: Passman . . .

President Johnson: For what?

Raupe: Not so much on the floor as a statement yesterday in which he indicated, says, "Every president I've talked to, including the President incumbent, knows himself that he doesn't know a damn thing about this bill,"—or not "a damn thing," "a darn thing," something to that effect. Not nearly as vitriolic as he was in committee the other day.

President Johnson: Did Halleck say anything about it this morning?

Raupe: Nope. Not a word about it. Matter of fact, he was kind of—he left the floor immediately thereafter, and he acted like he was a little ashamed, because he knew they were going to quote these quotes, you know, that we got together, but he—

President Johnson: Did Albert quote him?

Raupe: He hasn't. No, he hasn't yet. [*President Johnson acknowledges.*] And I guess he won't. He hasn't used them.

President Johnson: Mm-hmm. OK, you let me know.

Raupe: I will, sir. Good-bye.

2:01 P.M.: McGeorge Bundy brought French economic leader Jean Monnet by for a four-minute photo opportunity. Monnet was the visionary behind the creation of the European Coal and Steel Community in 1950 and the European Economic Community (known as the Common Market) in 1958.

2:06 P.M.: Johnson called Walter Jenkins on the personal line.

2:15 P.M.: Went over the afternoon newspapers with Jack Valenti and completed some paperwork on federal appointments.

2:25 P.M.–4:25 P.M.: Left for lunch with Jack Valenti, arriving at the Mansion at 2:30 P.M. One minute after arriving at the Mansion for the meal, they called Bill Moyers (unrecorded, 2:31 P.M.). Throughout the afternoon Johnson had unrecorded telephone

14. Thomas Morgan was a Democrat from Pennsylvania; J. Vaughan Gary was a Democrat from Virginia.

exchanges with speechwriter Horace Busby, (2:44 P.M.), White House Counsel Mike Feldman (2:48 P.M.), Walter Jenkins (3:47 P.M.), and House Majority Leader Carl Albert (4:25 P.M.).

4:55 P.M.: Returned to the Oval Office and immediately phoned George Reedy (unrecorded, 4:56 P.M.). After that, he checked in with the White House's chief congressional liaison.

4:57 P.M.

To Larry O'Brien[15]

The saga over foreign aid continued.

The President instructs the operator to place calls to both O'Brien and George Smathers. He will talk to one and hold for the other.

Jack Valenti: [*in office*] Senator [Everett] Dirksen would like to come in after you meet with these people at 5:30 or 5:40 [P.M.]. That's the . . .

Larry O'Brien: Hello?

President Johnson: Yeah, Larry, did you call me?

O'Brien: Yeah, that the [Otto] Passman amendment on the teller [vote] was defeated 171 [to] 151. [*Unclear comment by the President.*] They're on the so-called [Paul] Findley amendment now, and they're voting.[16] I'll have it for you shortly.

President Johnson: That tellers or roll call?

O'Brien: No, tellers. Tellers.

President Johnson: Will it be close on the Findley? That's just wheat.

O'Brien: Well . . . yeah, it's hard to determine, you know, it's . . . I think our boy is in pretty good shape.

President Johnson: Thank you, Larry.

O'Brien: OK.

---

15. Tape WH6407.01, Citation #4105, Recordings of Telephone Conversations—White House Series, Recordings and Transcripts of Conversations and Meetings, Lyndon B. Johnson Library.
16. Paul Findley, a Republican from Illinois, introduced a provision to prevent loans to Communist nations. In a teller vote, 119 supported the amendment, while 151 opposed. *Congressional Quarterly Almanac*, 88th Cong., 2nd sess., 1964, vol. 20 (Washington, DC: Congressional Quarterly Service, 1965), p. 314.

4:59 P.M.

To George Smathers[17]

Smathers, a Florida Democrat and secretary for the Senate Democratic Conference, was a close friend of the President's and his family, who often had frank exchanges with Johnson.[18] In this call, President Johnson gave Smathers a colorful analysis of the workings of Capitol Hill, voicing his concern about the parliamentary skills of fellow Democrats. Johnson was extremely upset about the Senate's handling of yesterday's food stamp bill passage, particularly the Senate Democratic leadership's inability to derail Republican Jack Miller's amendment to prohibit the use of food stamps to purchase Australian meat. This addition to the bill meant that the legislation now had to go back to Judge Smith's House Rules Committee before it could go to the floor for concurrence. Smith kept it bottled up until August 11. The House passed it that same day. Johnson signed it into law on August 31.

Smathers and Johnson also covered the excise tax battle, the Australian–New Zealand meat import issue, and the ongoing civil rights struggle in St. Augustine.

The President continues his office conversation about his schedule with Jack Valenti before the secretary reports that Smathers is on the line. Johnson speaks to Smathers over the speakerphone.

President Johnson: George? [Douglas] Dillon was really raving about how effective you were on excise tax bill, and I wanted to thank you for it.[19]

George Smathers: Well, I appreciate his being generous with me. I thought we came out very well. We did a poor job to start with, but it finally got straightened out.

President Johnson: Well, he said you were very effective, and it was largely due to you that an agreement was reached. And you were [*reading*]

---

17. Tape WH6407.01, Citation #4106, Recordings of Telephone Conversations—White House Series, Recordings and Transcripts of Conversations and Meetings, Lyndon B. Johnson Library.
18. For example, see the conversation between President Johnson and George Smathers, 9:01 P.M., 10 January 1964, in Germany and Johnson, *The Presidential Recordings, Johnson*, vol. 3, *January 1964*, pp. 419–20.
19. The bill to extend excise taxes on certain goods had passed the House on 17 June. An amended bill made it through the Senate on 25 June, and this version was accepted by the House and Senate on 30 June. Johnson signed it that same day.

"very successful in his assumption of personal responsibility in pushing for agreement on the House bill, and it would [be] most appreciated by me if you'd give him a ring on the telephone and thank him for what he did to help us."

Smathers: Well, that's wonderful.

President Johnson: I'm awfully grateful.

Smathers: Well, I appreciate it, and I appreciate his thoughtfulness too, so that's very nice.

President Johnson: George, I'm having a lot of problems, as you-all can watch. I don't want you to say I told you, but, we just . . . we are *inept*: What the House does, the Senate fucks up.

Smathers: Yeah.

President Johnson: Then the Senate does something and the House screws it up.

Smathers: Right.

President Johnson: We got 27 of the 30 bills, and they pass one house or the other, and we can't do anything with them.

Smathers: Right.

President Johnson: [*with Smathers acknowledging throughout*] I'll give you an example: We got the food stamp [bill], and it took us six months to get a rule on it. We got it through the House, after it finally got past that damned old . . . old man [Howard] Smith.[20] Well, it got over there [in the Senate], and [Allen] Ellender said, "I'll bring it up and I'll pass it."[21] He brought it up and passed it, but [Hubert] Humphrey left the floor, [and Jack] Miller put a little chicken shit amendment that you couldn't put any stamps on Australian beef.[22]

Now, nobody wants to put any stamps on Australian beef. If he'd asked us, we'd have told him we wouldn't put any on. But he puts an amendment on. Now, that makes you go back to the House, and the only way you can get through the House is by unanimous consent unless you get a rule.[23] So you can't get unanimous consent and you can't get a rule, so what goddamn good does it do for the Senate to act on it?

Smathers: Well, I agree.

President Johnson: [*with Smathers acknowledging*] Now, that just runs

---

20. Howard "Judge" Smith was chair of the House Rules Committee.

21. Allen Ellender was chair of the Senate Committee on Agriculture and Forestry.

22. Jack Miller was a Republican senator from Iowa and had been lobbying the President for most of the year to restrict meat imports.

23. This scenario had played out with the civil rights bill that had made it out of the Rules Committee on 30 June.

me nuts: *every*day something like that. [*Unclear name*] said yesterday the House screwed it up and, of course, you-all saved the day by concurring. But when the Senate screws it up, the House can't concur. It's got to have a rule to concur. And then the old man [Smith] goes out to his farm, and they won't get it.[24]

Smathers: We could have beat Miller pretty easy on the thing. I saw that transpire. I was waiting to take up that excise tax bill, and I saw . . . I'm sure it was just a case of not having thought it through very well, because I remember [Mike] Mansfield went over to Ellender and said, "Why don't you just take it and drop it in the conference," never . . . forgetting about what . . . having forgotten what the rules in the House were. Ellender didn't want to take it, you had Miller [who] didn't have a damn vote but his own, and—

President Johnson: That's all right, but Mansfield had four cowmen raise hell, and that just ruins the whole program.

Smathers: Yeah. . . . Yeah, he didn't want to, I guess, put people on record on that particular program.

Well, I'll try to—I will help out on that. . . .

President Johnson: We're going to have a hell of a record, an awfully good record, if we can just get the two coordinated. If we could get two leaders to really function together: if [Carl] Albert and Mansfield would really be alert and be on the phone with each other like [Sam] Rayburn and I used to do all the time.[25]

Smathers: Right. That's right. Well, that's what's needed, but that's what's lacking. They're not in as good a communication . . .

President Johnson: I sent them up a week ago these 30 bills and where they were, and I said, "Now let's program them and see right which one can do this and which one can do that," but I've been unable to get from either one of them, well . . . how we're going to coordinate. But we're moving and . . . we've—

Smathers: You're going to get them. Before it's over with, you're going to get all of it, and it's going to be because you just rode everybody's ass

---

24. Howard "Judge" Smith owned a dairy farm near Broad Run, Virginia, about 45 miles from Capitol Hill. One legendary tactic to prevent action on certain legislation was to leave the capital to tend to matters on that farm. See the conversation between President Johnson and Katharine Graham, 11:10 a.m., 2 December 1963, in Robert David Johnson and David Shreve, eds., *The Presidential Recordings, Lyndon B. Johnson: The Kennedy Assassination and the Transfer of Power, November 1963–January 1964*, vol. 2, *December 1964* (New York: Norton, 2005) p. 42.
25. Known as "Mr. Sam," Rayburn was a legendary Democrat from Texas and one of Johnson's cherished mentors. He served in the House from 1913 to 1962 and was Speaker of the House for nine congressional terms.

to do it. That's just what's happening, and that's [*chuckles slightly*] why you're going to have it, but that's the way it has to be done. So, it's just unfortunate—

President Johnson: Now, they tell me that you did a good job on St. Augustine, too. Lee White said that you . . . your man's been very helpful, and they worked out an agreement down there.

Smathers: Yeah. Well, it had. We've been worried about that. Poor Herb Wolfe, who's got no business undertaking this because of his age—he's got Parkinson's disease anyway—but he finally agreed.[26] We begged him and asked him would he be the chairman, and so he finally said yes, he'd do it. So that's the basis on which the whole thing has been worked out is because old Herb was willing to get back in there and do it.

President Johnson: Well, thank you so much, George.

Smathers: All right. Anytime.

President Johnson: Bye.

Smathers: Thank you.

5:02 P.M.

From Larry O'Brien[27]

Johnson's congressional liaison provided an update on last-minute developments on the foreign aid bill.

Jack Valenti: [*in the office*] If you want them to have a record, Mr. President, of the Latin American ambassadors.[28] I wouldn't think it would be. I think it—

The secretary reports that O'Brien is on the line.

Larry O'Brien: [Paul] Findley [amendment] was licked 151 to 119. The committee has risen, and they're now going to introduce the recommit motion.

President Johnson: Have a roll call then?

---

26. Smathers was apparently referring to the biracial committee that had recently been formed. Herbert Wolfe was the chair of the Quadricentennial Commission and the key white businessman involved in St. Augustine negotiations.

27. Tape WH6407.01, Citation #4107, Recordings of Telephone Conversations—White House Series, Recordings and Transcripts of Conversations and Meetings, Lyndon B. Johnson Library.

28. The President was entertaining 18 ambassadors the next day at 6:00 P.M.

O'Brien: Yeah, I think so. So they've moved a little faster today than I thought, however. They've gotten . . . they've risen earlier than I anticipated, and now I would think they would go with this recommit and passage, and here we are. This is on the record, though, so [*chuckles slightly*] we'll see.

President Johnson: OK. Bye.

O'Brien: This is [Otto] Passman recommit.

President Johnson: All right.

O'Brien: OK. Thanks.

> **5:05 P.M.:** The President took a quick unrecorded call from Walter Jenkins, then phoned George Reedy on the personal line (unrecorded, 5:10 P.M.).
>
> **5:12 P.M.:** Continuing to serve as the host of Costa Rican President Orlich, Johnson greeted him in the Cabinet Room. While there, Johnson made unrecorded calls to Jenkins (5:15 P.M.) and to McGeorge Bundy (5:17 P.M.).
>
> **5:25 P.M.:** On his way back to the Oval Office from the Orlich meeting, Johnson stopped to read some of the afternoon coverage of the struggle for a Republican presidential nominee.
>
> **5:30 P.M.:** Reached Jenkins on the personal line and then received another call from Larry O'Brien.

5:31 P.M.

From Larry O'Brien[29]

The deep-voiced O'Brien opened another report on the foreign aid bill before offering a broader summary of key matters before Congress. Johnson continued to fume about the procedural setback on the food stamp bill.

President Johnson: . . . That's pretty good, isn't it? Now, will they have any problem on passing?

---

29. Tape WH6407.01, Citation #4108, Recordings of Telephone Conversations—White House Series, Recordings and Transcripts of Conversations and Meetings, Lyndon B. Johnson Library.

Larry O'Brien: I wouldn't think so. Now we get a shift to Republicans, see, to passage that voted to recommit. Now, you know—and also, we'll have a little shift of our fellows off, but with the 208 to 198, we had 4 or 5 in the well, in reserve, if we had needed them.

President Johnson: Well, usually there's 40 or 50 Republicans [who] vote for the bill on passage, don't they?

O'Brien: Yeah. That's why I say now that we'll get that shift one way, and we'll have a few of our fellows that have gone as far as they can [who] will just shift the other way. So we ought to be all right. They're on the final passage roll call now.

President Johnson: That's good.

Larry, we're really going to have to caution these folks not to let these—Mike Mansfield just went to sleep yesterday and went down and insisted [Allen] Ellender let them add that food stamp amendment.[30] He didn't want to let them add it. [*O'Brien makes a scoffing sound.*] And it was no damn good. And it don't amount to a damn thing, but now we've got to get a rule, and can't get a rule.

O'Brien: Yeah, God.

President Johnson: And it's all because the [Democratic] leadership's inept. We got to get those boys together, the House and Senate.

O'Brien: What the hell would they want amendment for?

President Johnson: Huh?

O'Brien: Why would he do that, I wonder?

President Johnson: Why, he'd do it for [Jack] Miller just because he don't want to oppose him.

O'Brien: [*muttering*] Jesus. Fff—Boy. That's held up a damn important bill.

President Johnson: Yeah, damned important, and we could go with it, I just don't know.

[*with O'Brien acknowledging*] You might want to consider, if Carl Albert can't get it through, he ought to tell the Republicans it's a Republican amendment, and he ought to tell them that we don't want to sell the Australian meat in food stamp anyway. And the Democrats oughtn't to care if we're willing to accept it and just let them . . . except for unanimous consent, he can't get past them. He ought to get them to get a rule, but he says old man [Howard] Smith won't give them a rule now.

---

30. This was Jack Miller's amendment to prohibit the purchase of Australian meat with food stamps. See the conversation between President Johnson and George Smathers, 4:59 P.M., 1 July 1964, in this chapter.

O'Brien: [*muttering*] Geez.

President Johnson: And it doesn't do us a damn bit of good to pass them through one house and the other house screw them up.

O'Brien: I know.

President Johnson: It's what they almost did on [the] Mass Transit [Act].[31]

O'Brien: Yeah. Well, let me get ahold of Albert. He'll be free to discuss this in the next few minutes.

President Johnson: Now, your 30 bills, how many of them have been cut down? We know excise tax; we know [food] marketing; we know the debt limit; that's three.

O'Brien: Yeah. Actually . . . wait a minute, I don't even have the darn list in front of me, Mr. President, I'm sorry, at this point. When I give you the final passage, why don't I give you a quick count on that too?

President Johnson: All right, and the [federal employees] pay bill ought to be through today, oughtn't it?[32]

O'Brien: Yeah, they're on the pay bill. We had a little trouble today: Some of the boys thought maybe they ought to go along with [William] Proxmire on the congressional end of it, but that's been straightened away, and [Mike] Manatos and [Frank] Valeo did some work earlier today. So . . . and Bill was in it, so we're in good shape on that.[33] It may drag on pretty late and maybe even into tomorrow, but it's been going along OK.

President Johnson: OK, all right. Thank you.

O'Brien: OK, Mr. President.

---

31. The Urban Mass Transportation Act had passed the Senate on 30 June.

32. The Senate was considering a $556 bill to raise the salaries of federal employees. It passed the next day, 2 July, and then went into Conference Committee. The House and Senate agreed to the final version on 4 August, with the President signing it on 14 August. *Congressional Quarterly Almanac*, 1964, vol. 20, p. 416.

33. William Proxmire was a Democratic senator from Wisconsin who supported the federal pay raises, but had pushed an amendment to prevent the boosts for Congress. His amendment failed overwhelmingly. Mike Manatos was O'Brien's deputy. Frank Valeo was secretary of the Senate. "Bill" was not positively identified. *Congressional Quarterly Almanac*, 1964, vol. 20, pp. 416–23.

5:37 P.M.

To Ralph Dungan[34]

Ralph Dungan was the White House aide who handled most of the key federal appointments for the President. Here, Johnson spoke to him about filling positions on the National Food Marketing Commission. Of the fifteen commissioners, five were from the Senate, five from the House, and five from the public.[35] The two men then congratulated each other on the defeat of Otto Passman's attempt to trim almost $350 million from the final foreign aid bill.

After first asking for Myer Feldman and being told he was out of the office, the President asks for Dungan.

Ralph Dungan: Mr. President.

White House Operator: There you are, sir.

President Johnson: Ralph?

Dungan: Yes, sir.

President Johnson: Walter [Jenkins] told you that Albert Mitchell checked out all right.[36]

Dungan: Yes, sir! And I told—

President Johnson: You want to be sure to check him with the senators, though, so [Clinton] Anderson don't get his back up.

Dungan: Yes, sir.

President Johnson: And check him with the Republican senator [Edwin Mechem] too, and just say I'd like to know what he thinks of him.[37]

Dungan: All right. Have you talked to him at all, Mr. President? I don't want to duplicate—

President Johnson: No.

Dungan: You have not?

---

34. Tape WH6407.01, Citation #4109, Recordings of Telephone Conversations—White House Series, Recordings and Transcripts of Conversations and Meetings, Lyndon B. Johnson Library.
35. See the conversation between President Johnson and Orville Freeman, 12:00 P.M., 30 June 1964, in this volume.
36. Albert K. Mitchell was a Republican cattle farmer and businessman from New Mexico who had lost a bid for the U.S. Senate in 1940 and was currently the state's Republican national committeeman.
37. Clinton Anderson, a Democrat, was the senior senator from New Mexico. Edwin Mechem, a Republican, was the junior member and would be defeated in the November 1964 election.

President Johnson: No, I have not.

Dungan: All right, sir, I will.

President Johnson: I have not talked to any of them.

Dungan: All right.

President Johnson: You've talked to Judge [Marvin] Jones, haven't you?

Dungan: I have not directly.

President Johnson: Well, Walter said Judge Jones [was] over here, and you talked to him, and he said he'd take it.[38]

Dungan: No, Marvin Jones, I think was talked to by . . . [Orville] Freeman, but I have not talked to him directly.

President Johnson: Well, Walter said you had him over here, and you had a long talk with him, and he said that he would do it.

Dungan: No, sir, I think there was a bad communication there.

President Johnson: All right. Well, you ought to have him over and talk to him and get him set up, and we ought to try to announce it as soon as we can.

Dungan: All right, sir.

President Johnson: If he'll do it this afternoon—see if he'll do it— why, we can announce him as chairman when we name him.

Dungan: Right.

President Johnson: And you might clear out Albert Mitchell this afternoon. Now, do you know whether any of the—who else . . . what about Thurman Arnold?[39]

Dungan: Like . . . What about whom, sir?

President Johnson: Thurman Arnold.

Dungan: I just put a call into him, and I just got a call put into [William] Batten, the [J.C.] Penney fellow.[40] He's not in the office, and I was just about to make the call, as a matter of fact, to Thurman Arnold.

---

38. See the conversation between President Johnson and Orville Freeman, 12:00 P.M., 30 June 1964, in this volume.

39. A prominent Washington, D.C., attorney and a principal in the firm Arnold, Fortas, and Porter, Thurman Arnold was the law partner of Johnson's confidant Abe Fortas. He was not appointed to the Marketing Commission.

40. William Batten, a Republican, was president of J.C. Penney Company. By mid-July, the commission was full. In addition to Batten, Marvin Jones, and Albert Mitchell, Johnson appointed former Democratic congressman Fred Marshall (a man he described publicly as a "dirt farmer") and Elmer Kiehl, dean of the University of Missouri's Agriculture School. "The President's News Conference of July 10, 1964," *Public Papers, Johnson, 1963–64,* 2:851–58.

President Johnson: I may sign that tonight, and if I do, I'd like to name them when I can.

Dungan: All right, sir. I'll call Arnold and the rest of them right now.

President Johnson: All right. Now, I guess this is Lee White and Larry's [O'Brien's] department on civil rights, who we get to . . . that signature, but I guess it looks like we're going to be able to sign it tomorrow.

Dungan: Yes, sir.

President Johnson: We just won the vote 208 to 198 on [Otto] Passman.

Dungan: Oh, boy. Isn't that ter[rific]—That's the recommit?

President Johnson: Yeah.

Dungan: Boy, that's wonderful. My God.

President Johnson: 171 to 151 on tellers.

Dungan: Yeah. I heard that figure earlier, but I must say that the recommit motion is really great.

President Johnson: That's the first time anybody's ever rolled Mr. Passman.[41]

Dungan: Exactly. We're passing that word around. Mike [Feldman] and I were talking about that this afternoon. We—

President Johnson: I wish you would. That damn *Washington Post* ought to have a front-page editorial tomorrow morning. As mean as they and the *New York Times* are to me when I do something wrong, they ought to really go to town for us now.

Dungan: We'll try it.

President Johnson: OK.

Dungan: Right, sir. Bye.

5:40 P.M.: The President called Jack Valenti on the personal line.

5:50 P.M.: Met with George Reedy.

---

41. The *Washington Post*'s lead story was on the defeat of Passman, declaring in its opening line, "An era ended on Capitol Hill yesterday." The paper described the moment as "the most dramatic illustration of President Johnson's special touch." Richard L. Lyons, "Full $3.3-Billion for Aid Passes House, 231–174," *Washington Post*, 2 July 1964.

5:51 P.M.

From McGeorge Bundy[42]

One minute into a session with George Reedy, Johnson took a call from National Security Special Assistant Bundy, who wanted Johnson's feedback on a letter set to go out to Prime Minister George Papandreou of Greece. This sternly worded letter expressed worry that the situation in Cyprus was "near to the last hour" and implored Papandreou to negotiate with the Turks. Bundy commented to Johnson that the Greek Prime Minister "will not like this letter." The correspondence went out this evening at 9:17 P.M. The next day, Papandreou read the letter with a "serious even grim" face and then dismissed it as "more of the same."[43]

President Johnson: Yeah?

McGeorge Bundy: I've got a draft on this [George] Papandreou letter when you want it.

President Johnson: All right. Come right on.

Bundy: Fine.

President Johnson: I've got an appointment in five minutes. Come right on in.

Bundy: Right.

---

42. Tape WH6407.01, Citation #4110, Recordings of Telephone Conversations—White House Series, Recordings and Transcripts of Conversations and Meetings, Lyndon B. Johnson Library.
43. President Johnson to Prime Minister Papandreou, "Telegram from the Department of State to the Embassy in Greece," 9:17 P.M., 1 July 1964, U.S. Department of State, *Foreign Relations of the United States (FRUS), 1964–1968: Cyprus; Greece; Turkey*, ed. James E. Miller (Washington, DC: GPO, 2000), 16:170–71; "Telegram from the Embassy in Greece to the Department of State," 8:00 P.M., 2 July 1964, ibid., 16:172–73.

5:55 P.M.

From Jack Brooks[44]

Having acted as Johnson's eyes and ears in the House over the past few days, Brooks called with news on the final House vote on the foreign aid bill.

> **Jack Brooks:** Congratulations, Mr. President.
> **President Johnson:** Have you passed it?
> **Brooks:** You [are] goddamn right.
> **President Johnson:** What's the vote?
> **Brooks:** 231 to 174, final passage.
> **President Johnson:** Well, that's wonderful.
> **Brooks:** 231 to 174.
> **President Johnson:** OK. God bless you. I'll—
> **Brooks:** You got the vote on recommit [*unclear*].
> **President Johnson:** Yes, sir; yes, sir.
> **Brooks:** Well, I knew you were worried about it, so I kept telling them to hand you those little cards.
> **President Johnson:** Thank you, my friend.
> **Brooks:** Bless your heart, good-bye.
> **President Johnson:** All right, bye.
> [*speaking to someone in office while hanging up*] 231—

5:56 P.M.: Walter Jenkins called the President (unrecorded).

5:57 P.M.

From Larry O'Brien[45]

The delight over defeating Otto Passman continued as Johnson checked up on the administration's legislative scorecard.

---

44. Tape WH6407.01, Citation #4111, Recordings of Telephone Conversations—White House Series, Recordings and Transcripts of Conversations and Meetings, Lyndon B. Johnson Library.
45. Tape WH6407.01, Citation #4112, Recordings of Telephone Conversations—White House Series, Recordings and Transcripts of Conversations and Meetings, Lyndon B. Johnson Library.

Johnson is talking through the speakerphone.

President Johnson: Congratulations.

Larry O'Brien: Well, it's a good one to have over with, isn't it?

President Johnson: Proud of you. Proud of you. How many bills, now, have we cleaned up?

O'Brien: We have six that we can take off this thing. We're taking off now and revising our little memo here.[46] We have six additional ones in conference or ready for conference, and I'm sending you a memo on this that'll be down to you in a couple minutes.

President Johnson: Yeah, but I mean how many have we passed?

O'Brien: Six that we have passed and are down here that you have either signed, or you're awaiting . . .

President Johnson: Well, you said "in conference or ready for conference."

O'Brien: No, there's six more in conference or ready for conference.

President Johnson: And six already passed; that means twelve.

O'Brien: That's right.

President Johnson: And we had 30 to go?

O'Brien: We had 31.

President Johnson: So that leaves 19 that are still up there.

O'Brien: Right.

President Johnson: Uh-huh. And you don't count something like the pay bill?

O'Brien: No.

President Johnson: In the 12?

O'Brien: No.

President Johnson: Mm-hmm. Or the food—we have food stamp. You count that.

O'Brien: Yeah. I'll have a memo and send it right down to you.

President Johnson: Mm-hmm. . . . OK.

O'Brien: And let them list it.

5:59 P.M.: The President called Walter Jenkins on the personal line.

6:00 P.M.: Met with McGeorge Bundy about the Papandreou letter.

---

46. For O'Brien's weekly reports on pending legislation, see "Legislative Reports—Education, O'Brien Memos, Jan 1963–Sept. 1964" folder, Box 1, Special Files: Reports on Pending Legislation, Lyndon B. Johnson Library.

6:05 P.M.

To George Mahon and John Rooney[47]

Democratic congressmen Mahon and Rooney performed key roles in the struggle against Passman.

President Johnson: George?

George Mahon: Hello there, Mr. President.

President Johnson: That was a great victory. I . . . gosh, I [am] proud of you.

Mahon: Well, I'm proud of my President. I was glad to carry some wood and water, boy.

President Johnson: Well, you did a wonderful job. They just told me that nobody could have done it but you.

Mahon: Well . . .

President Johnson: Just said you had them all lined up, but it was a close call, wasn't it?

Mahon: I'm very, very happy about it.

President Johnson: Close call, wasn't it?

Mahon: Yeah.

[*to someone in office*] Tell John Rooney to stand out there just a minute, would you?

President Johnson: Yeah, tell him to come on. I'd like to thank him.

Mahon: Yeah, I'd like to put him on the line with you.

President Johnson: All right, do that.

Mahon: [*Unclear*] I'll tell you, Mr. President, this was a real interesting experience, and nothing except all this work could have done it.

President Johnson: Well, [*unclear*]—

Mahon: But having made this headway, I think it augurs well for the future.

President Johnson: Yes, I think so, and don't you be too damn kind to that guy [Otto Passman], because he's awfully mean, and we've got to let people know it. They can't be that way and play on the team.

Mahon: That's right; that's right.

President Johnson: We all got to be fair and reasonable, and I can

---

47. Tape WH6407.01, Citation #4113, Recordings of Telephone Conversations—White House Series, Recordings and Transcripts of Conversations and Meetings, Lyndon B. Johnson Library.

give and you can give and everybody can give, but a fellow that just says that a man that disagrees with him, is no damn good.

Mahon: Yeah, that's right. Well, it's been a great pleasure to work with you, Mr. President. It's been really wonderful. Here's John Rooney, and you said you wanted to say hello and thank him.

President Johnson: I sure do. . . . Thank you so much, George, and . . .

Mahon: OK, now.

President Johnson: Bye.

John Rooney: Mr. President, I'm just as delighted as you.

President Johnson: They tell me you did a smack-up job, and I—

Rooney: Well, I was in the corners, you know.

President Johnson: No, you weren't in the corners. They tell me you were out there slugging. [*Rooney laughs.*] Somebody told me you gave them a hell of a good speech.

Rooney: I'm a fairly good [*unclear*].

President Johnson: I'm mighty proud of you, and, by God, that shows them where we are, didn't it?

Rooney: That's right.

President Johnson: Thank you.

Rooney: It certainly does. You had to do it, and you faced up to it, and it's done.

President Johnson: Thank you, Johnny. [*Unclear comment by Rooney.*] Johnny, you touch base now with your newspaper people up there so that you get a good press on it. You tell—

Rooney: Oh, [*unclear*] intelligent people in my district, you know that.

President Johnson: I know that, but you—I mean these folks that hang around those House galleries that don't have anybody up there talking to them, and George will go to his office, but you see that they understand that this is the first time this guy's ever taken on and really met his masters.

Rooney: Well, he's been deflated.

President Johnson: OK, partner.

Rooney: Very good, Mr. President.

6:19 P.M.–6:35 P.M.: The President had a flurry of unrecorded phone calls with George Reedy (6:19 P.M. and 6:25 P.M.), McGeorge Bundy (6:20 P.M. and 6:35 P.M.), Bill Moyers (6:21 P.M. and 6:30 P.M.), and Walter Jenkins (6:32 P.M.). He also received word that an amended federal aid to highways bill had been reported

out of the Senate Public Works Committee and was scheduled
for a vote by the full Senate.[48]

6:38 P.M.

To Hubert Humphrey[49]

With the foreign aid bill sewn up, Johnson turned his attention to matters in the Senate. One involved speeding up consideration of the War
on Poverty legislation. The other was the food stamp bill. Here, Johnson
offered Humphrey a possible way to salvage the situation.

President Johnson: What reason did Lister [Hill] give you for not
being able to have that [Labor and Public Welfare] Committee today?[50]

Hubert Humphrey: Well, he gave me several, but we're going to meet
Tuesday morning, report the [War on Poverty] bill out Tuesday, and
have it on the calendar ready for action on Wednesday.

President Johnson: Mm-hmm. OK.

Humphrey: That's—I just got through meeting with Lister and with
Pat McNamara.[51] I told Lister that—he gave me the talk about these
hearings not being printed. I said that don't mean a damn thing. We don't
need any printed hearings. [*Chuckles slightly.*] So . . . but they are apparently no dice on tomorrow, and the boys don't get back in town here, they
figure, early enough Monday morning.

President Johnson: No. No, they won't ever come back Monday.[52]

Humphrey: But Tuesday they have 10:00 [A.M.], scheduled 10:00
meeting, and they promised me that they would report the bill out. I said,
"Now, look it, we're not going to have any dances around there, any mon-
key business, are we?" And they said, "Absolutely not. We'll have that bill

---

48. The bill passed the Senate on 2 July. The House took up the bill again and passed another
version on 28 July, with the Senate concurring that one on 31 July. Johnson signed it on 13
August. *Congressional Quarterly Almanac*, 1964, vol. 20, p. 514.

49. Tape WH6407.01, Citation #4115, Recordings of Telephone Conversations—White House
Series, Recordings and Transcripts of Conversations and Meetings, Lyndon B. Johnson Library.

50. Lister Hill (D-Alabama) was chair of the Senate Labor and Public Welfare Committee,
which had been considering the War on Poverty legislation and would report it out on 7 July.

51. Patrick McNamara (D-Michigan) chaired the Labor and Public Welfare Select Subcommittee
on Poverty that was handling the War on Poverty bill.

52. Johnson was referring to the long Fourth of July weekend.

out Tuesday, put it on the calendar, and we could take it up Wednesday."

President Johnson: All right, now you talk to [Mike] Mansfield and see—

Humphrey: I'm going to talk to Mike right now, and he wants to get the damn bill passed as fast as possible.

President Johnson: You tell him that that's one that you've got to pass.

Humphrey: Yes, sir.

President Johnson: He's busy working on these meat projects of his, and you just tell him this is one we've got to pass.

Humphrey: Yes, sir. Now, the other thing, on this food stamp thing, I got ahold of Carl Albert and talked with him. I reported back because I've been visiting with Mike Manatos. Carl just says that he just couldn't get another rule on that one. But I said, "Well, what about if you get a quick conference, and if we could get the conferees appointed, we could go to conference tomorrow and finish it and pass it."

President Johnson: You can't get a conference unless you get a rule.

Humphrey: Well, they got—I mean they can get a rule for a conference, but not a rule to accept the House amendments or the Senate amendments.

President Johnson: All right, just so we get a rule. I don't think he can do that. He called me.

Humphrey: Did he?

President Johnson: Said [Howard] Smith wouldn't give him a rule on anything. And Mike [Mansfield] went over and got poor [Allen] Ellender, who didn't want to do this damn thing, to take it, which nobody wants to use Australian meat in a food stamp anyway, and [Orville] Freeman wouldn't do it.

Humphrey: Yeah.

President Johnson: And those leaders of the Senate have got to know that when a bill passes the House, please don't add an amendment because it's just as . . . it's almost tantamount to killing it. Howard Smith with a rule.

Humphrey: Yeah, I know.

President Johnson: [*with Humphrey acknowledging*] So, I don't know what we do. You don't think that you might go to this damned . . . if we can't get a rule in the morning, you might go to [*unclear*] [Jack] Miller and say, "Now, we're not going to use Australian meat or any imported meat in a food stamp, and I'll give you administrative assurance." And we could check that out with Freeman and say, "Do you mind if I call that bill back and take that amendment off because it's going to kill the whole damn bill?"

Humphrey: I'll talk to Miller tonight. Maybe I could get a letter from Freeman to that effect to him.

President Johnson: Then you could move it back and take the amendment off and send it to the President like it should have been done with competent leadership before.

Humphrey: Yes, sir.

President Johnson: And that'll straighten us out.

Humphrey: I never knew that Miller had any damn amendment on this bill. There was nothing around—

President Johnson: Well, Ellender didn't want to take it, but Mansfield went over and urged him to take it.

Humphrey: Oh, for God sakes.

President Johnson: And our own leadership is killing it. We all have got to understand that this is an 81-year-old man.[53]

Humphrey: Yeah.

President Johnson: And he is determined to murder any bill he can.

Humphrey: Yes, sir.

President Johnson: And when we got it passed in rule before, we just did it with our eyeteeth. Now we got to go back and get it again, and, of course, he wants to save that money.

Humphrey: I'll tell—I'll get ahold of Miller tonight, and—

President Johnson: Yeah, tell him that you can get him assurance that his amendment will be in effect without putting it on the law.

Humphrey: Yeah.

President Johnson: Why do we want to take chances on killing the thing by law, and you'll get him a letter—

Humphrey: I'll tell you what, the other thing is, if he'd like it: He could . . . he could amend that resolution that's coming out of the Finance Committee on beef with his amendment on that. That Mansfield resolution is out of Finance.

President Johnson: Yeah, but he knows that it won't have as good a chance to pass as this one. The best one is, say, "Now, what you want accomplished is not to use imported meat."

Humphrey: Right.

President Johnson: "Now, if I gave you a letter that we won't put it in the plan at all, won't you let it pass the bill? Otherwise, we're liable not to have a bill."

Humphrey: All right. I'll get at him right—he's downstairs now.

---

53. Johnson was referring to Howard Smith. Smith died in 1976 at the age of 93.

President Johnson: All right.

Humphrey: All right.

President Johnson: Bye.

6:39 P.M.–6:42 P.M.: Ambassador for Protocol Angier Biddle Duke, Duke's wife, and Lady Bird waited for the President to finish looking over a speech draft for an anticipated Civil Rights Act signing ceremony. Disappointed in the version provided by Bill Moyers, Johnson returned it to his close aide.

6:45 P.M.: Johnson and his guests left for a reception at the Pan-American Union Building for President Orlich. They arrived two minutes later.

7:23 P.M.: Left the reception and returned to the Oval Office by himself.

7:26 P.M.–7:32 P.M.: Chatted with Lee White and education aide Douglas Cater.

7:40 P.M.: Had a drink with Yolanda Boozer and Jack Valenti.

8:00 P.M.: Called Walter Jenkins on the personal line.

8:30 P.M.: Sent word to Lady Bird that he would be in the Mansion soon and then called Jenkins again (8:35 P.M.) before actually leaving.

8:45 P.M.: In the Mansion, made an unrecorded call to Speaker of the House John McCormack.

9:00 P.M.–9:31 P.M.: Finished out his day of triumph with dinner and a movie with Lady Bird. Before heading to the White House theater for a pre-release screening of John Huston's *The Night of the Iguana*, however, he made unrecorded calls to Majority Leader Carl Albert (9:02 P.M.) and Congressman George Mahon (9:30 P.M.).[54]

10:50 P.M.: Returned to the living quarters and retired for the evening.

---

54. The film had made its world premiere the night before at the Lincoln Center in New York City, but would not be in open release until August. The premiere also doubled as a fund-raiser for heart disease research. Bosley Crowther, "'Night of the Iguana' Has World Premiere," *New York Times*, 1 July 1964; "Heart Fund Nets $102,519 from Premiere of 'Iguana,'" *New York Times*, 1 July 1964.

Thursday, July 2, 1964

If it's signed today, we are going to have a rather difficult weekend . . . with the Fourth of July and firecrackers going off anyway, with Negroes running all over the South figuring that they get the day off, that they're going to go into every hotel and motel and every restaurant.

—Robert F. Kennedy to President Johnson

If this thing blows up, I want to be in a position of saying I took precautions, and I put all the people that Edgar Hoover could spare down there to try to track down these violators and perpetrators of these crimes.

—President Johnson to J. Edgar Hoover

On June 11, 1963, President John Kennedy asked Congress—and the country—to support a new civil rights bill. He was the third president since the end of World War II to do so. Today, a fourth president signed that bill into law before a live television audience. With the East Room filled with over 130 leaders from civil rights organizations, labor unions, federal bureaucracies, and Congress, Lyndon B. Johnson inked his name to the Civil Rights Act of 1964. This landmark document signaled the end of legalized segregation of public spaces and gave the federal government powerful tools to challenge discrimination in schools, employment, and federally funded programs. Johnson saw the bill as a "time for testing" American character and hoped that it could "close the springs of racial poison."[1]

---

1. "Radio and Television Remarks Upon Signing the Civil Rights Bill," 2 July 1964, *Public Papers of the Presidents of the United States: Lyndon B. Johnson, 1963–64* (Washington, DC: GPO, 1965), 2:842–44.

The Civil Rights Act of 1964 had its immediate origins in the Kennedy administration and owed its passage to the Johnson administration.[2] Its history, however, was much older than that. The movement behind the legislation grew out of decades of struggle at the grassroots level, while the legislation itself evolved during almost 20 years of battles on Capitol Hill. In 1948, Harry Truman had backed a bill to implement the recommendations from *To Secure These Rights*, the report of his Committee on Civil Rights. Truman asked for the creation of a national Civil Rights Commission, a Civil Rights division in the Justice Department, and perhaps most important, a strong Fair Employment Practices Commission (FEPC).[3] His legislation also called for the enactment of federal antilynching statutes, better protections for the right to vote, the desegregation of interstate travel, and a prohibition on discriminating against immigrants from Asia. Although this omnibus legislation failed to pass Congress, it did set a legislative agenda for future generations.[4]

Dwight Eisenhower was not a vigorous advocate of federal civil rights solutions, but in 1957, his administration followed through on several of Truman's proposals. A testament to the lawmaking skills and consensus-building talents of then–Senate Majority Leader Lyndon B. Johnson, the Civil Rights Act of 1957 became the first civil rights bill passed by Congress since 1875. The Eisenhower-proposed legislation established the Civil Rights Commission and expanded the Justice Department's civil rights efforts into a full Civil Rights Division. The most controversial element of the law was Part IV. It expanded voter protections by giving the attorney general the power to file injunctions to prevent individuals from depriving others of the right to vote in federal elections. To make the overall bill more palatable to southern segregationists, this portion was weakened to allow individuals charged with criminal violations of the statute to go before a jury of their peers (effectively meaning southern white men) if fines or penalties exceeded $300. Three years later, the Civil Rights Act of 1960 offered some meager

---

2. The most concise congressional history of the Civil Rights Act is "Civil Rights Act of 1964," *Congressional Quarterly Almanac*, 88th Cong., 2nd sess., 1964, vol. 20 (Washington, DC: Congressional Quarterly Service, 1965), pp. 338–82; and this volume uses the vote totals and chronology from that source. Other key histories of the act are Charles and Barbara Whalen, *The Longest Debate: A Legislative History of the 1964 Civil Rights Act* (Washington, DC: Seven Locks Press, 1985); Robert Mann, *The Walls of Jericho: Lyndon Johnson, Hubert Humphrey, Richard Russell, and the Struggle for Civil Rights* (New York: Harcourt Brace, 1996).

3. In 1939, the Department of Justice had created a Civil Rights Section, but it had remained small.

4. "Special Message to the Congress on Civil Rights," 2 February 1948, *Public Papers of the Presidents of the United States: Harry S. Truman, 1948* (Washington, DC: GPO, 1964), 1:121–26.

provisions allowing federal judges in certain circumstances to appoint referees to investigate voter discrimination.[5]

Over the next three years, the effectiveness of southern resistance to sit-ins, Freedom Rides, boycotts, voter registration crusades, and other direct action protests showed the limitations of existing civil rights laws. Fearing the backlash of southern Democrats, Kennedy steered a cautious course. Violent white reaction to the Freedom Rides in March 1961 encouraged the administration to send in federal marshals, and the riot at Ole Miss on September 30–October 1, 1962 forced Kennedy to order the deployment of the 101st Airborne to Oxford just before midnight. In other action, the administration tried in 1962 to redirect civil rights activism toward more voter registration by helping to form the privately funded Voter Education Project (VEP) of the Southern Regional Council, and in February 1963, it proposed a set of measures that addressed school desegregation, voting, and an extension of the Civil Rights Commission.[6]

The Kennedy administration's approach to civil rights and the whole history of civil rights legislation took a dramatic turn in June 1963, partly because events on the streets of the Deep South could not be ignored, particularly in Alabama. In April and May, Martin Luther King Jr., Fred Shuttlesworth, several Birmingham civil rights leaders, and several civil rights organizations orchestrated an ambitious challenge in the South's steel city. The result became a defining moment of the southern freedom struggle and built momentum for strong national action. In the most intense confrontations, Public Safety Commissioner Theophilus E. "Bull" Connor ordered the use of dogs and high-pressure fire hoses to break up demonstrations and marches, many of them populated by children. Cameras captured the brutality and ensured that the southern problem became an international disgrace that demanded dramatic federal action. A month later, George Wallace, Alabama's unyielding segregationist governor and emerging conservative political star, openly defied Kennedy over the registration of two black students at the University of Alabama. On June 11, with dozens of reporters as witnesses and Deputy Attorney General Nicholas Katzenbach tilting forward in bent-necked exasperation, the tiny Wallace spoke unflinchingly about

---

5. "Annual Message to the Congress on the State of the Union," 10 January 1957, *Public Papers of the Presidents of the United States: Dwight D. Eisenhower, 1957* (Washington, DC: GPO, 1958), 1:17–30; The 1957 bill began as H.R. 6127, the 1960 bill as H.R. 8601.
6. "Special Message to the Congress on Civil Rights," 28 February 1963, *Public Papers of the Presidents of the United States: John F. Kennedy, 1963* (Washington, DC: GPO, 1964), 1:221–30.

states' rights, then jutted out his chin and chest and took his famous "stand in the schoolhouse door."

Later that evening, the Kennedy administration responded by unveiling its bold new plans. Speaking to the nation from the Oval Office, John Kennedy described the situation in the South, and then made an eloquent plea for equal access to public accommodations, for faster public school desegregation, and for several other elements designed to dismantle Jim Crow. Among those measures, he pressed for the power to end discriminatory voting tests and procedures, to send in registrars to places demonstrably practicing discrimination in voter registration, to give the attorney general the right to act on complaints in school desegregation cases, to withhold federal funds from entities practicing discrimination, and to create the Community Relations Service. In the area of jobs, he made some vague appeals to reducing black unemployment and to encouraging voluntary action against discrimination (largely through making permanent the President's Committee on Equal Employment Opportunity).[7]

After Kennedy's speech to the nation—in another Mississippi midnight—a white segregationist shot Medgar Evers in the back with a deer rifle. The Mississippi NAACP director was getting out of his car in the driveway of his Jackson home. He made it a few feet before collapsing; his wife and children had heard the shot and found him seconds later. He died about an hour later at a local hospital. The killer went free for 31 years.[8] Ninety miles to the north in Winona, several fellow activists were suffering from vicious beatings received two days earlier. Returning from a citizenship school and voting rights seminar, they had been arrested at a bus stop and taken to the local jail where, for several hours, police officers—and prisoners acting as their proxy—systematically attacked them with fists, boots, and billy clubs. Among the victims was Fannie Lou Hamer, the Sunflower County sharecropper who later stole Lyndon Johnson's spotlight at the August 1964 Democratic National Convention.[9]

From June 1963 until the signing of the Civil Rights Act in July 1964,

---

7. "Radio and Television Report to the American People on Civil Rights," 11 June 1963; and "Special Message to the Congress on Civil Rights and Job Opportunities," 19 June 1963, ibid., 1:468–71, 483–94.

8. Reed Massengill, *Portrait of a Racist: The Man Who Killed Medgar Evers?* (New York: St. Martin's Press, 1994), pp. 135–36; Myrlie B. Evers, with William Peters, *For Us, The Living* (New York: Doubleday, 1967; repr., Jackson: University Press of Mississippi, 1996), pp. 302, 358. Citations are to the University of Mississippi edition.

9. Fannie Lou Hamer, Affadavit before John D. Due Jr., Hinds County, Mississippi, 24 May 1964, Folder 15: "Depositions Montgomery County," Box 4, Council of Federated Organizations Records, Z/1867.000/S, Mississippi Department of Archives and History.

white southerners fought the mounting pressure for integration any way they could. At the local level, white extremists continued a clandestine reign of terror, often assisted by law enforcement officials (some of whom were initiates of the Ku Klux Klan).[10] The White Citizens' Councils extended their more upscale intimidation, keeping civil rights sympathizers in check through firings, financial harassment, and other economic reprisals. In Washington, D.C., segregationists had equally adept defenders who thrived on congressional seniority and in Senate filibusters a nearly unbreakable will at the podium. For them, parliamentary protocol proved more effective than the pistol or the pink slip.

From June until his death in November, John Kennedy had to contend with those powerful southerners and their shrewd understanding of Capitol Hill, as well as an energized civil rights movement that brought over 250,000 people to the Lincoln Memorial for a March on Washington. Kennedy's response was to target the House of Representatives first. In late October, a bill made it out of the House Judiciary Committee, but it actually went against the President's wishes. Judiciary Chair Emanuel Celler had pressed through a much stronger version that included provisions for a new, more powerful FEPC (known as the Equal Employment Opportunity Commission), for the Justice Department to initiate school desegregation suits without local plaintiffs, and several other tweaks that bolstered the executive branch's power to fight racial discrimination.[11] This new bill went to the House Rules Committee two days before Kennedy's assassination.

Lyndon Johnson wasted no time in seizing upon this legislation as both an homage to the fallen leader and as the basis for his own presidential legacy. Thanks in part to his cajoling and political acumen, the bill made it out of the Rules Committee on January 30 and was passed by the full House on February 10 in a vote of 290 to 130. On February 26, the Senate agreed to put the House version on their calendar for consideration. Debate began on March 9. The anticipated southern filibuster commenced on March 26 and continued for 57 days. On June 10, the

---

10. Roy K. Moore, FBI Special Agent in Charge, to Governor Paul B. Johnson, 23 September 1965, Folder 1: "Ku Klux Klan," Box 142, Series II, Sub-Series 9: Sovereignty Commission, Paul M. Johnson Papers, in Collection M191, Manuscript Collection, McCain Library and Archives, University of Southern Mississippi.

11. See President Kennedy, "Meeting with Eugene Carson Blake," 30 September 1963; and "Meeting on Civil Rights Bill," 23 October 1963, in Jonathan Rosenberg and Zachary Karabell, eds., *Kennedy, Johnson, and the Quest for Justice: The Civil Rights Tapes* (New York: Norton, 2003), pp. 174–93; *Congressional Quarterly Almanac*, 88th Cong., 1st sess., 1963, vol. 19 (Washington, DC: Congressional Quarterly Service, 1963).

Senate invoked cloture by a tally of 71 to 29, cutting cut off discussion and making a vote possible. Throughout the process, Johnson and his allies had stood by the original House version of the bill and held off any core compromises.[12] Nine days later, the full Senate passed the House bill with a few changes and sent it back to the lower chamber for concurrence. In the House, Judge Smith held it in his Rules Committee as long as he could, but he had to let it come to a vote on June 30. By overwhelming margin, the bill left Smith's hands, allowing for a final vote on this day in the House and the historic signing broadcast live on national television at 6:45 P.M. Even at this moment of triumph, the violence of the South seeped through. An hour before the ceremony, Johnson received word from the FBI about a plot to extort ransom money from the family of missing civil rights activist Andrew Goodman.

The White House was too busy this day for its occupants to bask in the glow of their impending civil rights victory. In addition to signing the Civil Rights Act, Johnson would hold ceremonies to swear-in General Maxwell Taylor as ambassador to South Vietnam, open the National Food Marketing Commission, and would greet 18 ambassadors from Latin American countries. He also had over half a dozen phone calls regarding meat imports and other matters before the Senate and took numerous pictures with Oval Office visitors. When it was all over, he and his family got on a plane and flew to Texas for the holiday.

> **9:00 A.M.–10:01 A.M.:** The day began with a family birthday break-fast for the Johnson's youngest daughter. Lady Bird described the 17-year-old Luci as "a beauty, much more grown-up and very much more a woman than I was at that age." Today was also the ninth anniversary of President Johnson's last heart attack, adding special significance to this morning's blood pressure check and exercises.[13] After that, the President made unrecorded calls to Secret Service Chief James Rowley (9:44 A.M.), Bill Moyers (9:50 A.M. and 10:01 A.M.), and George Reedy (9:54 A.M.) The first Dictabelt-preserved call went to a power-ful Republican concerned about the Civil Rights Act signing.

---

12. For a comparison of the original Kennedy bill, the House version, and the Senate version, see *Congressional Quarterly Almanac*, 1964, vol. 20, pp. 362–65.
13. Lady Bird Johnson, *A White House Diary* (New York: Holt, Rinehart, Winston, 1970), p. 173.

10:25 A.M.

From Clare Boothe Luce; President Johnson joined by Lady Bird Johnson[14]

Luce, a former congresswoman who was also married to Time, Inc., President Henry Luce, had read that Johnson planned to hold the signing ceremony on Independence Day. She wanted to make sure that the President knew that she thought it was "quite improper to inject a racial struggle into the Fourth of July." Johnson blamed reporters for the misunderstanding, and in a bit of irony considering Luce's family business, she joined the President in complaining about the press.

President Johnson: Hello?

Clare Boothe Luce: Hello?

President Johnson: Hello?

Luce: Oh, good morning, Mr. President, how are you? Clare Luce, here.

President Johnson: Fine, thank you.

Luce: I'm sorry I'm wasting your time. I called up because I heard yesterday that you were going to sign the civil rights bill on the Fourth of July, and it seemed to be such an appalling idea that I placed a call yesterday.

President Johnson: No.

Luce: And they've just put it through, and I've just read the newspapers. You aren't, thank God. Forgive me wasting your time.

President Johnson: No. No, I've never had any thought of doing that.

Luce: Well, it was in all the papers.

President Johnson: I know it, honey, but . . . [*Chuckles.*] I don't want to be critical of the press. [*Chuckles again.*]

Luce: I know. Well, do you mean to say they put that in without asking?

President Johnson: I mean no human being has ever discussed it with me, and I've never given any indication that I would do anything except sign it the first moment it was available, which would be Thursday. And it's very much like the great war speeches we make all the time, you know.

---

14. Tape WH6407.01, Citation #4116, Recordings of Telephone Conversations—White House Series, Recordings and Transcripts of Conversations and Meetings, Lyndon B. Johnson Library.

I made a speech out in Minneapolis the other day [June 28] for ten minutes, a thousand words on peace, but I said in order to have it, sometimes we have to risk war, and we have to be strong. And they took a half of a sentence [*chuckles*], and the peace went by the wayside, and the headlines were all that I was launching a new war.[15]

Luce: I know. It's terribly difficult. I don't know what's happened to the papers: They pick up first one thing, then the other. Well, I was worried—

President Johnson: You take my word: There's not one person out of 190 million that ever mentioned the Fourth of July *to* me, and I have not mentioned it to one.

Luce: Well, this was even the *New York Times.* [*Chuckles.*]

President Johnson: That's right.

Luce: And I thought, "No, no, I mean, that can't be, because he—"

President Johnson: I think what happened . . . I think what happened: Mr. [Charles] Halleck wanted to take off a week before the San Francisco meeting [Republican National Convention] so that some of his members could go and work on the platform, and I think that in the discussions on the Hill, they decided they'd try to get through this week, and it happens that the . . . I think the Fourth must be on Saturday and that this would be—that would be the end of the week when they would normally adjourn, so they would have to pass it by that time.[16]

Luce: Yes.

President Johnson: And therefore it'd be available. So the stories . . . I've watched them, and I'd say in fairness to the press, they've all [*belches*] originated on the House side of the Congress. And I think that's because it just happens that simul—that they will be adjourning, but they're not going to be adjourning Saturday, they'll be getting through Thursday. They've moved faster than they thought, you see.

Luce: Mm-hmm.

President Johnson: So I plan to sign it tonight, soon as it's available.

Luce: Oh, well, that is very good news. It would have been quite

---

15. Making top headlines in the major newspapers was Johnson's statement that "a nation must be prepared to risk war" if it wanted to keep its "freedom." See the conversation between President Johnson and Hubert Humphrey, 2:35 P.M., 29 June 1964, in this volume; "Remarks at the Annual Swedish Day Picnic, Minnehaha Park, Minneapolis," 28 June 1964, *Public Papers, Johnson, 1963–64*, 1:830–33.

16. Halleck was the House minority leader. See the conversation between President Johnson and Charles Halleck, 6:24 P.M., 22 June 1964, in Guian A. McKee, ed., *The Presidential Recordings, Lyndon B. Johnson: Mississippi Burning and the Passage of the Civil Rights Act, June 1, 1964–July 4 1964*, vol. 7, *June 1, 1964–June 22, 1964* (New York: Norton, 2011), pp. 535–43.

improper to inject a racial struggle into the Fourth of July. [*Chuckles.*]

President Johnson: Well . . .

Luce: Well, I'm sorry to have bothered you. How is Lady Bird?

President Johnson: Just doing fine. I'm mighty glad to hear from you, and—

Luce: I'd like sometime, if I can arrange it with her, to do an article on her with her [*garbled recording*].

President Johnson: Fine, here she is. I'll let her say a word.

Luce: Yeah.

Lady Bird Johnson comes on the line.

Lady Bird Johnson: Hello?

Luce: Hello! Listen, how are you? This is Clare Luce [*unclear*].

Lady Bird Johnson: Yes. Oh . . . fine. Struggling along, and just doing the best we can.

Luce: Well, one of these days when you're not too busy, perhaps you can give me some time, because I would like to do an article [*unclear*]. [*Lady Bird begins to speak, but Luce continues.*] I mean an interview. I know how busy you are now and all that, but I would like to do it on account of I'm so fond of you. [*Chuckles.*]

Lady Bird Johnson: Clare?

Luce: Yes?

Lady Bird Johnson: That's most intriguing, and I will sure try to sometime.

Luce: Well, then I will get in touch. I'm on my way out to the [*unclear*].

Lady Bird Johnson: Good. Have an exciting time. I know you will. [*Laughs.*]

Luce: I don't think there's much to it. I think it's pretty much all over, the shooting's all over it [*unclear, Lady Bird chuckles*]. But after I get back from that, and at the convention—I'm going to the Democratic Convention—

Lady Bird Johnson: Mm-hmm.

Luce: I was telling [*unclear*].

Lady Bird Johnson: Mm-hmm.

Luce: I'd like to get ahold of you, perhaps. If you're going to be there, we could put aside an hour or so.

Lady Bird Johnson: Well, I'm just waiting to get my instructions from our good friend here.

Luce: Yes, [*unclear*]—

Lady Bird Johnson: When and where we're going to be.

Luce: Anyway, you're . . . you're . . . you're sympathetic to the idea.

Lady Bird Johnson: OK.
Luce: OK, [*unclear*]—
Lady Bird Johnson: We'll try.
Luce: And we'll be in touch later.
Lady Bird Johnson: All right.
Luce: Good luck.
Lady Bird Johnson: Bye.
President Johnson returns to the line.
President Johnson: Clare?
The recording ends.

11:00 A.M. From the Mansion, the President had two unrecorded telephone exchanges with George Reedy, then placed a recorded call to the Attorney General from there.

11:19 A.M.

To Robert Kennedy[17]

For the past week, Robert Kennedy and his family had been on a trip to Europe, where the Attorney General had received an enthusiastic welcome. In Poland, crowds of cheering spectators were common, and according to the *New York Times*, Kennedy took to the streets "like an Irish politician running for Mayor of Boston," at one point speaking from the top of a car.[18] In this call, he reflected on his travels before trying to salve President Johnson's feelings about a controversial *Newsweek* interview he had given to *Washington Post* editor Ben Bradlee. After a terse, but diplomatic exchange on that matter, the two men turned to a subject of mutual satisfaction: the best time to sign the Civil Rights Act.

President Johnson: Hi, General.
Robert Kennedy: How are you, Mr. President.
President Johnson: Well, you're a world traveler. How you—You worn out?

---

17. Tape WH6407.01, Citation #4117, Recordings of Telephone Conversations—White House Series, Recordings and Transcripts of Conversations and Meetings, Lyndon B. Johnson Library.
18. Arthur J. Olsen, "Kennedy's Visit Jolts Regime," *New York Times*, 5 July 1964.

Kennedy: Well, no, not too bad. Gosh, that's very encouraging, though.

President Johnson: Must have been exciting.

Kennedy: Well, you know, it just makes you feel so good about the . . . you know, when you . . . when we talk about all our problems here in the United States and foreign aid and all that, and it's not doing any good, how . . . you know, and then you go to a country like Poland that's been hearing bad things from the people for 20 years about the United States and have the people as enthusiastic about our country as they are. You know, it's just . . .

I mean, what . . . how would we feel if Communists came over, [Nikita] Khrushchev's brother or some high official, and visited the Communist Party headquarters, and he has thousands of people getting . . . you know, the ordinary people that are turning out and cheering for him. [*Chuckles slightly.*] You know, that's what they must feel like: They been put[ting] all this effort in and had all this propaganda and this tight control and nobody allowed . . . no opposition allowed for 20 years, and then have an outsider, an American, come in and have the people all make *that* kind of an effort.[19] You know, I just think it's just a damn inspiring thing for the United States. I hope that after January that you're able to go to Eastern Europe and perhaps the Soviet Union. I just think it'd make a hell of a difference.

President Johnson: Good. Well, I'm sure glad you're back. Anybody [who] needs a little invigoration ought to leave Washington, oughtn't they?

Kennedy: Oh boy, what a difference. You see it when you're traveling around.

President Johnson: Sure.

Kennedy: I . . . I talked to Jack Valenti—before I bring that up, I just also yesterday, Mr. President, I read that . . . for the first time, read that article in *Newsweek*.[20] I talked to him [Benjamin Bradlee] for . . . you know, he took—made a trip with me and then, you know, I just spoke about all of these matters quite frankly and openly as I always have, and then he—I never thought he was going to quote me or get in . . . or take things out of context. Well, he wrote that article, and he said, you know, say, "Well, do you think anybody's for you?," and I'd say, "Well, I've

---

19. The *New York Times* reported that the Polish people's response to Kennedy had upset the Polish government. Arthur J. Olsen, "Kennedy's Visit Jolts Regime," *New York Times*, 5 July 1964.

20. Ben Bradlee, "What's Bobby Going to Do?" *Newsweek*, 6 July 1964.

worked for a long time on political campaign[s], so I know a lot of those leaders in the North." And then, you know, he puts—he couldn't . . . He didn't take notes, so he couldn't possibly get the quote correctly, and then I said I thought about it was Lyndon Johnson's administration and—after January—and that he would like to have it on his own, so I wouldn't think that he'd like to have a Kennedy directly associated with it. If I were he, I'd feel that way. So, you know, I just spoke in that context. As it came out, I didn't think it was very happy or very [*unclear*]—

President Johnson: No, I thought it was quite unfortunate. What they're doing, every one of them's playing it. I see this morning you've got—

Kennedy: Dave? Dave Lawrence.[21]

President Johnson: You've got the [*unclear name*], the ABC radio: "Some of the extremists backing Kennedy are challenging Johnson."

Kennedy: And of course, nobody's doing that, and—

President Johnson: David Wells of NBC and Lawrence and [Ralph] McGill and Dugman and O'Neil.[22] They're going to try to get us fighting. I hope we don't have to. I—

Kennedy: No, well, then you—and you know I'm not, hell . . . and I haven't done it and I, you know, I've talked to people for . . . [*sighs*] seven months, and nobody's ever done . . . written anything like that or nor has anybody ever come to you or . . . you know, because it'd be impossible for anybody to come and say anything like that because it hasn't been done. And I haven't done it. Now, people are going to write whatever they want to write—

Seven seconds excised under deed of gift restriction.

Kennedy: I mean, it's not—

President Johnson: Well, unfortunate, and let's forget it, and let's . . . there are too few left in the family—

Kennedy: Yeah.

President Johnson: —and let's hold together—

Kennedy: That's fine.

President Johnson: —as much as we can, and . . .

Kennedy: That's fine. Well, I, as they say, I've got—

President Johnson: We got so much more to be thankful for—

---

21. The syndicated columnist David Lawrence had written that the Bradlee interview was Kennedy's way of announcing his "receptiveness" to the vice presidency. Arthur Krock, "The Kennedy Interview," *New York Times,* 5 July 1964.
22. McGill is likely Ralph McGill, columnist for the *Atlanta Journal-Constitution.* Dugman and O'Neil are phonetic spellings and were not identified.

Kennedy: That's right.

President Johnson: —that we oughtn't to be worried about stuff like this, and I want you . . . you just tell these people [who] come to you that that's a matter that we'll all work out, and—

Kennedy: That's fine. [*Unclear.*] Seems too important to print, if you are not sure.[23]

President Johnson: We'll sit around the table and . . .

Kennedy: Well, I didn't want to get into a discussion about it now, but I just wanted to explain about what the . . . about that—

President Johnson: That's good.

Kennedy: —the background of that so that you would know, Mr. President.

President Johnson: Well, that's all right. I'll see you over at the Cabinet [meeting], I hope.[24]

Kennedy: Could I just take . . .

President Johnson: Yeah.

Kennedy: Take a minute. I talked to Jack Valenti, and I don't know whether this has gone down . . . gone too far, about the signing of the [civil rights] bill. This is a . . . You know, if it's signed today, we are going to have a rather difficult weekend, holiday weekend anyway, and whether . . . that . . . encouraging . . . whether that Friday and Saturday with the Fourth of July and firecrackers going off anyway, with Negroes running all over the South figuring that they get the day off, that they're going to go into every hotel and motel and every restaurant, whether if it's possible—and again, I don't know how far it's gone—whether it would be possible to postpone it until Monday and sign it so that it's in the middle of the week.

The other problem, of course, is that I met with Governor [LeRoy] Collins [of the Community Relations Service] this morning.[25] He really hasn't—he hasn't got any appropriation. He hasn't got his machinery set up, and so he doesn't—he won't be able to move in on any of these situations. There is an advantage if everything was equal, that there would be a great advantage in signing it at the beginning of the week, but as I say,

---

23. The volume editors believe that Kennedy said "I owe you." The audio is not entirely clear, however, and he may have said "I always do" or something similar.

24. Johnson had called a meeting of his Cabinet to discuss the Civil Rights Act. They met later on this day at 1:55 P.M.

25. Title X of the Civil Rights Act created a Community Relations Service in the Commerce Department to help mediate disputes over racial discrimination (primarily) in the South. Johnson's appointment of former Florida Governor LeRoy Collins had been a major point of conversation over the past ten days, particularly on 23 June.

I don't know whether it's gone so far that we . . . that . . . you'd feel that it's necessary to sign it today.

President Johnson: No, I don't think so. Here were the considerations that entered into it: They all announced . . . and we've got to stop that. You tell your publicity man over there, don't say a damn word about what I'm going to do. They've been—all these stories come out about who I'm talking to in the South, and what I'm doing, and kind of the thing we discussed but we didn't carry out, and there've been two or three columns written about it.

Well, the House did the same thing on me. They . . . some of their people up there planned on what the President is going to do. So they all got it pretty well scattered over the country that he was going to wait until July the Fourth to sign it, so that he'd tie it in with the Declaration of Independence. And that was pretty well accepted and generated all over the country before we could stop it. We never mentioned it, never opened our mouth, never said a word.

Kennedy: But, you know, I was thinking [*unclear*]—

President Johnson: [*with Kennedy acknowledging*] So then, some of them started coming back and saying, "Well, that's not fair. It's the [Charles] Hallecks and the rest of them who have participated in this thing are leaving, and they're going to their convention, and you just want to have it so you'll have [Senate Majority Whip Hubert] Humphrey and one or two of them up there taking all the glory and the people that helped do it . . . why do you wait?[26] Why don't you go on and do it when they pass it?"

So I asked them when they thought they'd get through with it, and they said they thought they'd get through by 3:00 or 4:00 [P.M.]. Now they tell me there's some debate that may go on later tonight. I told them that my plan would be to try to sign it as soon as the bill got to me. That I'd already told them how I felt about it. They knew that. There's no point of waiting until it's the Fourth of July. That I thought that was just [to] irritate a lot of people and unnecessarily, and then I didn't think we ought to wait two or three days. So that's kind of how we got off the hook on the Fourth of July by signing it when it gets to us.

Now when it gets to us, I don't know, but I think it'll be late today. We tentatively told them that we plan to do it today, before we heard about this, before I knew you—that you thought it'd be better to go over until

---

26. Humphrey was the floor leader for the bill.

next week. Now, we could back up on it, but I doubt the wisdom of it after we've said that, if the bill gets to us.

Kennedy: I see. I see, and I suppose all the Republicans will be gone next week.

President Johnson: Yes. Yes, they g—they're quitting tonight.

Kennedy: I see. Well then, I think we better go [*unclear*]—

President Johnson: I don't know whether they'll even come or not. I haven't invited them because we don't know what time. I told them, get Lee White and Larry O'Brien, put them in charge of the signings and get in touch with your people and see everybody that ought to be invited. Now, we'd try to have it in the East Room around 7:00 if the bill's here. If it's not, we'll have it whenever we get the bill, but we're kind of waiting until 2:00 or 3:00, see what time we—whether the bill—it got an hour on a rule when they come in at 12 [noon]—and if they make them read the record two or three times, why, it may be late.

But if we have it . . . I'd rather have it tonight than to have it Saturday, and if we have it passed Saturday, I think *they* would think that I held it up two or three days until they got out of town because they've been . . . they've . . . they've questioned. I asked them to stay next week and act on some of these important bills, and they said that wasn't fair play, that I was being unfair to them, that they . . . and they wouldn't pass civil rights [bill] unless I let them go. Well, I never did agree to let them go, but they kind of had an agreement among themselves to pass civil rights and then go. Now, if I held it over, I think they'd say that I was trying to take a little glory away from them on a bipartisan basis, don't you?

Kennedy: I see. Well, you mean because they won't be here?

President Johnson: Yeah, yeah.

Kennedy: Yeah, well, I think that is impossible. I do think that that's impossible.

President Johnson: I think it's important we extend them the invitation at a time when they can come—

Kennedy: Oh yeah. . . . Yes. I do too.

President Johnson: —even if they can't come. I don't know; Halleck may go fishing.

Kennedy: Yeah.

President Johnson: But one of them told me, I've forgotten who it was, I believe [Senate Majority Leader Mike] Mansfield called up and said that he was going to be in session tonight, he didn't know whether he could come or not.

Kennedy: OK.

President Johnson: But I believe that we ought to go ahead if . . . in light of the fact they'll be gone next week.

Kennedy: That's fine. I'd like to have a chance to talk to you about . . . you know, about Poland, some thoughts I had on that.

President Johnson: Fine. You can do it around Cabinet [meeting] . . . right after Cabinet, or right before today, or you can do it tomorrow, whenever you want to.

Kennedy: That'd be fine.

President Johnson: OK.

Kennedy: Thank you.

11:29 A.M.: Johnson showed up at the Oval Office briefly and then ventured to the Cabinet Room to sign a wage bill (H.R. 6041).

11:43 A.M.: On his way back to the Oval Office, he turned down an invitation from West Virginia Senator Jennings Randolph to attend a dedication ceremony in the Mountain State. Two minutes later, he had a photo session with Dr. Frederick Patterson, the president of the United Negro College Fund.

11:55 A.M.

From Clinton Anderson[27]

The low price of cows continued to be a major dilemma for the President. The day before, the Senate Finance Committee had voted 11 to 2 to report out the meat import quota bill. New Mexico Senator Clinton Anderson was a key Democrat on the Finance Committee and had a large population of ranchers in his home state.

President Johnson: Hello?

Clinton Anderson: Hello.

President Johnson: Yes?

Anderson: I think the Finance Committee did something foolish

---

27. Tape WH6407.01, Citation #4118, Recordings of Telephone Conversations—White House Series, Recordings and Transcripts of Conversations and Meetings, Lyndon B. Johnson Library.

yesterday, Mr. President. They reported out that [Carl] Curtis amendment to the meat bill. Now, Mike Mansfield had an amendment, which was endorsed by 26 other people, most of them Democrats.[28] It included support from Gale McGee and [Frank] Moss and those boys that are going to be in trouble out there in the West.[29] But instead of that, Curtis offered his amendment, and all the Democrats except Paul Douglas and me voted for it.[30] Mike's amendment should have carried; the Curtis amendment should never have carried. I wanted to know if you object if I go ahead and raise a little hell about this and suggest they hold up until they find out what the wishes of the administration might be between the two amendments.

Curtis's move is pretty political, I think, Mr. President. He hopes you'd veto it. Then they can go to these western states and say, "Johnson's against the cattlemen." With the other amendment, you at least might have a chance to sign it. I think you could sign it. I know the department's opposed to it, but I believe you could sign that one. I don't think it'd hurt too much, and that would help Moss, it would help McGee, and, I think, help you.

And I've talked to Mike this morning. He's a little sensitive about bringing up his own amendment again, but he said he would do it if he thought there was some hope of getting help on it.

President Johnson: Clint, I don't know the difference between the two, and I would be guided a good deal by your judgment on the matter. I know you know it. I'm . . . asked them to call you yesterday or last night about Albert Mitchell, and I think the boy got sick and didn't get a chance to.[31] But I'm going to name a couple of Republicans to this study group on prices, this investigation we're making of producer-food-chain-store relationships, and I can't really name somebody from the chain stores, from the . . . from the cattle industry. But he's retired, and his boy's running it, they tell me, and the Secretary of Agriculture would take him, and I—

Anderson: Yeah. . . . He's the Republican national committeeman [for New Mexico], but he's your friend.

---

28. The amendment by Carl Curtis (R-Nebraska) was more restrictive and based quotas on quarterly calculations. Mike Mansfield (D-Montana) was the Senate majority leader and had led the charge to establish the quota at an average of the past five years. He later lost the fight for an amendment that would have undone Curtis's quarter system. *Congressional Quarterly Almanac,* 1964, vol. 20, p. 137.
29. In the fall, Gale McGee (D-Wyoming) won reelection by almost 10 percent, Frank Moss (D-Utah) by almost 15 percent.
30. Paul Douglas was a Democratic senator from Illinois.
31. Johnson wanted to appoint Albert K. Mitchell to the National Food Marketing Commission and had asked his aide Ralph Dungan to check with Senator Anderson. See the conversation between President Johnson and Ralph Dungan, 5:37 P.M., 1 July 1964, in this volume.

President Johnson: Well, what I want is a Republican.

Anderson: Yeah.

President Johnson: That won't be . . . that'll try to help us find the real truth.

Anderson: He would.

President Johnson: So that's what I'm going to do.

Now, back to this amendment. I'm real interested in cattle, and I've had the best people in our state [Texas] in here. We produce more than any state in the Union. I've called in the Prime Minister of Australia [Robert Gordon Menzies] and the agriculture minister of New Zealand [Brian Talboys]. I've talked to the ambassador from Ireland [William Fay].[32] And we realize that imports, this year and last year, were excessive. They're not the real problem, but their people believe they are. [*Unclear comment by Anderson.*] So if they believe you are, why, that's just as bad as—[*unclear comment by Anderson*]—being almost. But what—we jumped our supply from 92 million to 106 [million], and until we eat it up, why, we just got that problem, and . . .

But we got Australia. We took this amendment—told them that Mansfield was shoving it and it was very dangerous and very difficult for the President on all these cattle states. And we ship $24 billion worth of stuff out of here every year and we only bring in 18 billion [dollars], so we can't raise too much hell about the people sending stuff in when we're sending it out ourselves and we got a 6 billion [dollar] balance. So we got them to agree voluntarily—Ireland and New Zealand and Australia, the principal importing groups—to reduce their imports—Australia reduces hers 38 percent; New Zealand, 23 percent—to where, by the end of this year—just what they're cutting back now, from June until January—that we will import less this year than the five-year average, which is what Mansfield's amendment covered.

We would achieve the same result as Mansfield without being on record right at the time when we're demanding to send agricultural products into Europe, saying we won't accept them in our own country, and it just screws us up on our trade policies and our trade bill and everything else. So we got them to voluntarily agree to it. Now . . .

Anderson: And it has worked?

President Johnson: [*with Anderson acknowledging*] And it's worked, and it's working now, and the price is up, and we're back. We're ahead yesterday: We got more for cattle than we did a year ago.

---

32. Johnson met with Menzies on 24 June, Talboys on 15 April, and Fay on 27 May.

So we moved it back, and it's going to get better all the time, and furthermore, we are just getting ready to put on the damnedest exporting campaign you ever saw. Our first ship has already landed, and they're eating their meat like nobody's business. And we're going . . . England and France are—Germany—are all short of beef—

Eight seconds excised as classified information.

President Johnson: So we're going to turn it around: Instead of us being importing here, we're going to export the hell out of it. And Australia and New Zealand are already diverting their shippers to the English market because they get more for it there than they do here, and they could afford to voluntarily agree to it. Now, if we come along and by legislation say, "We're going to cut out this," and they come along by legislation say, "Well, we'll cut off that much from America," and it just starts a damn gang war that we can achieve—we can get the same results without it. So that's what I hope.

Now they tell me [House Majority Leader] Carl Albert—he's a big cattleman, got a cattle district down there on the Texas-Oklahoma border.[33] He told me last night, said, "Now, I've held this thing up. I've done everything I can. They're trying to get an opponent for me, but I just see that it's suicidal for the United States to start legislating. We can't sell anything." Said, "Hell, we won't be shipping it . . . people won't be buying our cotton or anything else." And said, "What you've done is put that on as an amendment, and I can't hold it over here. It's an amendment to a House bill."

Anderson: That's right.

President Johnson: And said, "Anyone can apply for a rule and the Republicans will give them a rule, and when it votes, it'll be passed, and . . ."

Anderson: That's why it shouldn't pass the Senate.

President Johnson: Said, "It's just as dangerous as it can be, and I wish you'd get ahold of them in the morning." So I thought I'd call them this morning, see what I could do about it, but I don't know . . .

Anderson: Well, he ought to hold it up in any event, shouldn't he?

President Johnson: I'd hold it up as long as I could, Clint.

Anderson: Would you authorize me to tell Mike [*unclear*]—

President Johnson: Yes, sir; yes, sir. Just—yes, sir. Tell him that I

---

33. Carl Albert represented Oklahoma's Third Congressional District, which abutted Texas and Missouri and was known colloquially as "Little Dixie."

just think it would be disastrous. Tell him you called me; don't let him think I'm going around him.

Anderson: No, I did call you.

President Johnson: Tell him you called me, and I said that we're achieving the same results. We can prove to him that we are: I'll send the Secretary of State and the Secretary of Agriculture to show them if they have any doubt about it. But if this hits the House, it'll just be a Republican move, and they'll win the votes, and it'll hurt Gale McGee and hurt all of us.

Anderson: It would hurt him bad, too.

President Johnson: And it'll hurt me as a cowman having to veto it.

Anderson: That's right. All right, I'll—

President Johnson: And [Sam] Rayburn one time, he didn't want— he wanted [to] vote for the Taft-Hartley bill, but when [Harry] Truman told him he was going to veto it—or [Franklin] Roosevelt, whoever it was—he said he was majority leader, [and] he couldn't afford to cross ways with his president.[34] Now, that'd embarrass the hell out of me to veto something that my majority leader's for, you see?

Anderson: Yeah. Well, I—

President Johnson: But I don't know what I'd do with the rest of the world.

Anderson: You'd have to veto the Curtis rule, Mr. President. You just couldn't do otherwise. It's got pressed meats and everything else in it that the Mansfield amendment didn't have; it has no growth factor; it cuts it below what you could expect otherwise. The way you've worked it out now, the Argentines and New Zealanders wouldn't be too much offended by the Mansfield amendment. They wouldn't like it, but . . .

President Johnson: They say it would break our agreement. They entered into an agreement—

Anderson: I would. I'll stand under the gun and fire this stuff as long as I can to stop it.

President Johnson: All right.

Anderson: But Paul and I cast the only two votes against it.

President Johnson: Well, get up there and just raise hell, and tell them you're going to filibuster, you ain't going to let it pass.

Anderson: All right.

President Johnson: OK. Bye.

---

34. In 1947, Congress overrode Truman's veto of Taft-Hartley, a bill despised by labor unions for undermining the New Deal's Wagner Act.

12:05 P.M.

To Roy Wilkins[35]

Acting on Robert Kennedy's warnings about possible violence if the Civil Rights Act were signed before the holiday weekend, the President turned to the director of the national NAACP, one of his most frequent black advisers on civil rights issues. Johnson encouraged Wilkins to stay in close contact with LeRoy Collins and the Community Relations Service.

Johnson was talking on the speakerphone.
White House Operator: I had him holding, just a second.
President Johnson: Hello?
A 13-second pause ensues.
[*Johnson blows his nose.*] Hello? [*Break in the tape.*]
White House Operator: Hello?
President Johnson: Just answer me, honey, are you going to get him or not?
White House Operator: I'm trying to get him back on the line. He hung up on me. I'm sorry.
President Johnson: Well, cut in. I didn't know that you . . . when I place a call and I don't get it, you cut in and tell me, and I'll get off.
White House Operator: Yeah, well, you were talking to Senator [Clinton] Anderson. I hated to do that.
President Johnson: All right.
White House Operator: I'll have him [in] just a second.
A 25-second pause ensues.
Roy Wilkins: Hello? Hello?
President Johnson: Yes?
Wilkins: Yes.
Operator: Mr. Wilkins?
White House Operator: There you are.
President Johnson: Hello, Roy.
Operator: Mr. Wilkins.
Wilkins: Hello, Mr. President.

---

35. Tape WH6407.01, Citations #4119 and #4120, Recordings of Telephone Conversations—White House Series, Recordings and Transcripts of Conversations and Meetings, Lyndon B. Johnson Library.

President Johnson: How are you?

Operator: Just a moment.

Wilkins: Fine, thank you.

President Johnson: Roy, I need to have you do a little hard thinking for me.

Wilkins: Yes.

President Johnson: This [civil rights] bill looks like it'll be ready late today. They're trying to filibuster it some in the House, and it may not be, but word got out that we might have a big celebration and signing ceremony on July the Fourth. That came from some of the people on the Hill, and . . . we talked around here about it, and nearly everybody concluded that the wise thing to do was to sign the bill as soon as we could and name the conciliation director [Community Relations Service] as soon as we could after it became available. So we planned tentatively to do that this evening.

Wilkins: Yes.

President Johnson: Question has been raised now . . . I've talked to Louis Martin and some of the folks here, and they think we ought to sign it as soon as we can after it's passed.[36] But the question has been raised now that if we sign it that quick, that Saturday throughout the South is a big day when everybody's in town shooting firecrackers, and it's the Fourth of July and celebrating, and the fellows get a few drinks of beer, and we could kick off a wave of trouble that would wind up a lot of people getting hurt, and maybe we ought to wait until after the weekend.

Now, we've already tentatively announced that we're going to do it tonight—

Wilkins: Yes.

President Johnson: —if the bill's available. That is my better judgment, but I thought before I did it that maybe I better check with one or two of my friends and let them think about it and see what their judgment was. They know the situation better than I do maybe.

Wilkins: Mr. President, I think the idea, which has already been suggested, of signing it as soon as it's available is the correct idea. I think you have the right hunch here. I think a delay would simply mean that you felt that you . . . ought to delay signing it, you know? It would be interpreted that way.

---

36. Louis Martin, a former editor of the *Chicago Defender*, was a prominent African American adviser to President Kennedy and President Johnson. He was currently the deputy chairman of the Democratic National Committee.

President Johnson: I tell you another thing that worries me: The Republicans are leaving for their convention, and they're getting out tonight.

Wilkins: That's right.

President Johnson: Congress is not going to be in session in the House tomorrow.

Wilkins: That's right.

President Johnson: And I'm afraid, I don't know whether they'd come or not, but it was bipartisan, and I think that when the . . . We ought to have Republican legislators like [Thomas] Kuchel and like [Charles] Halleck just the same, [Everett] Dirksen, just like we have [Hubert] Humphrey.[37]

Wilkins: That was my . . . that was my second reason. The first one had to do with the problem, perhaps, of violence, but the second one is that the Republicans do deserve a chance at—

President Johnson: That's what I think, and I think they'd charge me with trying to be cute and put off signing after it was ready to sign until after they left town.

Wilkins: That's right. . . . That's right. That's right. And this is the overwhelming political reason. And that's what's being talked about in Washington—I was there last night—and they said the Republicans wanted a chance at it, and that's the reason it was being moved up, and I think it would be regarded as a gracious gesture on your part to sign it promptly so they could take part in the ceremony and go about their convention.

President Johnson: Yeah, all right. OK.

Now . . . I want you to be thinking how you can make good suggestions to LeRoy Collins. I've got . . . They haven't given me a final answer yet, but he has told me if his [National Association of Broadcasters] board will let him, he's going to come with me. . . .

Wilkins: He's a wonderful man.

President Johnson: And I believe it's the best man we could get.

Wilkins: Absolutely a wonderful man.

President Johnson: Will you stay close to him and give him suggestions from time—

---

37. Each of those Republicans had been vital to shepherding the bill through Congress. Thomas Kuchel, from California, was Senate minority whip and led Republicans in support for the civil rights bill.

Wilkins: I'll be happy to do anything I can, Mr. President. Anything I can.

President Johnson: All right. . . . Well . . . I need not reiterate that there's not anybody in this . . . in this cause that . . . and whose judgment I think is sounder than yours, so I just wish you'd take some initiative and not sit back and be too modest.

Wilkins: Very good, I'll . . . I'll endeavor to do anything I can to help out in this matter and to volunteer whatever advice I think will be helpful.

President Johnson: You think about folks like Ted Kheel, that general type, all over the South that you've found that are reasonable.[38]

Wilkins: Yes.

President Johnson: So you can make available some of those people's names to LeRoy, and I'll have him talk to you after he gets in.

Wilkins: Very good.

President Johnson: And I sure do thank you, Roy, and . . . [*unclear comment by Wilkins*]. Did our meeting come out all right with your board?

Wilkins: Yes, it did. I thank you.

President Johnson: Well . . .

Wilkins: I thank you for not only for what you said the other day with the board, but I thank you for what you did on this bill.[39]

President Johnson: Well, I have great confidence in you, and I think we'll . . . we've got a long, hard fight ahead, but if we work together, we can—we'll find the answers.

Wilkins: We'll do it.

President Johnson: Because we're right.

Wilkins: Yes, we'll do it.

President Johnson: We're right. Good-bye.

Wilkins: Thank you.

---

38. Ted Kheel was a New York attorney who had helped mediate railroad labor negotiations in April 1964. He had also assisted Johnson with the Civil Rights Act of 1957. See also the conversation between President Johnson and Luther Hodges, 2:28 P.M., 19 June 1964, in McKee, *Presidential Recordings, Johnson*, vol. 7, *June 1, 1964–June 22, 1964*, pp. 463–68.

39. The President met with the NAACP Board of Directors and vice presidents at the White House on 24 June.

12:09 P.M.

From George Reedy[40]

The press secretary asked for guidance on speaking to the media about the Cabinet meeting and the civil rights signing.

President Johnson is talking through the speakerphone.

George Reedy: Mr. President, one quick question: If they ask me about that Cabinet meeting, what should I tell them?

President Johnson: I'd tell them that we're going to have a Cabinet meeting and that . . . I'm going to go over the civil rights bill with them and general provisions, ask their . . . all of us cooperation . . . you . . . so that the government can all understand its obligations under the bill and leadership that we're expected to provide. I'll probably ask the . . . ask them to give, to get—help us every way they can.

Reedy: Right. OK, sir.

President Johnson: Anything else?

Reedy: No, that's all.

President Johnson: You heard any more about the signing?

Reedy: No, sir. I talked to Larry [O'Brien] about it, and Larry still seems fairly sanguine about 3 [P.M.]. He says it might even go earlier.

President Johnson: He think it ought to be signed today, or put over the weekend?

Reedy: I didn't ask him, sir.

President Johnson: Bobby Kennedy called up and said he thought it might cause a lot of violence in the South, but I don't think we ought to wait. . . .

Reedy: *No, sir.* I think it'd be very bad if you waited. It'd look like you're dawdling around just to get a big ceremony, or something like that.

President Johnson: And I think it'd look like we're waiting until we get out of town, too.

Reedy: Right. I agree. I think it's . . . I think you should handle this as an important bill, one that you aren't playing games with. You're having an appropriate ceremony, but you're having it right away because the

---

40. Tape WH6407.01, Citations #4121 and #4122, Recordings of Telephone Conversations— White House Series, Recordings and Transcripts of Conversations and Meetings, Lyndon B. Johnson Library.

world has been waiting. This country's been waiting 100 years for it. And there's no sense in playing around with it now and making what will look like a big public relations ploy. Actually, it will be, of course, but it won't look like it this way.

President Johnson: Any other news?

Reedy: No, sir, it's pretty quiet otherwise.

12:10 P.M.–12:26 P.M.: Johnson jotted down some birthday greetings to Luci before holding an unpublicized ceremony at 12:11 P.M. in the Oval Office to create the National Food Marketing Commission. Four minutes later, his guests departed, and he began a series of unrecorded calls to Walter Jenkins (12:15 P.M. and 12:26 P.M.) and Jack Valenti (12:16 P.M.).

12:28 P.M.

To Luther Hodges[41]

Johnson contacted the Commerce Secretary and former North Carolina governor to discuss possible reactions to the Civil Rights Act and for advice on a Community Relations Service appointment.

Johnson remains on the speakerphone.

President Johnson: Looks like we may sign this [civil rights] bill tonight.

Luther Hodges: Yes, sir.

President Johnson: And I don't know who they're inviting. You better talk to Larry O'Brien and see if anybody in your department ought to be invited that we don't think of. I don't know . . . We probably ought to announce [LeRoy] Collins, although it's been announced all over the damn lot.

Hodges: Yeah, but I guess we've got to go through the formality, Mr. President.

President Johnson: But I don't know whether we ought to do it on television or not. I guess so.

Hodges: I hope you can.

President Johnson: All right. Maybe you ought to have him there if we do.

Hodges: I'd like to have him there.

Now, I had planned to go out tonight and pick up some [*unclear*][42] tomorrow, but I'll stay if you think it'd be helpful if I stay.

President Johnson: Well, it doesn't make any difference. I'd be glad for you to. I just want to . . .

Hodges: It isn't necessary, is it?

President Johnson: No. I want to suggest this thought.

Hodges: All right.

President Johnson: The Attorney General called this morning, and he says that maybe we ought to wait until next week to sign it because the Negroes[43] through the South will be putting off firecrackers and raising hell and getting drunk.[44] We may have a lot of violence and that you-all are not set up to handle it, and Collins is not in office yet. I don't want to get us separated from Justice Department, but I didn't get that suggestion until we'd already announced—he's [Robert Kennedy's] been over in Poland—

Hodges: Yeah.

President Johnson: —that we were going to do this, and [it's] pretty hard to back up now. I've talked to Roy Wilkins and some of the leaders in that movement, Louis Martin and others. They think it'd be bad to hesitate and wait until next week.

Hodges: So do I, Mr. President.

President Johnson: And we certainly don't want to do it July the Fourth, like some of these leaders want us to, because I think that's rubbing it in, and I'm not going to do that.

Hodges: Well, I . . . I don't mind telling you: I was present when Bob—I went to Bob Kennedy this morning with Collins at Kennedy's request to talk over some transition matters, and he raised the question at that time and a little bit pontifically, and I said, "Bob, you can say anything you want to, to the President, but I don't believe with all the emphasis we've got now that he can hold this over several days. I think he's got to go. Now," I said, "of course, we're going to have trouble whatever day it goes out." So, Mr. President, I don't think you can hold

---

42. Here, Hodges may say "speeches," "peaches," "preachers," or another similar word.

43. One might also hear this as "Nigras."

44. See the conversation between President Johnson and Robert Kennedy, 11:19 A.M., 2 July 1964, in this chapter.

it up. If you hold it up, you're going to have to hold it up until Monday or Tuesday.

President Johnson: Well, that's what he suggests.

Hodges: Well, I don't . . . I don't . . . I don't believe you can get by with it because your whole surge forward, and I agree with you, we should have been talking about this two or three days ago, rather than this morning. I don't see how you can hold it up. Now, I don't . . . politically, I don't think you ought to get any flack out of it from him, and despite the fact he said it in front of three or four people over there [that] he was going to call you. But my judgment, politically, that you . . . although I know we're going to have problems. I don't see how you can hold it up several days with the emphasis that has been placed on it in the last few days.

President Johnson: All right. Now, if we're going to have Collins, how are you going to be prepared to handle it?

Hodges: Mr. President, it would be true, whatever day we bring it out. We've got meetings going on right now, and it's been going on night and day now for a week. There was an ad hoc group in Justice, as you probably know, working on this for some months, and they've been doing some of this, including St. Augustine and so forth. I told them this morning I wanted to quietly borrow any people they had, and although we were not legally set up yet, that we would keep in mind that this weekend—Collins and all the rest of it—would try to throw people in there and see what we could do.

If particularly they could reach the Negro leaders and say, "Please don't hurry about this thing and don't start getting arrested," I think this is one of the most important parts of it. It's really in the hands of the Negroes: If they would go at it slowly and not push it too much, we could handle it. But I'll have to say to you, sir, you may get a couple of hundred cases the first two days, and we're not prepared to handle in that, and neither is any other department of government able to do it. That's the reason that your wires and my letters are going out literally to several thousand people, is to try to prevent this kind of thing from happening. But I couldn't give you any assurance that this thing could be taken care of in a satisfactory way if you had a great bunch of them, Mr. President. Now, we'll do the best we can, that's [*unclear*].

President Johnson: Reckon you could ask Collins and the mayor of Charlotte [Stan Brookshire] and the mayor of Atlanta [Ivan Allen] and Dr. [George] Taylor and Ted Kheel in New York and maybe a dozen topflight conciliators to be available that you could dispatch into various areas if it got too tough, and have the Justice Department work closely with you over the weekend, so if something did come up that they wouldn't say that we were just totally unprepared?[45]

Hodges: Yes, we can, and I'm sure . . . I'm sure that's what's going to come out of this meeting. They will pick [*unclear*], and I think your suggestion is good. It reinforces what they're talking about: of trying to get from the few that we've got—with your wires having gone out, as I understand they did last night, about 200 wires, that theoretically prepares us to reach out and get all these people you're talking about— they're on the list, Ted Kheel and all the rest—so that we could call on them suddenly. But I think that . . . I'll follow your suggestion now and get with Collins in the next hour and see if we can't pick out a 10 or 12 of the blue-ribbon panel and maybe telephone them that they might be called on. That would be your idea, wouldn't it?

President Johnson: That would, and if you had a real roughhouse in St. Augustine or some place—Albany, Georgia.[46]

Hodges: Yes, sir.

President Johnson: If necessary, ask somebody to go in there and call them together and say let's take a look at this, stop and look at this and take a little time.

Hodges: Well, I've said this very thing, you know, sir, to Mr. Allen, the mayor, and told him we might have to call him the first day after you sign the bill, and he said, "I'll be prepared to go anywhere you say." And I've said the same thing to Brookshire of Charlotte, and we've got several others along the same line.

President Johnson: I think it's important, now, that whatever you do in this respect, that you tell Burke Marshall and ask him to go along with you because I don't want them saying that we played hell over in [the] Commerce [Department]. You follow me?

Hodges: I do, indeed.

President Johnson: And they're likely to after this got in the papers and everything that we're going to do it, then they come in and suggest another date.

Hodges: Yeah.

President Johnson: You follow me?

---

45. See the conversation between President Johnson and Luther Hodges, 2:28 P.M., 19 June 1964, in McKee, *Presidential Recordings, Johnson*, vol. 7, *June 1, 1964–June 22, 1964*, pp. 463–68.

46. Martin Luther King Jr.'s involvement in the Albany movement had thrust the small southwestern Georgia town into the media spotlight briefly in December 1961 and extensively in the summer of 1962.

Hodges: I do, indeed, sir. I know *exactly* . . . you don't have to spell it out. I know exactly what you mean. And if I thought this other thing you talked about was realistic, I would advise you to do it, but I don't think it's realistic, the thing they're asking for now.

President Johnson: Now, what I'd do if I were you, then, I'd call them and tell them that it looks like this thing is going to be signed and ask Burke Marshall what he thinks about this kind of a suggestion.[47] Don't tell him that I suggested, just say that you think that you ought to get Collins in, and will he have his group work with him, and what other suggestions does he have.

Hodges: Yes.

President Johnson: Wait just a minute, Luther.

Hodges: All right.

President Johnson: Wait just—

Johnson goes away from line for just over one minute to speak to Walter Jenkins, who was calling on another line.

President Johnson: Luther?

Hodges: Yes, sir.

President Johnson: Now, if we have to pay anybody, they want us to . . . they're talking about our taking a gamble on setting up this conciliation service. It's got no appropriation, and—

Hodges: That's right.

President Johnson: And spending 25[000] [to] 50,000 [dollars] out of the special emergency fund, which hasn't been appropriated. I've had our lawyers look at it . . .

Hodges: Yes, sir.

President Johnson: And they think that's very dangerous business. They think that they'd make an issue out of it up there, and it'd be illegal. What I propose to do would be to, say, set aside 25,000 [dollars] of my special projects fund here at the White House and just employ them as consultants to the White House until we get an appropriation.

Hodges: All right, sir. I looked over that letter that [Kermit] Gordon sent you. I think that's the safest thing. I wouldn't have worried about the other one, but if you can do that and your lawyers tell you that, then I think that's the thing to do.

President Johnson: OK. All right.

Hodges: Now, could I ask you two other questions, or did . . . what did—did Jack [Valenti] brief you about the possibility of Collins, who

---

47. Burke Marshall was assistant attorney general for civil rights.

talked yesterday with [Hubert] Humphrey, about him appearing before each convention if they would allow him to?[48]

President Johnson: Yeah, I told him I wanted to give a little thought to it. Seems like to me it's all right.

Hodges: I think it's all right if done in proper taste, which he'd do, it . . . If you can let us know about that [as] soon as you can, I'd appreciate it.

President Johnson: All right, I will. You check it out with the Attorney General, ask him what he thinks about it.

Hodges: I'll do that.

[Reverend] Billy Graham turned us down, Mr. President.

President Johnson: What'd he say?

Hodges: He simply said that he felt like he could do more good, and he said to tell you that he's going to try to have a crusade in St. Augustine and two or three other places in the South, including Mississippi, before long and he thought this other might detract from it.

President Johnson: That may be. OK.

Hodges: I didn't try to argue. Now, we can—what do we—do you have any suggestions from here? [William] Mitchell will not work.[49] [Willard] Wirtz and I both feel that he's not the way to turn, unless you feel strongly about it.

President Johnson: No, no. No, no. I don't.

Hodges: Now, Arthur Dean, who must know—you didn't want Lucius Clay—so Arthur Dean is a great mediator of worldwide reputation.[50] We could—I'm not sure you could get him. He's a lawyer now in New York.

President Johnson: [*with Hodges acknowledging*] All right. That's all right with me. I'd check with the Attorney General. Be sure that they

---

48. Hodges was referring to the Republican National Convention and the Democratic National Convention.

49. William Mitchell was an attorney from Arkansas. Johnson had considered him for the Civil Rights Commission in March 1964. See the conversations regarding that appointment on 2 March 1964 in Robert David Johnson and Kent B. Germany, eds., *The Presidential Recordings, Lyndon B. Johnson: Toward the Great Society, February 1, 1964–May 31, 1964*, vol. 4, *February 1, 1964–March 8, 1964* (New York: Norton, 2007), pp. 865, 872–82.

50. They were discussing candidates to head up the National Citizens Commission for Community Relations, a national advisory committee for the Community Relations Service. On 3 July, Johnson named Arthur Dean, a negotiator who had helped broker the 1963 Nuclear Test Ban Treaty. Lucius Clay was once the military governor of West Germany and the commander of U.S. forces in Europe from 1945 to 1949. See the conversation between President Johnson and Arthur Dean, 11:29 A.M., 3 July 1964, in this volume.

don't undercut us, and they don't tell the Negro groups that the South is taking over, and they've got nothing to do with it.

Hodges: All right. Fred Kappel would bother you if we couldn't get Dean?[51]

President Johnson: No, I'd like to have Kappel, but I don't think he'd do it at all.

Hodges: Yeah. Well, I'll try the both of those.

President Johnson: All right.

Hodges: I'll start working on it.

President Johnson: I don't know who else . . .

Hodges: Well, we've got . . . of course, Crawford Greenewalt I don't think would be the man.[52] And you'd have to go down the line, probably, with some good men, but not as well known. We could . . .

President Johnson: You be sure you clear it over there, and whatever y'all get together ought to suit me. I just don't want them undercutting you.

Hodges: I'll do that.

President Johnson: Bye.

12:36 P.M.–12:41 P.M.: Prior to speaking with Under Secretary of State for Political Affairs Averell Harriman, Johnson had two brief off-the-record photo sessions, the first with Fred Schwengel (R–Iowa) at 12:36 P.M., who was president of the U.S. Capitol Historical Society. The other session, with Adolf Berle Jr., the former assistant secretary of state (1938–1944) and Latin American expert who was a leading figure in New York's Liberal Party, began at 12:41 P.M., right before the call with Harriman. Harriman and Berle had known each other for several decades and had worked together at the State Department during and after World War II.

---

51. Fred Kappel was the president of AT&T.
52. Crawford Greenewalt was chairman of the DuPont Company.

12:42 P.M.

To Averell Harriman[53]

The prominent heir of a railroad family, Harriman was a well-known financier, diplomat, and politician. In addition to a stint as New York governor and failed bids for the Democratic presidential nomination, he had served as a key adviser to Presidents Roosevelt, Truman, and Kennedy. Harriman was also a close friend of the Kennedy family who had housed Jacqueline Kennedy after she left the White House. In this call, Johnson tried to assure the current under secretary of state for political affairs that his ideas were valued by the Johnson administration, while Harriman attempted to address an oversight regarding the invitation list to today's swearing-in of General Maxwell Taylor.

A brief office conversation [with A. A. Berle] precedes the call.
Unidentified: They're coming in, sir.
President Johnson: Hello, [*unclear*]. How are you? Nice to see you.
Adolf Berle Jr.: Good to see you again.
President Johnson: How are things getting along?
Berle: [*Unclear.*]
Unidentified: [*Unclear*], sir.
President Johnson: There's a little memo that . . . we're having the ambassadors in tonight [at 6:00 P.M.] from Latin America. Read that.
[*on phone*] Hello?
Berle: You've got a new one—
The operator connects the call.
President Johnson: Yes? Averell?
Averell Harriman: Yes, sir.
President Johnson: I just wanted to tell you I got your notes, and I particularly appreciate these little brief reports and suggestions you make and your passing on what you pick up at these meetings, and I think it's very good for you to send them. And the Michigan memo I was particularly pleased about, and I just wanted to . . . I didn't want you to think that I just read them and filed them and didn't—
Harriman: No.

---

53. Tape WH6407.02, Citation #4124, Recordings of Telephone Conversations—White House Series, Recordings and Transcripts of Conversations and Meetings, Lyndon B. Johnson Library.

President Johnson: —appreciate them because sometimes I don't get back to you immediately. But I do thank you, and I do think that it's extremely important, and I don't know anybody better equipped to do it than you are.

Harriman: Well, I'm grateful for you calling. I'm pretty careful about what I do. I make thoroughly political talks in a nonpolitical way or nonpolitical talks in a political way, and I think it does some good, and I've had a fair amount of experience with this over the last decade or so.

President Johnson: Well . . .

Harriman: Mr. President, General [Paul] Harkins is here with me for lunch.[54] He hasn't been invited to the swearing-in of General [Maxwell] Taylor. [It] must have been an oversight. May I ask him in your name?

President Johnson: Yes, I didn't know . . . I didn't know that it'd been arranged yet. Has it?

Harriman: Well, we've been told that the swearing-in is at 1:30 [P.M.]. Is that correct?

President Johnson: Yes, I guess so. I didn't know it. Yeah, sure, I'd invite him over.

Harriman: Well, can I invite him in your name? It has gotten up such a short time, and . . .

President Johnson: Sure, matter of fact I wasn't sure it [was] 1:30 myself.

Harriman: Yeah.

President Johnson: But if you're sure of that, why, do it, and—

Harriman: Well, I'll bring him over whenever the time is. I'll check and see what time it is.

President Johnson: That'd be good, Averell. I just wanted—

Harriman: Thanks a lot. I'm grateful to you for calling.

President Johnson: Thank you.

12:44 P.M.–12:54 P.M.: Immediately after the Harriman call, the President had two unrecorded phone conversations with Jack Valenti (12:44 P.M. and 12:51 P.M.). The ongoing photo session with Adolf Berle ended at 12:51 P.M., and then at 12:54 P.M., President Johnson began a 20-minute, off-the-record meeting with

---

54. On 19 June, General Paul Harkins had stepped down as commander of U.S. forces (MACV) in Vietnam. Johnson awarded him the Distinguished Service Medal on 24 June.

Matthew McCloskey, the former ambassador to Ireland and Democratic fund-raiser who had been implicated in the Bobby Baker scandal over the past year. A few minutes after their session began, Johnson phoned the Senate majority whip.

12:56 P.M.

To Hubert Humphrey[55]

Johnson continued to address the Senate's handling of meat imports. Midway through the call, the President switched to a discussion of the Civil Rights Act signing ceremony and other matters before the Senate. Humphrey had been the administration's floor leader for the civil rights bill.

Unidentified: If he was to win this one—[56]
An office secretary interrupts to report that Humphrey is on the line.
President Johnson: Hubert?
Hubert Humphrey: Yes, Mr. President.
President Johnson: I thought I ought to talk to you. Clint Anderson called me this morning, and he's awfully upset about that meat amendment that—
Humphrey: I know it.
President Johnson: —came out on [Carl] Curtis yesterday. He said they ought to be [Mike] Mansfield's. Now, Orville [Freeman] and [Dean] Rusk have got them to agree to limit their imports to less than the five-year average, and that's what they'll run this year. And we're getting by administrative agreement what we hope we wouldn't have to do by law because we send out 24 billion [dollars], and we take in only 18 [billion dollars], and if we go to passing laws saying we won't take in your stuff, they'll go to passing laws saying they won't take in our stuff. And we're routing these ships now: Instead of coming here, we're routing them to England and France, and then we're putting on a big export campaign ourself.
Six seconds excised as classified information.

---

55. Tape WH6407.02, Citation #4126, Recordings of Telephone Conversations—White House Series, Recordings and Transcripts of Conversations and Meetings, Lyndon B. Johnson Library.
56. This unidentified person may have been Matthew McCloskey.

President Johnson: [*with Humphrey acknowledging*] England's short of it, so we're going to be exporting it, and it's damn poor grace for us to say we won't take any, but we want you to take ours. And it's just going to have us in hell of a shape, me vetoing a majority leader's resolution or even Curtis's. Now, Carl Albert called me last night, said he's humiliated, said he's got more cattle than anybody.

Humphrey: Yes, sir.

President Johnson: [*with Humphrey acknowledging throughout*] But he just thinks it's outrageous. But he says he can't hold it: If the Senate passes it, it's coming right on to us.

And it looks like to me the Democratic Party's getting in worse shape in Pennsylvania, by God, with [Genevieve] Blatt and [Michael] Musmanno, just because we don't think.[57] And I think some of them ought to consider that. Maybe you could get Clint, and you-all could talk and agree to hold up Curtis's for a while and find some way that maybe Albert can work it out.

Humphrey: The . . . I talked to Carl this morning, and we are thinking about that. There are a couple of other little tactics that we could use. One of them is that if this bill went up to the Senate and passed, then somebody can file a motion, you know, immediately to ask that it be reconsidered and put . . . you know, just file a motion of reconsideration—that is, if they don't go through the business of tabling and all. Or to call the bill back. There are a lot of these little tricky ones that we can use.

I'll talk to Clint today, but I told Carl this morning, it'll pass this Senate like a dose of salts if we get it up here.

President Johnson: Well, now, what do I do? If it comes in here now? It'll be overriding your veto if that's what it does, and I'll tell you, it's a very bad thing nationally and internationally to do. Don't you think so?

Humphrey: I think it is. I'll . . .

---

57. Since the Democratic primary on 29 April, Genevieve Blatt and Michael Musmanno had been locked in a battle over who would challenge Republican Hugh Scott in the fall. Blatt was slightly ahead in the count, but Musmanno, a Pennsylvania Supreme Court justice on leave from the bench who was the favored candidate of the state Democratic Party regulars, was suing to include 6,000 votes from Philadelphia that had not been counted due to machine error. On 1 July, the day before this phone call, Musmanno took his case to his colleagues on the state Supreme Court. Eventually, on 28 July, the court would rule in Blatt's favor. Initially undeterred, Musmanno would continue to fight the ruling for two more weeks before giving up. Blatt went on to lose a close race with Senator Scott and actually launched her own challenge of those results. An investigation of vote fraud in the Blatt-Musmanno primary continued until July 1965. "Pennsylvania High Court Hears Musmanno Appeal," *New York Times*, 2 July 1964; "William G. Weart, "Miss Blatt Opens Senate Race After Claiming Primary Victory," *New York Times*, 15 August 1964; "Vote Inquiry Off in Pennsylvania," *New York Times*, 14 July 1965.

President Johnson: We talk about our great trade program, and we got [Christian] Herter over there in Geneva, and we're trying to . . .[58]

Humphrey: Yeah, and you see we passed this one "buy American" business on the transit thing. We got this Kennedy Round going over there, and it's all very bad. I agree with you. It puts us in a—

President Johnson: And you see what's happened since Mike got to demagoguing for these goddamn meat men. We got meat up above what it was last year.

Humphrey: That's correct.

President Johnson: The report last night shows that we paid $23.80, and it was $23 last year for 800-pound steers, so we're 80 cents a hundred more than they were getting this time last year.

Humphrey: Well, nothing's going to be done on this bill until after the conventions anyway.

President Johnson: Well, you just delay it . . .

Humphrey: I'll delay the hell out of it around here, and—

President Johnson: Now, another thing, Bobby [Kennedy] came in this morning and suggested we might not ought to sign that thing [the civil rights bill] tonight, maybe we ought to wait until next week. I'm afraid to wait until next week because . . . he said well, they might have some trouble Saturday, Negroes putting off firecrackers and everything. I talked to Roy Wilkins and some of them; they say we ought to sign it as soon as it gets available.[59] It oughtn't to be on July the Fourth, but go on and sign it as soon as it gets available. Another thing, I don't want the Republicans to think that I wanted to wait until they got out of town and then put on a public relation trick with just me and you.

Humphrey: I agree. I think you . . . that that would be very unfortunate. I think you ought to sign it either tonight or tomorrow, and . . .

President Johnson: Just as soon as it's available, not show any doubt or hesitancy.

Humphrey: No hesitancy at all, and it might very well be—I spoke to Mike Manatos and Larry [O'Brien] this morning about the fact that you have some people that ought to be invited into this ceremony. You may want to hold it up until tomorrow morning.

---

58. Former Massachusetts governor and secretary of state Christian Herter served as a special trade representative for the President at the General Agreement on Tariffs and Trade (GATT) talks. Known as the Kennedy Round, those talks had begun in Geneva, Switzerland, in May 1964.

59. See the conversation between President Johnson and Roy Wilkins, 12:05 P.M., 2 July 1964, in this chapter.

President Johnson: No, we want that night TV, is what we want.

Humphrey: You want the night TV. Well then, it . . . I mean, you could, you know . . . whatever you think is best.

President Johnson: We're going to try to shoot 7:00 if the House gets us the bill.

Humphrey: Yes, sir.

President Johnson: OK.

Humphrey: Well, I think that you ought to get the most out of it, and I'd sure—

President Johnson: When are you going to pass the pay bill?

Humphrey: We ought to pass it in the next three hours.

President Johnson: Mm-hmm.

Humphrey: And it's all in good shape; there's no problem here.

President Johnson: What else you taking today?

Humphrey: Gee, just some . . . we've got, I think the housing bill is being reported today. I [*unclear*]—

President Johnson: Be sure, now, you ought to feel Mike [Mansfield] out. Tell him it's going to be bad when the President and the majority leader go to vetoing each other's bills. [Sam] Rayburn one time wanted to vote for Taft-Hartley, but when [Franklin] Roosevelt told him he was going to veto it, why, he had to vote for it.[60] I sure hate for us to get separated that way, but I don't believe an American president ought to be signing a bill that says to Australia and New Zealand that we ain't going to let you ship stuff to us.

Humphrey: Right.

President Johnson: Do you?

Humphrey: I think not. Well, let me just—I'll delay this. I'll get on this with Clint. I'll talk . . . we'll—

President Johnson: Talk to Clint, and you ought to talk to Mike. Just let him see what this story is. Vietnam is bad enough for us to differ about. When we get . . . we go to . . . going back to Smoot-Hawley, why, it's pretty bad for a Democrat.[61]

Humphrey: Yeah.

President Johnson: I don't—

Humphrey: Let me, may I—may . . . one other suggestion. Now, I've

---

60. On this matter, see the conversation between President Johnson and Clinton Anderson, 11:55 A.M., 2 July 1964, in this chapter.

61. Passed in 1930, the controversial Smoot-Hawley Tariff Act raised tariffs dramatically on a wide range of goods. It is considered one of the most protectionist pieces of legislation in U.S. history.

been pushing hard to get this poverty bill through next week, and I think we can make it.[62] I think we are all right. We'll get the bill up. [Everett] Dirksen and the boys are going to raise hell about having this bill up, and . . .

President Johnson: *Why?*

Humphrey: Well, because their boys [are] going to be out of town, see; a lot of their boys. Now, I just want to make sure that any note that comes over here is very firm about us pushing to get this bill up.

President Johnson: Yeah, well, I sure hope it is. I'd love for it to. Y'all are going to be in session next week.

Humphrey: We're going to be in session, and . . .

President Johnson: And I would tell them that anybody who wants to pair on it, you'll give them a pair. Tell them you'll give them a pair yourself. You'll get him pairs for four or five people that are gone.[63]

Humphrey: Yes, sir.

President Johnson: But he agreed for the Senate to be in session. He didn't agree that it'd be in session and not do anything.

Humphrey: Well, they kind of talked about, you know, it's an easy cats and dogs stages around here. But I just talked with Mike, and he wants to bring it up next week, but I was worried that the pressure might get a little heavy here.

President Johnson: Well . . .

Humphrey: Now, the other thing is, we're going to report the foreign aid bill this afternoon, and it's in good shape.

President Johnson: Please don't let them cut. They cut 30 million [dollars] off that we beat [Otto] Passman on.

Humphrey: Yeah, well, we're not—we're in good shape here on the foreign aid bill. And the only question is, we could pass that damn bill next week except our friend Wayne Morse is *demanding* that this go over until after the Republican [National] Convention.[64]

---

62. The Senate Labor and Public Welfare Committee's Select Subcommittee on Poverty had been holding hearings on the poverty bill since 17 June. On 7 July, the full committee would vote to send the bill out to the Senate. The only two committee members voting against it were Barry Goldwater (R-Arizona) and John Tower (R-Texas). *Congressional Quarterly Almanac*, 1964, vol. 20, p. 224.

63. Generally, pairing is a procedure in which one Republican and one Democrat agree not to vote on a particular measure, thereby creating a "pair."

64. Wayne Morse (D-Oregon) was a member of the Senate Foreign Relations Committee who fought against the foreign aid bill and later successfully injected amendments to establish an appropriations ceiling of $3.25 billion. Also, in August 1964, he and Ernest Gruening (D-Alaska) were the only senators to vote against the Gulf of Tonkin Resolution. *Congressional Quarterly Almanac*, 1964, vol. 20, p. 307.

President Johnson: Why?

Humphrey: Well, because he's got to make some speeches out around the country, and he wants to file a minority report, and then he says you—he just told me over at the White House this morning, he says, "You're just not going to pass that bill when I'm gone next week. You just make up your mind to that, if I have to tie the Senate up into knots." Well, I don't know what the hell we . . . I want . . . I feel that we ought not to let one man just do this. He—

President Johnson: I wouldn't at all, but you-all are the boss. But I'd go—I made him go around on tidelands two nights, and I whupped his tail, but I don't know what you-all will do.[65] You can't do it by quitting at 8:00. I wouldn't let him do it at all.

Humphrey: We're going to have it out on the calendar, and it'll be reported tonight, and it'll be ready for action Monday.[66] I just think we ought to go ahead.

President Johnson: I would too.

You getting any appropriation bills?

Humphrey: Yes, sir. We'll have several of them ready next week. We'll have . . . oh, I guess about three of them. We'll be . . . We'll be in hellish good shape next week. Right down the line.[67]

President Johnson: OK.

Humphrey: Bye-bye.

President Johnson: Bye.

---

65. Oil-rich coastal states, particularly California and those along the Gulf of Mexico, had been battling with the federal government for several decades over the line where federal offshore waters began and state jurisdiction ended. In 1953, Senator Morse filibustered the submerged land bill for 22 hours and 26 minutes, setting what the *New York Times* claimed was a record for the "longest continuous speech" in Senate history. Johnson and other coastal senators backed the bill to return more land to state control. In the month after Morse's speech, they were able to push through the Submerged Lands Act of 1953. Disputes, however, continued for another two decades. In 1975, the Supreme Court ruled in *United States v. Maine* that federal waters began three miles from the low-water mark. *United States v. Maine*, 420 U.S. 515 (1975); John D. Morris, "Morse Sets Mark with 22-Hour Talk on Offshore Bill," *New York Times*, 26 April 1953.

66. On this day, the Senate Foreign Relations Committee reported out the foreign aid bill, although with $50 million less than the Johnson administration wanted. The Senate filed the committee's report on 10 July, began discussion of it on 1 August, and after a delay, passed it on 24 September. After a successful vote on the House/Senate Conference Committee version, the President signed the final bill on 7 October. *Congressional Quarterly Almanac*, 1964, vol. 20, pp. 296, 306–7, 311.

67. Senate hearings on foreign aid appropriations began on 21 July. *Congressional Quarterly Almanac*, 1964, vol. 20, p. 314.

1:15 P.M.: Before connecting with Larry O'Brien, Johnson talked (unrecorded) to Jack Valenti on the personal line.

1:16 P.M.

To Larry O'Brien[68]

Concerned about rewarding supporters of the Civil Rights Act, Johnson called his chief expert on the Hill about details for the anticipated signing ceremony. The President also explored responses to the meat import quota bill set to come out of the Senate Finance Committee on this day.

The President is using the speakerphone.
President Johnson: Larry?
Larry O'Brien: Yes, Mr. President.
President Johnson: What is our situation on the signing [of the civil rights bill], and . . . how . . . how are we going to avoid overlooking somebody?
O'Brien: Well, first on the signing, they're . . . they're debating the resolution right now. They should be able to . . . they should vote about 1:30 [P.M.], Claude [Desautels] tells me, 1:35. So that gets . . . we're all set on our end.[69] We've gone over these lists very, very carefully: lists submitted by Justice, lists that involve the Negro community, and, of course, obviously the appropriate congressional people. We felt that the format of the tax bill went reasonably well for a large signing ceremony and that we would have the key people that should be gathered around you in the East Room. We would have them properly placed so the appropriate people will have the proper recognition, and we won't have a mob scene of elbowing.[70] We—
President Johnson: And you look after the Republicans so we don't get cussed out about that.
O'Brien: That's the major part of the problem, are the . . . is the

---

68. Tape WH6407.02, Citations #4127 and #4128, Recordings of Telephone Conversations—White House Series, Recordings and Transcripts of Conversations and Meetings, Lyndon B. Johnson Library.
69. Claude Desautels was a legislative liaison working for O'Brien.
70. Johnson chose a prime-time television signing for the Revenue Act (or tax bill) on 26 February. See 26 February 1964, in Johnson and Germany, *Presidential Recordings, Johnson*, vol. 4, *February 1, 1964–March 8, 1964*, pp. 734–74.

[Kenneth] Keating–[Jacob] Javits part.[71] Now, [Thomas] Kuchel is another story. We thought we'd . . .

President Johnson: Kuchel–[William] McCulloch.[72]

O'Brien: Yeah. That we thought that we would place them, but nevertheless the Democrats would have the key spots. Now, in addition to that, when they . . . when you actually sign the bill and they're seated for your remarks, we're going to have name cards on the first two rows—there will be about 14 or 15 of them—key people who will be placed in the seats that we designate. The others gather, again, in seats behind them. We may have . . . I think we've got it geared, Mr. President, that number one: that people that should be at this ceremony—that I don't think, very honestly, we've overlooked anyone that would be key and would feel that someone was invited and if he were invited, why wasn't the other guy. I think we're in good shape that way. And secondly, I think the format that's been established—Claude and Jack [Valenti] have worked on it, and Claude and I have talked it over in detail—

President Johnson: Just as long as . . . just as long as you're . . . you know . . . you're in charge of it, I'll feel relieved, and I don't want to know—

O'Brien: All right. Well, I'll—

President Johnson: —anything about it. I just want you to run the show, and I know you'll do it right.

O'Brien: I'm taking the responsibility.

President Johnson: That's good.

Now, any other news?

O'Brien: No, nothing too much at the moment.

President Johnson: And [Wayne] Morse tells them that he's not going to let them bring up foreign aid until after the conventions, and he's not going to let them bring up authorization, and he's just having hell with them, they tell us.

O'Brien: Yeah.

President Johnson: Now on this meat thing, that can be disastrous to us. I don't know. You better talk to [Mike] Mansfield. [Carl] Albert called me last night. I talked to Albert to thank him, and he said it's just awful, that he's got a big beef district himself.

---

71. Republican senators from New York, Kenneth Keating and Jacob Javits had supported the civil rights bill.

72. William McCulloch (R-Ohio) was a key member of the House Judiciary Committee who was cultivated by the Kennedy and Johnson administrations. Thomas Kuchel was leading the Senate Republicans in support of the bill.

O'Brien: Yeah.

President Johnson: And they've added that to an amendment to a House-passed bill, and it doesn't even go to the committee, and that all they've got to do is get a rule, and all the Republicans will give them a rule immediately.

O'Brien: Yeah. Now, I talked to Albert this morning on this, and I didn't get the same reaction, but he sounded like a fellow who wanted to try somehow without being caught with his own fingers in the cookie jar to have this thing fade out over in the House. Now, however, [Orville] Freeman followed my call with him by a visit, and Freeman reported back that Albert was very, very tough on this, that—

President Johnson: [*with O'Brien acknowledging*] Well, he told me last night, and [Hubert] Humphrey told me this morning, that he just says if it passes the Senate it's long gone, and the only thing I can do is veto it. And I think if I go to vetoing stuff that Mansfield's interested in, it'd be terrible, and I can't afford to sign a bill that—we ship out $24 billion worth of stuff a year, and we only import 18 billion, and if we go to signing bills like that, well, other countries will go to sign them, [and] we'll loose 6 billion in trade ourselves. And we've already got the same agreement by voluntary means. The damn thing doesn't do . . . it just makes a law out of something we don't need a law on.

O'Brien: Yeah, now—

President Johnson: But I don't know how to stop Mansfield on it.

O'Brien: I . . . Now, I had asked Albert as a friend of the court, so to speak, to talk to Mansfield this morning. He did talk to him, and he reported to Freeman that Mansfield told him that he just was not going to budge; by God, the Senate was going to pass that.

President Johnson: Well, I think that's right, and I think it's a terrible mistake.

O'Brien: So I asked Freeman to get back directly with Mansfield and go over all these statistics that Freeman has showing price increases and a generally improved situation and report back again on how he made out in that conversation. And that's about where we stand, and—

President Johnson: [*with O'Brien acknowledging*] I think what you better do, Larry, you better call Dean Rusk, and ask Dean Rusk. And tell him to take the Secretary of Commerce on his trade if he wants to, or his trade expert, George Ball, and they'd better get up and have a meeting with the . . . ask the Senate leadership to have a meeting with [Clinton] Anderson, who's very interested in the subject, and Mansfield and Humphrey. And point out to them there's great dangers and how—

what will happen, and how it will ruin our Kennedy Round, and see if they can't have a meeting tomorrow.

O'Brien: All right, that's damn good. I'll—

President Johnson: Rusk is leaving town, taking a vacation, so he may already be gone, but I think you better get him and tell him that—

O'Brien: All right.

President Johnson: —this is so urgent that he and Ball better go into it swinging and say it'll destroy the Kennedy Round, it'll destroy everything. They'll have to recommend a veto, and there's no use letting this thing get going too far.

O'Brien: No. See, I had hoped that Mansfield might feel that he could go along with us a little on this, that he has shown some activity for his constituents and what have you, and that we could run this out on a time basis, but . . .

President Johnson: [*with O'Brien acknowledging*] Well, you see, if they hadn't have added this amendment, if they'd just passed the Mansfield bill. Now, Mansfield's got a good thing to insist that they can't—to tell him that the House won't even consider this if it's tied to their bill, but if they'll pass a separate bill . . . they can consider it. Then let Wilbur [Mills]—[he] could block it in the committee.[73] And by delaying. But it don't go to committee now. All it can go to [is] the Rules Committee, who's after us.

O'Brien: That's right; that's right. [*Unclear comment by Johnson.*] Well, let me—that's a damn good idea. Let me grab Rusk, if I can, right now and get this set up.

President Johnson: All right.

O'Brien: I will; I'll go right at it.

President Johnson: All right.

O'Brien: And thanks.

President Johnson: Now, Larry?

O'Brien: Yeah?

President Johnson: Be sure you check with Bobby [Kennedy] to see that whoever they want's invited.

O'Brien: Yeah, we already checked Justice and had them submit a written list to us. They've had—

President Johnson: Now, he called in and said that he wondered if we

---

73. Wilbur Mills (D-Arkansas) was the powerful chair of the House Ways and Means Committee.

oughtn't to put it off [until] next week, and I said, "Well I'd be glad to consider it, but we've . . . we've considered it, and I think it'd be pretty bad to wait and sign until the Republicans got out of town. They'd just say that we're a cheap bunch of public relations experts." And I talked to Roy Wilkins and some of the Negroes, and they agreed we ought to sign it as soon as we could.

O'Brien: Well, you mean Bobby didn't want it signed?

President Johnson: Yeah. He said, "Let's wait until Monday." Said there might be some trouble Saturday in these southern towns.

O'Brien: [*dismissively*] Oh . . .

President Johnson: But I think that Kuchel and McCulloch would think you'd really broken faith with the Republicans to wait until they got out of town to have a ceremony.

O'Brien: I agree with you; I agree with you. I think this is far . . . so far down the road that, God, we ought to go forward with this, this evening.

President Johnson: All right. You said most of the men [will] be out of town next week if we waited, you know.

O'Brien: That's right!

President Johnson: Well, you better bear that in mind when you talk to him. Just tell him that's why we had to go ahead because you can't let these Republicans think that we're being unfair.

O'Brien: No, we've got to go ahead today. My God. And even some of our Democratic friend—Manny Celler's called me twice this morning.[74] Christ, you know, these fellows, they want to be part of this. They . . . they just anticipate that—we've given them no specific time at the moment; we will be giving it to them shortly—and they just anticipate they're going to be in town here for a ceremony later this evening at some hour in the relative early evening, and, God, I think if we just started talking about next week or something like that, you'd be accused of all kinds of things.

President Johnson: OK. Thank you.

O'Brien: OK.

1:24 P.M.–1:29 P.M.: Johnson made unrecorded calls to Jack Valenti (1:24 P.M. and 1:29 P.M.) and Bill Moyers (1:25 P.M.).

---

74. Emanuel Celler (D-New York) was chair of the House Judiciary Committee and an essential proponent of a strong civil rights bill.

1:34 P.M.: Swore-in Maxwell Taylor as the newly appointed ambassador to Vietnam in a Rose Garden ceremony.

1:43 P.M.: Returned to the Oval Office, where he with Bill Moyers spoke to George Reedy on the telephone.

1:44 P.M.

To George Reedy; President Johnson joined by Bill Moyers[75]

While waiting for the call to Reedy to go through, the President comments to Bill Moyers in the office. The conversation was recorded through the speakerphone.

President Johnson: Now, our discussion of the civil rights bill, so then I read these—

The operator interrupts to announce that Reedy is on the line.

President Johnson: George?

George Reedy: Yes, sir.

President Johnson: Why don't you answer me in there? I—

Reedy: Because I was outside just stepping in as it rang, sir.

President Johnson: Yeah. All right. Now, tell me, I've got to announce to the Cabinet what time we have the ceremony and where and so forth. It's in the East Room, isn't it?

Reedy: East Room. The networks say 6:45 [P.M.] is the absolute best time, sir. We put—weighed it to them cold. And they say 6:45. Both NBC and CBS will carry live, and some of the ABC stations will carry live, and others will tape.

President Johnson: Well, I thought 7 [P.M.] was what we asked them to do because—

Reedy: It was. It was, and they'll do it, but we'll get better play at 6:45, they say.

President Johnson: Well, I don't believe that. That's cheaper time, and 7:00 is . . . See, 6:45 is 4:45 in a good part of our country, George.

Reedy: That's right, sir, but that'll, of course, will be replayed and taped.

President Johnson: No. Well, I mean that's not an answer to it. It—

Reedy: No, I know it's not.

---

75. Tape WH6407.02, Citation #4129, Recordings of Telephone Conversations—White House Series, Recordings and Transcripts of Conversations and Meetings, Lyndon B. Johnson Library.

President Johnson: —would seem like it'd be better to me in Texas to have something at 5:00 when people are getting off than it would be at 4:45.

Reedy: Right.

President Johnson: I mean, that 15 minutes, it . . . I don't see why it would be better at 6:45 than 7[:00]. I [*unclear*]—

Reedy: Because more of their stations will carry it live, that's why. [*Pauses.*] But they'll do it at 7[:00]. There's no question there. But they just say—

President Johnson: Think it's better at 7[:00]?

Reedy: I think it'd be better if they'd carry it, but fewer stations will carry it at 7[:00], they tell me.

President Johnson: I just don't believe anybody's going to turn down—

Reedy: I don't either, sir . . . I don't either.

President Johnson: —[*unclear*] 7:00, [*unclear*] I sign the bill. I just don't believe it.

Reedy: I don't either, but I'm pass[ing] . . . just passing on what the [press] pool said.

Bill Moyers: [*in the office*] They don't like to interrupt their 7:00 programs, [*unclear*].

President Johnson: I guess they don't want to interrupt . . . 7:00 news, NBC doesn't, and they get it on 6:45, and then I guess CBS doesn't mind that cheap time, but seem like to me—

Reedy: That's what they're after; there's no doubt of it, sir. They'll carry it, I think. I can't imagine their turning it down.

President Johnson: Well, now, what time are we going to announce it? That's what I'm—got to do. Let's think about it. We got—I don't want to do this in a hurry, and I don't know enough about it, and I don't think anybody in our outfit knows enough about the radio, television. I believe they're selfish bastards. They're like Jesse Kellam: He wants anything carried in the afternoon he can because he don't want to give up that night primary time.[76]

Reedy: That's right.

President Johnson: And, you see, if it's 7:00 here, it's 5[:00] in Texas, but if it's 6:45 here, it's just 4:45 there, and, hell, it's about 3:45 in California. And I just don't believe you're going to get much audience. I think the later in the evening you do it, the better, but now, that's my

---

76. Jesse Kellam was the manager of Johnson's radio and television stations.

offhand thought. Let's don't decide it; let's talk about it. Bill Moyers is in here, and let's just try to reason it out.

Are they united, or are they just . . . is this just a pool man, or who says? You asked for 7:00, and they told you [that] you [*sic*] thought that you'd get more at 6:45.

Reedy: They told me they thought they would get more stations to carry it live at 6:45 than they would at 7[:00], yes, sir. Now, my own judgment is that almost everybody will carry it live regardless. The pool man, John Lynch of CBS, and all he did was to query the networks on this matter, and that's the response that he got from them. [*Pauses.*]

Now, the California thing, of course, what will happen there is they wouldn't actually play it at 3:45. They would tape it [and] hold it, and they shove those programs back a bit.

President Johnson: Hold a minute. Let me ask Walter [Jenkins], see if he's . . . not out at lunch, see what he thinks.

The recording continues for almost two minutes, but the President does not return to the line.

1:47 P.M.–1:55 P.M.: Johnson called Walter Jenkins on the personal line, checked back with George Reedy, and then phoned Bill Moyers before heading off for the Cabinet Meeting at 1:55 P.M. The session lasted until 2:24 P.M. During that time, his office received positive updates on the passage of the Civil Rights Act in the House.

APPROXIMATELY 1:55 P.M.

Between Office Secretary and George Reedy[77]

An office secretary calls to inform Reedy that the President would like him to attend the Cabinet meeting, which has just started.

77. Tape WH6407.02, Citation #4131, Recordings of Telephone Conversations—White House Series, Recordings and Transcripts of Conversations and Meetings, Lyndon B. Johnson Library. The Daily Diary listed the time of this call as 2:05 P.M.

2:10 P.M.

Between Juanita Roberts and Carl Albert[78]

Carl Albert: Mrs. Roberts?

Juanita Roberts: Yes.

Albert: This is Congressman Albert. How are you?

Roberts: Fine. How are you?

Albert: [*with Roberts acknowledging*] Fine. Listen, Walter Jenkins called me, and would you call him—we're voting on the bill now, the civil rights, and it will be over in about 10 minutes here in the House, or 15 at the most. So the President can get ready to make any, you know, invitations or whatever he wants to do. They wanted as much time as possible. I should think it'd be down there by 3:00.

Roberts: All right.

Albert: Would you tell him that?

Roberts: I surely will.

Albert: All right.

Roberts: I'll be happy to—

Albert: We're past the danger stage now of any slipup.

Roberts: Good.

Albert: OK.

Roberts: Thank you.

Albert: All right.

Roberts: Bye.

2:10 P.M.: Apparently after the Carl Albert call, Juanita Roberts heard news of the final passage from White House congressional liaison Claude Desautels and then ferried the message to the President in the Cabinet Room. A delighted Johnson announced the results to the Cabinet.

2:24 P.M.: At the conclusion of the Cabinet Meeting, Commerce Secretary Luther Hodges and Attorney General Robert Kennedy accompanied the President to the Oval Office. On the way there, they peered at a headline speculating that Dwight Eisenhower would make a nominating speech on behalf of

78. Tape WH6407.02, Citation #4134, Recordings of Telephone Conversations—White House Series, Recordings and Transcripts of Conversations and Meetings, Lyndon B. Johnson Library.

William Scranton. Johnson doubted the news and asked Kennedy, "I'll bet he doesn't . . . do you want to bet he does?" Kennedy opted not to take the wager.[79] Back in the Oval Office, the men called Larry O'Brien about the Community Relations Service, which fell under the Commerce Secretary's authority.

2:26 P.M.

To Larry O'Brien; President Johnson joined by Robert Kennedy[80]

The President is meeting with Robert Kennedy and Luther Hodges at the time of the call. Johnson is on the speakerphone.

Larry O'Brien: Yes, Mr. President.

President Johnson: I have the Attorney General and the Secretary of Commerce listening to this conversation in my office.

O'Brien: Right.

President Johnson: We are thinking about talking to the Negro leaders about cooperating with us after we sign the law until we get our machinery organized for observance.

O'Brien: Right.

President Johnson: And we thought we might just informally get together quietly off the record after the signing ceremony this evening.

O'Brien: Mm-hmm.

President Johnson: Do you have any indication of who is invited and who will be there?

O'Brien: I don't at this moment, Mr. President, I'm outside the building. But Claude Desautels just called me a few minutes ago, and he is in the process of issuing the invitations, and I know it covers all the major Negro leaders, as suggested by Nick Katzenbach.[81]

President Johnson: OK. All right, then we'll see the ones that accept, and if the . . . the ones that do, we'll ask them to come upstairs, maybe, after the—

O'Brien: All right.

President Johnson: —signing, and . . .

---

79. Daily Diary, 2 July 1964, Lyndon B. Johnson Library.
80. Tape WH6407.02, Citation #4135, Recordings of Telephone Conversations—White House Series, Recordings and Transcripts of Conversations and Meetings, Lyndon B. Johnson Library.
81. Nicholas Katzenbach was deputy attorney general.

[consulting with guests in room] What? Will we come back over to the Cabinet Room after we . . .

Robert Kennedy: That would be fine. *[Unclear.]*

President Johnson: *[to O'Brien]* Come back over to the Cabinet Room right after the signing, and then we'll meet with them here.[82]

O'Brien: All right, fine.

President Johnson: Thank you.

O'Brien: Thank you.

2:29 P.M.

From Carl Albert[83]

Luther Hodges departed at 2:28 P.M., but Robert Kennedy remained. He and Johnson caught up with the House majority leader.

President Johnson: Sitting here with the Attorney General. We're about . . . looks like congratulations *[are]* in order. We want to salute you.

Carl Albert: Thank you, sir.

President Johnson: I guess you know that this probably this . . . you get more congratulations up here than you get at home.

Albert: *[Chuckles.]* Well . . .

President Johnson: Have you finished the bill?

Albert: Yes, sir! The Speaker's *[John McCormack's]* signed it. It's on its way to be—messaging in to the Senate right now. The clerk's already on his way.

President Johnson: How long will it take over there?

Albert: I wouldn't take it—I'm going to call Mike *[Mansfield]* now and tell him—I told your people it would be down there by 3:00, and—

President Johnson: That's wonderful; that's wonderful.

Albert: —I'm getting Mike to help me get *[unclear]*—

President Johnson: That's wonderful; that's wonderful.

---

82. Lee C. White, "Memorandum to the Files: Meeting with Negro Leadership Following Signing Ceremony," 6 July 1964, "HU 2/ST 5/25/64–7/16/64" folder, Box 2, White House Central Files: Human Rights, Lyndon B. Johnson Library.

83. Tape WH6407.02, Citation #4137, Recordings of Telephone Conversations—White House Series, Recordings and Transcripts of Conversations and Meetings, Lyndon B. Johnson Library.

Albert: It's past any problems.

President Johnson: That's wonderful; that's wonderful.

Albert: It's just a matter of signing it now.

President Johnson: Did anybody cause you any trouble today?

Albert: Not a bit. They hollered, but they didn't filibuster a bit. Just had one quorum call when we came in, and they let us read the journal. We had a very long journal. They could have kept us here until 6:00 on that journal alone, you know.

President Johnson: Mm-hmm.

Albert: If they made us read every word and everything because that foreign aid journal was pretty long. But we had no problems, none whatever.

President Johnson: Well, you sure—I wish you'd tell Vaughan Gary; I tried to get him last night, and I missed him. I got George Mahon, the Speaker, and you. But tell him I sure do appreciate it, and I'm going to call him the first time I have a moment this afternoon.[84]

Albert: All right.

President Johnson: I just got the Cabinet meeting, and I haven't even had my lunch yet, but I sure want to get to him, and I think that was a marvelous victory, and all of you are due a lot of credit.

Albert: Well, I think he did a marvelous job, too. And then . . . the . . . I—

President Johnson: I—

Albert: Walter [Jenkins] called me and said you-all wanted to know as soon as possible so you could set your time for signing that other thing—

President Johnson: Yeah. . . . Yeah, I think we'll set it at either 6:45 or 7 [P.M.], and they'll be back to you right away.

Albert: [*with the President acknowledging*] You can have people in that you want to invite and give them a little time. We didn't want him to do it before because they might have started a filibuster, you know. [*Unclear*] that now.

President Johnson: That's good. Now, are you going to get any rules tomorrow?

Albert: We got some rules today.

---

84. George Mahon, chair of the House Appropriations Committee, had been critical for passage of the foreign aid bill. J. Vaughan Gary, a Democrat from Virginia, was on that committee and had supported the President. Conversation between President Johnson, George Mahon, and John Rooney, 6;05 P.M., 1 July 1964, in this volume; conversation between President Johnson and Craig Raupe, 2:00 P.M., 1 July 1964, in this volume.

President Johnson: Today. You-all are getting out, then, tonight, aren't you?

Albert: Yes, sir.

President Johnson: All right. What rules did you get? SEC [Securities and Exchange Commission]? What else?

Albert: Yes, and another little one about health—public health disorganization.[85]

President Johnson: All right. Now, have you got any—

Albert: We got a big bunch of pretty important suspensions coming up,[86] including the nurses training bill, for when . . . as soon as we get back—[87]

President Johnson: On that list of 30, Carl, how many of those are you going to be able to pass?

Albert: Well, I—

President Johnson: All of them?

Albert: I think we'll pass all but one or two.

President Johnson: Mm-hmm; mm-hmm. All right. Now, have you talked to these eight members about the showdown we're going to have when we get back with [Howard] Smith again?[88]

Albert: Well, I've been talking to them today.

President Johnson: What do they say?

Albert: They think—

President Johnson: Are they ready to go?

Albert: I think if he doesn't show . . . if he shows an unwillingness when we get back, there will be no question about it.

---

85. Among other things, the Securities Acts Amendments required more public disclosure regarding securities. The legislation had come out of the House Interstate and Foreign Commerce Committee on 19 May. It passed the House on 5 August, the Senate on 6 August, and became law on 20 August. The public health training bill provided almost $70 million to fund university-level training programs. It emerged from the House Interstate and Foreign Commerce Committee on 9 July, the full House on 21 July, the Senate on 12 August, and Johnson's desk on 27 August. *Congressional Quarterly Almanac*, 1964, vol. 20, p. 245, 562–65.

86. The House could suspend the rules and bypass the Rules Committee with a two-thirds majority vote.

87. The House Interstate and Foreign Commerce Committee reported out the nurse training bill on 7 July, and the full House agreed to it on 21 July. It called for almost $300 million to expand nursing education as a way to address a shortage of nurses in the marketplace. An amended version came out of the Senate on 12 August, with the final bill passed on 21 August. Johnson signed it on 4 September. *Congressional Quarterly Almanac*, 1964, vol. 20, pp. 244.

88. Howard "Judge" Smith was chair of the House Rules Committee.

President Johnson: Mm-hmm. See what—
Albert: They don't want to do it, but they will do it.
President Johnson: No. . . . OK. All right. Thank you, Carl.

    2:35 P.M.–3:05 P.M.: Johnson held unrecorded calls with Walter Jenkins (2:35 P.M.), Jack Valenti (3:04 P.M.), and McGeorge Bundy (3:05 P.M.).

    3:07 P.M.: Met longtime Democratic adviser Clark Clifford for lunch in the Mansion. Clifford was a key link to Robert Kennedy, and on June 23, Johnson had asked Clifford to look into Kennedy's plans for the fall election season.

    3:57 P.M.: Took an unrecorded call from Robert Kennedy.

    4:30 P.M.: Sat down in the White House barbershop to get his hair trimmed for the early evening television appearance.

    4:44 P.M.: Chatted with Walter Jenkins and then went to the Mansion for Luci's birthday party and a rest. At her party, Luci had a piece of lemon cake and then took the rest of the cake down to the press for photos.[89]

    5:00 P.M.: Took an unrecorded call from Lady Bird, and then a recorded one from the FBI director.

5:02 P.M.

With J. Edgar Hoover[90]

Hoover phoned with news of an extortion plot in the Mississippi Burning case and with an update on opening an FBI office in Jackson, the state's capital. Most of the conversation involved Johnson's request that Hoover create the "best intelligence system" in the country to infiltrate the Klan in Mississippi, which the President considered "the most dangerous thing we have this year."

Johnson was speaking from the Mansion.

---

89. Lady Bird Johnson, *A White House Diary*, p. 173.
90. Tape WH6407.02, Citation #4138, Recordings of Telephone Conversations—White House Series, Recordings and Transcripts of Conversations and Meetings, Lyndon B. Johnson Library.

J. Edgar Hoover: . . . highway patrol are doing likewise, and we have had this lead, as you probably already have been told, in New York of the ransom demand on the [Andrew] Goodman family.

President Johnson: Mm-hmm.

Hoover: For $15,000. I think that's a fake, but we don't know. We're running that out. There have been three or four phone calls to the Goodman family demanding that they bring $15,000 to the Manhattan Beach Hotel, which [is] out on Long Island there, and the Goodmans have insisted upon either talking to the boy to make certain they're dealing with the right people or asking the boy the nickname of the grandmother of the family. The reply of the person calling, which has a Bronx accent, says that the boy is not there and that they got in touch with him where they have him, wherever they have him hidden away, and he refuses to tell them the nickname of the grandmother, which I think pretty clearly shows that that's a fake. We're running that down, though, on the grounds of extortion; that's a violation of the extortioner statutes.

President Johnson: Mm-hmm.

Hoover: So far as the Mississippi situation is concerned, I've got a conference on in Jackson this afternoon for the matter of space. We've located space down there, but there's a question whether the concern that owns the building will rent to an integrated agency because we're integrated in the FBI: We have Negro agents, although we haven't any in Mississippi per se.[91]

President Johnson: Mm-hmm.

Hoover: But that'll be thrashed out within the course of the next hour, and then it'll take us possibly maybe a couple of weeks to get the place set up properly. It's an entire open floor now, but in an air-conditioned building—an entire open floor—so that we can then make arrangements for the formal opening of the office.

President Johnson: Mm-hmm.

Hoover: And in line with the conversation with Walter Jenkins this morning, we can then reevaluate the need of my going down there.

President Johnson: Mm-hmm.

---

91. Hoover was taking liberties with the truth on the matter of the FBI having black agents. According to historian Kenneth O'Reilly, Hoover had employed black agents to spy on Marcus Garvey and the Universal Negro Improvement Association in the 1920s, but after that, the FBI had no "more than a token number of full-fledged black agents" while Hoover was alive. At the time of this call, the FBI had only a reported five black agents. One was Hoover's chauffeur and domestic helper, two worked as valets in Hoover's office, and the other two, according to O'Reilly, were "a mystery." Kenneth O'Reilly, *"Racial Matters": The FBI's Secret File on Black America, 1960–1972* (New York: Free Press, 1991), pp. 13, 17, 29–31. 97–100.

Hoover: I'm perfectly willing to do so. I think there are several aspects of that we want to keep in mind: First, whether these racists will yell that we waited until these three people had disappeared and then tried to plug the gap by suddenly opening an office at Jackson. But the answer in my mind to anything of that kind is that whatever you do, you're going to be damned.

President Johnson: Hmm.

Hoover: You can't satisfy both sides.

President Johnson: No, I have this feeling; I have this feeling: Ain't nobody going to damn you. Here's the feeling I have: You didn't create this situation; you didn't have anything to do with it; the FBI didn't have anything to do with it. Nobody but a few Communists and a few crackpots and a few—

Hoover: That's right.

President Johnson: —wild people are against you in this country. They're unanimous: If anybody in the country has got the respect, you have.

Now, what I think you ought to do. I don't want to urge you to go. I just want you to consider it, and then evaluate it, and then I'll be guided by your judgment because you've been at this a good deal longer than I have, and I don't want to put my judgment against yours.[92] But the thought just occurred to me that it would . . . you don't have to be blustering or threatening; you're dignified and quiet and modest and humble, and . . . but you have a perfect right to appear at your office. And you have been called on for extraordinary service, and there's . . . I think you ought to give serious thought [in the] next day or two—I may be gone; if not I'll talk to you Saturday; this is Thursday.

Hoover: Yeah.

President Johnson: See how many people you can bring in there, say, [*garbled recording*] Monday until we find this answer. I think the best— You ought to put 50, 100 people after this Klan and studying this from one county to the other. I think their very presence may save us a division of soldiers.

Hoover: Yeah.

President Johnson: Not throwing their weight around, or throwing their pistols—you don't hear criticism of any of your people—but if they are there. I think you ought to have the best intelligence system, better than you got on the Communists. I read a dozen of your reports last night

---

92. Hoover had been director of the FBI since 1924.

here until 1:00 [A.M.] on Communists, and they can't open their mouth without your knowing what they're saying.

Hoover: That's very true.

President Johnson: Now, I don't want these Klansmen to open their mouth without your knowing what they're saying. Now, nobody needs to know it but you, maybe, but we ought to have intelligence on that state because that's going to be the most dangerous thing we have this year.

Hoover: I think that's very true.

President Johnson: And I think if I have to send in troops, or somebody gets rash and we have to go like what we did in Little Rock, or something else, that it could be awfully dangerous.[93]

Hoover: I think it's important—

President Johnson: Now, nobody objects to the FBI, everybody, all the local people. Nobody really objects to the Navy boys; that was a master stroke when you got them.[94]

Hoover: Yes.

President Johnson: But I'm having these demands for 5,000 soldiers.

Hoover: Yes.

President Johnson: And all these groups are meeting all over the United States and sending wires. [James] Farmer has got a group out in Kansas City today.[95] They called up yesterday. Martin Luther King's getting ready. All this. So the only way I can answer them is to say, "Now, I have substantial people in every area of this state; that we are carefully studying this thing; we're carefully investigating it. And to send in a bunch of marshals, or send in—that have no law to enforce, that nothing [has] been violated—or send in a bunch of Army people, divisions, is just a mistake. But I've got ample FBI people."

And I would express the hope, even if I have to get a supplemental appropriation for it, that you figure out where you can borrow them in case of an emergency and let's put them in there for the next 30, 40 days while we're making this search and until this thing quietens down a little bit.

Hoover: We'll certainly work that out.

President Johnson: Now, you make an estimate. Call your district men, whoever you need to, and let me talk to you day after tomorrow and see how many we can put in there next week.

---

93. In 1957, President Dwight Eisenhower sent in the 101st Airborne to preserve order during the implementation of a federal order to desegregate Little Rock's Central High School.

94. Johnson was referring to the sailors attached to the naval base in Meridian who had been assisting in the search.

95. James Farmer was the director of the Congress of Racial Equality.

Hoover: And my idea was, if I went down there I would invite the governor and the attorney general of the state and the federal district judges to be present at the opening of the office.

President Johnson: Uh-huh . . . I sure would; I sure would. That'd be excellent. You've got them cooperating. You . . .

Hoover: Oh, they're cooperating.

President Johnson: You're getting voluntarily, after we talked to the governor, and you had him have that first press conference—

Hoover: Yeah.

President Johnson: —that's when he broke the ice—you're getting voluntarily what you'd try to get with a battalion of Marines.

Hoover: Exactly. Without the hostility.

President Johnson: That's right. Now, what I want you to do, though, I want you to put in 50, 100 men and scatter them—I want you to have the same kind of intelligence you have on the Communists. Now, this Klan could spread all through the 11 southern states and be—

Hoover: Oh, they are.

President Johnson: I know, but I mean it could be . . . You remember they were electing senators in Texas—

Hoover: I know they were.

President Johnson: —in 1924. Earle Mayfield came up here. Tom Connally beat him.[96]

Hoover: That's right . . . that's right.

President Johnson: [*with Hoover acknowledging*] And we've just got to see, because that outfit will be flogging people and be violating—this statute goes into effect. I'm going to sign it at 6:45 tonight. I'm going to make a television statement then. And I want to . . . If this thing blows up, I want to be in a position of saying I took precautions, and I put all the people that Edgar Hoover could spare down there to try to track down these violators and perpetrators of these crimes. And if it blows up, I want to be in a position to say this is what I did; if it doesn't blow up, I want to be sure I've got enough there to try to deter it.

Hoover: That's right.

President Johnson: Now, there's some talk about asking to get . . . 5,000 soldiers in there, and I've just told them I'm not going to do that now.

---

96. As the candidate of the Ku Klux Klan and the Anti-Saloon League, Earle Mayfield was elected to the U.S. Senate and served one term, from 1923 to 1929. Texas Democrat Tom Connally defeated him in 1928, beginning a 24-year career in the Senate. Connally died in 1963. Mayfield had passed away nine days before this call, on 23 June 1964. "Ku Klux Bid for Senator," *New York Times*, 20 August 1922.

Hoover: Oh, I think that'd be the worst move to make.

President Johnson: Well, let's send one-tenth as many FBI men: 50 FBI men instead of 5,000 soldiers.

Hoover: And of course we have the offer of the governor for the state national guard if we need any of that assistance as far as searching is concerned.

President Johnson: Yeah.

Hoover: I don't think they ought to be used for any military purposes.

President Johnson: No.

Hoover: But I think if we can confine—use them to the searching, that will release our men from the actual searching detail and get them into this Klan side, which will probably . . . may dig up some dirt.

President Johnson: Well, now, you consider where you're going to get 50, 100 to send in there, too, so we can say that we've sent three bunches in.

Hoover: All right, I will.

President Johnson: OK.

Hoover: Fine.

President Johnson: I'll talk to you tomorrow or [the] next day.

Hoover: Good.

5:15 P.M.–5:45 P.M.: Johnson lay down for a 30-minute nap. When he arose, he called Bill Moyers (5:44 P.M.) and Lee White (5:45 P.M.), both unrecorded.

6:00 P.M.–6:45 P.M.: Prior to his speech before the nation on the Civil Rights Act, Johnson attended a party with Lady Bird for ambassadors from Latin America.

6:45 P.M.: The ceremony for the Civil Rights Act began. Johnson delivered his historic remarks, continuing the theme from John Kennedy's inauguration that the torch of the American revolution had been passed to another generation, this time through "an unending search for justice within our own borders." The new law did not provide special privileges, Johnson assured his audience, but it did establish that "those who are equal before God shall now also be equal in the polling booths, in the classrooms, in the factories, and in hotels, restaurants, movie theaters, and other places that provide service to the public." In asking for compliance with the law, the President issued a religious-themed plea to "let us close the springs of racial poison" and "hasten the day when our unmeasured strength and our unbounded spirit will be free to do the great works ordained for this Nation by the just and wise God who is Father of us all."[97] He then said good night, scrawled out his name, and passed out dozens of pens to supporters who had crammed into the East Room.

During the ceremony, Lady Bird saw Robert Kennedy on the front row and reflected proudly that his brother's bill had "finally come to passage because, I believe, of the earnest, dogged work and the legislative expertise of Lyndon." She departed the East Room "feeling that I had seen the beginning of something in this nation's history, fraught with untold good and much pain and trouble."[98]

7:22 P.M.: In the afterglow of this triumphant moment, President Johnson returned to the Oval Office with Jack Valenti and Deputy Attorney General Nicholas Katzenbach to have a more intimate gathering with several civil rights leaders. Johnson emphasized the Justice Department's willingness to secure compliance and explained that the Civil Rights Act made "demonstrations unnecessary and possibly even self-defeating."[99]

8:25 P.M.–9:00 P.M.: Secretary Robert McNamara was hosting a party at his residence for Maxwell Taylor, and the President and Lady Bird mingled for approximately 40 minutes.

9:10 P.M.: Left for the White House, arriving seven minutes later.

9:25 P.M.–10:37 P.M.: For the next hour and a half, he made numerous unrecorded calls. The first two went to Vicki McCammon (9:25 P.M.) and Bill Moyers (9:27 P.M.), two assistants from Texas who were traveling with him to the LBJ Ranch later in the evening. The others were to speechwriter Horace Busby (9:30 P.M.), Speaker of the House John McCormack (9:33 P.M.), and Press Secretary George Reedy (9:35 P.M. and 10:37 P.M.).

---

97. "Radio and Television Remarks Upon Signing the Civil Rights Bill," 2 July 1964, *Public Papers, Johnson, 1963–64*, pp. 2:842–44.

98. Lady Bird Johnson, *A White House Diary*, p. 174.

99. Attending this meeting were A. Philip Randolph, James Farmer, Martin Luther King Jr., Whitney Young, Roy Wilkins, Rosa Gragg, Dorothy Height, Clarence Mitchell, Steven Currier, Robert Kennedy, Nicholas Katzenbach, Burke Marshall, Luther Hodges, LeRoy Collins, Louis Martin, and Lee White. Lee C. White, "Memorandum to the Files: Meeting with Negro Leadership Following Signing Ceremony," 6 July 1964, "HU 2/ST 1 5/25/64–7/16/64" folder, Box 2, White House Central Files: Human Rights, Lyndon B. Johnson Library.

10:40 P.M.: President Johnson and Lady Bird took a familiar helicopter ride to Andrews Air Force Base, where they boarded a small jet for the Texas Hill Country. Lady Bird described the departure as the "perfect beginning for a vacation," as she felt "exhilarated with that sense of adventure and youth and release." After a nap on the plane, Johnson and his entourage arrived at the LBJ Ranch (at 1:50 A.M., EDT). He received a quick update on the ranch's productivity and then went to bed. Lady Bird drifted off to sleep with a vision that this was "one of those rare nights, starry in every way, when one does not think about tomorrow."[100]

100. Lady Bird Johnson, *A White House Diary*, p. 175.

Friday, July 3, 1964

The New York Times *and NBC just made us look like a bunch
of barefoot hooligans who want to kill everybody we see.*

—Paul Johnson to President Johnson

You became President yesterday. That was your most wonderful hour. It only comes to a President about every 40 years.

—C. C. "Charley" McDonald to President Johnson

In the wake of his monumental Thursday, President Johnson spent most of the day relaxing at the ranch and at a nearby lake. He rounded up some old friends to help him break in a new boat and watch his daughter Lynda and others try to do some waterskiing—all while the national press tried their best to keep up. In more official matters, he touched base with members of the Kennedy family, reached out to two southern governors, and continued behind-the-scenes activities for his presidential campaign.

10:10 A.M.–11:07 A.M.: Having arrived in the early morning hours, the President and Lady Bird slept late and awoke to breakfast in bed. Soon, Bill Moyers came in to go over press release material, then left the two alone to finish their breakfast. Over the next hour, Johnson took two unrecorded calls from Press Secretary George Reedy (10:25 A.M. and 11:07 A.M.), who was 80 miles away in Austin. The second call concerned a July 4 message from Soviet Premier Nikita Khrushchev.

11:18 A.M.

From Robert Kennedy[1]

Worried about violence in the South in the aftermath of the Civil Rights Act signing, the Attorney General phoned with news of Mississippi Governor Paul Johnson's defiance. At a press conference the night before, the governor warned that implementation of the act presented "tremendous dangers." Ominously, he predicted "chaotic days" if civil rights activists did not proceed "with caution," while openly encouraging Mississippians not to comply until the courts decided the law was actually constitutional.[2]

Over the next three days, several hotels and restaurants in Mississippi desegregated, including Jackson's Sun-n-Sand Motor Hotel. The Sun-n-Sand, the facility that had hosted Allen Dulles on his recent trip, decided to close its pool, however, rather than allow African Americans to swim with whites. Even more dramatically, Jackson's Robert E. Lee Hotel closed its doors rather than have to accept black patrons.[3]

President Johnson: . . . Have you talked to your people, or—
Robert Kennedy: Yeah, our people.
President Johnson: That's good.
Kennedy: And they've been in . . . also in touch with the FBI, so—
President Johnson: The wires are good.
Kennedy: Yes.
President Johnson: They . . . We got about 20 percent of them [that] were from the South and were friendly. We got some unfriendly ones.[4]
Kennedy: Yeah.
President Johnson: It runs about 70–50 [*sic*]. I don't tell that figure to anybody, but I don't give it out, but just for you.

---

1. Tape WH6407.03, Citation #4139, Recordings of Telephone Conversations—White House Series, Recordings and Transcripts of Conversations and Meetings, Lyndon B. Johnson Library.
2. "South's Leaders Hold Bill Illegal," *New York Times*, 3 July 1964.
3. John Herbers, "Jackson Closes Hotel," *New York Times*, 7 July 1964; "2 Mississippi Hotels, Motel Deseregate," *Chicago Tribune*, 6 July 1964.
4. According to one internal document, the White House had 338 letters supportive of Johnson's signing the Civil Rights Act and his speech (63 of them southern) and 116 opposed (43 southern). Notes on White House stationery, 2:00 P.M., 8 July 1964, "HU 2/ST 1 5/25/64–7/16/64" folder, Box 2, White House Central Files: Human Rights, Lyndon B. Johnson Library.

Kennedy: Yes. That's fine.

President Johnson: And we like the ones from the South. I'm going to call . . . I thought I might call the governor of Mississippi [Paul Johnson] just to carry through today what we'd already started and not let him think we'd forgotten him, and then call . . .[5]

Kennedy: Now, he's sending his representative up here, and he's going to be here at 3:00 this afternoon.[6] That's the first point. The second point is, he call—did call for noncompliance in the state.

President Johnson: He did?

Kennedy: Yeah.

President Johnson: What'd he say? Resist it?

Kennedy: He said it should be tested and that we shouldn't . . . you just didn't have to comply until it was tested in the court.

President Johnson: Hmm. Well, that's . . . that's bad.

Kennedy: So . . . yeah. The only thing is, if we just stress that . . . I suppose even in view of that, that we want law and order and that when it *is* tested in the court and it is declared [constitutional], we'll all abide by the decision . . . if he'd make sure that he'd give some support to it then. And in the meantime that we don't have disorder or violence of any kind in the state. He could do *that* at least. I think it's too far to go back on the other, but at least ask him to do that. For the future.

President Johnson: Any others call for noncompliance?

Kennedy: No. I think that's the only one. I don't think the governor of Alabama [George Wallace] said anything, but I'm sure he'll say something similar to that.[7]

But it's been relatively calm, and for the first time in Jackson, Mississippi, they've got some of the Negroes and whites sitting down and talking over some of the problems, some of the people that are down there now.

So, you know, there's some promising things. I don't think we could

---

5. See the conversation between President Johnson and Paul Johnson, 3:17 P.M., 3 July 1964, in this chapter.

6. Dan Shell, a Jackson attorney and White Citizens' Council leader, was on his way to Washington, D.C. In Mississippi, three congressmen, including William Ryan (D-New York), were spending their holiday on a fact-finding tour regarding the Council of Federated Organizations (COFO) disappearance. Conversation between President Johnson and Paul Johnson, 3:17 P.M., 3 July 1964, in this chapter.

7. This morning, the United Press International reported that Wallace agreed with Paul Johnson. "South's Leaders Hold Bill Illegal," *New York Times*, 3 July 1964.

expect anything much different from the governor. I mean, I'm sure they went to him and asked him, and if he'd said, "Got to comply with the law," I'm sure it would have been very difficult for him. But if he now keeps stressing law and order, number one; and number two, the fact that when a court decision *does* come down that they are going to have to abide by the law and prepare people for that, that would be helpful.

President Johnson: OK. Any other news? [*Unclear comment by Kennedy.*] What are you going to do over the weekend? You going to—

Kennedy: I'm going to go to the Cape [Cod], I think, this afternoon.[8]

President Johnson: [I] see your daddy [Joseph P. Kennedy Sr.] went to see Teddy [Kennedy].[9]

Kennedy: Yes, he did.

President Johnson: Where is Joan [Kennedy]?[10] I got a call from her last night, but I didn't get through to her before I left.

Kennedy: She'll be up at the Cape.

President Johnson: All right, I think I'll call her this afternoon, if you . . .

Kennedy: If you have a chance, you might also call my father.

President Johnson: I will. Every time I call up there—Well, can you get both of them at the same time?

Kennedy: Uh . . . No. . . .

President Johnson: Have to be different.

Kennedy: [They're in] different houses, but they can get them quite easily. They have both of those numbers.

President Johnson: All right. Does he . . . does he realize I'm calling—

Kennedy: Oh, sure, sure.

President Johnson: —and does it . . . does it upset him, or is it good for him?

Kennedy: No, you know, he gets upset, but he . . . [*unclear*] him, and then, you know, it's awfully good for my mother [Rose Kennedy], too.

President Johnson: Yeah. Wonderful.

Kennedy: And having, you know . . . the fact that you're thinking of

---

8. The Kennedy family's compound was in Hyannis Port, Massachusetts, on Cape Cod.

9. Joseph Kennedy Sr. had been paralyzed by a stroke suffered in December 1961. He had limited mobility and speech. His niece, Ann Gargan, served as his nurse and assistant. She and the Kennedy patriarch had flown up to see his youngest son the day before. Sue Cronk, "Fastened Seat Belt Saved Kennedy," *Washington Post*, 4 July 1964.

10. Joan was the wife of Senator Edward Kennedy.

him makes a big difference. And, you know, the last time you called it helped a lot.[11]

President Johnson: Good. Well, I'll be happy to.

Kennedy: The fact that it's important. I think that if he could talk a little bit about what's going on. You know, about problems. Civil rights, you get that, but you still have the problem of Southeast Asia . . . and working on the [*unclear*], and the—

President Johnson: Did you get in time to talk to [Maxwell] Taylor?[12]

Kennedy: And the—you might then also [talk about how] the economy looks.[13]

I did a little bit, and I'm going to—he's going to come up tomorrow for the day. Cape. [*Unclear.*] His wife's going out for September, so that's nice.[14]

President Johnson: She's going out until September?

Kennedy: Well, she's going out then. You know, at first, she wasn't going to go at all.

President Johnson: Oh. . . . Mm-hmm.

Kennedy: So he was very concerned about that. But she's going now, and I think, at least, that makes a big difference for him. So . . .

So happy Fourth of July.

President Johnson: Same to you, Bobby.

---

11. The last recorded call was on 30 March 1964, and Ann Gargan did most of the talking on Kennedy's end. Johnson also received an update on Kennedy's condition on 11 May from Stephen Smith, Joe Kennedy's son-in-law, who was married to Jean Kennedy Smith and served as a trusted political adviser to the Kennedy family. He had told Johnson that his calling was a "great boost" for the elder Kennedy. Conversation between President Johnson and Ann Gargan, 11:55 A.M., 30 March 1964, in David Shreve and Robert David Johnson, eds., *The Presidential Recordings, Lyndon B. Johnson: Toward the Great Society, February 1, 1964–May 31, 1964*, vol. 5, *March 9, 1964–April 13, 1964* (New York: Norton, 2007), pp. 580–82; Conversation between President Johnson and Stephen Smith, 12:27 P.M., 11 May 1964, and between President Johnson and Ann Gargan and Joseph Kennedy Sr., 12:45 P.M., 11 May 1964, in Guian McKee, ed., *The Presidential Recordings, Lyndon B. Johnson: Toward the Great Society, February 1, 1964–May 31, 1964*, vol. 6, *April 14, 1964–May 31, 1964* (New York: Norton, 2007), pp. 541–47, 548–50.

12. General Taylor had been sworn in the day before as ambassador to South Vietnam.

13. Johnson would call the elder Kennedy on 8 July and talk in general terms about the economy and other matters. As in previous calls, the President communicated primarily with Ann Gargan. Kennedy remained mute throughout the call, with Gargan telling Johnson, "He gets rather emotional when you call." Conversation between President Johnson and Joseph P. Kennedy Sr. and Ann Gargan, 11:26 A.M., 8 July 1964, Tape WH6407.05, Citation #4180, Recordings of Telephone Conversations—White House Series, Recordings and Transcripts of Conversations and Meetings, Lyndon B. Johnson Library.

14. General Taylor had been married to Lydia Gardner Happer since 1925. Alben Krebs, "Maxwell D. Taylor, Soldier and Envoy Dies," *New York Times*, 21 April 1987.

Kennedy: Thank you.
President Johnson: Bye. [*Hangs up.*]
Kennedy: Say hello to Mrs. [Lady Bird] Johnson for me. Thank you.

11:22 A.M.: After the call with Robert Kennedy, Johnson asked his administrative assistant Vicki McCammon to set up afternoon calls to Ted Kennedy's wife, Joan, and his father, Joseph, then decided to try to contact Joan immediately.

11:29 A.M.

To Arthur Dean[15]

Arthur Dean had chaired the U.S. delegation to the Geneva Disarmament Conference until December 1962. Today, Johnson was appointing him to head the National Citizen's Commission for Community Relations, an advisory board created to assist the director of the Community Relations Service.

President Johnson: Hello?
Arthur Dean: Yes?
President Johnson: Arthur?
Dean: Yes, Mr. President.
President Johnson: I wanted to tell you I was . . . nothing happened to me yesterday that was more pleasing than to understand that you might be willing to help us.
Dean: Yes, I'd be very glad to.
President Johnson: Well, you're a great patriot. I've known that for a long time, but we never needed you more than now. And . . . I wish that you'd give all of your talents and thoughts to it, and let's hold this republic together.
Dean: Well, I'd be very glad to.
President Johnson: We've had a wonderful reaction to the broadcast last night, and—

---

15. Tape WH6407.03, Citation #4144, Recordings of Telephone Conversations—White House Series, Recordings and Transcripts of Conversations and Meetings, Lyndon B. Johnson Library.

Dean: I heard it, and I thought it was wonderful.

President Johnson: I know that we'll get a good response to your appointment, and I just wanted you to know that I considered it a very great personal favor to me.

Dean: Well, I will be delighted to work with you, sir.

President Johnson: Well, you'll—I'll be available to you at any and all times, and you try to think of some of the best people in the United States, and let's move forward.

Dean: All right.

President Johnson: Thank you, Arthur.

Dean: Thank you very much, sir.

President Johnson: Bye.

Dean: Bye.

11:30 A.M.: Before reaching out to Texas Governor John Connally, President Johnson made an unrecorded call to Press Secretary George Reedy.

11:38 A.M.

To John Connally[16]

Connally, perhaps best known for being shot during John Kennedy's assassination in November 1963, was seeking a second term as governor. Although he and Johnson were old friends and many Texans considered Connally a protégé of the President's, their relationship had cooled in February because of Johnson's support of Senator Ralph Yarborough, Connally's enemy in the Texas Democratic Party.

In this almost 20-minute conversation, Johnson invited him and his wife Nellie up to the LBJ Ranch for the holiday, discussed the presidential campaign, and offered suggestions on implementing the Civil Rights Act in Texas. Connally was at his own ranch near Floresville, Texas, a town just south of San Antonio. By automobile, his ranch was a little over two hours from the LBJ Ranch.

---

16. Tape WH6407.03, Citations #4145 and #4146, Recordings of Telephone Conversations—White House Series, Recordings and Transcripts of Conversations and Meetings, Lyndon B. Johnson Library.

John Connally: . . . what kind of?

President Johnson: My God, what kind of wire you got down there? Have you got a baling wire phone?

Connally: [*Unclear*] yes, sounds like it, doesn't it?

President Johnson: Sure does. Is that normal?

Connally: No. We had a real good connection awhile ago.

President Johnson: Well, let me see if this—we've got a ham [radio] operator here, maybe.

Connally: [*chuckling slightly*] No. The first call we had a real good connection. I can hear you all right.

The operator comes on the line.

President Johnson: [*to operator*] Give me a better connection to Governor Connally. You know I can't talk on one like this.

Operator: All right, sir.

A pause ensues while the connection is reset.

President Johnson: Hello, John.

Connally: Yes, sir, is that better?

President Johnson: Little better. Not much, though. How you getting along?

Connally: I'm real good. How you feeling?

President Johnson: Fine. Have you already been to the bar?

Connally: Yes, sir. I got back yesterday about 1:00, and then we came on down here early this morning.

President Johnson: That's—

Connally: I didn't know y'all were going to be coming in. . . .

President Johnson: Well, I got—I didn't know it, either, but I signed the Civil Rights Act last night, and I decided I'd go away and get a little Fourth of July [vacation] and hope that everything would go quietly. And it's going pretty good up to now.

Connally: Well, that's wonderful. Are you feeling good?

President Johnson: Feel fine. Just wonderful.

Connally: Well, that's—

President Johnson: I want to see you while I'm down here. I've got a lot of important things to talk to you about, and particularly about the [Democratic National] Convention and about . . . about the vice president and about some things like that.

Connally: All right. . . . What's your pleasure?

President Johnson: Just any time that you're free. I don't want to mess up your Fourth of July. But there's nobody here with me except one girl answering the phone [Vicki McCammon] and Bill Moyer[s], and he's going out tonight. I've got—[*Unclear comment by Connally.*]—I've got a brand new boat that I'm crazy to see, but I haven't, and . . .[17]

Connally: Well, why don't I come up there tomorrow?

President Johnson: All right.

Connally: Spend two or three hours.

President Johnson: That's good. Come up and—won't you spend the night with me?

Connally: Well, we're trying to build this house. . . .[18]

President Johnson: Yeah.

Connally: We probably . . . I probably won't spend the night. We just got down here, and the kids are all coming down.

President Johnson: Yeah.

Connally: But I'll come up there tomorrow.

President Johnson: All right. Bring Nellie [Connally] with you; [Lady] Bird wants to see her.

Connally: All right, and we'll just—If I can locate Bill [Willis].[19] I'm sure I can.

President Johnson: Well, if not, I'll send for you.

Connally: Well, if I can locate Bill Willis, we'll just fly. I've got a strip down here now. We could just leave here and fly up there.[20]

President Johnson: You haven't got one big enough for my jet, have you?

---

17. LBJ's Texas Broadcasting Corporation had recently purchased a 28-foot cabin cruiser that was moored at the Haywood Ranch on the Llano River. UPI, "New Cabin Cruiser Awaiting Johnsons," *New York Times*, 30 May 1964.

18. In February, Connally declined a Johnson invitation ostensibly because he had to see about his home's construction. At that time, the two men were feuding over the U.S. Senate race. See conversations on 1, 3, and 8 February 1964, in Robert David Johnson and Kent B. Germany, eds., *The Presidential Recordings, Lyndon B. Johnson: Toward the Great Society, February 1, 1964–May 31, 1964*, vol. 4, *February 1, 1964–March 8*, 1964 (New York: Norton, 2007), pp. 25–35, 131–33, 332–40.

19. Bill Willis was a pilot and airplane broker out of San Antonio. He had helped negotiate a sale of one of Johnson's airplanes to Connally. See the conversation between President Johnson and Bill Willis, 9:35 P.M., 1 January 1964, in Kent B. Germany and Robert David Johnson, eds., *The Presidential Recordings, Lyndon B. Johnson: The Kennedy Assassination and the Transfer of Power, November 1963–January 1964*, vol. 3, *January 1964* (New York: Norton, 2005), pp. 54–56; conversation between President Johnson and Bill Willis, 11:55 A.M., 8 February 1964, in Johnson and Germany, *Presidential Recordings, Johnson*, vol. 4, *February 1, 1964–March 8, 1964*, pp. 358–61; conversation between President Johnson and John Connally, time unknown, 8 February 1964, ibid., pp. 332–40; conversation between President Johnson and Bill Willis, 8:20 P.M., 30 March 1964, in Shreve and Johnson, ibid., vol. 5, *March 9, 1964–April 13, 1964*, pp. 588–89.

20. The Brown & Root Company recently constructed an airstrip for Connally. See the conversation between President Johnson and Jimmy Dillinger, 8:35 P.M., 4 January 1964, in Germany and Johnson, *Presidential Recordings, Johnson*, vol. 3, *January 1964*, pp. 140–41.

Connally: Yeah. No, I don't know. I'd be afraid to bring it in.

President Johnson: Five thousand feet?

Connally: No. No. We've got 4,200.

President Johnson: Huh?

Connally: What time tomorrow would suit you? What are you going . . . where are you going to be tonight?

President Johnson: I'm going to be here at the ranch all the way through, and if I'm not at the phone, the White House operator will get me. I'll be at A.W.'s [Moursund's] or out on the boat, and I've got a place there [Haywood Ranch].[21]

Connally: Well, we'll just plan to be up there about . . . oh, 10:00 in the morning?

President Johnson: That's good! Now, bring them—Bird says bring all the children if you'd love to.

Connally: Well, Johnny is on his . . . will be on his way down here. Mark will be here, but we'll probably leave him here with Merrill and Mary, I guess, and . . .[22]

President Johnson: Well, bring Merrill and Mary if you want to. Bring anybody you want to. We're by ourselves. Got lots of room. I'd like you to just sit on the deck with me and just talk for an hour or so, and I'd like to spend as much time as you'll spare.

Connally: Well, we'll just—

President Johnson: Of course, if you're a big shot and you haven't got any time to spend and forget your old friends, why, I'll understand that too.

Connally: [*laughing heartily*] Yeah. We'll be up there at 10:00 in the morning, and we'll stay through lunch. We'll spend whatever time— you haven't got too much time to devote to me, I know that, but we'll [*unclear*]—

President Johnson: Yeah, I've got all day and all night until I leave!

Connally: Yeah.

President Johnson: Have you got lights on your runway?

Connally: No. We have temporary lights, yes.

President Johnson: Mm-hmm.

---

21. A.W. Moursund was Johnson's business partner in several Hill Country ventures, including co-ownership of the sprawling Haywood Ranch and the Comanche Cattle Company.

22. Mark was Connally's young son. Merrill was Connally's brother. He was a former county judge who later enjoyed a modest acting career, at one point starring as Davy Crockett in *Alamo . . . The Price of Freedom.* Mary was the wife of Merrill.

Connally: But what we have: We have portable lights you can set out.

President Johnson: Yeah.

Connally: But we haven't . . . and I've landed here at night, but I wouldn't ask anybody else to. Although it helps with this 4,300 foot base [*unclear*] which you can equalize. So, it would be no problem—

President Johnson: How do you like your plane, John?[23]

Connally: Wonderful.

President Johnson: Isn't it the nicest plane you ever had?

Connally: Yes, sir, and I don't know why in the hell you ever traded this for that [Beechcraft] Queen Air, but that's your business.

President Johnson: Well, I [did it] primarily because these little trips over to the ranches and places where that one doesn't get in without a good runway, and then I have to have two people on it.

Connally: Yeah, yeah.

President Johnson: But I wouldn't *dare* do it if I was governor flying to these places around the state. And I wouldn't dare do it if I didn't have other transportation.

Connally: Yeah.

President Johnson: You know, like my Jetstar.

Connally: Right.

President Johnson: But I just . . . I love that plane more than any plane we ever had. I think it's the nicest appointed one and most comfortable one inside.

Connally: I'm crazy about it. It's the smartest thing I ever did. It'll break me, I guess, if I ever have to try to support it myself.

President Johnson: No, it won't. You go to practicing law, and you get you a client or two that can furnish you gasoline.

Connally: But, hell, we . . . I'm just crazy about it.

President Johnson: Do you use it much?

Connally: Oh, yeah, we've been using it quite a bit.

President Johnson: [*Blows nose.*] What do you fly in it—10 days a month?

Connally: Yeah. We've been using it that much.

President Johnson: Well, that's good.

Connally: Sure have. I used it, went down to the forest convention, and I went down to the [Rio Grande] Valley in it a day last week and

---

23. Johnson had recently sold an airplane to Connally. See the footnote regarding Bill Willis earlier in this conversation.

Dallas last week. I didn't go to Montana in it because it was too long a trip and I had a ride. But all over the state, we've been just enjoying it an awful lot. And it has . . . it was a lifesaver during the [primary] campaign and later. And I'm just tickled to death with it.

President Johnson: I wish you'd give a little thought to the permanent chairman and the keynoter and the chairman of the [Democratic National Convention] platform committee.

Connally: All right.

President Johnson: And I think we've got to give a little thought to our vice president. I . . . You know who's campaigning for it, and that's going to be a knock-down, drag-out, probably with Mrs. [Jacqueline] Kennedy nominating him [Robert Kennedy] and *all* the emotions and everything that are worked up in it. You can't tell what'll come there.

You've got to bear in mind—I don't know what the Republicans are going to do, but they'll probably name a Catholic as vice president, and we'll have that problem.[24]

Connally: Yeah.

President Johnson: As . . . Well, I need to talk to you about a good many of them. I'm going to . . . I need probably a dozen of the smartest, ablest men we've got that we know around the country to be working on some of these things now. I'm going to ask Jim Rowe to move in about the 10th and see if I can get some other folks and just assign them states.[25] Give each one of them six or eight states, and let them go and talk to them and visit with them and get their ideas and their plans on a series of questions, see what their thoughts are.

Connally: Good.

President Johnson: And—

Connally: Yes, sir, I will be thinking—matter of fact, I've been thinking. I haven't come up with any answer on the keynote [*unclear*]. I haven't even thought about the permanent chairman, but . . . or temporary, but I sure will be thinking.

President Johnson: I rather think the permanent one has got to be [Speaker of the House John] McCormack. I wished it was a young, able man, but it's got to be somebody that has parliamentary know-how, because

---

24. New York Congressman William Miller, the Republican National Committee chair and eventual vice presidential nominee, was Catholic and had graduated from Notre Dame University.

25. A longtime Washington, D.C., lawyer and insider, James Rowe was a friend of Johnson's from the New Deal and was a close adviser to Senator Hubert Humphrey.

he and [Clarence] Cannon—[Sam] Rayburn and Cannon are both gone.[26]

Connally: Yeah.

President Johnson: It's got to be—and the Speaker has traditionally had it all the years, so that's a problem.

Connally: Yeah.

President Johnson: I've got to get along with the Speaker.

Connally: I think that's all right; I think he'll do a good job.

President Johnson: I believe he's loyal to me.

Connally: Yeah, I would think so.

President Johnson: But although I really want young faces.

Connally: Yeah.

President Johnson: Because . . .

Connally: Well, I can understand your desire there.

President Johnson: I believe it will be somebody like [Barry] Goldwater and [William] Scranton, or Goldwater and [William] Miller, maybe.

Connally: Yeah. I think it'll be Miller. That would be my judgment. I think it will be Goldwater and Miller.

Is he a Catholic? He is, isn't he?

President Johnson: Yeah, he's a Catholic. [*Pauses.*] Who had you rather the Republicans nominate—Goldwater or Scranton?

Connally: I'd rather they nominate Scranton.[27]

President Johnson: Well, a good many of them had. I think from the southern standpoint it'd be better, but, *God*, if they nominate Scranton, we have all those newspapers and all that money.

Connally: Well, I agree with that. The only thing that Scranton won't do: He won't make a vicious fight out of it.

President Johnson: They say he's the worst in the world.

Connally: Well, maybe so.

President Johnson: They say he's a real character assassin, but he does it in a Brooks Brothers style.[28]

Connally: Well, then I don't know.

President Johnson: They say he's more vicious and more effective and

---

26. Sam Rayburn (D-Texas) and Clarence Cannon (D-Missouri) were legendary Democrats, Rayburn as Speaker of the House and Cannon as Appropriations Committee chair and as Democratic National Convention parliamentarian. Rayburn died in November 1961, Cannon a few weeks before this call, on 12 May 1964.

27. In 1971, Connally was appointed as secretary of the Treasury in the Nixon Administration and was rumored to be a replacement for Vice President Spiro Agnew. Connally officially became a Republican in 1973.

28. Brooks Brothers was a clothing company known for its expensive men's suits.

more character assassination. He just destroyed Gillwood—[*correcting himself*] [Richardson] Dilworth.[29]

Connally: Well, that may be. If he's that type, then I'd rather have Goldwater.

Approximately one minute and eleven seconds excised by the agency that originated the document and under deed of gift restriction.

Connally: I'm afraid—my knowledge of this—this is going to be the most personal, the most vicious campaign probably in this century.

President Johnson: Yeah, it will be.

Connally: And I think they're going to try to destroy you on that basis. I don't think they can do it. And I don't think it'll be effective. I mean, people will react to it. But, nevertheless, I think they'll try it. I think that's the type of campaign they're going to run.

Now, I know Gold[water]—I'm satisfied in my own mind Goldwater will run that kind. Whether or not Scranton will, I don't know it. But if he'll run that kind, then I'd rather have Goldwater.

President Johnson: Yeah.

Connally: And we can take Goldwater. He'll create more of a problem for us in Texas than Scranton would; there's no question about that, but it's not going to make that much difference.

President Johnson: Well, Texas is pretty belligerent, but I don't believe they want a fellow with the A-bomb that's ready to turn it loose like he is.[30]

Connally: That's right. He'll have trouble getting that [*unclear*].

President Johnson: Huh?

Connally: He'll have trouble getting into the press . . . the international[ist] Republicans all out for him. They would go all out for Scranton.

President Johnson: That's right.

Connally: You're right about that.

President Johnson: Yeah, and you take fellows like [William] McCulloch.[31] They'd have to go when [Nelson] Rockefeller and them turn the heat on.[32]

Connally: Yeah.

---

29. William Scranton defeated former Philadelphia mayor Richardson Dilworth in the 1962 Senate race.

30. Two weeks later at the Republican National Convention, Goldwater made his famous declaration that "extremism in the defense of liberty is no vice."

31. William McCulloch was a congressman from Ohio whose support had been crucial in the passage of the Civil Rights Act.

32. Nelson Rockefeller, a candidate for the Republican presidential nomination, was the governor of New York and a leader of the so-called liberal wing of the Republican Party.

President Johnson: And—

Connally: No doubt about it. They can [*unclear*] a little lip service, a little undiscovered after [*unclear*] out in front the other way.

President Johnson: Yeah.

Connally: [*Unclear.*] And of course that's the reason I never thought Rockefeller was going to get the nomination, because I thought when the powers—the financial power and the economic power and the press power—would turn loose on him, they'd cut him up, but they waited too long.

President Johnson: You mean Goldwater?

Connally: Yeah.

President Johnson: Yeah.

Connally: And I think he's gone now. I think he's going to be nominated.

President Johnson: I believe so.

Connally: I don't think they can stop him. They *could* have, if they'd have made this plea they're making now, if they'd have made it five months ago.

President Johnson: Yeah, I think that's right.

Connally: But they just waited too long.

President Johnson: Nobody would do it but Rockefeller, and he couldn't do it on account of his wife.[33]

Connally: That's right. He couldn't do it, and the rest of them were all waiting around to pick up the pieces with him wanting to be the nominee, and they thought he would get [it] together. [*Unclear*] before they knew what would happen.

President Johnson: Did you see—you didn't see my [civil rights] speech last night, did you?

Connally: No, I didn't. I heard it was *real* good, though.

President Johnson: Things pretty quiet in Texas.[34] What, are you going to have any problems with the [civil rights] law?

---

33. Rockefeller had a messy divorce in 1962 from his wife of 31 years. Soon after, he married his secretary Margaretta "Happy" Murphy, a woman who divorced her husband to marry Rockefeller. In late May 1964, on the eve of the California primary, she gave birth to their son. This issue was frequently discussed as a reason for Rockefeller's failure to become the Republican standard-bearer. Donnie Radcliffe and Jeannette Smyth, "Rockefeller's Divorce Hurt in '64," *Washington Post*, 21 August 1974.

34. The quiet in Texas did not last long. On 5 July, a small riot broke out at Lake Texarkana, a massive body of water not far from Lady Bird's hometown of Karnack. In a clash between black swimmers trying to use a traditionally segregated beach and white resisters, five people were shot (four of them were black) and 23 were arrested (all of them were black). "23 Negroes Held in Texas," *New York Times*, 7 July 1964.

Connally: No, I don't know. I don't think so. I may have to make some recommendations to the legislature, just so we'd have a state agency. But I haven't studied the bill well enough to know just what I am going to have to do. But I don't want to leave it wide open: I'm going to have some steps . . . between . . . well, some intermediate step that would [*unclear*] the community [*unclear*] people before the FBI or the federal board, control board came in. [*Unclear*] some state agency, I think that's what will happen. And I think . . . I think I'm probably going to have to recommend some to the legislature on it, but frankly I haven't studied it enough to know.

President Johnson: You know what I would do?

Connally: What?

President Johnson: I'd set me up a state conciliation service by executive order . . . immediately, and then I'd recommend that to legislature.

Now, the soundest, ablest men we've got recommended that. We've got it in this bill. I've got Arthur Dean on an advisory committee of 2[00] or 300—he's a member of a big Wall Street law firm and negotiated the disarmament stuff.[35]

Connally: Right. Yeah, I know him.

President Johnson: [*with Connally acknowledging*] And he's the best mediator we got. He gladly took over the chairmanship. LeRoy Collins is going to be the head of the mediation service, and Dean's going to be head of the committee of 2[00] or 300.[36]

Nobody can get mad about trying to conciliate, but the governors are having to conciliate it themselves now.

Connally: Yeah.

President Johnson: And [Florida Governor] Farris Bryant talks to us every day and gets our advice and suggestions, and then he goes in and tries to do it. And he has finally worked out St. Augustine.

Connally: Yeah.

President Johnson: The governor of Mississippi [Paul Johnson] has been talking to me pretty regularly, and he has come a *long* ways and has given me 200 extra patrolmen and now given me all the National Guard and personally going in himself and doing everything he can.

Connally: Yeah.

President Johnson: But if a big problem breaks out at any place, instead of their making you come in and send troops in, or instead of the

---

35. Arthur Dean was a partner at the firm of Sullivan & Cromwell.

36. See the conversation between President Johnson and Arthur Dean, 11:29 A.M., 3 July 1964, in this chapter.

federal government having to come in, you've *always* got a break and a cushion and a sponge to absorb it.

Connally: Yeah.

President Johnson: If you take a good man with a religious background and say, "Well, I'll send in a conciliator," and let him go and get the Negro—talk to him—and then get the white or the Mexican. And then talk to them separately and work around with them until he can get them together. And nine times out of ten, when they get together, you can work it out.

Connally: Yeah.

President Johnson: And the governor doesn't *have* to get in it, and the troops don't have to get in it, and the President, FBI don't have to get in it.

Connally: Sure.

President Johnson: And nobody . . . nobody has really ever objected to it except the civil rights people themselves, and they said it was just a southern strategy to keep from passing a good bill.

Connally: Yeah.

President Johnson: The service was really suggested by a boy named [Ted] Kheel, who's Eddie Weisl's friend, and who helped me settle the railroad strike, and who is a top conciliator in New York.[37] And that's the way they handle them all up there: When Bob Wagner gets anything hot, he just turns it over to a conciliator.[38]

Connally: Yeah.

President Johnson: And lets them cuss him.

Connally: Yeah.

President Johnson: But now, you've got some *awfully* good people in this state in this field.

Connally: That's right.

President Johnson: You've got Sam Bloom at Dallas.[39]

---

37. Theodore Kheel had been mentioned as a possibility to head the Community Relations Services. Edwin Weisl was an executive for Paramount Studios, a major insider in New York's Democratic Party, and a former attorney for several congressional committees once headed by Johnson. See the conversation between President Johnson and Burke Marshall, 3:51 P.M., 23 June 1964, in this volume.

38. Robert Wagner was the Democratic mayor of New York City.

39. Sam Bloom, the owner of an advertising agency, was a member of the powerful Dallas Citizens Committee. In 1961, he headed a biracial committee designed to maintain order during episodes of desegregation. His film, *Dallas at the Crossroads*, was played throughout the South and helped create the image that Dallas had peacefully desegregated its public schools. Gladwin Hill, "Dallas Follows Long Range Plan to Adjust Citizens to Integration," *New York Times*, 30 July 1961.

Connally: Yeah.

President Johnson: Who brought about the Dallas integration. You got this fellow, this preacher up there, this lay preach—

Connally: Holcomb.

President Johnson: Luther Holcomb.[40]

Connally: Yeah.

President Johnson: Who's real good, and you got—

Connally: Bob Storey would be good.[41]

President Johnson: Who?

Connally: Bob Storey.

President Johnson: Excellent. And you got folks like that that you could *make* take over this committee.

Connally: Yeah.

President Johnson: And the Negroes couldn't cuss a fellow like Storey or Holcomb or Sam Bloom, because they've made advances for them. And the conservative Republicans couldn't either. And you just . . . then you get a . . . you get a kind of a progressive outlook for acting; what they want is action. At the same time, you haven't imposed anything on them; you haven't done anything. Until there's a fire, you just send the fire engine.

Connally: Yeah. Well, I think that's sound.

President Johnson: Now, Bert Combs put in a public accommodation by executive order, and that's quite a different thing.[42]

Connally: Yeah.

President Johnson: But a conciliation [committee] by executive order, and instead of talking about compliance and enforcement. Don't ever use those words if you can avoid it.

---

40. Luther Holcomb, a liberal minister from Dallas, headed Dallas's Council of Churches. A passenger in the motorcade on 22 November 1963, in Dallas, he was scheduled to deliver the prayer at the official luncheon preempted by President Kennedy's assassination. President Johnson appointed Holcomb vice chairman of the Equal Employment Opportunity Commission. Luther Holcomb, Transcript of Interview by Dana Whitaker, 28 April 2000, http://www.eeoc.gov/abouteeoc/35th/voices/oral_history-luther_holcomb-dana_whitaker.wpd.html.

41. Robert Storey was a former dean of Southern Methodist University School of Law and a former member of the President's Civil Rights Commission. See the conversation between President Johnson and Robert Storey, 1:05 P.M., 1 December 1963, in Robert David Johnson and David Shreve, *The Presidential Recordings, Lyndon B. Johnson: The Kennedy Assassination and the Transfer of Power, November 1963–January 1964*, vol. 2, *December 1963* (New York: Norton, 2005), pp. 6–7.

42. Bert Combs, a Democratic governor of Kentucky from 1959 to 1963, issued this public accommodations order on 26 June 1963.

Connally: Yeah.

President Johnson: Talk about observance.

Connally: Yeah.

President Johnson: Everybody wants to *observe* the law.

Connally: Yeah.

President Johnson: When you go to *enforcing* something, a man gets his back up.

Connally: That's right.

President Johnson: And I talked to the Attorney General this morning, and we've had these spies in different states watching for trouble.

Connally: Yeah.

President Johnson: And it's *very* quiet over the country. And the response, the wires, are just *amazingly* good, particularly from the South, on the speech last night.

Connally: Yeah.

President Johnson: Because I didn't . . . I didn't cuddle up to them, but I wasn't . . . I wasn't the least bit critical or vicious or demanding, and I just appealed for us reasoning together.

Connally: Yeah. Well, everybody—I heard several reports on it, and everybody told me it was [an] excellent appearance that you made last night.

President Johnson: I had all the Republicans and all the Democrats. Had [Charles] Halleck and [Everett] Dirksen, and had all the liberals— [Jacob] Javits and [Hubert] Humphrey and all that group. But it was a pretty united group that was there.

Connally: Yeah. [*Pauses briefly.*] Well, I'll be up there tomorrow, and we'll just . . . we'll go into this and anything else that I can do.

President Johnson: Well, one thing I've got to get you to do is just take your plane or some other thing—first do it by telephone—and then pull these back where we were in Bob Kerr's funeral.[43] We've got to pull these 11 southern states where we know that, as against any challenges we have from up there, that they're all with us. They all are, but somebody might split them off and tell them something else.

Connally: Yeah.

President Johnson: And we can't do it in that way. We can't tell them that's the name, but we've got to be sure that's the result.

---

43. Robert Kerr, the 14-year Democratic senator from Oklahoma and former chairman of Kerr-McGee Oil Industries, had died on New Year's Day in 1963.

Connally: Right.

President Johnson: And we've got to try to hold them together, and I got to get your ideas on other parts of the country too.

Have you read *Newsweek* this week?[44]

Connally: Yes, sir.

President Johnson: Well, read that very carefully. Just take it and read some more sentences after lunch.

Connally: All right.

President Johnson: Take each sentence and analyze it.

Connally: All right.

President Johnson: OK.

Connally: OK.

President Johnson: See you at 10:00 tomorrow.

Connally: All right, sir.

President Johnson: Now stay as long as you can and don't have to hurry back.

Connally: All right. . . . Well, we'll spend the . . . we'll spend the day.

President Johnson: All right.

Connally: OK.

12:06 P.M.: Johnson continued to gather some of his old friends. After the Connally call, he used the radio system to contact his friend and business partner A.W. Moursund. A few minutes after that, the President's daughter Lynda Bird landed at the ranch with her date for the holiday weekend.[45] A half hour later, another close Texas associate reached the President.

---

44. Presumably, Johnson was referring to the Ben Bradlee piece on Robert Kennedy. Ben Bradlee, "What's Bobby Going to Do?" *Newsweek*, 6 July 1964.
45. The Daily Diary also listed her date, Dave Lefeve, as arriving the next morning aboard a courier flight. Daily Diary, 4 July 1964, Lyndon B. Johnson Library.

12:43 P.M.

From Jesse Kellam[46]

Kellam was the manager of the Johnsons' broadcast stations.

President Johnson: A.W. [Moursund] and I want you to come up and see us!

Jesse Kellam: Fine. I'd love to.

President Johnson: Well, just come anytime you can. We're going over to the [Granite Shoals] Lake. You can meet us up there.

Kellam: All right, sir. What time y'all going around over there?

President Johnson: You might bring somebody . . . Huh?

Kellam: What time are you-all going to be over there?

President Johnson: We're going over in the next hour.

Kellam: Have you got somebody to drive you?

President Johnson: A.W. says he can.

Kellam: All right. He can. He can. I'll be in communication with you by radio when I get up in that neighborhood. I imagine it will be, oh, 2[:00] or 3:00 before I get away. You all meet me up there.

President Johnson: All right. . . . You might ask Tom Miller and his wife, and if you know any other interesting men with good-looking wives that keep their mouths shut and would like to just really drive around and flirt with us a little bit, pick them out.[47]

Kellam: Well, how about Ed Rowe Jr.?[48] And Frank Erwin?[49]

President Johnson: Frank Erwin we know, so urge him to come.

Kellam: All right.

---

46. Tape WH6407.03, Citation #4147, Recordings of Telephone Conversations—White House Series, Recordings and Transcripts of Conversations and Meetings, Lyndon B. Johnson Library.
47. Tom Miller, a friend of Johnson's and longtime mayor of Austin, had died in 1962. This person is almost certainly his son, Tom Miller Jr. The "keep their mouths shut" statement can be interpreted in a number of ways. Here, Johnson may have been expressing his persistent desire for his friends and advisers not to talk to the press.
48. The spelling of Ed Rowe Jr. is phonetic. He was not positively identified.
49. A conservative Texas Democrat, Frank Erwin was a close adviser to Governor John Connally. The basketball arena at the University of Texas would later bear his name. See the conversation between President Johnson and Frank Erwin, 1:25 P.M., 1 February 1964, in Johnson and Germany, *Presidential Recordings, Johnson,* vol. 4, *February 1, 1964–March 8, 1964,* pp. 25–35.

President Johnson: If you think you want Ed Rowe Jr., you can ask him to come with Tom if you want to.

Kellam: All right.

President Johnson: But let's think of somebody else there, now. Who else do you think of?

Forty seconds excised under deed of gift restriction.

President Johnson: I thought Roy Butler and Bob Armstrong—find out what happened there.[50] I thought they were wanting to give me a party together, and then it wound up Roy is the only one that gave it.

Kellam: [*with Johnson acknowledging*] Yeah, I think there's a little bit of—Bob kind of had the idea that each man would buy a ticket or something, you know. Some misunderstanding there. So rather than press the issue, Roy claims he didn't want to give it. I haven't checked that out with Bob; it's a little too delicate. That's Roy's story. And there may be something to it. Bob might have been going to throw a party and let them all be Dutch—that will [*unclear*]. That's what Roy says.

I didn't talk to him, but Harry Jersig called this morning and talked to someone in the office.[51] They're going to send a picture of you—they're very anxious for you or [Lady] Bird to—or both—to see it. The one that's apparently going to be in the [state] capitol. If it comes up in time, when I come, would you like me to bring it?

President Johnson: Yeah.

Kellam: All right, sir. KWTX called a meeting for July the 15th, one of their regular meetings.[52] I haven't heard from them since we talked several weeks ago; I don't know what they've decided to do.

President Johnson: Did they go through with the old man's sale?

Kellam: Yes, they're going to go through with it, they say.

---

50. Roy Butler was a car dealer and businessman from Austin who owned a ranch nearby. In May, he had held a men-only barbecue for the President. He later served as mayor of Austin, from 1971 to 1975. Bob Armstrong was a progressive Texas Democratic Party insider who later served as the Texas land commissioner. Edward T. Folliard, "Receptions Show Home-State Pride in Johnson," *New York Times*, 1 June 1964.
51. Harry Jersig was the owner of the Lone Star Brewing Company and a civic leader in San Antonio, Texas. See the conversation between President Johnson and Harry Jersig, between 2:00 and 3:00 P.M., 1 January 1964, in Germany and Johnson, *The Presidential Recordings, Johnson*, vol. 3, *January 1964*, pp. 17–21.
52. The Johnsons owned 29 percent of KWTX, a station in Waco, Texas, that carried both CBS and ABC programs. The Johnsons secured the arrangement in 1954 in what the *Wall Street Journal* considered shady business dealings involving Johnson's influence with the Federal Communications Commission. "FCC Issues TV Grants" *Wall Street Journal*, 3 December 1954; Louis M Kohlmeier, "The Johnson Wealth," *Wall Street Journal*, 23 March 1964.

President Johnson: Uh-huh.

Kellam: How about Frank Denius, if his wife's around?[53] She's kind of cute.

President Johnson: Yeah, I'd like that.

Kellam: All right, sir. And you don't want over, I'd say, more than three couples, would you?

President Johnson: Three or four.

Kellam: All right.

President Johnson: If Don [Cook] wanted to, I'd have Don.[54]

Kellam: Don's not back yet.

President Johnson: All right.

Kellam: But I'll get Denius.

President Johnson: Where's Don—New York?

Kellam: Yes, sir. Would you want to try the Clarks if some of these others can't come?[55]

President Johnson: Afraid he'd talk too much. I went swimming with him once, and I've been reading about it ever since.

Kellam: What would you think, sir—how are you-all going over to Haywood [Ranch]?

President Johnson: Helicopter.

Kellam: What would you think—it would be a little trip—but what would you think about landing that thing at Nicholson [Ranch] and driving over from there?[56] I believe that it might not alert that damn . . .

President Johnson: Rhea [Howard]?[57]

Kellam: Rhea.

President Johnson: A.W. and I were talking about landing down [at] Mary Margaret's [Valenti's] place, or [th]at airport right back there, but there are probably more people around there than there are at the Haywood [Ranch].[58]

---

53. Frank Denius was a World War II hero, an alumnus of the University of Texas, and an Austin attorney. The University of Texas later named its football practice facility in his honor.
54. Donald Cook, the president of the American Electric Power Company, was a longtime friend and close adviser to President Johnson.
55. Edward A. Clark was a prominent Austin attorney and political supporter of Johnson.
56. The Nicholson Ranch bordered the Haywood.
57. Rhea Howard was a newspaper publisher from Wichita Falls, Texas, who had supported Johnson's political career.
58. Mary Margaret Valenti was the wife of Jack Valenti and a former secretary to President Johnson. The Valenti family had a vacation home on Granite Shoals Lake. The Johnson entourage spent part of the afternoon there on this day.

Kellam: I thought about landing at Mary Margaret's, and then, of course, you wouldn't want to do it with A.W., but if someone could bring the boat down to Mary Margaret's, and you and I [*unclear*] going down, that it might work a little bit better. You landing there at the Nicholson place would not . . . I don't believe it would alert anybody on the lake so much.

President Johnson: I think that's probably the best thing to do.

Kellam: And it's not a very far automobile trip if some of them could meet you over there. And then if we had somebody like Earl [Deathe] or somebody else to drive the boat down—[59]

President Johnson: Well, if Earl hasn't got anything to do, you just tell him to go on up there right now, and proceed immediately, just as soon as he can—

Kellam: And take the boat down there.

President Johnson: —to the Haywood, and get the boat down to Mary Margaret's, and then we'll worry about the rest of it.

Kellam: All right, sir. And then I won't come with him, but I'll come up a little later, and I'll call these people.

President Johnson: All right. [*Unclear*] invite the Baileys; they're good.[60]

Kellam: All right.

President Johnson: And tell her you want her to come out with you, and he can come out later.

Kellam: All right.

President Johnson: If she can't do it—I invited the [Homer] Thornberrys, but they're in Houston.[61]

Kellam: All the lawyers, I guess, are there now. They've got a law—

President Johnson: And I imagine that's where Frank Erwin is.

Kellam: Probably so. Probably so. I'll see if I can't get two or three or four of these couples, and I'll bring them up somewhere. It may be as long as [*unclear*] 4:00—

President Johnson: Don't get up after the day's over, because we won't have any fun!

Kellam: We'll try to get there by 4:00.

---

59. Earl Deathe worked for Johnson's broadcast stations and was well known as a problem solver. Some sources spelled his name as Earle. Transcript, Marie Fehmer Chiarodo Oral History Interview I, 16 August 1972, by Joe B. Frantz, Internet Copy, Lyndon B. Johnson Library, p. 8.
60. Charles William Bailey Sr. was one of the Johnson family's physicians from Texas.
61. Homer Thornberry was a federal judge for Texas's Western District. He took that position in December 1963 after almost 14 years as a Texas congressman.

President Johnson: They can come without you. You come on when-ever you can.

Kellam: All right, sir.

1:45 P.M.

To Joan Kennedy[62]

After trying earlier in the day, the President finally reached the wife of Ted Kennedy.

Joan Kennedy: Mr. President?

President Johnson: Yes?

Kennedy: Is that you? Hello?

President Johnson: Hi, Joan.

Kennedy: Oh, Mr. President. . . .

President Johnson: I'm so glad to hear your voice.

Kennedy: Well, I'm sorry to bother you down there, but I just feel like I haven't had a chance to thank you yet for your concern and all your thoughtfulness about, you know, about Ted.

President Johnson: Dear, you shouldn't do that at all. I just . . . I have as much at stake as you do almost, and I . . . I'm so happy that things are turning out better for you.

Kennedy: Oh, I think he's going to be all right. We're . . . we're so glad about that.

President Johnson: Well, both of you mean a lot to us and to the country, and you've got so much wonderful work to do ahead of you, and we want to do anything we can to lighten your burden.

Kennedy: Oh, well, you and Mrs. [Lady Bird] Johnson were wonder-ful. I . . . she was wonderful to call right away, and your flowers and tele-gram and . . . well, just everything . . . just wonderful, and I just wanted you to know we appreciated that very, very much.[63]

---

62. Tape WH6407.03, Citation #4148, Recordings of Telephone Conversations—White House Series, Recordings and Transcripts of Conversations and Meetings, Lyndon B. Johnson Library.
63. After hearing of the accident, Lady Bird phoned Teddy Kennedy's mother Rose and then reached Joan Kennedy at the hospital. The First Lady recounted that Joan was the "first person to use the word 'paralysis'" as a possibility for the senator, an outcome that did not develop. Lady Bird Johnson, *A White House Diary* (New York: Holt, Rinehart, Winston, 1970), p. 172.

President Johnson: We're just as close as a telephone, and please do let us know anything we can do, and I'm going to go to see him just as soon as it looks like it'll be all right.

Kennedy: Oh, well, thank you. And I hope you have a nice weekend.

President Johnson: Thank you, my dear, and give my love to Teddy.

Kennedy: [*Unclear*] Mrs. Johnson and your daughters Lynda and Luci, would you?

President Johnson: Sure will. And keep a big hug for yourself.

Kennedy: All right. Thank you.

President Johnson: Bye. Bye.

Kennedy: [*Unclear.*]

2:50 P.M.: Johnson went sightseeing for about 20 minutes in the Continental convertible with Lady Bird, Lynda Bird, A.W. Moursund, and Jesse Kellam. He returned to the house to call Mississippi Governor Paul Johnson.

3:17 P.M.

To Paul Johnson[64]

After chatting about the weather, President Johnson and Governor Johnson discussed the Chaney, Schwerner, and Goodman investigation and southern compliance with the Civil Rights Act. In the disappearance case, the governor continued to inject doubt that the three men were dead, telling the President that "everybody claims they've seen them."

President Johnson: Hello?

Paul Johnson: Hello?

President Johnson: Governor?

Paul Johnson: Yes, sir, [*unclear*].

President Johnson: How are things with you today?

Paul Johnson: [*chuckling*] Well, getting along pretty good. I was down here on the farm.

---

64. Tape WH6407.03, Citation #4150, Recordings of Telephone Conversations—White House Series, Recordings and Transcripts of Conversations and Meetings, Lyndon B. Johnson Library. The Daily Diary lists this call at 3:10 P.M.

President Johnson: Well, good. Well, you going to take a little Fourth of July off, huh?

Paul Johnson: Yeah, that's what I kind of need to do. I've got this legislature in session again, and it can wear you out pretty good, I guess. How have you been?

President Johnson: We've been doing pretty good. We had a good day yesterday, and things have been going . . .

Paul Johnson: Did you get any rain out your way?

President Johnson: No, we're just so dry, you can't do anything. Everything's burning up.[65]

Paul Johnson: Well, I wish we could send you some of this.

President Johnson: Have you been getting any?

Paul Johnson: Yes, sir. It's raining now.

President Johnson: Isn't that wonderful? You get about 55 [inches] a year, don't you?[66]

Paul Johnson: It's about that, [*unclear*].

President Johnson: We get about 25 [inches].

Paul Johnson: [*Unclear.*] Your cattle, though, when we bring them over to this country, they lose weight. I don't know what for. Those small stomachs, I guess.

President Johnson: Uh-huh. Well, we got a mighty good strong grass here, but it—[*unclear comment by Paul Johnson*] we . . . we don't get near enough rainfall.

How are your . . . how are your men getting along with our folks down there?

Paul Johnson: Well, they're getting along real good. The only incident that we have had at all where there was not complete cooperation that we know of was with the Indian agent.[67] He wanted to talk with the FBI, and he wouldn't talk with us.

President Johnson: Mmm. Indian agent?

Paul Johnson: Indian agent, yes, sir.

---

65. Johnson's conversation on 23 June with James Eastland opened with a similar discussion of the dry weather and its effect on crops and livestock. See the conversation between President Johnson and James Eastland, 4:25 P.M., 23 June 1964, in this volume.

66. Johnson was essentially correct.

67. The Mississippi Highway Patrol had met resistance in their efforts to determine the identity of the person who had found the burned car of the civil rights activists. They proved successful, however, on 1 July. Gwin Cole, "Report RE: Philadelphia Situation," 1:05 P.M., 1 July 1964, Folder 1, July 1964, Box 136, Series II, Sub-Series 9: Sovereignty Commission, Johnson (Paul B.) Family Papers, in Collection M191, Manuscript Collection, McCain Library and Archives, University of Southern Mississippi.

President Johnson: Uh-huh.

Paul Johnson: But it didn't amount to all that much. [*Unclear comment by the President under his breath.*] As a matter of fact, they've . . . everybody's been working as close as they possibly could.

President Johnson: You had any clues?

Paul Johnson: And the governors in all the states around me have called me practically every day.

President Johnson: Uh-huh.

Paul Johnson: And they're trying to help. They've got out—Their contacts are working in various big cities like Memphis and New Orleans, Mobile, different places.

No, we don't have anything we can definitely tie to. We got a report yesterday that the three were seen by a filling station attendant somewhere in north Mississippi, and, of course, we had out alerts for them up until a little while ago. We haven't been able to locate them, but we don't give much credence to that theory. [*Johnson acknowledges.*] Of course, everybody claims they've seen them, you know.

President Johnson: Mmm. Yeah. Yeah, I guess that's right.

Paul Johnson: Yeah, I heard from Alaska. [*The President chuckles slightly.*] Somebody's seen them up there.

President Johnson: Mm-hmm.

Paul Johnson: He told me that the bearded man was about the fastest one.

President Johnson: You've got a man going up to Washington today, haven't you?

Paul Johnson: Yes, sir.

President Johnson: Mm-hmm.

Paul Johnson: He left this morning. It's Dan Shell, who used to be with the FBI.[68] He's a practicing attorney, very reputable [*a telephone rings*] citizen of our state.

President Johnson: [J. Edgar] Hoover says his folks have been doing well, and been treating fine, and your folks have been cooperating with them, and I think it's left a mighty good—[*unclear comment by Governor Johnson*]—mighty good taste in their mouth.

Paul Johnson: Right. We have every way that we know how. We've been using our game wardens and all of their dragging equipment and their boats. We've really put on about the biggest manhunt they've seen

---

68. Dan Shell was a prominent Jackson attorney and a leader of the local White Citizens' Council.

down in that country in a long time. [*The President acknowledges.*] And, of course, we're continuing it.

Do you have anything that you-all feel that you are tied to at all?

President Johnson: No. No. I think that since [Allen] Dulles went down and came back and made a pretty good report and said he had dinner with you and had a good meeting and you wanted him to stay all night, everything.[69]

We get lots of pressure from these [civil rights] groups, as you can imagine, but we tell them there's not any use of our trying to do anything that you're already doing, and that you put on extra patrolmen and told us you'd put on wherever more are needed, and that you had the [National] Guard ready, if we wanted to use the Guard. You were ready to use as many FBI men and Navy as we wanted to in cooperation. And we've added to the FBI from—every few days add a few people. And we see no . . . nothing that marshals and divisions and battalions could do.

But they still denounce us and kind of send us wires and send delegations in and things of that kind. But up to now, I think that . . . I think you've left a mighty good impression. Ever since the Dulles thing came off, it's brought better understanding, I think, over the country, and they've been less violent in their attacks on me at least.

Paul Johnson: If we could just get this national news media off of us down here, Mr. President. They just . . . they have *really* made this thing look like it was the worst thing on earth. You know, you have 800 missing persons in New York . . . this year.

President Johnson: Yeah.

Paul Johnson: Yet the *New York Times* and NBC just made us look like a bunch of barefoot hooligans who want to kill everybody we see and look at a stranger like [*unclear*]. But that's our big problem down this way. We're not treated properly because of the national press.

President Johnson: Well, I think that you've been—

Paul Johnson: It just stirs our people up, you know.

President Johnson: It sure does, and I think you've been . . . I think you've done unusually well under the circumstances, and I've certainly said nothing or done nothing that I thought would add to it, and if I knew how to get away from all of it, I'd sure do it.

Paul Johnson: Do you have anything at all on this case that would even be worth discussing at all?

---

69. Johnson was referring to the former CIA director's fact-finding mission to Mississippi on 24–25 June.

President Johnson: Not at all. Nothing that . . . I talked to Hoover yesterday, told him to put some more men in Monday, Tuesday, whenever he could, so that we could tell them we had no use in going in with marshals and with other people as long as he and your patrolmen and you were doing it.[70]

He said that they'd had this rumor or two, but that . . . not anything that led to anything. I think somebody called up and said that they had seen them, or something like that, but there's not anything he puts any credence in.

Paul Johnson: But it's the most mysterious thing that I've ever heard of. It's as if they went straight up.

President Johnson: Yeah.

Paul Johnson: They've found no tracks leading from the—

President Johnson: We've had a pretty good—I talked over the country this morning. I've talked to some of the Justice officials in our [*a telephone rings*] office up there. Our wires were very good on the appeal I made last night. And I talked to the governor here [John Connally], and I talked to some others.

Things are relatively quiet, and they wanted me to sign this thing on the Fourth of July, and I thought that would be bad, and . . .

Paul Johnson: Yeah, that [*unclear*].

President Johnson: So I rushed it up as quick as I could and just got it in last night and then got out of town.

Paul Johnson: I think that was smart.

President Johnson: And . . . I have asked and hoped and sent word out to everybody I could: to the governors to be as helpful as possible, and to the groups and organizations not to be throwing their weight around over the weekend. Let's take this thing slow and easy and kind of adjust to it instead of making mass invasions and mass violations and things of that kind.

Paul Johnson: Yeah, that was more or less what I told them in a little press conference I had yesterday:[71] That the success of this thing depended upon how fast, you know, some of these big niggers[72] like to move, you know? And they could make it mighty, mighty rough.

---

70. See the conversation between President Johnson and J. Edgar Hoover, 5:02 P.M., 2 July 1964, in this volume.

71. The governor's interpretation of his message at his press conference diverged from that reported in the press and that conveyed by Robert Kennedy in his call to the President this morning.

72. Because of the similar ending sounds of "ras" and "ers," this word can possibly be heard as "Nigras."

President Johnson: Well, you keep a stiff upper lip, and if you need me, call me, and I'll—

Paul Johnson: We'll do it.

President Johnson: I'll be in touch with you, and don't hesitate to ring me anytime day or night, and I'll do the same with you. And I didn't have anything; I just wanted to visit with you and tell you—

Paul Johnson: I appreciate your calling. [*Unclear.*]

President Johnson: —how things are going, and I know . . . I know you've got a great problem, and I . . .

Paul Johnson: You're terrific. [*Unclear.*]

President Johnson: I sympathize with you, and I wished I could do something to help you.

Paul Johnson: I just . . . I wish I had you down here where you could help me. [*Chuckles slightly.*]

President Johnson: Well, I'll do everything I can from the distance. You know I know what a spot you're under and the problems you got, and you know mine, and we just have to work together best we can.

Paul Johnson: Fine, and I appreciate it so much.

President Johnson: Thank you, Paul.

Paul Johnson: Thank you.

President Johnson: Bye.

3:33 P.M.: President Johnson, friends, and family left the house at the LBJ Ranch for an afternoon on Granite Shoals Lake, the reservoir created by the Alvin Wirtz Dam on the Colorado River. One of Johnson's properties, the Haywood Ranch, had waterfront access (along a tributary known as the Llano River) where he kept a big new boat. The group took a helicopter to the Haywood, then a car to the house of Jack and Mary Margaret Valenti, where they met the group of Texans assembled by Jesse Kellam.[73] The younger members of the party did some waterskiing, while the others relaxed. Afterward, the group

---

73. This group included Kellam (whose wife had died in early February 1964), Mr. and Mrs. Earl Deathe, Mr. and Mrs. Tom Miller, Mr. and Mrs. Jack R. Maguire (who brought a book manuscript called "A President's Country: A Guide to the Hill Country of Texas" to show Johnson and Lady Bird), Mr. and Mrs. Charles Bailey, Mr. and Mrs. Jim McMullings, and Judge and Mrs. A.W. Moursund. Daily Diary, 3 July 1964, Diaries and Appointment Logs of Lyndon B. Johnson, Special Files, 1927–1973, Lyndon B. Johnson Library.

returned to the Haywood for a fish fry. Later in the evening, Johnson received a call from Wichita Falls.

8:14 P.M.

To C. C. "Charley" McDonald and Genie McDonald; President Johnson joined by Lady Bird Johnson[74]

Charley McDonald was an old Texas political hand from Wichita Falls who had finished third in Texas's 1934 Democratic primary for governor. He began this call by congratulating the President on his handling of the Civil Rights Act.

President Johnson: [*to someone in the room*] Need a pencil. You got one? [*to McDonald*] Hello?

C. C. "Charley" McDonald: Mr. President?

President Johnson: Yes, Charley, how are you?

McDonald: Oh, fine.

President Johnson: Glad to hear your voice.

McDonald: Well, this is from Genie and me. You became President yesterday.

President Johnson: Well, thank you!

McDonald: That was your most wonderful hour. It only comes to a President about every 40 years.

President Johnson: Well, you're mighty wonderful. I sure do appreciate your thinking so.

McDonald: Well, you'll see it 10 years from now.

President Johnson: Mm-hmm.

McDonald: And . . . I haven't written you. I haven't telegraphed you. I haven't done anything since you was elected. But I've followed it pretty closely.

President Johnson: I know you have, and [there is] nobody that I owe more to than I do you.

---

74. Tape WH6407.03, Citation #4151, Recordings of Telephone Conversations—White House Series, Recordings and Transcripts of Conversations and Meetings, Lyndon B. Johnson Library.

McDonald: I kept reaching you through Rhea [Howard] and [Gene] Chambers and the other boys.[75]

President Johnson: Yeah.

McDonald: But there were only two little clouds that I wanted to give you two suggestions to be thinking on.

President Johnson: Good!

McDonald: Don't debate [Barry] Goldwater!

President Johnson: All right.

McDonald: Every time I see some columnist wanting to stir up some debates.

President Johnson: Yeah.

McDonald: All you've got to do is, when he challenges you, tell him your answer would be found in his answer to [William] Scranton in Chicago.[76]

President Johnson: That's right.

McDonald: All right. Just end it.

President Johnson: That's right. That's what I'll do.

McDonald: The other thing is . . . you have two fine appointments down this way, just made under [the] Kennedy administration, probably, both of them, but they were yours too. That was Sarah Hughes and Barefoot Sanders.[77]

President Johnson: Yeah. Yeah. I named them both.

McDonald: Well, I didn't know just how it was.

President Johnson: Sure.

McDonald: Now . . . the—That [John Kennedy] funeral was the most wonderfully . . . most pressing thing that ever happened in the Republic. And when that widow [Jacqueline Kennedy] reached down and lighted that eternal flame and went off with two orphan children, you were that day elected.

---

75. Eugene "Gene" Chambers was an oilman from Wichita Falls, Texas. He and his wife, Dee, were friends of the Johnsons. Rhea Howard was an editor from Wichita Falls who had supported Johnson's political career.

76. On 29 June, Scranton had challenged the front-running Goldwater to a debate before the Illinois Republican Party in Chicago. Goldwater declined, deeming the "request" to be "ridiculous." Philip Benjamin, "Goldwater Calls Scranton's Bid for Chicago Debate Ridiculous," *New York Times*, 30 June 1964.

77. In 1961, President Kennedy appointed Sarah Tilghman Hughes as a federal judge in Texas's Northern District and Harold Barefoot Sanders Jr. as U.S. attorney for that district. On 22 November 1963, following the Kennedy assassination, Hughes gave Johnson the oath of office aboard Air Force One. Sanders was promoted to assistant deputy attorney general in 1965 and assistant attorney general for civil rights in 1966. In 1979, he became a federal judge in the Northern District of Texas.

President Johnson: Yeah.

McDonald: If you carried it out.

President Johnson: Yeah.

McDonald: That was the second point.

President Johnson: Yeah.

McDonald: Yesterday, you were a part of the image all the way. Yesterday, that image descended on you.

President Johnson: Yeah.

McDonald: And if there is any breach comes up, don't let it pull you loose from that family. I don't know what the cost will be or don't know if there is any, but that tie-in will go to Maine and New Hampshire and Massachusetts and places that don't even know you yet personally.

President Johnson: Yeah.

McDonald: And it's a combination that's fine.

President Johnson: Yeah.

McDonald: The greatest thing you have done personally was to enlist the support of the Protestant and Catholic churches of the whole United States on this thing before it was signed yesterday.

President Johnson: Yeah, yeah.

McDonald: And they've met down in the Methodist church in its quadrennial conference in Pittsburgh the other day.[78]

President Johnson: Yeah.

McDonald: Integrated.

President Johnson: Yeah.

McDonald: Presbyterians integrated.

President Johnson: Yeah.

McDonald: Baptists in the North integrated and left to the respective congregations in the South.[79]

President Johnson: Yeah.

McDonald: It's spread, you know.

President Johnson: Yeah.

McDonald: And old man [Richard] Russell of Georgia the other day,

---

78. The quadrennial General Conference of the Methodist Church had voted on 1 May to begin desegregating its governing structure, eliminating its black division.

79. The Southern Baptist Convention was the largest Baptist organization in the United States. The smaller American Baptist Convention represented congregations largely outside the South and was far more racially progressive. In May, the two groups had held their annual meetings at the same time in Atlantic City. While there, the Southern Baptists refused to accept a resolution in support of the civil rights movement. Paul Montgomery, "Southern Baptists Reject Move to Back Negro Rights," *New York Times*, 22 May 1964.

what he said, you was probably the hardest thing that went up against. If it was just [Everett] Dirksen and [Hubert] Humphrey, they'd be debating this Christmas. [*The President chuckles.*] I heard all that. He said there was one other cause, and that was that the ministers' march on Washington lost—cost them some votes.[80]

President Johnson: Yeah.

McDonald: That they professed to see a moral issue in it. He said there wasn't any, but they professed to see one.

President Johnson: Yeah.

McDonald: Well, the world sees one.

President Johnson: Yeah, they sure do.

McDonald: And I wanted you to know how happy I am, and then I want to—Genie and I both agree on one thing and want to tell you that: Your wife is the equal of all of them. Everywhere she goes.

President Johnson: Yeah.

McDonald: And your two daughters are coming right on. Over in Hawaii the other day.[81] That's fine.

President Johnson: Well, that's—

McDonald: And that Peace Corps, that exchange of students from one nation to the other, bringing the whole world closer together—if you just stay right there, and let them go out on the hustings, and you haven't got time to debate for some fellow [Goldwater] that's been against everything foreign and domestic that's been before Congress for 20 years. You've got work to do in Washington!

President Johnson: Yeah.

McDonald: That was what I wanted to tell you.

President Johnson: Well, you're right. Here's Lady Bird who wants to say a word, Mr. Charley.

McDonald: Well, Genie's waiting too.

President Johnson: All right.

McDonald: All right.

President Johnson: Let me talk . . .

---

80. Presumably, McDonald was referring to the August 1963 March On Washington for Freedom and Jobs.

81. Press coverage of a threat to Lynda Bird's flight out of Hawaii had irritated Johnson because of the appearance that military jets were escorting her plane. See the conversation between President Johnson and John Burns, 8:34 A.M., 21 June 1964, in Guian A. McKee, ed., *The Presidential Recordings, Lyndon B. Johnson: Mississippi Burning and the Passage of the Civil Rights Act, June 1, 1964–July 4, 1964,* vol. 7, *June 1, 1964–June 22, 1964* (New York: Norton, 2011), pp. 511–13.

Johnson hands the phone to Lady Bird while Genie McDonald comes on the line.

Genie McDonald: Mr. President? Mr. President? Hello?

Lady Bird Johnson: Mr. McDonald?

Genie McDonald: Lady Bird!

Lady Bird Johnson: How nice to hear you.

Genie McDonald: McDonald wants to speak with you too [*Lady Bird chuckles*], but I want to, too, Lady Bird. There's *nobody* that McDonald and I love and adore more in the United States than your whole family.

Lady Bird Johnson: Oh, how sweet, and—

Genie McDonald: Oh, everything in the paper we just love. Television, everything else. You are a wonder.

Lady Bird Johnson: Well, I thank you so much, and I want . . . I want to try very hard to live up to your expectations and those of all of Lyndon's friends.

Genie McDonald: But you . . . you have done it. But I've got to speak to Mr. President. I never have talked to a president before.

Lady Bird Johnson: [*Chuckles.*] Here he is.

[*to President Johnson*] Mrs. McDonald.

President Johnson returns to the line.

President Johnson: Hello, Charley!

Genie McDonald: Mr. President?

President Johnson: Hello, Mrs. . . . . Mrs. McDonald. How are you?

Genie McDonald: This is Genie.

President Johnson: Glad to hear you.

Genie McDonald: Nobody in the United States loves this family like we love your family.

President Johnson: Well, thank you very, very much.

Genie McDonald: And you just don't know what you-all mean to us.

President Johnson: Well, you mean a lot to us, Mrs. McDonald.

Genie McDonald: Now, McDonald wants to speak to Lady Bird just a minute.

President Johnson: All right. [*Tells Lady Bird Mr. McDonald would like to speak with her.*]

McDonald: Hello?

President Johnson: Just a minute, Charley.

McDonald: Yeah.

Lady Bird returns to the line.

Lady Bird Johnson: Hello?

McDonald: I'm proud of you.

Lady Bird Johnson: Oh, *thank* you, sir.

McDonald: You measure up to all of them.

Lady Bird Johnson: I've been proud of you ever since I heard—

McDonald: Now wait a minute.

Lady Bird Johnson: —you make a speech, must have been 12 years ago.

McDonald: You have two of the loveliest daughters. All over in Hawaii the other day, just anywhere they go. [*Lady Bird chuckles.*] It's fine.

Lady Bird Johnson: You know, you have more fun with your children after they get to be nearly grown than you do all of the young years.

McDonald: Absolutely.

Lady Bird Johnson: I guess it's just that "the year that is" is the most fun.

McDonald: That's right.

Lady Bird Johnson: Whichever one that is.

McDonald: Well, I told the President a minute ago his greatest hour was signing that bill last night.

Lady Bird Johnson: Oh, Mr. McDonald, you just don't *know* how good you make me feel! Because—

McDonald: Well, here's the thing. . . .

Lady Bird Johnson: I—

McDonald: I'd rather be president one term and have a secure place in history like old [Winston] Churchill. He had his great hour; everybody has them. But that came last night.

Lady Bird Johnson: Well, I was proud of it, and I also thought that I would have . . . and some of our southern and Texan friends might have their doubts. But to hear *you* say that, well, makes me feel *so* good. I thank you.

McDonald: Well, it's—everything's all right.

Lady Bird Johnson: All right, sir.

McDonald: [*chuckling*] All right, Lady. [*Hangs up.*]

Lady Bird Johnson: Well, bye.

The operator comes on the line to inquire whether they are through and Lady Bird replies that she had not realized that McDonald had hung up.

9:33 P.M.: After saying good-byes, President Johnson, Lady Bird, Lynda Bird, Vicki McCammon, and Jesse Kellam lifted off in a helicopter from the Haywood, landing back at the LBJ Ranch at 9:53 P.M.

9:55 P.M.: The group took the ranch's golf cart down to Cousin Oriole's to say hello and to watch the news, a frequent occurrence when Johnson was back home.[82]

10:23 P.M.: They left and were back at the main house four minutes later.

10:30 P.M.: The President received a massage and went to bed.

---

82. Oriole Bunton Bailey was an elderly maternal cousin of President Johnson's who lived on the LBJ Ranch. When he was home, he made frequent trips to visit her, often incorporating walks to her house into his exercise regimen. Transcript, Oral History Interview of Robert Baker, 11 October 1984, by Michael Gillette, Lyndon B. Johnson Library, pp. 45–46.

Saturday, July 4, 1964
Independence Day

You'll look marvelous with a sunburn.
> —Jacqueline Kennedy to President Johnson

I'm sorry he [Martin Luther King Jr.] was there. It was very unfortunate he was there, and don't you get hung in on it. And then you get it in transcript that he's [President Johnson's] been in continual touch with him. That's the last thing I want....And who is making all these mistakes in transcripts?
> —President Johnson to George Reedy

For this Independence Day, Lyndon Johnson was home. Amid the familiar landscape of limestone and live oaks, he continued his vacation, and as the Saturday sun warmed his Hill Country to the 100-degree mark, he took to the waters, relaxing on rivers he had once helped to tame. Six massive concrete dams with names like Wirtz and Miller and Inks rose up to pool the flow of the lower Colorado River, forging monuments to men who had helped make Lyndon Johnson more than an ambitious local.[1] As a Texas congressman in the 1930s and 1940s and as a senator after 1948, Johnson played a central role in turning this stretch of stream into a marvel of the modern world, bringing electric power and predictable water to a region ready to embrace new conveniences and

---

1. These dams were named for Congressman James P. Buchanan, Lower Colorado River Authority [LCRA] board member Roy B. Inks, attorney and New Deal administrator Alvin Wirtz, LCRA manager Max Starcke, Congressman Joseph J. Mansfield, and Austin Mayor Tom Miller.

new dreams. One of the new reservoirs was Granite Shoals Lake, the waterway that the Johnsons had been enjoying this holiday weekend. It would be their last Fourth of July on Granite Shoals, however, because the water behind the Alvin Wirtz Dam would be christened with a new name in April 1965—Lake Lyndon B. Johnson, or Lake LBJ as it would be more popularly known.

As much as Johnson was immersed in the Texas world he knew best, he was also surrounded on this day with reminders of the tragedy in Dallas that had elevated him to the presidency. He had John and Nellie Connally in for breakfast and lunch, and in the evening, talked on the phone with John Kennedy's widow and brother. For Johnson, most of his presidency lay in the future. Today marked his 226th day. Over 1,600 more lay ahead.[2]

All times referenced for this day were central standard time [cst], two hours behind eastern daylight time.

9:38 A.M. (CST)

To George Reedy[3]

Before greeting Governor John Connally and other guests for breakfast, Johnson spoke to his press secretary about securing supplemental appropriations to fund aspects of the Civil Rights Act, managing information about Mississippi, and being hounded by the press. Johnson was particularly upset by photographs published of his boating excursions the day before.

President Johnson: . . . I don't have anything for you this morning. The . . . the supplemental [appropriations] stuff, they're all working on it and getting it, but the House is not in session, and [*Reedy acknowledges*] it'll be ready for them when the House . . . the House will be asked to go

---

2. Johnson's administration lasted a total of 1,887 days, from 22 November 1963 to 20 January 1969.
3. Tape WH6407.03, Citation #4152, Recordings of Telephone Conversations—White House Series, Recordings and Transcripts of Conversations and Meetings, Lyndon B. Johnson Library.

to work on a supplemental for [LeRoy] Collins and Justice and the rest of them as soon as they come back.[4]

George Reedy: Well, if I can just say that, that it'll be ready as soon as they come back, that'll . . .

President Johnson: Well, I'd just say it'll be . . . it'll be transmitted as soon as they come back; it's ready now.

Reedy: Good. OK, sir. Have you had any other conversations?

President Johnson: No, I don't think of any. [*Pause.*]

Reedy: OK. [*Pause.*] I might be—could I say something like this: that you discussed the question of the appropriation with the staff members, and that there will be one ready to go back when . . . be ready to send up to Congress once they get back to . . .

President Johnson: Say I've discussed—yeah, that's all right. Yeah. It's ready now, as I say, George.

Reedy: Yeah.

President Johnson: We've got a request, and I'm going to use them even though we don't have appropriations right now, but . . .

Reedy: Mm-hmm.

President Johnson: See, Justice is going on—taking on its work, and . . . we'll . . . we'd send it today if it were . . . Congress were in session.

Reedy: Mm-hmm. I understand. OK, sir.

Did you ever get the governor of Mississippi [Paul Johnson], sir?

President Johnson: Yeah, I talked to him over the phone.[5] I don't think I ought to say more than we said yesterday: that I talked to him. I heard it on CBS news before I talked to him.

Reedy: Mm-hmm.

President Johnson: And I ran and grabbed the phone after I'd done it. I thought that I said I was going to talk to him, and . . . but you got it announced down there, and they got it out, and I was afraid it'd insult him. We got to be awfully careful in discussing what we say with him at

---

4. On 7 October 1964, Johnson signed a supplemental appropriations bill that provided almost $13 million to operate six programs under the Civil Rights Act. This expenditure for civil rights was the smallest in the bill. Among the other items approved were $800 million for the War on Poverty, $25 million for the food stamp program, $65 million for mass transportation, $45 million for the Small Business Administration, and $22.5 million for public housing. *Congressional Quarterly Almanac*, 88th Cong., 2nd sess., 1964, vol. 20 (Washington, DC: Congressional Quarterly Service, 1965), p. 175.

5. Conversation between President Johnson and Paul Johnson, 3:17 P.M., 3 July 1964, in this volume.

all, because that's inflammatory. One little word you say may kick off a revolution. So I'd just stay away from that as far as I could.

I indicated I was *going to* talk to him yesterday, but before I could get to it, why, the damn thing was on CBS that I *had.* So either you made a mistake there in briefing, or CBS is not reliable, whoever's traveling with you.

Reedy: Well, I thought you said you were going to talk to him as soon as you hung up from me, sir.

President Johnson: Well . . . I didn't get to, and it was on the thing that I had, and it will—

[*to aide*] Give me a piece of paper and bread.

Reedy: Do you have any plans today that I ought to tell them about, or just . . .

President Johnson: No. [*Pauses and begins to eat.*] AP [Associated Press] and *Life* [were] up here with a boat chasing us yesterday afternoon.[6]

Reedy: Yeah, they got a picture, sir.

President Johnson: Fine. I guess we can't go there anymore, so I don't know what we can do. I'd like to go over there. [*Pause.*]

Reedy: Well, I think if you'd just let them get one or two pictures, they'd leave it alone.

President Johnson: [*audibly chewing*] I don't particularly like to get pictures of [me] out in my shorts. [*Pause.*]

Reedy: No, but a picture, say, of you standing behind the wheel of the boat. Something like that.

President Johnson: But then I have to spend a year on the boat: who owns it, how much it costs, all that stuff.

Reedy: Well, they're going to ask me all that today, anyway. I'm just going to say I don't know.

President Johnson: Yeah. [*Pause.*]

Reedy: Anything I should tell them about church or anything like that tomorrow?

President Johnson: No, I'm afraid to go to church, afraid somebody

---

6. The press viewed the search for Johnson in semi-comical terms. One reporter wrote, "We're soaked, sunburned, and slightly seasick, but we haven't been able to catch up with President Johnson." Laurence Stern, "A Summer White House Is Found in Texas Maze," *Washington Post*, 6 July 1964.

will have a flat [tire].[7] Then they'll have screaming headlines that we just barely missed having a wreck with the President.[8]

Reedy: Incidentally, that business of [Dean] Acheson to Cyprus—not to Cyprus, but to be . . . I think they call it an observer in the talks, or something like that—is leaked. Murrey Marder had it nailed down in this morning's *Washington Post.*[9]

President Johnson: They gave out . . . the State Department gave out a statement.

Reedy: Yeah, I know it. They weren't supposed to give the statement out until tonight, but Murrey . . . Murrey got the thing last night.

An almost ten-second pause ensues as President Johnson continues eating.

President Johnson: I didn't know when it . . . when . . . But I don't guess it makes much difference, does it?

Reedy: No. It doesn't make much difference. The only important thing there is that the source be the State Department rather than the White House—rather the announcement come out of the State Department.

You've received Fourth of July messages from [Sir Alec Douglas-] Home and . . .

[*to Mac Kilduff*] Who else, Mac?

[*to Johnson*] Home and [Charles] de Gaulle, which are on their way down.[10] They may have gotten to you already; I don't know.

President Johnson: The courier just come in, but I haven't had a chance to look over his stuff. [*Reedy acknowledges.*] Have you?

Reedy: No, sir, it comes . . . they come direct—

President Johnson: I was asking Buzz [Horace Busby] here.[11]

Reedy: Oh. I'm sorry, sir.

President Johnson: [*to Busby*] I thought his briefing had to be at 10:30.

---

7. Johnson chose to break his routine of churchgoing on Sunday, opting instead for sightseeing and boating.

8. On Johnson's irritation with the Secret Service and his difficulties in getting to church, see the conversation between President Johnson and James Rowley, 11:25 A.M., 2 March 1964, in Robert David Johnson and Kent B. Germany, eds. *The Presidential Recordings, Lyndon B. Johnson: Toward the Great Society, February 1, 1964–May 31, 1964,* vol. 4, *February 1, 1964–March 8, 1964* (New York: Norton, 2007), p. 835.

9. Murrey Marder covered the international beat for the *Washington Post,* and this morning's paper carried his story that Johnson was sending Dean Acheson to help mediate the Cyprus conflict. Murrey Marder, "U.S. Sends Acheson to Geneva," *Washington Post,* 4 July 1964.

10. Sir Alec Douglas-Home was Prime Minister of Great Britain. Charles de Gaulle was President of France.

11. A redheaded Texan, Horace Busby had been a longtime aide and speechwriter for Johnson.

Horace Busby: [*Unclear*] tried to call [*unclear*] last night.

President Johnson: Well, I was calling you; I thought it was 10:30 now. I looked at the wrong clock.

Reedy: OK, sir.

President Johnson: How did AP's picture look?

Reedy: Uh . . . I have it here. It's . . .

President Johnson: Can you tell anything about it?

Reedy: I can't recognize anybody in the picture.

President Johnson: Well, that's good.

Reedy: Except you. [*Chuckles.*]

President Johnson: Can you recognize me?

Reedy: Yes, sir. It . . . it's taken from the port side of the boat, and it . . . it's just a broadside picture. There's a . . . there are a man and a woman seated in the bow that I don't recognize, although the woman might be Mrs. [A.W.] Moursund. Then there are three men, one smoking a pipe, sitting up in the . . . on the roof of the lounge, or whatever they call it. One of the men could be Billy Bailey, although I don't know.[12] Then on the starboard side, you can see two women standing. One has her hand half over her face, obviously shading her eyes, and might, I don't know, might be Lynda Bird, because it's quite tall. And the other one might be Mrs. [Lady Bird] Johnson, simply because the hair is very dark. Then you're sitting on the roof. Then there's a girl in a bathing suit to your right, a rather good-looking girl, although I can't make it out, who it is.

President Johnson: Lynda?

Reedy: No, sir. It's not Lynda. I think Lynda's standing in the other side of the boat. And there's a girl on your left—the girl on the right's in a bathing suit, the girl on the left in a dress; it looks like Mrs. Johnson is right behind you. The picture shows you [in] swimming trunks, white cap, and dark glasses, and you're looking up to the right.

Then there's a man standing behind the wheel of the boat that looks like A.W. And there are two or three other people in under that canopy, and I can't make them out at all. Then two Secret Service agents, Arthur Godfrey and Jerry Kibbitz, standing in the back.

A ten-second pause ensues, while President Johnson continues to eat.

President Johnson: How'd they know we were over there?

Reedy: They claim they didn't. They said that they were up there just to get some general pictures of the territory, and they knew you had a

---

12. Dr. Charles William Bailey and wife were guests of the Johnsons.

place at Kingsland.[13] And they wanted to . . . just get some general shots, and they spotted this boat.

Now, UPI [United Press International] also has a couple of pictures, but they can't identify anybody in it, including you.

President Johnson: Were they up there too?

Reedy: Yes, sir.

President Johnson: How'd they happen to be there—just taking general area [shots] too? They lying that way?

Reedy: This I do not know, because the UPI man who called me was not the one up there. He said that he had been called by a couple of these men who are from Dallas, UPI, and they told him they had this picture but couldn't identify anybody in it. This is Jim Sutherland, whom I think you know. UPI in Austin.

And he said apparently they were on the bank of the river and saw this boat. He said everybody up there had said it was Lyndon Johnson's boat, so they snapped some pictures of it. But they can't identify anybody in it.

President Johnson: Well, what does he want? What does he [want by] telling you about it? Just telling you that?

Reedy: He called me and said, "Was the President out in a boat yesterday?" and I said, "I don't know." And he said, "Well, we've got a picture of the President in a boat." [*Chuckles slightly.*] And I said, "Well, that's kind of a peculiar question to call me and tell me you got a picture of the President on a boat and was he in a boat." I said, "I don't know." He said, "Well, we can't identify it." I said, "Well, I don't know what good I can do you, then." [*An approximately ten-second pause.*]

President Johnson: Well, I don't know. I'd like to go over there this afternoon, or I'd like to go to the horse races, but I guess either one of them would be bad.

Reedy: I don't think so. Horse races at the county fair wouldn't hurt you in the slightest. And, on the boat, as I said, I think if you just let them get a couple of pictures of you standing behind the wheel or something like that, that'd be that. I haven't seen this picture printed anywhere, but I know they put it out in the wire last night. [*An approximately 20-second pause.*]

President Johnson: What are you going to tell them when they ask you about the boat?

Reedy: I'm just going to tell them I don't know anything about it.

---

13. Kingsland is a town along the upper end of Granite Shoals Lake.

[*Pause.*] Which I don't. I mean, all I know is the picture that I've got.

President Johnson: Jimmy Banks's story is awfully ugly.[14] Did you read it this morning?

Reedy: Yeah, and I thought that was the only bad one. I wouldn't say awfully ugly, but it was a bad one. The others, I thought, were very good.

President Johnson: Why does he have to be bad, you reckon?

Reedy: I don't know. I don't—I think that, for some reason I've never been able to fathom, Jimmy just never liked you, and I can't . . . I don't know why. It must be something that goes back a few years. [*A ten-second pause.*]

President Johnson: He's got a UPI boy that patrols the house: just rides up and down the road all the time. We have to keep one highway cop watching him to be sure he's the same one, that hasn't got a gun.

Reedy: Mm-hmm. There'll be an AP man staked out there somewhere, too, sir. If you haven't seen him, you just haven't been able to find him yet.

President Johnson: How do you know?

Reedy: Well, because it's a normal operation of a wire service. I mean, nobody's told me that, but they wouldn't have to. Any [*unclear*]—

President Johnson: That time we were in here before, it's just UPI.

Reedy: That's the same—well, they used to do it up at the Cape.[15] They just haven't found the AP man then, sir. This happens to every president. It's just as routine as posting . . . posting military guards at a fort. And questionably, they've probably got a couple of rooms up at Johnson City. [*President Johnson makes an unclear comment to someone with him.*] Or Fredericksburg. More likely Johnson City.

President Johnson: OK. I'll call you back at 10:30 if there's anything else.

Reedy: You bet, sir.

As they hang up, Johnson speaks to someone in the room.

10:05 A.M.: President Johnson and Lady Bird ate breakfast with a crowd that included Governor John Connally, the governor's brother Merrill, and their wives.

---

14. Jimmy Banks was a reporter for the *Dallas Morning News.* He later published *Money, Marbles, and Chalk: The Wondrous World of Texas Politics* (Austin: Texas Publishing, 1971).
15. John Kennedy had a compound at Hyannis Port, on Cape Cod.

11:00 A.M.–12:56 P.M.: The group left for the Lewis Ranch, returning at 12:56 P.M. to visit with some newly arrived guests: federal judge Homer Thornberry, former Texas congressman
Frank Ikard (currently serving as president of the American
Petroleum Institute), and their wives.

1:00 P.M.–3:00 P.M.: Johnson passed out some presidential mementos
to the group before they sat down to lunch at 1:15 P.M. The
Connallys excused themselves after lunch, but the others chatted until 3:00 P.M.

3:00 P.M.: President and Mrs. Johnson, with the remaining guests,
headed out for an afternoon of boating and skiing—all the
while trying to hide from the press.

7:05 P.M.: President Johnson and his guests arrived back at the LBJ
Ranch, and seven minutes later, he went to his office to take a
call from several members of the Kennedy family.

7:15 P.M. (CST)

From Robert Kennedy, Jean Kennedy Smith, and Jacqueline Kennedy[16]

The Attorney General delivered generally positive news about southern compliance with the Civil Rights Act but wanted the President to
be aware of some resistance from George Wallace and some likely resistance from South Carolina Governor Donald Russell. President Johnson
then said hello to Kennedy's younger sister Jean Kennedy Smith and to
Jacqueline Kennedy.

President Johnson: Hello?
Robert Kennedy: Hello?
President Johnson: Hi, General.
Kennedy: How are you?
President Johnson: Fine. Did you have a good day?
Kennedy: How's Texas?
President Johnson: Pretty hot.[17]
Kennedy: [*chuckling slightly*] Yeah. Well, listen, we had a good day.

---

16. Tape WH6407.04, Citation #4153, Recordings of Telephone Conversations—White House
Series, Recordings and Transcripts of Conversations and Meetings, Lyndon B. Johnson Library.
17. The temperature in some parts of the Hill Country reached 100 degrees.

President Johnson: Good.

Kennedy: And I think the most significant thing is that the Chamber of Commerce of Jackson, Mississippi, voted last night to abide by the law.

President Johnson: Good.

Kennedy: And I think there was one dissent out of 16; you know, 16 to 1, or something.

President Johnson: That's wonderful.

Kennedy: Yeah, and then beyond . . . Savannah, Atlanta, and all of these other cities went along. Birmingham, Montgomery. A lot of the cities went along very, very well.

President Johnson: All the newspapers spent all day interviewing Johnson City [Texas] motels.

Kennedy: Oh, really?

President Johnson: [*Laughs.*] They got the right answers, too.

Kennedy: Oh, well, that's good. But it's been very good.

President Johnson: Well, that's good.

Kennedy: Very, very good. I'm—You know, all the work, I think, that's been done in the last two months really paid off.

President Johnson: Well, that's good.

Kennedy: And so I think it's most encouraging.

President Johnson: Well, that's fine. How long—When are you going home—Sunday?

Kennedy: Yeah, Sunday. The one problem—and I think, I understand you've done something on it—is the governor of South Carolina [Donald Russell], you know, about seeing Governor [LeRoy] Collins and [Luther] Hodges.[18] But, you know, [George] Wallace said he wouldn't see them.

President Johnson: No. No, I didn't know that.

Kennedy: Yes. Well, you know, they sent telegrams to all these people. First place, I think the problem is if we could coordinate what we're doing out of there, I think it's helpful because it puts some of these governors in a tough spot who are—you know, I think maybe some of them we could feel out first.

President Johnson: Yeah?

---

18. Under the direction of the Community Relations Service, the Johnson administration had plans to send a team of racially moderate former governors, including Buford Ellington (Tennessee), LeRoy Collins (Florida), and Luther Hodges (North Carolina), to visit with current southern governors and seek compliance with the Civil Rights Act. George Wallace declined to see them. See Conversation between President Johnson and Luther Hodges, 7 July 1964, Tape WH6407.05, Citation #4171, Recordings of Telephone Conversations—White House Series, Recordings and Transcripts of Conversations and Meetings, Lyndon B. Johnson Library.

Kennedy: Like [Donald] Russell is a good man in South Carolina.

President Johnson: And what did he do?

Kennedy: Well, Wallace said that he wouldn't see them, and then Russell sa[id]—and he put the telegram out that he wouldn't see them.

President Johnson: Wallace said he wouldn't, wouldn't see . . .

Kennedy: Collins and Hodges.

President Johnson: All right. Now, what about Russell?

Kennedy: Russell wrote—sent them a telegram saying that he wouldn't see them. But he didn't put it out. Now, if we could just . . . if there were some way that we could get that, so that we don't have . . . put Russell in the . . . in a . . . [Governor Carl] Sanders in Georgia said he *would* see them. But if we could get Russell just to say that he, you know, out of courtesy he'd see them; he doesn't have to agree [*unclear, Johnson coughs*] see them. But I think we could isolate Wallace, and it would be very helpful.

President Johnson: Yeah.

Kennedy: I had understood that they had brought that to your attention.

President Johnson: No. No, I haven't heard from them. They haven't, they haven't told me; I haven't heard a word on it.

Kennedy: Oh, well, that's too bad.

President Johnson: Well—

Kennedy: They told me that you had . . . already were aware of it and were working on it.

President Johnson: No. No.

Kennedy: I think if we just . . . if somebody—Russell's a good man and . . . and . . . just as long as he understands it would be harmful if the telegram got out. And they don't have to come down and see him now; maybe they could see him later on. But just so that it wasn't publicized that he was in the same category as Wallace, that would be very helpful—

President Johnson: Did they contact all 11 [southern] governors?

Kennedy: Yes, they did.

President Johnson: And two of them said they wouldn't?

Kennedy: Well, you see, I don't know. I just—all I know is that Russell and Wallace did—

President Johnson: Yeah.

Kennedy: And I know Sanders said that he would.

President Johnson: Yeah.

Kennedy: But I haven't heard on the others.

President Johnson: Yeah.

Kennedy: But I think for the future that it would be well if . . . if, you know, they work with somebody in the White House who knew all those southern governors so that they could feel them out before they sent the telegrams.

President Johnson: Yeah.

Kennedy: So that we make sure that nobody gets . . . you know, for some of them it's . . . politically, it's difficult, as you know.

President Johnson: Yeah. . . . Yeah, I know that.

Kennedy: And we want to make sure that—

President Johnson: I'll talk to Hodges about it tomorrow.

Kennedy: Yes. But otherwise, this thing has been very good.

President Johnson: Fine. Well, I'm sure glad to hear it, and hope you have a good Fourth, and I'll see you Monday.

Kennedy: You want to talk to a couple of your girlfriends?

President Johnson: Sure would.

Kennedy: Jean and Jackie. Hold on.

After a 20-second pause, Jean Kennedy Smith comes on the line.

Jean Kennedy Smith: Hello?

President Johnson: Hello?

Smith: Hello?

President Johnson: Hello?

Smith: [*Chuckles.*] Hello?

President Johnson: Who is this—Ethel?[19]

Smith: Oh no, this is Jean.

President Johnson: Hi, Jean, how are you?

Smith: Oh, is this Mr. President?

President Johnson: Yes, ma'am. I'm glad to hear you.

Smith: This is the itty-bitty baby sister.

President Johnson: [*Chuckles, talks over Smith.*] Good to hear you, my dear. How are you?

Smith: Listen, I must tell you that Joan [Kennedy] was so excited.[20]

President Johnson: Well, I . . .

Smith: You said such nice things about Teddy [Kennedy] and [*unclear*].

President Johnson: Well, I enjoyed talking to her. She's a sweet girl, isn't she?

Smith: Yeah, [*unclear*].

---

19. Ethel was the wife of Robert Kennedy.
20. The President had called Joan Kennedy, the wife of Senator Ted Kennedy, the day before. See the conversation with Joan Kennedy at 1:45 P.M. on 3 July 1964, in this volume.

President Johnson: I . . .

Smith: So . . . oh, well, wait a minute, Jackie wants to talk to you.

President Johnson: Thank you, dear.

Smith: Hold on.

President Johnson: Thank you.

Jacqueline Kennedy quickly comes on the line.

Jacqueline Kennedy: Mr. President?

President Johnson: Hi, Jackie, how are you?

Jacqueline Kennedy: Happy Fourth of July.

President Johnson: Thank you, my dear. Did you have a good day?

Jacqueline Kennedy: Oh, yes. Are you in Texas?

President Johnson: What'd you do, go out on the boat?

Jacqueline Kennedy: Well, no, it's so rainy, nobody could. But General [Maxwell] Taylor came up, and then we saw him off.

President Johnson: Uh-huh.

Jacqueline Kennedy: Are you . . . are you at your ranch now?

President Johnson: Yes, I just came off the lake. I've been out in a boat all afternoon.

Jacqueline Kennedy: Oh, I'm so glad. So you get some rest?

President Johnson: I got a sunburn, and I'll probably be blistered now.

Jacqueline Kennedy: Oh no, don't. You'll look marvelous with a sunburn.

President Johnson: Well, I hope so. I hope you're doing all right.

Jacqueline Kennedy: Yes, I'm fine, Mr. President.

President Johnson: How are the children?

Jacqueline Kennedy: Oh, fine, thank you, and yours?

President Johnson: Good. Lynda's with us; Luci's in Washington having dates.[21]

Jacqueline Kennedy: I know! I noticed she didn't come. I thought it was something sinister like that.

President Johnson: You know, she came in and said that she wanted a very special [17th] birthday present on July the 2nd, and we asked her what it was, and she said she just wanted to go one whole day without an [Secret Service] agent. [*Kennedy laughs.*] What do you reckon happened?

---

21. The Johnsons left Luci in the nation's capital under the supervision of Willie Day Taylor, the longtime Johnson assistant who frequently took care of the children. Lady-Bird Johnson, *A White House Diary* (New York: Holt, Rinehart, Winston, 1970), p. 174.

Jacqueline Kennedy: And did you arrange it?

President Johnson: Oh yeah, I arranged it.

Jacqueline Kennedy: Good work!

President Johnson: What do you reckon happened?

Jacqueline Kennedy: [*Both laugh.*] I hate to think. And don't you.

President Johnson: [*Laughs again, and Kennedy chuckles.*] It's sure good to hear your voice, and I hope that you're feeling all right.

Jacqueline Kennedy: Oh, yes. Well, it's nice to talk to you. And give my love to Lady Bird.

President Johnson: Fine. I long to see you.

Jacqueline Kennedy: OK, we'll see you soon.

President Johnson: Thank you, dear.

Jacqueline Kennedy: Good-bye, Mr. President.

President Johnson: Bye. . . . Bye.

7:25 P.M. (CST)

To George Reedy[22]

In the last recorded conversation of the day, Johnson covered some press issues and discussed the difficulties involved in going to church services before launching into a brief critique of Reedy's description of the President's relationship with Martin Luther King.

Before the President comes on the line, White House Secretary Gerri Whittington and Reedy exchange greetings and discuss the details of a press release on the President's activities, particularly in international affairs. She asks Reedy to hold, and then after an approximately 35-second pause, the President comes on the line.

President Johnson: George?

George Reedy: Yes, sir.

President Johnson: Buzz [Horace Busby] has got a backgrounder [memorandum] I think's all right. You can add to it. He says we worked on Vietnam problems, and General [Maxwell] Taylor, and . . . and Greek/Turkish problems last week. And then we're having . . . he didn't

---

22. Tape WH6407.04, Citation #4155, Recordings of Telephone Conversations—White House Series, Recordings and Transcripts of Conversations and Meetings, Lyndon B. Johnson Library. The Daily Diary listed this call at 7:13 P.M.

say we're appointing these task forces, but we think in the future . . . I think it's all right.[23] I don't think it's too hot, but I don't think it's too bad.

Reedy: Good.

President Johnson: He's got a copy, but you can go over it and improve on it. I'd add to it that we met with all the Latin American ambassadors, and we also spent some time with President [Francisco] Orlich on plans for the Western Hemisphere, and [*Reedy acknowledges*] he thought things were going better than ever.[24] And [I] also had a good many conferences with private people interested in the Western Hemisphere. Let's have last week as kind of a Western Hemisphere week.

Reedy: OK, sir.

President Johnson: That's about all I know. I'm going over to A.W.'s [Moursund's] to eat dinner.

Reedy: Got it.

President Johnson: John and Nellie [Connally] and them came out and had lunch with us, and John's brother and his wife. Judge [Homer] Thornberry came up, but I don't think we need to tell them that.

Reedy: No. I've already told them about John and Merrill [Connally].[25]

President Johnson: All right. And they [the press] had some people scouring the lakes all afternoon, but I don't think that any of them ever ran into anybody.

Reedy: They did not. [*Chuckles.*] I know it. I'm—I've just been talking to some, and it's rather amusing.

President Johnson: What are they say[ing]?

Reedy: Oh, they're just kind of amused by it too. They went on up, and they went into Fredericksburg and attended the horse races, and they went on up to the lake, scoured around there and drove up and down the —oh, what is it?—Granite Shoals Highway from Johnson City north?

President Johnson: Yeah.

Reedy: But never did find you. They're kind of amused by it too. It's a game now, I think.

President Johnson: Who was it, UP[I] [United Press International]?

Reedy: No, it was Gordon Yoder.

President Johnson: Who is he?

---

23. Blue-ribbon task forces were key to planning Great Society legislation and programs.
24. Francisco José Orlich, the President of Costa Rica, had made an official visit to the United States from 30 June to 2 July.
25. Merrill was John Connally's brother.

Reedy: He's that . . . he's a freelance cameraman, movies, out of Dallas, who's usually hired by CBS. Or he might be hired by any one of a number of outfits. I think he's down here for CBS this time, although I haven't checked it. He comes down for a different outfit each time.

President Johnson: Who else? They said that there's—

Reedy: [*Unclear*] technicians.

President Johnson: They said there's a fellow from the UP[I] named Hamilton.[26]

Reedy: Oh, I don't know him. He may be somebody out of Dallas.

President Johnson: Mm-hmm. No, he's in Austin. [*Unclear comment by Reedy.*] He's a kid out of Austin.

Reedy: Might be. He must be somebody new, then; I don't know him.

President Johnson: Yeah, Hamilton.

Did everybody go to the horse races—all your reporter staff?

Reedy: Doug Kiker went to the horse races, and I think some of the local natives took him for his shirt.[27] He made some bets on the horses. [*Chuckles.*] Didn't lose a lot of money, but I think he lost five or six bucks betting with the citizens of Fredericksburg. I think they more went up to see the horse races than anything else. [*The President acknowledges.*] Right now they're all over—We're all over at Lakeview, which is a new lodge, on Lake Travis.[28]

President Johnson: Who's taking them over there?

Reedy: It's just sort of a general party that they wound up themselves.

President Johnson: They entertain themselves, or is TWA doing it?[29]

Reedy: Oh, they're entertaining themselves.

President Johnson: Somebody told me TWA had a big party on for them.

Reedy: Well, I think TWA organized it, yeah. [*The President acknowledges.*]

Then do you have any plans for tomorrow that I can tell them about, or should we just go our way?

President Johnson: No. No. No. Tell them I'd like to go to church, but I'm afraid that somebody down the road would have a flat, and I just don't

---

26. Hamilton was not positively identified.

27. Douglas Kiker was a White House columnist for the *New York Herald Tribune*.

28. Downriver from Granite Shoals Lake, Lake Travis was the largest in the string of reservoirs along the lower Colorado River.

29. TWA was not positively identified, but it was possibly Trans World Airlines.

want to get . . . startle the nation, and only . . . the best way to do is just sit at home, and . . . may have a little service here at home.

Reedy: OK, sir.

President Johnson: I'm afraid if Secret Service had a flat, they'd make headlines out of it.

Reedy: You are not going back tomorrow, though, are you, sir?

President Johnson: No.

Reedy: Right.

President Johnson: No, I'm not going back tomorrow, and if I go back Monday, it'll be late Monday.

Reedy: Right.

President Johnson: But I do not want to say that I'm going back.

You know, they all say that you didn't notify them I was leaving. I thought you told them—you told me you had to give them two hours' notice, and hell, I gave you about four before we left.

Reedy: What I did . . . no, I had it . . . as soon as you alerted me, as soon as you said there was a possibility, I set all the wheels in motion, so they didn't have to have those two hours. But I didn't . . . I told them you were leaving as soon as you told me you'd made up your mind.

President Johnson: Well, why do they lie, then, and say that they didn't know until I—

Reedy: They aren't lying; they're just confused over the situation, is all.

President Johnson: Well, they lied: They said that they weren't told that I was leaving until my plane had already taken off!

Reedy: No, they were told before that. That—your . . . That's some of them who weren't there at the time. Half of them know it, and half didn't; they're just confused by the situation.

President Johnson: Well, if you ain't going to get any credit out of telling them, we just don't have to tell them. Hell, we'll just go on. Doug Kiker's story says . . . he makes a big to-do about it.

Reedy: Well, Doug *wasn't* notified for the simple reason that he wasn't there. I was calling around frantically trying to find him and finally got him. But that was after you'd taken off.

President Johnson: [*softly*] Let the little son of a bitch stay at home, as far as I'm concerned. He . . .

Now, you say I've been in touch with Martin Luther King continuously.

Reedy: No, that's . . . that's a mis—at the time—mistake. I said that—

President Johnson: I haven't been in touch with him at all and don't want to be. You know his record.

Reedy: Yeah, I know.

President Johnson: It's the last thing. [*seeming to quote from some source*] "The President has been in *continual* touch with Dr. King."

Reedy: I know it; that's a mistake in the transcript which I've gotten corrected. I said, "From time to time he has seen Martin Luther King" is what I said.

President Johnson: [*testily*] Well, why do you say that?

Reedy: Well, you saw him at the ceremony—

President Johnson: Well, I say, *why* do you say it?

Reedy: Because I was asked and because they'd seen you there.

President Johnson: Well, all right, then, don't—just say if you've seen him. Just keep that out, though. I'm sorry he was there. It was very unfortunate he was there, and don't you get hung in on it. And then you get it in transcript that he's been in continual touch with him. That's the last thing I want. They're making an issue on you, and you'll hear from King before this campaign's over with.

And then you go to making an explanation, it won't do any good. So I'd just say . . . that you don't know a damn thing about who I've seen. And you don't. If they ask you if I've seen him, you tell them you don't know. Don't get in there that I'm in continuous touch with him. [*Pauses briefly.*]

And who is making all these mistakes in transcripts? Your transcriber?

Reedy: Well, there aren't many, sir. They come from time to time.

President Johnson: Well, I mean this one.

Reedy: He made that one. Yes, sir.

President Johnson: [*Pauses.*] Mm-hmm. OK.

Reedy: OK, sir.

This anxiety about Martin Luther King Jr. was the last recorded thought of the day. It underscored the precarious position that Johnson was staking out in his bid to be elected President in his own right. Concerned about alienating too many white southern moderates, especially in the states of the Upper South, President Johnson pursued a strategy of compromise that eventually left many civil rights activists feeling alienated, particularly after the confrontation between Johnson and the Mississippi Freedom Democratic Party (MFDP) at August's Democratic National Convention in Atlantic City.

The day's hostile remarks about King also highlighted a basic issue that remained unresolved. James Chaney, Michael Schwerner, and

Andrew Goodman were still missing. "It's the most mysterious thing that I've ever heard of," Mississippi Governor Paul Johnson had told the President on July 3. "It's as if they went straight up."[30] Their whereabouts remained a mystery for another month. On August 4, President Johnson and the rest of the world learned for sure that their bodies had not gone straight up or to Chicago or to some other place to laugh about the commotion they had caused. They had, in fact, been dumped into a clay farm-pond dam being built six miles southwest of Philadelphia, Mississippi. According to J. Edgar Hoover, an FBI informant—paid $30,000—divulged the location, and the FBI descended on Olen Burrage's farm with a backhoe and other equipment.[31] After the FBI confirmed the identity of the bodies, Lee White let the President know. Johnson immediately instructed his aides to inform the parents before the story broke in the news.[32] Coincidentally, the Gulf of Tonkin incident had just occurred, and Johnson was about to decide to ask Congress for sweeping power to carry out military action against North Vietnam. He also was coping with racially charged civil disorders in several New Jersey cities, a precursor to the long, hot summers to come.

---

30. Conversation between President Johnson and Paul Johnson, 3:17 P.M., 3 July 1964, in this volume.

31. Jerry Mitchell, an investigative reporter for the Jackson, Mississippi, *Clarion-Ledger* whose work earned him a John D. and Catherine T. MacArthur Foundation "Genius" Award in 2009, has been instrumental in bringing attention to civil rights murder cases, in several cases encouraging the re-opening of investigations that produced convictions, including the 2005 one of Edgar "Preacher" Killen. In 2007, Mitchell used new documents to identify Philadelphia resident and Klan member Pete Jordan as the informant who gave information about the bodies' location to Mississippi Highway Patrolman Maynard King (known as Mr. X within the FBI), who then informed the FBI. Mitchell also cites evidence that suggests that the FBI did not pay $30,000, but spread the story after finding the bodies as a way to put pressure on Klan members who might think one of their own was witnessing against them. In 2010, however, a retired FBI agent told Mitchell that the FBI gave the $30,000 in cash to Patrolman King to pass along to the informant. Jerry Mitchell, "Documents Identify Whistle-Blower: Who Told Where Bodies of Slain Trio Were Buried?" *Clarion-Ledger*, 3 December 2007; Jerry Mitchell, "New Details on the FBI Paying $30K to Solve the Mississippi Burning Case," Journey to Justice Blog [Internet], *Clarion-Ledger*, 15 February 2010. Available from: http://blogs.clarionledger.com/jmitchell/2010/02/15/did -the-fbi-pay-30k-to-locate-the-bodies-of-the-three-missing-civil-rights-workers/; Conversation between President Johnson and J. Edgar Hoover, 8:10 A.M., 26 March 1965, Tape WH6503.13, Citation #7162, Recordings of Telephone Conversations—White House Series, Recordings and Transcripts of Conversations and Meetings, Lyndon B. Johnson Library.

32. Conversations between President Johnson and Lee White, Time Unknown (evening, first two conversations) and 8:47 P.M. (last conversation), 4 August 1964, Tape WH6408.05, Citations #4694 and #4696; WH6408.06, Citation #4701, Recordings of Telephone Conversations— White House Series, Recordings and Transcripts of Conversations and Meetings, Lyndon B. Johnson Library.

Arrests in the Mississippi Burning case came four months later.[33] On December 4, FBI agents detained Neshoba County Sheriff Lawrence Rainey, Deputy Sheriff Cecil Price, and 17 others on federal charges of conspiracy to violate the civil rights of Goodman, Chaney, and Schwerner.[34] The men were soon indicted, but in February 1965, the charges were dropped by Federal District Judge Harold Cox, a native of Sunflower County and close friend of Senator James Eastland who earlier in 1964 had referred to black citizens trying to register to vote as "a bunch of niggers" and described them as "acting like a bunch of chimpanzees."[35] In 1966, the U.S. Supreme Court disagreed with Cox's decision in the case. The trial was set to proceed in October, but the Justice Department asked Cox to dismiss the charges because too few women served on the grand jury that had handed them down.[36] After new indictments, the case finally went to trial in October 1967, again with Judge Cox presiding.

On October 20, the all-white jury delivered guilty verdicts to seven of the eighteen defendants, including Cecil Price. Sheriff Rainey and seven others were acquitted. The jury deadlocked on three of the defendants. One of them, Edgar Ray "Preacher" Killen, escaped conviction because one woman on the jury refused to send a preacher to prison.[37] Killen avoided prosecution for over four decades. On June 21, 2005—exactly 41 years after the murders—he was convicted of manslaughter for his part in orchestrating the mob attack. So far, he has been the only defendant to stand trial in state court for the murders.

In 1964, the violence directed at civil rights activities in Mississippi did not stop with the murder of Chaney, Schwerner, and Goodman. The Council of Federated Organizations documented 175 episodes of harass-

---

33. On 3 October, Sheriff Lawrence Rainey, Deputy Sheriff Cecil Price, and three other local officers were arrested for violating the civil rights of seven black Mississippians, but not for the Chaney, Schwerner, and Goodman incident. John Herbers, "5 Mississippians Arrested by FBI on Rights Charge," *New York Times*, 4 October 1964.

34. The Justice Department used provisions from the Civil Rights Act of 1870 to prosecute the case. The pertinent parts were sections 241 and 242 of Title 18 of the U.S. Criminal Code. The use of these sections in 1960s era civil rights cases is explored in Michal R. Belknap, *Federal Law and Southern Order: Racial Violence and Constitutional Conflict in the Post-Brown South* (Athens: University of Georgia Press, 1987).

35. John Herbers, "U.S. Judge Voids a Major Charge in Rights Case," *New York Times*, 26 February 1964; "Judge Due to Rule on Suit to Speed Up Negro Registration," *New York Times*, 9 March 1964.

36. "Charges Dropped in Rights Death," *New York Times*, 7 October 1966.

37. Jerry Mitchell, "Jurors Recall Holdout Vote That Let 'Preacher' Walk Away Free," *The Clarion-Ledger* (Jackson, Mississippi), 7 May 2000.

ment or violence in the first month of Freedom Summer.[38] Beating, bombings, and burnings continued for years, and the slow march to justice for the defendants in the Neshoba County murders did little to diminish white violence. In fact, one of the principals in the Neshoba case, Sam Bowers, who was the Imperial Wizard of Mississippi's White Knights of the Ku Klux Klan, continued orchestrating a campaign of terror. Well over a year before Bowers was convicted of civil rights conspiracy for his part in Neshoba County, he ordered the elimination of Vernon Dahmer, a prosperous black businessman and farmer who supported voting rights efforts. In January 1966, two carloads of Klansmen assaulted the Dahmer home in the early morning, setting it ablaze and opening fire with guns. Dahmer seared his lungs in the attack and died later that day. After four mistrials, Bowers was finally convicted on state murder charges in 1998.[39] He died in prison. In February 2007, partly because of successful prosecution of decades-old civil rights murders and independent investigations by reporters such as Jerry Mitchell of Jackson, Mississippi, and groups like the Southern Poverty Law Center in Montgomery, Alabama, the U.S. Justice Department announced the expansion of its Cold Case Initiative to focus resources in almost 100 other cases.[40]

Between July 4 and November 4, the President signed the Food Stamp Act, the Economic Opportunity Act (the War on Poverty), the Wilderness Act, and the Land and Water Conservation Fund Act. In late-August, he endured the controversy over the Mississippi Freedom Democratic Party at Atlantic City and then completed a vigorous campaign. In early November, he achieved a victory equal to his towering ambition, defeating Barry Goldwater by one of the largest margins in modern American history. A little over three months later, he sent in the first American combat troops into Vietnam and then ordered Army men into Alabama to protect marchers going from Selma to Montgomery.

---

38. Mississippi Summer Project Communications Staff, "Mississippi Summer Project Running Summary of Incidents," 1964, Folder 25: "Depositions Summary, 1964," Box 3, Council of Federated Organizations Records, Z/1867.000/S, Mississippi Department of Archives and History.

39. For transcripts of the 1998 trial, see Boxes 39 and 40, Robert B. Helfrich Papers, Manuscript Collection, McCain Library and Archives, University of Southern Mississippi.

40. Alberto Gonzales, "Prepared Remarks of Attorney General Alberto R. Gonzales at the Press Conference on Civil Rights Cold Cases," 27 February 2007. Available from: http://www.usdoj.gov/ag/speeches/2007/ag_speech_070227.html; FBI National Press Office, Press Release, "Partnerships Established with NAACP, the National Urban League, and the Southern Poverty Law Center," 27 February 2007. Available from: http://www.fbi.gov/pressrel/pressrel07/coldcase022707.htm.

Tonight, though, was more sedate and the sunset more appealing. At 7:50 P.M., Johnson and his guests took a 19-minute helicopter ride over to old friend A.W. Moursund's house for the evening. He stayed until 10:42 P.M., then took to the air once more. Ten minutes later, he passed over his property on the Pedernales River and was back inside the LBJ Ranch house at 10:54 P.M. The President soon turned in for the night and readied for his 227th day in office.

Index